D0930537

DATE DUE

TOWARD A PSYCHOLOGY OF SITUATIONS:
An Interactional Perspective

List of Contributors

Michael Argyle, *University of Oxford, Great Britain*

Daryl J. Bem, *Cornell University, Ithaca, N.Y. USA*

Jack Block, *University of California, Berkeley, Calif., USA*

Jeanne Block, *University of California, Berkeley, Calif., USA*

Kenneth S. Bowers, *University of Waterloo, Ontario, Canada*

Nancy Cantor, *Princeton University, Princeton, N.J., USA*

Gösta Carlsson, *University of Stockholm, Stockholm, Sweden*

Kenneth H. Craik, *University of California, Berkeley, Calif., USA*

Norman S. Endler, *York University, Downsview, Ontario, Canada*

Donald W. Fiske, *University of Chicago, Chicago, Ill., USA*

Winfried Hacker, *Technische Universität, Dresden, GDR*

Joe McV. Hunt, *University of Illinois, Champaign, Ill., USA*

Lawrence R. James, *Texas Christian University, Fort Worth, Tex., USA*

Richard Jessor, *University of Colorado, Boulder, Co., USA*

David Magnusson, *University of Stockholm, Stockholm, Sweden*

Maria Nowakowska, *Polish Academy of Sciences, Warsaw, Poland*

Lars Nystedt, *University of Stockholm, Stockholm, Sweden*

Lawrence A. Pervin, *Rutgers University, New Brunswick, N.J., USA*

Richard H. Price, *University of Michigan, Ann Arbor, Mich., USA*

Ragnar Rommetveit, *University of Oslo, Oslo, Norway*

Julian B. Rotter, *University of Connecticut, Storrs, Conn., USA*

Barbara Sarason, *University of Washington, Seattle, Wash., USA*

Irwin G. Sarason, *University of Washington, Seattle, Wash., USA*

S. B. Sells, *Texas Christian University, Fort Worth, Tex., USA*

Lennart Sjöberg, *University of Gothenburg, Gothenburg, Sweden*

Daniel S. Stokols, *University of California, Irvine, Calif., USA*

TOWARD A
PSYCHOLOGY OF
SITUATIONS:
An Interactional Perspective

Edited by

DAVID MAGNUSSON

University of Stockholm

LEA LAWRENCE ERLBAUM ASSOCIATES, PUBLISHERS
1981   Hillsdale, New Jersey

Lawrence Erlbaum Associates, Inc., Publishers
365 Broadway
Hillsdale, New Jersey 07642

Library of Congress Cataloging in Publication Data
Main entry under title:
Toward a psychology of situations.

Papers presented at a conference on inter-
actional psychology, held June 16–22, 1979, in
Stockholm.
   Bibliography: p.
   Includes index.
   1. Personality and situation—Congresses.
I. Magnusson, David. [DNLM: 1. Interpersonal
relations—Congresses.   2. Social environment—
Congresses.   3. Psychological theory—Congresses.
HM 206 T737 1979]
BF698.9.S55T68   155.9   80-28493
ISBN 0-89859-061-2

Printed in the United States of America

Contents

Preface

The environment has become a focus of interest in many areas of psychology during recent years. In the field of personality, intense theoretical discussion and comprehensive empirical research have drawn attention to the environment, and especially to that part of it that is immediately available to us on every occasion, i.e., to the situation. A necessary consequence of an interactionistic position, which has drawn so much attention both in theorizing and in empirical research during the seventies, is an increased interest in the situations and situational conditions with which an individual is involved in a continuously ongoing, reciprocal interaction process. In this context, many researchers have emphasized that more sophisticated theorizing and more effective and systematic empirical research on situations are prerequisites for a more functional and effective psychology, both in theory and in applied areas.

In 1975 the first international conference on Interactional Psychology was organized in Stockholm (by D. Magnusson and N. S. Endler), resulting in the book *Personality at the Crossroads: Current Issues in Interactional Psychology.* The natural emphasis at that conference was on the person side of person-situation interactions. In the light of what has happened since, an equally natural theme for the second Stockholm conference on Interactional Psychology, held June 16–22, 1979, was "The Situation in Psychological Theory and Research." All 22 papers presented at the symposium are included in this volume. The introductory chapters constituting Part I were written especially for this book. The main aims of these two chapters are to discuss some basic conceptual and methodological problems in analyses of situations and environments, and to suggest some lines for future research. It should be underlined that the introductory chapters do not attempt to summarize major points of the papers presented at the conference. However, in writing the introductory chapters, I have attempted to refer to other papers in the appropriate places.

The book is organized into four parts. Part I consists of the two introductory chapters, written by the editor. In keeping with the discussion in chapter 1 of major problems in environmental analyses, the symposium papers themselves are grouped into three categories, constituting Parts II–IV. Each part is prefaced by an introduction and commentary. The heterogeneity of the field at the present state is reflected in the diversity of the issues, conceptualizations, and methodologies dealt with in the different papers, and because of this diversity the basis for the grouping of the papers into Parts II–IV is not self-evident. Many of the papers discuss problems and issues appropriate to several parts of the book, and other ways of categorizing the papers would have been possible.

The final grouping of the papers is relevant to the following main themes:

Part II: Actual situations and environments.
Part III: Perceived situations and environments.
Part IV: Person-situation interactions.

Since many of the authors have used the same sources, all references have been placed at the end of the book, for easy referral.

The participants' contributions to the symposium and to this book are highly appreciated. Their scientific attitudes and knowledge led to fruitful, stimulating and exciting discussions during the conference.

The symposium was made possible by a grant from the Swedish Council for Humanistic and Social Science Research. It was also supported financially by the University of Stockholm, and the Department of Psychology, University of Stockholm.

The final drafts of chapters 1 and 2 were written during a period when I was staying by invitation at the Netherlands Institute for Advanced Study, which offered a stimulating environment for scientific work. Valuable comments on a preliminary version of the two introductory chapters were given by participants at the symposium and by Vernon L. Allen, Anders Dunér, Charles D. Spielberger, Håkan Stattin and Bertil Törestad. However, I bear full responsibility for the final version of chapters 1 and 2.

I wish to thank Gunnar Backteman, Håkan Stattin, and Bertil Törestad for participating in the organizational work on the symposium, Anita Magnusson for cooperation in the tedious editorial work, Anne Simpson for secretarial help, and Barbro Svensson for her assistance in preparing the symposium and the manuscript of the book.

David Magnusson

ISSUES

Part I contains two chapters written by the editor. In Chapter 1, I have attempted to provide an environmental framework for the analysis of situations and a structure for the categorization of the chapters in this volume. Two different approaches to the study of environments are outlined: analysis of environments "as they are" and analysis of environments "as they are perceived." Four main classes of problems in environmental analyses are distinguished and briefly discussed.

Chapter 2 is concerned with five main themes: (1) conceptual distinctions, set within a historical perspective; (2) the role of situations in principal approaches to research in psychology; (3) the meanings and implications of formulations on perceived environments and situations and their role in person–environment interactions; (4) problems in description and classification of perceived situations; and (5) description and classification of individuals on the basis of interindividual differences in the way they perceive, interpret, and act in situations of different characters.

As pointed out in the preface, this chapter does not aim to be a summary of the other chapters of the book. It is an attempt to provide, in a historical perspective, a conceptual and methodological framework for systematic analyses of environments at the level of situations, to identify and discuss some main problem areas which need special attention,

1

and to indicate what I believe are fruitful lines of research in the future, based on my experiences of fifteen years of theorizing and empirical studies as person–situation interactions and on situations (Magnusson, Gerzén, & Nyman, 1968; Magnusson, 1971; 1974; 1976; 1978; 1980a). The chapter also, I hope, will serve as a framework for the following chapters.

1 Problems in Environmental Analyses—An Introduction

David Magnusson
University of Stockholm

We live in a total environment that forms a complex system of physical–geographical, biological, social, and cultural factors that interact continuously with each other and with the individuals involved. It can be considered on a continuum ranging from a macrolevel to a microlevel (Bronfenbrenner, 1977, 1979; Craik & Zube, 1976; Magnusson, Dunér, & Zetterblom, 1975; Moos, 1973; Stokols, 1977) or ordered along a dimension of its proximity to the individual perceiving it and acting in it (Jessor & Jessor, 1973; Pervin, 1978b).

The environment influences individuals in many ways, directly and indirectly. It is fundamental to the central issue of this book that the environmental influence on individual development and on actual behavior is always mediated via actual situations. It is in actual situations, with their physical–geographical and biological characteristics, that the cultural and social characteristics of the total environment are reflected and can be experienced by individuals. However, it is not just the information offered directly in specific situations that constitutes the environmental influence. Indirectly, great influence is also exercised by the cognitive structures, contents, affective tones, and coping strategies characteristic of an individual's conceptions of the total world and formed in earlier confrontations with various environments. In some sense, past environments are also present. And the norms, values, goals, paths, and other factors that determine the behavior of individuals in a given situation are embedded in and determined by the social and cultural environment at more distal levels.

The Environment "as It Is" and "as It Is Perceived"

There is a conceptual distinction between (1) the environment "as it is" and (2) the environment "as it is perceived," construed, and represented in the mind of an individual who is appearing and acting in it on a certain occasion. This is an old distinction in philosophy and psychology. Philosophers have for a long time discussed the existence of a "real world" outside and independent of the individual. In psychology the distinction was made by early theorists, using various terms to separate the two conceptualizations. For the environment as it is, Koffka (1935) introduced the term *geographical environment* and Murray (1951) talked about *alpha situations*. The perceived environment was referred to by Koffka (1935) as the *behavioral environment,* by Lewin (1936) as *life space,* by Murray (1951) as *beta situations,* by Tolman (1951b) as *the immediate behavior space,* and by Rotter (1955) as *the psychological situation.*

In other contexts, the distinction between the two conceptualizations has been discussed in terms of the *objective* and the *subjective* environment (Magnusson, 1978). As observed by Craik (Chapter 3, this volume), these two terms are inappropriate. The inadequacy of the term objective for the environment as it is is illustrated by the fact that it can be and has been used interchangeably in at least the following four senses, reflecting a mixture of definitions in terms of environmental *content* on the one hand and in terms of *methods* for analyzing and studying environments on the other:

1. As the physical and biological properties of the environment, which can be counted or measured directly by instruments (frequency, pitch, loudness, temperature, humidity, length, weight, density, etc.) and which can be varied and manipulated quantitatively. In this definition, cultural and social factors are excluded.

2. As all the factual conditions of the total, outer world, independent of interpretations by single individuals, with the potential of influencing the behavior of individuals, directly or indirectly. This definition includes, for example, cultural and social factors, such as religion, norms, values, goals, and paths, etc., that are available to the individual and constitute essential factors in his perceptions, interpretations, and conceptualizations of the world.

3. By standardization of the procedures and instruments for data collection.

4. As high consensus (high intersubjectivity) among observers (cf. Brunswik's [1956] discussion of ecological validity).

Taking for granted that an outer world exists and that it can be accounted for, analyzed, and investigated in effective, scientific terms, the old distinction between the world as it is and the world as it is perceived, construed, and represented in the mind of individuals will be maintained here. The former is designated *the actual environment* in the sense described in category 2 just noted and the latter *the perceived environment.* This distinction should be separated from the two kinds of empirical approach to the study of environments which, in Craik's (Chapter 3, this volume) terminology, can be called *technical* and *observational* assessments, respectively.

Three main kinds of *actual* environmental variables have to be distinguished: (1) physical–geographical, (2) biological, and (3) sociocultural. A room with its furniture, books, flowers, and so on may constitute exactly the same physical environment on two occasions but two different biological environments because of differences between the two occasions with respect to number, age, sex, and so on of those present. A certain classroom can define the same physical and biological environment for the pupils in two lessons, say singing and mathematics, but two different sociocultural environments because of differences in the rules, and so on prescribed for behavior in these two kinds of lessons. Theoretical and empirical analyses of actual environments can concern each of these three networks of variables or combinations of them.

For decades, the importance of considering environments and situations as they are *perceived* and *assigned meaning* has been underlined not only by psychologists advocating different theories but also by sociologists and anthropologists. Obviously, the real world in which we experience, feel, think, and act is the world as we perceive it (cf. Baldwin's 1969, term "the effective environment;" Block & Block's "functional situations", Chapter 6; Nowakowska, Chapter 14). According to Thomas (1928): "If men define situations as real, they are real in their consequences." Against that background, we can state that having an understanding of an individual's conceptions of the world and an understanding of his perception and interpretation of the specific situation in which he finds himself makes it possible to understand his actual behavior in that situation. Theoretical analyses and empirical studies on situation perception and the process involved in the transformation of situational information into inner and outer actions may yield results of essential import for psychological theory and application in a variety of central problem areas. Because of the importance of perceived environments and situations for theorizing and research in the field of personality, these issues will be given special attention in Chapter 2.

In the perspective discussed earlier, one important task for psychological theorizing and research is to investigate the relation between perceived and actual environments (in this volume, Hacker, Chapter 8; Nystedt, Chapter 23; Stokols, Chapter 24). Data for actual and perceived environments are complementary. It can be argued that one of the most important tasks in psychology is to explain how an individual's conceptions of the outer world are built up in confrontation with different actual environments in the course of development and how they function in relation to the specific actual properties of situations. In that perspective, also phenomenological data on situations (i.e., data for perceived situations) are of fundamental importance for further scientific progress in the field of psychology. There are no good reasons why such data should not have to be accepted as having enough scientific quality (Jessor, 1956, Chapter 19, this volume). The usefulness of situation–perception data for the elucidation of important psychological problems is discussed in Chapter 2.

Four Main Categories of Problems

The environment has come to the fore in much recent psychology. In theoretical analyses and empirical research, one can discern roughly four main classes of problems.

1. Analyses of Actual Environments and Situations.   This category of problems has been dealt with mainly in theoretical analyses. Most frequently, such analyses have been presented by anthropologists, chiefly interested in the environment at a macrolevel in terms of social and cultural factors (Arsenian & Arsenian, 1948; Chein, 1954), and by sociologists, for the most part interested in generalized situational settings (Ball, 1972; Cottrell, 1942; Goffman, 1974; Stebbins, 1969; Thomas, 1927, 1928). In psychology, Sells (1963a) argued for environmental analyses in physical–geographical terms, and Sherif and Sherif (1956) for analyses in terms of social factors. Lately, the importance of analyses of physical environments has been emphasized by Wohlwill and Kohn (1976), among others. Within the rapidly expanding field of environmental psychology, assessment is concerned with ''. . . the development and application of techniques for the systematic description and evaluation of physical and social environments (Craik, Chapter 3).'' In the present volume, Argyle (Chapter 5), Block & Block (Chapter 6), Carlsson (Chapter 9), Craik (Chapter 3), Fiske (Chapter 4), Hacker (Chapter 8), Price (Chapter 7), and Stokols (Chapter 24) deal with environments and situations in terms of actual properties.

2. Analyses of Perceived Environments and Situations.   In this type of analysis, environments and situations are described and classified in terms of person variables; perceptions, needs, motives, reactions, actions, etc. Empirical studies, dealing with different kinds of situations, directed at different kinds of person variables, and using different approaches to the presentation of the situations and the collection of empirical data, have been published along with theoretical analyses. (For a review, see Magnusson, 1978.) Most of the chapters in this volume deal with environments in person terms. This is especially the case with the chapters by Bem (Chapter 16), Bowers (Chapter 12), Cantor (Chapter 15), James and Sells (Chapter 18), Jessor (Chapter 19), Nowakowska (Chapter 14), Rommetveit (Chapter 10), Rotter (Chapter 11), Sarason and Sarason (Chapter 13), and Sjöberg (Chapter 17).

3. Description and Classification of Individuals in Terms of Situation Perceptions and in Terms of Situation Responses.   This approach to description and classification has a tradition in psychology, reflected in such clinical methods for observation as TAT, CAT, Picture Frustration Test. In these methods, individuals' interpretations and evaluations of a number of situations are used as a basis for diagnosis. That situation perception is an important person characteristic that can be used for classification of individuals was underlined in Magnusson (1971, 1976, 1978; Forgas, 1976). In this volume, Bem (Chapter 16) and Cantor (Chapter 15) point to the possibility of describing a person in terms of how he responds in a particular set of situations. However, it is of interest that not one of the authors in this volume has focused on this approach. In view of its potential value, classification of individuals in situation–perception terms is discussed more fully in Chapter 2.

4. Analyses of Person–Environment Interactions. The formulation of a dynamic interactional model of personality, stressing the continuously ongoing, reciprocal person–situation interaction process, has created a need for systematic theoretical and empirical analyses of the role of situations in that process (Endler & Magnusson, 1976a, 1976b; Magnusson, 1976, 1978; Magnusson & Endler, 1977a). Studies aiming at description and classification of situations in terms of person characteristics, especially those describing and classifying situations in terms of situation perception (see category 2, already mentioned), are highly relevant as a basis from which to understand the role of situations in the person–situation interaction process. Actually some of the chapters that have been referred to category 2 in this volume could as well have been referred to category 4. However, the chapters by Endler (Chapter 22), Hunt (Chapter 20), Nystedt (Chapter 23), and Pervin (Chapter 21) in particular deal with the situation in the frame of reference of person–situation interactions.

The problems to be handled in the four main categories are multifaceted and complex. This diversity of problems cannot be dealt with by a single theory, a single method for data collection, or a single model for data treatment. In each case we have to specify the problem under consideration before we can discuss the appropriate theory, the adequate methods for data collection, and the appropriate model for data treatment. One of the main aims of this book is to contribute to the identification of the important problems to be investigated.

The discrimination of four main categories of problems in environmental analyses has been used as a basis to the structuring of Chapters 3 through 24 in this volume.

As stated in the preface the grouping of the chapters has not been self-evident. Few of them deal exclusively with only one of the main types of problems, and most could be classified in more than one category. The grouping reflects the authors' main direction of interest in environments and situations: if it is in terms of actual properties, if it is in terms of perceptions and behaviors, or if it is in person–situation interactions. On this ground, each chapter has been referred to one of the following parts: Part II, Actual Situations and Environments; Part III, Perceived Situations and Environments; and Part IV, Person–Situation Interactions. (As noted earlier, not one of the authors has devoted his or her main interest to the study of individuals in terms of how they perceive and interpret situations and environments.)

2 Wanted: A Psychology of Situations

David Magnusson
University of Stockholm

THE SITUATION—A SUBJECT OF RESEARCH

This book, as its title indicates, is concerned cheifly with the analysis of what in everyday language is referred to as *situations*. There are several reasons for making situations a subject of analysis and observation.

First, analyses of situations are essential in a developmental perspective. It is in actual situations that we meet the world, form our conceptions of it, and develop our specific kinds of behavior for dealing with it. Situations present, at different levels of specification, the information that we handle, and they offer us the necessary feedback for building valid conceptions of the outer world as a basis for valid predictions about what will happen and what will be the outcome of our own behaviors. By assimilating new knowledge and new experiences in existing categories and by accommodating old categories and forming new ones, each individual develops a total, integrated system of mental structures and contents in a continuous interaction with the physical, social, and cultural environments. On the basis of and within the limits of inherited dispositions, affective tones become bound to specific contents and actions, and coping strategies develop for dealing with various kinds of environments and situations in a continuously ongoing learning process. Thus, physical, biological, social, and cultural aspects of the environment that an individual encounters in the course of development are of decisive importance for the development of his more permanent ways of conceptualizing and dealing with the actual world (Lewis, 1978; Matheny & Dolan, 1975; Runyan, 1978; Wohlwill & Kohn, 1976). In the present volume, Hunt (Chapter 20) gives this perspective special attention. Knowledge of the kinds of actual situations an individual has encountered and the physical, social, and cultural contexts in which they have been embedded

9

helps us to understand his/her world conceptions and his/her behavior in actual situations at different stages of development.

Second, behavior takes place in situations; it does not exist except in relation to certain situational conditions and cannot be understood and explained in isolation from them. Thus, the situation and all its elements must necessarily play a decisive role in any effective model of behavior. Knowledge of and models for the functional interrelations of the network of individual *and* situational factors operating in the continuously ongoing, reciprocal person–situation interaction process are prerequisites for understanding and explaining individual behavior in its situational context. For understanding "the individual *in* the situation," the main unit of research in an interactional paradigm, we need: (1) knowledge about the effective person variables and their interrelations; (2) knowledge about the effective situational variables and their interrelations in relevant terms; and (3) a theory linking these two networks of factors together in the framework of dynamic interaction (cf. Block & Block, ch. 6; Endler, ch. 22).

Connected with the second reason is a *third* one that concerns the role of situations and situational conditions in empirical research in psychology. On the environmental side, the traditional, experimental S-R approach has been mainly interested in *single* stimuli defined in terms of their physical properties which can be manipulated in quantitative terms, assumed to be similarly perceived by all subjects. Cognitively oriented psychology (information processing, decision making, cue probability learning, person perception, etc) has shown a surprisingly low interest in situational effects, both on the input and on the output side of mental processes. An integration of situational factors into the models would certainly contribute to more realistic and more functional models for cognitive processes. Researchers in personality are generally interested in molar, social behavior, and one implication is an interest in general aspects of situations and especially in perceived and appraised qualities.

In order to discuss the role of situational factors in personality research one has to distinguish two kinds of situational effects on behavior, namely (1) *general* effects, and (2) *differential* effects (see Magnusson, 1980a). When situational effects on behavior are general the rank order of individuals for a certain behavior is assumed to be the same across situations, independent of their character. Only the intensity of the behavior changes with variation in situational conditions, but in a monotonic way across individuals. When only general effects are assumed it is appropriate to aggregate data from observations from different situations, as is done in the traditional and very common type of *trait* inventories, in which raw data consist of subjects' answers to questions of the type "Do you usually . . . ?" Such data are generalized measures across situations, expressing each individual's position in a rank order of individuals for a certain type of behavior. This type of data is clearly bound to the trait measurement model, with its basic assumption about stable rank orders of individuals across situations for each type of behavior.

According to an interactional model the characteristic of an individual is in his/her unique *pattern* of stable and changing behaviors across situations of different character or, in terms of data, in his/her partly unique *cross-situational* profile for each of a number of relevant behaviors. This implies an assumption of *differential effects* of situations on individual behavior. In this framework we need situation bound raw data which can be used to express both general interindividual differences in main level of intensity of behaviors *and* the specific unique individual cross-situational patterns reflected in a person by situation matrix of data.

The importance of upholding the distinction between general and differential effects of situations on behavior and of considering their effects on data is demonstrated in the debate on personality consistency. It has been argued that some kinds of variables (cognitive variables such as intelligence, for example) are more stable than others (temperament variables, for example) (cf. Endler & Magnusson, 1976b; Mischel, 1973). This proposition, however, rests on an empirical basis that confounds types of person variables and types of data (Magnusson, 1980a). Most research on intelligence has used situation bound data, which makes it possible to consider differential situational effects, while research on temperament variables has used the traditional type of data from trait inventories, which reflect only general situational effects. This difference in data between the two approaches may have contributed to the reported differences in stability in data between the two types of person variables. The debate on personality consistency clearly illustrates the need for systematic knowledge about situations, so that situational conditions can be considered in a known, predictable, and controlled way.

A *fourth* reason for making situations the subject of observation and research is that more systematic and effective knowledge about the situations in which individuals function will also contribute to more effective applications of psychology. Bronfenbrenner (1977) recently drew attention to the importance and possibility of changing individuals' behaviors by changing crucial aspects of the environments, i.e., by means of so-called transforming experiments. An experiment by Sherif, Harvey, Hoyt, Hood, and Sherif (1961)—in which aggression and hostility amongst boys at camp were transformed into friendliness and cooperation by changes in the situational conditions—shows the effectiveness of the method and the social implications of transforming experiments. Allen and Greenberger (1978), in their theory of vandalism, regard the physical and social conditions under which vandalism occurs as one important source, suggesting the possibility of influencing the amount of vandalism by changing the environment. Stress origins in physical, biological, and psychosocial situations which the individuals experience as too demanding for their capacities (cf. Lazarus, 1966, 1971), and anxiety is a reaction to situations experienced as threatening (cf. Spielberger, 1977). In this volume, Price (Chapter 7) points to the importance—for effective prevention—of identifying situations that are potential generators of maladjustment of undesirable behaviors (cf. also, Hacker's discussion in Chapter 8 of work situations, and Sarason and Sarason's discussion, in Chapter 13, of stress situations). These examples illustrate the need for more and better knowledge about situations as a basis for effective transforming experiments and interventions and for the formation of an environment that is physically, socially, and culturally adapted to the needs and qualifications of individuals.

The implication of the reasons given previously for making situations the subject of research is that situational analyses are not a goal in themselves; they are motivated by the need for more effective theorizing, research, and application in psychology.

A Historical Perspective

As with so many ideas that have become popular in psychology, there is not much new in making the situation the subject of observation and analysis. Sociologists early called attention to the situation and situational conditions. Thomas (1927, 1928) eloquently discussed many of the problems that have been raised and dealt with in recent theorizing and empirical research on situations and that are featured in this book. He noted the distinction between actual and perceived environments and situations per se, discussed the problems connected with defining and demarcating a situation, stressed the developmental role of the situations as individual encounters, and argued that situational conditions must be incorporated in models of actual behavior.

Also, foreshadowing central issues in later psychological discussions, Cottrell (1942) suggested systematic research on situations as a basis for understanding actual behavior. However, in the same issue of *American Sociological Review,* Green (1942) employed the most common argument against making the situation—as perceived and interpreted by individuals—the subject of analysis and research. Social situations, he argued: "... often *mean* something different to the participants, are often *used* for something different, and therefore, often times, *are* different. This is why the study of social situations will never comprise an adequate method of investigating personality [p. 393]."

In psychology, the importance of considering the situation and situational conditions in models of behavior has been underlined by researchers from different angles since the twenties and later (e.g., Angyal, Kantor, Koffka, Lewin, Murray, Tolman, Sullivan). However, with few exceptions—Murray's (1938) suggestion that situations could be classified in terms of the "benefits" and "harms" they exert on the subjects with respect to a certain need, for example—there were no explicit propositions about making the situation the subject of analysis and research and no systematic empirical research on situations appeared until rather late. The first very comprehensive attempt at an analysis of situations and situational conditions was presented by Rotter (1954, 1955). In the frame of reference of social learning theory he discussed what he termed "the psychological situation'' (i.e., the situation as it is interpreted and assigned meaning by the subjects) and suggested that the main characteristics of situations are their ability to arouse *expectations* and their *reinforcement value*. He proposed that situations be empirically classified in terms of *similarity* in four main respects, namely the actor's *expectations,* the *reinforcement value* of the situations, the *actual behavior* of actors, and the *generalization potential* with respect to these three aspects. The similarity approach to the study of situations has subsequently become a main line for empirical investigations.

A potential framework for situational analyses in a dramaturgical perspective was suggested by Goffman (1959; cf. also Harré & Secord, 1972). It provides a conceptual framework in terms of plots, leading and subordinate parts, roles, audiences, stages (back and forth stages), scenery settings, and so on. Hitherto this approach seems to have drawn little attention in empirical work.

An influential contribution to the course of development came from Sells (1963a, 1963b), who at that time presented himself as a proponent of analyses of actual environments and situations. He compiled a comprehensive, detailed scheme for the description and classification of actual environments and situations in physical–geographical terms (1963a) and argued strongly for systematic analyses of situational dimensions. Although other researchers also produced theoretical arguments favoring systematic empirical analysis of situations (Abelson, 1962; Bieri, Atkins, Briar, Leaman, Miller, & Tripodi, 1966; Magnusson & Heffler, 1969; Miller, 1963), such studies were, with few exceptions, very rare until recently.

THE SITUATION AS THE SUBJECT OF ANALYSES

The situation *per se* can be made the subject of theoretical analysis and empirical research, without paying special attention to the role of situations in the continuously ongoing person-situation interaction process (see Chapter 1). Description and classification of situations raises a series of problems of which three main ones will be dealt with here, namely problems with respect to (a) units of analysis, (b) time and space demarcations, and (c) the characteristics than can be used for description and classification.

Units of Analysis

As stated in Chapter 1, the environment can be conceptualized and investigated along a dimension from a microlevel to a macrolevel. For effective theory and research on environments, and on situations in particular, we need to identify appropriate units of analysis along this dimension. Then, of course, any attempt to demarcate units of analysis are to some extent arbitrary; there do not exist any given, definite boundaries. This circumstance is reflected in the many different senses in which the terms *situations* and *situational factors* have been used by the authors in this volume and by others.

With these statements in mind, a few uses of the term *situation* that define different possible units of analyses are discussed. Each unit incorporates the more molecular ones. The concepts and definitions become broader and less specific along two dimensions: from the physical to the perceived properties of situations and from molecular to molar units.

The Actual Situation.   In *physical* and *biological* terms, a situation can be rather strictly defined as that part of the total environment that is available for sensory perception for a certain amount of time. To the physical and biological properties of places (churches, kitchens, clubs, ballrooms, buses, classrooms, laboratories, etc.) are attached *sociocultural* factors—norms, rules, roles, etc.—that contribute to a complete definition of an actual situation (Stokols, Chapter 24, this volume). Separately and in combination, these three types of properties can be used for descriptions and categorization of actual situations.

Within the frame of an actual situation, subunits of analysis can be distinguished. Here, two such units will be mentioned: (1) situational *stimuli;* and (2) situational *events*.

Stimuli—that is, a sound, a barking dog, a snake, etc.—function for a participant as signals in themselves (cf. the discussions of stimuli by Allport [1955] and Gibson [1960]). Description and classification of stimuli in terms of actual properties have been a central issue in research on fear (cf. Braun & Reynolds, 1969; Wolpe & Lang, 1964). In this volume, Fiske (Chapter 4) points to the importance of situational stimuli as units of analysis.

Specific parts of a total situation, which can be delimited in terms of cause and effect (e.g., what a person says or does in response to an immediately preceding act by another person or to a change in the physical and/or biological environment), can be called *events* (cf. Murray's [1938] discussion of "episodes" and Lewin's [1936] definition of an "event"). Events and sequences of events have been proposed as important units of investigation in person by situation interaction research (Golding, 1977; Peterson, 1977; Raush, 1977). An illustrative example may be fetched from studies on dialogues, where the end of one conversational turn and the beginning of a turn by the interlocutor forms the unit of observation and analysis in terms of actual properties (Duncan, 1969; Duncan & Fiske, 1977).

The Perceived Situation.   A perceived situation is defined here as an actual situation as it is perceived, interpreted, and assigned meaning or, in other words, as it is construed by and represented in the mind of a participant.[1] This formula-

---

[1]One distinction with possible consequences in further theorizing on perceived situations and environments is not dealt with here, namely, the distinction between a perceived situation (a) as it is represented in the mind of an observer, and (b) as the situation "out there", i.e., the actual situation with its perceived relations of stimuli and events, and meaning attributed to it by the observer (cf. Allport, 1955).

tion implies the existence of partly different perceived situations for one and the same actual situation, depending on each participant's interpretation.

As suggested in Magnusson (1976), two types of situational factors, constituting two levels of analysis of perceived situations, can be separated: (1) *within* situation factors; and (2) *overall* or *general* situation factors.

The continuous flow of situational stimuli and situational events, as they are interpreted in the mind of an observer, forms the within situation factors. Illustrative examples of research that focus on events and sequences of events in terms of perceptions and interpretations by the participants can be taken from modern work on the educational process for the understanding of what is going on in a classroom (Lundgren, 1977). In this volume (Chapter 17), Sjöberg's analysis of situations in terms of action episodes represents this level of analysis.

Overall or general situation factors are comprised of the perceived and interpreted characteristics of total situations, as frames of reference, steering a subject's selection and interpretation of specific stimuli and events as well as his expectations and predictions with respect to possible and adequate options for action. According to Raush (1977): "Situations are more than specific stimuli. They not only constrain the probabilities that certain behaviors occur and others do not, they also organize the patterning of behavioral sequences [p. 288]."

The Situation Type.   The situation type can be conceived of as the general class of a particular kind of actual and/or perceived situations, without specification of time and place, in contrast to *momentary situations.* For example the situation type corresponding to the momentary situation "being at Joe's barber shop at 8:30, June 29" would be "a barber shop," or "a barber shop in America." In this volume, Bem's (Chapter 16) and Cantor's (Chapter 15) discussions of situation prototypes are close, but not identical, to analyses of situational types.

The Life Situation.   In sociology and anthropology especially, but also in psychology, the term *situation* has been used to represent those parts of the total world that an individual can experience and interpret and does perceive and interpret as having reference to himself and his behavior. In his definitions of a situation, Lewin (1936) discussed both what he called the "general life situation" or "life space" and what he designated "the momentary situation." One side of the life situation of an individual is constituted by the actual conditions under which he lives: type of profession and work organization, family relations, socioeconomic standards, type of geographical area, and so on. Another side of his own experiences and evaluations of these conditions. In psychoanalytic theory, the perceived life situation is a key concept and this is even more the case in existential psychology (Frankl, 1973). World conceptions ("Weltanschauung"; cf. also "perceptions of reality," Schatzman & Strauss, 1966) have become an issue for theorizing and research as an essential aspect of an individual's subjective life situation.

A further breakdown of this unit of analysis can be highly appropriate for other purposes. For example, *behavioral settings* (Barker, 1965, 1968) and their perceptual–cognitive representations, *organizations* (James & Jones, 1974, 1976), and *institutions* (Moos, 1973, 1975; Insel & Moos, 1974) have formed units for analysis and research (cf. also Stokols' analysis of *"social fields,"* Chapter 24, this volume). At different levels, the life situation of an individual in his own interpretation forms one important frame of reference surrounding his choice of environments, organizations, and situations (insofar as he has alternatives) and for his interpretations of actual momentary situations and of what is going on within them.

In this volume, Jessor's analysis of perceived environments (Chapter 19), James and Sells' analysis of psychological climates of organizations (Chapter 18), Price's analysis of risky situations (Chapter 7), and Stokols' analysis of group–place transactions (Chapter 24) deal with these units of analysis.

Comments.   Naturally enough, in view of the character of their disciplines, psychologists, sociologists, and anthropologists have differed and still differ in their focus of interest in the environment. Psychologists have devoted themselves mainly to actual and perceived situations with their stimuli and events, whereas sociologists and anthropologists have been more interested in situational types and life situations as factors of importance for the behavior of individuals and groups.

The *individual* himself and his own reactions are, both in defining the total situation and as part of the continuous flow of situational stimuli and situational events during the situation process, influential parts of his perceptual–cognitive appraisal (Sheldon, 1951; Tolman, 1951b). For example, if a boy blushes during a conversation with a girl, this reaction may form an important element in his perception and evaluation of the situation and influence his reactions and actions in the next stage of the process.

With respect to perceived environments, the units of analysis can be discussed in terms of *figure–ground* (cf. also the discussion by Allport (1955) on *core–context* relationships). Then the more molar environmental units form the ground for the perception and interpretation of each underlying unit. For example, the momentary situation can be said to form the ground for the interpretation of situational stimuli and events, an organization forms the ground for interpretation of a momentary situation, and the total life situation forms the ground for the perception and interpretation of an organization, a behavioral setting, or a momentary situation (Rokeach & Kliejunas, 1972).

Most of the discussion in the rest of this chapter is formulated in terms referring to actual and perceived situations and situational types. This does not mean to say that there exist clear boundaries between the various units of analysis or that situational stimuli, situational events, and life situations are unimportant units of analysis. Much of what is said about actual situations and situational types also has a bearing on these issues.

The Horizontal Dimension–Time Demarcations

Inherent in the previous discussion of momentary situations is the time dimension. In the continuously changing flow of environmental conditions that an individual meets, a situation—as the unit of research—has to be demarcated in time; it has a beginning and an end. In some cases the time boundaries are rather obvious, and all participants would agree on when the situation starts and when it ends. This is the case for a dinner, a committee meeting, or a ball game, for example. However, in most cases the time boundaries are elusive and open for discussion. Actually, only limited parts of the continuously changing environment can be meaningfully defined as momentary situations along the time dimension.

For some types of situations, one basis for a meaningful definition of the time boundaries would be, for example, in terms of generative rules that dominate the scene under some particular circumstances for a particular part of time (Argyle, 1977; Chapter 5, this volume). Then a situation lasts as long as the same generative rules prevail under specified environmental conditions on a certain occasion. This is a demarcation of a situation in terms of actual sociocultural properties. A demarcation in perceptual–cognitive terms, leading to somewhat different definitions for different individuals, was proposed by Stebbins (1969). He suggested that a psychological situation prevails for an individual until he reaches ''the end he was pursuing when he entered the objective situation [p. 152].''

The Momentary Situation—A Space of Action and a Space of Observation

For some purposes, it might be fruitful to define a momentary situation as the interface of the ''vertical'' distal-proximal dimension and the ''horizontal'' time dimension, as illustrated in Figure 2.1. The figure illustrates the essential fact that a perceived situation cannot be discussed and investigated effectively without consideration of its context, both on the vertical and on the horizontal dimension (cf. Lewin, 1936; and Kelley, 1955, respectively). Three ways of dealing with the momentary situation jointly on the two dimensions will be distinguished.

1. As a Space of Action.   An actor is passing through a momentary situation in a process of continuous, reciprocal interaction with other elements. Among situational elements involved in the interaction, other individuals are especially important.

On the physical situation side the information available at each specific moment can be separated into three categories from the standpoint of the actor; (a) what is in the focus of attention, (b) what is considered but peripheral and not attended to, and (c) what is not considered at all. That which is in focus of attention changes continuously and depends upon the characteristics of the situa-

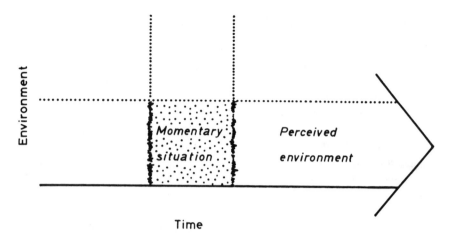

FIG. 2.1. The momentary situation as the interface of time and space.

tion and the character of the individual's problem at the moment. What is peripheral but considered, in the sense that it affects actual behavior, likewise changes continuously (cf. Nowakowska, ch. 14). There is also a continuous change with respect to the relative role of external factors in this process. Peripheral perceptions and interpretations function unreflectively but very effectively in many situations (cf. Bowers' discussion of the role of "unconscious factors" in chapter 12, and Cantor's discussion of "indirect" context effects, in chapter 15). It is common experience that one can walk as usual to work while thinking about a problem—which brings various sets of abstractions and conceptions into focus—and paying no attention to all the external cues that actually steer one's way and one's steps.

The temporal character of the dynamic person-situation interaction was underlined by Fiske (1977) and Raush (1977). What is in the focus of attention, and what is peripheral but considered are dependent at each specific moment upon what happened the moment before, and determine to some extent what will happen next in the process. Adjacent situations also influence each other; cognitive and emotional states in a situation may be influenced by knowledge of an approaching anxiety provoking situation and the applied expectations.

2. As a Space of Observation, with the Actor as the Observer.   On instruction, the actor himself may undertake to observe and account for his own perceptions, interpretations, reactions, and actions. This, however, renders the process reflective to an extent uncommon in everyday life. Such an instruction will affect—to an unknown degree—the very perceptions, interpretations, reactions, and actions that are under consideration. This gives rise to a problem of the validity of the data when one wants to describe and classify situations in terms of person variables and when situation perceptions, reactions, and actions are used as a basis for classifying people.

3. As a Space of Observation, with Another Person or Other Persons as Observer(s). In this case self-reports are not obtained from the actor(s). The object of interest is actual reactions and behaviors displayed by the actor(s) in relation to different aspects (especially other individuals), stable or temporary, of the situation.

Comments. The problems in defining a situation with reference to both dimensions at the same time and in observation within the frame of references of momentary situations are not unique to psychology. They arise in principle in other sciences too, when observations are made of processes in which different elements are in continuous reciprocal interaction with each other, as for example in thermodynamics in physics and in meteorology. A common problem lies in the effect, on the process studied, of procedures of measurement. One essential characteristic of the problem in psychology is that the object of interest in a momentary situation, namely the person, is an active intentional agent in the continuously ongoing, reciprocal person–situation interaction process.

Situation Characteristics

There is not one single characteristic or a definite set of characteristics that can be used for all purposes in analyses of situations. According to Rommetreit, in this volume, "The meaning potential of a given situation must hence be conceived of as a set of aspects and patterns of aspects [Chapter 10]." Depending on the problem, the approximate properties to be investigated vary. Among situation characteristics that have been discussed and can be used as fruitful bases for description and classification of situations, the following are of special interest (for a more elaborated discussion, see Magnusson, 1978; cf. also Block & Block, Chapter 6, this volume):

1. *Complexity* (cf. Schroder, Driver, & Streufert, 1967; Shalit's 1977 discussion of *differentiation;* and Rommetveit's discussion of *referential alternatives,* Chapter 10, this volume).
2. *Clarity* (cf. the *overt–covert* dimension discussed by Warr & Knapper, 1968; the *salience* dimension discussed by Stokols, 1979; and in Chapter 24, this volume, the *articulation* dimension discussed by Shalit, 1977, 1979; and *texture,* discussed by Jessor, Chapter 19, this volume).
3. *Strength* (Magnusson, 1974; Mischel, 1973).
4. *Promotion* vs *restriction* (Barker, 1968; Chein, 1954; Insel & Moos, 1974; Jahoda, 1961; Lazarus, 1974; Price & Bouffard, 1974; Proshansky, Ittelson, & Rivlin, 1970; Wallace, 1967; Wolk, 1976).

5. *Tasks* (cf. Sherif & Sherif, 1956; see the discussion of *demands* by Lazarus, 1974; and of *problems* by Goldfried & D'Zurilla, 1969; and by Goldfried & Kent, 1972).
6. *Rules* (Argyle, 1977, Chapter 5, this volume).
7. *Roles* (Cattell, 1963; Rotter, 1954; Thomas, 1927, 1928).
8. *Physical settings* (Barker, 1965; Craik, Chapter 3, this volume; Price, 1974a; Stokols, Chapter 24, this volume).
9. *Other person* (Block, 1952; Goffman, 1959; Golding, 1977; Peterson, 1977; Rommetveit, Chapter 10, this volume).

These characteristics mostly come under what were termed *actual situational properties* (p. 4). Situations can also be characterized in terms of *person-bound properties,* and among those discussed as having a potential value for that purpose are the following:

1. *Goals* (Argyle, Chapter 5, this volume; Fuller, 1950; Pervin, Chapter 21, this volume; Rommetveit, Chapter 10, this volume; Rotter, 1954; Sarason & Sarason, Chapter 13, this volume; Sjöberg, Chapter 17, this volume; Stebbens, 1969; Stokols, Chapter 24, this volume).
2. *Perceived control* (Allen & Greenberger, 1978; Averill, 1973; Stokols, Chapter 24, this volume).
3. *Expectancies* (Lazarus, 1966; Rotter, 1955; Wortman & Brehm, 1975).
4. *Needs and motivations* (Murray, 1938; Rotter, 1955).
5. *Affective tones or emotions* (Mehrabian & Russell, 1974; Pervin, 1977; Shalit, 1977).

Another distinction that can be made is between what might be called *structural* characteristics—such as complexity, clarity, strength, promotion versus restriction—and *content* characteristics—such as tasks, rules, roles, goals, expectancies, and motivations. The former kind of characteristics is more general and quantitative, permitting a rank ordering of environments at different levels of generality for each of a number of specified aspects. On the other hand, content variables are more situation bound, specific and qualitative in nature, implying suitability for qualitative analysis of situations and of dynamic person–situation interactions.

The most frequently discussed among the structural characteristics is that rank ordering environments and situations with respect to their *restrictive* versus *promotive* effect on various kinds of behavior. The restrictive effect on actual behavior of the physical, biological, cultural, and/or psychosocial aspects of some situations, settings, and environments (e.g., prisons, hospitals, poverty-stricken neighborhoods, religions, educational systems) can be very strong and prohibit exploratory behavior and constructive action and, instead, lead to passivity and reactive or even destructive behavior. This implies, among other things, that the restrictive versus promotive character of environments and situations is important in the analysis of developmental processes (Hunt's discussion in Chapter 20, this volume, about the role of environments in development). The character of restrictions and promotions, the types of behaviors that are restricted versus promoted, and the strength with which reinforcements and punishments are inferred play a crucial role in the learning process in which individuals' perceptions, interpretations, and ways of dealing with the external world are formed. On these grounds, analyses of environments and situations in terms of restriction promotion of various kinds of behaviors and of the effects on actual behavior and development of such characteristics are an essential task for psychological research.

Another central situation variable that has been especially underlined by several authors in this volume is *goals* or intentions. Intentions and goals are central steering factors influencing which situations an individual seeks insofar as he has alternatives, which cues he attends to, and which strategies he applies for dealing with situational information. Long-term goals are important factors in an individual's life pattern in a very broad and general sense, whereas short-term goals may be bound to specific types of situations and occasions and may differ at different stages of development. In the frame of field theory, Fuller (1950) suggested that situations be distinguished with respect to three main characteristics, all concerned with the actors' goals: (1) goal objects (field incentive); (2) obstacles between the organism and goal (field impedence); and (3) paths to goals (field complexity). Stebbins (1969) stated that goals in terms of *action orientation* are basic elements underlying the psychological structure of situations and suggested situational analyses in such forms.

PERCEIVED SITUATIONS AND ENVIRONMENTS

It is trivial to state that situations and environments influence individuals' thoughts, feelings, and actions. Such a statement has to be qualified. The individual is not a passive object for environmental forces. Even if environmental influence to some extent may be unidirectional, the basis for the discussion here is the assumption that the individual is the active, intentional subject in a continuously ongoing reciprocal person by situation interaction process. The person seeks some situations and avoids others. He is affected by the situations in which he occurs, but he also affects what is going on and continuously contributes to changes in situational and environmental conditions both for himself and for others. In this process, it is of decisive importance, in what way he selects situations, stimuli and events and perceives, construes and evaluates them in his cognitive processes. This makes situations and environments as they are perceived and appraised by individuals a crucial subject of analysis and research. The role of perceived situations and environments is reflected in the interest devoted to that subject in several of the papers in this volume.[2]

Momentary Perceptions—Persistent Abstractions

An individual's perception and cognitive evaluation of momentary situations. stimuli and events is determined by his rather persistent, integrated system of abstractions and conceptions of the world, including his self-conceptions. Various theories and models for cognitive processes, of interest for the present discussion, have been presented [cf. for example, the discussion of schemata by Piaget (1947), Neisser (1976), and Rumelhart (1976); of scripts, plans, and goals by Schank & Abelson (1977); of semantic networks by Woods (1975); of programs by Amasov (1967); coping strategies and skills by Bruner, Goodman & Austin (1956); and Lazarus & Launier (1978)]. Mischel (1973) suggested that cognitive processes in an individual's interaction with the environment should be discussed in terms of cognitive competence, encoding strategies, expectancies, subjective stimulus value, and self-regulatory systems and plans. They can also be discussed in terms of (a) *contents,* (b) *structures,* (c) *affective tones* and (d) *coping strategies and skills* (Magnusson, 1980b). An individual's total system of structured contents, with their affective tones, and with the coping strategies, constitutes an important basis for his way of dealing with situational information both in his "inner," private world and in his interaction with his environment. It contributes to determine which environments and situations he seeks or avoids, which situational properties he attends to and how he interprets them. Which contents and affective tones that are activated and which coping strategies that are brought into action in the cognitive process of a certain individual at a certain occasion depends, among other things, upon the situational conditions, stimuli and events and how they are perceived and evaluated by him. According to these formulations, perceptual and cognitive processes are central issues in personality theory and research, implying that the traditional separation of personality from cognitive theory is artificial and obsolete.

It is surprising to note how negligent many cognitive theorists have been of the importance in this process of the affective tones bound to specific situations, stimuli and events and their cognitive representations. Such tones become linked to particular situations, stimuli and events in the developmental process of learning and maturation (Piaget, 1947), and they contribute to determine an individual's seeking or avoiding situations and environments, and his interpretation of situational information, sometimes to a decisive extent. Also, in the continuously

---

[2]Analogous to the widely accepted use of the term "person perception," the term "situation perception" will be used here in a broad sense to cover the process by which situations and situational conditions are perceived, cognitively construed and appraised.

ongoing interplay between affective tones and physiological processes they play an important role.

An individual's system of self-conceptions and world abstractions and conceptions is formed and gradually changes in a continuous interaction with the environments that he encounters. In that process generalizations and discriminations in the perception of situations, stimuli and events develop, specially at early stages in the course of development. Experienced threat in, say, an achievement demanding situation may generalize to a wide range of similar situations, making way for avoiding behavior. In the process of learning and maturation—on the basis and within the limits of their inherited dispositions—individuals develop total mental systems that are partly unique with respect to contents and their organizations, with respect to the affective tones bound to specific situations, stimuli and events, and with respect to the coping strategies and skills for dealing with situational and stored information.

Common and Unique Situation Perception

The reasoning above leads to the conclusion that both the more permanent abstractions and conceptualizations of the world and the momentary perceptual-cognitive construction and evaluation of specific situations, stimuli and events are partly common and partly unique to individuals (cf. for example, Rommetveit's discussion of "shared social meanings" and "private worlds", Chapter 10, this volume).

It is understandable—in the developmental learning process—that *environments* that are partly similar and partly different for individuals contribute to abstractions and conceptions that are partly similar and partly unique. For the development of unique individual situation perceptions, *person factors* also play an important role. There are interindividual differences—from the beginning determined genetically but subsequently also due to learning—with respect both to vulnerability to some types of situations and to ability in receiving, interpreting, and using the environmental information that is important for the formation of environmental abstractions and conceptions. There are also important interindividual differences in *physiological* traits and states, learned and inherited, that contribute to influencing in a partly unique way the situations, events, and stimuli that an individual seeks and avoids, and how they are perceived, experienced, and reacted to.

What has been discussed in terms of common and unique situation perception implies the problem about *consensus* among actors that has been dealt with from various angles by different authors in this volume (Block & Block, Chapter 6; James & Sells, Chapter 18; Stokols, Chapter 24). Obviously, there is no simple answer to the question of whether high consensus is needed or not. If the main problem is to classify, as unambiguously as possible, a set of situations in terms of situation perception, as for example, in this volume, in Bem's study of situation templates (Chapter 16), in Cantor's search for situation prototypes (Chapter 15), or in Stokol's analysis of social fields (Chapter 24), high consensus among the actors obviously is wanted. On the other hand, low overall consensus is a prerequisite for categorizing individuals in terms of how they perceive, interpret or react in certain kinds of situations, say, anxiety provoking situations.

The fact that situation perception is to some extent individually unique has led some researchers to somewhat pessimistic conclusions about the possibility of describing and classifying situations in terms of situation perception. (Endler, Chapter 22, this volume; Green, 1942; Pervin, Chapter 21, this volume). However, the very fact that situation perception is both common and unique is the fundamental reason for using situation perception data for classification of both situations and individuals. In the domain of anxiety-provoking situations, for example, a series of important problems can be formulated and dealt with. Which situations are generally anxiety provoking for youngsters of a certain age? Which sex and age differences exist in that respect? Which situations are anxiety provoking for some but not for others? What aspects of situations make them generally anxiety provoking and what makes some situations anxiety provoking to some individuals but not to others?

SITUATION PERCEPTION—A FIELD OF RESEARCH

In Chapter 1, four classes of problems in environmental analyses were distinguished. With reference to three of those classes, situation perception can be discussed as an important field of theorizing and research: (1) As an intervening variable in personality theories and models of behavior. (2) As a basis for description and classification of situations, stimuli and events in person terms. (3) As a person characteristic, which can be used for description and classification of individuals.

The general idea of defining situations in terms of person variables, and individuals in terms of situation variables at the same time, is not new. In classical test theory the difficulty of single items (i.e., task-defined situations) is defined in person terms as the proportion of correct answers for each problem, and individual capacity for solving a certain kind of problem is determined in situation terms from the proportion of correct answers for the individual (cf. Magnusson, 1967). Thus the same data are used for measuring item difficulty (situations) and individual ability as a person characteristic.

Situation Perception in Models of Personality

The dynamic character of the continuously ongoing, reciprocal person—situation interaction process in which individual behavior is formed, and the role of individual situation perception in that process were underlined earlier. In an interactional model of personality, situation perception plays a key role, as an intervening variable by which actual situational conditions influence both "inner life" and actual behavior. According to such a model individuals differ in their *patterns* of stable and changing behaviors across situations.[3] The interindividual differences in cross-situational patterns of behavior are then explained by interindividual differences in the modes by which situational information is perceived, interpreted and treated in the actors' perceptual-cognitive processes. Most explicitly, the crucial role of how individuals perceive and appraise situational information as a determinant of actual behavior, has been discussed and investigated in research on stress and anxiety, in which perceived demands and threats in the environment are central concepts (see e.g., Endler, 1975b; Lazarus, 1966; Lazarus, Averill & Opton, 1974; Spielberger, 1972).

The key role of situation perception as "the point of engagement between organism and environment" (Pervin, 1978b, p. 83) in the person-situation interaction process makes research on the relation between situation perception and actual situational conditions, as well as on the relation between situation perception and reactions and actions, important fields of theorizing and research. It also implies a need for systematic analyses of situations, especially analyses yielding descriptions and classifications in terms of how situations are perceived, interpreted, reacted to and acted in.

Description and Classification of Situations in Person Terms

To a varying extent situations differ systematically with respect to how they are perceived and interpreted. Some situations are generally experienced as more threatening than others; some situations are experienced as ego-threatening while others are experienced as pain threatening, for example. This circumstance constitutes the basis for description of situations in terms of situation perception, and classification on the basis of similarity among situations in perceived and evaluated qualities. Among the first to classify situations empirically in terms of *situation perception* were Pervin (1968) using a semantic differential technique, and Magnusson (1971) using multidimensional scaling for analyzing similarity data. In this volume, analyses in terms of how individuals perceive and interpret situations are given special consideration by Bowers (Chapter 12), Cantor (Chap-

---

[3]An interactional model of behavior, stressing the cross-situational pattern of stable and changing behaviors as the characteristic of an individual, supports an idiographic approach to personality research, which might lead to a renewed interest in typologies (cf. Magnusson, 1976; in this volume Bem, ch. 16; Block & Block, ch. 6; Pervin, ch. 21). The fruitfulness of grouping individuals on the basis of their cross-situational profiles has been demonstrated empirically for various types of variables (see, for example, Magnusson, 1978; Magnusson & Ekehammar, 1975a; Magnusson & Stattin, 1978a).

ter 15), Jessor (Chapter 19), Rommetveit (Chapter 10), Rotter (Chapter 11), and Nystedt (Chapter 23).

As a consequence of differences among situations with respect to how they are perceived and interpreted, there are intersituation differences also with respect to other person bound factors that are involved in the dynamic person-situation interaction process and which are related to the individuals' perceptual-cognitive appraisal of situations. Description and classification of situations in such terms have mostly been performed on data for *affective reactions* (feelings), *somatic reactions* or *molar actions*. To give a few examples, Endler, Hunt and Rosenstein (1962); Ekehammar, Magnusson, and Ricklander (1974); and Magnusson and Ekehammar (1975a) studying situations in terms of somatic and affective reactions; by Mehrabian and Russell (1974), studying them in terms of emotions; and by, among others, Price (1974b), studying them in terms of actions. In the present volume, this approach is represented in empirical studies by Bem (Chapter 16), Block and Block (Chapter 6), and Sjöberg (Chapter 17).

Some of the problems of conceptualization and methodology in classification of situations have been dealt with earlier in this chapter (pp. 19–20) and elsewhere (Endler, Chapter 22; Magnusson, 1978; Pervin, 1978b). Here only a few problems of special importance are touched upon.

Situation Perception—Behavior.   Analysis of situations in terms of somatic or affective reactions or in terms of molar behavior and actions are of interest in themselves. Situation data of the latter sort are also noteworthy as indicators of how the situations are perceived and interpreted. This raises the question of the relation between situation perception and situation reaction data (Ekehammar, Schalling, & Magnusson, 1975; Magnusson & Ekehammar, 1975b, 1978; Stattin & Magnusson, 1978). The relation is of special relevance in an interactional model of behavior, in which interindividual differences in actual behavior are explained in terms of interindividual differences in situation perception. For such explanations to be effective, we need not only appropriate data for situation perception and for behavior but also an effective theory for defining the appropriate situation perception factors and behavior factors to be linked together and for formulating adequate hypotheses about the relation investigated (Magnusson & Endler, 1977a). This is important because there is not a one-to-one relationship between the two kinds of person factors (compare Hammond's [1955] discussion of equipotentiality and equifinality of person factors).

Data Collection and Data Treatment.   One important decision in analysis of situations in person terms concerns the way in which the situations under consideration should be presented to the judges. Most research hitherto has been performed on data for hypothetical situations presented *verbally*. Other feasible means of presentation take the form of *pictures* or *films* (Craik, Chapter 3, this volume). As argued by several of the authors in this volume, it is essential that research in this area be based, as far as possible, on data from *real-life situations*. Good examples of such research are presented in this volume by Pervin (Chapter 21) and Sjöberg (Chapter 17).

When person variables are used as the basis for systematic analyses of situations, the problems connected with data collection methods are for the most part the same as those in other psychological research, and the same arsenal of methods is at our disposal: direct observation, self-report, free description, interview, inventories, psychophysical methods, and semantic differential technique, the Rep Test, Q-sort, and so on, yielding quantitative and qualitative data.

It is similar with problems of data treatment. When the appropriate data have been collected, the structure of the data space with respect to dimensions and categories can be investigated with traditional methods.

In data treatment, the fact that situation perception is partly unique implies certain methodological considerations. The appropriacy of applying some multidimensional scaling methods—factor analysis, for example—to situation-perception data for groups of individuals depends on the extent to which the data matrix contains individually unique variance. If such variance is large, the factor pattern will be blurred and will seem confusing even though each individual matrix of data may have a clear, meaningful structure, as was demonstrated empirically in Magnusson (1971).

Definition of Situation Domains—Sampling.   To define the situation domain to be investigated is important on two counts. First, not all situations are of interest in psychological research—most of the time situations in which people appear are trivial from a psychological point of view. Second, in keeping with what might be assumed about objects in a cognitive space, it seems reasonable to assume that a certain situation derives its meaning not from its relation to all other situations in the individual's total cognitive space but rather from its relation to situations in a subspace, consisting of situations to which it bears some meaningful relations (Magnusson, 1971). Therefore, to introduce data for situations from quite different domains without meaningful relations in the same multidimensional scaling procedure, for example, might yield meaningless results.

The character of the situational categories and dimensions obtained in empirical analyses depends on, among other things, the generality-specificity of the situation domain investigated. Say social situations were to be analyzed at each of the following three levels of generality: (1) social situations in general; (2) social, active situations with peers; and (3) social, active situations with peers of own sex during leisure time. It is only natural and no source of confusion that the dimensionality and the categorization will differ among these domains of situations even though they all represent social situations. A special problem concerns the possible confounding of domains and level of generality in the sample of situations investigated. The importance of considering the level of definition of the situation domain in interpretation of empirical results is clearly illustrated in the work presented by Cantor in Chapter 15, this volume.

Having defined a situational domain, one faces the problem of adequate sampling (Magnusson & Heffler, 1969; Pervin, 1978b; Price, Chapter 7, this volume). Much of the research in certain areas—anxiety research, for example—has lacked generality and has contributed only confusion because the situations have been adopted for analysis without any attempt at systematic sampling. When interest is focused on situations in terms of person variables, one way to arrive at a representative, adequate sample of situations is to let individuals of an appropriate group describe situations belonging to the domain under consideration (Forgas, 1976; Janisse & Palys, 1976; Magnusson & Stattin, 1979; Pervin, 1976; Cantor, Chapter 15; Pervin, Chapter 21; Sjöberg, Chapter 17).

SITUATION PERCEPTION—A PERSON CHARACTERISTIC

The way situations, stimuli and events are perceived and cognitively construed is an important person characteristic, and situation perception is potentially one of the most meaningful and fruitful bases we have for characterizing individuals. A few examples of areas in which situation perception can be used for description and classification of individuals are discussed briefly.

Common Situation Perception—a Group Characteristic

As discussed earlier (p. 23), individuals belonging to a group raised or living and functioning in an environment that is to some extent homogeneous in essential physical, biological, social, and/or cultural respects will, to some degree, share common world conceptions and have some common situation perception variance (Stokols, Chapter 24, this volume). This is true for individuals belonging to the same culture, the same subculture, the same working group, the same peer group, and so on. This fact constitutes the basis for research directed at differences in situation perception for groups who differ with regard to some important characteristics such as (1) *age*; (2) *sex*; (3) *culture* (Magnusson, in press). Such differences are of interest both in themselves and as a basis for understanding actual behavior (Magnusson, 1971).

1. The way individuals perceive and interpret situations is formed in a process of learning and maturation and situation perception is thus a focal area for investigation in a longitudinal perspective. In such a perspective the relation between, on the one hand, situation perception—including perception of stimuli, events, and life situations—and on the other, cognitive, intellectual, and emotional factors is of special note. Jessor and Jessor (1973) have suggested that the study of age curves for situation perception is as relevant and needed as the study of age curves for intelligence. In a recent study, Magnusson and Stattin (1980)

investigated age differences with respect to two aspects of anxiety-provoking situations, namely, what *triggers* state anxiety and the *expected consequences*.

2. Sex differences in situation perception—say, in a certain type of situation such as anxiety or anger-provoking ones—are of interest in themselves too. Studies of such differences may also contribute to the understanding of sex differences in actual behavior and in physiological reactions which have been demonstrated in empirical research. Are, for example, sex differences in physiological reactions in achievement-demanding situations (Bergman & Magnusson, 1979; Frankenhaeuser, 1978) a consequence of differences in actual reactions to situations that are perceived similarly; or can they be explained in terms of differences in the perception and evaluation of such situations?

3. Hitherto, psychologists have displayed little interest in situation perception as a basis for understanding subcultural or cross-cultural differences in actual behavior. With few exceptions (Lazarus, Opton, Tomita, & Kodama, 1966), empirical psychological research has not allowed for the possibility that the perception of single situations may differ markedly across cultures, thus leading to differences in emotions, in reactions, and in molar behaviors. In a recent study by Magnusson and Stattin (1978b), results on anxiety reactions demonstrated striking cultural differences for specific situations. This is shown in Fig. 2.2. The most likely account of the cross-cultural differences in reactions is that they were

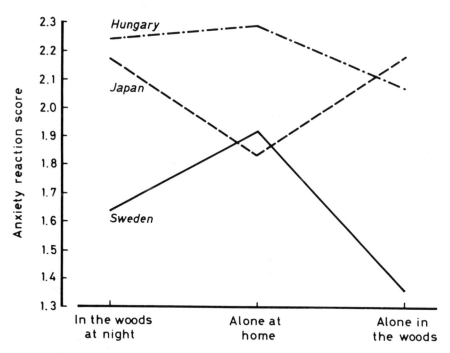

FIG. 2.2.   Cross-situational reaction profiles for teenagers from Hungary, Japan, and Sweden.

caused by differences in perceptions of the specific situations, arising from differences in the geographical, social, and cultural environments during the course of development.

Preliminary findings indicate that the patterns of reaction factors (a psychic and a somatic reaction factor) are very similar in Japan and Sweden, although the situation factors differ between the two countries. This indicates that when anxiety is experienced, the way in which it is expressed is similar in the two cultures, although there are differences with regard to the situations that arouse anxiety.

Unique Situation Perception—an Individual Characteristic

The uniqueness of situation perception makes this a useful tool for characterizing individuals in terms of deviations from what is common, in (1) clinical *diagnoses*; (2) *selection and guidance* procedures; and (3) studies of *effects of specific treatments*. Each individual's perception of a specific situation or of a certain set of situations is then seen in relation to what it has in common with and deviant from the perceptions of a relevant sample of other persons.

1. At the core of many neuroses and psychoses are misperceptions and misinterpretations of the outer world. This may be the case for the total environment, as in severe psychoses, or for certain situations, as in some types of phobias, for example, claustrophobia. Thus, to offer an individual a set of situations, including some that are hypothesized to play a central role in his conflict, and to compare his interpretations of them with those made by a relevant group of individuals is one method for getting at the core of a person's problem in order to plan adequate treatment (see the use of TAT, CAT, Picture Frustration Test, etc., in clinical diagnosis). In this context, empirical studies on interindividual differences in the perception of anxiety-provoking, anger-provoking and disappointment-provoking situations seem especially fruitful.

2. Professions and jobs—of, say, policeman, social worker, businessman, and teacher—differ in both the situations they offer and the demands they exert. Success in a job is very often a matter of a person's capacity to deal with its characteristic situations and their demands. To some extent, this depends in turn on how the situations are perceived and interpreted by the individual. This suggests that interindividual differences in perceptions and interpretations of crucial job situations are a valuable basis for guidance and selection.

3. One of the most convincing signs of a therapy's adequacy would lie in its ability to effect a real change in the perception of crucial situations. Expressed in terms of cognitive representation, the perception is supposed to change from what is deviant to what is normal for individuals of the same reference group. Thus situation perception data can be used in evaluating not only the effect of individual therapy but also group effects in so-called transforming experiments, for example.

CONCLUDING REMARKS

The discussion in this chapter has revealed a dire need for systematic knowledge, in appropriate terms, about environments and especially about situations: (1) for the understanding of actual behavior and development; (2) for the ability to control and deal with environmental and situational factors in a known and predictable way in empirical personality research; and (3) as a basis for effective temporary changes in undesirable environments as well as for the formation of physical, biological, cultural, and psychosocial environments that can offer individuals and groups situations in which they can develop all their potentialities and use them in an active, constructive way. To reach this goal we need a psychology of situations (Magnusson, 1978).

To make situations and situational conditions units of research involves many difficult and sometimes new problems. In this field we are now, in some respects, in the same position as psychology was at the beginning of systematic research on individual differences. Many of the problems are principally the same and, somewhat distressingly, so are many of the arguments against making the situation a field of research. However, in another respect the situation is different. As demonstrated in this chapter, much theoretical and empirical work has been done on situations, providing an important basis for further research. What seems to be essential now is to structure the problem area and to identify the most fruitful directions for further theorizing and research. The symposium at which the chapters in this volume were first presented aimed at such a contribution.

One issue of debate has been the problem of taxonomy of situations. It needs hardly be said that one cannot expect a single, definite solution. Jessor has stated in this volume, ''There is no single mapping of the content of the psychological environment that would make sense given the diversity of the enterprise of psychology [Chapter 19].'' There is not one given set of categories or dimensions that is appropriate for effectively resolving all the psychological problems that require knowledge about situations. Not all categorical or dimensional solutions are appropriate for every problem; but each problem may have its adequate solution. Then the essential basis for analyses of situations and situational conditions is the set of psychological problems that we formulate. Depending on the problem, the appropriate situation characteristic to investigate, the appropriate kind of data—quantitative or qualitative—and the appropriate method of data analysis, all vary.

Part of the discussion in this chapter has employed formulations about static situations as snapshots of available parts of the environment. Such analyses belong to a mechanistic person–situation interaction approach. A dynamic interaction model stresses the continuously ongoing person–situation interaction process in which individuals actively seek or avoid some situations, influence and transform situations and environments by their activities, temporarily and over time, and are influenced by situational and environmental factors at different levels of generality (Magnusson & Endler, 1977b). For the future, one of the more essential tasks is to analyze theoretically and to investigate empirically situations and environments in the framework of dynamic person–situation and person–environment interactions.

In forthcoming research on situations, we should learn from our experience of the fallacies in research on individual differences (Mischel, 1977b). Research on situations can never be a goal in itself; it is motivated by the contributions it yields to answering the psychological problems. For this it is essential that research in the field of situations is steered, not by the *methods* for data collection and data treatment to the extent that has occurred in research on individual differences, but rather by theoretical analyses and the formulation of psychological problems in a theoretical framework. If such a strategy can be followed, systematic analyses of situations and situational conditions will produce knowledge of basic import for a better understanding of human feelings, thoughts, and actions and for the formation of an environment that is adapted to the needs and potentialities of human individuals.

II
ACTUAL ENVIRONMENTS AND SITUATIONS

Although no single chapter is devoted to analyses of environments and situations in terms of only their actual (physical, biological, cultural, and social) properties, seven of them, in one way or another, deal with these aspects. They represent very different levels of environmental analyses, from Carlsson's very broad perspective in Chapter 9 to the microlevel advocated by Fiske in Chapter 4.

Craik (Chapter 3) discusses how the recently emerging field of environmental psychology can be usefully aligned with the analysis of the situation in psychological theory and research. Three main topics are addressed. First, developments in environmental assessment are reviewed and two kinds of environmental assessments distinguished and discussed: *observational assessment* and *technical assessment*. Second, parallels between environmental assessment and situational analyses are noted. Third, the conceptual linkages between the situation and the environment are examined. Joint consideration of the concepts of situation and environment points to the need for a broader perspective looking beyond psychology to interdisciplinary research.

Fiske (Chapter 4), in contrast to Carlsson, is interested in microlevels of situations. He advocates that the situation is best analyzed into objective constant features and changing stimuli. Each investigator's research approach determines his or her conceptualization of situations. That approach must strike a balance between seeking power and seeking generality. The search for generality of conceptual statements characterizes research on people's interpretive judgments about others, a domain with limited agreement between observers and hence limited sound generalization. The alternative approach, seeking powerful propositions, can be seen in work on the organization of ongoing behavior analyzed as action sequences, where observers can agree on the constants and generalization has an empirical basis.

Argyle (Chapter 5) includes physical–environmental and person factors (skills, for example), but his analysis is in terms of mainly sociocultural factors. He argues that discovery of the dimensions of situations does not reveal their full complexity and suggests instead that situations possess a number of basic features, goals, rules, elements, and so on. Of these, the *goals* are regarded as the primary reasons for the existence of a situation. Functional explanations can then be given for other features by showing, for example, how characteristic elements provide the means for attaining the goals and vary with the goals. Argyle discusses and presents results of empirical analyses of situations concerning various features of situations.

Block and Block (Chapter 6) are especially interested in the formal, abstract properties of situations as they exist independently of the perceptions and evaluations of a particular individual. Such properties of situations are reflected in high consensus among observers. Block and Block present an empirical analysis of *demand quality* or *evocativeness* of a number of experimental procedures, which were characterized using a situational Q-sort. Empirically, eight factors were identified. A number of situational parameters differentially associated with the situation factors were educed.

Price (Chapter 7) evaluates current theory and research on situations and underlines the problems connected with inadequate criteria for situational sampling, heavy reliance on the study of artificial situations, lack of a longitudinal perspective, insufficient attention to the context of the situation itself, and a frequent focus on problems of little social significance. He suggests that the study of situations that put people at risk in terms of psychological distress ("risky situations") helps focus attention on these problems and their potential solution (cf. Sarason & Sarason's discussion of social-support situations in Chapter 13). Possible dimensions for characterizing risky situations are suggested and generic strategies for situational intervention are proposed.

Hacker (Chapter 8) outlines interrelations between objective and subjective determination of working activities and the consequences of restrictive job situations on the development of personality, on the basis of field research (cf. James & Sell's analysis of psychological climate in work organizations in Chapter 18). The possible organization of working activities in terms of their surface as well as deep structure is determined by socioeconomic conditions including technology. In modern production, human activity is necessary at only special stages of the production process. The characteristics (*degrees of freedom*) of these technological stages determine the demands made on operators (i.e., determine the possible organization of their activity). On the other hand, motivation, knowledge, and skill determine the use made of given degrees of freedom by the redefinition of orders into subjective tasks and the style of coping with the job content.

Carlsson (Chapter 9) deals with the environment in a macro perspective. As an alternative to the traditional definition of the environment he suggests that it may be defined in terms of a stream of stimuli and signals, differing statistically between individuals. At least this appears reasonable for "historical environments," exerting their influence through the life history of persons. Historical environments may be supposed to shape a disposition to respond in a certain manner (allowing for possible genetic factors) when an actor is faced with a given situation. Referring to his random-walk model to depict the gradual change under the pressure of historical environment, Carlsson presents some empirical results from an analysis of environmental factors using the model. The environmental effects are shown not to be as strong as expected and possible explanations and refinements of the model are discussed.

3 Environmental Assessment and Situational Analysis

Kenneth H. Craik
University of California at Berkeley, USA

DEVELOPMENTS IN ENVIRONMENTAL ASSESSMENT

The present status of environmental psychology can be described as the invasion of an array of relatively distinct and mature research traditions, currently viable within scientific psychology, into the domain of person–environment relations (Craik, 1977). Each of these strands of normal science, guided by exemplary achievements and an agreed upon agenda of research, has discovered engaging puzzles and opportunities for paradigm extension and articulation within this new context (Kuhn, 1970; Masterman, 1970). This pattern is illustrated by such enterprises as: (1) ecological psychology; (2) environmental perception; (3) environmental assessment; (4) personality and the environment; (5) environmental cognition; (6) analysis of functional adaptations, and a number of other directions of research, many of them conducted through interdisciplinary collaboration with architecture, education, geography, landscape and regional planning, resources management, urban design, political science, social ecology, and sociology (Craik, 1973; Stokols, 1978). In order to focus discussion, primary attention will be given here to developments in environmental assessment but some note will be taken of ecological psychology and of environmental perception and cognition.

The aim of environmental assessment is the development and application of techniques for the systematic description and evaluation of physical and social environments (Craik, 1971; Moos, 1975). The full paradigm consists of: (1) a multidimensional taxonomic model providing descriptive or predictor variables; (2) a set of criterion or outcome variables; and (3) an arsenal of self-critical concepts and multivariate statistical techniques for gauging the reliability, validity, and utility of assessments and predictions, including incremental validity,

37

base rates, construct validity, and multitrait–multimethod analysis (McReynolds, 1971; Wiggins, 1973). Thus, the paradigm represents an extension of psychological assessment which has been developing for over four decades and is most familiar perhaps in its applications within personnel assessment, selection, and placement programs (Dunnette, 1966).

The places in which situations develop and transpire vary across many descriptive dimensions, such as scale (e.g., from kitchens to cities) and naturalness (e.g., from wilderness tracts to space capsules) (Craik, 1970). Two strategies that are clearly distinct but difficult to label properly can be used to assess physical and social environments. On the one hand, assessments can be based upon the impressions formed by observers of the environments. Observer judgments are often termed "subjective" (Payne & Pugh, 1976) or "perceived" (Pervin, 1978b) assessments and contrasted with "objective" assessments. These terminological options are unsatisfactory because observers are capable of yielding objective composite measures that display adequate levels of reproducibility and generalizability (Block, 1961; Wiggins, 1973). Perusal of systems that require a minimum of judgment by human observers and are usually termed "objective" measurements reveals a wide array of sources, ranging from standard metrics for weights and measures to geomorphology to organizational theory. For our purposes, environmental assessments based upon consensual impressions will be termed *observational assessments;* those based upon technical systems of measurement will be termed *technical assessments.*

Technical Assessment

In addition to the standard metrics for length and volume, an array of technical indices for the assessment of places is available, often drawn from other disciplines. For large-scale environments, geomorphological dimensions (e.g., relative relief, width of floodplain) and hydrologic characteristics (e.g., flood stage to flood peak interval) have been related in interpretations of natural hazards (Burton, Kates, & White, 1978) and to judgments of scenic quality (Zube, Pitt, & Anderson, 1975). Physical indices of air quality (Barker, 1976), water quality (Coughlin, 1976), and noise (Weinstein, 1976) have been employed in a variety of psychological studies. Within the built environment, physical variables have included lighting conditions (Hendrick, Martyniuk, Spencer, & Flynn, 1977), floor level (Fanning, 1967), ambient temperature (Berglund, 1977), and both interior and exterior colors (Küller, 1971; Sivik, 1974; Whitfield & Slatter, 1979).

Variations among places can reflect the assortment and location of material artifacts within them. At the regional and community level, the location of structures and activities on the earth's surface can be described by various land-use taxonomies and related to judgments of landscape quality (Zube, 1976). Within dwellings, Laumann and House (1970) used a Living Room Check List to record a physical description and inventory of objects (e.g., fireplace, wall mirror, trophies, stuffed furniture) for a sample of 897 living rooms. Smallest space analysis yielded two dimensions, one related to modern versus traditional style of decor and the other related to the social status of the owners. The location of tables, chairs, and other furniture and its influence upon interpersonal behavior has been studied by Sommer and others (Koneya, 1976; Mehrabian & Diamond, 1971; Sommer, 1967).

Both the social and spatial densities of places have been the focus of considerable research (Baum & Korman, 1976; Galle, Gove, & McPherson, 1972; Loo, 1978). Furthermore, the activity patterns of people in places offer additional assessment dimensions (Craik, 1970). The behavioral density of a place indexes the total frequency of all types of activity occurring within it during a standard period of observation. The range of different kinds of activities indicates the extent to which it possesses a diffuse or focal behavioral character. Finally, its activity profile depicts the relative frequency of specific kinds of activities. Given stable activity profiles over time and the application of the tools of numerical taxonomy (Sneath & Sokal, 1973), empirically identified typologies of places can be generated on the basis of their behavioral characteristics. Although originating in a different manner, the behavior setting approach of ecological psychology (Barker, 1968; Wicker, 1979) yields a similar system of places. A systematic procedure has been used to identify the public behavior settings of small communities in the United States (Midwest) and in England (Yoredale) (Barker & Schoggen, 1973), where behavior setting surveys have been conducted at two times, separated by a decade. The structure of such behavior setting inventories for communities can then be examined by factor analysis and cluster analysis (Price & Blashfield, 1975).

The comparative analysis of institutions offers a number of indices for assessing organizational structure (e.g., size, interdependence of subunits, centralization of decision making) and process (e.g., communication patterns selection procedures) (Forehand & Gilmer, 1964; James & Jones, 1974; Payne & Pugh, 1976). Systematic assessment procedures for these purposes include a set of structural indices for work organizations (Pugh, Hickson, & Hinings, 1969) and the Environmental Assessment Technique for educational institutions (Astin & Holland, 1961).

The use of a broad range of indices for assessing physical and social environments has been accompanied by conceptual distinctions between certain physical measures and related but quite different psychological constructs; for example, in the differentiation of crowding from physical density (Stokols, 1972), the differentiation between the perception of environmental quality and physical standards based upon public health and economic considerations (e.g., air quality indices) (Craik & Zube, 1976), and the distinction between organizational structure and process and organizational climate (Payne & Pugh, 1976; Schneider, 1975).

Observational Assessment

The human observer serves as an effective instrument in environmental assessment. Although observers can be used to estimate physical properties (Dawes, 1977), the value of observational assessment derives from its ability to tap differentiations among places that can be made only by human judges and that embody meaning within a social–cultural framework.

As in the case of our discourse about persons (Wiggins, 1973), there exists a rich fund of terms and concepts concerning places within everyday language and in more technical vocabularies (e.g., of architecture, design, geography, landscape analysis, organizational psychology, and social ecology). Several standard techniques have been introduced to record observational assessments of physical and social environments.

For the physical environment, there are Kasmar's (1970) Environmental Descriptor Scales; Mehrabian and Russell's (1974) affective response scales, Berlyne's (1974) set of collative dimensions; a variety of techniques for scenic analysis (Craik & Feimer, 1979); and Craik's (1972a, 1975) Landscape Adjective Check List, as well as the more comprehensive Environmental Adjective Check List and the Regional Q-sort Deck (Environmental Simulation Project, 1972a, 1972b).

For the social–institutional environment, devices have been developed to assess dimensions of social atmosphere and organizational climate (such as autonomy, competition, involvement, warmth, order) (Forehand & Gilmer, 1964; James & Jones, 1974; Moos, 1975; Payne & Pugh, 1976). Thus, the character of a given social environemnt may be summarized as it reflects the enduring norms, values, patterns of communication, expectations, rules, routines, and styles prevailing within it. Influenced by Murray's concept of environmental press (Murray, 1938), Stern (1970) pioneered in this form of social assessment. The College Characteristics Index (Stern, 1963, 1970) and the related College and University Environment Scales (Pace, 1963) provide assessment procedures for educational institutions. Moos and his associates have introduced a set of techniques for assessing social climate, including the University Residence Environment Scales (Gerst & Moos, 1972), the Family Environment Scale (Moos, 1975), the Ward Atmosphere Scale, the Community-Oriented Programs Environment Scale, and others (Moos, 1974). The Environmental Q Set (Block, 1961; 1971) was developed by Jack and Jeanne Block for describing childhood family contexts. For work environments, several instruments for assessing organizational climate are available, including the Organizational Climate Description Scales (George & Bishop, 1971; Halpin & Crofts, 1963), the Executive Climate Questionnaire (Tagiuri, 1968), the Agency Climate Questionnaire (Schneider & Bartlett, 1970), the Organizational Climate Questionnaire (Litwin & Stringer, 1968), and the Group Dimensions Description Questionnaire (Hemphill, 1956; Pheysey & Payne, 1970), as well as instruments for observer-based estimates of organizational structure (Hall, 1963; Payne & Pugh, 1976).

Observational Assessment and Environmental Perception

From a methodological standpoint, five facets of observational assessment have been identified: (1) characteristics of the observers; (2) transactional context; (3) medium of presentation of the environment; (4) response formats; and (5) physical indices and consensually judged attributes of the environments (Craik, 1968, 1971). Investigations of the influences of these classes of variables upon environmental descriptions and evaluations constitute contributions to the study of environmental perception (Ittelson, 1973; Porteous, 1977; Rapoport, 1977; Saarinen, 1976). In this instance, descriptions of the environment by each observer (e.g., "desolate," "enclosed," "colorful," "exciting," "orderly," "supportive," "competitive") are treated as *trait attributions* and factors affecting the judgments are examined. However, if many observers agree upon the assessment of an environment, the same descriptions and evaluations can be treated as *trait designations* and considered as properties of the places described, thus constituting useful forms of environmental assessment (Craik, 1971). Available evidence indicates that satisfactory levels of composite reliability can be obtained for observer-based descriptions and evaluations, while sensitivity of measurement is displayed by findings of statistically significant differentiation among places (Daniel & Boster, 1976; Kasmar, 1970; Moos, 1974; Oostendorp & Berlyne, 1978a, 1978b; Schneider & Bartlett, 1970; Zube, 1976).

Studies in environmental perception are informative regarding the technical functioning of observational assessment. The role of *observer characteristics* in accounting for individual variations in environmental description and evaluation has been examined (Craik, 1975; Mitchell, 1968). In addition, personality instruments assessing dispositions assumed to be closely linked to environmental perceptions and preferences have been introduced (Craik, 1976; Craik & McKechnie, 1977), including McKechnie's (1974, 1978) Environmental Response Inventory and Stern's (1963, 1970) College Activities Index. *Transactional variables* include cognitive and instructional sets that presumably prime the observer to attend to selective aspects of the environment (Leff, 1978) and such variables as prior familiarity with the environment (Appleyard, 1969; Oostendorp & Berlyne, 1978b; Sonnenfeld, 1969) and relative location in it, although the latter variable takes on quite different meanings for the physical environment (e.g., relative physical elevation) (Litton, 1972) and the social environment (e.g., status in the organizational hierarchy) (Schneider & Bartlett, 1970).

The environment can be presented to observers in many different ways (e.g., direct site visit, long-term residence, film and videotape tours, scale models and sketches, brief verbal descriptions). Techniques of environmental simulation in the form of various indirect *media of presentation* are widely used in studies of perception of the physical environment. Further, their importance in environmental planning, design, and management has been enhanced by recent innovations

in legislative mandates (e.g., environmental impact statements, public information programs) and parallel efforts to increase public participation (e.g.,
through earlier involvement of user–clients in the planning and design process
and improved procedures for public hearings) (Andrews & Waits, 1978; Appleyard, 1978; Craik & Zube, 1976). Recognition of these critical scientific and
applied functions has resulted in the emergence of research aimed at appraising the psychological effectiveness of various kinds of environmental simulation
and affording a better basis for informed use of them in research and in planning
(Acking & Küller, 1973; Gärling, 1970; Hendrick et al., 1977; Hershberger &
Cass, 1974; Seaton & Collins, 1972). The Berkeley Environmental Simulation
Laboratory, for example, has been developed to provide previews of alternative
environments for feedback in the planning and design process, for use in public
hearings and the preparation of environmental impact statements, and for experimental manipulations in environmental psychological research. The apparatus has as its centerpiece a remotely guided periscope with a tiny movable
lens. Supported by a gantry and control system the periscope can ''fly,''
''walk,'' or ''drive'' through physical models of buildings and landscapes under
either operator or computer control, projecting images onto closed-circuit television, videotape, or super-8- and 16-mm color movie film. A program of research
appraising its psychological effectiveness and exploring its application in environmental planning is underway (Appleyard & Craik, 1978; McKechnie,
1977). Most observational assessments of social environments have employed
direct presentations based upon residence, work experience, or site visits.

The *response formats* used by the observer can encompass varied kinds of
judgments and a range of reactions. Several recent analyses have found meaningful relations between the dimensions of environmental description and evaluation
yielded by factor analysis of bipolar verbal ratings of a sample of physical
settings and those yielded by multidimensional scaling of dissimilarity-similarity
judgments for the same settings (Gärling, 1976; Hall, Purcell, Thorne, & Metcalfe, 1976; Horayangkura, 1978; Oostendorp & Berlyne, 1978a; Ward & Russell, in press). The domain of verbal rating scales can itself be grouped into two
general classes: affective or evaluative terms and perceptual–cognitive or descriptive terms (Russell, Ward, & Pratt, 1978). Furthermore, when the factor
dimensions emerging from each of these domains are used in assessing a common sample of physical settings, the results from one set can be predicted from
the other to a substantial extent (Ward & Russell, 1978), suggesting that they
constitute sequential modes of response (with the affective evaluative responses
functioning as mediating variables) but at the same time that they offer alternative rating systems for environmental assessment.

The relationship between technical assessments and consensual observational
assessments of the same environments has been examined. Thus, a set of physical variables (e.g., relative relief, percentage of tree cover, presence of water
bodies) has been related to observational assessments of scenic quality (Zube,
Pitt, & Anderson, 1975). Technical indices of architectural design and of organi-

zational structure have been related to observational assessments of social climate in university residential environments (Moos, 1978). Indices of organizational structure have been related to observational assessments of organizational climate (Payne & Pugh, 1976). Except in cases in which observers are explicitly instructed to estimate a technical index (Dawes, 1977), it appears inappropriate to consider these studies as some form of validational appraisal of the observational assessments. Often, the observational assessment is tapping distinct environmental attributes that offer no one-to-one match to technical indices, either conceptually or empirically (Berglund, Berglund, Engen & Ekman, 1973; Moos, 1978). However, from a practical point of view, decision makers responsible for the planning and management of physical and social environments typically manipulate technical indices; thus, multivariate analysis of the relationships between technical assessments and observational assessments does possess pragmatic importance and may offer policy guidelines.

Evaluative Environmental Assessments and Applied Contexts

Environmental assessments can serve both descriptive and evaluative purposes. An important trend in research on environmental assessment is directed toward the identification of general standards of quality and the establishment of evaluative indices for monitoring purposes. In the case of the physical environment, indices of environmental quality have appeared based on both technical standards (e.g., indices derived from public health and economic impacts) (Inhaber, 1976; Thomas, 1972) and observer-based appraisals (Craik & Feimer, 1979; Craik & Zube, 1976). At the social level, emphasis has been placed upon broad societal indices, focusing more upon national and metropolitan than institutional units of analysis, although exceptions can be cited (Frankenhaeuser, 1977). Again, the distinction between appraisals of environmental quality based on technical indices (Bauer, 1968; U.S. Office of Management and the Budget, 1973) and observer-based indices (Andrews, 1974; Campbell, Converse, & Rodgers, 1976) can be discerned.

Complementing the effort to establish general standards of environmental quality, another trend in evaluative assessment takes a pluralistic perspective, recognizing individual and group variations in criteria for physical and social environmental quality. This approach is guided by the concepts of fit or congruence between individuals and their environment and by a stress upon mechanisms aimed at achieving a better match between the two and greater individual satisfaction. These strategies include selection and placement of individuals within environments, user participation in environmental changes, prechange simulations and impact analyses, and postchange evaluations (Appleyard, 1976; Appleyard & Craik, 1978; Campbell, 1965, 1975; Friedmann, Zimring, & Zube, 1978; Gerst & Moos, 1972; Holland, 1966; Payne & Pugh, 1976; Pervin, 1968; Walsh, 1973).

Conclusions

Several assertions regarding the current state of environmental assessment appear to be warranted. First, although the assessment of physical environments and social environments has tended to generate separate research literatures, they display a parallel methodological structure and can be usefully viewed as a common endeavor. Second, the systematic assessment of both physical and social environments derives from and gains strength through its place in the broader research tradition of psychological assessment. Third, environmental assessment takes two distinct and general forms, namely, technical assessment and observational assessment, each yielding important but to some extent incommensurate domains of environmental attributes. Fourth, notable progress has been made over the past decade or so, at both the physical and social level, in systematically identifying domains of environmental attributes and in developing standard techniques for their assessment.

IMPLICATIONS FOR SITUATIONAL ANALYSIS

If the distinctions drawn regarding environmental analysis are applied to situational analysis, we can differentiate among the technical assessment of situations, the observational assessment of situations, and situational perception. Much of the recent and most interesting research in situational analysis has dealt with situational perception (Argyle & Little, 1972; Forgas, 1976; Pervin, 1976; Price & Bouffard, 1974). Increasing knowledge of situational perception may form a basis for developing techniques permitting the observational assessment of situations. Brief comments from this perspective can be organized around the main facets of observational assessment.

The Observers.   Recent research has tended to stress the dimensions of individual variation among observers. From the vantage point of observational assessment, however, the degree of interobserver consensus and the level of composite reliabilities of situational descriptions also become matters of interest. Forgas (1976), for example, reports dimensional analyses but does not cite interrater reliabilities for the bipolar verbal ratings used in the situational descriptions.

Media of Presentation.   Brief verbal description appears to be the most frequently used medium for presenting situations to research participants (Bishop & Witt, 1970; Dworkin & Kihlstrom, 1978; Endler & Hunt, 1968; Forgas, 1976; Magnusson & Ekehammar, 1973). The usefulness of these findings and emergent dimensions for observational assessment of situations will be enhanced by comparisons with fuller or more direct presentations of situations. Possibilities worth exploring include: (1) more thorough verbal descriptions—perhaps selections from Proust and other writers (Heider, 1941); (2) observations of ongoing situations via videotape or film; and (3) participant observation with immediate debriefing (Murray, 1963). A second option in recent studies is to draw situations from the individual's experience (Epstein, 1977; Pervin, 1976). In these instances, it is not always evident whether a specific situation or class of situations is being described (Pervin, 1976).

Transactional Context.   Presumably, instructional set will prime observers to attend to selective aspects of ongoing situations (a method employed in technical assessments to enhance reliability). The location of the observer (e.g., whether out of the situation or participant observer) and the degree of prior familiarity with the physical and social environments, participants, and activities are also factors influencing situational descriptions. Surprisingly little research is available on these issues (Dickman, 1963; Duncan & Fiske, 1977; Newtson, Engquist, & Bois, 1977).

Response Formats.   Because of the stress in recent research upon individual variations in situational perception, bipolar rating dimensions have been based upon initial pools of free-description adjectives and phrases (Forgas, 1976; Pervin, 1976). For the purposes of observational assessment, movement toward a standard set of situational descriptors based upon this procedure would be valuable. Additional explorations of the interrelationships between multidimensional scaling of dissimilarity–similarity judgments and factor analysis of verbal descriptions for common samples of situations should also be encouraged.

Ultimately, the resources of situational perception, observational assessment, and technical assessment must be brought together to advance situational analysis. Here one can simply note the methods of technical assessment of situations that have been devised in social psychology; small group research; ecological psychology; industrial psychology; interactional psychology; behavioral analysis, and social ecology. Finally, one might note that in contrast to environmental assessment, little attention seems to have been directed toward developing standards of situational quality and indices for monitoring it.

CONCEPTUAL INTERPLAY BETWEEN SITUATION AND ENVIRONMENT

The Boundaries of the Situation

Situations, as they appear in recent psychological discourse and in the instances nominated by research participants, embody one or more actors, a social and physical setting, a sequence of acts, and (certainly as viewed under the aspect of eternity) a brief temporal span (e.g., "at a boring party," "mother refuses the gift"). A possible limitation of this boundary setting is that it seems to stress the here-and-now social interaction but tends to slight the cognitive-task facets of situations. On Friday, March 30, 1979, a member of the U.S. Nuclear Regulatory Commission might have recorded: "Attended a Washington meeting of the NRC dealing with the Three Mile Island problem." However, for that member and his colleagues, the situation was not simply the gathering of a group of individuals around a table in discussion but without doubt included the state of the hydrogen bubble in the top of the damaged reactor at Three Mile Island in Pennsylvania. Consequently, the situation included all the technical issues of nuclear risk assessment and the scientific understanding of the processes actually underway within the reactor, as well as matters raised by the societal management of technological hazards (Kates, 1977). Similarly, when foreign policy advisors gather during an international showdown, the situation consists partly in their social interaction but also in the nature of the crisis itself, for example, regarding such characteristics as the number of options it presents, the degree to which it was anticipated, the amount of decision time it affords, and the degree of threat it entails (Hermann, 1969). These contexts suggest that situational analysis requires attention to the cognitive tasks that form an important component of situations and also reminds us that the cognitive task often entails the problem of figuring out and doing something about the physical or social environment.

These examples were intentionally selected because of the self-evident technical complexity of the cognitive tasks they present. A simple fact of geography provides the punch line for Koffka's oft-told tale of the winter horse rider who raced safely across what he took to be a plain during a driving snowstorm only to drop dead away when informed by the innkeeper: "Do you know that you have ridden across the Lake of Constance?" (Koffka, 1935). Although psychologists and kindred researchers can study the beta press of those other, more complex situations of hazard and crisis (Fischhoff, Slovic, & Lichtenstein, 1978; Holsti, 1976; Kates, 1976), the fields of nuclear physics and international relations must be brought to bear upon the delineation of their alpha press (Murray, 1938).

But does not the same point hold for more mundane social situations? Take the case of a local school committee meeting hurriedly early on a drizzly overcast Saturday morning to determine whether or not to postpone the annual outdoor May Fair for a week. Consider the problems of social and meteorological inference and forecasting that face them as they weigh the consequences of the options available. The situations nominated by research participants (Forgas, 1976; Pervin, 1976) from their own recent experience fall into such categories as family, school, work, church, informal social gatherings, and public occasions. A full situational analysis will require collaboration with disciplines that can examine the alpha press generated by these contexts, such as administrative science, anthropology, family sociology and family therapy, organizational analysis, and sociology.

The Situation as Dependent and Independent Variable

Among the components of situations, the actors, the physical environment, and the social environment can be conceptualized as relatively enduring entities, whereas the acts and the situation as an episodic configuration are ephemeral events. Figure 3.1 depicts the individuals, the physical environment, and the social environment as entities with assessable characteristics, systemic properties, and historical–developmental trajectories (Craik, 1972b, 1976; Runyan, 1978; Smelser & Smelser, 1968). Their collision yields the situation.

The role of the situation as independent variable can take several possible forms: (1) the situation can result in decisions that transform the physical and social environments for subsequent situations; (2) the specific acts of the participants can mutually alter their personalities and their subsequent acts; and (3) the actors' perceptions of the situation as a whole can influence their subsequent acts. The third possibility raises two empirical questions: (1) to what extent does

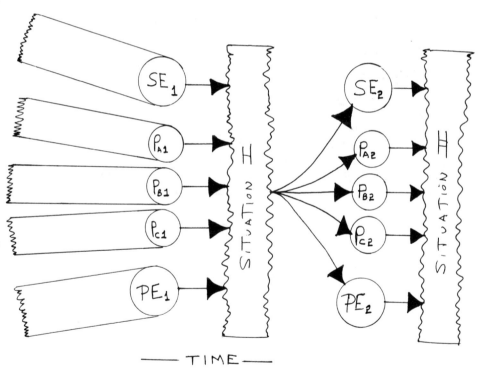

FIG. 3.1.   The situation as dependent and independent variable. Within the interior situational switchboard, of course, every independent variable is connected conceptually in potential interaction with every other. The interior of the situational switchboard is not depicted graphically here. (P = person; SE = social environment; PE = physical environment)

consensus or individual variation prevail in the perception of situations and (2) if significant and consistent individual variation is found, to what extent does it predict subsequent acts?

Multiple Perspectives and Approaches

As previously noted, establishing the alpha press in situational analyses will require multidisciplinary collaboration. Furthermore, even within the psychological analysis of situations and environments, many strategic options are available. For example, in studying behavior in environments, the behavior can be analyzed according to physical motoric and vocal movements (Duncan & Fiske, 1977) or treated as purposive-cultural acts (Allport, 1937; Alston, 1975; Hampshire, 1978), whereas the environment can be analyzed by the physical indices of euclidean geometry or according to social-institutional conceptualizations. Thus, borrowing an example from Hampshire (1978), four assertions about the same event are generated: The man is running through the 1 by 2 kilometer open space; The man is jogging through the 1 by 2 kilometer open space; The man is running through the university campus; The man is jogging through the university campus. In the first statement, the behavior and the environment are treated in terms of physical movement and measures; in the fourth statement, both the act and the setting are placed within a sociocultural framework. Given our diversity of scientific styles, strategic tolerance ought to characterize our own "research climate" as we seek to advance situational and environmental analysis. As Lawrence K. Frank (1943) recognized over thirty-five years ago: "It should be evident that we need a multidimensional conception and methodology for the study of human conduct, wherein all the disciplines may collaborate by helping to observe and, wherever possible, measure the many dimensions of man's environments and of his patterned conduct and feelings [p. 14]."

4 Situation and Generalization in Two Behavioral Domains

Donald W. Fiske
University of Chicago, USA

In a classical formulation, $B = f(P, S)$, that is, behavior is a function of factors within the individual organism and factors outside the organism. This formulation is, of course, a simplification for ease of conceptualizing. We all take it for granted that the effects of determinants originating outside the organism are mediated within the organism, that only influences within the organism's neural system directly affect behavior. Because we cannot observe those immediate influences, we construe some influences in terms of their sources outside the organism. Also, this formulation omits interactions between P and S. It is argued later that such interactions are best construed in terms of separate but related statements for different groups of persons.

Our primary concern in this chapter is not with P but with S. Commonly, S is analyzed into two parts—focal, immediate stimuli and everything else out there. Focal stimuli are those occurring just before the behavior of interest and usually are taken as eliciting or triggering the behavior. The situation is commonly taken as everything else, as all other factors out there, or as everything not singled out for special attention. The ''everything else'' includes stimuli that occurred some time previously—perhaps several minutes earlier. It also includes constant factors that potentially can affect the behavior being observed.

To make our conceptualization more explicit, we can write: $B/C = f(P, S)$. Given a set of constants, C, behavior is a function of P and S. Here, we interpret S simply as stimulation, so behavior at a moment is a function of the organism and preceding stimuli. What we are saying then is that, given an observed action or a nonoccurrence of an action, we are interested in what preceded that observation, both immediately and earlier. Space does not permit a detailed analysis of what we mean by stimulus. We can say only that a stimulus is a change in the physical world that is sensed by the person (or organism). (This is a slight oversimplification, because a steady stimulus may continue to have an effect after its onset before habituation sets in.) In addition to the obvious importance of the onset of a stimulus, the offset or termination of a stimulus is a change that can also have an effect, and an earlier stimulus, such as a task instruction, can still have residual effects even after its termination.

Although we are not examining P in this chapter, we should note that it may be clarifying to write P/C (P, given C) instead of P, because C may include factors in the state of the person or may affect such factors. More specifically, knowing the constants permits inferences about the general orientation of the person. For example, the investigator's instructions are assumed to produce a set to carry out the experimental or the testing task. Again, two persons seated near each other and talking to each other can, in the absence of any overt distractions, be assumed to be primarily oriented toward that conversation, or a mother duck sitting on a nest can be assumed to be oriented toward the hatching eggs if there are no predators around.

I am proposing, then, that we avoid the term *situation* and instead think about *constants* and *stimulation*. We should concentrate on the behavior being observed and on each preceding stimulus that we think may be relevant and so have included in our analysis, paying particular attention to the length of the time interval between each stimulus and the moment of observation. (Constants will be examined later.) For most of us, the primary focus is on behavior, with stimuli and situation being important only as they can be shown to affect behavior.

I am arguing that we can formulate some useful definition of situation in more or less formal terms. We should not seek to reach consensus on a substantive definition of situation per se. Instead, each investigator has to construe the term in a way that is appropriate for the particular class of behavior being studied. This is the way that investigators have been following, and it accounts for the range of construals evident in the literature (Magnusson, 1978, and Pervin, 1978b). What has not been made fully explicit by investigators are the links between their specification of situation and their particular research topic, the class of behavior they are seeking to understand.

POWER VERSUS GENERALITY

Implicit or explicit in the formulation of any research problem is the investigator's resolution of the dilemma between power and generality, between strength and breadth, adapting a contrast pointed out by Coombs (in a talk, November, 1978). This distinction applies to statements at all levels of abstraction, from low-level facts to abstract theoretical propositions. An investigator can seek to establish propositions that hold for all behavior, propositions that are broad and general. Such propositions will inevitably be weak. (For instances, consider the statements in the several classical theories of personality.) Alternatively, the investigator can seek powerful propositions, exact and precise statements. In the present stage of psychology, at least, these can be demonstrated as holding only under specific conditions or constants.

For most investigators, the choice of priority between power and generality is probably not made consciously—each investigator selects a research area on the basis of personal interest. A relative emphasis on power or on generality is only implicit in each research question because it is rare for such a question to be explicated completely or for an empirical finding to be stated with a full specification of its realm of applicability.

Many of us have been seeking generality. Typically, we have looked for covariations or differences that account for some of the variance in a broad class of behavior and then have tried to find factors that account for some of the remaining variance. This approach has not paid off well. In every instance, there is much variance that is not explained. Moreover, in those regrettably few instances where several studies have been carried out on the same problem, the proportions of variance associated with each factor have shown considerable variation. We are left with general statements, not strong and precise ones.

Part of the difficulty is that the behavior of interest in this approach is usually a rather heterogeneous class of behaviors that have been subsumed under some loose general label. Another source of difficulty is that there are ordinarily many factors that appear to affect that behavior, factors that we cannot pin down, factors to which we cannot assign precise values. In other words, we have not been able to cope precisely with all the components of S, with all the prior and relevant stimulation.

The previous description of those seeking general laws is probably overstated. When pressed, most of these investigators will grant that each of their general propositions holds only for some designated category of persons and some loosely defined set of conditions. What characterizes this approach is the relative neglect of these qualifications, the omission of any stated restrictions in the formulation of these general propositions. Such investigators appear to be thinking in terms of universal applicability of their statements.

An alternative strategy chooses to emphasize power. For instance, one can look for relationships that are invariant over some range of conditions. It is possible to identify, as the object for study, some kind of behavior that seems important and to specify some set of pertinent conditions. Thus, the domain of phenomena to be studied is restricted in a very explicit way. (Such examples as imprinting and conversational interactions are discussed later.) The specified conditions or constants will ordinarily include the kind of people (or organisms) and the activity in which they are engaged. Such specification must be at a simple, overt level so that everyone can agree with the accuracy of the several descriptive statements. But within this general approach, there are substrategies: for example, in each described situation, one can simply see what behaviors occur or one can examine the organization of behaviors.

The classical application of this approach is research in the laboratory. I dislike that tactic because of the well-recognized problems of generalizing to behavior outside the laboratory—the conditions in the psychological laboratory add factors that affect the behaviors observed and interfere with generalization. (Experiments in behavioral science show us what is possible, what some people will do, rather than showing us what happens in an ideal, simple case where some extraneous determinants are controlled.)

I prefer the alternative tactic of studying natural or naturalistic behavior. Here, either one can look at instances of some selected class of behavior or one can identify a situation, a set of constants, and then see what behaviors occur and how they are associated with each other. One can search for powerful, invariant relationships and then determine the limits within which they hold. If such a relationship holds for one group of studies but not for another, then one searches for the constants that are common to the first group but absent in the second. This approach could lead to an empirical taxonomy of situations, each class being defined by a set of constants and being identified in terms of the one or more relationships between behaviors that replicative studies have established to hold for that class.

Contained within the preceding discussion is an article of faith so important that it deserves restatement. We can discover an invariant relationship only when we have identified the relevant constants, the fixed conditions within which the relationship can be observed. The goal of science is the identification of laws, the formulation of each law stating explicitly the boundary conditions within which it holds.

DOMAINS OF PSYCHOLOGICAL PHENOMENA

As noted earlier, how one construes the term *situation* depends on one's research question. Let us consider that matter in more detail. Behavior constitutes a vast subject matter that has been rather arbitrarily classified into several behavioral sciences and into subfields within each of those. Although some such classifying is inevitable, I think these rather a priori differentiations have been very unsatisfactory and perhaps misleading. They certainly have not led to marked and rapid scientific progress.

Much of the confusion in psychology is due to the simple fact that various investigators and groups of investigators have been studying different domains of phenomena. Even when investigators apply a common label to their research topic, they often investigate separate sets of phenomena, as many review articles in the *Psychological Bulletin* demonstrate. We should come at the matter more systematically: We should carefully delineate the domain of phenomena we want to understand. Everything in science must be as explicit as possible, and certainly we must make explicit to ourselves and to others the domain of phenomena we study. In seeking to understand behavior, it is especially important to be explicit because we and others must know what connotations, what implications, and what construing we are carrying over from our prior everyday experience with behaving persons. A crucial aspect in specifying the domain of phenomena is a statement of the conditions under which those phenomena will be studied. What is the appropriate situation or, in terms proposed earlier, what are the constants within which the behavior will be observed?

We can start by identifying general classes of phenomena that people want to understand. Such a classification system has not been fully developed. Perhaps the most fruitful taxonomy of phenomena to be studied is a set of coordinate categories—perhaps it is a hierarchical system. In this chapter, I want to focus on just two major classes: (1) attributions made about persons, that is, interpretations of behavior; (2) actions as units of behavior (Fiske, 1978, Chapters 8–13). For purposes of empirical investigation, these classes can be indicated by two corresponding questions: (1) How is behavior interpreted? (2) How is behavior organized? Most work on personality asks the first question about the interpretation of behavior. Much work in other areas of psychology and in ethology asks about the organization of behavior. Thus, the domain and the question asked are linked together. Each domain poses its own basic problem for the investigator to solve.

As we shall see, situation is construed quite differently in these two domains. Much of the usual construing of that term has been at very gross levels, roughly parallel to the gross levels at which behavior has been construed as dispositions. Alternatively, situation can be used to refer to specific conditions at the moment. These are two points on a range of generality that is associated with the duration of the segments of behavior from which each datum is obtained (Fiske, 1978).

The Interpretation of Behavior.   In research in personality, in much of social psychology, and in some parts of other disciplines, the phenomena are interpretations of behavior. As they occur in the natural world, these interpretations may be more or less implicit and unverbalized. In our investigations, however, we elicit verbalized statements or attributions: An observer observes someone's behavior and interprets it, assigning a meaning to it. So research on these phenomena is concerned with the content of behavior as construed by people. Each datum used in such research involves a meaning assigned by the observer. So, instead of trying to discover meaning by finding and establishing empirical relationships, the investigator allows meaning to enter a priori.

Unfortunately, there is only limited agreement on such meanings or interpretations. The meaning assigned to behavior by an observer is determined to a large extent by the individual observer, and hence observers agree only modestly and are not interchangeable. There is at least as much disagreement as agreement. One consequence of these differences in meanings is that we have difficulty in generalizing. By what criteria can we conclude that two segments of behavior have the same meaning? How can such segments be shown empirically to be equivalent—when they have exactly the same relationship to other variables? (These and related problems are examined at length in Fiske, 1978.)

To assign meaning to a segment of behavior, one must also make an interpretation of the situation in which the behavior occurs. And the agreement of observers on the meaning of a situation is at least as limited as the agreement on the meaning of the behavior within it. In addition, there is the problem noted by Pervin (1978b) and Magnusson (1978): Are we attempting to assign an objective meaning to the situation (Murray's alpha press) or to infer the meanings of the situation as experienced by the persons (or organisms) being studied (Murray's beta press)? See also Rommetveit's discussion (Chapter 10, this volume) of meaning potentials in a pluralistic world.

There is a kind of confounding in our interpretations of behavior and of situation. We observe some behavior of a person, interpret it, and then say that the quality observed in the behavior is in part due to the person but in part due to the situation as we interpret that. But to interpret the behavior we invoke our interpretation of the situation, assuming that our interpretation is the same as the person's. Alternatively, we make an inference about the meaning of the situation to the person and derive our interpretation of the behavior from that construal.

Obviously, there is some overlap between several interpretations of a situation, but there are significant aspects of those interpretations that do not overlap. Just as we cannot build a science for personality phenomena on the basis of observations affected so much by individuality of observers that agreement is limited, so we cannot build a science on partial agreement about the nature of the situation in which the behavior occurs—about the constants and about the preceding stimuli discussed earlier. When the domain of phenomena is interpretations of behaviors, it includes interpretations of situations; both kinds of interpretations present obstacles to our efforts to understand the domain.

In more systematic terms: Where the phenomena are interpretations of behavior, we cannot form definite, explicit classes of behavior and classes of situations such that other investigators can confidently replicate our classifications. As a consequence, we cannot establish firm and strong generalizations but only rather vague ones, such as: "Persons who are high on dispositions of the kind I label as X will show behavior of the kind I call Y in situations that I classify as type Z."

Finally, we must note that the description of the situation must be coordinate with the temporal period of behavioral observation. If behavior during a given hour is being interpreted, then the situation must be described in terms of the conditions more or less constant throughout that period. In practice, investigators often emphasize a striking event that occurred during the period of observation and attribute a disposition on the basis of the subject's behavior following that event; the interpretive attribution is based primarily on a portion of the observation period and yet is generalized, first to the whole period and then to some unspecified longer period.

This discussion enables us to make explicit a fundamental obstacle in generalizing any interpretation of behavior. Each interpretation summarizes the sequence of behavior during a temporal period. When we generalize that interpretation to other time periods, we are assuming that the constants holding for the other periods are much the same as those for the period during which the observation of behavior was made. We are also assuming that the qualities and the patterning of stimulation experienced by the subject are much the same. Yet rarely or never do we have the overt evidence permitting us to test these assumptions. Instead, we implicitly assign the interpretive attribution to the subject who can clearly be identified as the same person in both the observational situation and in the later ones to which we make our generalization. This process illustrates the ''fundamental attribution error'' (Ross, 1977): the underestimating of situational effects, and the overestimating of dispositional effects.

The Organization of Behavior.   The other domain of phenomena to be examined here is the domain of actions: How is behavior organized sequentially, over time? What is going on? Behavior is behaving; behaving is change over time. An action is a change in activity (Atkinson, 1969), just as a stimulus is a change in the physical world outside the person. In fact, every action is not only a response but also a stimulus for other persons and for the actor. Behavior can be analyzed as a sequence of actions: For example, one person's action is a stimulus for another person's action, and the second action is a stimulus for the first person. It is all one world of behavioral phenomena. What we choose to view as response and as stimulus or as action and as preceding actions depends on the purposes of our analysis. We can establish a link between one action and a preceding one and then, separately, we can find other links to each of those actions. This is not so easy a task as such a verbal statement may suggest. The field of ethology is progressing in its study of actions, but only by slow, hard work. Intensive and extensive research within the behavior–theoretic framework has established several powerful propositions linking actions and subsequent events, propositions applicable to an important domain of behavior even though their generality remains to be delineated. Although I am not a Skinnerian, I do think that we must give Skinner much credit for his creative analysis of behavior and stimulation.

Actions are of course low-level constructs. Just as any scientist construes his phenomena as he studies and analyzes them, we construe behavior when we analyze it into actions. An action is identified as an instance of a class. Such a class can be described without imputing meaning to it. (For example, we can label an action as a gesture without assigning any specific meaning to it even though each of us may perceive a meaning in that gesture.) The meaning of the class of gestures can be determined empirically in terms of its observed relationships to other classes of actions, these relationships forming an empirical net that can be the basis for the subsequent development of a nomological net, a minitheory. More exactly, the class of gestures can be subdivided in terms of their association with other actions of the gesticulator and other actors present in the total situation. Gestures may be initiated as an auditor begins to take the speaking turn or at a later point in the turn (Duncan's speaker state and speaker gesticulation signals, respectively—see Duncan & Fiske, 1977).

In investigating the organization of behavior, researchers make two selections: They select the actions they will study; they also decide on the conditions under which the actions will be observed, these conditions being the constants identified earlier in this chapter. They are specified at a minimal level where there can be consensus among observers and where we can assume with reasonable confidence that such a consensus agrees with the description that would be given by the actors themselves, thus eliminating the problem of differences in the perceived meanings of the situation. The specification of conditions must, of course, be sufficiently complete to permit other investigators to replicate the conditions when confirmation of findings is desired.

When a body of relationships has been established for the specified set of conditions, the original investigator or others can determine empirically whether the relationships can be generalized to other sets of conditions. The goal then is to determine the boundaries of the area within which the relationships hold. Concurrently, other investigators will be studying other behaviors and delineating the limits of the areas for their topics. The ultimate result can be an a posteriori taxonomy of sets of conditions (situations, if you prefer), each tied to a body of established behavioral relationships.

In work on the organization of behavior, investigators make observations about the presence or absence of a single action, and so their period of observation for a datum is relatively brief, often just a few seconds or less. Such investigators specify not only factors that are constant over a longer period of time but also events, such as an action of another organism, that have immediately preceded the period of observation. Thus, they include both of the major components in our earlier definition of situation: recent stimulation and constant features.

Implicit in the notion of domains of phenomena is the idea that investigators in any one domain do not attempt to study all aspects of behavior, a fact that is quite evident in work on the organization of behavior. Let us look at some examples. A classical topic in experimental psychology is reaction time. Here, the constants include a single subject in a laboratory, isolated from distraction. Such subjects are given specific instructions and, from their behavior, the investigator can safely conclude that they understand and do as they are told. Along with researchers in that area, most of us are willing to believe that the findings in this area hold for reactions under the chaotic conditions of everyday living. It has long been established that reaction time increases with complexity of the task, with the difficulty of the discrimination, and with the number of alternative responses called for. The findings for reaction time are considered highly dependable and so reaction time or response latency is used as an objective index in research on cognitive processes, an index avoiding the problems associated with interpreting verbal or other cognitive responses of the subject.

In pupilometric responses (Hess, 1975), the primary datum is the maximum change in pupil size occurring within a short time after the presentation of the test stimulus. It is the difference between baseline (averaged over a short period of time) and the maximum departure from baseline. Irregularities in observed size between these points are attributed to error of measurement or to minor influences of no interest to the investigator. The general context is kept constant. Any effects on pupil size associated with context or prior events are presumed to be reflected in the baseline index.

Studies of imprinting specify the constants under which the observations are made and make no generalization to other sets of conditions. Thus, the mother duck is observed when in her nest during a short period (in minutes) before the incubated egg hatches, and her vocalizations are noted, following sounds from the egg. A few hours later, the exchanges between the duck and her hatched ducklings are observed. These are known to be different from what happens several days later.

In Duncan's work on the organization of interactions between two persons having a conversation (Duncan & Fiske, 1977, Part III), attention is centered on an action and on other actions occurring within two or three seconds before or after it. He has defined the active period for some signals, the period after an action when it is presumed still to be operative as a potential influence on the actions of the other person. In this work, the constants are two persons who are talking to each other, with nothing else going on (i.e., where the two are not doing something in addition to conversing). Here again, the constants are specified and no generalization is made to other sets of constants (such as three or more people).

In these latter two examples, imprinting and conversational interactions, it is assumed with good reason that the observing does not affect either the findings or their generalizability to other instances characterized by the same constants. In this kind of approach, the investigator determines empirically whether the findings from the observations can be replicated with other organisms under the specified set of constants. For example, Duncan's analysis of the organization of two-person interactions has been found to hold for paid research subjects who were previously unacquainted, for dyads that have known each other for some time, and even for marital partners arguing in a counseling situation. (Much further work systematically exploring the generalizability of Duncan's analysis must of course be done, including analyses of interactions observed unobtrusively and without subject awareness, but yet in some ethical way.) When investigators studying the organization of behavior obtain a high degree of replication, they can conclude that their explicit specifications of the constants do include all pertinent factors, all potential influences, and so there is no problem of the situation for them to resolve.

There are domains of phenomena in psychology where considerable progress has been made. In these areas, the research has been in a setting involving identifiable constants that can be described in terms on which we can all agree. These constants typically include the persons or organisms present; the state of those subjects insofar as it can be objectively described (for example, we can all agree that the duckling is about to emerge from its shell or has emerged very recently); the relationship between the subjects; pertinent physical factors—if any.

Mentioned earlier was a more abstract concept, the presumed orientation of the person or organism. This term can be defined by some set of the previous constants. Throughout the sequence of behavior being studied, each participant is oriented by some of the general constants, including the relationship between the participants and also the activity in which they are engaging. It may also be useful to think in terms of the immediate orientation of the participant at the point in time when an action of interest can occur or not occur. At this level, in addition to the features that are constant for the total sequence of behavior, there are other determinants that must be considered. Preceding events (especially actions of one participant or the other) that have taken place during the sequence of behavior can have effects during some period of time after their occurrence. What this more detailed analysis brings out is the fact that the description of *situation* as composed of constants and immediate stimuli is oversimplified. Although it is useful as a rough first approximation, it is not sufficient for a relatively extensive analysis of the organization of behavior. The wisest strategy is probably to begin by looking for invariant relationships within a specified set of constants for the entire behavioral sequence and then go further by bringing in factors with periods of influence falling between the periods for the constants and those for the immediate stimuli. There may well be only a limited number of invariant relationships that can be uncovered by the first, more simple approach.

TWO ASYMMETRIES IN THE ANALYSIS OF BEHAVIOR

Research on the organization of behavior has revealed two kinds of asymmetries. It looks as though the search for powerful statements in this domain and probably also in the domain for interpretations will be aided by looking for instances where these asymmetries occur. We psychologists may have been expecting to find very simple kinds of relationships, such as one variable covarying at a constant rate with another or simple 2×2 relationships—a value of one category, an A, being associated with a value of another category, a B, along with non-A being associated with non-B. Also, if A is found with B, we tend to expect that B will be found with A. Many patterns in behavior are not so symmetrical. If we are on the lookout for asymmetries and recognize them when they occur in our data, we may be able to understand behavior better.

An Action and a Nonaction Are not Necessarily Complementary.   If we find than an action R is always preceded by an S, we cannot conclude that non-R is always preceded by non-S (i.e., that if R does not occur, then S has not occurred). Here, we are taking S and non-S as mutually exclusive and exhaustive categories, and the same for R and non-R. The information associated with S cannot always be deduced from the information associated with non-S, and similarly with the information associated with R and that with non-R. The fact that two categories are formally complementary does not mean that the information associated with them is also complementary. For example, if the speaker in a two-person conversation is gesturing, we find that the auditor cannot start to talk (take the speaking turn) without simultaneous talking. If, however, the speaker is not gesturing and the auditor starts to talk, there can also be simultaneous talking unless the speaker has given the turn signal. As another example, in one 1978 senatorial election campaign, a candidate offered his hand to his opponent but his opponent turned away, refusing to shake it. The electorate reacted strongly to this breaking of an accepted rule. The information conveyed by this nonaction, this not shaking the proffered hand, could not be deduced from the information involved in a simple following of the custom.

This asymmetry seems rather straightforward, as described earlier. We can readily agree on the asymmetry between an action and a nonaction. But behavior is more complicated than that. Action and nonaction are arbitrary construals. Even the definition of an action may be somewhat arbitrary. Consider gazing: A person is almost always gazing. Four forms of gazing have been differentiated: turning the gaze toward the other person, turning the gaze away from the other, maintaining the gaze toward the other, and maintaining the gaze away. Each of these seems best construed as an action and, for some of these forms, relationships with other actions have been discovered. But insofar as these exhaust the possibilities, the notion of nonaction may not be useful here. This example brings out the fact that what we construe as an action must depend on what is going on at the moment, on the actional state of the actor. One action may preclude another: A person gazing at another person cannot shift his gaze toward that other person.

The same noncomplementarity can be found between the presence and the absence of a constant aspect of the setting. For example, student subjects have come to suspect that the experimenter will deceive them especially in the absence of any disclaimer by the experimenter. The experimenter's protestations of honesty and of the absence of any deception will not, however, remove these suspicions in all subjects. Again, having subjects sign their names on test answer sheets can reduce the candor of the responses. But eliminating that feature and using anonymous responses will not make the responses completely candid.

Relationships Are often Asymmetric.   Another intriguing asymmetry found in the analysis of behavior is the asymmetry of relationships. Thus, it may be established empirically that if an action R is observed, S invariably preceded it. If, however, we observe S, R may or may not appear. For example, if, when a duck egg is about to hatch, the mother duck makes certain sounds, one can confidently postdict that the duckling in the shell has made certain other sounds. But not all such duckling sounds are followed by those vocalizations of the mother. Again, if there is a smooth exchange of the speaking turn in a conversation, we can postdict that the speaker gave at least one of the actions that have been construed as cues in the turn signal. But not all such cues are followed by a smooth exchange: The auditor may not start talking; alternatively, if the auditor does start talking and if the speaker is also giving a gesticulation signal, there will be simultaneous talking. This kind of asymmetry occurs fairly widely in both human and animal behavior. It also occurs for the opposite type of relationship: Every instance of S may be followed by R, but the R may appear in the absence of the S. Thus, if you and I know each other and, as you approach me, you look at me and hold out your hand toward me, I had better hold out my hand and shake yours, and I almost always will. (Recall the senatorial candidate example, mentioned earlier.) But of course I am free to hold out my hand even if you have not already held out yours.

Note that the earlier formulation, $B/C = f(P, S)$, applies here. In each of the previous examples, we find that, given certain constants (C), one of two patterns of relationships holds: (1) if S', then R, but not all R's are preceded by an S'; or (2) if R, then S' preceded it, but not all instances of S' are followed by R. Each pattern is found for a set of specified constants. For example, the handshake may require that the two persons know each other and that they are facing each other so that each can see the other's hand. (The person, P, can be construed as affecting the occurrence or nonoccurrence of an action when the relationship is permissive, where there is an option. But the probability of some actions of P have been found to be affected by some additional action, S'', made by the other person—what Duncan, Brunner, & Fiske [1979] identify as a strategy signal.)

In studying the organization of behavior, then, we must expect to find complex relationships among complex variables. Behavioral variables seem most fruitfully construed as categorical. A nominal scale seems preferable to our usual ordered scales. The relationships we discover will often be complex contingencies, not symmetric associations.

Adapting a point made by Magnusson (1976) about situations, some relationships will involve action S' requiring action R, some will involve S' requiring non-R, and some will involve changing the probabilities: If S', then R is more likely; or if S', then R is less likely. For each of these, there is the opposite pattern starting with R and its relationship to a preceding S'. These relationships have been stated in simple terms, and we are likely to think about them for the condition under which S' and R occur within a second or a few seconds of each other, and quite appropriately because there are probably more relationships and stronger ones for such brief intervals. More difficult to discover and establish will be instances where one of these holds for an S' occurring some longer period of time before the R.

An interesting instance of asymmetrical relationship is found in the modifications of the classical hypothesis that frustration leads to aggression. Doob and Sears (1939) noted that, after frustration, the expression of aggression was contingent on certain conditions, rather than being invariant. Two years later, the original authors (Miller, Sears, Mowrer, Doob, & Dollard, 1941) stated the relationship in terms of the consequent being related to the antecedent but not necessarily the reverse: They proposed that, if aggression occurs, then frustration preceded it, but not all frustration leads to aggression. Later research (Bandura & Walters, 1963) demonstrated that aggression can be observed without frustration, as in children imitating adult models.

One final matter: It must be reiterated that the generalizability of our empirical knowledge about behavior must be determined by research studies, not by inference. We must establish empirically the limits within which each obtained relationship holds, within the field defined by the specified constant elements. When a relationship does not hold, then we must establish some new proposition that identifies some additional specification having a value different from that for the original studies and determine the limits for that proposition. Although I share the pessimism expressed by Cronbach (1975) about the psychological enterprise as now pursued, the presence of a so-called interaction should not discourage us unless it involves an organismic variable, especially a variable assessed through interpretations of a person's behavior. In the organization of behavior, there are what can be called *interactions*: R is preceded regularly by S; but where T is also present, that relationship does not hold. Why can we not treat such interactions as two or more relationships, each observable under an explicit set of circumstances? Very frequently, an interaction simply means that the sequence of actions being studied involves more than one relationship: S is followed by R if one additional stimulus, U, is present; if stimulus U is present and V is not, then S is followed by a different action.

ACKNOWLEDGMENT

Preparation of this chapter was supported by Grant No. MH30654-01 from the National Institute of Mental Health, U.S. Public Health Service to Starkey Duncan, Jr., and Donald W. Fiske.

5

The Experimental Study of the Basic Features of Situations

Michael Argyle
University of Oxford
Great Britain

Use of equations of the form $B = f(P, S)$ supposes that situations can be analyzed in terms of dimensions. A currently popular way of finding such dimensions of situations is by means of multidimensional scaling, in which subjects indicate how similar a number of situations are to each other, so that the underlying dimensions which they are using can be extracted statistically. Wish and Kaplan (1977) used this method for finding the dimensionality of eight different kinds of social events and eight role relations. He obtained the following dimensions: (1) friendly–hostile; (2) cooperative–competitive; (3) intense–superficial, (4) equal–unequal, (5) informal–formal, and (6) task-oriented–not task-oriented. They were not all independent; the first two are correlated, for example.

Although these dimensions are extremely valuable and have appeared in other studies, they do not tell the whole story, however. Consider the combination of *task-oriented, unequal, friendly, intense,* and *cooperatuve,* This includes such situations as going to the dentist, being psychoanalyzed, saying confession, having a tennis lesson, having a philosophy tutorial, discussing work problems with the boss, and discussing domestic problems with father. (It is difficult to assess them for formality). If someone has difficulties with one of these situations, as clients for social skills training often do, then they need to know more than the fact that the situation is task, unequal, friendly, etc. If we want to understand one of these situations to the point where we can predict or explain the sequence of events in it, we need to know more. What is it about situations that would be useful to know, and that would provide sufficient information for these purposes?

I propose to use games as models for other social situations. In each case the participants agree to follow certain rules; they pursue certain goals; and only certain moves are recognized as relevant acts. In his analysis of games, Avedon (1971) proposed features like purposes (i.e., how to win), rules, roles of participants, equipment required, etc.

The list of features of situations that I have been using, and which was developed independently, is as follows:

1. Goal structure.
2. Repertoire of elements.
3. Rules.
4. Sequences of behavior.
5. Concepts.
6. Environmental setting.
7. Roles.
8. Skills and difficulties (Argyle, 1976; Argyle, Furnham, & Graham, 1980).

These could be divided up differently. For example, roles could be a subdivision of rules, and sequences are closely linked with repertoire. I believe that these features are interdependent and form a system, so that only certain combinations of goals, rules, etc., are possible. I shall give a number of examples of one feature generating other features. In using the game analogy, I am using "game" in a rather general sense and want to underplay the element of competition, which is often absent from social situations. It can, therefore, include the kinds of situations that Harré and Secord (1972) call "rituals" and "entertainments".

A rather different view of situations is held by symbolic interactionists, who maintain that interactors are continuously renegotiating the shared definition of the situation. I agree that participants do alter the nature of situations along dimensions like friendly–hostile, or tense–relaxed, within a given situational framework (e.g., a tennis lesson or a visit to the dentist). They may also be able to modify the rules; for example, a series of seminars, or family meals, may develop a local modification of these. I also agree that participants sometimes change the nature of the situation entirely as when a philosophy tutorial turns into psychotherapy or a tennis lesson becomes a love affair. However, when this happens, there is a transition to another socially defined situational structure, rather like a change from tennis to squash; in each case there is a discontinuity. It is also true that new situations gradually evolve in the culture, as in the case of brainstorming, T-groups, and encounter groups. The same is true of the gradual development of games, like rugby football.

GOAL STRUCTURE

The needs, drives, and goals that are satisfied by a situation also form a *structure;* that is, a person may pursue more than one goal, or there may be more than one person there. We shall analyze situations in terms of the relations between two or more goals.

An Investigation of Goal Structure

A study was carried out in a college for occupational therapy. The first stage consisted of a few open-ended interviews to find the goals that the girls pursued in eight common situations. These interviews produced long lists of goals that were reduced to a smaller number of categories. In producing the final list, earlier lists of needs by Murray (1938) and others were borne in mind. The eight situations were:

1. Complaining to a neighbour whom you know well about constant noisy disturbances.
2. A friendly chat with a friend of the same sex, in the evening.
3. Being a hostess at a fairly formal meal at home with friends.
4. A first date with a member of the opposite sex whom you find attractive.
5. A class, including teaching and discussion.
6. A reception at a wedding of a relative whom you do not know very well.
7. Visiting a doctor, with whom you are familiar, when unwell.
8. An interview for a job or course.

In one study, 70 female students of occupational therapy rated each of the 18 goals on 5-point scales for their relevance to each situation. This showed which goals were thought to be most important. The ratings were put into a principal components analysis, producing more generalized goals. In a later study, another set of subjects rated the amount of conflict between the principal components. It was then possible to display the goal structures of several situations as shown in Fig. 5.1 and 5.2.

In criticism of this (Graham *et al.*, 1980) approach it could be objected that people may not be consciously aware of their goals. It would be possible to ask further questions like, "What would make you particularly satisfied (or frustrated) with situation X?"

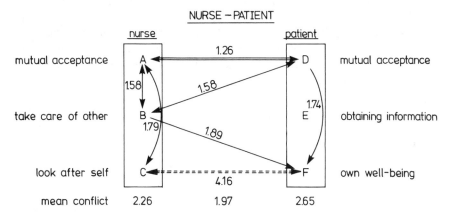

FIG. 5.1.   Goal structure of nurse–patient encounters.

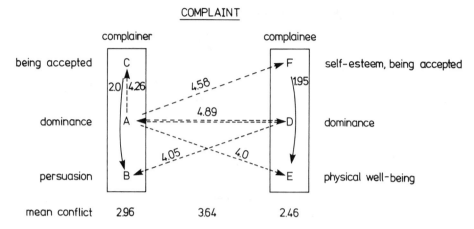

FIG. 5.2.   Goal structure of a complaint situation.

THE REPERTOIRE OF ELEMENTS

Research on personality-situation interaction produces equations of the form $B = f(P, S)$. Such equations are only possible, however, for forms of behavior that can occur equally well in each of a range of situations. These forms may be amount of anxiety, talk, conformity, or gaze, for example (Endler & Magnusson, 1976c). But they could not be level of bidding (i.e., at an auction sale), speed of running, or amount of alcohol drunk, because these forms of behavior only occur in particular situations. It follows that the $P \times S$ approach is limited to universally applicable categories of behavior and cannot incorporate forms of behavior unique to situations or groups of situations.

Early research on behavior in groups led to sets of categories such as those of Bales (1950) that were believed to be applicable to all kinds of behavior. In fact, later research on different social settings has produced quite different sets of categories for behavior in the classroom (Flanders, 1974) doctor–patient interaction (Byrne & Long, 1976), children at play (Blurton-Jones, 1972), and so on. The categories of behavior that appear to be useful for studying behavior in different situations are very different.

The hypothesis I want to develop is that each basic kind of social situation has a characteristic repertoire of elements. To some extent these elements follow from, and could be deduced from, the goals of the situation; the elements are the moves that are needed to attain the goals. Thus, problem-solving requires moves like "makes suggestion," "asks question," "disagrees," and so on. To some extent the repertoire is the product of cultural development in the course of which different ways of reaching the goals are worked out. This is reflected also in the emergence of different rule systems. Thus buying and selling can be done by auction sale with its special rules and limited number of moves by the buyers, who can only bid or not bid.

A further part of the hypothesis is that the semiotic structure of the repertoire is characteristic of the situation. What I mean by semiotic structure is the way certain acts are perceived and responded to as equivalent or similar, while others, perhaps equally similar in physical terms, are sharply contrasted. The hypothesis is obviously true in the case of games, where small differences in the way a ball is hit or thrown or the point at which it lands, make a great difference.

Psychologists have studied the sets of categories that have been found in several different fields—children's play, family interaction, group discussion and negotiation, the school classroom, doctor–patient, and psychotherapy interviews. How far are similar categories used? Several different kinds of categories are in use:

1. *Verbal categories, speech acts.* The Bales (1950) scheme has been widely used but generally abandoned in favor of more specialized ones. The interpersonal categories, or improved versions of them, can probably be used universally; the task categories, however, need special subdivisions (e.g., different degrees of interpretation by psychotherapists).

2. *Verbal contents.* It is widely found that speech act categories are not enough, and that account must be taken of the contents (e.g., of negotiation or teaching).

3. *Nonverbal communication.* The categories here are universal though categories are used at very different rates in, for example, committee meetings and children's play.

4. *Actions* (in relation to the task). These are highly task-specific, but it is conceivable that more general categories could be found.

5. *Larger units.* All situations have certain repeated cycles of interaction. Larger episodes are also found, related to the goals of the situation.

There are three ways of discovering the repertoire of elements:

1. *Construction by the investigator.* Numerous schemes have been developed, following the interests of different investigators, for social behavior in the classroom (Simon & Boyer, 1974) and doctor–patient encounters (Byrne & Long, 1976).

2. *Extraction by sequence analysis.* Small elements can be combined if they have the same antecedents and consequences (van Hooff, 1973) or if one very commonly leads to another (Dawkins, 1976).

3. *Perception by participants.* Items are grouped, for example, by cluster analysis based on ratings by observers.

We indicated before that the repertoires to some extent follow from goal structure, together with the cultural development of rule systems. Repertoires can also be manipulated independently. Shapiro (1976) carried out an experiment in which the experimental variable was a change of repertoire. He found that if questions were not permitted, special difficulties for interactors were created, in particular, in handing over the floor to another speaker.

There are also situational differences in repertoire at the level of language. Immigrants and other bilinguals may speak different languages at home and at work or school. There are often "high" and "low" forms of speech used on formal and informal occasions. The high version is more carefully planned and has more nouns, adjectives, and prepositions and fewer verbs, adverbs, and pronouns (Brown & Fraser, 1979). Different vocabularies are used for different topics, especially technical topics. Sometimes these are designed to remove emotional associations, as in nursing, and sometimes to prevent outsiders from understanding, as in criminal argots. The meaning of words varies considerably between situations. Grammar takes simpler alternative forms in low versions of a language and in dialects like Black English. Accent moves toward upper class pronunciation in formal situations. People speak louder when farther apart and when excited (Bell, 1976; Dittmar, 1976).

An Investigation of the Repertoire of Four Situations

We have carried out two studies in which the repertoires of different situations were compared directly.

Graham, Argyle, Clarke, and Maxwell (in press) studied the repertoire, as perceived by participants, in the following situations: (1) an evening at home; (2) visiting the doctor; (3) a sporting occasion with someone of the same sex; and (4) a first date. Interviews were held with a sample of members of the Oxford Psychology Department subject panel, who were female, married, and under the age of 35. Elements of three kinds were elicited: (1) activities; (2) types of utterance; and (3) feelings. A total of 194 elements was obtained for the four situations. In a second stage, a further sample of 10 subjects from the same subculture were asked to check the items that they considered normal and typical for each situation. There was no obvious cutoff, and we accepted all items that 40% of the sample agreed to, giving 91, 65, 76, and 91 items, respectively, for the four situations. The greatest differences between situations were for activities (e.g., at the doctor's). A substantial proportion of the conversation and feeling elements were common to all four situations though there were also items unique to situations (e.g., "ask if disease is serious," and "hope treatment will work").

A third stage of the study produced larger groupings of these items in terms of possible substitution. This followed a grammatical model, in which classes of words can be discovered by finding possible substitutes in sentences (e.g., in "the boy ate a bun," *boy* can be replaced by *girl* or *dog* but not by *bun, ate,* or *slowly*). A third sample of ten subjects were asked individually to group the elements for each situation in terms of possible substitution. The results were analyzed by hierarchical cluster analyses and dendrograms were obtained. A cutoff point of 65% agreement was selected; this reduced the numbers of items or clusters to 49, 53, 46, and 48. An example of a cluster was "sit and watch other people''/''read magazines.'' Perhaps the main result is that items do not fall into equivalence classes nearly as readily as words do, and to this extent the linguistic model is inapplicable.

A Study of the Semiotic Structure of Elements in Two Situations

Duncan (1969) contrasted experimental and structural approaches to social psychology. The following study combined both methods. Argyle, Graham, and Kreckel (1981) studied the ways in which elements of behavior were grouped and contrasted in two situations. The situations were a young man and a young woman, on a date and at work in an office. Twenty-six elements of behavior were used that could occur equally in either situation. Twenty subjects rated each element on ten rating scales, regarding each element as if it had been directed to them by the person of the other sex.

The data were analyzed by hierarchical cluster analysis. As predicted, there was a very clear separation of task and personal issues in the work situation but not in the date. For example, questions about work and private life fell into distant clusters for work but were seen as very similar for the date (Fig. 5.3) Although the main division for both situations was between positive and negative, in the work situation there were also work and social clusters.

RULES

Continuing the analogy between social situations and games, I want to propose that all social situations are rule governed. There could not be a game between a team following the rules of, say hockey, and a team following the rule of rugby football or between someone playing chess and someone playing tennis. Some of the rules can be described in terms of repertoire; they are rules about which moves are allowed and which are not. Closely related are ''constitutive rules'' that define what counts as a ''goal,'' a ''no-ball,'' etc. Rules are primarily regulations about how the game is to be played that must be agreed to and followed by all players (Collett, 1977). If a rule is broken, the game is usually stopped; and further rules prescribe what sanctions shall be imposed—a free kick, etc. Even the most fiercely competitive and aggressive games can only take place if both sides abide by the rules, of boxing or wrestling, for example. Rules are developed gradually as cultural products, as ways of handling certain situations; they can be changed, but changes are slow. The rules have to be learned, by children as part of their socialization, by new members of organizations, and by people from other cultures.

The rules of social situations may be discovered through: the observation of behavior, but it is very difficult to infer rules unless regular sanctions are used, as in games. Rules may also be ascertained through reports by participants. They

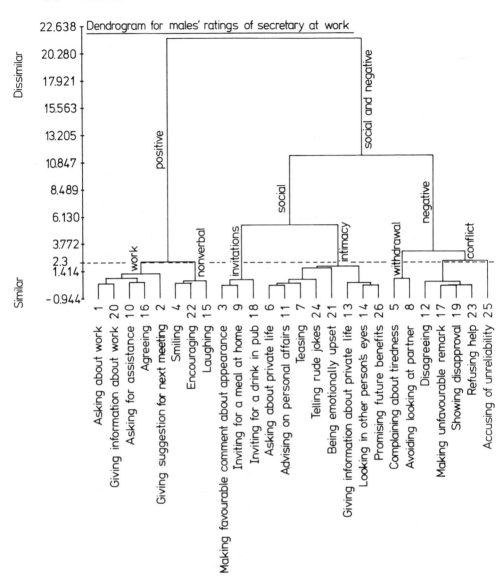

FIG. 5.3.   Semiotic structure of the repertoire for a secretary in an office.

usually can't state the rules, however. Reactions to rule-breaking also provide keys to the rules. The experimental breaking of rules was first used by Garfinkel (1963), in an experiment on noughts and crosses (tic-tac-toe) where the experimenter placed his mark on one of the lines. We have used this method in a more controlled experimental way to study the rules of interruption, an example of a sequence rule. Subjects were asked to judge experimentally varied instances of interruption. It was found that the latter is most acceptable at the end of a sentence rather than at the end of a phrase, though this was better than in the middle of a phrase. It was irrelevant how long the person interrupted had been speaking (Argyle, 1975).

Our procedure has been to take formal situations, in this case games, as models for less formal situations as recommended by Harré and Secord (1972). But are less formal situations governed by rules at all? Clearly some situations are more rule bound than others. Price and Bouffard (1974) asked subjects to rate the appropriateness of 15 kinds of behavior in 15 situations. It was found that the situations varied greatly in "constraint" (i.e., the number of things not permitted). At one extreme were church services and job interviews; at the other were being in one's own room or in a park. As the study reported later shows, however, even the most informal situations are governed by some rules.

It may be argued that the rules of situations are not fixed but changeable. Piaget (1932) showed that even children are capable of altering the rules of games. In the case of most games, however, the rules have developed very slowly in the course of history, as in the emergence of rugger from soccer, and tennis from real tennis. The same is true of formal social situations, like committees, lectures, interviews, and visits to the doctor. Less formal situations, with fewer intrinsic rules, are probably more subject to local variations and the emergence of local conventions concerning, for example, family meals or coffee at work. In both formal and informal situations there can be gradual changes, but these changes take place slowly, especially in the case of formal situations.

It must be emphasized that there is play within the rules. Just as the playing of football depends on individual and joint skills and strategies within the framework of the rules, the same is true of behavior in social situations.

Rules are developed so that the goals of situations can be attained. Some of these are common to many different situations, such as:

1. Maintaining communication—rules about turn-taking, the use of common language.
2. Preventing withdrawal—rules about equity, division of rewards.
3. Preventing aggression—rules about restraint of violence by rules of ritual aggression (e.g., among football hooligans, (Marsh, Rosser, & Harré, 1978).
4. Coordinating behavior—driving on the same side of the road, having morning coffee at the same time (Bach, 1975).
5. Achieving cooperation—keeping quiet at concerts (Bach, 1975).

When the goal structure of specific situations is examined, it is evident that more than one set of rules will do the job. For example, buying and selling can be done by barter, bargaining, auction sale, raffle, or in fixed-price shops; the latter can be further divided into supermarkets and personal selling. The goal of taking open-air exercise with a ball in a group of people can be met in a larger number of ways. Here the rules represent not so much a limited set of logical alternatives as in the case of selling but more a set of elaborate cultural constructions. The same could be said of some social situations like dinner parties, weddings, and religious ceremonies.

An experimental demonstration of goal structure leading to rule development is Thibaut and Faucheux's experiment (1965): When two players were given unequal power in a game-playing experiment, the more powerful initiated the establishment of rules for some degree of equity to ensure that the other player didn't withdraw from the situation. Mann (1969) carried out a field study showing the emergence of rules as a function of goals. The queues for Australian football games last for over 24 hours. Rules have developed about how much time out is allowed (2–3 hours at a time), staking claims by property (wooden boxes), and turn-taking in groups. Queue jumpers are rarely attacked but simply booed. They are kept out by the closeness of the queue. This is an example of the emergence and negotiation of local rules modifying more general cultural rules or deciding how they should be applied.

A Study of the Rules of Different Situations

Two studies were carried out by Argyle, Graham, Campbell, and White (1979). In each, a list of possible rules was obtained by pilot interviews, 124 rules in one case, 20 in the other. Samples of subjects were asked to rate the applicability of each rule to each of 25 and 8 situations, respectively. It was found that subjects could rate whether or not they considered that a rule applied to a situation. There was a greatly above chance degree of agreement on which rules applied. There were a number of rules which were almost universal (e.g., should be friendly, should not try to make other feel small). Some rules were specific to one or two situations (e.g., should dress smartly—wedding). Cluster analysis produced clusters both of rules and situations and showed the cluster of rules for each cluster of situations. Some situations had far more agreed rules on which subjects agreed than others (e.g., a tutorial versus a conversation with boy or girl friend), and some of the rules could be given a functional interpretation (e.g., at a tutorial "don't pretend to understand when you don't"). Others guarded against situational temptations (e.g., "don't touch" at a first date) or helped with difficulties common in a situation ("don't outstay your welcome" when visiting a friend in a college room).

SEQUENCES

Just as situations have characteristic repertoires of elements, so also do they have characteristic sequences of these elements. The sequence of acts forms the route to the goals of the interactors. In the case of games the sequence usually takes the form of alternate moves, each responsive to that immediately preceding, in an attempt to defeat the other player. An auction sale has a similar structure of alternating, competitive moves. So do sessions of boasting or storytelling. Most social situations, however, are more cooperative and less competitive. In selling, for example, there are such cooperative sequences between customer (C) and sale person (S) as:

1. C asks to see goods; S produces and demonstrates goods.
2. C asks for price or other information; S gives information.
3. C asks to buy and pays; S wraps up and hands over goods.

Sometimes longer sequences are needed to carry out the interpersonal task. For example, at a doctor–patient consultation:

1. The doctor establishes a relationship with the patient.
2. The doctor either attempts to discover or actually discovers the reason for the patient's attendance.
3. The doctor conducts a verbal or physical examination or both.
4. The doctor, or the doctor and the patient, or the patient (in that order of probability) consider the condition.
5. The doctor, and occasionally the patient, detail treatment or investigation.
6. The consultation is terminated usually by the doctor. [Byrne & Long, 1976, p. 21].

It would be impossible for these phases to be carried out in a different order.

We can partly analyze social behavior into two-step sequences. Some of these are universal to all situations: questions lead to answers, and instructions or requests lead to positive action or refusal. Some two-step sequences are based on special situational rules, like bidding at auction sales. Others are not so much rules as natural psychological tendencies, such as response-matching, the effects of reinforcement, and the effects of friendly and hostile behavior.

Three-step sequences are more complex:

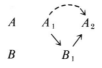

$$A \quad A_1 \quad A_2$$
$$B \quad B_1$$

In addition to the two-step linkages (A_1B_1 and B_1A_2), there is also a connection (A_1A_2). The A_1A_2 link reflects the persistence of A's planned social behavior. For example, he asks permission to smoke and does. The same occurs in four-step sequences when A_2 is a response to feedback and is a piece of corrective action. Examples of such corrective action can be seen in the social survey interview involving an interviewer (I) and a respondent (R) (Brenner, 1978).

I_1: I asks question.
R_1: R gives inadequate answer or does not understand question.
I_2: I clarifies and repeats question.
R_2: R gives adequate answer.

OR

I_1: I asks question.
R_1: R refuses to answer.
I_2: I explains purpose and importance of survey and repeats question.
R_2: R gives adequate answer.

In each case, I_2 is a modified version of I_1, as a result of R's move R_1, with the intention of eliciting a proper answer, R_2. There is continuity between I_1 and I_2, related to I's goals, based on R's feedback.

It is useful to distinguish between cases where one person has most of the initiative, as in interviewing or teaching, and cases of real negotiation or discussion where both can initiate equally well (Jones & Gerard, 1967).

Larger sequences of interaction can be generated by use of repeated cycles, closely reflecting the nature of the situation. For example, teaching uses cycles like:

teacher lectures, explains with examples, and asks question.
pupil   replies.

An encounter between two people getting to know one another might repeat the following cycle:

A: asks a question;
B: replies and asks A a similar question.

Interaction sequences can be divided into episodes or phases. There may be shifts of topic or other aspects of interaction. Committee meetings, meals, and formal occasions have clearer episodes than less formal ones. Episodes of different sizes can be located by asking observers to indicate the break-points while watching videotapes. Episodes may consist of repeated cycles, as in classroom interaction, or run through once, as in greetings. An episode involves temporary agreement to collaborate in a familiar sequence and is started by episode-negotiating signals that may be verbal or nonverbal. In an earlier example of the main episodes in doctor–patient consultation the order of the episodes follows from the nature of the task. In a selection interview, the main episodes are: (1) a welcome; (2) the interviewer asks questions; (3) the candidate is invited to ask questions; (4) an ending. Here the order of the second and third episodes is a matter of convention and could be reversed.

The basic method for analyzing sequences is to study transition probabilities (i.e., the probability that one act will lead to another representing a so-called Markov chain. Larger chains can be discovered by "chain analysis." If AB is the most common sequence, AB is called D, and the analysis repeated, with D as an element. This is repeated indefinitely (Dawkins, 1976).

A Study of the Parsing of Episodes

In a study of episodes three situations were described in outline, suggesting the goal structure. For example, one was a manager interviewing a girl for a job as secretary, who did not have very good typing skills but who was in other ways preferable to the other candidates. A page of *The Forsyte Saga* was provided, showing how a novelist might describe an encounter. Subjects were asked to write a description of how the encounters might develop. At a later stage they were asked to parse their own scripts in two stages, giving episodes and sub-episodes; and they were asked to describe the episodes. There was considerable agreement on the main episodes; these were described in fewer words than the sub-episodes, and the episodes fitted a five-part schema. In the case of purely social encounters it is not clear whether the task is omitted, or whether the "task" consists of, say, eating and drinking, or of information exchange. There was considerable agreement on the phase sequence for each situation. For example, when a wife calls on a new neighbor, it was agreed that the following episodes would occur: (1) greeting; (2) visitor admires house; (3) other provides coffee, etc.; exchange of information about jobs, husbands, interests, etc.; (4) arrange to meet again, introduce husbands; (5) parting.

ROLES

Most situations contain a number of different roles, that is, there are positions for which there are different patterns of behavior and different rules. The game analogy shows that in some games, like cricket, there are a number of different roles, but it does not show how these roles have come about. Roles are usually discussed in relation to social organizations, which have roles like doctor, nurse, patient, etc. Here we are concerned with roles in social situations, though these may be part of organizational roles. I also want to extend the idea of role to include informal roles (i.e., distinctive patterns of behavior that occur in the absence of independently defined social positions).

I suggest that situational roles come about for four main reasons.

Different Goals. When two people are drawn to a situation to pursue different goals, their roles will be different. Usually these goals will be at least partly complementary and cooperative, and the joint behavior satisfies the different goals. Examples are buying and selling, teaching and learning, doctor and patient.

Division of Labor.   When there is a joint task to be done, there is often division of labor. In a restaurant, waitresses, cooks, barman, and cashier divide up the work. Different industrial workers and their equipment are linked in "socio-technical systems." As organizations become larger, the more complex is the division of labor, and the more complex the possible situational role structure.

Social Control and Leadership.   One individual may have the power to reward or punish others in a situation. Teachers and interviewers, for example, have such power. "Equal–unequal" was one of Wish's dimensions of situations. How do such differences of power come about? A group of four can function quite well without a leader. Larger groups progressively need an informal leader, a formal leader, and then two or more levels of leadership. There is a rather crucial point at which the position of leader (or chairman) is established, and someone is formally appointed to this position. There is evidence that hierarchical role differentiation is functional. This reduces conflict; decisions can be made quickly, and the most skilled at the task have more influence over decisions. Organizations usually have a hierarchical structure, and positions differ in the power they command, in relations with other positions, in interlocking complementary roles, and in the style of leadership that is given and received. The extent of this hierarchical structure, such as the number of levels, is a product of sheer size and also of the nature of the technology. Under mass production, for example, there is a larger span of control and a flatter structure (Blauner, 1964).

Informal roles.   Informal roles are different. Because of the existence of different personalities in a situation, different people may react to it in different ways. However, the nature of the situation creates a limited and characteristic set of opportunities of this kind. In many groups there is a "socio-emotional" leader - who looks after the social as opposed to the task aspects of the situation. In juries and some work groups there is often a "leader of the opposition" (Argyle, 1969). Mann et al., (1967) found some interesting roles that often appeared in the Harvard variety of T-group, including "distressed females" and "sexual scapegoat"—a male who had doubts about his masculinity and invited the group to study him.

The role structure of a situation may be discovered in several ways:

1. *Books of rules.*   For formal situations like committees and games, the book of rules also describes the roles.

2. *Observation.* This is the anthropological method and can be used, for example, to describe the different roles in a ceremony.

3. *Interviews.* These will yield information about the less visible aspects of roles and information about expectations (i.e., the rules governing positions).

4. *Study of the socially mobile.* Anyone who has changed jobs, sex, class, or nationality can produce a wealth of information about rules governing positions.

Marsh, Rosser, and Harré, (1978) report on the roles that they found among football fans at British football grounds. These are: (1) rowdies, aged 12–17, who make the most noise, produce the most violent displays of aggression, and wear the most spectacular costumes; (2) town boys, aged 17–25, who have graduated from being rowdies and are quieter and normally dressed (they are deferred to by boys in the other roles); (3) novices, younger than the rowdies, set apart from them, and keen to join them; (4) part-time supporters, a varied group not so fully involved in aggressive displays and despised by the others; (5) "nutters," extremely aggressive boys, who often behave in a crazy way and break the rules accepted by the majority of fans.

CONCEPTS

In order to deal with people, individuals use personal constructs (Kelly, 1955). Individuals vary in the complexity of their constructs, using a larger or smaller number of independent dimensions. They use salient dimensions reflecting their main preoccupation—with race, class, intelligence, sexual attractiveness, and so on. The links between their constructs constitute "implicit personality theories," about how constructs are related to one another (e.g., race and intelligence). We should expect that people would be more socially competent in situations: (1) if they are cognitively complex (i.e., use a number of independent construct dimensions and (2) if their constructs are relevant to the situations in question. It is familiar in repertory grid research that constructs have a limited "range of convenience"; for example, false teeth cannot be rated as *religious* or *atheist* (Bannister & Mair, 1968). Similarly, small children cannot be rated as *radical* or *conservative,* and it would usually be pointless to rate members of a psychology conference as good or bad at croquet. Research on intergroup attitudes has shown that traits become salient to a group when they distinguish the group from other groups and by which they can be positively evaluated (Tajfel, 1970). For example, South African Hindus emphasize their spiritual superiority (Mann, 1963).

Other concepts are developed to handle aspects of the situation itself. Schank and Abelson (1977) have tried to formalize the conceptual equipment people need, for example, to eat a meal at a restaurant. They need to know about menus, tips, the order of courses, the roles of waiter and barman, and a great deal more in order to eat a meal and to understand such sequences as: "John went to a restaurant. He ordered a hamburger. It was cold when the waitress brought it. He left her a very small tip [p. 45]."

In order to deal with complex stimuli or problems or to perform skills it is necessary to possess the relevant concepts. In order to play cricket it is necessary to be familiar with such concepts as "out," "declare," "no-ball," and "l.b.w." In addition, the higher levels of skill may depend on the acquisition of additional concepts. In chess, for example, it soon becomes necessary to know about "check by discovery," "fork," and so on. These new concepts may refer to more complex aspects of the state of the game or to larger units of performance. In most skills the more skilled performer is able to run off larger strings of performance automatically, and these will be conceptualized. In Scottish country dancing it is essential to master sequences like "reels of three," "highland schottische," and "grand chain." The more advanced performer knows also about "rondel," "half Mairi's wedding," and "General Stuart setting step." Committee meetings require the mastery of a number of concepts like "straw vote," "casting vote," "nem con," "unanimous," "abstain," and so on. The concepts for everyday social interaction have not so far been much studied, but it is known that there are interesting cultural differences.

All the concepts that have been discussed so far could be deduced in principle from knowledge of the nature of the situations because they are needed to attain situational goals. However, there are other sets of constructs which constitute alternative constructions of social reality. Just as there are many different ways of playing with a ball, so there are several different ways of healing—western medicine, psychoanalysis, acupuncture, faith healing, etc.—each with its own set of concepts.

Two Studies of the Concepts Used in Different Situations

Forgas, Argyle, and Ginsburg (1979) studied a group of 14 research psychologists. Each person completed a set of 36 rating scales to describe the behavior of each person, including the rater, in four situations—morning coffee, going to the pub, seminars, and parties at the home of the senior member of the group. The ratings were analyzed by multidimensional scaling, to find the underlying dimensions being used. In the social situations there were two dimensions—extraversion and evaluation (as an enjoyable companion). In the seminar situation, however, there were three quite different dimensions—dominance, supportiveness, and creativity.

Argyle, Forgas, Ginsburg, and Campbell (1981) carried out a study with a group of housewives and a group of students, who were asked to rate the relevance of 36 bipolar constructs in four situations and for seven target groups.

Factor analyses showed that the constructs produced rather different factors in each situation. However, there was a friendly-extraversion factor in each situation, that was rated as highly relevant. Work-related constructs, like industrious, competent, and dependable, were much more relevant in work situations than in social ones. Different constructs were found relevant for different target groups. For example, the relevant scales for children were judged to be *well-behaved* and *noisy,* while for professional people the most relevant scales were *competence* and *high-status.* It appeared that the most relevant scales were those that reflected the nature of social interaction with different target groups.

PHYSICAL ENVIRONMENT

Barker and Wright (1954) defined their ''behavior settings'' as combinations of ''standing patterns of behavior'' (i.e., rules, roles and repertoire) and environmental setting. We, too, want to emphasize the physical setting as an important feature of situations. The environment causes behavior as is shown by studies of the effects of overcrowding, for example. The environment is also created for purposes of interaction, that is, in the pursuit of goals by architects, planners, and anyone who furnishes, decorates, or merely arranges a room. However, someone who, for example, arranges the furniture in a room, does so in the expectation that this will affect social interaction in some way; therefore we can concentrate on environment as a cause of behavior.

Several aspects of physical environment have been shown to influence behavior:

1. *Proximity* produces greater intimacy, or discomfort when past a certain distance, and progressive aversion of gaze.
2. *Crowding* produces high arousal, discomfort, aggressive behavior in males, laughter (tension release), withdrawal from social contact, and, if prolonged, emotional disturbance.
3. *Orientation.* Side by side creates a more cooperative and friendly relationship; facing opposite creates an atmosphere of competition and conflict unless two people are eating a meal.

However, environments affect behavior in another way via the perception or meaning of the setting:

1. *Furniture arrangement* produces various combinations of the factors above, together with creation of private spaces. Desks can be placed to dominate the room, chairs placed to suggest friendly chat. Sofas of different designs suggest varying degrees of intimacy.
2. *Color and decoration.* Colors affect emotional state—red and yellow for

warmth and cheerfulness, dark blue and brown for gloom. The nature of the furnishings can suggest interrogation, romance, office work, or important decision-making. People seen in a pretty room are liked more than the same people seen in an ugly room. Chairs placed by a fire suggest reading or chatting.

3. *Equipment.*   In many situations special equipment is needed, which extends the range of social behavior possible. These might include blackboard and chalk, pointer, and overhead projector, or bottles of drink and glasses, or various toys and games. Some of these features of environment can be looked at as "behavioral residues." The equipment indicates what is usually done there.

The physical environment is of particular interest in the analysis of situations as this is the easiest part of situations to change. Sommer (1969) was able to increase the amount of interaction among the inmates of an old peoples' home (see later). Harold Cohen found that fighting in a prison mainly took place at the corners of corridors and was started by inmates bumping into one another. He reduced the amount of fighting by rounding off the corners so that people could see each other coming.

A number of cooperative toys are now available that, like see-saws and table tennis, require two players, thus reducing one major form of conflict between pairs of children.

SKILLS AND DIFFICULTIES

Every social situation presents certain difficulties, and needs certain social skills in order to deal with it. The same is true of games. Polo, high diving, pole vaulting, each present obvious difficulties and require special skills. They also create some degree of anxiety that must be controlled. There are a number of general skills that are used in several games riding horses, swimming, hitting balls, etc. The same is probably true of social skills (Argyle, 1969).

Social competence can be assessed by measures of effectiveness (e.g., goods sold by a salesperson), observation of role-playing, ratings in real-life situations, tests of social competence, and various kinds of self-rating. Self-reports show primarily how comfortable versus how anxious a person feels in a situation, which is not quite the same as his effectiveness (Argyle, 1980).

There have been a number of studies of the situations which people find difficult or uncomfortable. The factors or clusters that are obtained vary with the range of situations studied and the statistical procedures used. The common areas of difficulty are as follows: (1) assertiveness situations (e.g., having to stand up for your rights); (2) performing in public; (3) conflict, dealing with hostile people; (4) intimate situations, especially with the opposite sex; (5) meeting strangers; (6) dealing with people in authority; (7) fear of disapproval, criticism, making mistakes, looking foolish (Richardson & Tasto, 1976; Stratton & Moore, 1977).

Our previous analysis can help us to account for these difficulties and also suggest the skills that would solve the problem. We showed the goal structure for complaining, with various conflicts. The solution might be to avoid dominance and to increase the interpersonal rewards provided. Difficulties with strangers (i.e., making friends) and with the opposite sex are very common among candidates for social skills training. The trouble is that they have failed to learn certain basic social skills, such as rewarding behaviors, nonverbal communication (e.g., for liking), and sustaining conversation (Trower, Bryant, & Argyle, 1978).

There are theoretical grounds for expecting other forms of social difficulty that did not appear in the studies cited earlier, perhaps because they were not included in the lists of situation studied. *Unfamiliar situations* where the rules, goals or concepts are unknown is an example of these and includes visiting a foreign country, joining a new organization, first visits to an encounter group or a psychoanalyst. *Complex situations,* where a number of different people have to be attended to at once, several different goals pursued, and the like, were also excluded.

APPLICATIONS

Social Skills Training

Social skills training (SST) by means of role-playing and allied methods is widely used for socially inadequate neurotic patients, for teachers, salesmen, interviewers, and other professional social skills performers, as well as members of the public who want to improve their skills. I believe that these forms of training can be made more effective by making use of our understanding of social interaction processes, including the analysis of situations.

A considerable number of the neurotic patients to whom we have given SST have reported difficulty with quite specific situations—often more specific than the factors listed earlier. In some of these cases we discovered that the patient had failed to understand correctly certain features of the situation in question. People who were afraid to go to parties didn't know what parties were for (goal structure) or what you were supposed to do at them (repertoire and rules). Candidates at interviews commonly mistake the goals and think that interviews are for vocational guidance or get the rules wrong, and think that they are going to ask the questions. For such people we have given instructions about the features of the situations in question. Sometimes this has been done didactically, drawing partly on published findings and partly on the experience of the trainers. Another approach has been to work with a group of individuals, all of whom have difficulties with, for example, dating. The experience of those present in the group is used, and it is necessary to have some people who are confident that they can handle the situation. In the course of an hour it is possible to arrive at an agreed-upon list of the main goals, rules and repertoire, and the main difficulties and how they can be tackled.

It may, in addition, be necessary to give behavioral SST, so that trainees can master some of the skills needed in the situation. Where the optimal skills are not known from the literature, analysis of the features of a situation can sometimes suggest ways of dealing with problems involved, as we showed previously in the case of assertiveness.

Debugging Problem Situations

Behavior is more affected by situations and by P $\times$ S interaction than it is by personality factors alone, yet emotionally disturbed and delinquent behavior is dealt with almost entirely by trying to change persons. We now know how situations might be changed instead, and here are some examples.

Change the Elements.   Brainstorming groups for stimulating creativity were produced by ruling out part of the usual repertoire of group discussion—criticism and disagreement. T-groups are groups in which the only topic of conversation permitted is what is happening in the group; this means that the normal repertoire is extended to allow direct personal comments. Encounter groups, too, involve an extension of the usual repertoire, to include bodily contact between strangers.

Change of Roles.   In one case Whyte (1948) solved the difficulty of waitresses giving orders to the higher status cooks in restaurants by the introduction of a spindle. Waitresses wrote their orders and pinned them to the spindle. The cooks looked over the orders and prepared them in whatever order was convenient.

Uneducated psychiatric patients think that all that is required of them is to take a pill and wait to get better. This is not the view of psychiatrists. To resolve this problem some hospitals now provide pretherapy training for psychiatric patients.

Changing the environment.   Sommer (1969) improved things in an old people's home by moving the furniture. Previously the chairs were in rows round the walls of large dayrooms, and the inmates sat in a stupor staring into space. Sommer grouped the chairs around coffee tables, which greatly increased the level of social interaction.

Changing communication structures.   Several of the studies by the Tavistock Institute for Human Relations involved redesigning socio-technical or work-flow systems. For example, Longwall coal mining was reorganized by including on each shift men who did the three main jobs of cutting, filling, and stonework; whereas before they were on different shifts and were often uncooperative (Trist, Higgin, Murray, & Pollock, 1963). These are one or two examples of examples of changing situations. When a situation has been analyzed in terms of the features introduced in this chapter, many possible ways of modifying it can be suggested.

6

Studying Situational Dimensions: A Grand Perspective and Some Limited Empiricism

Jack Block and Jeanne H. Block
University of California, Berkeley
USA

The recently renewed interest by psychologists in conceptualizing the environment cannot but be salutary in its consequences. For too long now the current cohort of personality psychologists has been controlled by methods and measures ignoring of the fine grain and fine influence of environmental context upon the perception and behavior of individuals. Although the accomplishments of personality psychology in assessment applications have been important and useful in their own right (c.f., Block, 1977; Gough, 1976; Hogan, DeSoto, & Solano, 1977; Stagner, 1977), these accomplishments have employed approaches to analysis and evaluation predicated upon or, in effect, expressing a view of personality as no more than a bundle of unconnected dispositions, a set of differing probabilities to respond in different ways without regard for the specific environmental context operative for the perceiving and responding individual. The typically calculated correlation coefficients relating personality characteristics over time or connecting assessment behaviors to criterion behaviors have reflected only an average *in vacuo* of relationships that exist for persons *in situ*. Given these constraints on possibility, it may well be surprising that personality psychology has progressed as far and as well as it has. But recent years have shown personality psychology to be on a plateau. Where once there was enthusiasm and a sense of prospect, the field now may be characterized as confused and downhearted, awaiting a sufficiently new paradigm.

Social psychology, as it has developed over the last quarter century, has in our view committed the reciprocal error. It has been preoccupied with models and techniques of situational influence and has avidly neglected the reliable but complex contribution of individual character structure to the perceptions and behaviors forged in social settings. The principles of attribution and of learning thus adduced have been instructive to bring forward and to articulate. But these principles, by virtue of their proclaimed universality and simplicity, have implied a view of people as remarkably homogeneous and situationally controlled in their everyday lives. Only recently has there begun to be the recognition among contemporary social psychologists that their experimental findings, when better analyzed, support "situationism" and social learning theory only in demonstrational and far from sufficient ways. This humbling awareness at once points the conceptual direction social psychology must go—study of the motivation-serving principles different individuals and different classes of individuals characteristically employ in what ostensibly are equivalent situations. The implementation of this theoretical reorientation has been slow in coming. Where the voice of social psychology once was assured and facile, it now seems uncertain and stuttering. Arriving from different points of the geographic and theoretical compass, we now bring hard won recognitions regarding the problem of understanding the person *in situ* but mill around regarding specifically productive ways of how to proceed.

This chapter is largely a presentation of some beginning efforts to describe in psychological terms the nature of various problem-solving, conflict-integrating, and cognition-demanding situations; to identify the congruences among these situations so as to establish a tentative taxonomy; and to conceptualize the situational parameters that may be said to underly the several types of situations we have discerned. But before plunging into the details of our method and analysis and results, it will be orienting to the reader to indicate our perspective on "the situation in psychological theory and research."

A GRAND PERSPECTIVE

In our view, it will be interesting, useful, but not enough simply to balance previous overemphasis on personality dispositions by developing analogous listings of situational dimensions or to study more and better the personality correlates of the individual differences observed in social situations. We will have to move on and give conceptual meaning and empirical specificity to the "interactional paradigm" talked about these last several years, more to acknowledge positions abandoned than the direction now to be taken.

We distinguish, not uniquely, three different levels of situational analysis. These three analytical levels reflect successive stages of interpretation of the situation by the experiencing individual. There is, first, what we call the *physico-biological situation*, the infinitely detailable, perceptually unfiltered and uninterpreted, sensorily available intakes by the individual. The physico-biological situation has something of an autochthonous structure—it is not entirely inchoate—as a function of evolution-ingrained perceptual and action schemata that the ages have by now wired into the human nervous system.

There is, second, what we call the *canonical situation* (the alpha press of Murray, 1938), the consensually defined, consensually constructed, or consensually accepted situation. It is the psychological demand-quality or structure of the situation as specified by widely established categories of objects, concepts and relations, rules, standards, and normatively provided expectations. The "blooming, buzzing confusion" that is the physico-biological situation, after the achievement or imposition of commonly evolved or commonly held organizing, structuring, interpretive principles, becomes the ordered, encompassable, communication-enabling psychologically prevailing canonical situation. How this happens, how a convergent differentiation of the physical world (and the then apparent social world) comes about has received a good deal of, but still not enough, psychological attention. The demarcation of objects must be agreed upon by the individual. The principles guaranteeing their constancy must be formulated. The cognitive economies to be realized by incisive categorization must be gained. Highly abstract or nonmaterial concepts must be arduously educed or constructed, and the relations characterizing a fuzzy world must be discerned (see, for example, Gibson, Brunswik, Rosch, Bruner, Bateson). For all of us, the raw, boundless, and even overwhelming physico-biological world is conditioned to become much less, but also much more, than it was, namely, a world structured to exclude certain possibilities and to emphasize others. Then, wonder of wonders, because of our common humanity, the perceptual and cognitive ontogeny of individuals proves to be surprisingly and strongly similar. To the extent that developing views of the world attain consensuality, they may be said to have canonical form and the canonical form can be identified. It is only rarely that "the doors of perception" are "cleansed" (as in hypnagogic moments or when under the influence of a psychotomimetic) and individuals can apprehend again the physico-biological world in its unfiltered and astonishing form and formlessness.

Third, there is the *functional* situation (the life space of Lewin, the beta press of Murray), the psychological demand-qualities and structure of the immediately pressing situation as it effectively registers on or is construed by the particular individual at the particular moment under scrutiny. It is the functional situation to which the individual reacts and responds, nothing else. Where the canonical situation represents the stimulus context as generally understood and, therefore, as it "should" register or be understood by any individual, the functional situation represents the stimulus context as it indeed registers or is effectively understood by the particular individual being evaluated. The differences between the canonical situation and the individual's functional situation is, logically, attributable to the operation of the individual's personality structure (the individual's developmentally achieved perceptualizing schemata) as further influenced by the immediately present motivational state of the individual.

Each of the three situational levels—the physico-biological, the canonical, and the functional—encounters or generates important and exciting psychological problems. However, historically, the three levels of analysis have not always been kept clearly distinguished. Further, because each of the three levels is so obviously of psychological interest, there has been a tendency on the part of conceptualizers and workers at any one level to ignore the claims on psychology that fairly follow from concern with other points along this analytical sequence. Although our focus in the present essay is of necessity primarily on the canonical situation, we acknowledge the fascinating problem and necessity of understanding the relationships between levels.

What should be the form of the interactional paradigm towards which the psychology of personality should aspire? Tersely put, it is our suggestion that: (1) if the parameter values of what we call the canonical situation can be specified; and (2) if the parameter values of the personality structure and the motivational state of the individual can also be specified; then (3) given a bit of theory, it should be feasible to predict various parameter values of the behavior of the particular person in the particular situation.

For this aspiration, an ultimate one, to be realized or to move even somewhat toward its realization, the characteristics of the normatively described, consensually received canonical situation must be defined independently of any one person. Otherwise we are mired in an oft-remarked, science-preventing tautology: On the one hand, we can know the *functional* situation of the individual only afterward, through observing the individual's subsequent behavior; on the other hand, we are presumably trying to study, before the fact of behavior, the effects of the situation on the individual's response. Thus, we understand the situation from the behavior and the behavior from the situation! The usual recourse to escape this circularity has been to define the situation in clean, indisputably independent, physicalistic or architectural terms (Davis, 1953). But physicalistic, architectural descriptions of the situation being encountered by the individual too often fail, embarrassingly, to express the prescriptive and proscriptive significance of what is impinging on the individual, the psychologically normative meaning of the surround that can be captured by the canonical definition of the situation.

It follows, of course, that the characteristics of the person must be defined independently of the canonical situation. Otherwise, we are burdened by the other side of the preceding tautological coin: We can know a person only through the behavior manifested in a particular situation while, simultaneously, we are trying to discern, before the fact of behavior, the implications of a person's character for the behavior formulated in a particular situation.

But beyond these logical necessities, several conceptual conditions must be satisfied if we are to have a paradigm of consequence:

1. A psychologically nontrivial set of situational parameters must be formulated to characterize the range of canonical situations encountered. To provide commensurability and, therefore comparability, among canonical situations pa-

rameters of the canonical situation will have to be defined in formal, abstract, content-free terms.

2. A psychologically nontrivial set of personality and motivational parameters must be formulated to characterize the range of personality structures and motivational states encountered. Such parameters of personality and motivation will also have to be expressed in formal, abstract, content-free terms.

3. A psychologically nontrivial set of behavior or action parameters, again must be formulated to characterize the range of behaviors or actions forged by individuals.

4. All three sets of parameters must conceptually mesh or be mutually reciprocal (existing within the same metaphorical system) so that: (a) the parameters of the canonical situation can be understood to register on the person: (b) the personality-motivation parameters of the individual can be understood to process and transform the canonical situation into the individual's functional situation; and (c) the individual's functional situation, as further processed or weighed by the individual's motivationally influenced cognitive and action schemata, can be understood to permit or to formulate the parameterized behaviors.

5. There should be a theoretical dynamic psychological system-goal being served that entails specific psychological relationships and changes over moments in the way an individual will behave in (apprehend and respond to) the canonical situation as a consequence of particular person-canonical situation conjunctions.

The preceding five interrelated points derive from a prior conceptual orientation worth remarking on. In turn, these five points, if they are to have consequence, must guide and be justified by explicit efforts to implement this approach. The prior conceptual orientation is simple enough to convey. We view the field of personality psychology as having permitted itself, quite unfortunately, to be defined as the static study of individual differences with respect to various arbitrary variables. Efforts to reduce the arbitrariness of the variables studied by means of factor analysis and related procedures have proven largely unavailing for technical as well as egocentric reasons. Consequently, the journals report relationships, often of interest, that aggregate without cumulating, that are inundating but not integrating. The study of environmental or situational psychology may well be proceeding, or be about to proceed, along similar lines—with arbitrary lists of situational variables to be used to order situations, with taxonomies of situations, and with an empiricism of appreciable psychological interest that, nevertheless, is without apparent or imposable organization.

Since variables can be created endlessly, why should we study one variable distinguishing people or situations rather than another? On what grounds can one list of variables proposed for describing differences among people or situations be viewed as more useful or important than another list? How can we achieve a nonarbitrary and incisive way of discriminating the psychological differences among people and among situations?

An attractive way of attaining a compelling set of variables for the description of between-individual or between-situation differences involves moving toward a psychology that studies and seeks to specify *the system properties of the person in situ*. If we can specify the parameters *within* a person and *within* a situation (and their dynamic interrelationships) that underly an individual's perceptions and actions, we have a theory of behavior for the individual. Then, almost as a by-product, the behavioral differences *among* persons can be understood as due to the different values held by each individual on the system-relevant personality parameters and the differences among situations can be understood as due to the different values of the system-relevant parameters characterizing the different situations. The variables underlying interindividual or intersituational differences are far less arbitrary if they are manifestations of parameters fundamental to a systematic, dynamic account of any person's behavior within any situation. In short we believe that the unhappy state of the psychology of individual differences requires a turn (or return) to the psychology of intraindividual functioning.

A related feature of our basic orientation is our attitude toward the psychological meaning of situations, experience, and behaviors. How exquisitely meaningful should we be, or can we be, in an approach to a scientific psychology? The experience of each human being is unique; we are insulated by solipsism from appreciating the meaning of any person's experience in all its ramifications and richness. Yet, efforts to deal with meaning, to gain a sense of it, and to declare it are personally satisfying and perhaps even introspectively necessary as we lead our everyday lives.

We cannot truly deal with meaning, but perhaps we can deal usefully with aspects of it. But which aspects? A basic division of the domain of meaning is between *the psychological content* of situations, experience, and behavior and *the formal, abstract properties* of situations, experience, and behavior. In our view the incorporation of psychological content into a system or theory of psychological functioning is not conceptually feasible. Psychological content is simply unmanageable it is too raw, too diverse, and at the wrong classificatory or metaphorical level to be fitted into a cognitively economic and coherent theoretical system. Content can be reported but before it can be scientifically employed, it must be parameterized. Such parameterization escapes from the details and diversity of content, leaving instead the recognition (perhaps only a definitional achievement!) of generalizations and uniformities spanning situations, experiences or behaviors that insistently naive or sensitive eyes could construe as endlessly unique. Is the tradeoff worthwhile, the abandoning of rich psychological content in order to reach a parsimonious, but perhaps intuitively unreal, system of explanation? It is difficult to say. The answer depends in large measure on how generative the parsimonious theory can prove to be. Sparse relationships from a parsimonious theory certainly provide little support for conceptual stinginess. Choice regarding the merits of a content-free versus a content-laden approach to psychology will depend on esthetic preference and how one wishes to place one's bets on the intellectual directions likely to prove fruitful.

The present chapter is an initial effort to address the first of the five conceptual requirements we have specified: to identify some of the parameters in terms of which to characterize a range of psychologically interesting situations.

SOME LIMITED EMPIRICISM

Since 1968 we have been conducting a longitudinal study tracing the development of particular ego functions—ego control and ego resiliency—and cognitive competencies in a sample of approximately 130 young children who were assessed initially as three-year-olds and who were evaluated subsequently at ages four, five, seven, and most recently, at eleven.

One of the important motivations for undertaking our longitudinal study was to test, from a developmental perspective, certain of our conceptualizations about persons in situ. This intention and our methodological preferences mandated the inclusion in our assessment battery at each age level of many experiment-based, standardized situations varying in their psychological demand qualities. (See Block & Block, 1979, for an explication of the methodology and its rationale).

Over four assessment periods, at ages three, four, five, and seven, the children in our sample have been experimentally evaluated in 54 different standardized situations. The experimental contexts employed will be conveyed later but include, for example, at one extreme, a naturalistic free play situation and, at the other extreme, a standard intelligence test.

The research approach employed here involved, first, describing the various features and psychological qualities of each situation and then analyzing the set of situations, seeking to classify them into a taxonomy and to identify the psychological parameters underlying situations as they impinge on the experiencing individual. The approach is not unlike that advocated by Frederiksen (1972) but deemed impractical by him for most psychological investigations. In discussing methods for developing a taxonomy of situations, Frederiksen noted, "Data that permit one to perform such an investigation (Person × Situation interaction) are rare because we do not in one investigation ordinarily evaluate many aspects of performance in each of many situations" (p. 121). Our research program provides one of those rare opportunities.

The California Situational Q-set (CSQ)

In order to describe situations according to their formal demand qualities a set of Q-items was developed to describe the various facets and the evocative potential of the various psychological situations included in the several test batteries. In formulating the initial items, we were influenced by dimensions posited by

Arsenian and Arsenian (1948), Chein (1954), and Lewin (1936, 1951c) to describe goals, pathways, and constraints in the psychological environment (e.g., numerosity, clarity, accessibility, acceptability, impedance). The item pool was further expanded to include various psychological "pushes" and "pulls" deemed present in the particular measures included in our test battery. After pretesting and several revisions, the current, but still tentative, set of 54 situation-relevant items was settled upon. Examples of items included in the CSQ are conveyed later in the section describing the results of a factor analysis of the CSQ as applied to the situations in our assessment battery. It requires noting that the CSQ in the form reported here is limited in its generality because its content was deliberately restricted to, and therefore determined by, the specific situations included in the assessment batteries designed for young children aged 3 through 7. These batteries evaluated performance largely in cognitive and problem-solving situations. For the most part the CSQ does not sample social situations extensively in the version being reported here. The data from our assessment of the children at age 11 will be used to extend the CSQ set further to include items descriptive of the demand qualities of the more social situations studied at this later age and to include more items reflecting situations that, for example, evoke introspection, require presentation of the self, assess emotional responsivity and sensitivity to metaphor.

Developing Observer-Based Consensual Descriptions of Psychological Situations

In order to obtain reliable descriptions of the demand qualities or evocative potential of the many psychological situations included in the assessment batteries, persons who had administered, or had observed regularly the administration of a particular procedure, either in the context of our own study or in studies conducted by other collaborative investigators, were contacted and asked to contribute to the present study. Fifteen experienced experimenters could be reached and all agreed to complete the CSQ descriptions for each of the procedures with which they were familiar. Each observer independently described a particular situation by using a forced, nine-step Q-sort distribution, placing six items in each category on a continuum ranging from most salient to least salient. It proved possible to obtain CSQ descriptions of 54 experimental situations; the mean number of experimenters describing each situation was 2.5 (range from 1 to 7). The average level of interjudge agreement reached acceptable levels (mean of .50), and therefore it was warranted to composite the independent observer descriptions where multiple Q-sorts existed. The composited experimenters' descriptions can be viewed as a consensual or canonical characterization of the psychological demand qualities of the various experimental situations. Obviously this effort to make operational a canonical definition of situations via consensus is limited by the small size and perhaps special character of the experimenter population available. However as a beginning effort to make sense of a well-traveled but still uncharted domain, our approach can have some usefulness.

The Dimensional Structure of Our Situations

The composited observer descriptions of the 54 psychological situations included in our test battery were submitted to inverse factor analysis, with unities entered as communality values. Thirteen factors meeting the conventional eigen value criterion of unity or more were extracted and rotated using the varimax procedure. Five of the factors were defined by only one experimental procedure and will not be considered further although, in their reliable uniqueness, they may well be important in their own right. The experimental situations with loadings in excess of .45 on each of the eight multiply-defined factors are presented in Table 6.1. Together the eight factors account for 88% of the communal variance.

Factor I.   The first factor is comprised of situations that include the Peabody Picture Vocabulary Test, the Wechsler Preschool Scale of Intelligence, and the Wechsler Intelligence Scale for Children, the Ravens Progressive Matrices, the Picture Arrangement Test, the Rod and Frame Test, the Matching Familiar Figures Test, the Embedded Figures tests, Conservation of Number, and an adaptation of Piaget's "Three Mountain Problem." The CSQ items most differentially descriptive of this factor include the following:

16. Performance in the situation emphasizes a wide store of previously acquired information.
24. Performance in the situation emphasizes speed in behavior.
20. Performance in the situation emphasizes manipulating abstract symbols, secondary processes of thought.
26. Performance in the situation emphasizes the use of convergent thinking.
23. Performance in the situation emphasizes accuracy in behavior.
28. Performance in the situation emphasizes the ability to extrapolate, to infer.

The common features of the tasks constituting Factor I as they are reflected in the CSQ descriptions include the necessity of a sufficient level of knowledge and memory, the requirement of analysis, manipulation, and extrapolation of this knowledge, and task demands that emphasize convergent modes of thought. From a personality standpoint the CSQ items suggest that among the ego functions facilitating performance on Factor I is the ability to control impulse in order that attention may be focused and sustained and ego resiliency in order that integrated performance may be maintained under conditions of failure and the stress of evaluation.

TABLE 6.1
Experimental Tasks Defining Factors Obtained from Analysis of the California Situational Q-sort

Factor	Task
I	Wechsler Preschool Scale of Intelligence
	Peabody Picture Vocabulary Test
	Ravens Progressive Matrices
	Conservation of Number
	Preschool Embedded Figures Test (Coates)
	Children's Embedded Figures Test (Karp & Konstadt)
	Matching Familiar Figures Test (Kagan)
	Portable Rod and Frame Test
	Piaget's Three Mountain Problem (adapted)
	The Picture Arrangement Test
II	Instances Test (Instances of Round Objects)
	Lowenfeld Mosaic Test (adapted to assess creativity)
	Alternative Uses Test
	Differentiation of Affect
	Standardized Free Play Situation
	Concept Evaluation Test (McReynolds)
	Physiognomic Perception Test (Ehrman)
	Parallel Lines Test (Torrance)
	Word Association
III	Competing Set (Resistance to)
	Simon Says
	Delay of Gratification
	Distractability (Resistance to)
	Level of Aspiration
	Motor Inhibition Test
	Satiation Box
IV	Barrier Box
	Barrier Drawer
	Barrier Door
	Partial Reinforcement
V	Memory for Narrative
	Digit Span
	Stanford–Landauer Memory Test
	Incidental Learning
VI	Moral Reasoning Test (adapted from Selman)
	Sharing Task (Rutherford & Mussen)
	Adjective Self-descriptive Q-sort
VII	Percept Formation Tests
	Role-taking Tasks (Flavell)
VIII	Sigel Object Sorting Test
	Unstructured Object Sorting Test (adapted from Gardner)

Factor II. The second factor is defined by situations that include the Alternative Uses Test, the Physiognomic Perception Test, and Free Play the Instances Test, the Parallel Lines Test, and a test of Affect Differentiation. The CSQ items most differentially characterizing tasks in Factor II include the following:

8. The context evokes creativity, imagination.
24. Performance in the situation emphasizes speed in behavior.
12. The context encourages the use of primary-process thinking.
20. Performance in the situation emphasizes manipulating abstract symbols, secondary processes of thought.
35. Performance in the task emphasizes introspection.
16. Performance in the situation emphasizes a wide store of previously acquired information.

The demand qualities of situations loading high on Factor II, as conveyed by the composited CSQ descriptions, place fewer restraints upon the responses of the child, encourage alternative and associative approaches, emphasize fluent, scanning thinking, and de-emphasize cognitive evaluation. The ego functions benefiting success on tasks defined by Factor II may be expected to differ according to the latent meaning of the score used to express the child's behavior in these situations. If fluency, regardless of the quality of response is emphasized in the score employed, then person characteristics associated with lesser control of impulse, under-control, would be important—spontaneity, ease of association, tolerance of ambiguity, broadly permissive categorization standards, and so on. If, however, the child's responses are scored according to a qualitative criterion of relevancy or appropriateness, then the ability to evaluate the adequacy of one's productions and to monitor one's behavior, an aspect of ego resiliency, also assumes importance.

Factor III. The experimental situations defining the third factor include Delay of Gratification, Resistance to Competing Sets, the Motor Inhibition Test, Resistance to Distractability, Satiation (operationalized as time spent performing repetitive tasks), and Level of Aspiration (operationalized to represent the establishment of realistic goals). The CSQ items most differentially describing situations loading high on Factor III include:

21. Performance in the situation emphasizes the inhibition of immediate response.
6. Few intellectual demands are made upon the subject by the situation; context is not challenging intellectually.
42. Failures in the situation are readily apparent to the subject.
2. The nature of the situation is ''lifelike'' or realistic.

1. The context evokes docility, tractability (N.B. low placement implies context evokes independence and manifestations of autonomy).

39. Performance in the situation emphasizes good motor coordination.

Common to the situations encompassed by Factor III, according to the CSQ descriptions, is a clear definition of task demands that are cognitively uninteresting and a clear directive definition of what behaviors will be viewed as "successful." Both the ability to control impulse, ego control, and the ability to monitor or regulate one's behavior in accordance with competing situational requirements, ego resiliency, would appear to be salient personality characteristics in Factor III situations.

Factor IV. The fourth factor is defined by three tasks in which the child unexpectedly encounters some type of barrier blocking the achievement of a goal and a fourth task, partial reinforcement that measures the number of nonreinforced trials required to extinguish a learned response in a conventional partial reinforcement experiment. The CSQ items most differentially descriptive of the situations defining Factor IV include:

42. Failures in the situation are readily apparent to the subject.

7. Performance in the situation emphasizes continuing and frequent reassessment of strategy by the subject in the light of newly available information.

5. Performance in the situation emphasizes risk-taking behavior.

8. The context evokes creativity, imagination.

14. The context evokes frustration.

49. The situation is difficult for most same-age peers.

These CSQ items indicate that the tasks defining Factor IV require the child to restructure a situation that is not consistent with prior expectations and to develop, in ambiguous circumstances, alternative modes of solution (i.e., finding ways to surmount the barriers or developing new hypotheses consistent with changed reinforcement contingencies). Although hypothesis generation and hypothesis testing are required in these situations, the child must also be sufficiently open to the expression of impulse so that ideas can be translated into actions. Given that the Factor IV situations will evoke unease because they lack clear structure and yet are constraining, the overly controlled child would be expected to be relatively inhibited and immobilized.

Factor V. Four tasks clearly involving memory define Factor V. Digit Span, the Sanford-Landauer Memory Test, Incidental Learning, and Memory for Narrative. The CSQ items most differentially describing this factor include:

37. Performance in the situation emphasizes the "chunking" or organization of large amounts of information.

33. Performance in the situation emphasizes an effective, short-term memory.

3. The context provides extrinsic rewards.

34. Contextual orientation or situational instructions are *not* simple, straightforward.

15. The context encourages guessing.

23. Performance in the situation emphasizes accuracy in behavior.

The demand qualitites of the tasks loading high on Factor V require effectively organized concentration and an eager acceptance of (or docility before) the memorial burdens of the tasks. The ability to resist distraction and maintain focused attention, aspects of ego control, and the ability to maintain integrated performance under conditions of increasing difficulty, aspects of ego resiliency, would be expected to be associated with successful performance on the tasks included in Factor V.

Factor VI.   The three tasks defining Factor VI are moral reasoning, an adjective Q-sort self-description, and a sharing task in which the child is asked to distribute rewards between self and an anonymous peer in accordance with a sense of fairness, given that there were quantitative differences in the contribution of each child to the completion of each of a series of tasks. The CSQ items most differentially describing Factor VI include:

11. The context requires the subject to be trusting.

9. The context encourages the subject to reveal or expose self, to express feelings, and/or to discuss personal matters.

35. Performance in the context emphasizes introspection.

37. Performance in the situation emphasizes the "chunking" or organization of large amounts of new information.

30. The situation encourages the subject to behave in a socially desirable way or to manifest socially desirable values.

16. Performance in the situation emphasizes a wide store of previously acquired information.

The demand qualities of the situations loading high on Factor VI appear to actuate inner life and value contemplation, require some degree of trust that self-exposure will not have catastrophic consequences, and tap the breadth and integration of the life experiences of the participating subject.

Factor VII.   Factor VII is composed of two types of tasks, Percept Formation and perceptual Role-Taking tasks. The Percept Formation task requires the child to identify initially unrecognizable pictorial stimuli as soon as possible when additional pictorial information is given incrementally over a series of projected slides. The Role-Taking tasks were developed by Flavell (1968) and require the child to consider how given pictorial arrays would be seen when viewed from a different perspective. The CSQ items most differentially describing these tasks include:

54. Performance in the situation emphasizes spatial transformations.
46. Performance in the situation emphasizes an interactive, zeroing in approach.
52. The context is structured so that subject perceives the other(s) as supportive (e.g., encouraging subject when the situation is difficult).
5. Performance in the situation emphasizes risk-taking behavior.
28. Performance in the situation emphasizes the ability to extrapolate, to infer.
19. Performance in the situation emphasizes evoking pictorial images.

The demand qualities of the situations included in Factor VII reflect the importance of pictorial imagery, the pressure for successive, self-monitoring inference, and a willingness to take chances to achieve early accuracy. In addition to the cognitive competencies essential for successful performance on these tasks ego resiliency would be required as well. In this context resiliency would permit the necessary relaxation of one's modal standards for evaluating percepts in the service of extrapolation and inference.

Factor VIII.   Two conceptualization tasks load highly on Factor VIII, the Sigel Object Sorting Test and a modification of Gardner's Unstructured Object Sorting Test. The CSQ items most differentially describing this factor include:

37. Performance in the situation emphasizes the "chunking" or organization of large amounts of new information.
8. The context evokes creativity, imagination.
44. Performance in the situation emphasizes following through a series or sequence of steps.
7. Performance in the situation emphasizes continuing and frequent reassessment of strategy by the subject in the light of newly available information.
31. The situation emphasizes close analysis of detail.
13. The context permits the subject to establish own goals or standards.

The situations encompassed by Factor VIII appear to require creative abstraction and conceptualization where the child is free to use self-set criteria for what shall be called a solution. The particular cognitive demands include abstraction and conceptualization; ego functions beyond those essential for maintaining integrated performance under conditions of unstructure and ambiguity (i.e., ego resiliency) are less relevant.

Some Situational Parameters

The preceding descriptions of the various types of situations issued by our analyses require some summary abstractions before this approach can begin to have broader and conceptual implication. We have educed seven situational parameters differentially associated with our types of experimental contexts.

1. Structure.   The parameter, structure, if its value is high, can be said to imply a canonical situation wherein goals, tasks, and roles are well-defined, and the pathways leading to goal attainment and task accomplishment, and the rules for social interactions, are clear and directive.

2. Convergency.   The parameter, convergency, if its value is high, can be said to imply a canonical situation usually, but not necessarily, cognitive in nature wherein the defined goal, task, or problem permits of but one correct or acceptable solution.

3. Divergency.   The parameter, divergency, if its value is high, can be said to imply a canonical situation wherein the defined goal, task, or problem permits an open-ended number of alternative solutions. Although a situation cannot simultaneously be divergent and convergent, it may be neither.

4. Evaluation.   The parameter, evaluation, if its value is high, can be said to imply a canonical situation wherein the accuracy, desirability, or appropriateness of behavior is explicitly or implicitly understood to be evaluated by another person who is in a position of status or judgment.

5. Feedback.   The parameter, feedback, if its value is high, can be said to imply a canonical situation wherein information about the effectiveness, appropriateness, or desirability of one's behavior is explicitly provided by another or is readily available through observation of the indisputable effects of one's efforts.

6. Constraint.   The parameter, constraint, if its value is high, can be said to imply a canonical situation wherein the defined goal, problem solution, or social interaction is constrained by the presence of a barrier, either physical or psychological in nature.

7. Impedance. The parameter, impedance, if is value is high, can be said to imply a canonical situation requiring a high degree of exertion, cognitive, physical, or affective in nature.

Each of the parameters described above, besides deriving from the characteristics of the several types of situations, also connects with dimensions earlier posited by others to describe characteristics of psychological environments (e.g., Arsenian & Arsenian, 1948; Chein, 1954; Lewin, 1936, 1951c). In addition, reference to certain CSQ items and close further reflection on some of the experimental tasks suggests four additional situational parameters worthy of consideration.

8. Malleability. The parameter, malleability (after Wapner, Kaplan & Cohen, 1973), it its value is high, suggests a canonical situation which admits of change by the person. Change may be alloplastic and effected by locomotion (Lewin) in the real world, or change may be autoplastic and effected by the individual's restructuring of the registering functional environment. Malleable situations, then, are those that permit locomotion and/or restructuring. In the present context, the barrier tasks exemplify malleable experimental situations.

9. Galvanization. The parameter, galvanization, if its value is high, can be said to imply a canonical situation that is attractively arousing, stimulating, or has incentive value. In galvanizing canonical environments the "average expectable person" can be expected to be highly motivated and engaged. Within our set of situations, the curiosity box, the barrier tasks, and most of the tasks comprising Factor III illustrate this contextual property.

10. Familiarity. The parameter, familiarity, if its value is high, can be said to imply a canonical situation wherein the physical, interpersonal, cultural context, together with the task and social demands of the situation, are known to and are predictable by the "average expectable person."

11. Differentiation. The parameter, differentiation, if its value is high, can be said to imply a canonical situation that is highly articulated, with a great number of "discriminanda" (Chein) or "regions" (Lewin).

None of these situational parameters should be viewed as exclusively defining a situation. As already noted, each situation can or should be characterized by a set or constellation of parameter values. When varying combinations of these situational parameters are considered, certain formal derivations begin to come forward. For example, following the early example of the Arsenians' definition of the formal characteristics of "tough" and "easy" cultures, it is possible to define the formal properties of "tough" and "easy" situations as experienced by the "average expectable person." A "tough" context is one that lacks structure, offers energetic impedance, is evaluative, unfamiliar, containing, unmalleable, highly differentiated (presenting a large array of alternatives), and excessively galvanizing. An "easy" situation would be one reversing the parameters of the "tough" situations. Other kinds of situations can be defined as well. A number of conceptual and predictive benefits should follow from the ability to characterize, in formal terms, the qualities of situations independently of the situation-experiencing individual.

Some Next Steps

Looking ahead to our own personal research agenda, we shall be relating parameters of the person to some of the situational parameters identified in our analyses. The connection of specific personality and cognitive characteristics to performance as a function of specifiable situational parameters will make the study of the person *in situ* much more interesting.

After developing a set of situational parameters deemed interesting and sufficient, it will then be feasible to examine the personality characteristics associated with behavior as a function of different parameter values, taken singly or in constellation. We will also be in a position to test some predictions derivable from our conceptualization of personality functioning, relating parameters of ego functioning (ego control and ego resiliency) to behavior in situations characterized by differing parameter values. We would expect, for example, that, holding intellectual level constant, individuals high on the ego-control continuum—individuals characterized as overcontrolling impulse—would manifest personally higher levels of performance in situations characterized by structure, convergency, familiarity, and low malleability than in situations not so characterized. We would expect also that individuals low on the continuum of ego resiliency—individuals characterized as brittle and unadaptive in the face of stress—would manifest personally lower levels of performance in experimental contexts characterized as evaluative, and low on feedback, than in situations not so defined.

Before moving on to this effort, however, we propose to improve upon the preliminary efforts here reported to identify situational parameters defining experimental contexts. First, we will be enlarging the sample of situations. The assessment of our sample of children at age 11 recently having been completed, we will be able to add 23 different standardized procedures to our sampling of situations, greatly extending the range and ecological validity of the groupings and parameters subsequently achieved. Second, we will be revising and extending the items of the CSQ to incorporate additional situational dimensions and demand qualities found to be lacking as our experience with the CSQ has grown. We will include dimensions relevant to the tasks administered at age 11 that are not now represented, and sharpen the meaning of some of the existing items. Third, we will be increasing the sample of judges by enlisting more psychologists outside our project and articulate lay people to describe the psychological features and impact of particular experimental situations or procedures. These three kinds of improvements should make the next set of situational parameters of finer differentiation and greater consequence and perhaps afford a sufficient basis for going on to the personalogical analyses we have outlined. The journey toward a new and useful paradigm for the person in situ has just begun. The goal has become clearer but the pathway is *unfamiliar, unstructured, difficult, evaluative,* and *impeding*. Fortunately, it is *galvanizing* as well.

ACKNOWLEDGMENTS

This chapter was written while the authors were Scholars-in-residence at the Bellagio Study and Conference Center of the Rockefeller Foundation during May, 1979. We are deeply grateful for the Bellagio opportunity. The research reported is being supported by a National Institute of Mental Health Research Grant MH 16080 to Jack and Jeanne Block and by a National Institute of Mental Health Research Scientist Award to Jeanne H. Block.

We wish to express our appreciation to the current and former members of our research staff and to the other researchers who completed the California Situational Q-sort descriptions: Richard Arend, Jessica Ball, David Buss, Judy Casaroli, Adrienne Gans, Per Gjerde, Sandy Gove, Mark Haarz, David Harrington, Joy Moore, Andrea Morrison, Miriam Rosenn, Judy Schiller, and Myrna Walton.

7 Risky Situations

Richard H. Price
University of Michigan
USA

There is now a fairly large body of theory and research on the nature of psychological situations and person-setting interactions (Magnusson & Endler, 1977a). The growth of this literature has been fueled by controversies concerning the question of whether situational variables or individual differences account for more variance in behavior, and advocates have argued in favor of individual differences, situations, and a variety of interactionists' views. In recent years, I have begun to look at some of my own work in this area (Price, 1974a,b; Price & Blashfield, 1975; Price & Bouffard, 1974) with some misgivings. I began to wonder whether I was working on a problem that was merely intellectually interesting or whether it had any real significance for actual people living in real situations. I began to worry about the ecological validity of the work. What was the relationship between this work and the situational world in which people actually work, learn, and live?

We all know that these are forbidden thoughts to the serious, basic researcher, or theorist. As theorists, we simplify the complexities of the social world for conceptual clarity. We admit (sometimes I think all too readily) that real-life situations are much too complex to understand and much too messy for the conduct of research with unambiguous outcomes. Still, my forbidden thoughts persisted. Most of them focused on my misgivings about what I have come to regard as our core theoretical problem: the defining characteristics of the situation itself. Much of the research seemed to sacrifice too much for the sake of clean experiments and elegant, yet simple, conceptualizations. Worst of all, there seemed to be almost no intuitive resemblance between the "situations" I was studying and the world in which I and others were living. Most of my misgivings seemed to be focused on five troubling questions.

AREAS OF CONCERN

The first of these had to do with the question of situational sampling and the ecological validity of our research. Typically, situations were sampled at the convenience of the investigator or theorist. There seemed to be no clear metric for deciding whether the situations we sampled were actually representative of any particular social world. Consequently, the external or ecological validity of the results we produced and the conclusions we drew seemed very much in doubt. In this context, the question of whether situations or persons account for more variance has little meaning since differential sampling from either realm has a direct impact on the proportion of variance accounted for by persons, situations, or their interaction.

A second misgiving had to do with the fact that in many cases we seemed merely to be studying cognitive representations of artificial situations and not situations themselves. Social psychology has turned very much in the direction of developing new cognitive representations of the social world, and this is indeed an important contribution. Nevertheless, there is a real distinction between studying people's cognitive representations in actual situations and studying a subject's response to a written description of a situation or merely a word denoting a situational context. We seemed all too ready to settle for a subject's response to a questionnaire item rather than the subject's response in some behavioral setting.

My third concern about the situations we were studying had to do with the lack of a clear temporal aspect. Most of the situations we studied seemed to have a diffuse temporal boundary or be of only momentary psychological significance. Consequently, the effects of these situations on behavior over time were either difficult to infer or trivial. We seemed to be missing an important longitudinal aspect of situations and therefore could not possibly understand the adaptation of individual behavior over time to a particular setting or a sample of settings.

A fourth misgiving had to do with the fact that we were often ignoring the context of the situation itself. Situations usually occur in the context of some social institution with its own norms, roles, and expectations for behavior, and yet the institutional and historical context of the situation was almost invariably ignored.

Finally, I was concerned that too often we failed to distinguish between intellectually interesting problems and problems of real human significance. I seldom saw in the literature any discussion of the role of situational variables as they applied to contemporary social problems. If my pessimistic view of the development of this field is correct, then we may be building theories of situations that: (1) are merely cognitive representations of hypothetical situations; (2) lack historical or institutional context; (3) ignore the temporal dimension; (4) are of dubious ecological validity; and (5) are of little consequence in understanding real human and social problems.

The easy answer to this dilemma is to argue simply that we don't yet know enough. As our theories become more powerful, so this argument goes, their human significance will become evident. Only then will our theories be able to address social problems in any detail. This is comforting, but I am not yet convinced that it is the case. Let me suggest an alternative strategy, one that was pioneered by Kurt Lewin. Lewin was convinced that in many cases it was most fruitful to try to understand a theoretical problem in the context of some concrete set of real-life situations. Only in this way, he argued, could a bridge be built between psychological theory and real human problems. In what follows, I will consider the question of the risky situations and the prevention of psychological distress. My goal will be to see how situational thinking can illuminate this problem.

RISKY SITUATIONS AND PREVENTION

The Logic of Prevention

Throughout the history of the mental health profession in the United States, the principal efforts of practitioners have been directed to the treatment of psychological distress rather than its prevention. There are compelling reasons, however, to indicate that a treatment-oriented strategy will in the long run be a losing cause in dealing with psychological disorders. Even leaving aside the question of how effective current treatment methods actually are, resources allocated to treat psychological disorders will surely not grow as rapidly as the incidence of psychological dysfunction itself. There will, therefore, be an ever-widening gap between the need for treatment resources and our ability to deliver them.

As a result of this state of affairs, a great many writers in the field of mental health, including Bloom (1977), Cowen (1977), Goldston (1977), Heller and Monahan (1977), Kessler and Albee (1975), have argued that attempts to *prevent* psychological dysfunction and therefore reduce the rate of occurrence of disorder in the population is, in the long run, the only acceptable strategy. In general, it is argued, prevention activities should be aimed at groups and communities of individuals who have not yet shown signs of psychological dysfunction, and the purpose of these activities should be to prevent the occurrence of disorder rather than merely to limit its duration once it has already occurred (Bloom, 1977; Bower, 1969; Price, Ketterer, Bader & Monahan, 1980). The preventive approach to psychological disturbance has now been strongly endorsed in the United States by the President's Commission on Mental Health (1978) despite substantial conceptual vagueness about the actual nature of preventive activities. In fact, it is perhaps most accurate to say that prevention is a *goal* that can be met in a wide variety of different ways, and there is not yet clear agreement on precisely how that goal should be met.

Despite the unclarity in the current thinking about prevention, there is agreement about one aspect of the conceptual problem. It is generally agreed that some groups of individuals seem to be more at risk for the development of psychological disorders than others and that it is on these groups that we should concentrate our efforts. Spouses and children experiencing a divorce, recently widowed individuals, people entering retirement, people experiencing a death in the family, children of psychologically disturbed parents, and recently unemployed individuals, for example, are all groups of people who are subject to a much higher risk of psychological disturbance than the general population.

What has all this to do with the situation in psychological theory and research? The answer, I believe, lies in the fact that those of us who have been thinking about the psychological impact of social environments would do well to turn our attention to the conceptually underdeveloped area of prevention. I believe that there are contributions to be made to the prevention effort by a situational orientation.

A Situation Orientation to Risk Groups

Let us return to the concept of a "high-risk" group. I suggested that a high-risk group was any group that, on the basis of epidemiological evidence, showed a higher probability than the general population of developing psychological distress or disorder. It is tempting to assume that people are members of high-risk groups because of some individual characteristics they possess.

But let us look at high-risk groups more closely. Children of divorce, children of disturbed parents, recent widows, all may be equally well thought of as groups coping with a life situation that places very high demands on the person's adaptive capacity. I would like to suggest that implicit in the concept of a high-risk group is a situation that may be placing very great demands upon the individual for coping and adaptation. It follows that it is the situation that we must focus upon if we are to discover some of the factors that place a person at risk for the development of emotional disturbance.

Although this proposition may seem self-evident to some of us, for many it is not. Caplan and Nelson (1973) have made it quite clear that person-centered attributions of the cause for social problems tend to be quite common irrespective of the evidence. Once established, such definitions have very powerful implications for both the problem and the decision to take any ameliorative action.

Arguments Against the Situational Orientation to Risk Groups.   Before we go further, let us examine some possible objections to this position. The first of these objections is simply a reassertion of the dispositional—or trait—assumption regarding high-risk groups. This argument asserts that there are people who are at risk because of individual difference factors and that we cannot afford to ignore this. A compelling example would be schizophrenia. We know that a child with two, or even one, parent who has been diagnosed as schizophrenic has a very substantially elevated risk for the development of schizophrenia. This would seem to suggest that a situational orientation to this risk group is untenable or even misguided.

But it is still quite possible that situational interventions would be appropriate for disorders having a substantial biological substrate. Consider for a moment Meehl's (1962) theoretical account of the broad outlines of the developments of schizophrenia. Meehl suggests that we consider the concept of specific etiology. By this he means that causal condition which is necessary but not suffient for a disorder to occur. Thus, there may indeed be a genetic constellation that is important and perhaps even necessary for the development of schizophrenia. Even so, it does not follow that this dispositional trait necessarily produces the clinically observed disorder, nor does it follow that the course of the disorder can be affected only by procedures that are directed against the specific etiology. Furthermore, the largest source of variance in symptoms is not necessarily due to the specific etiology and may indeed be due to situational factors even though the specific etiology is necessary for the disorder to occur. Thus, there is no necessary simple cause–effect relationship between causal factors and the ultimate development of a disorder. There may in fact be a large number of links in the causal chain and a correspondingly large number of points for intervention between some specific causal factor and the ultimate display of symptomatology.

Let us make the point very clearly. Even for disorders that have a specific etiology of genetic origin, situational factors may still determine to a very large degree whether the disorder in question will actually occur or not. Therefore, situational factors may be critical both in precipitating and in preventing the development of the disorder.

Interactionists may view the situational orientation to high risk groups as unduly simpleminded. Certainly, they might argue, a conceptual model for high risk groups, whatever its final form, must take into account individual differences, situational factors, and their interaction. Thus, according to this view, the most fruitful paradigm for studying high risk groups surely must be a person-by-setting interaction paradigm. It follows from this that our job is to search for the interaction between person and setting factors that will ultimately be relevant to the prevention of psychological disorders.

My answer to this argument is to concede that, in principle, it is highly plausible. It is only when we turn to the practical and methodological problems associated with pursuing a person-by-setting interactional approach to the study of high risk groups that we begin to realize how limited our knowledge really is.

Consider for a moment Nisbett's (1977) arguments in favor of a ''main effect'' rather than an interactional approach to the study of personality and situations. He argues that it makes no sense to look for interactions until we are sure of the main effects and that psychology is not the mature sort of science that is in a position to search for those interactions. Nisbett argues that we are in a position comparable to that of preclassical physics before the Newtonian revolution and that ''it is premature to search for interactions, as premature as it would have been to argue in 1400 that one should look for the interaction between gravity and levity [p. 237].'' He also suggests that interactional hypotheses have usually been developed in the context of inconsistent main effects, are difficult to refute with new evidence, create a sense of false precision, and require inherently complex designs to test.

These disadvantages of interactional approaches to high risk groups at the current state of our knowledge seem to me to be very real. The advantages of main effect studies including their generalizability, their refutability, their comprehensability, and their potential ecological validity need to be taken very seriously. In our current discussion, I will focus largely upon main effects that can be discovered by an examination of the situation in which high risk groups find themselves.

Advantages of the Situational Orientation.   Redirecting our attention to the situation of the person at risk for psychological distress has two further advantages. The first advantage is that our assumptions about cause or etiology will strongly condition our ideas about appropriate interventions. Caplan and Nelson (1973) argue:

> What is done about a problem depends on how it is defined. The way a social problem is defined determines attempts at remediation or even whether such attempts will be made by suggesting both the *foci* and the *techniques* of intervention and by ruling out alternative possibilities. More specifically, problem definition determines the change strategy, the selection of a social action delivery system and the criteria for evaluation.
>
>   Problem definitions are based on assumptions about the causes of the problem and where they lie. If the causes of delinquency, for example, are defined in *person centered* terms (e.g., inability to delay gratification, or incomplete sexual identity), then it would be logical to initiate *person change* treatment techniques and intervention strategies to deal with the problem . . . If, on the other hand, explanations are *situation centered*, for example, if delinquency were interpreted as the substitution of extralegal paths for already pre-empted conventionally approved pathways for achieving socially valued goals, then efforts towards corrective treatment would logically have a *system change* orientation. Efforts would be launched to create suitable opportunities for success and achievement along conventional lines; thus, existing physical, social, or economic arrangements, not individual psyches, would be the targets for change [p. 200-201].

Thus, our attributions about the causality of a social or psychological problem may strongly condition both whether and where we intervene. This is not merely an interesting observation. It suggests that social policy affecting large numbers of people may be affected by whether or not we take a situational orientation to the prevention of psychological distress for high risk groups.

There is a second advantage to the situational approach to prevention. Such an approach is more likely to focus us on *movable* variables. As researchers, we have been particularly interested in the percentage of variance accounted for by personal variables, situational variables, and their interaction. We have, however, been much less interested in the question of how moveable or how easily manipulated these variables are for the purposes of intervention. But, a focus on intervention requires that we search for moveable variables. I would argue that we will be more likely to uncover variables that ultimately can be manipulated in the context of a program or policy decision if we focus on situational variables.

SOME POSSIBLE CHARACTERISTICS OF RISKY SITUATIONS

A situational orientation to risk for psychological distress requires: (1) that we have at least a provisional description of what we mean by a "situation" in this context; and (2) that we have some plausible hypotheses about what makes the situation "risky."

The kinds of situations I have in mind have several distinguishing characteristics. First, they occur over relatively long periods of time. Rather than for a few seconds or minutes, their natural course may run for weeks, months, or even years. Second, the meaning of these situations and their impact is greatly affected by the larger social and institutional context in which they occur. Third, the adaptive demands of these situations are highly complex, occur over the long run, and require a mix of task and interpersonal skills. They are situations that occupy a large portion of the psychological life of an individual for relatively long periods of time and perhaps might best be called "life situations."

Consider two examples of risky situations recently described by Sidney Cobb (1979). In the first, Cobb and his co-workers studied the changes in blood pressure and the death rate for NASA engineers and staff over the period covering the preparation and launching of Project Mercury, Project Gemini, and Project Apollo. As the deadline for launch approached for each of the three missions, the blood pressure and death rate for project staff sharply increased and fell off again dramatically after the mission was safely launched. Cobb calls this "dying under pressure."

In another study Cobb examined the changes in death rate for married men over age 54 for 7 years following the death of their spouses. Compared with the base rate for mortality of men of the same age, the death rate was 40% higher at the end of 1 year and then fell back to approximately the base rate level after 4 years.

Other life situations that may be risky and deserve careful examination include retirement, the discovery that one is pregnant, the beginning of a new job, the birth of a child, and divorce. Certainly these examples suggest that the situations I have in mind are molar and will not lend themselves easily to precise analysis. But I believe they are also the sorts of life situations most likely to have substantial psychological impact on the individual.

Can we describe the characteristics of risky situations? An examination of the literature on the social psychological dimensions of settings suggests to me that no single theoretically derived set of dimensions currently exists that encompasses all of the effects in which we might be interested. There is, as yet, no universal taxonomy of situations. But we do have research on settings from several different theoretical traditions or perspectives that is instructive.

Research on the social climate characteristics of the various settings including student living units, military companies, high school classrooms, and other settings suggests in general that settings that are low in participant involvement and social support but high in competition, task orientation, and restrictive control, tend to produce higher levels of illness, physical symptomatology, and absence. Thus, social climate characteristics may be one way of defining "risky situations."

It is important to note in this context that Moos and VanDort (1979) suggest there may be no single social climate dimension that defines risk. Instead, there may be an interaction between social climate dimensions themselves such that one combination produces risky situations while others do not. Specifically, Moos suggests that where high demands for achievement and high levels of control occur in a supportive milieu, support may buffer the stressful impact of these other dimensions. On the other hand, social environments that demand high productivity, are very controlling, and involve little social support may indeed be stressful, risky situations. This is an intriguing hypothesis and deserving of careful research.

Another critical dimension for defining risky situations may be that of social support. Cobb (1976) suggests that we may define social support as information leading one to believe that he or she is cared for, esteemed, and belongs in a network of commitment and mutual obligation. Certainly, it is plausible to imagine that life situations may vary considerably along this dimension.

There is some evidence to suggest that life situations low in social support may make individuals more vulnerable to depression (Brown, Bhrolchain, & Harris, 1975). Furthermore, there is suggestive evidence that social support may have an ameliorative effect in the context of a stressful event such as job loss. Gore (1973) found that social support by family and friends was associated with less depression and fewer complaints of illness among men having recently experienced job loss.

However, in a careful review of the literature on social support, Heller (1979) points out that virtually every study is correlational in nature and therefore open to rival hypotheses about the relationship between social support and psychological dysfunction. For example, it is equally plausible that persons experiencing low levels of social support show higher levels of disturbance because they lack the social competence to develop supportive relationships rather than because the lack of social support in itself increases stress for the individual. Heller's point is well taken, but as a candidate for an overall dimension underlying many sorts of "risky situations," social support stands as a major area for inquiry.

A number of other dimensions of life situations also suggest themselves as candidates for characteristics of risky situations including controllability (Seligman, 1975) and undermanning (Barker, 1968; Price, 1976). The point is that it is, in principle, possible to characterize life situations using dimensions that may predict the degree to which a person in such situations is at risk for psychological distress.

If our understanding of what makes situations "risky" is some time away, scientifically based interventions are still farther off. However, I have recently suggested (Price, 1979) that systematically collected information about the psychological impact of situations can be used in at least three ways in developing social intervention strategies. First, situational information can provide a guide about which settings to select to maximize personal gains. Second, information on the characteristics of a setting can be fed back to participants to provide a stimulus for setting change. Finally, environmental information can be used as a guide to designing and planning new settings with some assurance that the setting, once implemented, will have the desired effect.

In summary, it is possible and even desirable to conceptualize the problem of the prevention of psychological disorders in situational terms. Focusing our attention on the situational context of high risk groups may provide us with important information about stressors in the situation that precipitate and maintain psychological disturbance. In addition, taking a situational view of the problem increases the likelihood that we will be able to diagnose high risk situations and design social interventions: (1) to select lower risk situations; (2) to alter the characteristics of risky situations; or (3) to plan new settings that minimize the risk of psychological disturbance.

SITUATIONAL THEORY AND SOCIAL PRACTICE

I have suggested that our thinking about situations can have implications for social intervention in the life situations of people who are at risk for psychological disorders. I have, in fact, suggested that there can be a fruitful relationship between theory and practice (Price & Politser, 1980).

Cartwright (1978) has recently given us a portrait of one of the original interactionists, Kurt Lewin. Lewin was continuously preoccupied with ways in which social psychology could best contribute to the improvement of social practice. In fact, Lewin was convinced that the interests of theorists and practitioners were inextricably interrelated. Cartwright reminds us that Lewin's (1951c) famous quotation "Nothing is so practical as a good theory," is really part of a longer quotation regarding the relationship between practitioners and theorists. The longer quote states that close cooperation between theoretical and applied psychology "can be accomplished . . . if the theorist does not look toward applied problems with highbrow aversion or with a fear of social problems, and if the applied psychologist realizes that there is nothing so practical as a good theory [p. 169]." Thus, Lewin's famous dictum applied equally to practitioners and to theorists. But, as I scan the theoretical developments in psychology and the world of practice, I see very few of our best researchers and thinkers attempting to bridge the gap between theory and practice.

Cartwright (1978) notes that the current development of social psychological theory and research attempts to explain behavior with highly abstract concepts such as social class, ethnicity, social role, socialization, or personality. But these concepts cannot be unambiguously related to the situations in which behavior actually takes place. As a consequence, they do not provide much useful guidance to the practitioner in the design of social programs.

In fact, Cartwright's assessment of social psychology today suggests that it now focuses primarily on cognitive processes within individuals. In effect, social psychology has become increasingly less social. As important as these theoretical developments in cognitive social psychology have been, cognitive phenomena represent only one of the many determinants of behavior. By themselves they cannot form a solid basis for what Lewin would have prescribed—truly useful theory. Cartwright calls for the development of new concepts to describe the situation so that they can show in specific detail how the environment influences behavior and is affected by it.

Lewin was remarkable in his ability to maintain an interest simultaneously both in the highly abstract issues of theory and in the concrete problems of social action. There is an inherent tension in these two apparently conflicting preoccupations. And yet Cartwright (1978) suggests that it was that tension that stimulated much of Lewin's creativity; as Cartwright notes:

> His deep concern for the ills that beset mankind kept him in close touch with social reality so that he was able to see the difference between a merely interesting intellectual problem and one of substantial significance. And his belief that the solution of social problems requires a scientific understanding of the nature of these determinants motivated his deep concern with the issues of theory construction. Since Lewin's day, we have been able to build few rather primitive bridges between theory and practice. And these have served us well. But what is more important, they have demonstrated that it is possible for social psychology to construct the kind of practical theory that Lewin was beginning to envision some 40 years ago [p. 180].

If these remarks accomplish nothing else, I hope that they arouse some of that tension which Lewin was too courageous to avoid. For I believe that it is out of that tension that truly useful and truly creative theory about the situation in psychological theory and research will develop.

8

Perceptions of and Reactions to Work Situations: Some Implications of an Action Control Approach

Winfried Hacker
Technische Universität
Dresden GDR

The main issue of this contribution is the utility of the situation approach for applied work, especially for human-centered job design. A main interest in this frame of reference is to test the possibility of an integration of an action control approach into the personality × situation conceptualization. The reason is that working activities are conscious goal-directed actions altering both the physical and social environment in a more or less intended mode and include some special traits of personality. The work environment may be conceptualized in terms of job characteristics, leader behavior, role ambiguity and conflict, work group characteristics, and organizational characteristics (James and Sells, Chapter 18, this volume).

This chapter stresses only the aspect of job characteristics, in general, and task requirements, in particular. Task requirements are referred to as job content relating primarily to job satisfaction, motivation, prevention of dequalification, and performance. In the literature on work environment statistics abstract macrodimensions prevail. These are generalized interpretative constructs or aggregates of perceptions of the environment. For job characteristics, such general dimensions are autonomy, variety, importance of tasks, and challenge (James and Sells Chapter 18, this volume). A search for the actual microvariables, that are globally condensed in these aggregates of perceived job characteristics, and an attempt to analyze them more precisely in terms of individual actual task requirements are the present objectives.

Until now, little attention has been given to the analysis of the properties of actual task requirements. In investigations of work environment perceptions verbal reports prevail. These perceptions were employed almost exclusively as independent variables. Interest here, on the contrary, is in the perceptions of job characteristics (esp. task requirements) as *dependent variables*.

It is a widespread belief that individuals respond primarily to cognitive representations of environments and tasks rather than to environments or tasks per se. Nevertheless, our objective is *job design* and not selection. What are the reasons favoring situational orientation in comparison with a purely person-centered selection approach? We shall assume that the psychologically based design of actual task requirments may alter cognitive representations of these requirements, which are the base of the individual's response. This would be practically essential because any job has two different types of consequences: (1) it brings forth products, thus having a productivity requirement; (2) it reacts upon the working individual, ultimately having the long-term power of altering personality traits. For instance, a job may bore, disqualify one or, on the other hand, generate a further development of one's abilities, due to the demands of learning.

For these two aspects of labor (i.e., the aspect of productivity and that of personality development), psychology has assumed a new role in the past decade. This discipline is no longer concerned only with the search for behavior-regulating laws, but rather increasingly endeavors to make contributions to the design of working conditions in the same way as the engineering sciences do. Maybe, in the not so distant future, this will give rise to a technology that is based on psychology, too.

Job design today, first of all, means designing the mental or cognitive task components that are decisive for productivity because they control the visible parts of the tasks, the overt motions. According to the character of the cognitive processes as information-processing operations, the predominant aspect of job design is the optimization of information processing, not minimization of energy expenditure. The consequences for psychology are that psychological analysis and design of industrial tasks have attained an important function in productivity.

Still more obvious is the increased importance of psychological factors for the second aspect of labor mentioned, personality. Despite the reduction in working time, the job is for most adults the sphere of greatest influence in personality development. Schleicher (1973), in a cross sectional study, examined the variation of memory capacity and intellectual abilities with age. He carried out his investigations on a large sample and stated that the type and the degree of change of such mental abilities depend on the demands made on them by the job over many years. The largest deterioration was found among unskilled workers who performed jobs that made only minimum cognitive demands, that could be learned in a few days or weeks at most and that were narrow and monotonous. Skilled workers indicate only a slight deterioration with growing age. For engineers and scientists improvements in steadily trained, verbal cognitive abilities are even to be found. Such different trends of development can be verified by means of more sophisticated approaches (e.g., in the case of population samples having comparable intellectual levels at the end of their schooling. It is evident that the cognitive job demands, to a certain degree, are responsible for the intellectual development of adults.

Interests and activities in leisure time are also correlated to job content. A study made on workers and engineers in the electronics industry resulted in finding significant interrelationships between the degree of responsibility in the job and the assumption of social responsibilities, for instance, in trade unions or in political organizations in factory or community. On every qualification level, persons who possess more autonomy (i.e., more degrees of freedom for decision-making in their tasks) are engaged in social activities to a higher degree. Substantial correlations exist between cognitive job demands and responsibilities and social or political responsibility on the community or society level (Hacker, 1978).

In accordance with the involvement in the design of job content as an important aspect of work situations this approach is *task-centered*. Therefore the main dimensions of description used here are goal structure, action sequence, and possibilities for decisions on procedures with differing efficiencies (versus prescribed algorithmic rules). In all types of real-life situations tasks are an important component. Tasks are accomplished through purposeful actions. A decisive link in action control are the *cognitive representations* of the task demands with their conditions of implementation. The literature on work environment and job design stresses that basic research is needed to identify the representations that different individuals employ to represent the same environment. Significant differences were found in cognitive representations and the strategies based upon them, depending on both the cognitive style parameters and job experience. From the viewpoint of an action control approach these differences in task representation should be responsible to a significant degree for different performances.

ASSUMPTIONS UNDERLYING THE TASK-CENTERED RESEARCH ON WORK SITUATIONS

A number of methodological assumptions underlie the field and laboratory research in the task requirement aspect of work situations.

1. The starting point for the analysis of the perception of and reaction to work situations is the investigation of the actual or objective features of the situation. The possible differences between these objective characteristics and the perception of situations (esp. the internal representations of the presented task and the conditions of its implementation) and the rules generating these differences will be discovered only by a comparison of the two aspects. For example, the redefinition of a presented task into an individually preferred one will become evident by the comparison of the presented task and the actually accomplished task. As a

consequence, the actual or objective conditions, (i.e., in this context, task and working conditions) should be the starting point of the analysis of situations. For that reason, the description in terms of the cognitive and motor operations required is more suitable than that in terms of personality traits. If an actual description of the conditions under consideration is intended, usually consensual verbal reports based upon impressions, using questionnaires and experts' ratings, are employed. Their validity is mostly unknown. An example of attempts in employing more objective technological data will be given later.

2. The analysis of *real situations* is differentiated from that of verbally presented ones. The perception of verbally presented situations may depend on additional variables, such as consent and the ability to imagine adequately the characteristics and consequences of a given description. For example, many workers are unable to describe completely the necessary operations involved in tasks although their practical solutions succeed without omissions or failures (Görner, 1968). Consequently, the analysis of *real* situations is indispensable.

3. The third assumption: Real situations differ as to the amount of various possible coping activities. These possibilities are the ''degree of freedom'' of a situation, and in work situations are characterized according to the dimension of autonomy. Autonomy is an essential feature of job content, since it determines the possibility of obtaining personally relevant goals within a job, for example, and the chance of getting control of the workers' own activities. Therefore the amount of degrees of freedom that a situation offers for coping with or changing it should be a main topic of the analysis of work situations. A distinction among objective, perceived, and used degrees of freedom seems to be necessary.

4. Fourthly, the comparison of the perception of a situation and its actual features reveals the information-processing procedures and is a necessary condition for the prediction of individual behaviors. An important type of situation perception is redefinition. For example, with the degree of freedom given, the redefinitions of problem-solving tasks seem to minimize the psychophysiological effort, especially short-term memory (STM) load. Moreover, personality variables modify this general direction of redefinitions. Consequently, in the case of situations including presented tasks, situation perceptions in the special sense of redefinitions are of central interest. Task redefinitions can only be identified through a comparison of actually presented and perceived or implemented tasks.

5. Situation perceptions are a base of reactions to, or actions in, situations. Purposeful, conscious, goal-directed actions are controlled by situation perceptions and cognitive or memory representations. It is noteworthy that the cognitive representations determine the momentary situation perceptions. Thus, the regulative representations constitute the essential component in action control. For example, the more adequate the cognitive representation of a presented task (i.e., the goal) the better is the result of work in terms of failures and time consumption (Hacker & Clauss, 1976). Consequently, reactions to, (i.e., actions in) situations should be analyzed in terms of action control approaches, in general, and the

regulative role of mental representations, in particular (Hacker, 1978; Miller, Galanter, & Pribram, 1960). Questions of main interest are how the representations develop, how they depend on task requirements, and how they regulate the sequence of operations.

6. People may react to real situations passively or actively. An *active reaction changes the situation*. This type of reaction may depend on the nature of the situation as well as on personality variables. For example, workers differ with respect to their planning of future operations. Plans are a means of the determination of the sequence of future events, that is, of situational features. Consequently, the analysis of person × situation interaction should include the aspect that is of main interest in applied work, the goal-directed changing of real situations.

7. In analyzing reactions to situations, perceived reactions must be distinguished from actual ones. They may or may not correspond. For example, a perceived fatigue may differ significantly from the actual psychophysiological state of the organism. As a consequence, a comparison of perceived and actual reactions to a situation may give useful additional information.

8. Finally, in using the situation × personality interaction approach in industrial psychology, the following network of variables is taken into consideration: (a) the *task* and the *conditions* of its implementation; (b) the *perception* of the task and conditions, including task redefinitions; (c) the *activities demanded* and those actually *executed*; (d) the workers' *perceptions* of their activities; (e) the *results produced* and the changes of the workers' *psychophysiological state*, well-being, satisfaction and experience; and finally (f) the *perceptions* of these two kinds of outcome.

The remainder of this paper is devoted to an overview of the issues that seem to be most challenging: the action control approach, in general, and the regulative functions of cognitive representations, in particular; the task dependency of cognitive representations as a situational problem; some aspects of task redefinition in the case of degrees of freedom or autonomy; and an attempt at an objective description of tasks (i.e., a description not based entirely on consensual impressions, see Craik, Chapter 3, this volume).

SITUATION DESCRIPTION IN TERMS OF ACTION CONTROL

Regulation of Goal-Oriented Actions

Tasks are important components of real-life situations and are accomplished by means of actions. We are in need of a theory on the cognitive and motivational control of action. It is simply impossible to practice industrial psychology successfully when conceiving it as an applied discipline of psychology exclusively. Theoretical bases and correlations with general and personality psychology are indispensable. In reference to Miller, Galanter, and Pribram (1960), it is necessary to bridge the gap between cognition and action and to describe how actions are controlled by an organism's internal representation of its universe. This theoretical rethinking will help us to get away from the barrenness of the mentalist/behaviorist controversy.

We all have learned that it is impossible to describe labor to an adequate extent in terms of the stimulus-response scheme. The elements even of plain, narrow jobs are no passive reactions but conscious actions that are controlled by consciously set goals and guided by anticipations and internal representations that are built up by cognitive processes. More complex actions are programmed and organized by means of more or less sophisticated individual plans as results of problem solving. The action is something like the psychological unit or "molecule" of activity. Normally, actions are regulated by the anticipation of their results. This anticipation together with the intention of implementation is the goal. More complex goals are achieved via partial results that are anticipated as subgoals. Together with the necessary procedures, these subgoals may form the programs or plans of actions. The programs are organized simultaneously in a sequential and hierarchic mode (for details see Hacker, 1978).

Although these statements seem to be compelling, some of them are more or less hypothetical. For example, the existence of motor programs in addition to the anticipation of results, has not been verified experimentally (Heuer, 1978). On the other hand, some further components of this approach are verified sufficiently. This holds, for instance, for regulation by anticipation. The question arises here how labor may be described in detail as a system of goal-oriented actions.

The following three aspects have to be distinguished in the analysis of industrial work operations (Fig. 8.1): (1) immediately visible is the sequence of movements only. The classical time and motion studies describe only this surface structure of work operations; (2) the logical structure of the task to be performed may be represented above this sequence of movements; it subdivides the task to be solved into partial tasks, considering thereby, besides motor elements, cognitive components within the meaning of the testing and modification steps of algorithm descriptions; (3) however, the psychological or depth structure proper that is of interest here is not identical with this logical structure. The nodes are symbols of the hierarchy of partial aims in representing it as a graph. The arrows correspond to cognitive processes that further break down or recode the superordinate parts of the task.

A new action firstly demands an orientation for the purpose of programming. The required steps of this program must be stored. Then they have to be recalled in the necessary sequence. Finally, they must be arranged into the *superordinate*

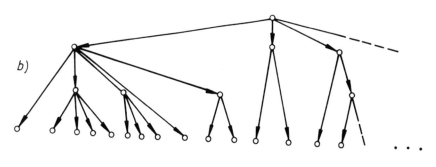

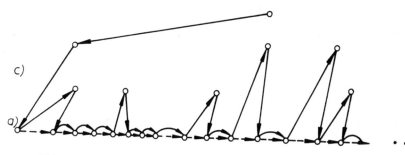

FIG. 8.1.   Aspects of the analysis of work activities (example): (a) sequence of movements (-→); (b) logical structure of the presented task; (c) hierarchical sequence of cognitive activities: psychological structure (→).

program in such a way that they are its dependent component. The question of psychic regulation leads to this depth structure.

Reverting to Tomaszewski (1964), we assume that the following five aspects are necessary for the analysis of the action control processes:

1. The redefinition of the task as a goal, dependent on the motivation.
2. The orientation toward the conditions of the activity in the environment and within the data of the memory.
3. The designing or reproducing of the subgoal sequences and the action programs, for instance, of the strategies. These are operations at the cognitive or memory representation level.
4. The decision for an individual program variant in the case of existing degrees of freedom, which is likewise an operation at the cognitive representation level.
5. The control of the goal and program implementation by feedback; this feedback indicates the cyclical nature of the process (Fig. 8.2).

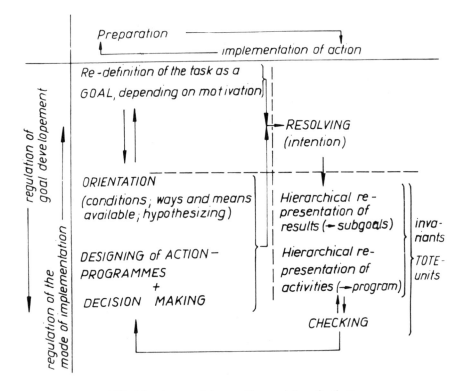

FIG. 8.2.   Aspects of the cognitive regulation of actions.

For the control of the activity, functional units form consisting of intentions and activity programs as well as feedback control operations. As is known, Miller, Galanter, and Pribram (1960) designate them, due to their characteristic structure, as test-operate-test-exit units, or properly speaking, as comparison-change-feedback units. In complex actions such units are hierarchically inter-laced.

By these deliberations we do not depart from actual practice in industry, but we obtain means for a more profound analysis with more pinpointed modification. For numerous labor activities in various industrial branches it can be demonstrated that workers of high performance standard distinguish themselves from those of a low performance level by establishing differentiated goals, by a more independent and creative approach when designing the activity programs, and by more competent cognitive representations of the technological process. Accordingly, the efficiency can be raised by means of mental training of these representations or by the design of the information offered. To put it differently, in spite of its hypothetical components this conception has proven successful as a guide for a purposeful analysis and for the modification of job processes.

Along with these general features, working actions show some percularities, especially:

1. In industry, working actions are dependent parts of the technological process. Their organization is determined by these objective technological conditions.

2. Working actions relate to prescribed tasks. They can be redefined into subjective tasks, if degrees of freedom are given.

3. Working actions are evaluated in advance and their organization is modified due to this predictive evaluation. The most important evaluation criterion is efficiency. Efficiency is the ratio of effort and result.

Some of the consequences of these pecularities will be discussed below.

Determination of the Organization of Actions by Technology: Situational Promotion or Restriction

The organization of actions is determined by socioeconomic conditions, including technology. In modern semi-automatic or even automatic production, human actions are only necessary at special stages of the production process. The characteristics of these technological stages determine the requirements made on the operator and, thus, the possible organization of human actions. In Fig. 8.3 the white boxes labeled a, b, etc., illustrate these stages with human components. Some of them may offer various possibilities of suitable operations or

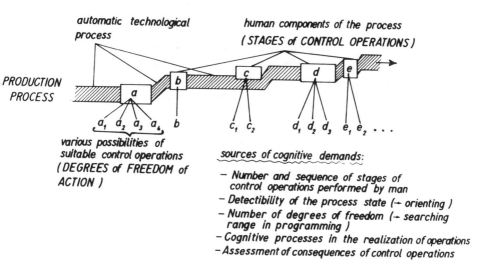

FIG. 8.3.   Main sources of cognitive job demands in man-machine systems.

degrees of freedom of actions; others may not. Their characteristics, determining the possible organization of actions and, thus, the cognitive requirements, are:

The number and sequence of such stages of human actions at all.
The detectability and discriminability of those process stages that are critical for actions.
The number of possible actions, i.e., the degrees of freedom, indicating the difficulty of decision-making and of program development.
The cognitive operations in carrying out the programs.
The predictive evaluation of possible consequences.

The influence of perceived or subjective degrees of freedom (frequently labeled "autonomy") on the organization of action is essential. With the number of different ways to achieve a goal, the requirements made on *decision processes* are increasing. And different decisions will generate different mental regulation processes. Therefore, an analysis of the organization of actions must start with the analysis of the conditions of actions, including the objective degrees of freedom.

Field studies show that the best workers identify the objective degrees of freedom of their jobs more adequately and cope with them more effectively than less efficient workers. In these field studies we were interested in the "real" degrees of freedom of workers in carrying out their jobs. By means of work studies with a flow diagram technique we sought those degrees of freedom that determine possible goal-setting. We found the following scale (Rothe, 1978):

Jobs without any degree of freedom for individual decision-making or goal-setting.
Jobs with degrees of freedom allowing goals concerning the *speed* of action.
Jobs with goals concerning the *sequence* of operations.
Jobs with goals concerning *means and procedures*.
Jobs with goals also concerning the *characteristics of the result*, too.

In the last two cases the goals are part of a problem-solving procedure.

Recently, Rothe (1978) demonstrated that, with increasing number and complexity of degrees of freedom, an activity also becomes more complex in terms of the number of different operations (variety). This conincides with decreasing perceived fatigue, monotony, and saturation and with increasing work satisfaction (Table 8.1).

Thus, human-centered job design means designing the degrees of freedom for the individual who performs the job. In industry, a few ways of altering the degrees of freedom proved to be successful. Figure 8.4 illustrates this for a special problem of job design, the division of labor. On the other hand, job design is only one source of the cognitive structure of actions. The other source is

TABLE 8.1
(Rothe, 1978): Perceived Effects of Work Situations: Assembly-Tasks with
Different Job Autonomy and Variety
(Boxed figures: critical values in the BMS-I-survey [Plath and Richter 1978])

Principle of Production	Time per Product	Number of Different Operations	Degrees of Freedom for	Perceived Fatigue	Monotony	Saturation	Job Satisfaction (−2.0 . . . +2.0)
Conveyor belt assembly task	5 min	1	0 speed	41.7	52.3	46.5	−0.1
Serial assembly task	1 . . . 2 days	6	0 speed 0 sequence	43.3	46.7	48.6	+0.4
Complex assembly task	> 30 days	15	0 speed 0 sequence 0 procedures 0 features of product	50.1	52.4	54.9	+0.7

related cognitive training. What are the reasons for this fact? Personal development understood here as the development of potential abilities in the job process,
requires the full use of the degrees of freedom available for mental activity.
There is a considerable number of degrees of freedom available in most branches
of industry. For instance, for more than 80% of the control operations in the
chemical industry there are several possibilities of decision-making. Hence the
operator can, by means of a complicated mental analysis, make the most appropriate choice.

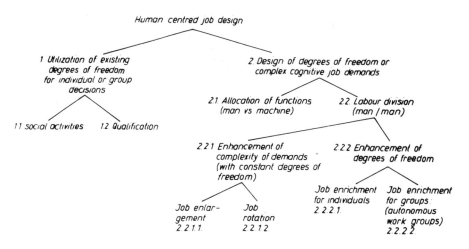

FIG. 8.4.   Some possibilities of a human-centered job design.

Task Redefinition: Perception of an Essential Situation Component and Its Effects

A second peculiarity is the determination of the organization of working actions by their *expected effort*. If a presented task offers degrees of freedom, it will be redefined in a task suitable for the individual. In the industrial working process this redefinition leads to tasks with an acceptable ratio of effort and result. The redefinitions reducing the perceived effort were experimentally analyzed in in-formation integration (multiple–cue-probability learning) tasks (Kasvio, 1978; Hacker, and Meinel, 1978; Matern, 1976), rule-learning tasks (Hacker, 1977b); and the classification of ill-defined categories (Hacker, 1978). The dependent variables were behavioral and performance criteria of strategies (e.g., information seeking, failures, reaction time, sinus arhythmia) and reported strategies.

Results, common for the three categories of tasks, are:

1. Subjects avoid strategies stressing complex logical, or mathematical rules even if they are highly skilled in their use and know them by heart. Instead, they prefer mixed strategies (i.e., combinations of very simple rules, categorizations, or even rough estimations). This holds even in the case of obvious deteriorations of the task accomplishment.

2. The preferred strategies show less perceived difficulty, perceived fatigue, and activation measured by means of the heart period time (Kasvio, 1978).

3. The reduction of effort seems to result from a simultaneous reduction of the number of long-term memory (LTM) items, STM items, and processing operations.

4. The saved mental capacity seems to be used for generalization as can be shown by transfer experiments.

Thus, the regulative depth-structure of actions is determined to a decisive extent by the predictive assessment of effort. Table 8.2 illustrates this for an assembly task, which could be accomplished by means of three hierarchically organized rules: repetition, inversion, change of the type of the sequence of elements. (For details see Hacker, 1977a). All subjects (36 students) succeeded in learning these rules and their nested hierarchic organization. Nevertheless all of them preferred several types of mixed strategies for reasons that can easily be identified in the table.

This general tendency of task redefinition may be modified by *personality traits* (e.g., variables of cognitive style). In a multiple–cue-probability learning task, using two groups of subjects (extreme field dependence versus independence) we found: Field-dependent subjects significantly ($p = .05$) preferred rough approximative strategies of information integration whereas independent ones preferred analytic rule strategies.

We conclude: Man never bears load passively. Working people anticipate load. Consciously or unconsciously, they modify their goals or their strategies to

TABLE 8.2
Procedures in a Hierarchically Structured Assembly Task and Their
Mental Requirements (Notice that mixed procedures reach the lowest
total requirements. The figures result from logical task analysis.
For details, see Hacker 1977b).

Procedures / Requirements	LTM-Items	Cognitive Operations Required	STM-Load per Step of Reconstruction	Identification of Deep-Structure
A. Rote learning	80	0	0	not required
B. Complete re-construction by means of all rules	5	26	4	Indispensable
C. Reconstruction by means of rules, applied on great chunks	5	4	8	
D. Mixed proce-dures (e.g., remember-ing of small chunks and use of 1 or 2 rules for reconstruc-tion)	7 .. 12	4 .. 5	2 .. 4	Partially indispen-sable

cope with load. Expected load does not, therefore, change only the surface structure of an action, but also—and primarily—the generating and regulating depth structure.

Regulative Cognitive Representations: Task Dependency as a Situational Impact

Cognitive or memory representations are the decisive link of mental control of actions. All phases of action are guided by them. It proved useful to classify these representations into three types (Fig. 8.5): (1) the goals or the desired values; (2) the representations of the conditions of implementation; (3) the representations of actions themselves (i.e., of the required operations) transforming the given state into the desired one. The goal as the essential kind of an internal representation, that is, an anticipated result of the action, is the indispensable constant of every goal-directed process, as Ashby and Conant (1970), Bernstein (1967), and Anochin (1967) have demonstrated. The goals are relatively stable memory representations that act as the necessary desired values in the compari-

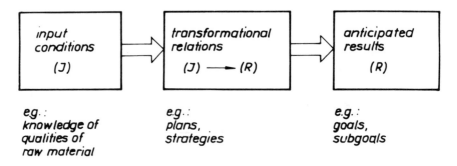

FIG. 8.5.   Possible contents of internal representations.

son between the actual and the desired state during the implementation of an action. In the feedback processes mentioned, the actual state attained at every time is compared with the goal as the required state.

Memory representations have an irreplaceable function in the preparation of actions. This holds, first, for the designing and testing of action-programs: internal representations of properties of the technological process, the means of production, or the raw materials enable internal program-testing before their implementation in practice. Furthermore, internal representations represent the base for the selection of action programs as far as degrees of freedom for a differentiated approach exist. They serve for the prognostic evaluation of the consequences of possible steps and the decision on the path to be taken. Thus, internal representations are the "material" on which the decisive steps of information-processing in the organization of goal-oriented actions are performed.

Orientation, too, is influenced by the quality of the internal representations. Different memory representations will result in different hypotheses on the present state of a technological process, thus inducing other search strategies and the selection of other sources of information.

In our field research it was shown that the more elaborated these representations are the more effective is performance. For example, the most effective workers: (1) developed a more sophisticated network of goals and subgoals; (2) used more effective signals to inform about future states of the technological process; (3) knew better the probability of important events (e.g., faults) thus using more effective strategies of fault finding; (4) predicted the future course of processes more adequately or a wider range of possible steps of a program including its consequences and alternatives. Thus, on the basis of a more elaborated system of representations, a planned (versus momentary) type of the organization of action may take place, that will enable a higher efficiency without increasing the work-load.

The following example contrasts the objective occurrence frequency of faults at machinery with the frequency that is expected personally. It can be seen that workers with a high performance level are better aware of the objective fault probabilities than other workers. Due to this knowledge, the workers of the first group reduce their search time and can even avoid the faults more methodically (Table 8.3).

Since more appropriate cognitive representations enable a more rational execution of work, they reduce the mental and physical work load at the same time. It could be shown that the teaching of optimum representations by means of modern cognitive and verbal training methods increases the output, while simultaneously the fatigue perceived is not increased. Ultimately, adequate representations also permit the development of efficient individual working strategies. Thus, they contribute to the utilization and training of cognitive abilities.

Regulative cognitive or memory representations in working activities are characterized by specific characteristics, determined by their functions in the control of actions. One of these characteristics is *task dependency or compatibility*. Remember that every action accomplishes a task. We assume that all mental processes and representations are organized in such a way that they permit a successful and efficient accomplishment of tasks. We also suppose that the task-dependent structure and code of the regulating mental processes and representations is one of the main characteristics of actions. It is well known that the regulation of actions by memory representations is more effective than the regulation by momentary input processing. However, different representations in memory are possible with different consequences for the efficiency of actions:

Hypothesis 1. The memory-model represents the *untransformed input*. Transformations between input and representations are saved.

Hypothesis 2. By means of feedback, the internal representation represents the information necessary for *response organization*. Transformations between internal representations and response-organization are saved. This is the point of task-dependent memory representations.

Hypothesis 3. The memory model represents the information in a *memory-specific code*, such as a code suitable for rehearsal.

We studied an assembly task common in the production of electronic equipment. The main independent variable was a different presentation of the necessary information for the required task (e.g., in the form of a completed product, a compatible or incompatible scheme, a typed or tape-recorded list of instructions. For details see Hacker and Clauss (1976). Results showed that before memory representations are established, the assembly time per element is a monotonically increasing function of the number of cognitive operations required. In the last repetition of the training procedure, a memory representation was developed.

TABLE 8.3

Comparison of Objectively and Subjectively Expected Frequencies of Six Types of Machine Failures for Two Differently Experienced Groups of Workers (correct expectation in the diagonal)[a]

Highly experienced workers

	Rank Order of Frequency of Six Types of Failures Expected by the Workers (R_E)						$\Sigma n_i \lvert R_o - R_E \rvert$
Objective rank order of failure frequency (R_o)	1	2	3	4	5	6	
Objective 1	2	2	1				4
rank 2		3	2				3
order of 3		1	3	2			2
failure 4		1	1	2	2		5
frequency 5				2	2	1	3
(R_o) 6					1	4	1
							18

Newcomers

	Rank Order of Frequency of Six Types of Failures Expected by the Workers (R_E)						$\Sigma n_i \lvert R_o - R_E \rvert$
Objective rank order of failure frequency (R_o)	1	2	3	4	5	6	
Objective 1	1	2	2				6
rank 2	2	2	1				4
order of 3		2	1	1	2		5
failure 4	2	1	1		1	2	9
frequency 5				2	1	2	4
(R_o) 6					2	3	2
							30

[a] The example illustrates the higher concordance for experienced workers in the fabric production (for a greater sample the difference was significant at $p = .05$).

This was verified by free recall. In this case, the dependence of time on cognitive complexity disappeared more and more. This reduction of time is due to the saving of those cognitive processes that initially produced the high differences. Therefore, the learning rate increases with the number of cognitive transformations between memory and response that become superfluous after having developed compatible memory representations.

For a further verification we asked whether, on the contrary, an identical information presentation may produce different memory representations in the case of different strategies of task accomplishment. Cavallo (1978), also using assembly-tasks, verified this hypothesis in her experimental study. The subjects were asked to assemble different types of electronic components at the adequate locations on circuit boards. Using identical information as to components and locations, one group of subjects was instructed to fit the components strictly following the columns on the circuit boards (local strategy); another was instructed to assemble one type of components after the other (categorical strategy). In the first trial, both the assembly time and the number and type of failures did not differ significantly between the two strategy groups. However, with increasing repetitions both parameters became significantly different. Moreover, they proved significantly different in transfer experiments, too.

Thus, the task-dependent structure of memory representations, which regulate actions, seems to be verified. However, a number of more analytic questions as to the nature of that effect remain unanswered.

Analysis of Objective versus Perceived Work Situations: Illustration of Field Research

Two distinctions need to be made: First, we have to distinguish the "situation 'as it actually is', defined by its objective physical and social characteristics, independent of any observer, from the situation as it is perceived" (Magnusson, 1978). Secondly, the situation "as it is" can be analyzed and assessed, on the one hand, by means of consensual impressions of observers (e.g., experts) or, on the other hand, by means of counted or measured data based on the technological instructions, schemes, schedules, algorithms, or other types of regulations of the workers' activity patterns at the work places under consideration ("technical assessments", Craik, Chapter 3, this volume).

In the following study we tried to simultaneously apply these different, but hopefully supplementary, approaches. The study is part of a project dealing with methods of analysis and evaluation of the job content. The main purpose of the present study was to find suitable indicators of the real and perceived job content and its effects, and to try to differentiate between similar work situations, by means of these indicators. In the case of work, the umbrella concept of "situation" may concern the task and the conditions of its realization, or this together with the workers' actual activity patterns, or all this together with the effects as to the result produced and the modifications in the workers' psychophysiological state and well-being. We decided on the broadest version.

Situations and Subjects

Three work situations (lathe operations with different machines, tasks, and workers) were investigated with regard to: (1) actual job demands; (2) perception of job demands; (3) actual reactions of the workers; and (4) perceived reactions. The three groups (20 workers) are relatively homogeneous. The three situations are referred to as N, S, and R.

Method

Job demands were analyzed by work-study methods, using a flow diagram technique. For perceived demands, ratings and inventories with interval scales (Hurrelmann & Stach, 1973; Kasielke, Möbius, & Scholze, 1974; Plath & Richter, 1978) were employed. For details, see Hacker and Jatzlau, 1978. Some results follow.

Technical Assessment Approach.   Table 8.4 demonstrates the frequency of cognitive and motor operations and the prevailing time allowances, Table 8.5 the frequency of different cognitive and motor operation patterns (variety). These data together with additional time studies show that the time percentage of 3% of

TABLE 8.4
Frequency of Cognitive and Motor Operations

	Different Types of Lathe Operations					
	S		R		N	
Operations	a	b	a	b	a	b
Signal processing	104	4600	52	4680	15	6750
Control by feedback	24	1080	8	720	2	900
Recoding	56	2520	26	2340	3	1350
Use of knowledge	76	3420	41	3690	6	2700
Identification of degrees of freedom	20	900	15	1350	2	900
Decision/reasoning evaluation	41	1845	28	2520	3	1350
Development of programs	41	1845	26	2340	3	1350
Physical operations	161	7245	46	4140	14	6300

a ... per series (S vs N vs R: $p \leq .05$)
b ... per shift
Prevailing piece rate: $\sim$ 10 min $\sim$ 5 min $\sim$ 1 min

TABLE 8.5
Variety in Frequencies
of Cognitive and
Motor Operations

Operations	S	R	N
Use of knowledge	16	15	4
Identification of degrees of freedom	10	9	2
Physical operations	22	17	7

the intellectual demands (e.g., decoding, reasoning, decision-making) in situation N is very low, compared with 20% in situations S and R. Moreover, the variety of operations in situation N is also small. Thus, the job content of situation N seems to be restrictive (i.e., without any essential autonomy and variety). This restrictive job content in situation N results from the elaborate division of labor: Demands made on the workers by organization, maintenance, repair, inspection, or cooperative activities are extremely low.

Expert Observation Approach.   A group of production engineers and supervisors rated the job content of the three situations according to a set of rating scales (see Fig. 8.6). The set included different versions of similar items for methodological reasons. The same set was used for the workers' ratings of perceived job content. There was a sufficient correlation between experts to allow the data to be summarized across the group. The experts' estimates significantly differentiate situations S and R from N, but not situation R from S.

Perceived Situation Approach.   All workers rated job content according to the same set of ratings. Again the data could be summarized across the group. With reference to the complete set of ratings, the workers' estimates differentiate situation S from N and R from N, but not situation R from S. (For the sake of legibility in Fig. 8.6, situation R is omitted.) Moreover, the screening inventory of the perceived mental strain shows a tendency to underload in situation N, and to overload in situation S (due to an occasional time pressure).

A comparison of the three approaches shows that the perception of job content seems to be adequate. For example, in work situation N anticipation and planning, decision making or individual intentions are estimated as unnecessary. This is exactly right (see Tables 8.4 and 8.5). In some directions these workers perceived even more autonomy and higher demands than the experts did for that job. This disagreement may be due to differences in qualification and can thus be discussed in terms of person × situation interaction. This is supported by the difficulty ratings for the different situations, which roughly indicate the relationship between job demands and qualifications of the raters.

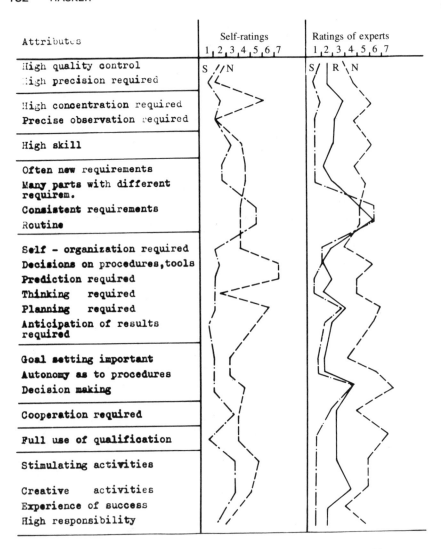

FIG. 8.6.   Mean ratings of work situations for workers and experts (labels of the alternative poles are omitted here).

In analogy with the distinction made between "objective" and perceived situation characteristics a similar distinction was made between reactions: We distinguish observable behavioral or "objective" reactions from verbally reported or "subjective" ones:

Objective Reactions or Effects.   These differ between situation R on the one hand, and situations S and N, on the other hand. Although there are no essential differences between S and N, in situation R the sickness rate is significantly lower and the workers' involvement in innovation proposals and social or political affairs is more frequent.

This coincides with the fact that reported general work satisfaction, satisfaction with working-conditions, and satisfaction with the job are not significantly different between situations S and N, but are significantly higher in situation R as compared with S and N. No essential differences exist in perceived momentary fatigue, monotony, and saturation (Subjective Reactions).

To sum up, the proposed distinctions seem to be essential for the assessment of work situations in general and for the job content in particular. The "technical" or objective approach to a situation assessment should be elaborated more thoroughly.

IMPLICATIONS FOR FURTHER RESEARCH

There is a considerable body of implications for further theoretical and empirical research in the situation × personality approach applied to work. An urgent need for further research exists as to the following topics.

Active Coping and Altering

In real-life situations man tries actively to cope with conditions and to alter situational aspects due to his or her internal model of a desirable solution. Therefore, people accept prescribed tasks or define new action goals. To this purpose, people have to take into consideration the characteristics (e.g., laws of nature) of the ongoing technological processes that they are going to alter.

Person × Situation Interaction Mediated by Actions

The essential link between personality traits and situation properties is constituted by actions. Along with their formal structure, their content, depending on socioeconomic conditions (ownership, employment chance, technology), has to been taken into consideration.

Depth Versus Surface Structure

The mediating actions are psychologically relevant as to depth structure, but not to overt surface structure. The levels-of-processing (Craik and Lockhart, 1972) or the multilevel-processing (Posner, 1973) approaches are important to the analysis of the depth structure of actions.

Regulating Cognitive Representations

Cognitive, especially memory representations are the decisive component in action control. Therefore, results and issues of memory research (e.g., semantic networks, propositional versus iconic storage, task-dependent memory processes) are indispensable for the explanation of goal-directed activities. However, it still seems to be impossible to describe exactly how actions are controlled by an organism's internal representation of its universe, as Miller, Galanter and Pribram stated two decades ago.

Styles of Coping

A considerable body of results has verified individual differences in situation perception, but only a few steps have been made in analyzing individual differences in coping with or altering situations. Along with cognitive styles in information processing, styles of coping in a broader sense, not restricted to stressful situations, are of practical importance.

More Objective Assessment

People do not interact with their situation perception, but with the actual, objective situation "as it is." An observer consensus is a weak argument in favor of the objectivity of situation descriptions. For instance, people will have similar geometric illusions in common; however, these misperceptions are in no way veridical. Thus along with methods for the analysis of situation perception and for the consensual observation of situations, more objective methods are necessary. The well-known methods of industrial psychology (e.g., the Position Analysis Questionnaire (PAQ), McCormick, Jeanneret, & Mecham, 1969; or the Job Diagnostic Survey (JDS), Hackman & Oldham, 1974) do not fill up this methodological gap, because they do not offer differentiated guidelines for the design of situations (i.e., prevention or job design). Further methodological research on this topic is necessary.

Psychological Participation in Intervention

The involvement of psychology should not end with the analysis of situations but should participate in the preventive aspect in the design of settings. It seems to be helpful to conceptualize preventive design in situational terms.

9 Environment and Response

Gösta Carlsson
University of Stockholm
Sweden

ENVIRONMENT IN SOCIOLOGY

Perhaps we may agree that "environment" serves its most useful function as a pointer word. That is to say, it shows the general direction to an area of research and theory-building but leaves the precise boundaries of this area and the details of its internal topography rather vague. Even the recent literature on "ecological" or "environmental" psychology forms no clear-cut exception, for definitions are usually framed within the limits of a particular tradition, say ecology, and are even then relatively vague (Ittelson, Proshansky, Rivlin, & Winkel 1974; Stokols, 1977).

It will be more productive to look at the approaches followed in different disciplines and subdisciplines when environment is studied, and the definitions are implied by research operations, if not explicitly stated. The writer is a sociologist with an interest in social and differential psychology (the interests in psychology more actively pursued in the past than currently), and the emphasis in the following treatment will be laid accordingly. This paper, therefore, differs in approach and theoretical style from most of the others presented in this volume. It is important to determine how the preoccupations of sociologists help to fashion their concept of environment, what they see and what they neglect. Also, attention should be directed to the related questions of consistency in human behavior, and the role of situational factors versus stable dispositions or traits (Magnusson & Endler, 1977a).

First, a reminder: sociologists usually have to tease out their answers without recourse to experimental methods. There are exceptions to this rule but they become numerous only if experimental social psychology is included. For the main part sociology looks for its data in real-life settings, often seemingly complex. Statistical operations on these data have to serve as substitutes for randomized assignment of treatment modalities. There are both strengths and weaknesses in this procedure, but at least it must be recognized that an element of doubt often remains with regard to the final interpretation. Are we dealing with straightforward, unidirectional causality flowing from stimulus conditions to response distributions, or with the manifestations of selective exposure, or again with interaction between environment and the person or persons responding? Do alleged indicators of environment really deserve this label? Education, amount of schooling, is one such case where both the simple effect perspective, and that of selective exposure can be applied.

It is a moot question whether sociologists, as such, should be more involved in uniform standardized behavior, or look for human variability. They are clearly concerned with social norms, that is, regulated and to that extent invariable, conduct. Especially when the focus moves in the direction of the cultural dimension, the relevant feature is uniformity within a culture (unless sex roles, age roles, etc. enter) and differences between cultures. In the shape of subcultural theory this type of analysis can be extended to patterns of variation within modern society. In passing, it may be noted that subcultural and personality factors are far from easy to keep apart in the explanation of certain behaviors, such as crime, violence, or addiction; the possibility of selective membership in groups and subcultural assemblages is clearly there.

However, it would be quite misleading to suggest that a hard and fast line exists, dividing matters sociological from the domain of psychology. Sociology is what concerns sociologists, and thus viewed it has much more in common with other types of behavioral research than might be inferred from a norm-oriented, or group, definition. In particular, a fair proportion of all published research can be brought under the heading of "behavioral" or "social epidemiology." Though it is not customary to use these labels, they appear to convey as well as any other term the spirit behind numerous studies in which the distribution of a given behavior or attribute in different strata of the population is studied. In methodology it is not far removed from differential psychology; some varieties have been called "differential class-behavior," or "differential life chances."

Indeed, sociologists in general would feel quite at home with most of the items in the following list of problems in the psychology of individual development:

> Thus, even the 'behavior setting' which may regulate our actions in accordance with the demands of a particular milieu, does not account for individual differences within the setting—why some pupils learn more rapidly or are more cooperative than others; why Bill drinks too much at the country club dance whereas Bob is a model of sobriety; in brief, why different persons use the same setting in quite different ways, still conforming to the setting's indicated behavior pattern. . . .

Behavior in any situation reflects the type of person we are, and this, in turn, involves our parental upbringing, the socio-economic class to which we belong, the values of our society, our religious and ethnic background, the influence of significant figures on our lives, accidents of fate . . . . All these factors, in the very broad sense, are part of our environment (Ittelson et al. [1974, p. 168].

It is hard to handle accidents of fate in any systematic theory and sociologists may be less interested than psychologists in the presence or absence of significant figures in the lives of the people they study. With socio-economic class or religious and ethnic background we are dealing with standard indicators of environment in sociological research that fall within the category of behavioral epidemiology. Such indicators may be called structural; correspondingly, we may speak of a *structural* (definition of) *environment*. Social classes are part of the social structure. They exist or can legitimately be postulated as relatively fixed and enduring features, according to this line of thinking. The place of a person within the structural framework becomes an index of the environmental forces acting on the individual. It is a static concept. Time and change do not figure in any direct and obvious manner though some allowance can be made for mobility between structurally defined positions (more about this later). It is, without doubt, standard procedure in the sociological analysis of environment and its impact. What degree of success has attended this methodology?

A STORY OF WEAK EFFECTS

An important theme in current thinking on man and society is that of sociological determinism. The question next to be addressed concerns the substance and validity of the rhetoric of environmental fate. However, it will be necessary to limit the scope to the belief that human differences within a given society are, in fact, accountable to a large extent in terms of known environmental conditions. How successful have sociologists, psychologists, and epidemiologists actually been in fulfilling this promise, real or imputed? Following the principles just laid down, we have in mind, then, accountability by reference to phenomena such as social class, the status and nature of the family, income, character of the local community, and other indicators of this type.

The standard of evaluation will then be the variance accounted for by the classification scheme examined or the correlation between an index of environment and the dependent response (the square of the coefficient being equivalent with the variance accounted for). By a technique described elsewhere (Carlsson, 1977), relationships are referred to the normal correlation surface (essentially the method of tetrachoric correlation). Even with this understanding there is no fully satisfactory way of answering the major question about established accountability. The wealth of data is enormous, scattered all over the literature. To the writer's knowledge no systematic inventory has been taken; the task is truly staggering. For the purpose at hand a short and perhaps dogmatic-sounding summary will have to do, supported by a few references to the available evidence, before we move on to consider models of environment.

The general picture is one of weak to modest relationships. With one or two exceptions the association between structural environment and the response or characteristic studied rarely reaches the level of .5, or even .4, evaluated as a correlation. It is quite appropriate in this context to cite data on environment and health. Though this is not a question that usually concerns psychologists; it is nearer to the interests of sociologists. In any case general health (or its opposite, illness) should be a good example of a property that is subject to numerous environmental influences reinforcing and counteracting one another through time. The present writer has recently concluded a search for socio-economic effects on overall health (as a part of an ongoing study of the medical and sociological aspects of health). For published data the relationships rarely seem to reach the level of .3. In a Nordic study of welfare dimensions (covering the four major countries) there were only weak correlations between health and income, or occupational status (Allardt, 1975). Indeed, the effects of the environmental indicators as revealed by correlation matrices are generally rather weak, including those on certain attitudinal scales bearing on happiness and satisfaction with life.

The relation between the IQ of children and parental status, or the resources of the home measured by the conventional indicators of income and occupation, hardly forms an exception to the rule. Jencks (1972) reports .35 as a reasonable estimate of the correlation, an appreciable part of which has a genetic background, rather than environmental. Wherever one looks, in the writer's experience, at people's behavior, choices, or life-styles, the story appears to be much the same. Deviant behavior falls into the same pattern in Sweden (Carlsson, 1977); spot-checks on American data (Wolfgang, Figlio, & Sellin, 1972), reveal no striking difference.

To this two remarks should be added, the first on the nature of the results so far reviewed. The associations involved are environment-behavior, not behavior-behavior. In other words, we have not examined, let alone rejected the notion of consistency, or stability, in response. To that subject we shall return shortly. Also, the exceptions to the rule need to be kept in mind, for something can be learned from them. As far as the author is aware the well-documented cases are limited to the areas of internal relations among so-called stratification variables on the one hand, and to class effects on political behavior on the other. Obviously not all relations within the former complex are purely environmental, for example, the education-occupation one; nor are they uniformly strong. But at least it should be noted that parent-child correlations within this area approaching and occasionally surpassing 0.5 have been observed (Jencks, 1972). The association between social class and party voting is also fairly strong in many European countries (though not in the USA), and may exceed 0.5 (Uusitalo, 1975). Historical reasons can be found for the last-mentioned finding, and it is of limited interest as such in the present context. It shows, however, that the methods of observation and classification of environment and response are not beset with errors of such a magnitude as to preclude any appreciable correlation.

STABILITY OF RESPONSE

In this section "response" is used in the wide sense that makes it almost equivalent with "effects of environment." And it should be noted that we are speaking of stability through time—which is not identical with "consistency" as sometimes understood—meaning, roughly, agreement or harmony among traits, or certain traits like attitudes and overt behavior. We may have low attitude-behavior consistency and yet a high degree of stability of behavior and attitudes.

The simple point to be made here is that, in actual fact, there seems to be a farily high degree of stability of response, thus understood, notwithstanding the difficulty of explaining the genesis of response in structural terms. For evidence, the monograph on stability and change of human characteristics by Bloom (1966) may be consulted. It covers a wide range of traits and dispositions, from physical development (height) and intelligence to interests and attitudes. It would be too much to say that the level of correlation over time, indicating stability, is invariably high. It is not new that personality characteristics, other than intelligence, present a formidable problem of measurement, and this, no doubt, has left its marks on some of the stability estimates. For several areas, however, the level is quite high. This is true of physical development, of IQ, values, and interests. With traits like aggression and competitiveness, or conformity and passivity, the impression is more mixed, though some high correlations are reported (Bloom, 1966, pp. 148–153). We shall have to return to interpretations, but the element of stability needs to be kept in mind. The time intervals occurring in these studies range from 1–2 years to a decade or more.

RANDOM WALK MODELS

In an earlier paper (Carlsson, 1972) the writer has proposed a random walk model to account for some of the observed features of the environment-response nexus. A few salient points will be recapitulated for the reader's convenience. It should be stated at once, however, that simple random walk proves insufficient to account for all the facts; its shortcomings in this respect will be the topic of the later parts of the chapter.

We have, then, a number of units (e.g., persons) each of which is subjected to a series of "shocks", or discrete events, shaping its behavior or propensity, denoted Y_t, where the subscript places the value in a sequence: $1, 2, \ldots, n$. Let the shock at time t be x_t, and assume, furthermore, the following simple relation (where subscripts indicating individuals are left out):

$$Y_t = Y_{t-1} + x_t \ (t = 1, 2, \ldots, n) \tag{1}$$

If Y_1 is put equal to x_1, we obviously have

$$Y_t = x_1 + x_2 + \ldots + x_t \tag{2}$$

Behavior or propensity, the state of the responding units, becomes equal to a sum of random variables, x. With respect to the terms one may choose between different sets of assumptions: equal or unequal variances of the x's, correlation of either sign or lack of correlation among the x's. In the simplist case the terms are taken to be mutually uncorrelated and of equal variance, σ_x^2. It then follows that the variance of Y_n, denoted $\sigma_{y(n)}^2$, is given by

$$\sigma_{y(n)}^2 = n \ \sigma_x^2 \tag{3}$$

Thus, the variance of the dependent, emerging state is proportional to the length of the series, and the standard deviation, $\sigma_{Y(n)}$, to the square root of that length. As the process continues variability among units, (e.g., persons) increases. It also follows from these assumptions that the correlation between current state, Y_n, and most recent environmental "dose", x_n, will be quite weak if n reaches any considerable size; the longer the series (the larger n) the smaller the correlation. On the other hand, there will be an appreciable correlation between continguous states, say Y_{n-1} and Y_n, if n is of any size; most of their constituent parts are identical.

In its simplest version, then, the random walk model contains one explosive feature, an ever-growing variability among units. There is, on the other hand, nothing explosive with regard to the stability of rank orders or positions of individual units relative to one another. Conventional techniques, for instance, of the test–retest type, would point to stable differences among individuals though they have responded to stimuli sampled from a common universe and randomly assigned.

In brief, the model explains both weak effects of current or recent environment and behavioral–dispositional stability through time. It may well strike the reader as oversimplified and remote from the complex causal matrix of the real world. About its problematic sides more will be said later, but at this point it should be noted that not all objections are equally serious. The explosive aspect, the ever-increasing variability among units, in our case, persons, can be removed by stipulating a limited length of the series or successively diminishing variances of the x's, corresponding to a gradually lessening impact of environment. This would strengthen the stability of response and make late environmental conditions even worse as predictors. One may also question the assumption of uncorrelated environmental doses, the x's of the equations. Perhaps most appealing, intuitively, is the contrary assumption of cumulative processes with positive intercorrelations. Persons will select and avoid stimuli according to previous experience and a gradually developing disposition. Conceivably this could hold equally for attitudes and certain skills; once the formation of certain dispositions has got under way the process will be quickened by selective exposure. The possibility of the selective environment is a complication to be reckoned with in many areas. The case of education, IQ, and later occupation is only the most obvious example. However, this principle is of little help in accounting for weak or nonexistent environmental effects as studied by customary methods. Variable exposure is reconsidered in a later section, within a somewhat different perspective.

RESPONSE AND DISPOSITION

As the reader may have noticed, the nature of the phenomenon to be explained, the outcome, has not been very clearly defined. The terminology has been intentionally elastic. Thus we have spoken both of response and disposition. A similar vagueness surrounds the events, the stream of environmental influences, the totality of which determines outcome. It is more important, for the moment, to clarify the first of these two points.

The appropriateness of a set of terms, and behind terms, mode of thinking, will depend on the precise nature of the problem at hand and the observational data. Sometimes we want to analyze the choices and decisions that people make and wish to stress the bounded and discrete character of the phenomenon by using a language of events rather than states. As to response, there appears to be no compelling reason why the term could not be used to cover both discrete events and more gradual change under the impact of environmental forces, and therefore be regarded as neutral in this respect.

In the majority of cases it will probably be most appropriate to work with a two-component model in which the outcome, momentary behavior, is a function of an underlying relatively stable disposition and the immediate situational factors, immediate environment. In sociological nonexperimental research there is a body of findings pointing in this direction (apart from its support in psychological theory and common sense). Time-ordered observations do not conform to the pattern one might expect; the series do not represent simple Markov chains. One manifestation of this is that the size of the correlation between observations does not diminish with increasing separation in time. Studies of voting behavior (Converse, 1966) give results that can best be understood as an effect of transient conditions superimposed on a stable disposition, "the normal vote". If Y_t denotes the stable and e_t, the transient component, while Z_t stands for the resulting behavior, we have

$$Z_t = Y_t + e_t \tag{4}$$

and

$$Z_{t-1} = Y_{t-1} + e_{t-1}$$

and similarly for Z_{t-2}. If the disposition changes little or not at all through time, Y_t, Y_{t-1}, and Y_{t-2} may all be replaced by a common value, Y. On the assumption that e_t, e_{t-1}, and e_{t-2} are mutually uncorrelated it follows that Z_t and Z_{t-2} will be as highly intercorrelated as Z_t and Z_{t-1}, or Z_{t-1} and Z_{t-2}. This is, in fact, what can be observed.

One way of summarizing the argument is to distinguish between historical and immediate environment. The former concept stands for the chain of events and conditions that have gradually shaped dispositions and propensities. Immediate environment stands for the more transient features or situational factors, of importance for momentary behavior but less important, perhaps, in the long run. It would seem that the structural approach has little relevance in the study of immediate environment; it may or it may not be relevant to historical environment.

STRUCTURAL AND HISTORICAL ENVIRONMENT

As should be clear by now, if not at the outset, standard methodology is better suited to confirm than to refute environmental explanations. Should response prove to be associated with customary indicators all is well. If not or only weakly, a more frequent outcome in empirical research, little has been demonstrated about the effects of environment in a generic sense; we may well have missed the true environmental forces by a wide margin. The sequence of doses or shocks deterministically adding up to response, or to a disposition observable in response, is a theoretical construction. It cannot be translated into observables as such; the elementary events elude our observation. Structural concepts can only do very imperfect justice to the underlying realities. It would be unnecessary to dwell on this point were it not for the fact that much confusion is caused by its neglect. Denial of the predictive value of structural categories quickly, but erroneously, becomes identified with a rejection of environmental explanation in general, an issue that easily acquires an ideological coloring.

In regard to the main question, two ways out of a threatening impasse suggest themselves. One may either try to adjust field methods to concepts or concepts to field methods. The former solution would mean finding new methods of studying environment minutely and as a flow of impulses rather than statically and summarily. Though this is a possibility not to lose sight of, it is the second solution that will be explored first. If the events of historical environment cannot be observed and accounted for in detail, researchers may accept this and look for a statistical manner of handling environment, rather than a deterministic one. The terms of the previous equations, standing for the chain of historical environment, are random variables. The means of these variables define environment and differences between environments. Specifically, the averages could vary among structurally defined categories. Structural environment is historical environment viewed statistically (or stochastically). Given certain assumptions about the distributions of the elementary variables, what follows for the aggregate outcome within structural environments? In the next section it will be shown that this is a solution that leads to new problems.

STRATIFIED ENVIRONMENT

In the following a simple case of two strata, or subpopulations, will be assumed to be defined in structural terms; for convenience they are taken to be equal in size, each containing one half of the total population. Within each stratum environment determines behavior or disposition according to the random walk model described earlier. That is to say, within a stratum the individuals can be regarded as drawing their environmental doses from a common universe. Their historical environment, the particular sequence of events, may differ considerably as well as the end result, even though events, the environmental doses, are randomly distributed. On the other hand, a systematic difference is assumed between strata; the expected value of the elementary terms is different. As before, unit variance characterizes these terms within a stratum.

Under these conditions it is easy to see what happens as the series of events, elementary terms, grows in length. The standard deviation of the outcome variable, Y, will increase by the square root of the length of series (n), while the difference in mean outcome grows linearly with n. In other words, with a relatively long developmental history strata will draw apart in terms of amount of overlap in outcome distributions. A convenient measure of this process is variance in outcome Y accounted for by strata effects. This will depend on length of series n and difference in mean dose, d. Two examples are given in Fig. 9.1. The shaded area in the graph shows the range, in terms of accountability or correlation, in which environment-response relations mostly fall as reported earlier. It is noticeable that the curves pass through that region, in one case very quickly, though they start at a very low level of stratum differences. For single doses stratum effects have been assumed lower than the typical range. A rough translation into correlation level can be obtained by taking the square root of variance accounted for.

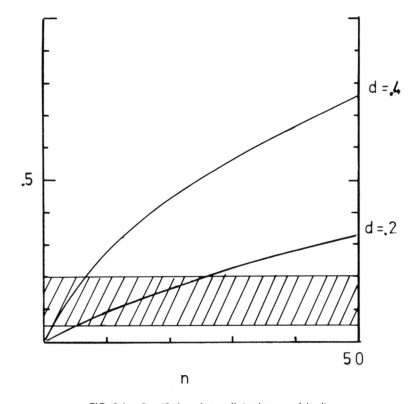

FIG. 9.1.   *Stratified random walk* (variance explained).

MODEL AND REALITY

We have seen that a simple random walk model, with modest strata differences added to the assumptions, would lead to quite considerable outcome differences between the strata if the history of the responding units, the length of the sequences of elementary events, reaches any appreciable length. This is true even if there is practically complete overlapping in distributions for the elementary events, the environmental doses or shocks. This result runs counter to the experience of most research on the behavioral effects of structural environment as discussed earlier in the paper; epidemiological effects are mostly unimpressive. So here is a difficulty; at least it seems so.

Something may be learned from the failure of models as well as from their success but only to the degree that they have a basis in sound reasoning and represent something more than sheer guesses. There is no denying a strong speculative component in the present case, and it is not easy to find operational translations of the abstract variables occurring in the models. Yet, the fundamental approach, with its emphasis on gradual development and growth of behavior dispositions, would seem plausible and agree with our intuitions in these matters. To that extent the conflict with observable facts presents a challenge. There are, of course, several ways out of the difficulty. Environmental effects may be weakened by mobility; current environment is often a poor indicator of lifetime or long-term exposure, even within the frame of structural categories. This, at least, is something that can and ought to be checked more carefully than has been the practice so far. It is unlikely, however, that environmental mobility will prove sufficient as an explanation, so we shall have to dig for deeper reasons. Perhaps developmental histories are not as long as suggested here. Or rather, they may contain only a limited number of significant events and learning episodes. Another way of expressing this idea is to say that the texture of human experience is more coarse-grained than supposed. In reality the sequences of our models will contain relatively few terms. If this is true, much of the noted discrepancy between model and observational data will disappear. Strata differences will not have time to build up, relative to individual variability. What amounts to much the same thing is an assumed positive correlation among the elementary terms, for this means that there is less independent variation.

The most fundamental question about the models concerns their solution of the summation problem. One might also call it the accretion problem. There is ground for a suspicion that this solution is a bit too simpleminded. Basically the philosophy underlying it has been a behavioristic one as is natural to sociologists of a statistical inclination. Stimuli, environmental shicks, have been treated as given physical facts, objective and external, not as a part of a perceived world. There is surely a place for both perspectives, and sociologists may perhaps be excused if they hesitate before the second alternative, and the demands it puts on observation and analysis. The question remains, however, if we have the right to impose the kind of summation employed in the models. Even if this simplification is allowed, at least provisionally, we still lack the proper method of observing and recording environment as a stream of events. Perhaps some inspiration can be fetched from the manner in which symbolic environment is studied, that is to say, the content of the popular media like TV, radio, or newspapers. Here there is a method, at any rate the beginnings of one. And the conceptual apparatus is designed to deal with this kind of environment as an ongoing process (Gerbner, Gross, Jackson-Beeck, Jeffries-Fox, & Signorielli, 1978). This is not to deny the formidable difficulties that remain, most notably the rare but crucial event easily missed in routine sampling.

III

PERCEIVED SITUATIONS AND ENVIRONMENTS

Part III contains 10 chapters. The first five—by Rommetveit, Rotter, Bowers, Sarason and Sarason, and Nowakowska—analyze the environment at the level of situations, in mainly theoretical terms. The next five papers are both empirical and theoretical in nature. Cantor, Bem, and Sjöberg are concerned specifically with situations and events, whereas James and Sells devote their interest to work organizations, and Jessor analyzes proximal perceived environments, without specification of level.

Rommetveit (Chapter 10) explores the possible implications of a consistently pluralistic outlook on "meanings," interaction, and communication. The point of departure is a framework for analysis of dyadic states of social reality in encounters between people representing different *private worlds*. Different "meanings" are in part analyzed as different aspects of a multifaceted entity. Which aspect will become salient, moreover, is in part contingent upon the *position*—as determined by engagement, background knowledge, interest, etc.—from which the situation is viewed. The problem of *shared meaning* may under certain conditions be approached in terms of *which one* of two different private worlds is going to be publicly valid when they interact with respect to or talk about some state of affairs. Intraindividual consistency in behavior across situations is discussed in terms of the individual's unique and limited set of possible interpretations of situations.

Rooter (Chapter 11) reviews a number of principles of a social-learning theory of personality dealing with the psychological situation and the interaction of situational and personality variables. Four problems inherent in the use of the psychological situation for purposes of prediction are reviewed. (1) How can the psychological situation be defined independently of the person? (2) How can one deal with the complexity of situational cues? (3) How much variance in a person-situation interaction results from personality variables and how much from situational variables? (4) How can situational similarity be measured? The present way of dealing with these problems in social-learning theory is discussed and illustrated.

Bowers (Chapter 12) evaluates two different and seemingly contradictory views on environmental influences on behavior; (1) formulations emphasizing the importance of, on the one hand, *conscious* representations of the environment as cognitive mediators of environmental influence; and (2) the proposition by Nisbett and Wilson (1977) that the causes of behavior are never immediately available to consciousness, and in this sense, that behavior is always unconsciously determined, on the other. Bowers presents an analysis in which information may or may not be consciously represented, depending on a host of environmental and organismic factors to be delineated. Clinical and experimental evidence is marshaled in support of the claim that information can have an impact on action without being represented in consciousness. However, it is also argued that some information *must* be consciously represented in order to have any impact on action at all.

Sarason and Sarason (Chapter 13) examine the role of mediating processes and moderator variables in stress situations. They advocate that stress does not inhere in situations, but in the ways in which they are perceived and interpreted. The paper is then devoted to an analysis of the concept of stress in the context of recent research on life-stress events and deals with the following factors: (1) the objective properties of situations confronting the individual; (2) the personal characteristics of the individual (such as coping skills, strengths and weaknesses); (3) the ways in which an individual attends to and interprets features of situations; and (4) social support that aids the individual in meeting situational demands.

Nowakowska (Chapter 14) presents her model of action as a model for analysis of situations. The paper consists of two parts. The first presents an algebra of situations and its mapping into the *linguistic space* (descriptions, self-instructions, modalities, evaluations) as a result of sorting in the motivational space. The second part concerns the study of strings of actions generated by situations and/or objects, in particular of mixed verbal and nonverbal strings, and examines the conditions for their consistency and satisfiability as well as the structure of strings that satisfy a certain promise. Next, the analysis concerns an algebra of goals, means, and conflicts.

Cantor's paper (Chapter 15) is concerned with the hypothesis that social behavior may be cognitively mediated by generalizations and expectations that the naive observer has about the nature of situations. The paper is structured around three issues. It is suggested that cognitive generalizations about the social world may be conceived, organized, and written in a compound, integrated person–situation language, a language constructed so as to emphasize the typical behavior and feelings that people have in specific situations, as well as the unique characteristics of people that emerge as salient in a particular situational context. Moreover, at least for "some people (some of the time)," categorical knowledge about situations—including, as it does, a large percentage of behavior-oriented information—may serve as guidelines for social behavior.

Bem (Chapter 16) devotes his paper to a presentation and discussion of the template-matching technique that characterizes situations in the language of personality description. A situation is characterized by a set of template-behavior pairs, a set of personality descriptions (Q-sort, originally developed by Stephenson, 1953) of hypothetical "ideal" persons, each one associated with a particular behavior. The behavior of a particular individual then can be predicted by matching his or her own Q-sort description against each template and predicting that he or she will display the behavior associated with the most similar template. Variations and extensions of the basic technique are described, with the suggestion that the technique is capable of prompting both personality and social-psychological theories to emerge as genuine theories of person–situation interaction.

Sjöberg (Chapter 17) examines situations in terms of episodes. Central concepts in his analysis are individual goals and actions. Results are presented from an empirical study using self-reports in actual realistic situations. Three kinds of actions are distinguished: *situational,* determined by situational conditions, *instrumental,* aimed at reaching a certain goal, and *consummatory,* valuable in themselves for the individual. An action can reflect the life situation of the actor or aim at a change. Consummatory actions usually reflect the life situation, whereas instrumental actions aim at a change. Sjöberg discusses cross-situational consistency of behavior and advocates that it can be explained better in terms of stable life situations than in terms of stability in basic personality traits (Wachtel, 1977).

James and Sells (Chapter 18) address the bases for individuals' perceptions of work environments from the perspective of psychological climate (cf. Hacker's analysis in Chapter 8, concerned mainly with actual characteristics of working conditions). Psychological climate is defined as the individual's cognitive representations of relatively proximal situational events. A review of the development of the psychological-climate approach includes an integration of psychological-climate concepts with related concepts from environmental psychology, interactional psychology, and social-learning and cognitive–social-learning theory, expressed in terms of assumptions for psychological-climate perceptions. Illustrations of empirical research are presented, and include the measurement of psychological climate and studies of person–by–situation interaction and perception–attitude reciprocal causation as important components in the formulation of environmental perception.

Jessor (Chapter 19) emphasizes that behavior is invariant with the perceived environment, the environment that is most proximal to experience and that has immediate significance for the actor. In order to elaborate the nature of the perceived environment, it is contrasted with two other environments of interest to psychologists—the demographic and the social structural environments. In addition, several conceptual properties of the perceived environment are described, including its *depth*, its *texture*, its *enduringness*, its developmental *change*, and its *content*. Finally, a particular variable in the perceived environment—its conduciveness to problem behavior—is operationalized and examined empirically in two independent studies of adolescent problem behavior.

10 On Meanings of Situations and Social Control of Such Meaning in Human Communication

Ragnar Rommetveit
University of Oslo, Norway

INTRODUCTION

The essential features of modern interactionism have been summarized as follows (Endler & Magnusson, 1976a);

1. Actual behavior is a function of a continuous process or multidirectional interaction (feedback) between the individual and the situation that he or she encounters.
2. The individual is an intentional active agent in this interaction process.
3. On the person side of the interaction, cognitive factors are the essential determinants of behavior, although emotional factors do play a role.
4. On the situation side, the psychological meaning of the situation for the individual is the important determining factor [p. 968].

Because "meanings" of situations are generated by "reciprocal causation" in multidirectional interaction, moreover, they are to some extent ideographic. Apparent behavioral inconsistency across situations hence at times may be due primarily to unwarranted monistic presuppositions embedded in traditional research paradigms, i.e., to the misfortune that, according to Bem and Allen [1974]: ". . . behaviors do not sort into the equivalence class which the investigator imposes by his choice of behaviors and situations to sample [p. 509]." As Bowers (1973) puts it: ". . . interactionism argues that *situations are as much a function of the person as the person's behavior is a function of the situation* [p. 327]." And meanings of situations are thus, according to modern interactionism, engendered by *persons interacting in those situations* (Wachtel, 1973).

The purpose of this chapter is to explore whether fragments of a conceptual framework for analysis of human communication can be brought to bear upon some of these central issues within current interactional theory of personality. More specifically, my aim is to examine some implications of a consistently pluralistic outlook on communication for the assessment of the psychological meaning of the situation and explore how shared meanings are generated in encounters between different "private worlds."

THE SITUATION: ITS ASPECTS, MEANING POTENTIAL, AND POSSIBLE DOMAINS OF REFERENTIAL ALTERNATIVES

My point of departure for analysis of human communication is a critique of explicitly held and/or tacitly endorsed monistic assumptions about our language and the world within the linguistics, psychology, and philosophy of language (Rommetveit, 1974; 1978a; 1978b; 1979; 1980). Such assumptions, I have argued, are revealed in Searle's notion of unequivocal "literal" meanings of verbal expressions (Searle, 1974) as well as in Smedslund's notion of objective "public" meanings of acts (Smedslund, 1969).

I have tried to show, however, that vagueness, ambiguity, and incompleteness—and hence also versatility, flexibility, and negotiability—are inherent and essential characteristics of meanings of situations as engendered by human beings as well as of linguistically mediated meaning. There is accordingly no natural end to our explication of meaning either in the form of literal semantic interpretation or ultimate knowledge of the world. As Garfinkel puts it (1972): "... no matter how specific the terms of common understanding may be—a contract may be considered the prototype—they attain the status of an agreement for persons only insofar as the stipulated conditions carry along an unspoken but understood et cetera clause [p. 28]." This must be so simply because human discourse *takes place in* and *deals with* a multifaceted, pluralistic, only fragmentarily known, and only partially shared social world.

The *meaning potential* of any given situation (event, act, or state of affairs) in a pluralistic world, however, may be explored systematically in terms of a set of experiential possibilities or *aspects*. The very term "aspect" stems from *aspectus*, the perfect participle of the Latin compound verb *aspicere* (*ad* + *specere*), "to look at." And Wittgenstein (1968) maintains: "... what I see in the dawning of an aspect is not a property of the object, but an internal relation between it and other objects [p. 212]." Which aspect(s) of an object will acquire saliency and be put into words in simple tasks of verbal labeling is hence contingent upon *the range of other objects from which the referent must be set apart.*

The object S in Fig. 10.1 is thus unequivocally identified as the *white* one in context 1, as the *big* one in context 2, and as the *triangle* in context 3. How

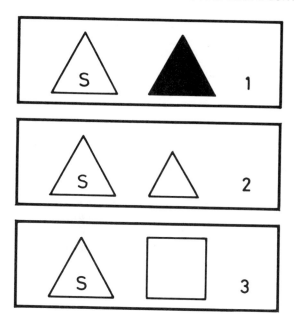

FIG. 10.1.   The same object *S* in different referential domains.

different explicitly introduced such referential domains affect linguistic encoding and decoding has been cogently demonstrated in psycholinguistic experiments by Olson (1970) and Deutsch (1976). And there is no reason to believe that such referential domains are of less significance when they are tacitly taken for granted: for instance, when two persons approach the "same" situation from different "private" positions as determined by background knowledge, presuppositions, interest, and personal engagement. The situation is in such a case rendered "meaningful" relative to a privately provided range of possible alternatives, as *similar to* and/or *different from* other situations. Its potential aspects acquire saliency and significance in a process of comparison (Tversky, 1977). And the issue of different meanings of situations engendered by persons interacting in those situations, I argue, may hence in part be explored in terms of different tacitly taken-for-granted referential domains.

Schutz (1951) maintains: "If I, with respect to an element *S* of the world taken for granted, assert: "*S* is *p*"", I do so because for my purpose at hand at this particular moment I am interested only in the *p*-being of *S* and I am disregarding as not relevant to such purpose that *S* is also *q* and *r* [p. 167]."

The assertion "*S* is *p*", in conjunction with the fact that aspects *q* and *r* are disregarded, implies, in the terminology of Mannheim (1952) and Hundeide (1978), that the state of affairs *S* (the situation) is experienced from some particular *position* and—in the terminology of Bateson, Goffman and Minsky—as enclosed within a certain *frame*. Its "meaning" when experienced from that position at that particular moment is thus generated from *some particular premises for interpretation* (Bateson, 1973, p. 60), *a certain background understanding* (Goffman, 1974, p. 22), and *a given collection of questions to be asked* (Minsky, 1975, p. 245). The cognitive factor on the person side of the person-situation interaction, accordingly, may in part be explored in terms of his sustained presuppositions, tacitly taken-for-granted referential domains of alternatives, and repertory of possible perspectives across a range of inherently composite and multifaceted situations.

Let us at this stage try to examine the meaning potential of one particular such inherently multifaceted situation, namely Menzel's mystery case: "What was Mr. Smith doing behind the lawn-mower?" (Menzel, 1978). Mr. Smith, who lives in a house in the suburbs of Scarsdale, is seen, very early on a Saturday morning, pushing a machine around on the grass. The machine is a lawn mower, and Menzel (1978) comments upon the meanings of that situation as follows:

> . . . while it is (almost unquestionably) true that Mr. Smith is mowing his lawn, there are a number of other things which he is also doing by the same behavior:
> he is beautifying his garden;
> he is exercising his muscles;
> he is avoiding his wife;
> he is conforming to the expectations of his neighbors;
> he is keeping up property values in Scarsdale;
> and he is angering his new neighbor, Mr. Ifabrumliz, who prefers to sleep late, and feels that Smith's mowing is a criticism of his, Ifabrumliz', unkept lawn [p. 147].

Menzel shows by this and a number of additional examples that most streams of behaviors can be conceptualized as *acts* in more than one way, and the multi-faceted nature of the situation he describes can be spelled out in terms of a set of aspects such as those indicated in Fig. 10.2.[1] The "making-the-lawn-neat-looking" aspect is thus apparently of primary significance to Mr. Ifabrumliz who feels guilty because of his own unkept garden. The physical exercise component, on the other hand, acquires saliency when the situation is viewed from the position of a neighbor who is seriously concerned with his own obesity and bodily decay. The horizontal range of "meanings" at each vertical level in Fig. 10.2 thus may be read as a set of potential aspects of what is going on in Mr. Smith's garden (i.e., as a set of *meaning potentials*).

The vertical scope of Fig. 10.2 illustrates what Feinberg (1965) has aptly labeled "the accordion effect" in the attribution of meanings to acts. What Mr. Smith is doing may be squeezed down to the trivial minimum *mowing the lawn* or even some component of that such as *using his muscles*. But it also may be

---

[1]Another, more complex version deals with instances of "genuine ambiguity" as well (Rommetveit, 1979b).

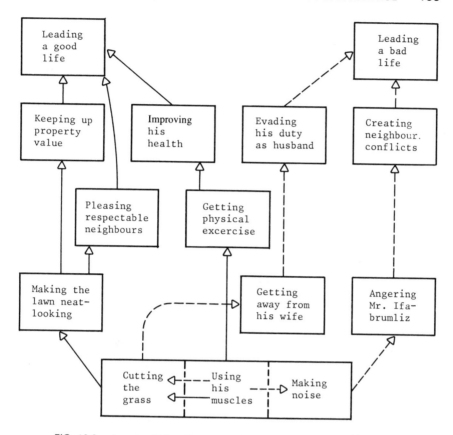

FIG. 10.2.   Aspects of Menzel's mystery situation: What was Mr. Smith doing behind the lawn mower?

stretched out in terms of successively more inclusive means–ends–structures and causal or quasi-causal textures. And Davidson (1971) maintains: "The accordion, which remains the same through the squeezing and stretching, is the action; the changes are in aspects described . . . [p. 22]."

The possible solutions to Menzel's mystery are thus, if we are searching for Mr. Smith's "true" intention or the "real" meaning of the situation, legion: Mr. Smith may actually be in a happy and exceptionally unreflective state of intrinsically satisfying bodily activity; he may be suffering the pain and entertaining the hope of the good Protestant torturing his flesh in anticipation of remote rewards; he may be avoiding his wife and/or annoying Mr. Ifabrumliz, etc. What remains invariant across the entire range of such "meanings," however, is the trivial, and in some sense public, minimum that he is *mowing the lawn*.

But even such a trivial minimum meaning of the situation is contingent upon some background understanding. It makes no sense at all to a visitor from an isolated rural area, for instance, who is entirely unfamiliar with suburban ways of life and takes it for granted that grass is something to be harvested and fed to the sheep. The expression "mowing the lawn," however, serves in a lawn-mowing but otherwise pluralistic community the very important public function of *identifying reference*. It imples nothing about "intentions" or "psychological meanings" of the situation such as those indicated in Fig. 10.2, yet entails them all as *possibilities*. The expression is accordingly as *opaque*—and as *useful*—as a proper name (see Rommetveit, 1974, p. 49–51).

Our task is not, however, to assess the "real" meaning of the situation but to explore which "psychological meanings" are engendered when it is assimilated into different "private worlds." It may well be that Mr. Smith is doing only some of the things indicated in Fig. 10.2 *intentionally* and that others (for instance making noise) are things that "befell him" (Davidson, 1971). He may even "actually"—if God's truth about intentions were revealed and his (Mr. Smith's) notoriously low level of reflectiveness forgiven—be in a genuine state of *intrinsic motivation* and doing nothing but using his muscles (Eckblad, 1977). The predicament of life in a pluralistic social world is such, however, that even if such were the case, *he cannot prevent uninformed passers-by or maliciously prying neighbors from reading, e.g., good citizenship or wife avoidance into the situation*.

What happens as we proceed from bottom toward top in Fig. 10.2 is thus that a *public* "trivial minimum meaning" of the situation branches off into different, yet in some sense successively more meaningful, *private* entities. What strikes a member of the Scarsdale establishment who happens to pass by the Smith residence is thus that Mr. Smith at such early hours actually is mowing his lawn rather than, for example, *staying in bed with a hangover after a Friday night of excessive drinking at the pub*. The fact that his gardening is a solitary activity, the whereabouts of Mrs. Smith, and the noise of the lawn mower are of no concern to him whatsoever. These are very salient and significant aspects of the situation, however, when it is viewed from the position of a neighbor prying into Mr. Smith's marital affairs and personal feuds with Mr. Ifabrumliz.

Composite private meanings of the situation entail aspects at different vertical levels in Fig. 10.2. The implications of what Mr. Smith is doing may for instance be captured in chains of attribution of *intention* and/or *reason* and/or *responsibility*, and the situation in that way is imbued with meaning from successively more inclusive and inherently meaningful patterns. Composite meanings accordingly may be revealed in different *accounts* of what is going on (Harré, 1978). The member of the establishment who happens to pass by may thus make sense of the situation by an account such as:

A_1:   Mr. Smith is using his muscles cutting the grass in order to make the lawn nice and neat-looking. While in that way pleasing respectable neighbors and keeping up property values in the area, he is at the same getting some outdoor physical exercise and improving his health and, all in all, leading the good life of a decent Scarsdale citizen (solid lines in Fig. 10.2).

The story Mr. Smith's prying neighbor tells us about what is going on, however, may be as follows:

A_2: Mr. Smith is using his muscles cutting the grass at such early hours merely because he want to get away from his wife and in order to anger Mr. Ifabrumliz by the noise he is making. He is thus evading his marital obligations, ruining interpersonal relationships between neighbors, and leading a bad life (broken lines in Fig. 10.2).

These are composite as opposed to *single-aspect* accounts of the situation such as "Mr. Smith is getting some physical exercise" or "Mr. Smith is getting away from his wife." Accounts A_1 and A_2 are thus strikingly different with respect to selection of aspects, yet similar with respect to level of reflectiveness and vertical scope. Which potential aspects of the situation will acquire saliency and *be accounted for,* moreover, is in each case apparently contingent upon a particular range of tacitly provided alternatives. The prying neighbor's interest in the situation thus is flavored clearly by what he already knows or presupposes about Mr. Smith. His account (A_2) answers questions such as:

Why does Mr. Smith, who has plenty of leisure time but because of his wife's odd working hours hardly any time to chat with her, decide to work alone in the garden at these early hours when for once they are both at home?

Why doesn't he invite Mr. Ifabrumliz to tea rather than disturbing his morning sleep by the noise of the lawn mower?

The incidental passer-by, on the other hand, is preoccupied with the general virtues of good Scarsdale citizenship rather than Mr. Smith's private affairs. His account (A_2) entails tacit comparisons such as

making the lawn neat-looking versus letting the garden grow wild, and working in the garden at such early hours versus staying in bed with a hangover.

The two divergent accounts thus answer *different sets of questions.* The situation is accordingly imbued with meaning from different personal perspectives and *relative to different tacitly taken-for-granted referential domains of alternatives.*

MEANINGS OF SITUATIONS, SHARED MEANINGS, AND SOCIAL CONTROL

What any particular solitary observer "sees" going on in Mr. Smith's garden that Saturday morning is actually an entirely private affair. But it can be *talked about* and hence—at least under certain conditions and in some sense—become *a temporarily shared social reality.* The solitary observer thus may try to transform his "private" outlook on the situation into a social reality simply by telling some other person about it. Once the other person accepts the invitation to listen and engage in a dialogue, he leaves behind whatever his preoccupations might have been at the moment "silence was transformed into speech (Merleau–Ponty, 1962, p. 182)." From that moment on the two of them are jointly committed to a temporarily *shared* social world, established and continually modified by acts of communication.

A prerequisite for establishing intersubjectivity across different private worlds, moreover, is *reciprocal role taking*. The speaker monitors what he says in accordance with what he assumes to be the listener's background information and premises for comprehension whereas the listener tries to make sense of what he is hearing by adopting what he assumes to be the speaker's perspective. There is thus in acts of human communication an *inbuilt circularity*.

This does not imply, however, that the two participants assume equal responsibility for what is being "meant" or "referred to" in the conversation. The speaker—or, more generally, the participant who introduced whatever is being talked about at any particular stage of the dialogue—has the privilege of determining what is going to be jointly attended to at that stage. And this is the case *even when he fails to make himself understood*. Only he—not the listener—can decide what he himself intends to make known and *whether it is being misunderstood*. Control of the temporarily shared social reality of a dialogue is thus under conditions of symmetry between conversation partners in principle determined by *dialogue role* or *direction of communication*.

William James (1962) maintained about human interaction in a pluralistic social world: "You accept my verification of one thing, I yours of another. We trade on each other's truth [p. 197]." And let us now examine how the incidental passer-by's personal meaning of the lawn-mowing situation may be transformed into a social reality and become *his wife's "truth" about it as well*. The story he tells her when he returns home is possibly as follows (see account A_1, p. 156, and Fig. 10.2, p. 155:

> A Saturday morning walk through Scarsdale is really a treat. It's so nice here, a real paradise compared to some other places. I remember driving through the East River district one early Saturday morning last year. What misery: ugly houses, unkept gardens, half-naked kids running around while their parents were probably sobering up after last night's booze . . . But people here in Scarsdale deserve their good fortune. We are hard-working people who care about our properties and like to keep the neighborhood nice and clean. I walked by Mr. Smith's residence, and *Mr. Smith was indeed already busy mowing his lawn.*

What he tells *about Mr. Smith* is in this case "the truth, the whole truth, and nothing but the truth." It entails hardly more than the "trivial minimum" meaning of the situation and therefore—when detached from the preceding hymn to Scarsdale—can be endorsed by Mr. Smith's prying neighbor also. What very likely is made known to his wife, however, is that *Mr. Smith seems to be a very conscientious and respectable Scarsdale citizen,* and this is possibly also what she will remember when the details of her husband's Saturday morning report are forgotten. Her immediate response to gossip about the Smith's leading a Bohemian life hence will probably be one of protest: How can that be? Didn't she hear from the mouth of her own very trustworthy and credible husband some time ago that Mr. Smith is such a very decent and respectable fellow?

An entirely different "truth" may emerge, however, in a dyad composed of *Mr. Smith's prying neighbor and a visiting friend of his* who knows nothing about the Smiths or any other couple in that neighborhood. The two of them are looking out the window, and the pryer says while pointing in the direction of Mr. Smith and the lawn mower (see account A_2, p. 157, and Fig. 10.2, p. 155):

> He has all the time in the world for gardening, but early Saturday morning is the only opportunity for a little family life in that house because of Mrs. Smith's odd working hours. And *she* is so keen to make the most of that opportunity. Imagine how she feels right now, left alone there in the kitchen! And think of Mr. Ifabrumliz, their next door neighbor on the other side, who is trying to get some sleep!

What is "pointed out" by the pryer is thus *a Mr. Smith evading his marital duties and angering a neighbour.* And this will also very likely be the gist of the story about what went on in Mr. Smith's garden that the visitor later on tells *his* wife.

These two cases indicate how a *shared* meaning of an inherently ambiguous and multifaceted situation may be attained in dyadic interaction. The interaction is in both cases characterized by a definite actual asymmetry ($p_1 > p_2$ in Table 10.1) in the sense that one participant (p_1) has background information about talked-about states of affairs that the other participant (p_2) lacks. The passerby (p_1) has thus actually *seen* what happened in Mr. Smith's garden whereas his wife (p_2) has not, and the pryer (p_1) *knows about* Mr. Ifabrumliz' sleeping habits as well as the Smiths' rare opportunities to be together, whereas his visiting friend (p_2) is entirely ignorant about those states of affairs and has no background information of his own about the situation.

The psychological meaning of the lawn-mowing situation S for the incidental passer-by may perhaps be summarized as

> S is A_1: Mr. Smith's mowing of the lawn is a manifestation of good, conventional Scarsdale citizenship.

This, however, is mediated to his wife in terms of *referential alternatives* such as "unkept gardens," "keep the neighborhood nice and clean," "sobering up after last night's booze." It is *presupposed* rather than *asserted,* and his wife has of course a priori neither any alternative outlook nor any notion about the meaning potential of the situation (see Fig. 10.2). A situation that per se resembles an isolated polysemous or even homonymous verbal expression is thereby

TABLE 10.1

Transformations of Dyadic States of Social Reality Under Different Conditions of Actual and Reciprocally Assumed Presuppositions and Communication Control. I. Passerby to his Wife; II. Pryer to Friend; III. Passenger to Driver; IV. Passerby to Pryer and Pryer to Passerby

		Meaning of S (Presupposition)				Control Pattern		
		Personal		Reciprocally Assumed		Actual	Assumed	
		for p_1	for p_2	p_1:(p_2)	p_2:(p_1)		by p_1	by p_2
(I)	1.	S is A_1	—	S is A_1	—	$p_1 > p_2$	$p > p_2$	$p_1 > p_2$
	2.	S is A_1	—	S is A_1	(S is A_1)	$p_1 > p_2$	$p_1 > p_2$	$p_1 > p_2$
	3.	S is A_1	S is A_1	S is A_1	(S is A_1)	$p_1 > p_2$	$p_1 > p_2$	$p_1 > p_2$
	4.	S is A_1	S is A_1	S is A_1	S is A_1	$p_1 > p_2$	$p_1 > p_2$	$p_1 > p_2$
(II)	5.	S is A_2	—	—	—	$p_1 > p_2$	$p_1 > p_2$	$p_1 > p_2$
	6.	S is A_2	S is A_1	S is A_1	(S is A_2)	$p_1 > p_2$	$p_1 > p_2$	$p_1 > p_2$
	7.	S is A_2	S is A_2	S is A_1	(S is A_2)	$p_1 > p_2$	$p_1 > p_2$	$p_1 > p_2$
	8.	S is A_2	S is A_2	S is A_2	(S is A_2)	$p_1 > p_2$	$p_1 > p_2$	$p_1 > p_2$
	9.	S is A_2	S is A_2	S is A_2	S is A_2	$p_1 > p_2$	$p_1 > p_2$	$p_1 > p_2$
(III)	10.	S is A_i	—	—	—	$p_1 = p_2$	$p = p_2$	$p_1 = p_2$
	11.	S is A_i	—	—	(S is A_i)	$p_1 = p_2$	$p_1 > p_2$	$p_1 > p_2$
	12.	S is A_i	S is A_i	—	(S is A_i)	$p_1 = p_2$	$p_1 > p_2$	$p_1 > p_2$
	13.	S is A_i	S is A_i	S is A_i	(S is A_i)	$p_1 = p_2$	$p_1 > p_2$	$p_1 > p_2$
	14.	S is A_i	S is A_i	S is A_i	S is A_i	$p_1 = p_2$	$p_1 = p_2$	$p_1 = p_2$
(IV)	15.	S is A_1	S is A_2	S is A_1	—	$p_1 = p_2$	—	—
	16.	S is A_1	S is A_2	S is A_1	S is A_1	$p_1 = p_2$	$p_1 > p_2$	$p_1 > p_2$
	17.	S is A_1	S is A_2	S is A_1	S is A_1	$p_1 = p_2$	$p_1 > p_2$	$p_1 = p_2$
	18.	S is A_1	S is A_2	S is A_2	S is A_1	$p_1 = p_2$	$p_1 < p_2$	$p_1 < p_2$
	19.	S is A_1	S is A_2	S is A_2	S is A_1	$p_1 = p_2$	$p_1 = p_2$	$p_1 = p_2$

brought to her attention *in an already disambiguated version*. It enters her mind as a talked-about, social reality enclosed within a frame provided by her husband, and the incidental passer-by's presupposition becomes thereby his wife's *belief*.

What happens in this case can be described in terms of a transformation of dyadic states of social reality (see Table 10.1).[2] The passer-by (p_1) enters the conversation with his own particular personal meaning of the situation (i.e., with the presupposition that S *is* A_1). Let us assume, moreover, that he is a somewhat shielded and innocently egocentric member of the Scarsdale establishment with a monistic outlook on lawn mowing. This implies, more specifically, that he also takes it for granted that others—and, in any case, *his wife*—share his perspective [S is A_1 also in column p_1:(p_2) in Table 10.1]. Correspondence between columns p_1 and p_1:(p_2) thus means that p_1 engages in communication with p_2 from an

---

[2]This table is derived from a combinatorics yielding a "dialogical truth table" of 19,200 different states of dyadic social reality (Rommetveit, 1979, 1980).

assumption of *assumed similarity* and, in the extreme case, on the firm yet un-reflected assumption that the other person's private world is a duplicate of his own.

The passer-by's wife (p_2) is entirely ignorant about what happened during his morning walk until she is told about it. She is in a state of complete agnostic innocence as far as Mr. Smith's lawn mowing is concerned and knows of course nothing about her husband's presupposition. The column for p_2's personal mean-ing of S and the column p_2:(p_1) are thus, when she starts listening to his story, *empty*. The actual control of the temporarily shared social reality of their conver-sation, moreover, is $p_1 > p_2$, since p_1 is the one who observed what actually happened. He is also the speaker and has as such the privilege of conveying what actually happened as it appeared to him within his private world. The wife's (p_2's) commitment *qua listener* is to make sense of what he tells her by adopting *his*, p_1's, perspective. Control of *what is meant by what is said* is thus recipro-cally, by p_1 as well as by p_2, assumed to be $p_1 > p_2$.

The long introductory part of the passerby's story serves under these condi-tions to establish a *shared referential domain* for the lawn-mowing situation. What happens before the wife even hears about Mr. Smith is thus that her husband's presupposition is mediated to her *in disguised form*, as (S is A_1) in column p_2:(p_1). The good-Scarsdale-citizen aspect, for that reason, acquires saliency the very moment she is told what Mr. Smith did in his garden, in principle in the same way as object S in Fig. 10.1 becomes the *white* one the moment it is inserted in the referential domain (1). The presupposition S is A_1 is hence hardly recognized or reflected upon as a presupposition at all (i.e., as only one of a set of possible interpretations), but immediately endorsed by p_2 as part of a shared social reality.

What happens from the moment the passerby p_1 starts telling his story until the story is finished and his wife p_2 has understood what he meant accordingly can be described as a transformation of states of dyadic social reality from Row 1 through Row 4 in Table 10.1. The main character in this pedantic version of the story is p_1's presupposition that S is A_1. This presupposition constitutes at the final stage (Row 4) part of a perfectly shared social reality in the sense *that both p_1 and p_2 believe that S is A_1 and each of them assumes the other to hold that belief.* But p_1's presupposition that S is A_1, we remember, is nothing but the passerby's "personal meaning" of the lawn-mowing situation in condensed form. Rows 1 through 3 in Table 10.1 thus may be read as a systematic account of how the psychological meaning of a situation for one particular person, p_1, can enter a conversation as a presupposition in *disguise* and, in the absence of alternative meanings and under conditions of asymmetric communication con-trol, be transformed into a perfectly shared social reality. The asymmetric pattern of actual control, however, remains the same throughout such a transformation. This implies that the wife's resultant belief that S is A_1 remains contingent upon the credibility of her husband. And she will also, as already indicated, probably be made aware of that fact if her "truth" later on happens to be challenged: Didn't she hear from . . . her husband . . .? (see p. 159).

The psychological meaning of the lawn-mowing situation S for Mr. Smith's prying neighbor may be summarized as

S is A_2:   Mr. Smith's mowing of the lawn is a maneuver by which he manages to get away from his wife and make Mr. Ifabrumliz angry.

What is achieved by the pryer's (p_1's) comments when he calls his visiting friend p_2's attention to S is that this meaning enters their shared social reality as a presupposition in disguise (see Rows 5 through 9 in Table 10.1). His friend p_2 can of course see for himself what actually is going on. But the lawn-mowing situation has no psychological meaning for him at all (i.e., none whatsoever beyond the trivial minimum) until it is *commented upon and pointed out* to him by the pryer. The situation S then acquires meaning also for the visiting friend (p_2), but within a frame of referential alternatives provided by the pryer (p_1).

Episodes I and II are thus very similar, but different with respect to the speaker's initial assumption about the listener's perspective on the situation (see column p_1:(p_2), Rows 1 and 5 in Table 10.1). The innocently egocentric passerby takes it for granted that the wife shares his outlook whereas the pryer cannot possibly expect his visiting friend to know in advance what he takes for granted about Mr. Smith's reasons or intentions. If he tells him, however, he also takes it for granted that p_2 will endorse his perspective on the situation S once he is informed about Mrs. Smith and Mr. Ifabrumliz. The psychological meaning of the situation for the pryer is thus transformed into *a perfectly shared social reality* the moment he correctly assumes the visitor to share his belief (i.e., in Row 8 in Table 10.1).

Notice, however, that the pattern of actual and reciprocally assumed control of the shared social reality also in this case remains $p_1 > p_2$ and that the visitor's resultant opinion of Mr. Smith for that reason will be a socially contingent "truth." William James' claim that "we trade on each other's truth" will hence be corroborated if *the pryer's visiting friend* and *the passerby's wife* later on should happen to meet and engage in conversation about Mr. Smith, one suggesting that he is actually a nasty fellow and the other that he is such a nice and conscientious fellow citizen.

But the psychological meaning of a situation for one particular person may be transformed into a perfectly shared social reality also under conditions of symmetric interaction or equality with respect to actual control. Imagine, for instance, two people driving by the Smith residence in a car. Both of them observe what is "actually" going on and neither knows more than the other about it. The passenger may remark, however, the moment Mr. Smith and the lawn mower attract their attention: "I wonder how my neighbors feel about me and my messy and wild-growing garden." Or he may, alternatively, merely point his finger at the driver's protruding belly. And the topic of discourse in the car may in one case become whether or not to please respectable neighbors, in the other case obesity and physical exercise (see Fig. 10.2).

The two alternative, hypothetical variants of interaction serve as illustrations of a very general paradigm: An initially yet-not-attended-to or "virginal" situation S is commented upon or responded to by one person p_1 and *eo ipso* rendered "meaningful" to another person p_2 as well within some frame of referential alternatives provided by p_2. Some aspect A_1 of the multifaceted situation S that has acquired saliency for p_1 is then also under certain conditions of symmetry with respect to actual communication control transformed into a dyadic state of perfectly shared social reality (see Rows 10 through 14 in Table 10.1). An essential common feature of episodes I, II, and III is *the* absence of competing referential alternatives on the part of p_2 at the initial stage of interaction (Rows 1, 5, and 10). Reciprocally assumed control of what is being meant, moreover, is unequivocally determined by direction of communication. Joint commitment to a temporarily shared social reality implies therefore that p_2 in every case must make sense of what p_1 says or does concerning the situation S by adapting *his* (p_2's) perspective (Rows 2–3, 6–8, and 11–13). A distinctive feature of episode (III), however, is the actual and reciprocally assumed equality with respect to control of their shared social reality at the outset of the dyadic interaction as well as when "speech is transformed into silence" again (see control pattern in Row 10 and row 14).

The main character in the pedantic versions of all three stories, I have argued, is *a presupposition in disguise* of the general form S is A_1. But let us now explore what happens in dyadic communication if p_1 tacitly takes it for granted that S is A_1, whereas S makes sense to p_2 in terms of some alternative aspect A_2. Imagine, for instance, that the incidental passer-by (p_1) and Mr. Smith's prying neighbor (p_2) meet, and that the encounter takes place shortly after both of them have observed what is "actually" going on in Mr. Smith's garden. Their conversation may then possibly proceed as follows:

p_1 (passerby): It's nice here in Scarsdale, isn't it? I remember driving through the East River district one early Saturday morning last year. What misery: ugly houses, unkept gardens, half-naked kids running around while their parents were probably sobering up after last night's booze . . . But people here deserve their good fortune. We are hard-working people who care about our properties and like to keep the neighborhood nice and clean. I just walked by Mr. Smith's residence, and Mr. Smith is indeed already busy mowing his lawn.

p_2 (pryer): So you think Mr. Smith is a nice citizen caring for his garden and his family and the neighborhood, eh? Do you know that he has all the time in the world for lawn mowing, and that early Saturday morning is practically Mrs. Smith's only opportunity for a chat with her husband and some family life? What is she feeling left alone there in the kitchen? And what about Mr. Ifabrumliz, Mr. Smith's next door neighbor, who is trying to get some sleep?

Some main features of this conversation are captured in the formalized and pedantic version of it in rows 15 through 19 of Table 10.1. The passerby (p_1) engages also in this case in the dialogue on the innocently egocentric assumption that his conversation partner shares his outlook. His "background understanding" of what is going on in Mr. Smith's garden entails personal experience of Saturday morning life in a slum area. The pryer's (p_2's) personal background information has to do with proximal states of affairs such as Mrs. Smith's odd working hours and the sleeping habits of Mr. Ifabrumliz. The passerby's (p_1's) assumption that *he* is in control of a temporarily shared social reality once he has told his story (in Row 17) is thus false. The pattern of communication control is symmetric rather than unilateral, and there are no actual constraints upon interchangeability of dialogue roles: The Scarsdale establishment's outlook on gardening and the good life is indeed part of Mr. Smith's neighbor's repertory of *potentially available* perspectives, and the incidental passerby is also perfectly *capable* of adopting the position of a pryer into private affairs.

What happens as Mr. Smith's prying neighbor p_2 listens to the passerby p_1 is thus that p_2's perspective on the situation S temporarily is expanded so as to include aspect A_1 *as a possibility*. This latter meaning potential has been entirely disregarded and beyond his very restricted field of vision until the moment when the incidental passerby p_1 in the introductory part of his Saturday morning report provides a frame of referential alternatives for Mr. Smith's lawn mowing very different from his own. What is tacitly taken for granted by p_1 (that S is A_1) is accordingly not at all endorsed by p_2 as a shared social reality, but immediately recognized *as a presupposition on the part of p_1* (Row 16), and questioned (Row 18). The switch of dialogue roles, moreover, implies that the passerby p_1 now has to listen to what p_2 has to say on *his* (p_2's) premises. The resultant dyadic constellation (Row 19) is hence a *partially shared social reality* that entails, in a way, two different preestablished personal perspectives on (or "psychological meanings" of) the situation.

The passerby's presupposition that S is A_1 which becomes his wife's *belief* is by the pryer immediately unveiled as a *presupposition,* and his meaning of the situation can apparently be introduced in the form of a presupposition *in disguise* only in the absence of competing referential alternatives. Common to the three types of episodes I, II, and III in which the psychological meaning of S for p_1 becomes a fully shared meaning is that S remains "virginal" to p_2 until brought to his attention by p_1. The latter can for that reason profit from the innocence of silence *and* the efficiency of speech.

SOME GENERAL IMPLICATIONS OF A CONSISTENTLY PLURALISTIC SET OF ASSUMPTIONS CONCERNING HUMAN INTERACTION

The main features of my preceding rather detailed analysis of meanings of situations in dyadic interaction may be condensed into a general "theory of relativity." Situations are in a pluralistic social world necessarily multifaceted. The meaning potential of a given situation S hence must be conceived of as *a set of aspects and patterns of aspects.* A given aspect A_1 of S is generated by comparison and acquires saliency when S is attended to as enclosed within some more or less well-defined frame of referential alternatives. The psychological meaning of a situation S for a person p may be described in terms of some single aspect or patterns of aspects. Such meanings are engendered by persons responding to, commenting upon, and/or interacting in particular situations and must accordingly be specified relative to (frequently, tacitly taken for granted) domains of experiential possibilities or referential alternatives.

People differ, however, with respect to sustained presuppositions about and repertory of potential perspectives on situations. Intrapersonal behavioral consistency across variant situations hence may in part be described in terms of constraints on experiential possibilities and referential alternatives with respect to situations, and an individual's personality may from a purely cognitive perspective in part be described in terms of his *range of* and *prevalance among* such referential alternatives. Personality differences may accordingly in part be assessed as "private worlds" differing with respect to prevalent perspectives and availability of referential alternatives.

Such private worlds are by no means solipsistic. They intersect, first of all, in very important "trivial minimum" meanings of situations (p. 155). A person's repertory of potential perspectives is such, moreover, that his perspective on a situation may be expanded so as to entail as experiential possibilities aspects that are visible only from the position of his conversation partner. States of partially shared social reality are thus under conditions of adequate role taking in accordance with the primary rule of communication control attained in encounters between different private worlds. The psychological meaning of a particular situation for a given person may even, as we have tried to show, under certain conditions be transformed into a perfectly shared social reality.

Berger and Luckmann (1967) maintain: "It can . . . be said that language makes 'more real' my subjectivity not only to my conversation partner but also to myself [p. 38]." And Bateson (1973) defines *ego weakness* as "trouble in identifying and interpreting those signals which should tell the individual what sort of a message a message is . . . [p. 167]." The issue of "shared meanings" of social situations, moreover, may become in human interaction an issue of whose private world is endorsed by others as well, accepted as the basis for joint or collective action, and hence in some very important sense made publicly valid. The transformation of the incidental passer-by's meaning of the lawn-mowing situation into a perfectly shared social reality when he tells his wife about it represents thus, in a way, *a social validation of his subjectivity.* And repeated instances of such social validation may indeed in part explain his innocent egocentrism in interpersonal relations.

Social validation serves to confirm and sustain the basic assumption that (Schutz, 1945) ". . . the world is . . . an intersubjective world common to all of us . . . [p. 53]." Its subjective quality and contingency upon personal referential alternatives are brought to the foreground only under very exceptional conditions such as, for instance, when one of George Kelly's clients attempts to account for important characteristics of people she knows well in terms of "Mary-ness" (Kelly, 1955). What is meant by that word is entirely bound to her subjective experience of one particular friend of hers, Mary. And the bipolar nature of language as a bridge between different private worlds is reflected in its composition: The component "Mary" is intelligible only in terms of one particular referential alternative whereas the component "-ness" is comprehensible to everybody yet nearly devoid of experiential content.

Issues discussed under headings such as "ego weakness" and "social validation of one's subjectivity" may thus within a consistently pluralistic conceptual framework be rephrased in terms of meaning potentials of situations, different domains of referential alternatives, and social control of temporarily shared social realities. *Personal flexibility,* for instance, may in part be assessed in terms of an individual's *range of possible perspectives on situations* and *capacity to take the roles of "different others."* And *ego* or *personality strength* becomes in some cases of dyadic interaction a question of *whose personal "meaning" of a given situation is accepted as a temporarily shared social reality in encounters between different private worlds.*

Such questions, however, cannot be settled by recourse to traditional indices of communication control such as, e.g., who is doing most of the talking in a group of people. A brief introductory remark may indeed under certain conditions suffice to establish a shared frame of referential alternatives for the sustained topic of a long group discussion. The person who made that remark is then in some very important sense in control of the interaction *even if he remains silent during the remaining part of the discussion.* The interpersonal climate of a "virginal" social situation, moreover, also may be affected significantly by one single participant's tacit presupposition and initial move in the social game. A person p_1, for instance, may treat and/or talk to a person p_2 whom he had just met as if p_2 were already a member of his inner circle of friends, and such an apparently erroneous presupposition is under certain conditions in itself conducive to intimacy (Rommetveit, 1974, p. 87). Even a highly prestructured situation of human interaction, moreover, remains virginal and ambiguous to some extent until its meaning for the participants is specified relative to certain optional aspects. The host and expert player of a bridge party may thus by his general introductory comments and/or initial social move set the stage for a relaxed social event or a competetive intellectual ordeal.

The case of Mr. Smith mowing his lawn has been thoroughly exploited in a systematic analysis of meanings of situations and social control of such meaning. It sheds hardly any light upon person–situation interaction of the kind suggested by the example of the bridge party, however. Nor is it particularly suitable as a point of departure for analysis of general "substantial" dimensions of either persons or situations. Very little probably is gained by defining, e.g., prying as a "personal predisposition" to transform multifaceted and inherently ambiguous social situations into talked-about private affairs and interpersonal intrigues.

More is possibly gained by examining abstract person–situation dimensions (e.g., vertical scope of meaning potentials of situations, see Fig. 10.2). This implies, on the person side of the interaction, an exploration of vertical scope of referential alternatives. Some persons may tend to "stretch out" very trivial events and imbue them with meaning from inclusive means–ends structures. Others may be inclined to "squeeze down" even the most tragic situation to a triviality. Such potentially significant person characteristics cannot easily be assessed in verbal reports, however, because "meaning" most often emerges within tacitly taken-for-granted frames of referential alternatives as people respond to and/or interact in situations. A main asset of a consistently pluralistic conceptual framework, though, is the explication of the conceptual interdependency between person and situation dimensions in interaction psychology.

ACKNOWLEDGMENT

I am indebted to colleagues and friends in Oslo for helpful comments during the preparation of this chapter and, in particular, to Dr. Finn Tschudi for his illumination of general theoretical issues in the intersection of interactional psychology and semantic theory.

11

The Psychological Situation in Social-Learning Theory

Julian B. Rotter
University of Connecticut

In 1954 the author published a social-learning theory of personality and complex human behavior that attempted to integrate the two major traditions in psychology—the S–R or reinforcement theories on the one hand, and the cognitive or field theories on the other. Whereas the basic assumptions of the theory have not changed in the intervening years, various aspects have been added to or refined and new elements added. The purpose of this chapter is to summarize the present status of the psychological situation as a theoretical variable in this theory.

This chapter first presents briefly some of the basic theoretical propositions regarding the nature of the psychological situation; then it presents four problems inherent in the use of the psychological situation as a *predictive* theoretical construct. The present way of dealing with these problems in social-learning theory are explicated.

SOME GENERAL PRINCIPLES REGARDING THE PSYCHOLOGICAL SITUATION IN SOCIAL-LEARNING THEORY

1. The first basic postulate of social-learning theory according to Rotter (1954) is: "the unit of investigation for the study of personality is the interaction of the individual and his/her meaningful environment [p. 85]." This is clearly an interactionist position. It was stated earlier by Lewin (1935), Kantor (1924), and Murray (1938). Coutu (1949) in the field of sociology and Brunswik (1943) in his analysis of the field of perception expressed a similar principle. It should be noted, however, that all these theorists have had great difficulty in using the

169

concept of the psychological situation, meaningful environment, life space, and so on systematically in a predictive fashion, because they have stressed the subjective or learned nature of the environment. The term *meaningful environment* as used here refers to the acquired significance or meaning of the environment to the individual. It is the psychological, not the physical, description of the environment that is important.

2. All variables in social-learning theory are situationally bound; that is, to be useful or meaningful within the theory they have to be considered as limited by a specific described situation or class of situations (Rotter, 1955). This is expressed in the general formula for behavior potential, as follows:

$$BP_{x,s_1,R_a} = f(E_{x,R_a,s_1} \ \& \ RV_{a,s_1})$$

The formula reads: The potential for behavior x to occur in situation 1 in relation to reinforcement a is a function of the expectancy of the occurrence of reinforcement a, following behavior x in situation 1, and the value of reinforcement a in situation 1. For this predictive formula to work there must be a way of reliably describing the nature of the psychological situation prior to the occurrence of the behavior x.

3. How is the situation defined in social-learning theory? Of course most, if not all, theorists accept the idea that external influences in some ways affect specific behaviors, but the systematic use of these external influences presents a problem that often is either ignored or actively avoided. To use the psychological situation as a theoretical variable requires, to begin with, a careful definition. Only with such a definition can we determine whether or not any attempt to describe, identify, or measure the psychological situation is reasonable and logical.

In social-learning theory we define the psychological situation as a complex set of interacting cues acting upon an individual for any specific time period. *These cues determine for the individual the expectancies for behavior–reinforcement sequences and also for reinforcement–reinforcement sequences.* Such cues may be implicit as well as explicit; that is, they may be thoughts, ideas, or internal stimuli such as pain, pleasure, excitement, or fear. Implicit responses may be carried over from a prior experience and not be related to what are considered present external cues. It is *not* necessary that the person be able to express verbally conscious awareness of these cues but only that it can be demonstrated that he/she was reacting to them. In order to make the concept of the psychological situation operational, implicit cues must be identified by inference from immediately prior events or by inference from behaviors in the situation other than the one we are predicting, including physiological observations that serve as indirect measures of the psychological state of the organism.

We define the psychological situation as the interacting cues perceived by the individual over any defined time unit; thus, we may be interested in cues over a period of a moment, an experimental hour, or much longer periods of time, as when we talk about a person's job situation or marriage situation. The definition, then, is not precise. What we call *personal variables* and what we call *situa-*

tional variables is in part an arbitrary decision, and what we call *present situational variables* can extend over long periods of time. The overall definition has to be in part arbitrary and relativistic, but it can be made workable and useful. The alternatives of either trying to predict behavior without paying attention to the present cues to which the individual is responding or of trying to predict behavior without taking into account what the individual brings into a situation in terms of relatively stable characteristics limits one to extremely low levels of prediction. In other words, a useful distinction between person and situation is one that defines personal variables as a set of relatively stable characteristics and defines situational variables as the set of meaningful cues to which he or she is reacting at the present. Both sets of variables are presumed to be determined by past learning.

4. In social-learning theory, an expectancy for a behavior-reinforcement sequence is considered to be a function of an expectancy built up in the same situation over past experience (E') and generalized expectancies (GE) from relevant classes of similar situations. The generalized expectancies may be of many different kinds (Rotter, Chance, & Phares, 1972). Thus, in the case of a student discussing a problem with a teacher, significant generalized expectancies may include one for being put down by an authority figure, one for being able to understand the subject matter, one for trust of others, and so on. The relative influence of the generalized expectancies is determined by the degree of novelty of the situation and is represented in the formula that follows as some function of (N_{s_1}), where N stands for the number of previous experiences in that situation.

$$E = f(E'_{s_1} \ \& \ \frac{GE_1, GE_2, \ldots GE_n}{f(N_{S_1})}$$

There are a number of implications of this formula for understanding the role of the psychological situation in predicting behavior. One of these is the considerable importance of novelty. If the formula is correct, then personal characteristics based on generalized past experience are likely to play a much greater role in a novel, ambiguous, or unstructured situation than in one with which the individual has great familiarity. Another implication is for the great complexity of situational analysis, inasmuch as the variety of cues present may bring into play a series of relatively independent generalized expectancies.

PROBLEMS INHERENT IN THE TREATMENT OF THE PSYCHOLOGICAL SITUATION AS A SYSTEMATIC VARIABLE

1. How Can the Psychological Situation Be Defined Independently of the Person?   If one defines the psychological situation as meaningful or as truly psychological rather than physical or as subjective rather than objective, then the situation is a function of the person. We have already indicated that this is not a necessary barrier to problems of analysis, because we can treat situational variables as one aspect of the person and stable accumulated effects of experience, or personality variables, as a different aspect of the person. However, this does not tell us how to use the situation predictively.

In social-learning theory this problem is treated by identifying the situation in the commonsense terms of the social group, subculture, or culture. In other words, we can make clear the objective referent for what we are talking about and still treat the environment as a psychological, meaningful, or subjective environment. The subject's reaction to the environment and the scientist's descriptions of the environment need not be identical. In fact, the social scientist often is busily engaged in using the latter in order to understand the former. In this way we can talk not only about differences among situations but about individual differences in response to the same objective situation. For example, we generally can obtain high agreement when we identify a situation as a classroom situation, a party, an authority situation, a frustration situation, and so on. These are in themselves abstractions of a variety of cues but at the commonsense level. Note that we are not referring to an average of interpretations but to a descriptive level that will allow for high agreement among observers. If necessary or desirable, much more elaborate and detailed descriptions of the situation can be made, but always in the commonsense terms of the subculture. Once we have identified a given situation, we then can make predictions about differences in behavior of individuals within that situation, differences of behavior of a group of individuals in one situation versus another, and interactions of the two. This is, of course, what social psychologists and clinical and personality psychologists have been doing for a long time. We are stating here explicitly what others have done implicitly over many years. By describing how situations can be identified objectively, we have opened the way but have not solved the problem of identifying or discovering the important dimensions of situations that can be used in defining classes of situations.

2. *The Complexity of Situational Cues.*   As we have indicated earlier, most "real-life" situations involve a bewildering variety of cues that in themselves may interact, thus making both classification and prediction extremely difficult. The problem can be illustrated by an analysis of the effect of the testing situation on test behavior, using a projective test such as the Rorschach. Considerable research and clinical data with the Rorschach indicate that a wide variety of cues will affect test results. Some of this early literature has been summarized by Rotter (1960) and Masling (1960).

Probably the most significant variable in affecting test responses is the purpose of the test. Subjects may hypothesize about the purpose from a variety of cues or they may be told about the purpose via instructions. In the case of the Rorschach test the subject may believe that he or she is merely a research subject and that the experimenter is not interested in him or her personally; that he or she may be a patient and believe that the test administrator is trying to determine the extent of his or her psychopathology; that he or she is being tested for creativity, as the instructions imply, or for his or her general intelligence; that his or her responses will reveal unconscious ideas; or that the test is being given to determine whether or not he or she should be hired or promoted. All of these cognitions will significantly affect the subject's test responses.

We know that the examiner's characteristics will have an effect: whether the examiner is male or female, an authority figure or a peer; whether he or she is warm and friendly or cold and distant; whether he or she is physically attractive or not. In addition, these characteristics interact with the subject's sex, age, and belief about the purpose of the test.

We know that the instructions will make a difference, not only for the Rorschach but for all tests, and that changing only a few words in the instructions may have significant effects on test results.

The format and items of the test and, in the case of the Rorschach, the nature of the inkblots do affect test behavior. A different set of items may change not only the differences between groups but the order of individuals in a group. The physical location and surroundings may affect test results. For example, different results have been obtained in a gymnasium versus a classroom for a questionnaire about preferences among reinforcements; and, with the Rorschach, differences have been obtained by the display of X-ray pictures on the walls, pickled organs prominently displayed in jars around the testing room, and so on.

Implicit cues also must be considered. The subject's illness, use of alcohol, or even an overheated room are likely to affect test responses. Such implicit cues may not be considered part of the situation in other kinds of analyses, but in this analysis they are situational variables. Finally, some nonobvious cues that the examiner may not be aware of affect test responses.

Contrary to the belief of many Rorschach experts, but following from our E' and GE formula, if the Rorschach represents a relatively novel test situation, it is more likely rather than less likely to be affected by a large variety of otherwise relatively unimportant cues. In other words, a number of generalized expectancies are brought into play that have a more powerful effect in this situation than in a relatively familiar one.

When one considers that interactions among the great variety of cues we have already mentioned can be demonstrated, the problem of even *describing* the relevant cues in a given testing situation becomes formidable and a general classification of all situations seems impossible. No overall list of situations parallel to a list of traits such as Cattell's (1957) or of needs such as Murray's (1938) are going to represent adequately the great variety of cues and interactions necessary to deal with all kinds of psychological problems.

The solution in social-learning theory is to attempt the analysis of some significant situational variables for a specific problem or problem area. But how is one to select significant situational dimensions without a great deal of trial and error? The answer lies in having some theory about the behavior being studied. An excellent example is Jessor and Jessor's (1977) successful analysis of situational variables in the study of adolescent problem behavior. Nevertheless, their situational variables, although useful and predictive for such problem behavior as drinking and drug usage, might have little overlap with and relevance to a study of the significant situational variables in investigating the nature of therapeutic milieus in mental hospitals.

In general, in social-learning theory we look for those cues that are likely to affect seriously expectancies and/or the reinforcement values of the behavior-reinforcement sequences in which we are interested. As one requires stronger or more accurate predictions, one must look for both additional variables and more specific ones.

A parenthetic note might be added here. In the study of person–situation interactions, the relevant variables in the situation that require initial investigation are generally dictated by theory. The same is true when one is interested primarily in situational variables, as are many social psychologists, but who also elect to study personal variables primarily to determine whether or not there are significant interactions. These investigators may include personality variables in order to discover whether they need to limit the generalizations that they might make from observing situational differences. For example, one might study attributions of luck versus skill following success or failure in an achievement situation. Clearly, the selection of the personality variables needs to be dictated by some kind of theory; otherwise one can select personality variables and tests that are essentially irrelevant to the behavior being studied. An omnibus test, such as the MMPI, may show no significant relationships to the attribution data. However, if one's theory leads one to predict that attributions for failure are likely to be defensive in nature, at least for many subjects, this would suggest the need for a specific test of the kinds of defenses likely to be used by the person (e.g., a scale of defensive externality and/or a test of the tendency to repress and/or a scale that measures the tendency to seek sympathy).

3. How Much Variance in a Person–Situation Interaction is Due to Personality Variables and How Much Variance is Due to Situational Variables?   From the point of view of social-learning theory, this question has to be regarded as a pseudoproblem. Although in the recent past many investigators have been interested in this issue, most now recognize that the question is essentially meaningless, because both the personality variables and the situational variables depend on the person's previous experience. If we seek the answer to some specific practical problem, the question may have some significance. For example, we may wish to know how much effect may be expected in measuring intelligence or school achievement when the examiner is black or white and the subjects are all black.

If one does ask the general question, there are at least seven aspects of the experimental design that will affect the answer.

The first of these is the homogeneity of subjects. If we are studying adjustment under conditions of mild and/or no stress, then an unselected group of college freshmen is a much more homogeneous sample than a group of subjects who range from hospitalized psychotic patients through the professional personnel who work at the institution. In the latter case, it is obvious that more variance will be attributable to people than to situations.

The second aspect is the question of what is being measured, or the criterion behavior being studied; that is, if we want to see how Moslem and Protestant Americans respond to success and failure situations, a measure of attributions to fate will probably show stronger between-group (personal) differences than will a measure of perseverance.

The third experimental consideration that affects the relative importance of situational and individual differences is the degree of situational homogeneity. If we are examining the effects of success and failure on behavior and design our experiment to include passing or failing on a test of arithmetic reasoning given to high school subjects for "research purposes," with confidentiality of test scores assured, the situational variable will not account for as much variance as when we are studying the effects on behavior of passing or failing an examination in which failure would lead to the exclusion of any further educational goals.

The fourth variable affecting the relative variance attributed to behavior by situational and personality variables is the nature of the culture or subculture. This may be regarded as a special case of the first variable, namely, homogeneity of subjects. For example, consider a study of attitudes toward big-time athletics in college in which individual differences were predicted from a measure of need for achievement. The study is done in two colleges, one in which the football team has just won a national championship and the other in which they have just lost the national championship. With these situational and personality measures we might expect the degree of variance contributed by the individual difference variable to be much higher for females than it is for males or for seniors than it is for freshmen. In relation to specific situations and when studying particular behaviors, one subculture may be much more homogeneous than another.

We already have noted that many studies usually done by social psychologists with a secondary interest in individual differences often show little or no contribution of these individual differences to the prediction of criterion behavior. The variable implicit here is the relevance of the individual difference measure to the criterion behavior. In many studies of person–situation interactions the individual-difference measures employed by the investigator often are invalid or irrelevant. In part, this is the result of the lack of good measures developed for specific purposes. The development of such measures requires years of careful work and modern test-construction theory and technology. It is relatively easy to construct two situations that differ clearly and markedly in the degree of threat they present or in the kinds of reinforcements that it is possible to obtain. It is not nearly so easy to find a good measure of individual differences relevant to the criterion behavior being studied. And it is both difficult and time-consuming to construct such a measure and to validate it carefully. Literally hundreds of studies have "thrown in" a scale for measuring attitudes toward internal versus external control of reinforcement, as an afterthought in a study whose main focus is situational differences. But I believe that in a significant proportion of such studies it can be reliably established that the measure was, in fact, irrelevant to the behavior being studied.

The sixth variable, similar to the one just discussed, is the relevance of the situational variable that is being manipulated to the criterion behavior. If we are studying the interaction of academic aptitude and the sex of the examiner during the giving of final examinations in a math course, then it is common sense that the situational variable—sex of the examiner—will have little or no effect on the criterion behavior—grade on the examination. It is not a relevant dimension for the criterion of examination grade in a math course, although it would be a relevant dimension if the test were a Rorschach test being given to college students for research purposes.

Finally, the seventh dimension is the degree of familiarity or novelty of the situations used in the experiment. For example, Schwarz (1969) has shown that several measures of a generalized expectancy for success on a relatively novel motor-skill task correlated significantly with the first trial on the task. The correlation was lowered eventually to zero with increasing massed trials. In social-learning theory this follows from our formula that an expectancy is a function of a specific expectancy learned in that situation and related generalized expectancies. The generalized expectancies have less influence on the situation as the number of trials increases.

It is clear from the previous analysis that one can easily design an experiment to maximize variance accounted for either by personality measures or by situational differences in some specific person–situation interaction.

4. How Can Situational Similarity Be Measured?   If it is true that it is never the same river, then it is equally true that it is never the same situation. The passage of time and intervening experience alone makes some difference in the perceived situation. And what has happened in a situation once before makes it a different situation when it occurs again. Even if we deal only with the objective identification or description of a situation, it is impossible to duplicate exactly in every detail a complex life situation. But there are degrees of similarity or degrees of sameness. On the basis of such degrees of sameness, we can make better-than-chance predictions. If we are going to use the psychological situation as a predictive variable at all, then we must have some way of identifying relatively similar situations. Even if we eschew some grand classification and limit ourselves to some of the important situational variables for a given problem area, we still need to be able to measure or discover situational similarity.

If situational variables in social-learning theory are objectively identified by the commonsense language of the culture rather than by physical descriptions, what then are the bases for determining that two situations are at least in some degree similar?

Some six slightly overlapping methods of identifying situation similarity seem feasible. One such method is by expert judgement. This is the method that is normally used, although it is sometimes done carelessly and is not necessarily always labeled as such. If we read an experiment in which the author contrasts success and failure situations in a skill task and discovers some differences in behavior of subjects, we simply extend these results to predictions in other situations in which success or failure occurs and that we deem as similar. If it is necessary to ask whether these are equivalent situations, we discuss it informally among our colleagues. However, such procedures can be formalized, and descriptions of complex situations can be rated along dimensions of similarity by people who understand the culture, keeping in mind some general problem to be investigated or criterion behavior to be studied.

We may do the same thing by having the potential subjects, individuals who are members of the culture or subculture being studied, compare a set of situations in terms of similarity, using ratings, paired comparisons, or other methods.

A third method involves the analysis of the frequency of specific kinds of behaviors in specific situations. This involves a post hoc kind of analysis; but once degrees of similarity are empirically demonstrated, they then can be used predictively, at least for the same culture.

Similarly, we can measure *expectancies* for certain kinds of reinforcements to occur or for the efficacy of behavior–reinforcement sequences in various situations and base our similarity dimension on similarity of the expectancies. So, for example, a subject may expect to be socially rejected by others in some situations and accepted by others in other situations for the same behavior such as boasting in front of parents or peers. Such grouping based upon the similarity of expectancies for a particular reinforcement constitutes one kind of situational similarity.

Another method for determining situational similarity is by determining the predominant reinforcement likely to occur in the situation. Both the nature of the reinforcement (such as academic achievement, dependency, affection, or dominance) and the sign of the reinforcement, whether negative or positive (in social-learning theory what some others refer to as punishment is referred to as negative reinforcement) or both may be important. The dominant reinforcements can be established by subjects' judgments, by experts' judgments, and, in laboratory situations, by the use of instructions.

Finally, although it is cumbersome, we may study the gradients of generalization of changes that take place in behavior, expectancies, or reinforcement values. For example, we could measure an individual's expectancy for success in a variety of tasks. Following this, the expectancy for one of these tasks is lowered by giving a failure experience. We could then measure *changes* in expectancy for success in the other tasks as a function of the person's failure in the first one. The gradient of generalization would be the gradient of similarity.

SUMMARY

In summary this chapter presents four general propositions regarding the use of the psychological situation in the prediction of behavior:

1. It is possible to utilize a concept of meaningful, subjective, or perceived situation that can be considered as an independent, or partially independent, set of variables. Such variables interact with another set that may be called personality variables, although both may be regarded as aspects of the person.

2. Situational variables, although subjective, are not independent of the stimulation arising from external stimuli. Such external stimuli can be *identified* reliably by using the commonsense language of the culture. These objective descriptions are necessary in order to use situational variables predictively. In this way, individual differences in reactions to the same situation and group differences in reaction to different situations can be predicted.

3. There are practical limitations both to the prediction of individual differences in behavior in the same situation and to group differences in behavior in different situations, because both are based upon the generalization of a large number of related previous experiences. Inasmuch as all situations involve a variety of interacting cues, it is practically impossible to identify all the relevant cues and all the relevant previous experiences.

4. Because situational variables and personality variables are themselves complex and involve *within* and *between* interactions, useful grand classifications of all psychological situations do not seem feasible. However, it is possible to identify some of the relevant situational variables for specific problems and to discover or measure perceived situational similarity.

5. When selecting both personality and situational variables, prediction of behavior can be improved in studies of interaction when the variables selected are relevant to the criterion behavior. Such relevance is ideally determined by the use of sound psychological theory or at least, in the absence of good theory, by good common sense.

12
Knowing More Than We Can Say Leads to Saying More Than We Can Know: On Being Implicitly Informed

Kenneth S. Bowers
University of Waterloo, Canada

Traditionally, there have been two schools of thought about how to conceptualize the situation. One school has emphasized the physical, measurable properties of the environment, whereas the other has stressed the importance of the situation as perceived (Pervin, 1978b). The latter conceptualization is psychologically closer to behavioral outcomes (Jessor, Chapter 19, this volume), but there are nevertheless problems with this view.

The first difficulty is that identifying the situation with a person's perception of it brings us perilously close to a solipsistic position that threatens the very notion of an objective science of psychology. One way of dealing with this problem is represented by the Blocks' (Block & Block, Chapter 6, this volume) conceptualization of the "canonical situation," which consists of the "consensually defined, consensually constructed, or consensually accepted context [p. 87]." This is an important and entirely legitimate escape from potentially idiosyncratic perceptions of the world but does not safeguard against the remoter possibility that the consensus is simply wrong. Partly, this chapter is an attempt to supplement the notion of a canonical situation in a way that recognizes the individual's ability to be informed by aspects of the situation and of the world that are not yet consensually grasped.

Another problem or ambiguity inherent in the notion of the perceived situation is this: To what extent is the perceived situation one that is consciously represented? A major portion of this chapter is devoted to an examination of this question, because it has profound implications for the study of personality. To put the issue in historical perspective, consider the fact that even the most unreconstructed behaviorists would readily agree that the situation has to be perceived in order for it to reinforce and shape behavior. But they would stead-

179

fastly reject the claim that such perceptions have to be consciously represented in order to be effective movers and shapers of behavior. In other words, for an arch behaviorist, consciousness of the situation is not implied by the perception of it. Rather, consciousness of the situation is considered to be only one possible effect of perceiving it and is in no way necessary for the environmental control over behavior.

Recent formulations of personality have historical roots in behavioristic psychology but have nevertheless foresworn the mindless for the mindful and have emphasized the importance of cognition and higher processes as crucial antecedents of behavior (Mischel, 1973). Moreover, there is a strong implication that consciousness of the situation is part and parcel of what is meant by the perception of it. In fact, neobehaviorist or cognitively oriented psychologists interested in personality are rather averse to the possibility that unconsciously processed information is of any importance in the determination of human thought and behavior (Mahoney, 1980). So when these psychologists talk of perceptions, stimulus meanings, appraisals, plans, and so on, it is typically assumed that people are conscious of these determinants, at least in principal.

There is, of course, a clear methodological advantage to the assumption that the important antecedents of behavior are consciously represented. For it is but a small step to the conclusion that people can access the determinants of their thought and behavior by introspection, and they can communicate the results to an interested psychologist. And, in turn, this possibility implies that questionnaires, rating scales, and similar self-report devices are sensible and rational approaches to the understanding of people's behavior.

However, the assumption that the determinants of action are as accessible to introspection as they are influential has recently come under attack in a deliciously provocative article by Nisbett and Wilson (1977). These authors argue that cognition supplements and reconstructs the antecedents of action in a manner that may or may not be veridical. In a series of clever studies, they demonstrated that people are often quite mistaken about the actual determinants of their behavior, and in a manner that makes it difficult for the mistake to be identified. According to Nisbett and Wilson, people account for their behavior in terms that seem sufficient to the action, either because the alleged antecedents are readily available (e.g., salient) factors in the environment and/or because they seem representative of factors that ordinarily explain such behavior (Tversky & Kahneman, 1973). In other words, people often invoke the most plausible explanation for their behavior, even under experimentally controlled circumstances where the most plausible account is demonstrably false.

The empirical basis for the Nisbett and Wilson (1977) position has been criticized on technical grounds (Smith & Miller, 1978), but the basic thesis is a controversial one because it constitutes an attack on the presumed bastion of self-knowledge, viz., introspection. The authors assert that people have no (or at most very limited) privileged access to the determinants of their own action and that knowledge claims about oneself are *inferences* based largely, if not entirely, on overt behavior that is as available to an observer as it is to the perpetrator of the action. Further, Nisbett and Wilson argue that the subjective sense of certainty often conveyed by introspection (regarding the reasons for one's own behavior) is often thoroughly misleading. Indeed, Nisbett and Wilson (1977) imply that introspection is the dupe of the availability and representative heuristics, so that even when people are accurate in accounting for their behavior, they are only "incidentally correct [p. 233]." In other words, such accuracy as there is in self-understanding derives from an accidental correspondence of available and/or representative reasons offered by the actor for his behavior, and the real reasons for it (as discoverable by experimental inquiry).

The essence of the Nisbett and Wilson argument thus seems to be that people cannot identify the determinants of behavior that are "invisible" to introspection, and they cannot distinguish between salient and/or representative factors that do determine behavior from salient and/or representative factors that do not. Consequently, introspection seems to them seriously deficient as a basis for identifying the actual determinants of action.

If the Nisbett and Wilson (1977) analysis is correct, it would seem that the possibilities for growth in self-knowledge are more or less limited to the increasing possibility of being accidentally correct in accounting for one's behavior. Instead of becoming more genuinely sophisticated about ourselves, it appears that we may only become more adroit sophists. It is the apparent cynicism implicit in this view of self-knowledge that I believe is one of the chief reasons for its controversial status. Thus, an important goal of this chapter involves examining in what sense sophistication about oneself and others may be possible in light of the Nisbett and Wilson critique.

There is a related but more immediate concern, however, for psychologists who stress the importance of the perceived situation as the proximal determinant of thought and action. For the Nisbett and Wilson (1977) article raises with renewed insistence the ambiguity presented at the outset of this chapter, viz.: To what extent is the perceived environment consciously represented and accessible to the perceiver? Insofar as consciousness of the situation is not entailed by the perception of it, people would not necessarily have introspective access to the antecedents of their actions, and much of their behavior could therefore be caused by determinants outside of awareness. In turn, such a state of affairs would potentially have devastating implications for research in the area of personality. For example, the use of subject inquiry and questionnaire devices would be highly suspect as a way of obtaining veridical information about why people behave the way they do.

To summarize, Nisbett and Wilson's "neocognitive" position asserts that people say more than they can know about their behavior. I first examine this assertion more carefully and then attempt to show how it articulates with an older claim that people often know more than they can say about themselves and the world. The integration of these two propositions will help us understand the strengths and limitations of the Nisbett and Wilson (1977) analysis insofar as it pertains to self-knowledge and introspective accounts of one's behavior. Finally, I examine the relevance of these considerations for an understanding of the "perceived situation" as an important determinant of behavior.

PROBLEMS IN SELF-KNOWLEDGE

There are surely a variety of factors that influence behavior that do not necessarily influence the experience or explanation of it. This is the problem of subtle control (Bowers, 1975; Kelley, 1967), whereby people simply find it difficult to identify the truly controlling features of a circumstance that are operative in a particular situation. Similarly, there are factors that influence the conscious experience and explanation of the behavior under consideration but that do not necessarily influence the behavior itself. These latter influences are largely due to distortions in memory introduced by interrogation format (Barber, Dalal, & Calverley, 1968), self-serving biases in memory (Ross & Sicoly, 1979), self-deception (Sackheim & Gur, 1979), motivated suppression and repression (Erdelyi & Goldberg, 1979), the often misleading cognitive heuristics of availability and representativeness (Tversky & Kahneman, 1973), and so on.

The previous factors can often make it difficult to access the actual determinants of behavior, but they do not render it impossible in principle to do so, for when the actual determinants are reasonably conspicuous and there are no biasing factors operating on memory, we can legitimately claim introspective access to the true determinants of action. Nisbett and Wilson's evident denial of this possibility is a mistake (Adair & Spinner, 1979; Ericsson & Simon, 1978). Their error is in failing to distinguish between the possibility of having introspective access to the actual determinants of a given action, and the impossibility of having introspective access to the causal connection between these determining antecedents and their behavioral outcomes. In order to clarify this distinction, consider the following passage written by David Hume in 1748:

> When we look about us towards external objects, and consider the operation of causes, we are never able, in a single instance, to discover any power or necessary connexion; any quality, which binds the effect to the cause, and renders the one an infallible consequence of the other. We only find, that the one does actually, in fact, follow the other. The impulse of one billiard-ball is attended with motion in the second. This is the whole that appears to *outward* senses . . . There is not, in any single, particular instance of cause and effect, anything which can suggest the idea of power or necessary connexion [cited in Rand, 1936; pp. 328—329].

This argument (which, ironically, is introspectively achieved) has passed the test of time—with honors. Causal necessity is simply not available to observation; nor does introspection reveal the causal link between a particular action and its determinants any more than the single observation of one billiard ball colliding with another reveals the causal connection between them.[1] Moreover, the subjective sense of certainty that antecedent X caused behavioral outcome Y does not constitute evidence for the causality of the connection between X and Y; being certain is simply not the same thing as being right, as any impartial witness to fanaticism can hardly fail to appreciate.

It would seem, therefore, that knowledge in general and self-knowledge in particular does not derive from direct and unmediated discernment of causal necessity. Rather, such knowledge is an extension of how events are conceptualized, either implicitly or explicitly. Yet theory and conceptualization do not just connect observed events (Bowers, 1973); to a very considerable extent, it creates the events to be explained. Thus, home runs, royal flushes, epileptic seizures, homosexual panic reactions, moon shots, and black holes are events, observations, or phenomena that reflect our understanding; indeed, to varying extents, they exist and can be observed for what they are because of our understanding of them (Kaplan, 1964; Kuhn, 1962). In effect, we are informed not only by nature but by our understanding of it; what we observe is shaped by our understanding of what we see (Bowers, 1977).

One implication of this inescapable state of affairs is that inadequate understanding often leads to inadequate observation (and introspection). One must already have a reasonably accurate understanding of a phenomena before observations of it are apt to extend our comprehension further. Someone who believes the earth is flat is unlikely to venture forth in search of its edges—lest s/he fall off. And so the question emerges: Whence come the more adequate, "well-rounded" understandings that permit ever more venturesome and probing explorations and observations of nature, and of oneself?

IMPLICIT RESPONSIVENESS AND INTUITION

Clearly, an emerging understanding of the earth as round is not simply deduced from the articulated, explicit evidence that it is flat, any more than Einstein's universe is logically implied by Newton's. Rather, the emergence of new understandings springs from roots that are not easy to articulate at the outset. Vague dissatisfactions with old understandings, worrisome, anomalous observations that don't fit the conventional view, a host of relevant life experiences, and

---

[1] I would like to acknowledge briefly that it is by no means necessary to adopt a causal account of purposeful human action. Indeed, many philosophers (Peters, 1958) have argued that it is inappropriate to depict such action in causal terms and instead submit that *reasons for action* are different from and not reducible to *causes for behavior*. Although the reason–cause distinction has relevance for the present analysis, I have chosen to ignore it simply because it unduly complicates my present task.

familiarity with the phenomena under investigation—all subtly guide and influence one's thinking (Pantin, 1969).

Indeed, Polanyi (1964) has argued quite effectively that our growing comprehension of nature emerges out of a background of "tacit", unarticulated knowledge; that is, people know a great deal more than they can say, and they sometimes conduct their personal and professional lives in accordance with information that is not consciously represented, but which is nevertheless registered and trusted as an important clue to reality. Because of their unarticulated origins, productive insights, actions, and decisions guided by tacit considerations are often regarded as intuitive, or, less exotically, as the outcome of good judgment. The exercise of good judgment or intuition is appreciated and rewarded at least in part because the weight of presently "articulated" evidence does not tip the balance clearly in favor of one or the other alternative courses of action and so would not "compel" the same decision by anyone or everyone familiar with the issues. In effect, decisions often go beyond the information articulated and so depend a great deal on the abilities of the decision maker to be sensitive and responsive to information that is tacit and not clearly represented in consciousness, at least at the outset.

Notice that, under circumstances where a choice has to be made despite insufficient or contradictory evidence of an explicit sort, the postdecision reasons offered for the choice do not necessarily make it a good one, for they are very often the same reasons that were articulated prior to the decision but seen at that time as somehow insufficient for it. The postdecision rationalizations do serve to make the course chosen sensible and understandable to oneself and others. However, a person who consistently makes (what turn out to be) wrong decisions for sensible sounding reasons would soon be looking for other work—except of course if s/he were a politician.

Good judgment or intuitiveness in a vast array of human endeavors is thus often times less a matter of reasons proffered than of sensitivity to information presaging a desired outcome. Though this information is not necessarily implicit and unarticulated, I wish to maintain that often times it is. The intuitive scientist who seems to have a "private pipeline" to nature, the experienced diagnostician who can sense the presence of neurological damage before s/he has clear evidence of it, the banker who has a better than average track record in sizing up the risks and benefits of lending large sums of money, the baseball scout who frequently sees potential in baseball players overlooked by his less perspicacious colleagues, the clinician who senses a real suicide threat before it is articulated by the patient, and the generally abrasive husband who (for once) thinks twice before making a sarcastic remark to his wife may all, to some degree, be responding to features of their environment that they might have difficulty specifying precisely.

Notice that the previous comments in some measure ratify the Nisbett and Wilson (1977) position. However, there is a clear difference in emphasis between their position and the one here being proposed. Whereas Nisbett and Wilson emphasize the *inability* of people to discern the causes of their behavior, I have emphasized the *ability* of people to respond productively and empathically to information that is not fully specified or represented in consciousness. I do not wish to argue that their emphasis is incorrect. Quite the contrary, if they were entirely wrong in their arguments, I could not possibly be correct in mine. For the possibility of being intuitively responsive to information that one cannot specify precisely presupposes that people do in fact often behave in particular ways for reasons that are not readily accessible. Consequently, insofar as Nisbett and Wilson have presented empirical evidence for a theory of action that does not necessarily "know" its antecedents, they have also provided data that is consistent with a theory of tacit knowledge, implicit responsiveness, and intuition.

It must be immediately acknowledged, however, that with one or two exceptions, the kind of evidence that Nisbett and Wilson forward in support of their ideas is only consistent with a theory of implicit responsiveness, intuition, and tacit knowledge but does not constitute strong evidence for it. This is true because such a theory is more interested in showing how a person's thought and action can be implicitly *informed* by the context in which it occurs, whereas Nisbett and Wilson are more interested in demonstrating how people's explanations of their own behavior are often *mis*informed and misled by a host of contextual features. Although the data base for these two kinds of claims is related, it is not exactly the same, as we soon see.

NISBETT AND WILSON REVISITED

Consider, first of all, the implications of the following rather extended quotation taken from Nisbett and Wilson's (1977) article:

> The reader is entitled to know that the stimulus situations were chosen in large part because we felt that subjects would be wrong about the effects of the stimuli on their responses. We deliberately attempted to study situations where we felt that a particular stimulus would exert an influence on subjects' responses but that subjects would be unable to detect it, and situations where we felt a particular stimulus would be ineffective but subjects would believe it to have been influential. It is even more important to note, however, that we were highly unsuccessful in this attempted bias. In general, we were no more accurate in our predictions about stimulus effects than the subjects proved to be in their reports about stimulus effects. Most of the stimuli that we expected to influence subjects' responses turned out to have no effect, and many of the stimuli that we expected to have no effect turned out to be influential [p. 242].

What is interesting about this quotation is that being poor predictors of their subjects' behavior was of so little hindrance to the theoretical argument the authors wished to make. For the fact is they were much less interested in predicting how their subjects would behave than in showing how their subjects would mistakenly account for action even if no one was able to predict it. On the other hand, a ''tamed'' theory of implicit responsiveness (i.e., one having experimental support) would be much more interested in showing how subjects were, in fact, predictably but implicitly responsive to experimentally manipulated factors in the immediate environment.

In their own research, Nisbett and Wilson do not worry much about the predictability of their subjects' implicitly informed behavior. However, they do cite research by others for whom this was an important concern. Preeminent among these is the work they cite by Norman Maier (1931) on the string–pendulum problem. In this experiment, subjects are required to join two strings that are hanging from the ceiling too far apart from each other for a subject to grab both of them at the same time. Yet the problem posed for the subject is to tie the two strings together. One of the several possible solutions to this problem was very difficult for the subjects to achieve spontaneously (i.e., without an implicit ''clue'' provided by the experimenter). This clue consisted of the experimenter's casually bumping into the string and setting it into motion. Within a fairly short period of time, many subjects exposed to this clue were able to achieve the correct solution to the problem by tying a weight to one of the strings and swinging it toward the other string. This enabled the subject to run to the stationary string, hold on to it, and simply await the arrival of the swinging string.

Nisbett and Wilson's approach to the Maier string problem emphasizes that subjects in the experiment often could not identify (and in fact often misidentified) the crucial antecedent of their insight; that is, few of the subjects recognized consciously the importance of the casually bumped string to their own eventual solution of the problem. What seems curiously underplayed in their account of this classic experiment is the fact that subjects were tacitly but productively informed by a contextual feature that was not explicitly represented in consciousness. But surely the fact that the solution was tacitly achieved is at least as interesting, psychologically, as the fact that people could not accurately identify the antecedents of their solution to this problem.

IMPLICIT RESPONSIVENESS: A REVIEW OF SOME EVIDENCE

Many psychologists are suspicious of unconscious factors at work on human behavior (Mahoney, 1980). Because the ability to have thought and action informed by factors that are not consciously represented is obviously a form of unconscious influence, the next section of this chapter briefly reviews evidence pertinent to this claim, most of which goes considerably beyond the experiments cited by Nisbett and Wilson in demonstrating the possibilities for being implicitly but effectively informed, without being conscious of the information (or even, sometimes, of its effect).

One further caveat is required before proceeding. Although I have up to now stressed the advantages of being able to respond to information that is not consciously represented (referring to this possibility as intuition or good judgment), this is clearly a truncated view of the matter. There is always a nether side to humanity's best possibilities. So if it is possible to be implicitly informed in a positive, productive manner, then it must also be possible to be similarly "informed" by factors that are irrelevant and/or potentially destructive and debilitating—unless, of course, one wants to posit a kind of supersensitive censor that filters out implicit information having a potentially bad impact while permitting the passage of implicit information engendering only positive and desirable outcomes. Such a censor does not seem to me to be a necessary part of a theory proposing implicit responsiveness. So although such responsiveness may be the basis for some of mankind's highest creativity and achievement, some of the examples to be discussed reveal the potential for pathology that resides in implicit responsiveness. In fact, let us begin with such an example.

Responsiveness by Unconscious People.   Levinson (1967) reported on a patient who had undergone surgery, only to emerge from general anesthesia with a rather prolonged, weepy, and totally inexplicable depression. Only after some rather extraordinary measures involving hypnosis were taken was the patient able to recover the surgeon's comment (uttered in the midst of surgery) that a small lump in the patient's mouth might in fact be malignant. It was this previously unremembered comment that had resulted in the patient's dysphoria. A subsequent experiment involving 10 surgical patients confirmed that eight of them were similarly responsive to standardized but emotionally laden information administered while they were under (pentathol-induced, EEG-confirmed) general anesthesia. Yet another study (Pearson, 1961) demonstrated that positive and hopeful suggestions delivered by earphones to anesthetized, surgical patients led to their speedier release from the hospital than was true for control subjects, who had received only music. Subjects in this experiment were run under double blind conditions, such that neither the surgeon nor the releasing physician were privy to the patient's status as an experimental or control subject.

Although the evidence regarding responsiveness to meaningful information under general anesthesia has not gone uncriticized (Trustman, Dubovsky, & Titley, 1977), there seem to be growing reasons to believe that being unconscious does not automatically render one insensible to informational input. For example, in a long and careful review of sleep-assisted instruction, Aarons (1976) cautiously submits that learning while asleep does occur, especially in subjects who are highly motivated to learn and who are set during waking periods to receive information while sleeping.

Perhaps the most convincing evidence of responsiveness to information received by "unconscious" (i.e., sleeping persons) is a series of studies conducted by Fred Evans and his colleagues (1972). These investigators were able to demonstrate repeatedly that people were responsive to suggestions delivered during alpha-free, stage I sleep. To illustrate, a sleeping subject would be told that whenever the cue word *itch* was presented, s/he would reach up and scratch his/her nose. About 20% of the time, sleeping subjects acted in accordance with the suggestions. Such suggestibility was not limited to the same alpha-free, stage I sleep in which the suggestion was originally given. People also responded to the cue word during later episodes of stage I sleep on the same and subsequent nights. Moreover, such sleep suggestibility was correlated with hypnotic ability, implying the importance of individual differences in the extent to which people are responsive to information that is not consciously represented.

Space does not permit a more extensive review of evidence regarding the responsiveness of "unconscious" people to external information (Aarons, 1976; Bowers, 1976, Chapter 8; Evans, 1972), but it is clearly the case that if sleeping or anesthetized persons are demonstrably responsive to information, consciousness of the information (in any ordinary sense) is not necessary to the effect. Consequently, research in this relatively exotic domain establishes the principle that people can be informed by and responsive to meaningful material that is not represented in consciousness.

Responsiveness to Unattended Information.   Support for implicit responsiveness is not confined to sleeping persons. Indeed, a number of contemporary investigations in cognitive psychology are concerned directly or indirectly with the problem of whether and to what extent peripheral or unattended features, which are not themselves consciously represented, nevertheless influence a person's behavior and perception. For example, MacKay (1973) presented ambiguous sentences to one ear and disambiguating words to the other ear of people participating in a dichotic listening task. Thus, the sentence, "They threw stones toward the bank yesterday," was disambiguated by presenting the word *river* or *money* on an unattended channel at the same instant that the word *bank* was presented on the attended channel. Such unattended words, though not consciously heard, disambiguated the subjects' interpretation of the sentences in the predicted direction. A somewhat similar finding is reported by Lackner and Garrett (1972).

A particularly good example of the practical implications of implicit responsiveness has been demonstrated by Willows and MacKinnon (1973). These investigators used a reading task in which every other line of the material to be read was irrelevant; the subject selectively attended only to the relevant lines of the story and skipped over and ignored the irrelevant lines. Contained in the irrelevant lines, however, was information semantically related to the attended passage. After completing the passage, subjects were to choose which answer (of the several provided) constituted the correct response to a question about the passage they had just read. Information from the unattended lines constituted one of the available options. Compared to an appropriate control condition, subjects in the experimental condition made more "intrusion" errors (i.e., their answers more often reflected information that had appeared in the irrelevant lines of the passage they had just read). This erroneous use of unattended material occurred despite the fact that subjects had virtually no conscious recall for any of the material appearing in the irrelevant lines.

In a clever and well-controlled extension of the previous investigation, Willows (1974) ran good and poor readers to see the effect of unattended information on their reading speed and comprehension. Not surprisingly, good readers read faster than poor readers. What was surprising is that good readers showed *more* (not fewer) intrusion errors than the poor readers; that is, on tests of comprehension, semantically related information contained in the unattended lines was appropriated as an answer more often by the good than by the poor readers. However, poor readers made more "irrelevant" errors than the good readers, which is to say that the poor readers made more errors of comprehension that did *not* reflect information appearing on the unattended lines. So although it is true that good readers made more intrusion errors, this was not due to a generally higher error rate. Evidently, good reading is at least in part aided by implicit information that is not focally attended or consciously recalled but that nevertheless contributes to one's understanding of the material being read.

It is perhaps worth pointing out that most of the investigations concerning the impact of unattended information imply the importance of memory in determining whether an environmental event has an implicit impact on perception and behavior; that is, many of the experimental studies on unattended information do not permit us to conclude that people literally never consciously perceived such information in the first place. With a few possible exceptions (Lewis, 1970), the most these studies permit us to say is that people do not *recall* the unattended information. In other words, what people recall determines to some considerable extent what they are conscious of. If an activating event cannot be recalled (even if it occurred just moments earlier) (Glucksberg & Cowan, 1970; Norman, 1969), then it has had what can legitimately be termed an *unconscious impact* on perception, behavior, or affect. This is not the place to dwell on the subtleties of memory for a theory of unconsciousness (Erdelyi & Goldberg, 1979). But perhaps it is relevant to point out that such "immediate forgetting" of supraliminal but unattended (peripheral, contextual, etc.) information makes it unnecessary to presuppose the existence of subliminal perception (Dixon, 1971) for a viable conceptualization of implicit responsiveness, (i.e., responsiveness to information that is not consciously represented).

Whereas most of the studies cited previously involve highly controlled circumstances in order to demonstrate the impact of information that is not consciously represented, there is at least one investigation that reveals the same state of affairs in a more complex, interpersonal setting. In a study on the detection of deception reported by Krauss, Geller, & Olson (1976), subjects' judgments about whether they were being deceived were essentially uncorrelated with the attributes they thought revealed attempted deception. And features that did in fact discriminate deceptive and nondeceptive communications were not typically identified by people who were successful in detecting deception at above-chance levels. To quote the authors directly: Subjects "both fail to use the cues they are likely to name and fail to name the cues they appear actually to use."

I hope that this brief review of evidence is sufficient to persuade the reader that people can indeed be sensitive and responsive to information that is not well represented in consciousness and that is therefore not accessible to introspection in an articulate, communicable form. And in the last study by Krauss et al. (1976), we have in addition further evidence of a sort initially presented by Nisbett and Wilson, to the effect that people will often misidentify the antecedents of their decisions and actions in a manner that leads to an erroneous accounting of their behavior. I would like to supplement this possibility for misexplanation and misunderstanding with one final and especially illuminating example of it from my own research.

In an experiment on the conditioning of picture preferences (Bowers, 1975), one young lady demonstrated a substantial increase in the selection of landscapes—the reinforced category of response. After the conditioning trials were completed, I inquired about her perceptions of the experiment, and the conversation went something like this. E: Did you pick landscapes or portraits more often? S: Landscapes. E: Did you notice that I said "good" only when you picked landscapes? S: Sure. E: Do you think your tendency to pick landscapes was influenced by my reinforcement of them? S: Of course not! I picked the landscapes because I liked them better than the portraits. Besides, you only said "good" after I made my choice, so it couldn't possibly have influenced my selection of pictures.

Such a charming mistake would not be possible if the determining character of particular antecedents were necessarily and automatically as self-evident to introspection as it is influential. Incidentally, the possibility for such mistakes is another kind of evidence that unconsciously determined behavior is conceptually nonproblematic. For whenever the determinants of action are not identified or accepted by the person as the cause of his/her behavior, they have, in effect, unconsciously influenced it.

SOPHISTICATION OR SOPHISTRY

Where do the previous considerations lead us in our concern for the two issues introduced at the outset of this article, viz.: (1) What is the basis for sophistication about oneself and others? (2) To what extent is the perceived situation (as the most proximal determinant of behavior) represented in consciousness?

With respect to the first issue, we have seen that Nisbett and Wilson (1977) are simply in error insofar as they claim that people necessarily have no introspective access to the determinants of their behavior. What is true is that people do not necessarily have such access. The research reported by Nisbett and Wilson (1977) and in this chapter supports the latter conclusion, but it does not support the former, much stronger claim.

There remains, however, an important problem, the essence of which Nisbett and Wilson (1977) have seen quite clearly, viz.: The causal connection linking antecedents to their behavioral consequences is *never* directly available to introspection. This is true even when there is no difficulty in accessing both the action and its activating antecedents. To illustrate, a person may have access to the determinants of his/her action and yet not regard them as the cause of action. This was the problem exemplified by the woman who incorrectly dismissed reinforcement as influential in her choice of pictures and instead attributed her choices to preexisting preferences. On the other hand, even when the actual determinants of behavior are introspectively accessed and experienced as the subjectively compelling cause of behavior, such feelings of conviction and certainty are not in and of themselves evidence of causality. After all, believing something does not make it so, or else every fanatic would be correct in his/her beliefs.

In light of the foregoing comments, sophistication clearly involves something less than direct introspective access to the causal connections between action and its antecedents. On the other hand, it surely involves something more than sophistry implicit in the notion that people can only be accidentally or incidentally correct about the determinants of their behavior. Specifically, sophistication involves having a reasonably adequate theory or understanding about likely causes of one's behavior.[2] The theory need not be formal and explicit, or even correct in some ultimate sense. Rather, a sophisticate's understanding or "theory" about his/her behavior should be well informed by a host of relevant considerations derived from broad life experience and from education of both a formal and informal kind. Of course, there is no guarantee that such theory will always generate correct explanations for the phenomena or behavior under consideration; indeed the possibility for error is built into the very idea of a theory. On the other hand, when a person does provide a correct account of his behavior, it is unreasonable to assert that s/he has only been incidentally correct—unless one is willing to attribute the same somewhat dismissive qualifier to all instances of corroborated theory.

Sophistication also implies openness to novel information of both an explicit and implicit variety. Such receptiveness permits a deeper and more comprehensive understanding of oneself and of the world generally, thereby altering, at least potentially, the way one behaves in the future. Let me give but one small

---

[2] I would like to acknowledge that in a revised version of the original Nisbett and Wilson (1977) position, Nisbett and Ross (1980) have come to essentially the same conclusion.

illustration of what I mean. In the study of verbal conditioning cited earlier (Bowers, 1975), one group of subjects, who were ego involved in their picture preferences, resisted the influence of contingent reinforcement when they viewed it as an attempt to influence their choices. On the other hand, a comparable group of ego-involved subjects did not react against the reinforcement of their choices as an influence attempt.

What was it that rendered reinforcement ineffective for the first group of subjects? The people who did not resist the reinforcement had very little exposure to the facts of operant conditioning in their introductory psychology class, whereas those who did resist had been enrolled in a psychology course in which operant conditioning had been emphasized and withal, the role of reinforcement in behavior change. Thus, when people had been explicitly informed about the importance of reinforcement as a means of altering behavior, they were less subject to its influence. Evidently, being formally educated or otherwise informed about the potential determinants of thought and action permits critical appraisal of them. As a result, such potential influences can be accepted as warranted or resisted as unwarranted constraints on behavior.

Such considerations (see also Neisser, 1976, Chapter 9; Scheibe, 1978) make it reasonable, perhaps, to argue that the disciplined study of psychology is in part a "consciousness raising" enterprise that attempts to identify in an articulate, explicit way the various kinds of implicit influences on human behavior, perception, and thought that have no automatic access to consciousness and introspection. Moreover, the accumulation of such educational and broad life experiences permits the sophisticated person to detect potential influences operating on his own behavior and to assess critically the costs and benefits of acting in a particular way in the context of the constraints that are judged to be operative in the situation. In this way, becoming sophisticated about (previously implicit) influences on one's behavior can minimize or entirely disarm the "power" of such influences to control behavior, as evidently occurred for the people in my picture preference study who had been informed about the impact of reinforcement on behavior.

It is precisely because such explicit knowledge can undermine otherwise subtle influences on behavior that social psychologists in particular are so anxious to obtain naive subjects for their experiments rather than advanced students in psychology or otherwise well-informed people knowledgeable about the hypotheses and issues under investigation. It is in order to preserve naivete about such subtle implicit influences that deception, misdirection, and other camouflage techniques are often employed in such studies. In effect, the investigators of cognitive dissonance, attribution theory, self-perception theory, and so on, intuitively recognize and exploit the possibility for the implicit control of human behavior; but at the same time their use of deception, misdirection, and other related techniques constitutes defacto recognition that such implicit, unrecognized control is by no means necessary or inevitable and can, in fact, be undermined by the use of sophisticated subjects or by employing manipulations that are too salient and figural to remain unrecognized for what they are.

All in all, it should no longer be surprising that carefully nurtured naivete can lead people to respond to subtle aspects of the experimental situation without having conscious access to the determinants of their response and/or without appreciating the extent to which accessed antecedents are in fact determinative. It is not entirely fair or persuasive, however, to turn around and use the mistaken accounts of such naive persons to suggest that people are ordinarily unaware of why they behave the way they do, for it remains to be demonstrated that people are usually (or always) naive and unable to recognize the basis of their behavior before one can confidently assert that implicit responding is typical (or inevitable). Nisbett and Wilson (1977) certainly did not establish that this was the case. Rather, they demonstrated that the determinants of behavior are not necessarily represented in consciousness and relied on their very considerable powers of persuasion to bring themselves and their readers to the empirically unsupported conclusion that people are almost always unable to access introspectively the determinants of their behavior.

THE PERCEIVED SITUATION

The previous comments concerning sophistication segues readily into a brief consideration of our other main concern; that is, to what extent are perceived situations consciously represented? We must first acknowledge that the evidence and arguments reviewed to this point clearly document that not everything that is perceived and effective in generating behavior is represented in consciousness. To the extent that this is true, people will of course have difficulty in identifying the situational determinants of their action. Moreover, because people do not enjoy behaving in ways that they cannot explain, they will sometimes misidentify, as the basis for their behavior, aspects of the perceived situation that *are* consciously represented and, in some sense, perceived as sufficient to explain the behavior in question.

Having said this, however, it is also clear that a person whose sophistication more or less matches the complexity of the situation s/he is confronting has a reasonably good chance of identifying the actual determinants of his/her behavior. Nevertheless, no matter how sophisticated, well motivated, and candid the person may be, what is said by way of self-explanation is in effect a theoretical statement about the likely causes of behavior and has no special claim to the truth of the matter. Introspection simply cannot access the ''true'' causal connections between action and its determinants any more than observation can discern the causal connection between external events.

So, ultimately, the subjective reports of any experimental subject must be judged in terms of other available data. To the extent that a verbal account fits into and extends an emerging pattern of coherent evidence, it has every right to be taken seriously. If, on the other hand, there are reasonable grounds for doubting the veracity, competence, or sophistication of the person reporting or if what is stated seriously violates other known facts, one is entirely justified in being cautious about accepting the report at face value, though it may have evidential value of other kinds. Unless I am badly mistaken, this is pretty much the way in which sophisticated psychologists deal with verbal report data already, and I can do no more than endorse this practice.

CONCLUSION

In the absence of automatic access to the causal link connecting behavior with its antecedents, there can be no absolute guarantees about why one behaved in a particular way. However, critical reflection, combined with relevant life experience and formal or informal education, enhances the likelihood of coming to a reasonably accurate understanding of one's behavior. To ask for more is to ask for the impossible.

Moreover, the fact that conscious access to the determinants of behavior is not necessary and/or automatic makes it possible for thought and action to be implicitly informed by information that is not consciously represented. And, in turn, the possibility for such implicit responsiveness is an important source of intuition and good judgment. So Nisbett and Wilson's (1977) stimulating but radically skeptical portrayal of people as irrational and self-deceived is tempered and complemented by humanity's possibilities for creativity and intuitive common sense. All in all, it may not be a bad bargain.

ACKNOWLEDGEMENT

I would like to thank Patricia Bowers, Lynda Butler, and Donald Meichenbaum for their helpful comments on earlier drafts of this paper.

13 The Importance of Cognition and Moderator Variables in Stress

Irwin G. Sarason
Barbara R. Sarason
University of Washington, USA

Despite extensive study of stress and anxiety, many researchers remain dismayed at the large amount of interindividual and intraindividual variability in response to challenging situations. One attempt to solve this problem of too much unexplained variance has been the use of an interactional approach that assesses how the characteristics of the individual and those of the situation work simultaneously and in interaction to produce behavior in a stress-causing situation. This chapter suggests a cognitive paradigm that emphasizes the role of moderator variables, both individual and situational, as a method of better understanding this interaction.

PERSONS AND SITUATIONS IN INTERACTION

Efforts to cut down the variability of responses among individuals in particular situations have for the past few years concentrated on the interactive effects of various types of individual differences and particular environmental situations. From this perspective, a key concept is *salience,* the perceptual "pull value" of situations and their motivational significance. The universally salient situation evokes a standard response because it is compelling to everyone. Some situations are universally salient because most people have learned the same meaning for a particular cue. For example, when a stop light turns red, most automobile drivers stop. Other situations are universally salient because their overwhelming characteristics evoke similar stress reactions in large numbers of people. Severe earthquakes, catastrophic fires, bridge collapses, mass riots, and nuclear explosions are examples of this type of stress-producing situation. Sometimes, however, when environmental conditions are not stereotyped or extreme, *personal sali-ence* plays a major role in influencing behavior by directing attention to the particular elements of a situation that have personal significance. Hearing a particular song may evoke a grief reaction or feelings of nostalgia or a relaxed state depending on whether it was associated with someone who died recently, with someone who is away and whose return is uncertain, or with happy memories of a high school romance.

Thus, some situations may not initially be experienced as stressful but, be-cause of learning that subsequently takes place, become capable of arousing stress responses. Both the classical conditioning situation and the operant paradigm deal with the ability of past experience to provoke stress responses in an originally nonstressful situation. The following classical conditioning situa-tion illustrates this point.

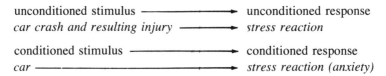

Although the car was originally not a stressful stimulus, it takes on that charac-teristic because of the conditioned stress reaction resulting from the earlier accident. Many stimuli experienced daily in the environment take on stress-producing characteristics for the individual as a result of this classical con-ditioning process. An operant learning situation with a discriminative stimulus can also be the basis for a stress response. An animal in an avoidance conditioning situation learns that jumping to the other side of the shuttle box will allow escape from the discomfort of an electrified grid. A light is introduced as a discrimina-tive stimulus. Now the animal learns that the grid will be electrified only when the light is turned on. Conditioning has produced a stress response to the light. Even if the animal uses illumination as a cue to jump and therefore escape the shock, the illumination produces a heightened physiological state.

Behavior that is strongly influenced by genetic or ontogenetic processes tends to unfold in an orderly manner, except under abnormal conditions. However, when environmental conditions are not stereotyped or extreme and when heredity or development does not play a dominant role, personal salience is a major influence on behavior because it directs attention to the particular elements of a situation that have personal significance. An interactional approach must be concerned with what characteristics of people contribute to personal salience, how these characteristics are shaped and modified by experience, and how situa-tions can be arranged so as to increase or decrease personal salience.

Researchers and theorists might agree completely about the importance of personal salience and yet direct their attention to quite different person and situation variables. Agreement about the importance of person × situation interactions does not provide answers to such questions as: How do you assess personal characteristics? Which situational elements are likely to evoke high levels of salience? Which are the most relevant response measures? Answers to these questions do not so much flow from the application of general methodological principles as from the judgments and hunches of researchers.

A COGNITIVE VIEW OF STRESS AND ANXIETY

Anxiety and stress have figured prominently as variables in studies using the person × situation approach. Because writers have attended to different things taking place in the interaction, theories of stress and anxiety have ranged widely in their definitions of these variables.

Stress

Stress, for example, has been defined variously as a stimulus, a response, and a hypothetical state. The preponderant view at the present time seems to be that it is something occurring within the organism rather than a characteristic of the situation. Stress, then, can be understood in cognitive terms. It involves two kinds of appraisals: of situations or tasks and of the individual's ability to deal successfully with them. These appraisals are arrived at in response to a *call for action,* defined as a situational demand, constraint, or opportunity of which the individual seeks to take advantage (McGrath, 1976). Calls for action vary in urgency and become stressful when they lead to such cognitions as: ''I'm on the spot,'' and ''I've got to do something,'' and where success is not certain. Although stressful cognitions, like other cognitions, involve information processing, they are influenced particularly by the need to act and uncertainty about the outcome.

The most adaptive response to stress is a task orientation that directs the individual's attention to the task at hand rather than emotional reactions. The ability to set aside unproductive worries and preoccupation seems to be crucial in functioning well under pressure. There are wide individual differences in the frequency and preoccupying character of stress-related cognitions. Some of the problems of stress are problems of personal salience of situations. Whether danger will be seen in a situation depends as much on the individual as on the situation. Consequently, an understanding of the effects of stress and prediction of individual behavior must take into account the individual's perceptions both of the demands of the situation and his or her ability to meet them.

The chain of events involved in stress begins with a problematic situation. A call for action is issued when either the environment or personal concerns identify the need to do something. What is done varies widely. Stress follows the call for action when one's capabilities are perceived as falling short of the needed personal resources. For example, in automobile driving, personal ability is usually perceived as commensurate with the situational challenge and the call for action is handled in a routine, task-oriented manner. However, stress may well up on treacherous mountain roads among persons who are not confident of their ability in that situation. Although some people are able to maintain a task orientation in the face of the call, for others, self-preoccupation often interferes with realistic planning and weighing of alternatives. Anecdotal evidence from many sources also suggests that individuals use different cognitive patterns in stressful situations and that these cognitions may be important in determining the level of adaptability of ensuing behavior.

John Johnson (1956), Britain's top fighter ace in the Second World War, has provided an interesting illustration of personal salience in combat. In characterizing pilots on the ground immediately before a mission, he noted that they fell into two groups: "It is fascinating to watch the reactions of the various pilots. They fall into two broad categories; those who are going to shoot and those who secretly and desperately know that they will be shot at . . ." [p. 101].

Johnson proceeded to describe how most of the pilots tie on their mae wests, check their maps, study the weather forecasts, and engage in last minute conversation with their ground crews or wingmen. He labeled these men the "hunters." The others are then described:

> The hunted, that very small minority (although every squadron possessed at least one), turned to their escape kits and made quite sure that they were wearing the tunic with silk maps sewn into the secret hiding place; that they had at least one oilskin-covered packet of French francs, and two if possible; that they had a compass and a revolver and sometimes specially made clothes to assist their activities once they were shot down. When they went through these agonized preparations they reminded me of aged countrywomen meticulously checking their shopping lists before catching the bus for the market town [p. 101].

It seems likely that these two groups' differing behavior was accomplished by very different cognitions concerning the outcome of the mission.

Whereas the research focus for many years had been on the conditions under which stress is generated, emphasis recently has been on understanding coping mechanisms. In Vaillant's (1974, 1977) report of a study of college students' adjustment over a 30-year period after leaving school, evidence is presented suggesting that pervasive personal preoccupations are maladaptive in various areas, including work and marriage, and that successful adjustment is associated with a task orientation and suppression of other cognitions. One of the best examples of the ability to maintain a dispassionate task orientation in the face of severe challenge is Winston Churchill's account of events in *The Gathering Storm* shortly before becoming Prime Minister in the face of war: ". . . by the afternoon I became aware that I might well be called to take the lead (office of Prime Minister). The prospect neither excited nor alarmed me. I thought it would be by far the best plan [p. 661]."

Although there is good reason to emphasize the role of preoccupying thoughts intervening between situation and response, how these personal preoccupations are formed and their physiological correlates are factors of great importance. Because personal preoccupations cannot be observed directly, objective bases for drawing inferences about them are necessary. Research on test anxiety illustrates that a laboratory approach can play a useful role in this inferential process. Perhaps the regularities uncovered in this research are due to the relative ease with which evaluative situations can be defined.

Anxiety

Whereas stress is a call for action determined by an appraisal of the properties of situations and personal dispositions, anxiety is a self-preoccupying response to perceived danger and inability to handle a challenge or unfinished business in a satisfactory manner. The anxious person feels unable to respond to that call for action. This view of anxiety as a state marked by heightened self-awareness and perceived helplessness is similar to Freud's concept of anxiety. Some situations may be anxiety provoking for most people. Their demands may be so great that few people perceive themselves as able to cope. Other situations may produce this feeling of inability to respond only in certain types of people, those who are characteristically anxious or people who are anxious only because of some specifics of the situation, for example, those who are anxious in evaluative or testing situations. This self-preoccupation of the anxious person, even in apparently neutral or even pleasant situations, may be due to a history of experiences marked by a relative paucity of signals indicating that a safe haven from danger has been reached. For the anxiety researcher, the challenge is to relate individual difference in cognitive appraisals of situations and then to build competencies based on this information.

People come to terms with their anxieties in different ways. Some highly anxious individuals are helped by learning to be less demanding of themselves. Others benefit when they revise their expectations about the consequences of failure. They catastrophize less and attend to the task more. Still others need to strengthen their behavioral repertory in specific ways such as strengthening study skills.

A cognitive method to reduce the negative effect of anxiety on performance has been found to be a successful approach. In one study (Sarason, 1973), subjects differing in text anxiety were given the opportunity to observe a model who demonstrated effective ways of performing the task. Using a talk-out-loud technique, the model displayed several facilitative thoughts and cognitions. The major finding was that high test anxiety subjects benefited more from the opportunity to observe a cognitive model than did low test anxiety scorers.

When interventions are successful in reducing evaluative anxiety, there is a commensurate increase in self-efficacy. Bandura (1977a) has described persons high in self-efficacy as seeing themselves as personally effective and able. These positive self-appraisals presumably result from personal successes and reinforcements following the successes. Persons experience increments of self-efficacy when they observe connections between their behavior and tasks that are successfully completed. One reason why these highly anxious persons are low in self-efficacy is that they are so preoccupied with fear of failure, catastrophizing, and blaming themselves. Put another way, they attend too often to what is going on within themselves and become diverted from the step-by-step approach needed in meeting problematic situations.

MODERATOR VARIABLES

Although the person × situation interaction approach and the emphasis on cognitive factors have helped to clarify this complex situation of differential reaction to stressful situations, yet another aspect of the problem, moderator variables, must be explored. These moderator variables may be situational or external to the individual such as social supports, or they may be personal characteristics such as trait anxiety and sensation seeking or even internal physiological states such as that which occurs during menstruation. Several writers have pointed to the possible role of internal moderator variables (Dohrenwend & Dohrenwend, 1974; Rabkin & Struening, 1976; Rahe, 1978). This chapter expands the definition of moderator variables to include variables in the environment as well. Both groups of moderator variables may help in better predictions of the effects of life stress.

The term *life stress* is usually used to refer to life changes that are stress arousing and that are calls for action. Examples of these changes include death or illness of family members, divorce, pregnancy, and marriage. Research has shown that whereas all persons experience life changes, high levels of change experienced within a relatively short period of time often have deleterious effects (Johnson & Sarason, 1979). Life changes, and particularly negative life changes, have been linked to many physical indicators including heart disease, complications associated with pregnancy and birth, tuberculosis, multiple sclerosis, and diabetes, as well as the seriousness of several other conditions. Life changes also correlate negatively with academic performance, effectiveness in work situations, and job satisfaction.

Unfortunately, although many studies have found statistically significant relationships between life stress assessed by a life change score and a host of stress-related variables, these correlations have usually been quite modest. This finding suggests that life stress accounts for a relatively small proportion of the variance in the dependent measures employed and that *by themselves* life stress measures are not likely to be of value for purposes of prediction. Although this poor ability to predict may be due, in part, to the inadequacies of life-stress measures, it is likely that other factors are also involved.

It seems reasonable to assume that the effects of life stress are not the same for all persons. Some persons may be greatly affected by even moderate levels of life stress, and others may show few effects even when experiencing high levels of change. A major limitation of research studies seems to be a relative lack of attention given to moderator variables, those which might mediate the effects of life change.

Situational Moderator Variables

One of the earliest life stress studies to consider the role of moderator variables was conducted by Nuckolls, Cassel, and Kaplan (1972) who examined the relationship between life stress and pregnancy and birth complications. Women were administered the Survey of Recent Experience (Holmes & Rahe, 1967), a measure of life change, and a specially designed Psychosocial Assets Scale during the thirty-second week of pregnancy. The latter measure was designed to assess the degree to which the women possessed social support systems in their environment. Information concerning pregnancy and birth complications was also obtained for these women. Significant relationships between life change and complications were found only when the psychosocial assets measure was taken into account. For subjects with high levels of psychosocial assets, no relationship between life stress and complications was found. Life stress was, however, related to complications among those women with low levels of social supports. Given high life-stress scores before and during pregnancy, women with low levels of psychosocial assets had three times as many pregnancy and birth complications as high life-stress women with high psychosocial assets scores. These findings suggest that a high level of social supports in one's environment may moderate the effects of life stress.

Henderson and Bostock (1975) reported what would appear to be a particularly dramatic example of the role social supports play in how adults cope with stress. They described how seven crewmen of a small cargo vessel survived after their ship sank off the west coast of Tasmania. The men boarded an inflatable life raft and drifted for 9 days, experiencing wet, cold, and rough seas. One man died while they were in the life raft and two other crewmen died shortly after reaching shore. Only a limited supply of fresh water and biscuits was available in the life raft. Henderson and Bostock interviewed the men and obtained extensive information from them because of the unusual life-threatening experience they had lived through. Special attention was paid to the survivors' descriptions of behavior they considered to have been useful in maintaining morale and promoting effectiveness.

The most conspicuous aspect of the information obtained about the survivors was that while on the raft they were preoccupied with thoughts about persons (wives, mothers, girlfriends) who represented significant social supports. The survivors both thought and talked among themselves about their closest family members. The combination of social supports in their personal lives together with the social supports they provided each other seemed to have had survival value. In this case social supports ameliorated the immediate situational stress but were not sufficiently potent to protect against delayed effects. Henderson and Bostock (1977) followed up the survivors for 2 years after their rescue and found that five of the seven had sought help for various types of psychological problems. The other two in contrast, were living satisfying lives and looked back on their miserable experience as a personally strengthening experience. The problems of the five who sought help included insomnia, nightmares, depression, and anxiety. The post-stressor problems suggest that the experience of short-lived extreme stress may carry a price in terms of subsequent self-preoccupation and maladaptation to life, even if social supports are important in immediate survival.

Sarason (1979) has recently demonstrated the potential of a laboratory approach to social supports. This series of experiments, discussed in a later section of the chapter, showed that the effect of a social support could be produced either by discussion groups designed to foster group feeling or by a vicarious experience in which subjects witnessed a worried student being reassured about his ability to meet a coming intellectual challenge. In the vicarious experience, subjects observed the experimenter's unconditional acceptance of the subject.

Individual Difference Moderator Variables

In addition to external or situational moderator variables, individual difference variables or personality characteristics moderate or intensify the impact of certain other personal characteristics. For example, it is well known that while intelligence level is related to many types of performance, anxiety level can also influence that relationship.

Anxiety

A number of test anxiety experiments have demonstrated that highly test anxious subjects perform as well as low anxious subjects in certain situations in which either the task appears easy or performance demands are not emphasized. On the other hand, if the subject perceives the task as a difficult one, then the personality characteristic of anxiety is detrimental to good performance.

But even responses of the subject that seem unrelated to task performance may be affected by this interaction of test anxiety level and situational stress. Differing cognitions characteristic of high and low test anxious subjects may affect such seemingly unrelated behavior as time estimation. In a series of studies, Sarason and Stoops (1978) used the Test Anxiety Scale (TAS) in testing hypotheses about both performance and cognitive processes. The investigation comprised a series of three experiments concerning subjective judgments of the passage of time. After being given either achievement-orienting or neutral instructions, subjects waited for an undesignated period of time, after which they performed an intellective task. The achievement-orienting manipulation involved telling the subject that the task was a measure of intelligence. The dependent measures were subject's estimates of the duration of the waiting and performance periods and their scores on the assigned tasks.

The experiments were aimed at providing information about the way in which individuals differing in anxiety fill time. In two experiments not only was the performance of high TAS subjects deleteriously affected by achievement-orienting instructions, but these subjects also tended to overestimate both the duration of the test period and the period during which they waited to have their ability evaluated. This appears analogous to the tendency to exaggerate time spent in such places as a dentist's waiting room and office. Anticipating and going through unpleasant, frightening, or threatening experiences seem to take up a lot of time. If this interpretation is correct, the question arises: Do individuals differing in anxiety fill time periods in similar or dissimilar ways? The third experiment dealt with this question.

In the third experiment of Sarason and Stoop's study, college students worked on a digit–symbol task prior to a waiting period and then were asked to solve a series of difficult anagrams. Finally, the subjects responded to a questionnaire dealing with their cognitive activity during the anagrams task. The subjects were 60 female undergraduates. The experimental design encompassed two factors: (1) high, middle, and low TAS scorers; and (2) achievement-orienting and neutral instructions. Each subject worked on the digit–symbol task for 4 minutes. This was followed by a 4-minute waiting period. At the end of the waiting period, subjects performed for 18 minutes on the anagrams. The experiment concluded with subjects responding to the Cognitive Interference Questionnaire that assessed how often preoccupying thoughts occur.

Waiting-period time estimates were positively correlated with anxiety and there was a significant interaction between test anxiety and the instructional conditions. This was attributable to the higher time estimates mean obtained by the high TAS group that received achievement-orienting instructions. Table 13.1 presents the means of the four dependent measures for all groups in the experiment.

The analysis of estimates of duration of the anagrams task yielded the same two significant factors, for Test Anxiety and Test Anxiety × Conditions. Again, the significant results were related to the relatively large time estimates given by the high TAS achievement-orientation group (see Table 13.1).

When an analysis was performed on the number of correct responses to the anagrams task, only the Test Anxiety factor was statistically significant. As the means in the third column of Table 13.1 show, this effect was due mainly to the relatively poor performance of the high TAS group receiving the achievement orienting instructions.

Test Anxiety and Test Anxiety × Conditions also produced significant results in the analysis of Cognitive Interference Questionnaire scores. Again, most of

TABLE 13.1
Mean Waiting Time and Task Time Estimates, Anagram Performance
Scores, and Cognitive Interference Scores (Sarason & Stoops, 1978)

	Waiting Time Estimate (seconds)	Task Time Estimate (seconds)	Anagrams Score	Cognitive Interference Score
H-E	357.0	1354.1	3.3	33.2
H-C	286.5	1114.0	4.8	24.6
M-E	266.3	1031.5	5.5	18.2
M-C	274.4	1103.5	5.7	21.6
L-E	266.5	1172.0	5.0	19.8
L-C	265.0	1140.5	5.0	21.4

Note: H, M, and L refer to levels of test anxiety; E and C refer to experimental (achievement-orientation) and control conditions.

the interaction effects were due to the high scores obtained by the high TAS achievement-orientation group. Results for separate analyses of individual questionnaire items were in every case in the same direction as the results presented for the questionnaire as a whole.

An item appended to the questionnaire asked the subjects to indicate on a seven-point scale the degree to which their minds wandered while working on the anagrams task. An analysis of variance of these scores also yielded significant factors for Test Anxiety and Test Anxiety × Conditions.

These results demonstrate that individuals for whom danger in evaluative situations is particularly salient (high test anxious people) tend to overestimate to a greater degree than do others both the time during which their performance is evaluated and the period during which they are waiting for the evaluation to take place. Highly test anxious subjects performed at significantly lower levels than low and middle scorers when emphasis was placed on the evaluational implications of performance. Perhaps this can be explained by cognitive interference occurring during both the waiting and evaluation periods. Highly test anxious scorers, more so than low and middle scorers, attribute to themselves preoccupations about how poorly they are doing, how other people are faring, and what the examiner will think about the subject. Although a measure of cognitive interference during the waiting period was not obtained, it seems likely that similar preoccupations would have characterized highly test anxious subjects then, too.

Sensation Seeking

Another individual difference moderator variable has been suggested by the results of a recent study conducted by Smith, Johnson, and Sarason (1978). In this study subjects were administered the Life Experiences Survey (LES) (Sarason, Johnson, & Siegel, 1978), a measure of recent positive and negative life events, and the Sensation Seeking Scale (Zuckerman, Kolin, Price, & Zoob, 1964). The sensation seeking measure employed is an instrument designed to assess the tendency of individuals to engage in thrill-seeking, risk-taking activities. High scorers on this measure seem to like high levels of stimulation, and those scoring low on the scale define a low level of stimulation as most optimal. Thus, low-sensation seekers are thought often to try to minimize arousing stimulus input. Smith et al. reasoned that if the sensation seeking measure, in fact, reflects one's optimal level of stimulation or arousal, low-sensation seekers should be more adversely affected by life stress than high-sensation seekers who are presumably more tolerant of change. Results in line with this hypothesis were obtained. A later study using a different measure of sensation seeking replicated these results (Johnson & Sarason, 1979).

Locus of Control

The degree to which the person perceives events as being under his/her personal control may also serve as a moderator for life change events. Johnson and Sarason (1979) recently reported results that support such a relationship. In that study subjects were given the Rotter (1966) Locus of Control Scale, the LES, the State–Trait Anxiety Inventory (Spielberger, Gorsuch, & Lushene, 1970), and the Beck (1967) Depression Scale. The Locus of Control Scale assesses individuals' perceptions of control over their environment. Low scorers (internals) are thought to perceive environmental reinforcers as being under their personal control. High scorers (externals) are believed to view reinforcers as being controlled by fate, luck, or powerful others. There is considerable evidence that this measure reflects subjects' perception of their own control over environmental events.

Because experiencing life changes that persons feel unable to control might be expected to result in increased anxiety and depression, it was expected that the highest levels of anxiety and depression would be found with high life-stress subjects external in their locus of control orientation. A high level of negative life changes was found to be significantly correlated with measures of both trait anxiety and depression, but only for externals. Although it is difficult to infer cause and effect relationships from them, these findings are consistent with the notion that people are more adversely affected by life stress if they perceive themselves as having little control over their environment.

Experimental work such as the Sarason and Stoops study illustrates that even behavior that does not seem logically related to test anxiety may be affected by this individual difference variable. Other research suggests that the effects of individual differences may be even more subtle. The importance of these individual difference variables invades even the insulated sanctuary of the well-controlled psychology laboratory where research on topics such as memory and attention is carried out. Broadbent (1977) and Neisser (1976) both recently discussed the role of individual differences in *preattentive* processes, seemingly automatic features of information processing involved in the detection and analysis of information. Broadbent (1977), for example, has referred to factors other than those resulting from experimenter's instructions that: "... may not always be reportable, and which nevertheless may cause attention to be caught by this stimulus rather than by that, in a way that is systematic rather than random [p. 110]." What subjects bring to the laboratory (attitudes, predilections, fears, information) exert influences over their performances and they may be as unaware of these influences as is the experimenter. Thus, individual difference variables may affect performance in ways most theorists have not even considered. An interesting possibility would be to approach this problem from the standpoint of the factors that inhibit a person's ability to attend to potential sources of danger in the environment. Defense mechanisms can be reformulated in terms of cognitive styles defined as the predominance of a variety of rigid, limiting constructions of events and plans for action. It is perhaps because of the individual differences in these cognitive styles that Neisser (1976) has called for a widening of cognitive psychology's purview to include events of everyday life.

Physiological State Moderator Variables

A classic experiment by Schacter and Singer (1962) demonstrated that the heightened physiological state produced by administration of adrenalin affected subjects' reactions to an emotion-producing situation. This was true, however, only when the subjects were misinformed about the expected effects of the injected adrenalin. When they were aware of the expected effects, their behavior did not differ from that of control subjects. The physiological state of the misinformed subjects served as a moderator variable that affected what behavior was shown under stress. Similarly other physiological states may serve as moderators of stress reactions. It seems likely that the physiological changes caused by periods of sleep deprivation or by nutritional state serve as moderators of the person × situation interaction.

In one experiment that has addressed this topic, Siegel, Johnson, and Sarason (1979) investigated the relationship between life stress, as assessed by the LES, and menstrual discomfort. A significant relationship between negative life change and discomfort was obtained, but only for women not taking oral contraceptives. The relationship between life stress and menstrual discomfort seems to vary with oral contraceptive usage.

THE INTERACTION OF MODERATOR VARIABLES

Not only do moderator variables serve as mediators between the situations and individual's responses, but moderator variables sometimes interact. Study of these interactions can further clarify what is occurring in the person × situation interaction and enable researchers to predict outcomes more effectively for groups differing in specific situational and personal characteristics.

In a recent series of experiments, Sarason (1979) studied subjects who differed in test anxiety and whose social-support level was experimentally manipulated. Subjects with high, middle, and low scores on the Test Anxiety Scale (TAS) (Sarason, 1978) performed on a difficult anagrams task either under a neutral or experimental condition. The experimental condition emphasized that ability to solve the anagrams was related to intelligence and likelihood of success in doing college-level academic work. Previous research had shown that highly text anxious people perform relatively poorly under this condition and that their performance is hindered by excessive self-preoccupations concerning failure and its consequences (Sarason & Stoops, 1978).

A second experimental variable was the opportunity for social supports or its absence. Although half the subjects performed only on the anagrams, subjects under the social-support condition participated in a prior 20-minute group discussion. These discussions were attended by six subjects who were asked to discuss a series of questions about their academic experiences. The questions asked by Sarason (1979) included: ''Are stress and anxiety about exams important problems here at the University of Washington?'' ''How often do you share your worries about tests with other students?'' ''What are the barriers to this sharing of personal concerns?'' ''Do you feel this discussion has brought you closer to people who otherwise would just be 'other' students?'' [p. 24]

Except for suggesting the specific topics, the discussions were freewheeling. In addition to the six subjects, two confederates were present at the discussions. Their roles were to: (1) stimulate discussion and keep it going if necessary; (2) reinforce positively comments made by participants and build group feeling and a sense of sharing; and (3) at the end of the discussion to say that the discussion had been valuable for them, comment on the degree of compatability among the group members, and suggest that the members get together after completion of the experiment to see if an informal meeting could be arranged for continuing the discussion. This condition was designed to heighten the sense of social association and shared values among group members.

Consistent with findings of previous research, the high TAS subjects performed more poorly under the condition which emphasized the evaluative aspect of subjects' performance. Subjects who participated in the group discussions performed at a higher level than did subjects who did not. Of particular interest was the Test Anxiety × Social Support interaction (see Fig. 13.1). Comparisons for each of the three levels of test anxiety yielded a significant difference between the social supports experimental and control groups only for high TAS subjects. Although the TAS × Instructions × Social Supports interaction only approached a statistically significant level, for subjects in the high test anxiety group who received the evaluative instructions, those who also participated in the group discussions performed on the anagrams at a higher level than those who did not.

Earlier, anxiety was depicted as a self-preoccupying reaction to stress. Among the hallmarks of anxiety are thoughts of personal inadequacy and helplessness.

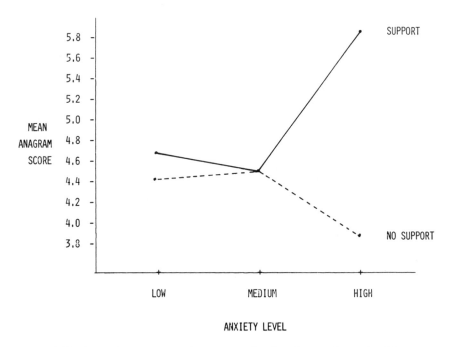

FIG. 13.1   Mean anagram performance as a function of test anxiety and social supports (Sarason, 1979).

The results of this experiment suggest that association with others and hope of its continuation may reduce the potency of these thoughts even when the threat of evaluation is present. As anxious self-preoccupation decreases, the opportunity for task-oriented thinking increases with consequent improved performance.

In the social-supports experiment just described, the factor studied was group association. A second experiment explored another dimension of social supports, acceptance. Test anxiety scores were again used as a measure of individual differences in self-preoccupation aroused by an evaluative call for action. An anagrams task administered in groups and instructional conditions similar to the ones employed in the experiment just described were used. Social support was provided vicariously for half the subjects. This was done by having a confederate raise his hand after the experimenter had introduced the anagrams task and say: ''I don't think I can work these problems. They get me all upset. I'm no good at them.'' The experimenter responded with: ''You're not the only person who clutches up in this kind of situation. I can tell from the fact that you took the initiative to tell me how you feel that you're an intelligent person. Just do your best. That's all anybody can expect. I think you have more ability than you give yourself credit for.''

There were four experimental groups each treated with one of the following conditions: (1) evaluative instructions; (2) social support; (3) evaluative instructions and social support; and (4) a control condition. The 16 subjects under each condition were divided into high and low TAS groups. The effects for social support and the interaction between test anxiety and social support were statistically significant ($p < .05$ and $p < .01$, respectively). Table 13.2 gives the cell means for the eight groups. Although high TAS subjects performed more poorly than the low TAS subjects under the evaluative instructions, their performance was equal to or better than the low TAS groups for the two conditions in which support was present. What was the nature of the support provided? The intention was to create a condition in which the subjects could observe a peer who was listened to with respect and interest. The emphasis was on the experimenter's unconditional acceptance of the subject. This was based on the idea that when a person feels valued, anxious self-preoccupation will be reduced. Although the evidence presented here obviously does not provide information about other self-preoccupying thoughts such as anger, similar results might be found for them.

CONCLUSION

A cognitive approach can be valuable in more clearly specifying what goes on in a person × situation interaction. It is beginning to lead to research that will help to clarify the factors involved in such an interaction and also to suggest coping techniques for rendering situations less stress engendering for the individual.

Moderator variables, personal (related to personality characteristic or physiological state) or situational, can play a major role in individual response to a stress-producing situation. Personality characteristics, such as sensation seeking and locus of control, and physiological states seem to function as a moderator of the effects of stressful life events. Social supports, a situational variable, seems to perform the same function. Of even greater interest is the interactive effect of these moderator variables. This type of interaction was illustrated by

TABLE 13.2
Mean Anagram Performance as a Function of Test Anxiety
and Experimenter's Supportive Comments (Sarason, 1979)

Test Anxiety	Conditions			
	Evaluative Instructions	Experimenter's Support	Evaluative Instruction and Experimenter's Support	Control
High	2.9	6.5	5.0	3.8
Low	5.4	4.4	4.8	3.8

experimental work that assessed the effects of a stressor on subjects who differed in test anxiety level, an individual difference moderator, and experimentally constructed social supports, a situational moderator.

It seems reasonable to conclude that a number of specific variables may mediate the effects of stress. To the extent that these moderator variables influence the effects of stressors such as life change, the finding of low correlations between measures of the stressor and dependent measures is to be expected when such variables are not taken into consideration.

14

Structure of Situation and Action: Some Remarks on Formal Theory of Actions

Maria Nowakowska
Polish Academy of Sciences, Warsaw, Poland

INTRODUCTION

The theory has an interdisciplinary character; it integrates within one system the psychological linguistic, logical, and decisional aspects of behavior. In short, one can say that this formal action theory is a system that unifies thought and action.

The idea underlying the construction of the theory is that composite actions are sequences of simpler, "elementary," actions and that the latter cannot, in general, be performed in arbitrary order. This observation alone suffices to draw a linguistic analogy: There must be a class of meaningful orders in which the actions can be performed, in the same way as there is a class of meaningful orderings of letters under which they form words—as opposed to nonsensical strings—and also a class of meaningful orderings of words into sentences—as opposed to syntactically incorrect utterances.

This analogy has numerous fruitful consequences, because it allows us to use the concepts of formal linguistics for the study of actions. One could call this study "formal grammar of actions."

Moreover, when uttering sentences, one usually wants to express some meaning. In a similar way, actions, whether composite or elementary, are performed in order to attain some goals, simple or composite, that is, to cause the occurrence of some events at specific times.

One may say also that actions are treated as "words" in a certain vocabulary and admissible strings of actions as expressions in the "language of actions." Furthermore, outcomes of strings of actions are regarded as "meanings" and hence constitute the semantics of the so-defined language of actions.

211

This is the starting point of the system, which—for the first time in the literature—analyzes thoroughly, in a unified, precise, and formal way, the verbal and nonverbal aspects of behavior. Thus, the central idea is that of extension of the concept of language to actions and nonverbal behavior (Nowakowska, 1973a).

The main primitive concepts of the system form a quadruplet

$$\langle D, L, S, R \rangle \tag{1}$$

where

D stands for the "vocabulary of actions,"

L is the "language of actions" (i.e. the set of all admissible strings of elementary actions),

S is the set of outcomes, and

R is the relation connecting strings of actions with outcomes from the set S.

The set D consists of elementary actions, with one particular action distinguished and denoted by $\#$, to be interpreted as *pause*—i.e., any action that is outside the scope of interest in the description of a given situation being analyzed. Next, one introduces also the function ϕ, representing the duration of an action [i.e., $\phi(d)$ is the time needed to perform action d]. For simplicity, one may always assume that $\phi(\#) = 1$, with longer pauses represented as strings $\#\#$ ... $\#$.

The concept of elementary action is taken as a primitive and left undefined.

The composite actions are, by definition, strings of elementary actions $d_1 d_2 \ldots d_n$. Which actions should be taken as elementary and which are composite in any context is largely a matter of convenience for a particular goal one has in mind when applying the system to a description of a real situation.

In the approach presented, the starting point is the recognition of formal analogy between the set of composite actions and language, as stated at the beginning. Accordingly, in the class D^*, that is, the class of all finite strings of elementary actions, one distinguishes those that are admissible in some specified sense; combinations of these strings, by definition, make up the language of actions L (so that L is a subset of D^*). Admissibility of a string may be interpreted in a number of ways, depending on the goal of analysis. Thus, L may be interpreted as the set of strings of actions that are:

1. Physically admissible, that is, physically possible to perform. This leads to a structural analysis of various specific-action situations, in particular those studied in the psychology of work.

2. Psychologically admissible for a given person. The class of all such "languages of actions" may constitute a basis for creating a special-personality theory, in which the concept of personality would be explicated and taxonomized in terms of "grammatical rules" for various languages of actions.

3. Socially admissible (i.e., consistent with a given social role). Here the analysis might provide structural characterization and taxonomy of social roles.

4. Organizationally admissible (i.e., acceptable in a given organization). This analysis might lead to a foundation-of-organization theory based on linguistic theory of actions. As opposed to the ''language of social roles,'' based mostly on intuitive acceptance or rejection of a given string as consistent or inconsistent with the considered social role, here the criteria for a string of actions to belong to L are expressed formally by norms, regulations, and customs of a given organization.

5. Admissible for a given object. The idea here is that each object generates a set of appropriate strings of actions, admissible in view of the structure of the object. In other words, one can speak of actions that are ''grammatical'' for a given object and those that are not grammatical (as an example, one can think here of an object such as a computer and the actions of operating it).

In the case of a certain configuration of objects related in some ways among themselves (by relations such as being a part of, domination, etc.), there arises a problem of relations between the ''languages'' associated with these objects, possibly expressible in terms of set-theoretical operations. It might seem that configurations of larger numbers of objects, with complicated relational structure, would impose more constraints on the generated actions and hence lead to a smaller class of admissible strings of actions than would ''looser'' configurations, with fewer objects. Easy examples, however, show that it need not be so in general.

A particular case of a configuration of objects is the environment; it generates a set of appropriate actions. All other actions from outside this set are therefore diagnostic in the sense that they represent those aspects of activity that are related to internal factors of the acting person, his motivation, his plan of actions, etc.

A further particular configuration of objects (stimuli) is the problem, generating solutions as its sets of actions—though possibly this set is empty or consists of only one element. Thus one can consider ''grammars'' of problems, that is, algorithms of solving them.

6. Admissible in a given methodology or theory. This interpretation applies especially when one treats scientific activity within the framework of system 1; that is, one can interpret scientific methods as sets of well-defined and structured procedures (strings of actions). This allows one to consider every method as a separate language of actions L or, alternatively, to treat it as a ''sublanguage'' of a universal language of actions L of a given theory or set of theories. Such an approach allows construction of a formal theory of research (Nowakowska, 1977).

The remaining two primitive concepts of system 1 have the following interpretation. An action, composite or not, leads generally to certain results (outcomes); accordingly, the set of all outcomes that are of interest in a given context will be denoted by S. The pairs (s, t), where $s \in S$ and t is a moment of time, will be referred to as time results, and (s, t) will be interpreted as occurrence of s at time t. The connection between actions and results will be expressed by postulating that each string of actions in L leads to the occurrence of some (usually more than one) time results. In formal terms this is the relation R, the last primitive concept of system 1, holding between strings of actions in L and time results (s, t). The symbol $uR (s, t)$, where $u \in T$, $s \in S$, and t is a particular moment in time, means that performing u leads to the occurrence of s at the time t (counting from the moment of originating the string u). Naturally, one string of actions may lead to several time results, and, similarly, one time result may be brought about by various strings of actions so that the relation R is, in general, not one-to-one.

Comments

Contrary to the S–R or S–O–R paradigm, in a formal theory of actions the central idea is to study not single instances of pairs such as stimulus–response or behavior–outcome but the whole class of such pairs at once. Moreover I propose to study not any class observed in a given experiment but a conceptually distinguished class of all behaviors or actions, verbal or nonverbal, that are feasible or admissible or possible in a given situation.

Let us for a moment leave the question of empirical access to such a class, and agree that in any given situation it may be conceptually distinguished. Let us think how such a class can be described and analysed. The next crucial step in the analysis concerns "discretization" of behavior, thinking about it in terms of some elementary units. One needs to distinguish—at least conceptually—the building blocks from which all other behavior in a given situation can be composed. There are several very important problems connected with discretization of behavior. Firstly, there is a group of epistemological problems. One of them concerns the level of generality. From the formal point of view, the behavioral unit is a primitive notion, and for the theory it does not really matter how it is explicated in a given context. The only postulate here is that the choice should match the desired generality level of description. If one's goal is to describe behavior and its results in very broad and general terms, then there is a natural limit beyond which further atomization of behavior is unnecessary or even meaningless. On the other hand, if one wants to describe more specific outcomes, it may be necessary to choose finer units of behavior.

The second epistemological problem is that of dimensionality. The behavioral units are, by their nature, multidimensional. In particular, a unit may contain two basic components—verbal and nonverbal—that is, utterance and some nonverbal action, performed simultaneously. The nonverbal part may in turn be decomposed further, if necessary, so that eventually on the desired level of generality one usually obtains some vector-valued, or multidimensional unit.

Still another important epistemological problem is that of asymmetry between action and nonaction. These two are conceptually distinct and not merely complementary. I was aware of this in my theory and introduced a convenient formal device of "behavioral pause." This pause does not mean abstaining from any activity. The pause is simply any action that is inessential from the point of view of the goal of description. If for some reason one wants to analyze a person's smoking behavior, then anything he does between smoking cigarettes will be a behavioral pause. Finally, putting aside all epistemological problems, there is a purely empirical problem—how to define behavioral units in a given context, situation, or class of situations.

It appeared (Nowakowska, 1973a) that they should be defined in terms of the relation between strings of actions and their outcomes, interpreted as meanings. It is also possible to go further and introduce, as shown in Nowakowska (1978a), strings of multidimensional units of simultaneous actions and define fuzzy relations connecting them with outcomes (meanings). In this context, the unit is defined as the shortest string of behavior that still carries some meaning.

As already mentioned, the class of all conceptually possible strings of units of behavior has all the formal features of a language. For environmentalists, this approach allows identification of situations, or environments, with a specific-action language—and, in turn, an analysis of situations in terms of a rich set of concepts-of-action theory.

What is most important, however, is the assumption lying at the foundation of the theory, that nonverbal behavior has a linguistic character, so that the concept of extended language, as introduced in the theory, allows one to describe the whole behavior in one system in a unified way by one set of concepts. It is worthwhile to point out that a recent program of Piaget (1976) also is concerned with the concept of extended language.

For environmentalists, the theory offers powerful tools for studying such aspects of behavior as its motivational consistency—in particular, consistency in mixed strings (i.e., verbal and nonverbal streams of behavioral units) such as keeping promises and fulfilling plans—and further, its decisional and predecisional aspects, especially the sequential features of decision making.

Concepts in the theory such as complete possibility, decisive moments, and attainability of outcomes appear quite often in contemporary characterizations of human actions.

Of course, the concept of action itself has been analyzed for a long time already, especially in the philosophical literature but until recently not as a deliberately chosen methodological tool, and there was no formal theory of actions with the exception of the partly formal considerations of von Wright (1968).

There is general agreement that until now, in the studies of situation, the motivational aspects have not been sufficiently represented. It seems that such notions of action theory as motivational space, with its linguistic representation, and motivational calculus, allowing classification, inference, and linguistic measurement of actional objects, can find fruitful applications in situational psychology. Especially, the motivational space is identified with decisional space in which judgments of courses of actions are represented.

This is the way strings of actions are combined with cognitive processes and linguistic descriptions, in particular with justification or looking for reasons for actions, explication, and so on, rather than searching for the elusive causes of actions.

THE MAIN DIRECTIONS OF RESEARCH

The formal analysis using this system 1 can be carried out independently of the possible different interpretations, though it is, of course, guided by them. The main lines of research (Nowakowska, 1973a) are the following:

1. Analysis of the structure of language of actions L, through application of some concepts borrowed directly from formal linguistics (generative grammars, distributional classes, parasitic strings, etc.): These concepts then acquire an action-theoretical interpretation and become useful tools in explicating the "grammatical" features of action situations.

In particular, parasitic strings (roughly, those strings that neither are admissible nor can constitute fragments of admissible strings) provide valuable information about the structure of L. In the case, for instance, when L is the language of actions consisting of strings that are "psychologically admissible" for a given person, the parasitic strings reflect the person's "inner constraints" that make it impossible for him to behave in certain ways. Through such an analysis one may arrive at a formal description of behavioral characteristics of personality.

2. Analysis of attainability of some outcomes or, generally, some configurations of outcomes (composite goals): If a given goal is attainable (i.e., there is at least one string of actions leading to this goal), the natural topics of study are various types of effectiveness and optimality. If a given composite goal is not attainable, but various attainments of various parts of it are possible, one obtains a model of internal conflict of motives.

A rather unexpected result here is that a relatively simple conflict of four competing motives, which cannot (say, because of situational constraints) be satisfied jointly, can take on one of 113 nonequivalent forms, depending on which of the pairs or triplets of motives are jointly satisfiable and which are not. The conflict theory, based on combinatorial analysis and its interpretation, is shown in Nowakowska (1973a, pp. 216–224). In psychological applications, just such a conflict of four motives forms the most typical scheme, which may be described generally as:

—occurrence of an event one wants to occur;
—nonoccurrence of an event one wants to avoid;
—performance of an action one ought to perform;
—nonperformance of an action one should not perform.
    This allows the characterization of internal conflicts of the type "approach–

approach," "approach-avoidance," and "avoidance-avoidance," as well as conflicts within the id domain or between the id and superego domains in dynamic psychology.

It is interesting to compare the theoretically possible 113 types of conflicts with the number of those for which it is possible to find real-life examples. The latter class is very limited: It contains only a few conflicts, and attempts to find examples of situations (in psychology) of a conflict of a given type leading to situations artificial and difficult to imagine. Thus, despite the richness of real situations and the theoretical possibility of 113 categories, there seems to exist in fact only a very limited number of types of internal conflicts.

This limitation is probably related to the restrictions imposed by "grammars of situations" and by learning, which lead to a tendency toward reduction of all situations to "binary" conflicts.

Of course, this limitation concerns only the psychological conflicts; in other cases (e.g., organizational planning or the solving of organizational problems, where the conflict lies in the lack of joint satisfiability of some four conditions), one can easily point out examples of all 113 types of conflicts.

If a given time result, or a composite goal, is attainable, there often may be more than one way of achieving it. In such cases, it is of some interest to impose appropriate criteria of optimality, or estimated values, on strings of actions so as to be able to select those that are "best" in some sense or other. Such a construct is of importance both for normative purposes, when the system is used to describe some action situation and when one is interested in the best ways of attaining a certain goal, and also as one studies actual behavior in real situations, comparing it against the optimal behavior.

One such criterion of optimality is provided by praxiology. Roughly, the criterion is reached when one goes about attainment of a given goal by performing only those actions that are essential (for economy of effort) and performing those strings of actions having the shortest duration (for economy of time). Accordingly, in the set of all strings of actions that bring about the goal $f(c)$, one may distinguish the subsets Prax $f(C)$ and Prax min $f(C)$.

3. The analysis of verbal behavior and its relation to nonverbal. Here we note that the "vocabulary of actions" D contains a subset, consisting of actions having the form of utterances. By restricting the latter to those in which a person evaluates, explains, justifies, and so on his past or future actions, one obtains a fragment of natural language that constitutes a linguistic representation of motivation.

It is worthwhile to point out that in this research, for the first time in the literature (dominated by the ideas of Chomsky, 1957), the analysis of verbal behavior is directed primarily toward the surface of the language. The example of the linguistic representation of motivation illustrates a methodology for the study of various classes of such representations in terms of both aspects of their semantic organization and aspects of logical laws of inference from natural language, as well as of the various aspects of approximate reasoning that may be observed in natural language.

Another advantage of this approach lies in the fact that it relates, on the one hand, the structure of linguistic, semantic, and logical aspects of language with, on the other, the underlying decisional space.

The principal lines of research in point 3 concern:

3a. The decision model based on the assumption that choice is determined by evaluation of the alternatives on various scales of "motivational space". The idea here is to consider the space spanned by the dimensions (scales, psychological continua such as subjective probability, or utility) as corresponding to various criteria, so that the choice alternatives may be ordered along each of the dimensions. Such space has been called *motivational space* (Nowakowska, 1973a); in that context it was spanned by cognitive scales represented by certain functors, such as epistemic (e.g., "I know that," "I am certain that"), emotional (e.g., "I am glad that"), motivational (e.g., "I want"), and deontic (e.g., "I must"). These functors were abstracted from an analysis of those utterances that explain, justify, evaluate, etc., the decisions that had already been taken or were being planned. The linguistic representation of such cognitive scales (psychological continua) as subjective probability, in the form of epistemic functors such as "I am certain that," "I think that," or "I doubt that"—the richness and sensitivity of this representation—was examined in decisional context for the first time in the 1973 book.

The decision criterion, by definition, must assign to every feasible set of points in the motivational space (i.e., to a set of orderings along the dimensions) a final ordering, or at least the first element of it (optimal decision). It may be shown that the formal structure of individual decision is exactly the same as that of group decision and, consequently, Arrow's *I possibility theorem* (Arrow, 1963) applies to it. It turns out that such an interpretation yields certain important psychological consequences about the process of decision making, simply by observing that people must divide into various categories, depending on which of the five postulates of Arrow (lack of dictatorship, sovereignty, independence of irrelevant alternatives, and so on) is broken. Each of these categories, in turn, acquires a suitable psychological interpretation.

The theoretical and empirical importance of identification between individual and group decisions, and the resulting application of Arrow's theorem to the former, is the following: For theoretical research, it stresses the importance of ordinal types of continua, which may intervene in the process of decision-making and which are traditionally left out in the decision models. Secondly, it leads (among other things) to the definition and taxonomy of internal conflicts, mentioned in the foregoing.

For empirical research, it suggests the following goals: the identification of: (1) those classes of situations where the criteria are not aggregated into a transitive relation; and (2) if they are so aggregated, a search for those of Arrow's axioms that have been violated in order to attain transitivity. The ultimate purpose of the latter study is to identify the types of decision problems that are most likely to lead to violation of a given axiom; such knowledge would, in turn, allow restriction of the class of decision criteria that could be employed by the decision maker.

3b. Motivational calculus, which describes the schemes of inference from utterances in natural language: The intuitive background for this calculus is the fact that there exists a sufficiently common feeling of correctness for such inference.

The basic primitive concept on which the construction of inference schemes of motivational calculus is built is that of inadmissibility of a sentence. Intuitively, an expression is inadmissible if there is no context in which it may be meaningfully applied, or if it could be applied only in very unusual circumstances. This concept permits definition of the notion of semantic implication $A \underset{s}{\rightarrow} B$ (A semantically implies B) if the sentence "A and not B" is not admissible. This calculus in effect initiated a very popular analysis of the logic of natural language, in particular of everyday reasoning. It was the first system in which a large set of functors was treated at once.

The notion of semantic implication is fuzzy in the same way as the notion of admissibility. If the latter were given in the form of membership function, one could define the strength of semantic implication $A \underset{s}{\rightarrow} B$ by postulating that the sum of this strength and the value of admissibility of "A and not B" is 1:

(strength of $A \underset{s}{\rightarrow} B$) + (admissibility of A and not B) = 1

An analysis of sentence schemes involving epistemic, emotional, motivational, and deontic functors (e.g., "I know that," "I am glad that," "I want," or "I ought to") leads to the construction of a calculus, which describes everyday inference. Examples of such rules are

$$D_p \rightarrow T(-p) \ \& \ -Cr(-p)$$

("I doubt that p" implies "I think that not p, but I am not certain that not p") or

$$W(p \ \& \ q) \rightarrow Wp \ \& \ Wq$$

("I want p and q" implies "I want p and I want q").

By contrasting a set theoretical model, it was shown by Nowakowska (1973a) that the obtained calculus is consistent.

In effect, these semantic implications (in the form of transformation rules from sentences involving motivational functors) constitute the rules of approximate reasoning, the approximation resulting from the fuzziness of the underlying concept of semantic admissibility.

In the construction of the motivational calculus, in order to achieve greater generality, the traditional way of listing the primitives and laying down the rules of construction of composite sentences was deliberately omitted, It should be clear, however, that giving such rules would restrict the considerations to a specific language and would also require the specification of the sense of the motivational functors. The latter task is still not completely solved for any single functor—though there are some results in this direction (Hintikka, 1962)—let alone for the whole set of functors at once. It appeared more promising to provide a set of inference rules directly and to prove the consistency of this set.

One can argue that such an approach is closer to natural language, inasmuch as laying down the construction rules for composite sentences would allow long sentences, acceptable logically but not linguistically.

The knowledge of the laws of motivational calculus allows formulation of the laws of motivational consistency by combining decisions (actions) with utterances. Such laws permit determination of the classes of conclusions (utterances or actions) that are consistent with a given utterance and thus also allow us to make some inference about the person's behavior in such a way that his or her decision becomes motivationally consistent with the combined utterances (tacit and not). In such a case, the added premises reflect the (unuttered) motive of a person. Clearly, the less the freedom resulting from such an addition of premises, the more certain the inference being made about the person's motives.

The rules outlined above may provide formal methods of inference in psychological diagnosis.

In sum, the central idea of motivational calculus, which seems to have some importance for semantic and psycholinguistic studies, lies in the introduction of the linguistic representation of a situation. Inferences are made about this situation and successive transformations are applied to it, based on linguistic competence and intuition. It is assumed here that the lexical units have certain admissible logical properties that allow observation and study of differences between linguistic and logical scope of inference. Finally, the studies of linguistic inference supply arguments against syntactic conceptions of the language by stressing the fact that in the dynamics of linguistic transformations an important role is played by both syntactic and semantic aspects or, in other words, by interactions between logical and semantic properties.

MOTIVATIONAL CONSISTENCY AND STRUCTURAL PROPERTIES OF SETS OF STRINGS OF ACTIONS THAT FULFILL OR BREAK A PROMISE

The situation and its meaning can be represented on different levels by different systems. The representation in focus so far has been the actional one. The situation was represented by a corresponding system of languages of actions, each generated by a different principle of admissibility of strings of actions.

The underlying different criteria of admissibility form an interesting organized system of sets of norms, laws, rules, customs, etc. In other words, the situation may be represented not only directly on the level of actions but also indirectly by systems of principles or criteria that imply some language, or languages, of actions.

Another, still more general, system by which situation can be represented is the set of values for which a given situation exists and/or that implies a given situation. Or, still differently, it may be represented by the values realized in a given situation.

Whereas the system of criteria determines what is admissible and what is not, the value system plays the explanatory and justificatory role, determines what is "good" and what is "bad," organizes the sequences of values, and sets up the time horizons for them.

In this sense, the value system itself is a social product and serves as a possible repertoire of goals for individual actions.

Another higher-order system that is also a representation of the situation is the sign (or semiotic) system of this situation.

The semiotic system is a certain form of "notation" of the meaning of the situation, through some more or less abstract objects (signs). Such objects allow a quick identification of the situation.

The relationship between the situation, its meaning, and its signs is fuzzy, (i.e., signs represent situations and their meanings in varying degrees).

This fact has important consequences for the degree of precision of identification of the situation and is responsible for possible misinterpretations and inadequate recognitions.

A further essential factor in identification of the situation is knowledge about the situation, understood here as the potentiality for complete reconstruction (on the basis of the semiotic system of the situation) of the remaining systems related to this situation such as the system of values, the system of norms and criteria, and finally action systems (languages of actions).

For environmentalists, the interesting questions concern various distortions of knowledge for various types of situations.

Another interesting problem is to what extent explicit knowledge guarantees efficiency of action in a situation and whether the learning of languages of actions is intuitive to the same degree as the learning of natural languages; in other words, the efficiency of using languages of actions does not depend on explicit knowledge of its grammar rules.

Also, it seems that in situational research the influence of existing systems of values and norms on the generation of new situations has not been analyzed nor have the potentials for new values, norms, plans, rules, etc., to be formed from situations. The changeability of systems of norms and situations has not been considered either.

The most fruitful research area for environmentalists seems to be, however, the research on particular types of situations and actions, to be called *situations enforcing promises and obligations* and hence also *actions implied by them* (e.g., marriage vows or military oath). In other words, these will be situations in which performing some actions or refraining from some actions is necessary.

Whereas in some enforcing situations one has the freedom to enter the situation or not, in more extreme cases one does not have such freedom and is situationally compelled to act (by commands, orders, psychological or physical pressure, and so on) or is blocked from some actions (by destroying or suppressing the conditions necessary for actions).

Obviously, various forms of enforcing situations differ by sanctions: punishments or rewards that are separately regulated by norms, laws, or procedures.

One can, of course, distinguish a group of situations that are obligation-neutral to varying degrees and in which obligatoriness depends on the psychological or social context brought in by the actors, that is, such situations that do not impose on the actors any type of promise or obligation but in which promises can be formed.

Looking over the situations, from obligation-neutral to promise-enforcing, the common underlying characteristic is the expectation of motivational consistency between a person's uttered promise or plan of actions (for a formal theory of planning behavior, see Nowakowska, 1973a) and his or her fulfillment of the obligation or plan. This is the most general postulate of rationality of behavior—a certain ideal expected pattern, which in social awareness is strongly connected with truthfulness and reliability.

Thus motivational consistency is to some extent expected to be context-free.

Breaks in motivational consistency take various forms; they may arise from lying, cheating, unreliability, and so on.

The analysis of situational conditions under which motivational consistency is preserved or broken should be of great interest for environmentalists. The structural properties of strings of actions that are consistent or inconsistent with a given utterance have been analyzed by Nowakowska (1973a). This analysis, which by itself is a contribution to deontic logic, shows that the set of all strings that fulfill a promise (or break a promise) forms a so-called context-free language, in the sense of Chomsky (1957). These facts, obtained deductively, have deep implications; for instance, it follows from them that some social norms, especially the ethical ones, are (as a rule) formulated without specific references to situations that may serve as a context of their applicability. Thus, taking religion as an example, a sin is defined as a specific act, and its presence in a string of actions determines the qualification of this string (with few exceptions) regardless of the preceding or subsequent actions (i.e., regardless of the context [situation] in which the sin occurs).

Law may be thought of as somewhat more flexible, in the sense that it occasionally provides classes of contexts (situations) in which a given action constitutes an offense and classes of contexts in which it is not so. This amounts to the specification of strings of actions together with surrounding circumstances as offenses rather than as isolated actions. Again, however, the presence of a string constituting an offense qualifies the string of actions in which the offense is embedded. The preceding and subsequent actions may serve as a factor determining the punishment but (as a rule) not as a factor in qualification of the actions as an offense per se. The most serious offenses, such as murder, rape, arson, or theft, are qualified as offenses regardless of the context in which they occur. In this sense one can say that the theorems in question reflect certain general regularities of the treatment of social norms, namely the relative universality of contexts to which they apply.

POSSIBLE APPLICATIONS AND EXTENSIONS OF FORMAL ACTION THEORY: THE CONCEPT OF LANGUAGES OF SITUATIONS

Because of the aforementioned flexibility of the system of the basic concepts in the formal theory of actions, the theory has many possible applications. Among the most useful domains for different aspects of situational analysis are:

1. The theory of group actions, with the main concepts being cooperation, blocking, and conflict, leading also to a formal theory of organization (Nowakowska, 1973b), to a theory of social change (Nowakowska, 1978a), and in particular to a formal theory of alienation and freedom (Nowakowska, 1978b, 1979a).

2. Formal analysis of verbal actions (utterances), especially dialogues, thus explicating the structure and nature of the various ties operating in a dialogue (i.e., of semantic interrelations between consecutive utterances or of ties resulting from change of topic). Within the formal theory of actions it is also possible to analyze dynamically the person–situation interrelation (metaphorically, dialogue with the situation).

3. The multidimensional nature of the language of actions manifested in communication (Nowakowska, 1978c), in which the concepts of the multidimensional unit, meaning generation, support, inhibition, cancellation, etc., constituting the basic notions of dynamic semantics, are formally explicated.

All these notions, together with the concept of pragmatic semantics, can serve as useful tools for the analysis of different aspects of situations.

The recent development of the system of actions consists of "fuzzifying" its basic concepts (Nowakowska, 1980a). The central notions of the thus extended system are those of state, history (a sequence of state), and event (a set of histories), as well as the fuzzy relation of "causing" allowing a degree of control over changes of states. The novelty here lies in the introduction of families of languages of actions, with varying degrees of admissibility, allowing a rich analysis of the problems of attainability.

Formal action theory, based on algebraic linguistics, has, further, a dual function (Nowakowska, 1977, 1980a) in terms of automata and programs. In these contexts, the theory accepts other primitives, and it is possible to express all the concepts of action theory, including that of the language of actions.

Given the concept of the situational unit, one can introduce the interesting notion of the language of situations, in which elementary words are distinct basic situational units (relative to the goal of description), and expressions are strings of situations, satisfying some constraints on production of such strings, resulting from conventions, social procedures, and so on. A good illustration here is a sequence of situational units in education, profession, and so on, where there exist various rules for passing from one situation to another. This language of situations (i.e., admissible strings of situations) is of course fuzzy; that is, the notion of admissibility is graded. One has, therefore, a family of situational languages, with various admissibility levels.

Because these languages are goal-dependent, they are of local character, some of them independent and some partly ordered, forming certain hierarchical trees. The basic notions characterizing the strings of situations in such languages are those of complete possibility, positive and negative decisive moments, and so on. These notions give a description of man's fate, depending on the choice of situational language.

In a formal theory of actions each situation is identified with a language of actions, specific to the situation in question. In the present context, where strings of situations are the issue, one obtains, consequently, strings of action languages that constitute the strings in situational language.

Naturally, one can treat the present setup as before, as an underlying situation with its corresponding language. The situation is understood here as the set of constraints imposed by one's sex, social class, family wealth, and so on and hence is of a rather general character, and all elementary actions are choices of situations (e.g., choice of school or profession). This language of actions is therefore a set of admissible strings of special-action languages that one encounters or is restrained by in one's life.

At such a high level of generality, it is of course meaningless to speak of such notions as complete possibility, simply because the special-action languages that would play the role of time results have a nature different from "ordinary" results, understood as occurrences of some events. Nevertheless some notions of syntactics character can be transferred to the present case, such as positive or negative decisive moments (with respect to a given action language). For example, to become a ballet dancer (i.e., to acquire the "language of actions of ballet") one has to start sufficiently early, and if one has not entered ballet school by the age of 10 or so, the decisive positive moment has passed.

The language of situation results from specific action languages that during his or her life an actor learns not only to perform but also to organize into a higher-order language, which is constantly being developed, refined, improved, and so on. Languages of actions of different situations are of local character, even if they are on a high level of generality.

Languages of situations, as languages of higher order, allow analysis of the constraints on the transitions from one action language to another, that is, of a whole class of situations at once.

Two more remarks: First, situational psychology seems to be insufficiently interested in the problems of change. The main research questions concern significant aspects of situations. Perhaps one would have to introduce the concept of the core of the situation, which would enable a search for situational invariants, for various classes of transformations of situations, permitting the inclusion of some blurring or changing of the situation in time—but under the assumption that it has some fixed meaning. One would assume then that the standard fuzzy situational unit has some admissible temporal variability, such that it still allows recognition of the unit as having a given meaning.

Both the language of actions and the higher-order language of situations take into account the context of action and situation, which are so often missing in situational research.

Second, although the usefulness of the analysis of the structure of situations is beyond discussion, it is nonetheless necessary to look more carefully at the cognitive value of situational research. There exists a danger of overrating environmental constraints and of disregarding the fact that actors are thinking people, able to reason and to imagine. The essence of consciousness lies in its potential in a given situation to produce new possible situations, implied either by the actual situation or entirely independent of it; potential for continuous intervention in what is possible and what is impossible, for comment, for dialogue between situation and consciousness, and, most of all, for the possibility of leaving the given situation for some imagined "world"—that is, for some freedom of consciousness—that is only partly constrained by the actual and concrete. Thus, the miracle of consciousness gives ontological freedom in a situation.

In other words, the reality of man involves both surrender to conditions and also complete freedom from them—complete not in the aspects of reality but in the aspects of meaning, which is man's true reality.

The borderline between what is purely external and what is entirely internal does not really exist; if there is such a borderline, its existence is merely apparent and arises from simplifications and mental constructions. What is internal is to a large extent only a reply to the situation and is relative to it. What is external operates only through its meaning for a man, his will, and his decision.

Up to this point, this chapter has shown a number of possible approaches to and lines of development of situational research. It appears that formal semiotics (Nowakowska, 1967, 1976, 1978a, 1979b, 1980b) can offer a new type of paradigm that complements, extends, and modifies the actional paradigm already introduced.

The starting point is the aforementioned relationship between an object (situation) and its various representations on different levels of abstraction (conventional or not), which enables analysis of the structural and logical properties of objects–situations, and understanding of their pragmatical and incentive functions.

The analyses of perceived objects and their mappings into a set of descriptive sentences are the primary and simplest models in the study of situations— understood as sets of objects connected by certain relations—that is, as relational systems of objects. All other research of a statistical or even modeling type is derived from this first and basic step of the mapping of an object into a set of sentences constituting a verbal replica of it. The latter has the structure of a conjunction of classificatory statements, as well as presuppositions implied by the set of basic sentences, among them the most important being statements about the meaning of the objects. Some of these presuppositions may have causal character, whereas others may concern possible future states of the situation, and so on. These sentences constitute the basic material used later for construction of tools of measurement of objects by various psychological techniques (e.g., evaluatory scales or questionnaires).

The conditions under which the set of basic and derived sentences constitutes a measurement are in each case specified by various requirements imposed by the theory of scale construction; first of all, the principal requirement is monotonicity with respect to the trait measured.

It is possible to introduce (Nowakowska, 1979b) an algebra of objects, that is, a calculus of attributes that are composed of more elementary ones; such an algebra allows one to speak in a parsimonious way about the attributes–situation of many objects at once and about language of descriptors, that is, a mapping of some—but usually not all—composite attributes into elements of a certain vocabulary.

A verbal replica of an object (situation), expressed in a given language, is simply a specification of the attributes of this object, meeting the constraints of the language. It usually either has or is reducible to its normal form (i.e., the form of a conjunction of propositions "x is 1," where 1 is a term admissible as a descriptor for a compound attribute).

In general, such classificatory propositions are fuzzy and therefore lead to a fuzzy classification of objects in the space of attributes—that is, they lead to linguistic measurement of the object.

Now, a copy is faithful if all terms of the conjunction in its normal form are true. It is exact if it allows the object to be singled out unambiguously from the set of other objects on the basis of its verbal replica only. Exactness is, of course, a very strong requirement and usually is stronger than necessary; that is, it is sufficient to have the possibility of differentiating the given object from some other preassigned objects.

The possibilities here are very strongly language-dependent. To use a somewhat artificial, but illustrative, example, take an attribute such as length, which can take on a potentially infinite number of values. Suppose, however, that our "language" contains only two basic expressions: $1_1 = $ shorter than a matchbox, and l_2 = shorter than a pencil. The language thus contains l_1, l_2, their negations, conjunctions, etc. The composite descriptors would then be expressions such as l_2 and not $-l_1$ = shorter than a pencil but longer than a matchbox.

Clearly, within this allowed language, it is possible to characterize objects in terms of their lengths only to a certain extent, inasmuch as it permits just five categories: shorter than a matchbox, equal in length to a matchbox, longer than a matchbox but shorter than a pencil, equal in length to a pencil, and longer than a pencil.

This simple example, artificial as it may seem, shows the deep problem of attaining adequate descriptions of situations and the impossibility of going beyond the constraints imposed by the type and richness of the assumed languages.

It should be noted, incidentally, that a restriction as severe as that illustrated in the foregoing results from the fact that we have used a "poor" class of objects for comparison and also because we have allowed algebraic operations only on propositions and not on objects themselves. The limitations of language disappear almost completely if one is allowed statements of the form "longer than two pencils and one matchbox end to end" and so on.

This, however, is the case with such measures as length only; for measurement of personality, attitudes, various characteristics of situations, and so on we still face linguistic restrictions imposed by the vocabulary of elementary traits, attitudes, and so on. The language here imposes an upper bound that cannot be overcome by any statistical techniques, corrections, and so on. The process of inference, therefore, is constrained also by the accepted or existing vocabulary.

Another constraint, connected with the structure of the language of description (choice of basic notions), is imposed by the subset of possible meanings assigned to a given situation. For experimental purposes, one would want to deal with only those situations whose intersections of possible meanings across persons are large in number, that is, with those situations that one person interprets in much the same way as do others. Most often, such situations do not in fact obtain, both for psychological reasons, and, most of all, because the unit of situation is defined arbitrarily by social conventions, rules, law, function, and so on, and these are usually relative to the aim and context of study. Despite the fact that each situation has fuzzy boundaries and is a fuzzy unit changing in time, it is nevertheless sensible to speak of such units, defining them through specification of their cores (i.e., attributes of aspects that remain invariant under description and temporal changes).

15
Perceptions of Situations: Situation Prototypes and Person-Situation Prototypes

Nancy Cantor
Princeton University, USA

INTRODUCTION: BEHAVIOR, COGNITION, AND SITUATIONS

Students of social behavior have become increasingly attuned to both the *cognitive* and *social-situational* forces that shape and constrain behavior in social interactions. The cognitive generalizations about people and about situations that an actor brings to a social interaction can shape that interaction (Jones, 1977; Rosenthal, 1974; Snyder & Swann, 1978; Snyder, Tanke, & Berscheid, 1977). Social norms for behavior in particular situations and social models in a situation can further constrain an actor's behavior in a social setting (Bandura, 1977b; Mischel, 1968, 1973; Rotter, 1954). Social behavior is determined in large part by an interaction between cognitive and dispositional characteristics of the person and social and situational characteristics of the environment (Magnusson & Endler, 1977a).

These converging positions emphasize the *dynamic* character of personality; people adapt their behavior to fit their own expectations about a social situation and the expectations of others in the interaction. Cognitive generalizations about the self (Kelly, 1955; Markus, 1977; Rogers, Kuiper, & Kirker, 1977), about different types of people whom one encounters in social interactions (Cantor & Mischel, 1979; Cohen, 1977; Hamilton, 1979), and about the nature of social situations (Magnusson, 1974; Pervin, 1977; Price, 1974a; Schank & Abelson, 1977) all play a considerable role in determining social behavior. People's responses to other people may be determined in large part by their "set" to see certain kinds of behavior in certain situations and from certain types of people; behavior may emerge through a cognitive filter containing generalizations about

229

the self, others, and the situation drawn from past experiences in similar circumstances.

To the extent that social behavior is cognitively mediated, the personologist needs to pay increasing attention to the cognitive generalizations about the world that the lay perceiver maintains. The present chapter is concerned with one such set of generalizations; the shared beliefs about the nature and diversity of social situations in everyday life. The first section is concerned with the expectations that people have when they enter everyday life situations. It is concerned with psychological situations;[1] that is, the perceptions, feelings, and attitudes that lay people have in different social situations. The second section of the present discussion is devoted to the role that situational context and generalizations about situations may play in the perception and interpretation of social behavior. It questions the extent to which lay persons (actually) use knowledge about situations and attend to the particular features of a situation when interpreting the behaviors of other people. The final section of the present chapter returns to the lay psychologist's role as actor in social interactions. It focuses on the use of information about situations in planning and executing social behavior. In particular, individual differences in the maintenance of and reliance on cognitive generalizations about everyday life situations are hypothesized and discussed. Cognitive–behavioral strategies are proposed in which the lay person uses generalizations from past experience as well as social cues in the present situation to guide his/her own choice of behavior in social interactions.

1. The Intuitive Psychologist's Categorical Knowledge of Situations

Recent research (Bem & Funder, 1978; Frederiksen, 1972; Magnusson, 1974; Pervin, 1977; Price, 1974a; Schank & Abelson, 1977) suggests that the lay psychologist perceives situations as having "personalities"; that is, people expect certain kinds of behavior to occur in certain kinds of situations, certain types of people to be found in particular situations, and certain physical and social structures to be encountered in specific situations. For example, Price and Bouffard (1974) have found that people perceive some situations to be particularly restrictive in the kinds of behavior appropriate in the situation (e.g., church or job interview) and other situations (e.g., park or own room) to be relatively unconstraining. There also seem to be relatively standard behavioral scripts associated with many common situations (e.g., the birthday party script) and people seem to have relatively clear senses of the kinds of dispositional attributes

---

[1]The reader should note that I am using situation in a broadly defined sense to include all features (both physical and social) that the lay perceiver associates with a particular kind of situation. So, the associations to the psychological situation *being at a party* may include as many features of the people who inhabit parties as of the physical layout of the party situation.

likely to be exhibited in a large variety of common everyday situations (Cantor, 1978; Schank & Abelson, 1977). These data collectively suggest that lay people share a relatively extensive set of beliefs about situations.

Walter Mischel and I have recently investigated the lay perceiver's categorical knowledge about everyday situations; the nature and richness of the features commonly associated with different kinds of situations. Our strategy of research in this area has been to draw an analogy between the properties of categories used to label and describe common objects (like tables and chairs) and those used to classify everyday situations. In particular, we have borrowed extensively from recent "revisionist" perspectives on natural language classification (Smith & Medin, 1979). According to the revisionist position, categorical knowledge is structured around, and represented in long-term knowledge as, a *prototype* which captures the meaning of the category. The prototype serves as a symbol and reference point for the category. The category prototype can take on many forms depending on the domain: For instance, prototypes have been variously defined as (1) the central tendency of a set of geometric forms, defined as the mean value of the set of stimulus objects on each relevant feature dimension (Posner & Keele, 1968; Reed, 1972); (2) an abstract set of features commonly associated with members of a category, with each feature assigned a weight according to degree of association with the category (Cantor & Mischel, 1979; Cantor, Smith, French, & Mezzich, 1979; Rosch & Mervis, 1975; Smith & Medin, 1979); (3) or a representative set of exemplars of the category (Ebbesen & Allen, 1979; Medin & Schaffer, 1978; Smith & Medin, 1979; Walker, 1975). The abstract feature set prototype has been the one most extensively studied and used in investigations of natural language categorization (Rosch, 1978; Rosch, Mervis, Gray, Johnson, & Boyes-Braem, 1976). Cantor and Mischel (1979) and Cantor et al. (1979) have also found this form of the prototype model to be useful in characterizing the naive observer's beliefs about different categories of persons like extraverts, manic–depressives, and comic-jokers.

The prototype view (as articulated by Rosch, 1978; Smith & Medin, 1979) has provided a research strategy and a set of questions for the study of the naive observer's categorical knowledge of situations. In keeping with this approach, Mischel's and my strategy for investigating perceptions of situations has been as follows: (1) Establish taxonomies of commonly used situation categories. (Obtain agreement from naive subjects that these taxonomies represent hierarchies.) (2) Ask subjects to generate *prototypes* for each category in each taxonomy. Then extract the features listed by various subjects to describe the same category so as to obtain a *consensual prototype* for each situation category. (3) Examine these consensual prototypes to test hypotheses about the *richness* of situation prototypes, the *hierarchical orderliness* of situation taxonomies, and the *content* of the features commonly associated with everyday situations.

For example, in one study, we used the four situation taxonomies illustrated in Table 15.1. These taxonomies were chosen to "match" four taxonomies of

TABLE 15.1
Three-Level Situation Taxonomies

Ideological	Social	Stressful	Cultural
Being in an Ideological[a] Situation	*Being in a Social Situation*	*Being in a Stressful Situation*	*Being in a Cultural Situation*
Being at a Demonstration for a Cause[b]	*Being at a Party*	*Being Imprisoned*	*Being on a Tour*
Being at an antiwar[c] demonstration	Being at a fraternity party	Being in a county jail	Being on a tour of old English castles
Being at a save-the-whales sit-in	Being at a cocktail party	Being in a state penitentiary	Being on a tour of European museums
Being on a union picket line	Being at a birthday party	Being in a hospital for the criminally insane	Being on a tour of Roman ruin
Being at a Religious[b] Ceremony	*Being on a Date*	*Being at an Interview*	*Being at the Performing Arts*
Being at Sunday Mass[c]	Being on a first date	Being at a job interview	Being at the symphony
Being at a revival meeting	Being on a double date	Being at an admissions interview	Being at the ballet
Being at a bar mitzvah	Being on a blind date	Being at a psychiatric interview	Being at the theater

[a] = superordinate level

[b] = middle level

[c] = subordinate level

common personality categories used in previous work (Cantor & Mischel, 1979; Norman, 1963). The four situation taxonomies seem to cover a wide variety of the types of situations encountered in everyday life or communicated about in books or movies or television. Each taxonomy is a three-level hierarchy. We refer to the most inclusive categories like *social situation* as *superordinate* categories, categories like *party* as *middle*-level categories, and the lowest-level categories like *birthday party* as *subordinate* ones. Naive subjects were asked to verify (in a card-sorting task) the hierarchical (superset–subset) relations within each of the four taxonomies.

Using these taxonomies, we asked subjects to describe in their own words the features common to and characteristic of situations that belong to categories at different levels of abstraction. In this way, subjects generated for us ''prototype'' descriptions for situation categories that vary in inclusiveness from very superordinate categories like *social situations* to more moderate level categories like *parties* to very subordinate ones like *fraternity parties*. From these lists of features we then extracted the consensual features (excluding unique features listed by only 1 subject) listed as characteristic of each category of situations—this final list served as a *consensual prototype* written in the language of the naive observer to describe their perceptions of different types of situations. Three sample consensual prototypes are illustrated in Table 15.2.

The consensual prototypes suggest that people share relatively rich sets of beliefs about the characteristic features of a wide variety of different types of situations. Categories at all levels of abstraction in the four taxonomies had rich consensual prototypes (an average of 12 features). It is clear that consensual prototypes can be generated easily for common everyday situations. Such prototypes provide us with a view of the cognitive expectations associated with different types of situations. These data also resemble data collected on the prototypes for common object categories like tables and chairs and for person categories like extraverts and emotionally unstable persons (Cantor & Mischel, 1979; Cantor et al., 1979; Rosch et al., 1976). The finding of notes in those other domains is that the main increase in richness (number of features) in the consensual prototypes occurs between the superordinate and middle levels of inclusiveness in the taxonomies; the increase in richness levels off between the middle and subordinate levels of inclusiveness. Moreover, the prototypes for middle-level categories (both in our data and in data from other domains) tend to be more distinctive, sharing fewer features in common with neighboring rival categories than do those for the subordinate categories. Rosch and her colleagues (1976) have suggested that an optimal, *basic* level of categorization provides the observer with rich prototype information, although at the same time minimizing the redundancy in the information contained in the prototypes for neighboring categories. In this sense, then, ''middle-level'' situation categories (like parties and dates) may best conform to Rosch's criteria for basic-level categorization.

In addition to obtaining rich situation prototypes, we also found that the situation prototypes conformed well to criteria for taxonomic orderliness. The

TABLE 15.2
Sample Consensual Situation Prototypes

Being in an Ideological Situation (Superordinate)
    Arguing
    Discussion—talking
    Hard feelings—anger
    Stubbornness
    Aware
    Skepticism
    Priest
    Mutiny—desire revolt
Being at a Religious Ceremony (Middle)
    Candles
    Incense
    Silence
    Solemn people
    People dressed up
    Prayer
    Thinking—thought provoking
    Singing
    Boring
    Dark surroundings
    Alter—podium
    White robes
    Listening to priest
    Organ music
    Happiness
    Lots of people
    Church
    Books—Bibles
Being at a Revival Meeting (Subordinate)
    Preacher
    Togetherness
    Hallelujah brother
    Chanting
    Singing
    Bibles
    Emotion
    Refreshments
    Hot room—sweating
    Socializing
    Stupidity
    Loud—shouting
    Mind storming—faith healing
    Purpose in mind—dedication
    Fat men
    Obnoxious
    Clapping—dancing

prototypes for categories within the same branch of a taxonomy had more features in common ($\bar{x} = 4.42$) than did prototypes for categories within different branches ($\bar{x} = 1.05$) (p<.01) of the same taxonomy. For example, the prototypes for fraternity party and cocktail party shared more features than did those for fraternity party and double date. Similarly, prototypes for categories related by class inclusion relations shared greater numbers of features ($\bar{x} = 5.71$) than did pairs of categories from different levels *and* different branches ($\bar{x} = 1.21$) (p<.01) in a single taxonomy. For example, the prototypes for party and fraternity party were more similar than were those for party and double date. The orderliness of these situation prototypes is particularly impressive given that different subjects were always used to generate the prototypes for the categories used in these comparisons.

Analysis of the content of these situation prototypes revealed a very interesting fact about people's categorical knowledge about situations. In this and other similar studies, we found that a substantial percentage (averaging over 50%) of the features in the situation prototypes were actually features that described dispositional and behavioral characteristics of *people* commonly found in these situations (e.g., happy people at parties who dance and talk). Situation prototypes included both physical and dispositional descriptions of people, in addition to the expected physical and atmospheric descriptions of the actual setting. A substantial part of the consensual knowledge about situations is "psychological" in nature; it includes details about the most appropriate behavior for a situation, the feelings associated with "being in a situation" and the typical reactions and behavior of others in the situation. Situation prototypes, whether generated by asking people to imagine themselves in the situation or simply to describe such a situation, seem to be conceived and written in a very person-oriented language. In fact, it appears that *situation* prototypes are really *person-in-situation* prototypes; prototypes that provide the perceiver with information and expectations about the most likely and/or socially appropriate behavior for different types of everyday situations. These cognitive structures would seem to be ideal tools for the actor as he/she enters a social interaction and plans behavior for that situation.

Situation prototypes are not only rich in useful social content, consensual and well structured, but they are also easy for subjects to access. For instance, in a reaction time-imagery paradigm, Cantor, Mischel and Schwartz (1980) found that subjects were substantially quicker at forming an image of a typical situation (e.g., an athletic event) than of a particular type of person (e.g., an athlete); the "situation images" were also richer in content than were the "person images." Again, over 50% of the material in the situation images was descriptive of persons typically found in the situation. However, it seems to be easier for subjects to organize and access this knowledge via *situation* labels (e.g., an athletic event) than via either *person* labels alone (e.g., an athlete) or even *person-in-situation* labels (e.g., an athlete at an athletic event). Situation categories and situation prototypes seem to be very powerful and useful cognitive guides for structuring, describing, and perhaps interacting in the social world.

2. Attention to Situations: The Perceived Utility of
Context Information

People seem to have fairly rich and well-structured information about different types of situations. Is this information used and attended to in social interactions? Do the cognitive expectations that people have about the nature of situations influence their perceptions of the behavior of people in these situations? In recent years attribution theorists (Jones, Kanouse, Kelley, Nisbett, Valins, & Weiner, 1972; Ross, 1977) and social judgment theorists (Nisbett & Ross, 1979; Tversky & Kahneman, 1974) have suggested that lay observers insufficiently acknowledge the situational constraints that shape the behavior of other people. In their verbal reports, observers seem consistently to underestimate the power of the situation, locating the causes of behavior in the person rather than in the situation. When asked to predict the behavior of another person, observers seem to ignore information about the most typical behavior for the situation, focusing instead on the personality of the target individual. These results pose something of a paradox. Why would people have the kinds of knowledge about situations revealed in our data and in the data of other investigators (Magnusson, 1974; Price, 1974a; Schank & Abelson, 1977) and yet totally ignore this information in their conscious interpretations of the causes of other people's behavior?

There is at the present time no clear reconciliation of these apparently discordant findings. However, some progress toward a resolution seems to lie in a distinction between *direct* (consciously acknowledged) and *indirect* (implicit, unrecognized) effects of situational context on behavior perception. A *direct* effect occurs when a person interprets the behavior of another person as resulting directly from pressures in the situation. So, if a person is believed to have fallen because the stairs were slippery and not because he/she is clumsy (Jones et al., 1972; Ross, 1977), this interpretation would represent a direct effect of situational information on the attribution process. Similarly, if one were to predict another person's behavior in a situation directly on the basis of statistical baserate information, this too would suggest a *direct* use of situational information. In contrast, an *indirect* effect is a bit more complex and harder to identify. The indirect effect occurs when the perceiver explicitly focuses on the person's *personality or behavior* but makes an interpretation of this behavior that varies with changes in the context of observation. So, although not consciously attributing the causes of behavior to the situation, the perceiver's attributions about the other person's personality may be influenced nonetheless by aspects of the situation. For instance, if I observe some person acting cheery and friendly at a party, I may use the trait *extraverted* as a description of their personality. However, the same behavior observed at a funeral might lead me to revise my interpretation of this person's character, describing his/her behavior as weird rather than friendly (Jones & Davis, 1965). It is this sort of indirect context effect that seems most consistent with our knowledge of the ways of the intuitive psychologist (Ross,

1977). Knowledge and beliefs about the nature of situations may come to influence people's conscious interpretations of behavior only indirectly, in an implicit, unacknowledged manner.

A few brief examples of *indirect* context effects may help illustrate my point. Taylor, Fiske, Etcoff, & Ruderman (1978) have repeatedly shown that group composition influences the interpretations that perceivers will make of the behavior of a single individual in the group. So, for example, a single male in a group of females is perceived as more "macho" than when the same man is observed performing the same behavior in a group of other males. These results can be interpreted using a model developed by Tversky (1977).[2] According to Tversky (1977), when the solo male is viewed among the group of females the attribute of *gender* becomes *diagnostic* with regard to distinguishing between subgroups within the total group context. Having focused attention on the diagnostic attribute (gender) in the solo-group condition, the perceiver comes to exaggerate the differences between the subgroups on this dimension. In contrast, in the all-male group, gender is no longer a diagnostic attribute and attention will be focused on other attributes which serve to distinguish between group members or subgroups within the total context. Hence, by simply changing the group composition, a relatively slight change in context can come to have a powerful, albeit unacknowledged, *indirect* influence on person perception and the interpretation of social behavior. The perceiver is, then, unaware of the degree to which his/her perceptions were sensitive to subtle contextual cues.

Another demonstration of the indirect influence of situational context on the interpretation of behavior occurred in my own work on perceptions of person prototypicality (the degree to which a target person is perceived to be a good example of a certain type of personality). I (Cantor, 1978) asked subjects to read stories about target persons and to rate the degree to which each person was a prototypical example of an extravert (or, in another condition, of a bright, intelligent person). Each target person was described in three episodes and each episode occurred in a different situation. The subjects' interpretations of the behavior of these characters depended on the particular context in which the character was observed. For instance, a character who was described as *outgoing* in three situations that commonly elicit outgoing behavior (e.g., party, carnival, and pep rally) was rated as *less* prototypically extraverted than one who performed the same outgoing behavior but in situations in which such behavior is less common (e.g., library, bus stop, and post office). Subjects were willing to make the inference that the character who was outgoing at the library, post office, and bus stop would also be outgoing at the party, carnival, and pep rally. However, they were not as sure that the other character (the one observed at the

---

[2]We should note that this interpretation is somewhat different than the one provided by Taylor and her colleagues in their explanation of these data.

party, rally, and carnival) would be as outgoing if observed at the library, bus stop, and post office. This second character was perceived as less likely to be cross situationally outgoing and hence received a lower prototypicality rating. In these and other comparisons it became increasingly clear that the ratings of prototypicality with respect to *personality* attributes were being influenced by the *situational* context in which the target person was observed (see Cantor, 1978 for a fuller report of those data).

A recent study conducted by Judith Schwartz and myself provides another example of an indirect effect of information about the situational context on the interpretation of social behavior. In this study we asked subjects to read about interactions between two persons. The subjects were asked to play the role of one of the participants in the interaction, ignoring their own personality and assuming the stated character of this person. So, for example, they might be asked to play the role of a customer in a store trying to cash a check. Next, they were given three "clues" (bits of information about the interaction) and asked to rank order these clues in terms of their utility (informativeness) for predicting the outcome of the interaction. In the previous example this would mean that they were to rank order the clues as to their relative utility for predicting whether the cashier would cash their (the customer's) check. Subjects were told that another subject would actually be estimating the likelihood of the stated outcome on the basis of the one or two clues that they chose as most informative. The three clues were always of the following sort: (1) A *self* clue described the character of the person whom the subject was role playing. So, in the previous example, the customer might be described as very genuine and sincere, leaving a good first impression. (2) An *other* person clue described the personality of the other person in the interaction. So, the cashier might be described as a sweet trusting soul. (3) A *situation* clue described relevant features of the situation. For example, the store might have a very strict check cashing policy. Subjects always received one self clue, one other person clue, and one situation clue for each interaction item. However, these clues were varied according to the degree to which they were positive predictors of the occurrence of the relevant outcome. Each clue could be either a *positive* predictor of the outcome or a *negative* predictor of the outcome under consideration. For example, the situation clue described earlier is a negative predictor, or inhibitor, of the outcome in question (cashing the check) and the self and other clues are both positive predictors, or facilitators, of this outcome. Various different combinations of inhibiting (negative) and facilitating (positive) self, other, and situation clues were used in the experiment.

On the basis of previous research in the attribution tradition, we expected that subjects would not choose the situation clues over the self or other-person clues in this study. The data conformed to this prediction. A clear preference was found for self and other clues over situation clues under all circumstances. There was, thus, no *direct* preference exhibited for situation information—subjects were clearly not willing to ascribe much predictive utility to situational factors in social interactions. However, also as expected, an *indirect* effect of situation information on the relative preference for self versus other-person clues was observed. The self and other clues were perceived as equally informative *when* all three clues were either positive or negative predictors of the outcome of the interaction. However, when the situation clue was negatively related to the outcome and the other two clues both positively related to the outcome, the other-person clue was suddenly preferred over the self clue. This shift in preferences occurred on the basis of a single change in the situation clue, with the other two clues remaining the same. Again, whereas the information about situations was not *directly* perceived to be as informative for predicting the outcome of an interaction as self or other-person information, the situational information did influence the relative perceived utility of information about the self and the other person in the interaction. The lay perceiver attends to situation information, but only indirectly.

The three studies mentioned in this section suggest that the lay perceiver does not directly acknowledge the powerful influence that situational constraints can have on the nature and outcomes of social behavior and social interactions. The intuitive psychologist is by no means a situation theorist. Information about situations is not considered particularly important in predicting the outcome of a social interaction; people do not attribute the causes of other people's behavior to forces in the situation, and even when their perceptions are actually influenced by the nature of the observation context, this fact is not recognized by the lay theorist. Yet the lay perceiver is not solely a person theorist either. People are perceived in social contexts and their behavior is interpreted (perhaps automatically and without awareness) against this situational background. Interpretations, attributions, and attentional-focusing strategies change with alterations in the situational context. The lay psychologist is closest to a person-in-situation theorist.

3. Planning Social Behavior: Individual Differences in the Use of Information about Situations

Naive psychologists are not always in the role of (passive) interpreters of other people's behavior. They must also plan their own behavior in social interactions, respond to the behavior of others, and change/shape their behavior to fit the ongoing dynamics of the interaction. It is in this role as planner and actor that lay persons may draw (more or less consciously) on their vast store of knowledge about the prototypic configuration of behavior for different situations. In fact, one way to ''plan'' social behavior would be to focus on the interaction situation and shape behavior to fit with generalizations drawn from past experiences about the most ''ideal'' behavior for the situation. In other words, one could aim to be the ''prototypic person'' for that type of situation. What conditions might be conducive to the use of this situation-focused strategy? One of the classic findings in attribution research has been the tendency for actors to explain their own behavior in *situational* terms and to use more *dispositional* language to describe the behavior of other people (Goldberg, 1978; Jones & Nisbett, 1972; Nisbett, Caputo, Legant, & Maracek, 1973). In fact, the "actor" component of this actor–observer difference is one of the few examples in the literature of a *direct* effect of situational information on the interpretation of behavior. It is clear, then, that actors do occasionally use situational explanations when they think retrospectively about the causes of their own behavior. But, what about the prospective use of knowledge about situations in anticipating, planning, and executing social behavior?[3]

The recent trend in personality research to think in person × situation interactionist terms seems to be based in part on the assumption that people (again, more or less automatically) use information about situations to moderate and shape their behavior (Magnusson, 1971; Magnusson & Ekehammar, 1978; Magnusson & Endler, 1977a; Pervin, 1977). Although this seems to be an intuitively plausible and widely accepted assumption, really very little research has been conducted to attack directly this problem. One of the few lines of research on this topic is the work of Magnusson and his colleagues on the influence that perceptions of anxiety-arousing situations have on subjects' reports of the feelings that they would anticipate having in these situations (Magnusson & Ekehammar, 1975b, 1978). In a variety of paradigms they have shown that the same factors that account for subjects' perceptions of situations also emerge when subjects rate their likely behavior in these situations. This research suggests that perceptions of situations may in fact mediate people's (conscious or unconscious) choice of behavior in a situation. Another approach to this problem focuses on individual differences in the use of information about situations in social behavior.

One of the persistent themes in the study of individual differences has been the notion of an internality–externality dimension (Riesman, 1950; Rotter, 1966). A basic assumption in such research is that people differ in the degree to which they plan their behavior on the basis of external cues (e.g., are influenced by situational factors) as opposed to turning inward to some internal standard or disposition. One personality scale directed at measuring responsiveness to and reliance on external (internal) cues to behavior is the Snyder Self-Monitoring Scale (Snyder, 1974, 1979). The self-monitoring scale assesses the degree to which people monitor their self-presentation in order to fit the requirements of the situation, the external cues to social appropriateness. The high self-monitoring individual reports that he/she tries to be the "right person" for each new situation, paying attention to all external cues in the environment (emanating from other people or events in the situation) and trying to shape his/her behavior to fit

---

[3]It should be noted that I do not intend to convey the impression that people are necessarily "consciously" strategizing or "purposely" using knowledge about situations—planning social behavior to fit the requirements of a situation may well be a well-learned and fairly automatic process (see Bowers, Chapter 12, this volume).

in best in each new situation. Such individuals tend to change their behavior from situation to situation (Snyder & Monson, 1975), pay close attention to what other people do in the same situation (Berscheid, Graziano, Monson, & Dermer, 1976; Snyder, 1974), control their self-presentation through variations in their expressive behavior (Lippa, 1976), and exhibit minimal correspondence between their stated beliefs and their actual behavior (Snyder & Tanke, 1976). In contrast, low self-monitoring individuals place special value on their own beliefs, attitudes, feelings, and personal characteristics (Snyder & Tanke, 1976). The low self-monitoring individuals report that they try to be "true to their self-images and inner states," often ignoring external social comparison information (see Snyder, 1979, for a general review).

For the present purposes, self-monitoring is of interest in that it may represent a mediating factor in an individual's reliance on cues in the situation and generalizations about typical and/or appropriate behavior in such a situation. The high self-monitoring individual would seem (at least from self-report) to be the ideal candidate for the type of person who would focus on and make extensive use of information in the situation to guide behavior in social interactions. The high self-monitoring individual would seem to be the one most likely to make use of the kinds of categorical knowledge about situations documented in the earlier sections of this chapter. In particular, such a person is likely to be constantly in the position to draw on information about the "prototypic set of behaviors for a situation" in order to shape his/her own behavior according to these prototype guidelines. In fact, Snyder and Cantor (1979) have suggested that the high self-monitoring individual may plan behavior in a social interaction by forming a dynamic image or scenario of a person exhibiting the prototypic behaviors in such a situation and then simply "play out" (so to speak) the scenario in his/her own behavior. So, one can imagine the high self-monitor at a party forming a generalized image of an extravert at a party and acting according to this image, whereas the same person at a faculty meeting might turn serious and thoughtful according to the image of the prototypic academician at a faculty meeting. From situation to situation, such an individual would appear like a chameleon (Snyder, 1979), changing his/her behavior in accordance with the image of the prototypic set of behaviors for each situation. The social behavior of such a person would be directly shaped by generalizations that he/she had previously drawn about the nature of the situation and the ideal behaviors for such a situation. In other words, this is the kind of person who would use the situation-based focusing strategy described earlier.

Snyder and I have recently begun to test our hypothesis that the high self-monitoring individual will have and use a rich set of information about the nature of different types of social situations, the requirements implicit in such situations, and the prototypic configuration of behaviors for such situations. For example, in one study (Snyder & Cantor, 1979), we asked high and low self-monitoring individuals to consider their own self-image on a particular trait dimension (self-image condition) *or* an image of a prototypic-ideal person for that trait (prototype-image condition). They were asked, for example, to think about their own degree of extraversion *or* to imagine a prototypic extravert. For each of 20 trait dimensions, subjects were told to form their image (self or prototype) and then generate a list of *situations* in which either they or the prototypic person would be likely to exhibit the trait in question. The dependent measure was the number of situations listed per dimension and the prediction was for an interaction between self-monitoring and image condition; that is, we expected that high self-monitors would list greater numbers of situations (than low self-monitors) on the task involving prototypic-external images and that low self-monitors would list correspondingly more situations (than high self-monitors) on the task involving self-images. This is exactly the pattern of data obtained in this experiment. High self-monitoring individuals generated significantly greater numbers of situations in which a prototypic other person would be likely to exhibit a particular trait than did low self-monitoring individuals. And low self-monitors generated significantly greater numbers of situations in which they would exhibit a particular trait than did high self-monitoring individuals. As expected, high self-monitors seem to have richer knowledge (or more accessible knowledge) about general associations between traits and situations (as measured in the prototype condition). Low self-monitors seem to have correspondingly richer sets of knowledge about "internal" relations between their own behavior and situations in which they perform that behavior (as measured in the self condition).

The previous study is an indirect investigation of the use of knowledge about situations on the part of high and low self-monitoring individuals. It begins with images of types of *people* (self or prototypic people for various trait dimensions) and asks the subject to place those people in an appropriate situational context. To study more directly the self-monitor's use of situational knowledge, Snyder (personal communication, 1980) recently gave high and low self-monitoring individuals the chance to choose situations in which to participate. As expected, high self-monitors were more influenced in their situation choices by the clarity of the situational demands (situation-prototype clarity) than by any stated predispositions of their own. The reverse pattern obtained for low self-monitoring individuals. Individuals do seem to differ in the use they make of information about situations to plan social behavior.

CONCLUSIONS: PERCEPTIONS OF PERSONS IN SITUATIONS

The research summarized in this chapter presents something of a paradox. Lay people seem to have ready access to a rich and well-articulated set of structured knowledge about situations (Section 1). Yet, they do not appear to focus *directly* on the situation and use this knowledge when verbally interpreting the behavior of another person or in predicting the outcome of a social interaction (Section 2).

As pointed out before (Jones et al., 1972), the intuitive psychologist is a person-oriented theorist, one who focuses on persons and interprets behavior in dispositional and personal terms. The perceptions and interpretations of the lay psychologist are, however, not really context-free. People shape their interpretations of the behavior of other people according to the situation in which they observe the others' behaviors. Their tendency to focus on their own or other people's dispositions in predicting the outcome of a social interaction is similarly affected by the nature of the interaction situation (Section 2). Whereas the lay observer is primarily an observer of people and personality, he/she thinks in person–situation terms and is influenced (if only in an indirect way) by the situations in which a person is observed. Actually, it should be no surprise that the role of situation information in person perception is often an indirect one. As is clear in our studies of categorical knowledge about situations (Section 1), the lay perceiver has a very person-oriented set of generalized beliefs and thoughts about the nature of situations. Perhaps, then, it would be more appropriate to say that the lay person thinks about the social world in compound person–situation terms.

In their role as actors, intuitive psychologists do sometimes attend directly to the character of the situation in which a social interaction takes place. Interpretations of their own behavior are often framed in "situationist" terms, even as they look to personological explanations for the causes of another's behavior (Jones & Nisbett, 1972). Moreover, we know that at least some people look quite attentively to the external environment for cues to socially appropriate behavior in social interactions (Rotter, 1966; Schachter, 1964; Snyder, 1979). High self-monitoring individuals, for example, search the environment for cues as to the most socially appropriate behavior for each new situation (Snyder, 1979). Their attentiveness to situational cues is reflected in the richly developed set of cognitive generalizations that they have (drawn from past experience) about the nature of situations and the kinds of people typically found in particular situations (Section 3). However, even for these "situationists," knowledge of situations is framed in personological terms. So, for example, the high self-monitoring individual looks for cues as to the prototypic type of person or behavior for the situation at hand (Section 3). Knowledge about situations is used in the service of planning behavior and therefore it must really be person oriented (situational knowledge) in order to be of use to the perceiver and to the actor.

The moral of this story (if there is one) is that investigations of the role that cognitive generalizations about situations serve in social perception and social behavior must be tricky and sophisticated. One should not necessarily expect to find the lay perceiver and actor relying directly on these cognitive generalizations about situations in their interpretations and actions. Precisely because this knowledge is used in the service of interpreting *people's* behavior and planning a *person's* actions, it cannot be studied separately from its role in *social* interactions. The lay psychologist's knowledge about situations is not primarily physical or structural but psychological in nature. It is this psychological knowledge about situations, then, that we must study. However, this moral should be neither a surprise not a bitter pill to take. After all, as personality theorists ourselves, we would not be interested in the intuitive psychologist's knowledge about situations unless this knowledge served a psychological function in the interpretation and execution of social behavior. It is the *person* in situational knowledge that makes cognitive generalizations about situations interesting and important to study.

ACKNOWLEDGMENT

I would like to express my appreciation to the following people for their comments on earlier versions of this manuscript: E. E. Jones, Mark Snyder, John Kihlstrom, and Walter Mischel, as well as to David Magnusson and the members of the Stockholm Conference, June 17–22, 1979.

16 Assessing Situations by Assessing Persons

Daryl J. Bem
Cornell University, U. S. A.

The familiar assertion that behavior is a function of both the person and the situation is now as tiresome as the parental admonition that "it will never heal if you pick at it." But this was not always so. The belief that behavior is person-determined and transsituationally consistent is rooted in antiquity. Thus, Theophrastus (372–287 B.C.) inform us:

> A Penurious Man is one who goes to a debtor to ask for his half-obol interest before the end of the month. At a dinner where expenses are shared, he counts the number of cups each person drinks and he makes a smaller libation to Artemis than anyone.... If his wife drops a copper, he moves furniture, beds, chests and hunts in the curtains.... [Quoted in Allport, 1937, p. 57].

The situationist challenge to this personological view did not appear until 19 centuries later (an excessive publication lag even by today's standards), and the first situationist to rush into print appears to be Michel—(de Montaigne, not Walter):

> It has often seemed to me that even good authors are wrong to insist on weaving a consistent and solid fabric out of us. They choose one general characteristic, and go and arrange and interpret all a man's actions to fit their picture .... The surest thing, in my opinion, would be to trace [our actions] to the neighboring circumstances without getting into any further research and without drawing from them any other conclusions.... [pp. 118, 120]. Michel deMontaigne "Of the Inconsistency of Our Actions" (1580/1943).

Now because this is a volume on situations, and because I am known as a social psychologist, truth-in-packaging considerations compel me to declare at the outset that I have always been a closet personologist. It has now been 6 years since I came out, embracing not only personology but its most oppressed variant, idiographic personology. The tactical problem I faced at that time was how to declare an affectional preference for an idiographic approach to personality without appearing vulnerable to the situationist arguments of friends and colleagues like Mischel (Walter, not de Montaigne). At the time, my options were limited. I could punt. Or I could finesse (Bem & Allen, 1974):

> The failure of traditional assessment procedures and the belief that person–situation interactions will account for most of the psychologically interesting variance in behavior have led several recent writers to emphasize that personality assessment must begin to attend seriously to situations. We agree. We have merely chosen to emphasize the perfectly symmetric, but perhaps more subtle point that personality assessment must also begin to attend seriously to persons [p. 518].

With that holding action in print, I then sat down to ponder how one could incorporate the assessment of situations into the personological enterprise in some systematic fashion. In particular, I wanted some way of characterizing both persons and situations in a directly commensurate language (Murray, 1938).

In selecting such a language, I deliberately sought an assessment technique that would conform to the injunctions dictated by an idiographic approach to personality, a technique that would assess the relative salience and configuration of variables within individuals rather than the relative standing of individuals across variables. Accordingly, I chose the Q-sort technique, utilizing the items of the California Q set devised by Block (1961/1978). This Q set consists of 100 descriptive personality statements (e.g., "is critical, skeptical, not easily impressed") that are sorted by the assessor into nine categories, ranging from the least to the most characteristic of the person being described. Although not derived from any particular theoretical orientation, many of the items have a psychodynamic flavor, and both phenotypic and genotypic levels of description are included. An extensive description of the Q-sort methodology in general and a detailed history of the California Q set in particular will be found in Block (1961/1978).[1]

Q Sorts and Situational Description

The possibility that Q sorts might be useful for characterizing situations as well as persons has long been implicit in the work of Jeanne and Jack Block themselves; they have frequently characterized individuals who behave in particular ways in a setting by listing the Q items that correlate with the behavior (e.g., Block & Martin, 1955). For example, in an earlier Stockholm conference, Block

---

[1] All Q-sort materials used in our research and a 1978 reissue of J. Block (1961) are available from Consulting Psychologists Press, 577 College Avenue, Palo Alto, Calif. 94306.

listed several theoretically meaningful Q items that correlated with children's delay times in an experimental setting designed to assess delay of gratification. At the same time, he noted that a slightly different experimental procedure yielded no such meaningful pattern (Block, 1977). This suggests that Q-sort information sometimes can provide valuable knowledge about the experimental setting itself and perhaps help pinpoint the sources of behavioral inconsistency across seemingly similar situations.

To explore this possibility more systematically, David Funder and I also conducted a delay-of-gratification study, using a deliberately modified version of the paradigm that assesses how long children will wait in order to receive a preferred snack rather than a less preferred one available immediately (Bem & Funder, 1978). Q sorts of the children were provided by their parents, using the same California Child Q set devised and employed by Block and Block (1969). Each of the 100 items in the Q set was then correlated with the children's delay times. The resulting list of significantly correlated items is presented in Table 16.1.

TABLE 16.1
Q-Item Correlates of Delay Scores

Item	r
Positively correlated	
Has high standards of performance for self.	.48[a]
Tends to imitate and take over the characteristic manners and behavior of those he/she admires.	.39[b]
Is protective of others.	.39[b]
Is helpful and cooperative.	.36[a]
Shows a recognition of the feelings of others, empathic.	.35[c]
Is considerate and thoughtful of other children.	.34[c]
Develops genuine and close relationships.	.31[c]
Negatively correlated	
Appears to have high intellectual capacity.	−.62[a]
Is emotionally expressive.	−.56[a]
Is verbally fluent, can express ideas well in language.	−.50[a]
Is curious and exploring, eager to learn, open to new experiences.	−.49[a]
Is self-assertive.	−.47[b]
Is cheerful.	−.43[b]
Is an interesting, arresting child.	−.43[b]
Is creative in perception, thought, work, or play.	−.40[b]
Attempts to transfer blame to others.	−.37[b]
Behaves in a dominating way with others.	−.34[c]
Is restless and fidgety.	−.31[c]
Seeks physical contact with others.	−.31[c]
Is unable to delay gratification.	−.31[c]

[a]$p < .01$ (two-tailed).
[b]$p < .05$ (two-tailed).
[c]$p < .10$ (two-tailed).

The positively correlated items listed in the table draw a portrait of the long-delaying child that, according to Mischel, is quite consistent with the developmental literature on ego control and prosocial behavior (personal communication; Mischel, 1974). Thus we see a child who, through identification ("tends to imitate and take over the characteristic manners and behavior of those he/she admires"), adopts high standards of performance; becomes protective of others; and is helpful, cooperative, empathic, considerate, thoughtful, and capable of developing close relationships. Additional support for an ego-control interpretation comes from some of the negatively correlated items, including, of course, the crucial item "is unable to delay gratification." For example, the long-delaying child is seen to be emotionally unexpressive and not restless or fidgety, attributes consistent with the expressive and motoric inhibition implicated in the development of ego control (Mischel, 1966).

But the remainder of the portrait sketched in Table 16.1 introduces a more dissonant note, a picture of the long-delaying child as not very intelligent, not verbally fluent, not eager to learn, and not open to new experiences; a child, moreover, who is not self-assertive, cheerful, interesting, or creative. The very strong negative relationship between delay and rated intelligence is particularly inconsistent with theories of ego control, and Mischel reports that he finds delay time to be positively correlated with rated intelligence in his own work (personal communication). Indeed, the gestalt that emerges from this entire set of Q items suggests that the child who delays in this situation is as accurately described as one who is dull, passive, and obedient to adult authority as he or she is described as one who possesses a large amount of self-control.

The important point to be emphasized here is how this Q-item portrait points rather directly to the properties of the situation that appear to be both salient to the children and functionally controlling. Thus it would appear that the presence of the experimenter and the implicit social desirability of delaying are as salient to the children in this setting as the differential attractiveness of the two food items, the stimulus that, on theoretical grounds, is supposed to be the controlling variable. This illustrates how the Q sort can function as a valuable instrument for detecting theoretically extraneous features of an experimental situation that are affecting the subjects' behaviors.[2]

It is instructive to contrast this Q-sort portrait with the one presented by Block (1977). In the Blocks' experiment, the child was shown a gaily wrapped gift and was told that it was to remain unopened until he or she completed a puzzle. The measure of "delay of gratification" was the length of time the child waited

---

[2]In a further illustration, Mischel has now rerun the Bem-Funder procedure on a fresh sample of children, children who had not had the kind of previous experience in this setting that our sample had. The theoretically congruent Q items again emerge as significant correlates of delay times, but the dull-passive-obedient cluster of items does not (Mischel, personal communication), suggesting that possible practice effects need to be taken into account in these kinds of experiments. Again the Q sort serves as a valuable diagnostic tool.

before reaching out and taking the gift. Table 16.2 shows the Q items that were most highly correlated with delay in this setting.

As seen in Table 16.2, the item "is unable to delay gratification" is the best single predictor of the children's delay time. Moreover, several of the other items appear to support the interpretation that this situation is, in fact, tapping a dimension of impulse control: "planful, thinks ahead"; "attentive and able to concentrate"; "is reflective; thinks and deliberates before acting."

But it is clear that Tables 16.1 and 16.2 draw very different portraits of the long-delaying child; even the items relevant to the construct of ego control in the two tables show very little overlap, and the dull–passive–obedient cluster of items that emerged in our experiment is completely absent from the Blocks' data. What we have here, then, are two situations that appear conceptually equivalent but that are functionally quite different, and it would appear that different subsets of children are delaying in the two settings. One typically learns only that behavior across two theoretically similar situations is disappointingly inconsis-

TABLE 16.2
Q-Item Correlates of Gift Delay Times
(After Block, 1977)

Item	r
Positively correlated	
Is planful, thinks ahead.	.37
Is reflective, thinks and deliberates before acting.	.35
Becomes strongly involved in what he/she does.	.31
Is attentive and able to concentrate.	.31
Uses and responds to reason.	.30
Is shy and reserved, makes social contacts slowly.	.27
Is protective of others.	.27
Tends to keep thoughts and feelings to self.	.26
Has an active fantasy life.	.25
Negatively correlated	
Is unable to delay gratification.	−.47
Attempts to transfer blame to others.	−.37
Has rapid shifts in mood, emotionally labile.	−.33
Is aggressive (physically or verbally).	−.32
Tries to take advantage of others.	−.31
Has transient interpersonal relationships.	−.28
Is restless and fidgety.	−.26
Emotional reactions are inappropriate.	−.26
Overreacts to minor frustrations, easily irritated.	−.26
Is stubborn.	−.25
Expresses negative feelings directly and openly.	−.25

Note. All correlations in this table are estimates based on the sex-separate correlations reported by Block (1977). I have reproduced here the 20 items with the largest estimated mean correlations.

tent. By collecting Q-sort data, however, one can see in exquisite detail the nature of that inconsistency and draw plausible inferences about its source in the nonoverlapping features of the settings. At the very least, Q-sort information provides valuable guidance to the investigator who needs to redesign an experimental procedure so that it serves its intended conceptual purposes. Even psychologists who have no particular interest in individual differences per se should welcome this entree into the phenomenology of the situations they have created.

The Template-Matching Technique

The delay-of-gratification studies described previously illustrate that Q sorts themselves can provide valuable knowledge about an experimental setting after the fact, in a "context of discovery." The next step was to deploy this tool more conceptually, so that it could serve to assess situations in the "context of justification" as well. This was the origin of the template-matching technique, a formalization of a procedure we use often in everyday life to describe situations (Bem & Funder, 1978).

Consider, for example, a student who wants to know how he or she would fare at a particular college. Note that this is a question about person–situation interaction in that the student is not interested in his or her potential performance at colleges in general or in how students in general do at this particular college. What the student seeks is information about how his or her unique characteristics mesh or interact with the unique characteristics of that particular college. One particularly common way to give such a student information about the college is to describe how several types of students fare there: "Students with varied interests tend to get caught up in extracurricular activities, have a marvelous college experience, but get rather poor grades; students who work hard but are somewhat shy obtain good grades but are unlikely to have much interaction with the faculty; students who . . . , " and so forth. With this kind of description in hand, the student has only to match his or her own characteristics to the various "templates" we have provided in order to predict his or her probable outcome at the college. Rather than describing the college in terms of the physical plant, faculty–student ratios, graduation requirements, and so forth, we have instead characterized it in terms of a set of template-outcome, or template-behavior pairs. The language system used to characterize the situation is the same system the student uses to characterize himself or herself. (See Cantor, Chapter 15 this volume for evidence that laypeople themselves categorize situations in this way.)

What Bem and Funder (1978) proposed formally, then, is that situations be characterized as sets of template-behavior pairs, each template being a Q-sort description of an idealized "type" of person expected to behave in a specified way in that setting. One then predicts the behavior of particular persons in that setting by comparing their own Q sorts with each template in turn and predicitng that they will display the behavior associated with the template of closest match or greatest similarity. The nice feature of Q sorts in this context is that two sorts can be compared with one another simply by computing a Pearson product-moment correlation across the items, thereby expressing directly and quantitatively the degree of similarity between the two profiles. Thus if one has constructed a Q sort of some hypothetical ideal personality—our "template"—one can correlate the Q sorts of actual individuals with this idealized sort in order to assess their similarities to the template. Although a Q sort of an individual is obtained by having an assessor actually sort the items into categories, constructing a template requires a different method for assigning numerical values to the items because only a small number of items will be relevant to any particular template. The actual method for constructing a template once one has identified the subset of relevant items is described in Bem and Funder (1978) and discussed further by Green (1980).

Probing the Ecological Validity of the Mixed-Motive Game

One of the first tests of the template-matching technique as a conceptual tool for assessing situations was a study by Bem and Lord (1979) designed to probe the ecological validity of a classical experimental setting in social psychology, the mixed-motive game (e.g., the Prisoner's Dilemma Game). We selected the mixed-motive game as a testing ground because it is widely used, frequently criticized, and the debate between its proponents (e.g., Kelley, Shure, Deutsch, Faucheux, Lanzetta, Moscovici, Nuttin, Rabbie, & Thibaut, 1970) and its critics (e.g., Knox & Douglas, 1971; Nemeth, 1972; Pruitt, 1967) appears to epitomize the field's more general concern with the issue of ecological validity: Do people behave in real life as they behave in our laboratories?

It will be recalled that in the mixed-motive game, two subjects simultaneously are required to make a series of decisions independently of one another and with no communication between them. The payoff to each subject is contingent upon both of their choices. Thus in the Prisoner's Dilemma Game, the most familiar of the mixed-motive games, when both subjects select the "cooperative" response, their joint payoff is high; when both select the "competitive" response, their joint payoff is low; when one subject selects the cooperative response and the other the competitive response, the latter (the "defector") earns points or money at the expense of the cooperator.

We used the so-called "decomposed" versions of mixed-motive games introduced by Messick and McClintock (1968). These games enable investigators to move beyond the simple cooperative–competitive dichotomy and to distinguish three distinct strategies of play: a strategy in which a player attempts to maximize the joint gain of both players; a strategy in which a player attempts to maximize his or her own absolute gain; and a strategy in which a player attempts to maximize his or her gain relative to that of the other player. Typically it is found that individuals adopt one of these strategies consistently throughout an experiment.

We constructed templates for the mixed-motive game situation by supplying a written description of the three strategies to five judges along with the list of Q-sort items. Each judge went through the list and rated each item in terms of how characteristic it was of a person following the strategy. For example, the item "behaves in a giving way toward others" was given a high rating by all the judges when they were characterizing the strategy in which players attempt to maximize the earnings of both themselves and the other player. The judges were directed explicitly not to be personality theorists (i.e., not to speculate about remote personality correlates of the behavior) but rather to judge only whether an item might or might not characterize the behavior involved in the strategy itself. This procedure was repeated for each of the three strategies, yielding for each a template characterizing the hypothetical ideal person who pursues that strategy.

We then recruited subjects to participate in an actual mixed-motive game experiment. Q sorts of the subjects were obtained from their roommates, and these were correlated with each of the three templates. The results supported the ecological validity of these mixed-motive games: The subjects' Q sorts were correlated significantly higher with the template characterizing the strategy they actually adopted in the laboratory than they were with the templates characterizing the alternative strategies. These individuals did, indeed, behave in real life as they behaved in the experimental laboratory.

As in the delay-of-gratification studies, the Q-sort data provided insight into the subjects and the strategies well beyond the success of the template-matching procedure itself. We found, for example, that the woman who pursued the highly competitive strategy in which the major concern is beating the other player by the widest margin was described by her roommate as subtly negativistic, tending to undermine, obstruct, or sabotage; keeps people at a distance; avoids close interpersonal relationships; does not behave in a sympathetic or considerate manner; and so forth. In contrast, these women characterized themselves as tending to arouse liking and acceptance in people, to be personally charming, and feminine, and to have social poise and presence. Not surprisingly, their roommates rated these women significantly lower than they rated themselves on the item "has insight into her own motives and behavior." Note that Q sorts provided us with three distinct kinds of information: peer perceptions, self-perceptions, and discrepancies between the two.

Testing Competing Theories of Situations

To show that the template-matching technique could serve even more explicitly theoretical ends, Bem and Funder (1978) deployed it as a vehicle for testing competing social–psychological theories against one another. Again we chose a classical experimental setting, namely, the forced-compliance experiment. In such an experiment, individuals are required to advocate attitudes contrary to their own positions. The classical finding is that, subsequent to their compliance (and under theoretically specified conditions), individuals report attitudes that are closer to the advocated positions than were their initial attitudes. Several theories offer explanations for this effect. Cognitive dissonance theory, the original source of the paradigm, asserts that an aversive state of "dissonance," aroused by the discrepancy between their behavior and their contrary attitudes, motivates subjects to change their attitudes (Festinger & Carlsmith, 1959). Self-perception theory (Bem, 1967, 1972) proposes that the subjects observe their own behavior of advocating the designated position and then infer their final attitudes from that behavior in much the same way that an external observer of their behavior would do. A third group of theories emphasizes the self-presentational demands of the setting and suggests that the final attitude reports given by subjects are motivated primarily by an attempt to make a particular impression on the experimenter (Tedeschi, Schlenker, & Bonoma, 1971), evaluation apprehension (Rosenberg, 1965, 1969), or a desire to project a particular "situated identity" to themselves as well as to others (Alexander & Knight, 1971).

First we derived a separate template for each theory, a Q sort of the hypothetical person who, according to each theory, should show the most attitude change in that situation. This was accomplished by having three psychologists who have been active researcher/theoreticians in the forced-compliance paradigm independently select those Q-sort items that would characterize the attitude changer according to each theory.

College undergraduates then participated in a classical forced-compliance experiment, and Q sorts were obtained on each subject from two of his or her acquaintances. Each subject's Q sort was correlated with the template constructed for each theory, and the template-similarity scores obtained for each theory were then correlated with the attitude-change scores; the higher this correlation, the better the theory was predicting attitude change. In this way, the theories were pitted against one another in predicting the individual-difference variance in attitude change.

The results showed that cognitive dissonance theory was not successful at predicting attitude change, the template-similarity scores actually correlating negatively with attitude-change scores, $r = -.25$; self-perception theory was moderately successful, $r = .35$, $p < .10$, two-tailed; and, self-presentation theory was the most successful of all, $r = .53$, $p < .005$, two-tailed.

As we noted, the study did demonstrate that the self-presentation template accounted for more of the individual-difference variance in attitude change than the other templates, but it might be that some theories are simply more capable of generating individual-difference predictions than others, and a greater ability to predict person effects does not strictly imply a greater ability to predict situation effects. Thus we ran only the "choice" condition of the typical forced-compliance experiment, and our contest required the theories to account for within-cell variance (person effects); conceivably our winners and losers could have fared differently in a battle over the between-cell variance (situation effects). Indeed, most social–psychological theories are designed to predict treatment differences, including the theories tested in our study. It was only we who coerced them into playing the unaccustomed role of personality theories.

But this points up the real value of the template-matching technique: If personological theories have not lived up to expectations because they have limited themselves to person effects in a world populated by person–situation interactions, then neither should we be hopeful about theories that limit themselves to situation effects. The template-matching technique thus provides a potential tool for expanding such social–psychological theories into genuine theories of person–situation interaction. Additional studies have pursued this potential capability of the technique. For example, Funder (1979) employed template matching in a forced-compliance experiment that required the theories to address both within-cell and between-cell variance. Ransen (1980) used the procedure to probe the possibility that different theories account for the debilitating effects of extrinsic rewards on intrinsic motivation at different ages. Although it is still too early to tell, the hope is that the template-matching technique might provide a systematic way of going beyond the simple detection of interaction effects to their explanation and hence begin the development of integrated theories of persons-in-situations.

Assessing Persons by Assessing Situations

As noted at the outset, the template-matching technique was devised in order to preserve and defend my enthusiasm for idiographic personology against the challenge that one must "attend seriously to situations." But a funny thing happened on the way to the clinic: I seem to have lost my client, the individual person. The first clue was that my research appeared to have a number of useful things to say to experimental social psychologists, including those who have no interest in personality variables whatever, but vanishingly little to say to those personologists whose ranks I thought I had joined. Worse, after presumedly renouncing my former life-style as a social psychologist, I had continued to have brief encounters of the 60-minute kind with my subjects, running them through mixed-motive games and—God forbid—yet more forced-compliance experiments!

It was Stanford colleague Curt Hoffman who made the first suggestion for getting the enterprise back to the "perfectly symmetric, but perhaps more subtle" problem of attending seriously to persons. Hoffman proposed that we should pursue the mirror image of the template-matching technique: Rather than characterizing situations with templates couched in the language of personality, we should characterize persons with templates couched in the language of situations. Rather than describing a situation in terms of how a set of hypothetical ideal persons respond within it, we should describe a person in terms of how he or she responds in a set of hypothetical ideal situations. For example, we might give an individual a set of items describing properties of situations (e.g., "is unstructured"; "encourages or demands independence"; is characterized by the presence of an authority figure") with the instruction to construct a template or prototype that describes the idealized situation that makes him or her the most anxious; a second template might characterize the hypothetical situation that would evoke the most self-confidence or the greatest sociability; and so forth. If one wished to predict the individual's responses in a novel situation, one would match that situations's characteristics to the person's several templates and predict that he or she would display the responses associated with the most similar template. This, then, is a scenario that responds to my earlier self-injunction to go forth and be idiographic.

It is also a scenario that can respond to injunctions from several other personologists who achieved grace before I did. For example, by asking individuals to construct prototypes of situations that evoke particular affects in them, we can heed Pervin's observation that affective rather than behavioral reactions probably mediate the degree to which individuals respond to situations as similar to one another (Pervin, 1977). (It is pertinent to note that behavioral therapists employ a special case of this procedure when they seek to construct a client's stimulus hierarchy for anxiety.) Similarly, by asking individuals to construct templates or prototypes of situations they generally approach or avoid, we can attend to Wachtel's reminder that persons in real life do not have situations imposed on them by experimenters but exercise considerable choice over the circumstances that influence their behavior (Wachtel, 1973).

The construction of templates or prototypes is but one possible variant of the general approach being advocated here. We also can ask the individual to characterize particular situations. Just as we have used the California Q set to characterize both hypothetical ideal individuals (the templates) as well as actual individuals, so too, we can use the same set of situation-feature items to characterize both the individual's situational proptotypes as well as his or her definition of particular concrete situations. To put this a bit more formally, we can define a situation as an unordered or unweighted feature list (our item set) and define the psychological or "interpreted" situation as the individual's own salience ordering or weighting of those items. By extension one can intercorrelate several such "situational Q sorts" from an individual and construct his or her situational-equivalence classes from the resulting similarity matrix. This, in fact, constitutes yet another alternative for arriving at an individual's prototypes. If the situations to be characterized by this technique are drawn from each individual's own daily life, we then arrive at a technique quite similar to Pervin's method of factor-analyzing situations according to the person's reactions to and situation-trait ratings of those situations (Pervin, 1977).

These last suggestions, however, raise a more general issue concerning the meaning of similarity among situations. The models of similarity employed in most of the research on situations are the familiar metric and dimensional models to which we have become accustomed in psychology (Magnusson 1978). Indeed, this is the implicit model behind the template-matching technique as well. In my view, however, situations are similar to one another in ways that violate these models and conform more closely to the set-theoretic, feature-matching models introduced by Tversky (1977) and by Ortony (1979). For example, most models of similarity require that the similarity of A to B be the same as the similarity of B to A. We already know that this does not hold for similarity measures based on trait implication. Thus the probability that a person is witty, given that he is intelligent, is not the same as the probability that he is intelligent, given that he is witty (J. Block, private communication). Similarly, Little Hans reacted to horses as if they were similar to his father; he did not react to his father as if he were similar to a horse. In general, the similarity of two situations would seem to be a function of the number of salient features they share with one another, the number of features unique to one or the other of them, and the distinctiveness of both their shared and unshared features within the context of all the situations in the comparison set. This is precisely the kind of similarity embraced by the Tversky and Ortony models, models that can handle even qualitatively different kinds of similarity simultaneously—including the symbolic and metaphorical similarity exemplified by Little Hans.

The case of Little Hans also points up the fact that the present set of suggestions is as deficient as most other current research programs in this area at meeting Wachtel's challenge that we include the assessment of unconscious processes in our schemes (Wachtel, 1977). Like most current research programs, those I have advocated rely heavily on conscious self-report and would have to be supplemented by other assessment techniques to meet this challenge. It is unlikely that Little Hans would have generated the situational feature "reminds me of dad" or that any a priori list of situational features would contain such an item. Perhaps we can devise something short of inviting each individual's therapist to be a coparticipant in the research.

And finally we need to consider the role of theory in this enterprise. The research in this area seems long on clever methods and short on substantive theory. The template-matching techinique is just that, a technique. So, too, are the suggestions made in this last section. As we have seen, however, the template-matching technique can, in principle, adopt any of several existing theories of situations—social–psychological theories of conditions producing attitude change, for example—and push them to expand into theories of person-situation interaction. In analogous fashion, the mirror-image template-matching technique, using a set of situational descriptors, can adopt an existing personological theory and push it to incorporate situational factors. I regard Jeanne and Jack Block's theory as one very promising candidate for this purpose (Block & Block, 1979). It is a theory in the grand tradition; it is idiographic in that it deals with an interacting system of variables within the individual; it can handle unconscious as well as conscious processes; the Blocks' own longitudinal work has already shown that it can make pinpointed predictions about situational factors; and, finally, the Q-sort technique is, not accidentally, an intergral part of the research on their theory.

As for Michel de Montaigne (1580/1943), to whom I referred at the outset, even he came around a bit to personology in his essay, while ending with a refreshing alternative to the usual call for more research: "It is not a matter for a calm mind to judge us simply by our outward actions; we must sound the inside and see what springs set us in motion. But since this is a high and hazardous undertaking, I wish fewer people would meddle with it [p. 126]."

17

Life Situations and Episodes as a Basis for Situational Influence on Action

Lennart Sjöberg
University of Göteborg, Sweden

In interactionistic research on personality the study of how situations influence action has become a topic of central interest (Endler & Magnusson, 1976a, 1976b; Magnusson & Endler, 1977b). A basic theme in interactionistic approaches is to conceive of behavior as a function of person and situation (Ekehammar, 1974). The situation is often seen as possible to describe in much the same way as persons are described, and such descriptions may be useful in accounting for behavior together with person variables. Indeed, Magnusson (1978) conceived of a differential psychology of situations, to be developed along the lines of the established differential psychology of persons. Pervin (1978b) also gave an extensive review of work on situations with this particular orientation. The present paper discusses a different approach, where the person as an active agent is in focus. Action is studied in situations rather than as a function of situations. Situations are considered in different roles, depending on how they influence action. Additional comments on other approaches are, however, in order.

If our purpose is to study the influence of situations on behavior, we must start by defining situations with reference to some conceptual framework. Three alternatives may be mentioned. First, situations may be described to the individual and he may be asked to report his experience with the situations or his imagined experience with the situations or a combination of these two. This is a common approach in the study of person–situation interaction. There are two obvious problems with this approach: (1) situations are not fully brought into mind because the experimenter can describe them only at the surface and externally; and (2) various conceptual and memory distortions may strongly influence the judgments made by the subject. In my view, it is regrettable that so much work is still being carried on with conceptions of behavior and situations rather than actual studies of real actions in real situations. The study of conceptual systems is, of course, important, but it cannot be a substitue for the study of real actions. The second approach is to define situations externally but to study actual behavior rather than the conceptions or expectations that people have about their own behavior in such situations. This would involve studying, say, emotional responses in a threatening situation rather than asking what emotional responses one expects to emit in such a situation. The trouble with this approach is that it still defines the situation from external considerations only. People may for several reasons experience and interpret any set of external circumstances in very different ways, and their actions may have little to do with a particular set of external conditions at any point in time. The actions, rather, may reflect ongoing internal events superseding any external conditions within a considerable range of such conditions.

So far the term *behavior* has been used when referring to previous work and *action* has been used as a preferred alternative. What is the difference? "Behavior" is a very broad concept, and the term has many connotations. It can refer to any organismic process studied by psychologists: movement of muscles, thoughts, feelings, etc. And it can be described by means of many conceptual systems but most often in terms of performance. I prefer "action" because the term has fewer denotations (and mentalistic rather than mechanistic connotations). An action is a process of goal-directed mental activity. It is often largely conscious and is then experienced as something being done. A natural way of describing action is to start by questioning a subject about what he is doing. One could, naturally, also describe actions in performance terms but then a problem arises (Sjöberg, 1971). How can one evaluate success if one does not know what was intended? So in order to study performance one really needs well-grounded knowledge about intentions or there is a risk that one must rely on overtly simplistic instructions.

All mental activity is not action according to the definition given. Dreams, day dreams, and emotions constitute obvious cases of other types of mental processes.

A third approach in the study of situational influence on action would involve studying people in naturally occurring situations and finding out what their actions in such situations are, an approach favoured by Harré and Secord (1972). Here the set of external conditions at any point of time constitutes only one part of the whole situation the individual finds himself in.

External conditions are both physical and social and they may instigate, facilitate, guide, or block action. People differ greatly, of course, in terms of what problems or possibilities external conditions may offer to them and also in terms of what facilities or blockings that conditions constitute once action is started. Normally, basic needs are satisfied by the person through his organizing events and resources in stable ways. Possibilities for stability may be ecologically quite accessible, even if the needs of any person are relatively unique. This means that the person partly creates his own stability.

Brunswik's (1956) requirement of ecological representativity of situations studied (see also Sjöberg, 1971) did not involve an attempt to specify just *how* situations may influence action. In so-called ecological psychology (Pawlik, 1978), Barker (1968) has suggested that behavior is strongly influenced by norms and physical conditions organized in behavior settings. This assumption appears to be well-justified but cannot account for the choice of which settings to enter. Such choices apparently reflect plans of individuals and cannot be explained directly by situational influence on action.

The individual's life situation may be defined as a relatively stable set of needs, abilities, conceptual structures, and external conditions (Lewin, 1935, 1936, 1951c). Conceptual structures may be differentiated according to values and knowledge, and the relation between beliefs and values is an interesting problem of its own (Sjöberg, 1976, 1978). Action at the internal level is triggered off by a constant interaction of wishes arising from needs and values (Persson & Sjöberg, 1978; Sjöberg & Johnson, 1978; Sjöberg & Samsonowitz, 1978). In the process, abilities and knowledge are utilized to attain goals in interaction with external conditions. Plans are formed and carried out (Miller, Galanter, & Pribram, 1960; Schank & Abelson, 1977).

Because actions are goal-directed, they may be defined as existing from the time they are instigated until the goal is reached or the attempt is finally given up. Any action thus defines a certain interval of time as an episode (Harré & Secord, 1972). Certain episodes may be very brief and others may be very long. Because several actions may be processed simultaneoulsy, there is often a set of episodes that are being pursued at the same time.

In any episode we may assume that there is a chain of various subacts and that early subacts tend to be seen as instrumental and of value only in leading toward the goal, which constitutes some kind of consummatory action that is seen as a value in itself. This does not mean, however, that activity is purely instrumental or purely consummatory, only that it may be dominated by one or the other of these two aspects. We would, however, expect activity to be instrumental more often than consummatory, inasmuch as we live in a world in which all desired things have a price.

Rommetveit, Chapter 10, this volume, pointed to the intricacies involved in interpreting actions and stressed, in particular, the muliplicity of possible accounts for any given act. Nevertheless, it seems useful or unavoidable to persist in the belief of the existence of one true interpretation, even while admitting the difficulty of finding it in any concrete case.

Some acts are triggered in an obvious and compelling way by external conditions. Such acts, strictly speaking, may also be instrumental, but because they are perceived in a special way as contingent on external conditions it may be more fruitful to classify them as situationally caused. It also seems likely that actions that are seen as situationally caused may be considered as less significant in terms of their importance in the life situation and ongoing episodes of the individual.

An action may reflect the present life situation of an individual. Such an action is presumably seen as characteristic and relatively common in the life of the individual. Alternatively, an action may constitute an episode of change. It may be seen as a way of brining about some kind of desired change. An episode directed toward bringing about change may be seen as meaningful or significant rather than as characteristic or common. In both cases, actions may be seen as instigated externally or internally and as blocked or facilitated internally or externally.

There are several other aspects of actions that may be of importance in understanding their relations to external instigation and external conditions. One of these is the emotional mood in which the action is carried out. Another is the moral evaluation of the action.

Let us now summarize the conceptual framework for studying actions and external influence on actions. It was suggested that recourse should be made to phenomenological data, (i.e., how actions are experienced). A natural categorization would then be to classify actions into those caused by instrumental reasons, consummatory reasons, or externally instigated ones. In each of the three classes action may reflect the life situation or an episode of change. If the life situation is mostly reflected the action is to be seen more often as characteristic or common. If an episode of change is reflected the action is to be seen more often as meaningful or significant.

As a preliminary test of the framework and in order to obtain some notion about the ecological relevance of various categories, a preliminary study of a sample of actions was carried out, as reported in the following. In this preliminary study, data were also obtained on moral evaluation and mood states in which actions were carried out. An attempt to differentiate external conditions into instigating, facilitating, or blocking conditions is reported in a follow-up study.

STUDY 1

Method

Subjects.   The subjects were introductory level psychology students, six men and 13 women. The average age was 24.5 years. They were guaranteed complete anonymity in all their responses.

Procedure.   Each subject was given eight copies of the questionnaire, a pocket-size alarm clock, and written instructions that stated eight points in time distributed across 2 days. The times were 11, 13, 19, and 21 hours for a Saturday and 10, 14, 17, and 19 hours for a Monday. The subjects were instructed to set the alarm clocks to those times and asked to carry them always at the occasions where they would be needed. When the alarm was heard, the subjects were to register and note what they were doing at that very moment. Later, at their convenience, they were to use the questionnaire and rate each of the eight actions. The idea of the alarm clock, of course, was to sample activity in the natural stream of actions of a given subject.

Questionnaire. The first part of the questionnaire was to give the subject an opportunity to penetrate and analyze his or her actions. The subject was asked first to state what he or she was doing and then the reasons for his or her doing so. (The assumption made here was that people will report their ongoing actions if they are asked what they are doing). Secondly, the subject was to consider his or her answer and to respond further why these were reasons for action. He or she was then to consider again his or her reasons and to penetrate them further four more times. The subject of course was to penetrate only as deeply as he or she felt it was meaningful.

In the second section of the questionnaire the subject was asked to give several ratings of each action. First, it was asked whether the action was carried out because it would lead to something desirable and in such a case what that goal was and why it was desirable. The subject was also given a chance to state any additional goals of the action. Then he or she was asked whether something in the action itself made him or her carry it out (for example, was it pleasant or exciting), what was attractive about the action, whether external conditions had contributed to or instigated the action, and to state those conditions. He or she was also given a chance to state any reasons other than the three mentioned and, finally, which of the reasons was the most important one.

The subject was then asked to rate several aspects of the action:

1. Was the action replaceable with some other action? If yes, which other action?
2. Would your life be changed if you do not get a chance to pursue such an action?
3. How often do you carry out this type of action?
4. Do you consider the action significant?
5. Is the action characteristic of your life pattern?
6. Do you think other people should act in the same way in a similar situation?
7. When you reconsider the action, do you feel satisfied or do you regret it?
8. Were you concentrated in carrying out the action?
9. Was the action pleasant or unpleasant?
10. Was the feeling you had strong or weak?
11. Did the action give rise to some other specific emotional experience? Please describe! Was your emotional experience strong or weak?

12. How was the action instigated? Was it due to your own initiative or were you driven by external conditions?
13. Do you consider your action as meaningless or meaningful?

The rating scales used five categories and ample space and opportunity was given to the subject to give comments to his ratings and to the whole set of questions.

Results

Data were obtained for a total of 147 actions and were coded by two persons independently of each other. Actions were classified as instrumental, consummatory, or situational. Discrepancies between the judges were small and insignificant.

The mean number of reasons given for each action was 2.98 ($\sigma = 1.31$). The most important reason given was *instrumental* in 55% of the cases, *consummatory* in 18%, and *situational* in 27%.

The actions were considered on the whole pleasant in 49% of the cases and on the whole unpleasant in 6%. In 11% of the cases they were stated to be simultaneously pleasant and unpleasant and in 34% they were neutral in this respect. The large percentage of "pleasant" actions is of some interest, especially when it is considered that only a few actions were conceived as mostly consummatory and that most actions were conceived as instrumental.

Significant correlations between rating scales and the number of reasons of instrumental, consummatory, or situational type are given in Table 17.1.

The correlations are generally low but some interesting conclusions may be drawn. First, situationally caused actions were seen as infrequent and the number

TABLE 17.1

Significant Correlations ($p < 0.05$) Between Number of Reasons of Different Types and Ratings of Actions

Aspect	Type of Reason		
	Instrumental	*Consummatory*	*Situational*
Life change			
Commonness		0.19	−0.18
Significance			
Typicality	0.23	0.25	
Should others act like this		0.16	
Regret		0.18	
Concentration	0.20		
Pleasantness		0.18	
Own initiative		0.19	−0.20
Meaningfulness	0.25		

of situational reasons did not correlate with any of the rating scales. This is in contrast to the number of instrumental or consummatory reasons. These two variables correlated with several rating scales. Consummatory actions were seen as more common and characteristic, morally justified, and satisfactory. Instrumentally generated actions were seen as more meaningful (but also, contrary to expectation, as characteristic).

One may tentatively suggest that instrumentally generated actions reflect change episodes whereas consummatory actions mostly reflect life situations. Situationally instigated actions seem to be relatively rare and perhaps rather insignificant, inasmuch as they do not reflect any of the aspects of action sampled here.

Female subjects rated their actions as morally more justified than did male subjects and also as more strongly colored by emotional mood. Older subjects gave more instrumental reasons for each action and considered their actions as more meaningful and significant. There was a tendency, on the whole, for more reasons to be given for actions carried out on a Saturday than on a Monday. However, actions carried out on a Monday were more significant.

Because the group was composed of students it was not inconceivable that their weekday activities were more oriented toward their life episode of eduction and that their free time was spent on activities within their life situation.

Discussion

The fact that people often cannot account for the causes of their behavior (Nisbett & Wilson, 1977) does not mean that their reasons are without interest or validity. Structural properties of data provide possible criteria for the evaluation of verbal reports; external relations provide other criteria. According to structure the present data make sense; hence, the claim to validity is supported.

If people are asked for reasons for their actions they must try to make their goals clear and conscious. This does not mean that goals need always be conscious while actions are being carried out. It is interesting to speculate as to possible sources of individual differences in self-knowledge of this type.

There were few cases of situational attribution of causes in the present data, somewhat in contrast with findings cited by Jones and Nisbett (1972), who claimed that one's own behavior is more often explained by situational reference and others' by personality characteristics. Note, however, that character was not available as a causal category here, whereas Jones and Nisbett apparently considered personal references as more permanent personality traits, not so much intentions, so the contrast may be only apparent, not real. Still, several authors have claimed that people seriously underestimate situational influence on behavior (Cantor, Chapter 15, this volume). Situational influence may be a powerful, perhaps self-evident, source in accounting for behavior without this fact normally being brought into awareness. Examples of subtle, unnoticed, but powerful influences on behavior are given by Rommetveit, Chapter 10 this volume, Cantor, Chapter 15 this volume and Bowers, chapter 12, this volume. In many cases such influences may be seen to affect *how* something is done rather than *what* is done. Reasons for action often refer to why one chose to enter a situation in the first place rather than to how action is regulated and maintained within the situation. Further study of the issue requires more data on the perception of situational influence on behavior, as reported in Study 2, which follows. In particular, there was clearly a need to differentiate among various types of situational factors.

In Study 2 an attempt also is made to decrease possible demand characteristics that may have arisen due to the somewhat cumbersome alarm clocks used in Study 1, although there were no strong indications that the clocks caused much of a problem with demand characteristics.

Futher discussion of the findings of Study 1 is postponed until Study 2 has been presented.

STUDY 2

The purpose of this study was to try to replicate the major findings of Study 1 and to investigate in more detail any situational influences on behavior. Any possible demand characteristics from using the alarm clocks in Study 1 were to be diminished by the use of more discreet wrist watches. The questionnaire used for rating the actions also was improved.

Method

Subjects.   15 subjects participated in this study; five men and 10 women. The average age was 30 years. Three of the subjects were undergraduate students of psychology, ten were students of social anthropology, and two were teachers of social anthropology. They were paid a small fee for their participation in the study.

Procedure.   Each subject was given eight copies of the questionnaire, a wrist watch with an alarm, and written instructions that started eight points in time, distributed across 2 days. The times were 10, 14, 17 and 19 hours. Two weekdays were to be used but, due to a misunderstanding, two subjects sampled their actions on a holiday for one of the days. The subjects were instructed to set the alarm to the times stated and always to carry it with them when needed. When the alarm was heard the subjects were to register and note what they were doing at that very moment. Later they were to use the questionnaire at their convenience and to rate each of the eight sampled actions.

Questionnaire.   In the first part of the questionnaire the subjects were asked to try to penetrate their reasons on five different levels, as in Study 1. In the second section the subjects were asked first to rate to what extent the action was carried out for what it might lead to (instrumentality), to what extent for its own sake (consummatory action), or to what extent it was caused by external circumstances (situational causation). In cases judged to be to a large extent caused by external circumstances, the subjects were asked to describe those circumstances. They were also given a chance to give reasons other than the three types stated. Furthermore, the subjects were asked to rate to what extent the external circumstances were facilitating, blocking, or steering (guiding). The subjects were then asked to rate their moods at the time of carrying out the action according to the mood dimensions described by Sjöberg, Svenson, and Persson (1979). They rated pleasantness, activity (concentration), confidence, tension, and sociability. The subjects then rated whether the action was typical, to be regretted, significant, usual, efficient in providing the hoped-for result, meaningful, and morally negative or positive.

The rating scales used five categories throughout the questionnaire. Mood ratings and the rating of moral value used bipolar scales, whereas the other rating scales were unipolor. Bipolar scales were converted to a unipolar format before proceeding to data analysis.

Results

Data were obtained for a total of 120 actions. The mean number of reasons given to each action was 2.97 ($\sigma = 1.58$). There was a tendency for the distribution of the number of reasons given for an action to be bimodal, with large numbers of cases given five reasons (34) and many given one reason (29).

The mean rating of instrumentality was 4.08. The ratings of the other two types were considerably lower: 2.58 for consummatory reasons and 2.92 for external circumstances. The distributions were very skew for instrumental and consummatory reasons and, interestingly enough, bimodal for external circumstances (see Fig. 17.1).

So far, indications are that there is a group of actions for which external circumstances are seen as important. Because ratings were obtained as to what way external circumstances influenced actions, we may say something more about this finding. Both facilitating and steering factors were rated rather high (3.37 and 3.15, respectively), whereas blocking effects were rated as rare (1.53). The distribution of ratings of steering effects was bimodal and resembled the distribution of external effects in Fig. 17.1.

Mood ratings are given in Table 17.2. It is particularly interesting to note the relatively few cases of negative mood. Only the dimension of sociability gives any indication of a large number of negative moods, and that only in roughly one-third of the cases.

The other scales will be mentioned only briefly. Actions were rated, on the average, as being mildly typical, significant, usual, efficient, meaningful, and

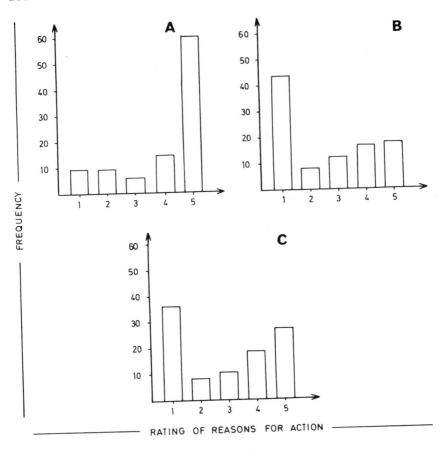

Figure 17.1   Distributions of ratings of strength of reasons in Study 2: Instrumental (A), Consummatory (B), and Situational (C).

morally positive. Only rarely did subjects indicate that they regretted what they had done.

In Table 17.3 there is a summary of significant correlations obtained among the numbers of reasons, the ratings of different types of reasons, and various rating scales applied to actions. The correlations are, on the whole, quite low. In particular, no significant correlations were obtained for situational reasons. Instrumentality and the total number of reasons had similar correlational profiles and correlated negatively with consummatory reasons. There was a tendency toward instrumentally motivated actions being seen as more meaningful and significant and less common. A corresponding mirror pattern for consummatory actions can be expected on more stable data because there is a clear negative correlation between instrumentality and consummatory reasons, but it did not appear in the present data. Thus, only rather weak support was obtained in this

TABLE 17.2
Mood Ratings in Study 2 (Percentage)

	Positive	*Neutral*	*Negative*
Pleasantness	48.3	39.2	12.5
Activity	46.7	35.0	18.3
Relaxation	60.5	26.1	13.4
Confidence	42.0	47.9	10.1
Sociability	26.3	36.4	37.3

and the previous study for the distinction between life situations and life episodes.

The correlations between mood ratings and reasons for actions are given in Table 17.4.

Both instrumental reasons and the total number of reasons correlate negatively with mood, whereas consummatory reasons tend to be positively related to pleasantness. Again, situational reasons do not correlate with the other variables. The pattern obtained for the instrumentality and consummatory reasons seems to make sense, however.

The correlations among situational determinants are given in Table 17.5. It is interesting to see that the total rating of external factors correlates rather strongly with the rating of these factors as steering or guiding (0.46) and also to some extent with rating them as facilitating. Steering and facilitating intercorrelate (0.36).

TABLE 17.3
Significant Correlations ($p < 0.05$) Between Reasons for Actions
and Ratings of Actions in Study 2

		Type of Reasons		
Aspect	*Number of Reasons*	*Instrumental*	*Consummatory*	*Situational*
Typicality				
Regret				
Significance	0.26	0.19		
Commonness	−0.18			
Efficiency		0.24		
Meaningfulness	0.23			
Moral value	0.22		0.18	
Number of reasons	—			
Instrumental		—		
Consummatory	−0.34	−0.54	—	
Situational			−0.19	—

TABLE 17.4
Significant Correlations ($p < 0.05$) Between Reasons for Action and
Mood Scales, Mood Scales Being Scored in the Positive Direction,
in Study 2

Mood	Number of Reasons	Type of Reasons		
		Instrumental	Consummatory	Situational
Pleasantness	−0.27	−0.30	0.27	
Activation				
Relaxation	−0.37			
Confidence				
Sociability	−0.25	−0.19		

Other correlations will be mentioned only very briefly. Expected correlations were obtained between ratings of meaningfulness and significance and between typicality and commonness. Some meaningful correlations were obtained also between mood ratings and ratings of situational determinants. Sex differences were obtained in that men rated their actions as more often instrumental than did women, whereas women had a tendency to rate their actions as more morally justified.

Summing the correlational data, the following picture emerges: there seem to be two clusters of actions that may be termed instrumental and consummatory. Instrumental actions tend to be deeper in intention and to be carried out in somewhat more tense and unpleasant moods. They tend to be seen as more meaningful and less usual or typical than consummatory actions. Situational determinants correlate very little, if at all, with other ratings made of actions. The major finding here was the finding that situational reasons correlate rather more strongly with the particular aspects of steering than with facilitation or blocking.

As noted in Fig. 17.1, there was a sizeable group of actions that were rated as situationally determined. It was decided to make a closer investigation of actions

TABLE 17.5
Significant Correlations ($p < 0.05$) Among Situational Determinants

	Situational Reasons	Facilitating	Blocking	Steering
Situational reasons	—			
Facilitating	(0.16)	—		
Blocking		−0.34	—	
Steering	0.46	0.36		—

that were rated as extremely well characterized by one of the three aspects, and in particular to study actions that were seen as clearly determined by situational factors.

Of a total of 120 actions only 32 were not rated as being influenced to a very high degree (a rating of 5) in at least one of the three scales of instrumental, consummatory, and situational factors. Purely instrumental reasons were seen for 43 actions and purely consummatory reasons for nine actions, whereas purely external factors were seen as responsible for only six actions (5%). However, there were also combinations. External and instrumental factors were seen as jointly responsible in 19 cases and external and consummatory factors as jointly responsible in one case. This means that a maximum rating of external factors was given to a total of 26 actions (disregarding ratings of one subject who rated all of the reasons as extremely high in those particular four cases).

A further scrutiny of the 26 actions being highly rated in external causation showed that the actions were very rarely rated as being blocked by external factors. They were rated, rather, as being facilitated or guided.

Of the 26 actions, external circumstances were described by the subjects in 24 cases. The circumstances most often denoted either some physical problem or a socially compelling context or a combination of these two. Physical problems were alluded to in 10 cases, socially compelling contexts in 12, and a combination in two. Examples: One subject gave for the action of baking bread the external circumstances that she had the necessary ingredients available (physical) and that she expected guests (social). This was a clear case of the combination of physical and social circumstances. Another subject had a shower because of the hot weather. This was a case of physical circumstances. In another case a subject was checking a list of course books and stated that the external circumstances for this were that she had been told to do so. This was a case of socially compelling circumstances.

It is clear, then, that subjects sometimes see external circumstances as affecting their actions. However, they conceive of such circumstances as constituting in some sense problems or opportunities. There were no cases of other types of conceptions of situational influence on action. One may wonder whether or not our subjects were realistic in evaluating how much their actions were influenced by situational factors. To answer, there is a need for a criterion against which our subjects' interpretations can be evaluated. No such criterion appears to be available at the present time.

GENERAL DISCUSSION

Attempts at sampling activity in the ongoing stream of events have been reported before. An interesting example is the thought-sampling work described by Klinger (1978). Now, it may be problematic to define just what a thought is—but in any case it seems natural to conceive of a thought as a smaller unit than an action. Normally, many thoughts arise in the course of pursuing an action. The work on situation perception by Pervin (1976, 1977, chapter 21, this volume), is in some ways similar to the present study, but Pervin interviewed his subjects about which situations they encountered and did not perform an actual sampling of situations or of actions. Informally, however, Pervin confirmed the prevalence of instrumentality of action (Pervin, Chapter 21, this volume).

Action sampling has been reported by Csikszentmihalyi and his co-workers (Csikszentmihalyi & Graef, 1979; Csikszentmihalyi, Larson, & Prescott, 1977; Larson & Csikszentmihalyi, 1978). The general orientation of this work is similar to the present one, but the distinction between instrumental and consummatory actions is not made, nor is there an attempt to study the goal structure involved in an act or to specify the factors of situational influence. Hence, comparing results is not altogether easy, but some convergence can be noted, most notably that voluntary actions were more frequent than coerced actions (Csikszentmihalyi et al., 1977; Csikszentmihalyi & Graef, 1979). In the last-mentioned paper validity of action sampling was supported by successfully comparing action sampling data to results previously accumulated in time-budget studies. The careful and pioneering work by Csikszentmihalyi should inspire to further developments of the technique of action sampling.

In further work, one should probably distinguish between the different types of nesting of actions. First, there is vertical nesting, which refers to the hierarchy of values accounting for the value of an action at any given point in time. Second, there is horizontal nesting, which refers to conception of instrumental subacts, as outlined in the introduction. A purely consummatory act is not horizontally nested, but may well have a complex vertical nesting. An interesting example is discussed by Rommetveit (Chapter 10, this volume). Likewise, a purely instrumental act has not vertical, only horizontal, nesting. And many actions carry some components of both types of nesting.

The results of the study indicate the feasibility of using this general framework for studies of action. Classification of actions into the three categories of instrumental, consummatory, and situationally caused was relatively straightforward. The rating scales were not altogether successful in describing the aspect of life situation and episode of change but some positive suggestions came out of data.

Several ecological aspects of the data also deserve some comments. First, it is striking that so much of the activity was seen as instrumental in its orientation and that several reasons (on the average about three) were given for each action. This, in connection with the overall pleasant emotional mood of the subjects, seems to indicate that we studied a population of instrumentally oriented and well-adjusted people in pursuit of their goals. A natural extension would be to apply the approach to people from other cultures or with signficantly different life situations (e.g. drug addicts or alcoholics).

Why are so few actions unpleasant? Do we live in the best of all possible worlds? Pervin (Chapter 21, this volume) suggests that emotions have been somewhat neglected in learning approaches. Perhaps people strive less for the satisfaction of needs or the fulfilment of value-based commitments than they strive to avoid unpleasant actions and situations. Emotions may possibly have an adjustment value best understood in phylogenetic terms (Toda, 1979).

Some methodological comments are in order. First, asking people what they are doing may suggest that they must come up with some action. (Note, however, that there is no clear reason why they should feel pressed to give it a high instrumental rating). One perhaps should make provisions for the reporting of other types of mental activity than actions. Second, one may wish to study also if people feel they influence situations, not only that situations influence them. Third, one could ask for actions carried out over a longer interval of time (or ask for time ratings of the actions being carried out). Presumably, such an approach would also bring up different conceptions of situations. Fourth, instrumentality is not the same as freedom. The experience of being free is worthy of study in relation to the experienced determinants of action. Perhaps the Rotter (1966) scale of internal–external locus of control is related to perceived causes of action. Another personality dimension of possible relevance is the Snyder (1979) variable of self-monitoring. Csikszentmihalyi and Graef (1979) were specifically concerned with the experience of freedom. They found it to be clearly related to a question they assumed to measure intrinsic motivation, viz. if the subject wished he had been doing something else. One may be doubtful as to the validity of the question. It seems to be hard to interpret in the case of instrumental action, which is the dominant type of action in the present data.

Finally, a few comments on a controversy in interactionistic psychology are called for. A central problem is to what extent behavior may be accounted for by invariant personality traits (Mischel, 1973, 1977a; Bowers, 1977). Conceiving of action as goal-directed, as a sequence of episodes of variable length, intensity, and content, leads in a natural manner to a different perspective. Person-bound variables are potent in accounting for behavior without necessarily being invariant over time as traits should be (what Mischel [1973] calls ''self-regulatory systems and plans''). Hence, one may be led to underestimate the importance of person-bound information from the fact that trait concepts have met with only very modest success. However, stability also may be caused by stability of the life situation rather than by person stability. It seems likely that people actively search for conditions that serve their basic needs—and once such conditions have been found, one is strongly discouraged from leaving them. Personal stability may simply reflect to what extent one stays within a certain life situation.

ACKNOWLEDGMENT

The author is indebted to Bengt Jansson for data collection and analysis in Study 2.

18 Psychological Climate: Theoretical Perspectives and Empirical Research

Lawrence R. James and S. B. Sells
Texas Christian University, U. S. A.

Psychological climate refers to individuals' cognitive representations of proximal environments, expressed in terms that represent the personal or acquired meaning of environments to individuals. Psychological-climate theory was developed primarily to study individuals' perceptions of *work* environments (James & Jones, 1974, 1976), although as discussed throughout this report, the assumptions underlying psychological-climate theory were derived from many areas of psychology and the assumptions themselves are not limited to work environments. Nevertheless, to maintain consistency between assumptions and empirical research, the discussions and illustrations presented focus on work environments, although, the implications drawn from these discussions and illustrations are extended easily to environmental perception in general.

The formal definition of psychological climate is: the individual's cognitive representations of relatively proximal situational events, expressed in terms that reflect the psychological meaning and significance of the situation to the individual (James, Hater, Gent, & Bruni, 1978). A central postulate of psychological-climate theory is that individuals tend to interpret situations in psychological terms; that is, to assign psychological meaning to environmental attributes and events (Ekehammar, 1974; James et al., 1978; Schneider, 1975). The focus of measurement of psychological climate is thus directed toward assessments of interpretative, abstract, generalized, and inferential constructs such as ambiguity, autonomy, challenge, conflict, equity, friendliness, influence, support, trust, and interpersonal warmth. It is also important to stipulate that psychological climate is regarded as an attribute of the individual. This stipulation is necessary because the psychological meaning and significance that an individual assigns to an environment often may involve idiosyncratic interpretations, generalizations, and inferences. As discussed in more detail later, psychological-climate perceptions are believed to be a function of historical components, namely cognitive schemata that reflect idiosyncratic learning experiences.

Over the last few years, the present authors and several colleagues have developed a research program to investigate the bases for and the results of psychological-climate perceptions (Hornick, James, & Jones, 1977; James & Jones, 1974, 1976, 1979; James, Gent, Hater, & Coray, 1979; James, Hartman, Stebbins, & Jones, 1977; James et al., 1978; Jones & James, 1979; Jones, James, & Bruni, 1975; Jones, James, Bruni, & Sells, 1977; Sells, 1976). This paper presents an overview of the psychological-climate research program. Sequentially, the discussion includes first a brief review of the assumptions underlying psychological climate, followed by illustrations of empirical research, including: (1) the measurement of psychological climate; (2) tests of the generalizability of psychological-climate dimensions; (3) the roles of situational variables, person variables, and person by situation (P × S) interactions in perceptual/cognitive processes underlying psychological-climate perceptions; and (4) an investigation of reciprocal causation between psychological-climate perceptions and attitudes. The concluding section addresses implications of current psychological-climate theory for future research on environmental perception.

ASSUMPTIONS UNDERLYING PSYCHOLOGICAL CLIMATE

The assumptions that follow reflect attempts to integrate postulates of psychological-climate theory with those of basic perception and cognition (Erdelyi, 1974; Wyer, 1974), environmental psychology (Ittleson, Proshansky, Rivlin, & Winkel, 1974), interactional psychology (Bowers, 1973; Ekehammar, 1974; Endler & Magnusson, 1976a), and social-learning and cognitive–social-learning theory (Bandura, 1978; Mahoney, 1977; Mischel, 1973, 1977b; Rotter, 1954; Stotland & Canon, 1972). A summary of this integration, which is treated more extensively in James et al. (1978), is as follows.

1. Psychological-climate (PC) perceptions reflect the psychological meaning and significance of the situation to the individual. PC represents a perceptually based, psychologically processed description of the work environment. In effect, the environment that an individual "knows" is a product of cognitive constructions, reflecting various forms of filtering, abstraction, generalization, and interpretation. Of particular salience to our concept of PC is that this processing ultimately results in cognitive representations (interpretations) that reflect the psychological meaning and significance of the work environment to the individual (e.g., the extent to which the environment is regarded as ambiguous, challenging, supportive, warm, and so forth).

The interpretation of environments in terms of their psychological meaning and significance is thought to be a result of higher-order cognitive information processing and the development of *higher-order schemata, or beliefs,* about situations (James & Jones, 1976; James et al., 1978). An important component in the development of higher-order schemata is an awareness of relationships or recurring patterns of configurations among lower-order, more descriptively oriented perceptions (e.g., job tasks vary from day to day) and psychological events (e.g., experienced mental challenge). This awareness allows individuals to process information further and to impute psychological meaning and significance to perceived situational attributes and events. For example, a cognitive association between perceived nonrepetitiveness of tasks and experienced mental challenge serves as a cornerstone for the development of a higher-order schema (belief) that the job is challenging.

In the present context, psychological climate involves perceptual/cognitive constructs that are designed to be indicators of higher-order schemata (HOSs) of work environments. When viewed in this manner, several implications are salient regarding HOSs, and therefore PC. An important implication is that HOSs reflect only abstract generalizations about situations, and thus may not be tied directly to situational attributes and events (Stotland & Canon, 1972). Furthermore, intrinsic to the concept of higher-order information processing is the rationale that individuals are active agents in the construction and reshaping of cognitive environments. In other words, individuals have the capacity not only to process information and cognitive associations, but also cognitively to manipulate information and associations to create new knowledge. Information processing is illustrated when perceived situational events and associations among situational and psychological events are redefined and restructured to protect self-esteem or to preserve cognitive consistency with other beliefs. Examples of the creation of new knowledge and the susceptibility of HOSs to distortion are discussed later. We wish to emphasize, however, that: (a) PC measures are designed to represent HOSs; no stipulation is made that PC perceptions are veridical descriptions of environmental attributes and events; and (b) the HOSs included in PC measurement reflect the assumption that the individual is an active agent in constructing cognitive representations of environments.

2. PC is historical, reflecting a continuing antinomy between: (a) the openness of the HOSs underlying PC perceptions to change; and (b) the tendency to preserve abstract, familiar, and valued beliefs about situations. HOSs are learned (i.e., based on developmental experiences) and are products of continuously interacting cognitive processes of perception, learning, memory, and recall. This suggests not only that PC perceptions have historical antecedents, but also that individuals with different learning experiences and synthesizing capabilities may employ different HOSs to interpret the same environmental attributes and events and thus experience different PC perceptions. It is noteworthy that once learned, HOSs may be relatively impervious to change because: (a) they are abstract and

generalized and often not highly influenced by inconsistencies between existing HOSs and specific situational events; (b) they are familiar; and (c) they are valued by the individual (Jones & Gerard, 1967).

The desire to preserve abstract, familiar, and valued HOSs is evident in the assumption that HOSs, and therefore PC perceptions, are predisposed toward the construction of a subjective reality that is compatible with such factors as existing (or desired) needs, values, and self-concepts (Erdelyi, 1974; Jones & Gerard, 1967; Stotland & Canon, 1972). This implies that individuals with different needs, values, and self-concepts, which in part reflect different learning experiences, will be cognitively predisposed to differ in what they judge to be (i.e., perceive as) challenging, fair, friendly, supportive, etc. In effect, measures such as needs, values, and self-concepts reflect underlying cognitive structures, and their roles in perception/cognition are evident in perceptions that display the results of processes such as assimilation, restructuring, redefinition, and selective attention (Bowers, 1973; Erdelyi, 1974; Jones & Gerard, 1967; James et al., 1978; James et al., 1979; Stagner, 1976, 1977). Thus, if it is assumed that individual characteristics such as needs, values, and self-concepts are relatively stable, at least over identifiable time periods, then a basis is established for suggesting that HOSs and PC perceptions are a function of person variables and person by situation ($P \times S$) interactions.

It is important to note, however, that HOSs are subject to change particularly for the "functional" purpose of achieving a "fit" with the work environment by apprehending, ordering, and gauging the appropriateness of behaviors (Schneider, 1975). This suggests the likelihood of conflicting orientations generated by the desire to preserve abstract, familiar, and valued schemata, on one hand, and openness to change in the interest of achieving adaptive and functional person–environment fits, on the other (Jones & Gerard, 1967). The extent to which HOSs are open to change for functional/adaptive purposes, as opposed to being relatively impervious to change, is likely a function of a number of factors. As reviewed by James et al. (1978), a nonexhaustive and non-mutually exclusive list of these factors is as follows:

(a) the degree of incongruity between existing HOSs and requirements for adaptive fits; (b) the adaptability of existing HOSs to specific situations; (c) the degree of ambiguity and uncertainty in situations [where individuals may either fall back upon existing HOSs to interpret ambiguous situations or attempt to reduce the ambiguity by seeking new information]; (d) the desire to maintain cognitive consistency; (e) the level of cognitive complexity, where high cognitive complexity suggests a high tolerance for ambiguity and a low need for certainty; (f) the number of and extent to which defense mechanisms are called into play; (g) the extent to which action is required; (h) attribution of cause–effect; and (i) the extent to which important needs and values are served by changes in cognitive schemas [p. 795].

It is evident that PC perceptions are a function of what can be complex sets of interrelated cognitive processes. Given unique histories of individual learning experiences and the relative imperviousness of HOSs to change, perceptions of the same situation are likely to differ among individuals and the *reasons for these differences are psychologically important*.

3. Environmental attributes that appear to exercise major influence on PC perceptions are those that have relatively direct and immediate ties to individuals' experiences in the environment. Environmental attributes and events represent stimulus information that affects PC perceptions by activating cognitive activities that if attended to following processing, transformation, and interpretation, serve to support/reinforce existing HOSs or, as a function of the considerations discussed above, provide a basis for reality testing and change of existing HOSs. Environmental attributes and events include not only specific stimuli but also more complex stimulus patterns as well as the contexts in which specific stimuli and stimulus patterns are presented (e.g., leader behaviors in an uncertain environment—Bronfenbrenner, 1977). Environmental perceptions of major interest in the measurement of PC are those that reflect the more global and enduring aspects of environments, namely stimulus patterns and environmental contexts. It is believed that the stimulus patterns and contexts of most importance to individuals are those they experience directly and immediately in their proximal (work) environments. Proximal-stimulus patterns and contexts that appear to be of major interest in organizational-behavior research are those associated with roles, jobs, immediate levels of leadership, work-group interrelationships, and selected components of subsystems and organizations, such as reward dynamics (e.g., pay). The variables representing proximal-stimulus patterns and contexts are to be differentiated from more "distal" environmental variables (e.g., organizational size), which are viewed as more remote from individual experience and require more numerous and complex linkages to influence perceptions than proximal environmental variables.

4. The underlying causal model linking PC to attitudes, behaviors, and environments is one of reciprocal causation. In the process of constructing cognitive representations of environments, there appears to be a continuing reciprocal interaction between psychologically meaningful and significant perceptions of the environment, on one hand, and emotional (affective, evaluative) responses to the environment and behaviors in the environment, on the other (Bandura, 1978; Bowers, 1973; Endler & Magnusson, 1976a; James et al., 1978; Mahoney, 1977; Mischel, 1977; Pervin, 1968). The causal flow from PC perceptions to emotions and behaviors is based on the widespread belief that individuals respond primarily to cognitive representations of environments rather than to the environments per se. The salient question is, therefore, the reciprocal causal flow from emotions and behaviors to PC perceptions.

With respect to emotions, an area of major concern has been relationships between PC perceptions and job satisfaction. Whereas it is known that PC perceptions affect job satisfaction (e.g., a job that is perceived as important leads to satisfaction of ego needs), it is also extremely likely that existing (or desired) levels of job satisfaction influence PC perceptions. For example, existing (or desired) levels of job satisfaction may cause the individual: (a) to attend selectively to environmental information in the interest of increasing (or decreasing), maintaining, or confirming existing levels of satisfaction; (b) to impute desirable/undesirable attributes to a job (or leader, work group, organization, etc.) that the individual already regards as satisfying/dissatisfying; (c) cognitively to restructure and redefine environmental information in such a way as to increase the probability that it will be interpreted as satisfying/dissatisfying; and (d) cognitively to restructure the environment to make it consistent with learned expectations as to whether this type of environment should be satisfying/dissatisfying (James & Jones, 1979).

Reciprocal causation between PC perceptions and behavior is observed most clearly in the self-regulation of behavior in relation to self-evaluative consequences, such as self-satisfaction, self-pride, self-criticism, and self-incentives (Bandura, 1977a, 1978; Mischel, 1973, 1977b). As discussed by Bandura (1978), self-evaluative consequences are viewed as conditional on self-appraisals of accomplishments resulting from behavior, whereas self-appraisals are a function of achieved goal accomplishments in relation to personal standards and objectives (i.e., what is important to the individual). Environmental perceptions affect behavior in the sense that perceptions that are psychologically significant to self-regulatory functions (e.g., perceived outcomes of behaviors, such as reinforcements/punishments from a supervisor) stimulate self-evaluative and self-regulatory influences. The reciprocal effects of self-evaluative and self-regulatory influences on PC perceptions are seen not only in the indirect linkages from self-evaluation/self-regulation → behavior → outcomes → perception, but also by direct effects of self-evaluative/self-regulatory functions on perceptual/cognitive processes. For example, self-regulatory processes affect perceptions directly in the sense that individuals are selectively attentive to environmental information that is salient to self-conceptions, personal standards, and behavior–performance and performance–outcome expectancies. Moreover, the individual cognitively may construct new environments in the interest of formulating such things as self-observations, behavior–outcome contingencies, self-appraisals, self-generated consequences, and self-regulated incentives (Bandura, 1978).

Reciprocal causation between persons and environments takes a number of forms. It has been demonstrated that perceptions of work environments are in part caused by environmental attributes and events (James et al., 1978), and thus our primary concern is with the reciprocal effects of persons on environments. These reciprocal effects are believed to include the following components: (a) the environment is an inseparable function of the person who is perceiving it; this implies that the individual may change the environment he or she experiences by means of idiosyncratic cognitive constructions; (b) selectivity, in which individuals may select the environments in which they participate (e.g., the place of employment, a union, an informal group); this implies that environments are affected differentially by those who choose and who do not choose to join and/or participate; and (c) direct reciprocity, in which individuals may actively affect the character of environments, as for example when subordinates affect the behaviors of their leaders toward them as a function of their (the subordinates') performance levels, cooperativeness, absences, and attitudes toward the leader (Bandura, 1978; Bowers, 1973, Ekehammar, 1974; Endler & Magnusson, 1976a; Graen, 1976; James et al., 1978; James, Irons, & Hater, 1978; Mahoney, 1977; Pervin, 1968).

Cognitive/perceptual factors are involved, either directly or indirectly, in each of the above forms of person–environment reciprocal causation. It is also important to note that the environmental events that are most amenable to change as a function of individual influences are those of a social or process nature (e.g., social norms, leader behaviors). Nevertheless, it is also possible that environmental attributes of a more stable and structural nature (configuration of organizational hierarchy) are subject to change as a result of individuals' influences, especially over long periods of time.

ILLUSTRATIONS OF EMPIRICAL RESEARCH ON PSYCHOLOGICAL CLIMATE

Measurement of Psychological Climate

Quantitive information on individual PC perceptions may be obtained by several different strategies, including direct procedures, such as self-reports on questionnaires or responses to interview questions, and indirect procedures, such as inferences from ratings by observers or responses to experimental treatments. The completion of questionnaires by organizational incumbents is by far the most popular strategy for collecting PC data inasmuch as it provides: (a) direct, self-report measures of perceptions; (b) a method for standardizing the climate items and modes of response; and (c) a practical way to obtain data on a large item pool for large samples. Consequently, we have focused on the use of questionnaires to collect PC data.

In the development of the PC questionnaires, an attempt has been made to develop a comprehensive measure of the perceptual domains that are psychologically meaningful and significant for most individuals in work environments. The selection of domains was predicated on prior reviews and research, which suggested five domains of principal concern with respect to work environments (Campbell, Dunnette, Lawler, & Weick, 1970; Hellriegel & Slocum, 1974; Indik, 1968; James & Jones, 1974, 1976; Jones & James, 1979; Payne & Pugh, 1976; Schneider, 1975; Sells, 1963a, 1968). These five domains are:

1. Role characteristics, such as role ambiguity and role conflict.
2. Job characteristics, such as job autonomy and job challenge.
3. Leader behaviors, including goal emphasis and work facilitation.

4. Work-group and social environment characteristics, including cooperation and friendliness.
5. Organizational and subsystem attributes that are proximal to individual experiences, including fairness of the reward system.

Several forms of a PC questionnaire have been developed and employed in a continuing program of research. These include a long-form questionnaire of 35 PC variables (145 items), in which each PC variable was based on a composite of homogeneous PC items, and several short-form questionnaires of 17 to 24 variables (80 to 115 items). The short-form quesionnaires were developed by combining highly correlated variables from the long-form questionnaire and by retaining only those items that contributed strongly to composite homogeneity and internal consistency. A list and brief description of the PC variables included in the 24-variable questionnaire is presented in Table 18.1.

TABLE 18.1
Twenty-Four Psychological-Climate Variables

Characteristics of Role	
1. Role ambiguity	Degree of perceived ambiguity in demands, criteria, and interfaces with other jobs–tasks–roles
2. Role conflict	Degree to which role performance is seen as affected by pressures to engage in conflicting or mutually exclusive behaviors
3. Role overload	Degree to which role performance is seen as affected by inadequate time, training, and resources
Characteristics of Job	
4. Job autonomy	Degree of perceived opportunity to determine the nature of tasks or problems and to act without consultation or permission
5. Job challenge	Degree of perceived opportunity to make full use of abilities, skills, and knowledge
6. Job importance	Degree to which job is perceived as making a meaningful contribution and is important to the organization
7. Job variety	Perceived range of tasks, equipment, and behaviors involved in job
Characteristics of Leader Behavior	
8. Leader support	Degree to which leader is perceived as aware of and responsive to needs of subordinate and shows consideration for feelings of personal worth
9. Leader goal emphasis	Degree to which leader is perceived as stimulating subordinate's involvement in meeting group goals
10. Leader work facilitation	Degree to which leader is perceived as providing resources, guidance, problem solutions, and aiding subordinate in achieving planned goals
11. Leader interaction facilitation	Degree to which leader is perceived as encouraging development of a close, cohesive work group
12. Leader trust	Degree of confidence and trust in leader
13. Psychological influence	Degree of influence that subordinate perceives himself/herself as having on decisions made by leader
14. Hierarchical influence	Degree to which a leader is perceived as successful in interactions with higher levels of management

TABLE 18.1 *(cont.)*

Characteristics of Work Group	
15. Work-group cooperation	Degree of perceived cooperative effort among work group members to carry out tasks
16. Work-group friendliness and warmth	Degree to which warm, friendly relations, trust, and mutual liking among work-group members are perceived
17. Work-group esprit	Degree to which work-group members are perceived as showing pride in their group, their fellow members, and their accomplishments as a group
Characteristics of Subsystem and Organization	
18. Openness of expression	Degree to which organizational atmosphere is perceived as fostering expression of ideas, dissent, criticism, opinions, suggestions, and other information upward
19. Openness of information	Degree to which information is perceived as being communicated to subordinates on matters affecting their work, status, and feelings of well-being, including advance knowledge of impending changes in procedures, policies, etc.
20. Subsystem conflict	Degree to which subsystems are perceived as being uncooperative and in conflict over goals and resources
21. Management awareness	Degree to which management is perceived as attempting to assess and to respond to employees' needs and problems
22. Opportunities for growth and advancement	Degree to which the organization is perceived as providing career paths, training, and recognition to afford growth in responsibility and advancement in job status over time
23. Organizational identification	Degree to which organization is perceived as performing an important function and, in comparison to other organizations, offering greater rewards
24. Fairness and objectivity of the reward system	Degree to which organization is perceived as determining the award of recognition, promotions, and other types of rewards based on merit rather than favoritism and bias

Dimensions of Psychological Climate and Generalizability

As discussed in several recent articles (Hornick et al., 1977; James et al., 1977; Jones & James, 1979), each of the PC variables typically has demonstrated construct validity; many of these variables have long histories of research and development in organizational and social psychology. It was reasonable to assume, however, that the PC variables were intercorrelated and that a smaller, more parsimonious number of dimensions could be employed to describe PC. Of additional concern was the question of whether the PC dimensions obtained in any one sample would be generalizable to other samples, especially samples that differed in respect to organizational, job, and role characteristics. A demonstration of generalizability across diverse samples would suggest that a common core of PC dimensions is employed by individuals to perceive a variety of work environments. This would have the important implication that the PC dimensions provide meaningful constructs for assessing perceptions of a large and varied group of work environments.

Dimensions of PC have been determined for and compared across a large number of samples, including U. S. Navy enlisted personnel, production-line workers, supervisory and management personnel, firefighters, and systems analysts and computer programmers. The dimensions of PC have been found to be highly similar, regardless of the PC questionnaire employed and the samples used to ascertain generalizability. In general, we have found that the PC variables reduce to six dimensions in each sample, based on principal components analyses (Jones & James, 1979). Five of these components (dimensions) are generalizable across samples, whereas the sixth component is idiosyncratic to the sample studied. The idiosyncratic component typically accounts for only a small proportion of the variance, but does indicate that sample-specific dimensions are needed to describe unique aspects in the perceptions of different work environments (Schneider, 1975).

The five components of PC with demonstrated generalizability are: (1) conflict and ambiguity; (2) job challenge, importance, and variety; (3) leadership facilitation and support; (4) work-group cooperation, friendliness, and warmth; and (5) organizational concern and identification. Interestingly, these five components tend to match the five domains of PC variables reported in Table 18.1. This suggests that these five domains represent meaningful categories for differentiating among the major dimensions of PC. The results suggest further that individuals are able to differentiate among different aspects of their work environments in their cognitive representations of situations.

The Proximal Environment and Correlates of Psychological Influence

Data from both field and experimental studies of climate perceptions suggest that individuals in the same workgroup do not assign closely similar meanings to their work environments. For example, as reviewed by Hater (1977), James et al. (1978), and Jones and James (1979), the range of indices of perceptual agreement generally varied between .06 and .35, with a median of about .12. A number of potential reasons for this lack of perceptual agreement has been presented; these reasons, however, focused on individual differences in information processing and idiosyncracies in perceptual/cognitive filtering and interpretation. Of perhaps equal importance is the likelihood that individuals in presumably the same work environments might *not* have been exposed to the same set of situational attributes and events (James et al., 1978; Schneider, 1975).

To illustrate the problem, the formal work group often is employed as the basis for defining a work environment operationally. It is quite possible, however, that at least some individuals in the same work group: (1) have different role requirements, especially those of a more informal nature such as "acting supervisor" when the formal supervisor is absent; (2) perform different job functions (e.g., a surgical nurse and surgeon are part of a work team but have different functions); (3) are recipients of different leader behaviors from the supervisor, as discussed later; (4) have different social relationships with other work-group members; and (5) receive different levels of pay as a function of merit or seniority. Moreover, it is not uncommon to find studies in which the same work environment is defined as the same subsystem or the same organization. This may be highly questionable if perceptual agreement is assessed on samples of individuals from highly heterogeneous roles and organizational positions, not to mention the fact that work groups and subsystems in the same organization often differ substantially in regard to contexts, structures, and processes (James & Jones, 1976; Payne & Mansfield, 1973).

Stated directly, it is essential to define specifically what it is that constitutes proximal work environments in relation to work-environment perceptions. Unfortunately, little attention has been given to this question. While it has often been noted that environmental perceptions may be nonveridical, few attempts have been made to ascertain how the perceptions occurred because the perceptions were employed almost exclusively as independent variables (e.g., predictors of performance, satisfaction, or turnover,) and *not* as dependent variables. The comparatively few studies that have addressed situation-perception relationships have generally: (1) accounted for only small proportions of the variance in the perceptions; (2) employed either distal rather than proximal situational variables or situational variables that were confounded with individual differences (e.g., tenure, which reflects mutual and interactive influences of both the individual and the organization); or (4) in a few cases have relied on the same individuals as measurement sources for both the perceptual and situational variables, thus introducing a high probability of methodological confounding.

A few recent studies have shed light on what appears to be a significant improvement in the measurement of proximal work environments (Dansereau, Graen, & Haga, 1975; Graen & Schiemann, 1978; James et al., 1979). These studies questioned the prevailing concept that leaders employ a common or standard set of behavior (i.e., a leadership style) toward all of their subordinates. Rather, it was hypothesized that leaders tend to employ different behaviors toward different subordinates, and that these differences would be related to subordinates' perceptions of their leaders. This suggested that at least that portion of the proximal work environment associated with leader behaviors may be different for different individuals in the same work group, and that differences in subordinates' perceptions of the same leader are in part a function of differences in situations (i.e., the leader behaviors).

Tests of the hypotheses implied above typically are based on ''leader–subordinate vertical dyads,'' where leaders' descriptions of their behaviors toward *each* of their subordinates are related to the subordinates' perceptions of their leaders. The results of the vertical dyad studies have shown consistently that leaders tend to employ different behaviors toward different subordinates, based on reports from both leaders and subordinates. It has also been shown that the descriptions from leaders are related significantly to subordinates' perceptions of the leaders. However, these relationships have not been of large magnitude, which connotes that factors other than (self-described) leader behaviors may be involved in subordinates' perceptions of leaders. A synopsis of relevant results of a study designed to investigate these concerns is presented in the following.

The study was conducted by James et al.(1979) to identify correlates of subordinates' perceptions of psychological influence, defined in Table 18.1 as the degree of influence that a subordinate perceives himself/herself as having on decisions made by a leader. The samples consisted of 126 subordinates in high-level technical jobs (e.g., computer programmers and systems analysts—the Information Systems sample) and 205 subordinates in low-technology, production-line jobs (the Production sample). Data on perceptions of psychological influence and a number of person variables (Table 18.2) were obtained for all subordinates. Work-group supervisors (ns = 21 and 23, respectively) provided data on leader behaviors employed toward each of their subordinates. The leader behaviors of interest were direct and indirect indicators of subordinates' opportunities to participate in or otherwise influence leaders' decisions.

Results demonstrated that supervisors did in fact tend to vary their leader behaviors toward different subordinates in the same work group. Moreover, as shown in Table 18.2, the supervisors' descriptions of their behaviors were related significantly to subordinates' perceptions of psychological influence, although the correlations were not large. At this juncture, the results replicated prior research on leader–subordinate vertical dyads (Graen, 1976).

Two additional hypotheses were proposed regarding correlates of subordinates' perceptions, based on the PC assumptions discussed earlier. First, it was

TABLE 18.2
Correlations Between Subordinates' Perceptions of Psychological
Influence and Leader Behaviors and Subordinate-Person Variables

Variables	Information Systems (n = 126)	Production (n = 205)
Leader Behaviors Toward Each Subordinate		
1. Like to have subordinate's opinion	.25**	.12
2. Set high goals for subordinate	.38**	.20**
3. Encourage subordinate to act on own	.24**	.21**
Subordinate Person Variables		
4. Achievement motivation	.10	.19**
5. Job involvement	.27**	.42**
6. Externality	−.35**	—[a]
7. Anxiety	−.28**	−.26**
8. Education	−.04	−.17*

[a]The externality variable had insufficient reliability to be employed in the production sample.
*$p < .05$
**$p > .01$

postulated that individuals would assimilate perceptions of psychological influence toward existing cognitive dispositions, represented by needs (achievement motivation), beliefs (job involvement, externality), affect (anxiety), and differences in background (education). As shown in Table 18.2, this hypothesis was substantially upheld; subordinates' perceptions of psychological influence generally were correlated significantly with the subordinate person variables. The assimilation hypothesis received further support from a hierarchical regression analysis, where it was demonstrated that the person variables contributed significantly to the prediction of psychological influence after controls had been effected for the leader behaviors. For example, in the Information Systems sample, the addition of the significant person-variable correlates to the set of leader behaviors raised the multiple correlation for psychological influence from .38 (p < .01) to .59 (p < .01), a highly significant increase. As discussed in detail by James et al. (1979), these results could not be attributed to statistical artifacts such as methodological confounding.

The second hypothesis addressed the assumption that PC perceptions are a function of PXS interactions. This hypothesis was operationalized in terms of selective attention; it was predicted that a person-variable moderator—rigidity—would affect the attentiveness of subordinates to the leader behaviors in the process of formulating perceptions of psychological influence. It was also expected, as noted earlier, that contextual factors in the work environment might affect relationships between situational variables and perceptions. Consequently, a second, contextual moderator—certainty of environment—was included. Based on significant differences on measured indices of job complexity, work-group stability, and work-group structure, subordinates in the Informations Systems sample were classified as working in "uncertain environments," whereas subordinates in the Production sample were regarded as working in "certain environments."

The predictions based on the person-variable moderator (subordinates' rigidity) and the contextual moderator (environmental certainty) were as follows:

1. Positive relationships would exist between the leader behaviors and subordinates' perceptions of psychological influence for: (a) high rigids in uncertain environments; and (b) low rigids, regardless of the certainty of the work environment. The former prediction was predicated on the logic that high rigids in comparatively uncertain environments (Information Systems) would manifest needs for certainty and thus be attentive to opportunities to increase the clarification and control brought about by participation in decision making. The latter prediction was based on the rationale that low rigids would be attentive to opportunities for nonauthoritarian, human-relations styles of leadership and autonomy, irrespective of the work environment.

2. Low and nonsignificant relationships would exist between the leader behaviors and subordinates' perceptions of psychological influence for high rigids in certain environments. This hypothesis was predicated on the logic that high

rigids in comparatively certain environments would not manifest needs for certainty, and thus should not be attentive to opportunities to increase the clarification and control brought about by participation.

The statistical tests for these predictions were based on a subgrouping moderator analysis. This analysis involved comparison of the leader behavior–psychological influence relationships for high rigids in certain environments, where the relationships were expected to be low and nonsignificant, with the leader behavior–psychological influence relationships in the remaining three subgroups, in which positive and significant relationships were expected. The results of the analysis, shown in Table 18.3, generally supported the predictions.

In summary, the results of the psychological-influence study suggest the following conclusions: (1) it may be necessary to define and to measure the proximal environment for *each* individual, at least for leadership-related attributes and events; (2) variations in perceptions among members of the same work group are in part a function of situational differences; (3) individuals have capacities to construct psychological environments that reflect assimilations to-

TABLE 18.3
Moderated Correlations for Psychological Influence

Leader Behaviors	Moderator Subgroup		t
	Low Rigids—Certain Environment	High Rigids—Certain Environment	
Like opinion	.29*	.04	1.73*
Set high goals	.32*	.13	1.34
Act on own	.42**	.09	2.39**
	High Rigids—Uncertain Environment	High Rigids—Certain Environment	
Like opinion	.52**	.04	2.83**
Set high goals	.43**	.13	1.73*
Act on own	.20	.09	—
	Low Rigids—Uncertain Environment	High Rigids—Certain Environment	
Like opinion	.17	.04	—
Set high goals	.36**	.13	1.79*
Act on own	.25*	.09	1.21

Note: Sample sizes were as follows: Low Rigids—Certain Environment = 62, High Rigids—Certain Environment = 140. Low Rigids—Uncertain Environment = 88, High Rigids—Uncertain Environment = 37.

*p < .05
**p < .01

ward cognitive dispostitions and differential attention to selected aspects of situations; and (4) situational contexts (i.e., certainty of environment) may have important influences in perceptual processes.

Reciprocal Causation Between Job Perceptions and Job Satisfaction

A study by James and Jones (1979) was designed to investigate the assumed reciprocal causation between PC perceptions and attitudes, as well as several other assumptions intrinsic to the PC approach. The assumptions were operationalized in terms of job perceptions and job-satisfaction attitudes, and the following three hypotheses were addressed:

1. Satisfaction with job/task events (job satisfaction) and perceptions of job challenge, autonomy, and importance are reciprocal causes of each other.
2. Perceptions of job challenge, autonomy, and importance are caused directly by situational attributes/events and individual dispositions.
3. Job satisfaction is caused directly by individual dispositions, but only indirectly by situational attributes/events; that is, individuals rely on job perceptions rather than situational attributes for information in the process of formulating job satisfaction attitudes.

The perceptions of job challenge, autonomy, and importance (see Table 18.1 for definitions) were regarded as indicators of the psychological meaning and significance of jobs to individuals. The three job-perception variables were correlated and thus were combined to form one composite, designated simply as *job perceptions*. Job satisfaction was considered an affective/emotional evaluation of perceptions of job events, reflected by an emotional state varying from positive (high job satisfaction) to negative (low job satisfaction). The prediction that the job perceptions and job satisfaction are reciprocal causes of each other (Hypothesis 1) was predicated on the beliefs that: (1) job satisfaction attitudes are caused directly by psychologically meaningful and significant job perceptions because such perceptions convey directly opportunities to satisfy needs for mental challenge, self-determination, and recognition; whereas (2) job perceptions are caused by job satisfaction because, as discussed earlier, job satisfaction may serve as a major cognitive filter that predisposes the individual to construct and maintain a psychological climate that is consistent with existing or desired levels of job satisfaction.

Hypothesis 2 reflects the assumptions that PC perceptions are functions of proximal environments and person variables. In regard to person variables, the assimilation assumption discussed in the prior example, for perceptions of psychological influence, was again believed to be operational; that is, the job perceptions are believed to be predisposed toward the construction of a subjective

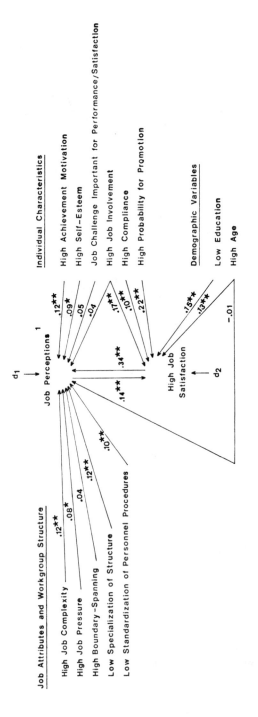

FIG. 18.1. A nonrecursive model relating job perceptions to job satisfaction.

environment that is compatible with factors such as needs, values, and self-concepts. A similar prediction is made for job satisfaction in Hypothesis 3, namely that job-satisfaction attitudes are viewed as being predisposed toward cognitive congruency with more basic values and norms (Rokeach, 1968, 1971). However, person variables that are causes for job satisfaction are not necessarily the same as those for the job perceptions. Finally, it is predicted that situational attributes and events do not affect job satisfaction directly, but rather that in the formulation of job-satisfaction attitudes, individuals rely on their job perceptions for environmental information. This suggests that the formulation of job-satisfaction attitudes, in comparison to job perceptions, requires additional stages of information processing that results in more personalistic, emotional states, further removed in the information-processing sequence from situational attributes/events.

To test these hypotheses, data were employed for a sample of subjects that differed significantly in regard to job attributes and work-group structure variables. The sample (n = 642) consisted of the production-line personnel and systems analysts/computer programmers described in the prior example, as well as subsamples of municipal firefighters, salespersons, accountants, secretarial/clerical personnel, computer operators, and printers. The empirical tests of the hypotheses were based on the structural equation method of two-stage least squares (2SLS), designed specifically to analyze reciprocal causation (James & Singh, 1978). Given that cross-sectional, correlational data were employed, the primary goal of this analysis was to identify (and to reject) causal hypotheses that appeared untenable. On the other hand, if major causal hypotheses are not rejected and if the structural model is shown to be logically consistent with the data, then a meaningful basis for causal inference will have been achieved (Heise, 1975).

The results of the 2SLS are presented in Fig. 18.1, which is a structural (causal) model designed to reflect the causal hypotheses. The values associated with each arrow in the model are estimates of standardized structural parameters, often referred to as "path coefficients." A summary of the results in relation to the hypotheses is as follows:

1. The (estimated) path coefficient for the job perception → job satisfaction causal relationship was significant (.14), as was the path coefficient for the job satisfaction → job perception causal relationship (.34). These results indicated the job perceptions and job satisfaction could be considered as reciprocal causes of each other, thus supporting Hypothesis 1.

2. Hypothesis 2 received partial support. In regard to the proximal-environment variables, the job perceptions were influenced causally and positively by higher levels of job complexity and job pressure and lower levels of specialization (a measure of the division of labor) and standardization of procedures. The job perceptions also were influenced causally and positively by per-

son variables, namely achievement motivation and self-esteem. It should be noted that large path coefficients were not expected inasmuch as multiple sources of causation were assumed.

3. Hypothesis 3 received strong support. It was found that individuals who were more favorably disposed toward their jobs, as reflected by higher levels of job involvement and compliance with traditional work norms, higher probabilities for promotion, and higher ages, were more likely to be satisfied with their jobs. In contrast, more highly educated individuals, who may well have greater mobility in the job market, were not as satisfied with their jobs. Tests of logical consistency of the model with the data (see James & Jones, 1979) demonstrated that job satisfaction was not caused directly by any of the proximal environmental variables. This supported the assumption that job satisfaction, in contrast to the job perceptions, required additional stages of cognitive-information processing and was more emotional and personalistic than the job perceptions.

In summary, the key implications of this study were: (1) that perceptions that reflect psychologically meaningful and significant interpretations of a job environment are related reciprocally to attitudes toward the job environment; and (2) that statistical methods such as 2 SLS can be adapted for use to study psychological problems that involve reciprocal causation (see also James & Singh, 1978). It should be noted that moderator analysis was not indicated in this study. That is, unlike the study of psychological influence, relationships between the proximal-environment variables and the job perceptions, as well as the job perception–job satisfaction relationships, were not moderated by either person variables or situational contexts. This indicates that the presence of PXS interactions may be a function of the particular domain of PC investigated as well as the criteria of interest.

IMPLICATIONS OF THE PSYCHOLOGICAL-CLIMATE APPROACH FOR RESEARCH ON ENVIRONMENTAL PERCEPTIONS

The concluding discussion addresses implications for future research based on theory and empirical studies on psychological climate. Hopefully, these implications will be of interest to other research endeavors in which emphasis is placed on environmental perceptions such as environmental psychology, interactional psychology, and social-learning and cognitive–social-learning theory. The most salient implications are summarized in the following:

1. Individual differences would be expected to be operative in perceptions that reflect the psychological meaning and significance of the work environment

to individuals. Consequently, the question must be asked whether it is meaningful to aggregate perception scores across individuals in presumably the same work environment in order to obtain a description of that environment. Clearly, if individuals do not agree, then the aggregate perception measure is not representative of all, or perhaps even most, of the individuals in the environment.

2. Differences in perceptions among individuals in the same or similar work environments have psychological significance. A serious need exists to address work environment perceptions as functions of person variables and PXS interactions. The list of possible studies is infinite, but some broad lines of research include the following.

(a) Basic research on the HOSs that individuals employ to represent work environments. To illustrate one line of research, the PC variables listed in Table 18.1 represent constructs that generally have a long history of demonstrated importance in the study of work environments. Thus, the typical question is not whether these constructs are generally represented in cognitive systems of all or most individuals but rather whether different individuals: (1) employ the same constructs (e.g., leader support) but attribute different values to the constructs; or (2) employ different constructs, although *all* the constructs are generally present in the cognitive systems for all individuals in defined populations. The issue that different individuals might *not* have the same sets of HOSs to represent work environments was not raised until recently (James et al., 1978). As recommended by James et al. (1978) for work environment perceptions and by Mischel (1973) for environmental perceptions in general, basic research is needed to identify the schemata that different types of individuals employ to represent the same environments.

(b) Studies are needed of the perceptual/cognitive processes that are involved in arriving at work environment perceptions. It is believed that individuals are unable, by introspection, to describe accurately their perceptual/cognitive operations such as selective attention (e.g., the processes are partially nonconscious—[Erdelyi, 1974]). Nevertheless, it is possible to infer whether perceptual/cognitive operations have occurred by examining individuals' reports on the end products of perceptual/cognitive processes (Nisbett & Wilson, 1977). In the studies presented, hypotheses were advanced and tested with respect to the processes of assimilation of perceptions toward cognitive predispositions, selective attention based on predispositions and situational contexts (PXS interactions), and reciprocal causation between perceptions and attitudes. Prior research also has demonstrated that work-environment perceptions are related to behavior–performance expectancies, performance–outcome instrumentalities, and valences of outcomes (James et al., 1977). However, empirical evidence remains sparse, and the need exists to demonstrate empirically that the perceptual/cognitive filtering, abstraction, generalization, and interpretation reflected in environmental perceptions are functions of processes such as assimilation, selective attention, restructuring, redefinition, and reciprocal causation between perceptions and factors such as attitudes, expectancies, and components of the self-regulatory system. Finally it is important to note that the situational contexts in which these processes occur may provide powerful moderators. Consequently, factors such as the following need to be considered: certainty and stability of the environment, situational constraints and requirements for action, acclimatization, stress and overload, and social factors, such as the presence of significant others.

3. Proximal-environmental correlates, preferably causes, of work-environment perceptions need to be identified. Of particular concern is the question of what constitutes a proximal environment for an individual, or, from a related perspective, what it is in the proximal environment that the individual experiences. The latter question connotes that it is impossible to divorce the person from the environment inasmuch as the environment that an individual experiences is in part a function of cognitive representations. Nevertheless, it is possible to identify environmental attributes and events that stimulate the occurrence of and provide information for cognitive processes. In part, these attributes and events should include variables that are broadly applicable to all or most individuals in a particular environment (dress codes, vacation schedules, selection standards, seniority systems, formal group goals and objectives, formal communication lines, physical environments, and so forth). On the other hand, many environmental correlates/causes of perceptions may have to be identified for *each* individual. This applies especially to variables of a "process" nature (i.e., variables easily amenable to change) such as leadership (as shown in the example for psychological influence), the content of verbal communication, performance evaluations, informal control and discipline procedures, acclimation and socialization processes, informal status and power relationships, procedures employed for conflict resolution, informal and some formal aspects of boundary-spanning activities, many aspects of resources, and social interrelationships.

Of additional importance is the likelihood that environmental attributes and events are related to perceptions in the framework of a reciprocal causation model. As discussed and illustrated by Bandura (1978), individuals engender much of their environments through their behaviors. This is especially, but not exclusively, applicable to process variables such as those discussed in the foregoing. The reciprocal causation model appears to be extremely promising, although, as noted earlier, there is little empirical evidence to support this contention. Hopefully, the availability of analytic procedures such as 2SLS, three-stage least squares, and limited and full-information maximum likelihood estimation programs (Duncan, 1975; Heise, 1975; James & Singh, 1978; Johnston, 1972; Jöreskog, 1978) will stimulate psychologists to conduct empirical tests of theoretical reciprocal causation models.

The three implications presented in these concluding remarks indicate a broad outline for research but are not meant to be exhaustive. Emphasis was placed on identifying the bases of environmental perceptions because this has not been a subject of strong research endeavors in the past. It would seem straightforward, however, that one cannot understand how perceptions are related to behavior/affect until one explains how the perceptions occurred in the first place. Thus, we chose to emphasize environmental perceptions as dependent variables throughout most of this chapter.

ACKNOWLEDGMENTS

Support for this project was provided under Office of Naval Research Contract Number N00014-77-C-123, Office of Naval Research Contract NR 170-840, and by the National Institute on Drug Abuse, Department of Health, Education, and Welfare, Grant Number H-81-DA-01931-01. Opinions expressed are those of the authors and are not to be construed as necessarily reflecting the official view or endorsement of the Department of the Navy or the National Institute on Drug Abuse.

19

The Perceived Environment in Psychological Theory and Research

Richard Jessor
Institute of Behavioral Science
University of Colorado

How to conceptualize the environment of human action continues to be a problematic enterprise in contemporary psychology. The most basic psychological term for the environment—the stimulus—still eludes consensual definition (Gibson, 1960; Jessor, 1956); environmental descriptions borrowed from other disciplines—physics, geography, sociology—appear in psychological research as if their appropriateness were self-evident; and when environmental concepts at very different levels of abstraction are employed in a study, the analysis often fails to consider their causal or logical heterogeneity.

COMING TO TERMS WITH SUBJECTIVITY

Despite this appearance of intellectual disarray, an evolutionary shift in thinking about the environment can be discerned in the more recent history of psychology and, indeed, of related disciplines. The key dialectic underlying this change seems to have been a recognition of and a coming to terms with the role of subjectivity in science. The ''intrusion of subjectivity'' (Kessel, 1970) in physical science can be widely documented but, for psychologists raised on the objectivism ostensibly inherent in operational definition, it is perhaps most telling to quote from the last book written by Bridgman (1959), the father of operationism: ''Here I shall only reiterate my opinion that a proper appreciation of [first-person report] will alter the common picture of science as something essentially public into something essentially private [p. 237].''

In sociology, concern for the subjective had long been a preoccupation of the symbolic interactionists (Blumer, 1966; Rose, 1962; Wilson, 1970) who argued that the environment of action is, in the last analysis, *constituted by the actor.* The classical environmental concept in this perspective is "the definition of the situation" (Thomas, 1928), and it yielded the well-known apothegm: "If men define situations as real, they are real in their consequences [p. 572]." Renewed support for this orientation emerges from a recent review of trends in social psychology; the author (Stryker, 1977), a sociologist, singles out the most important trend as: ". . . the general surge . . . of phenomenological thinking," and he concludes that ". . . the subjective has become respectable [p. 157]."

Within psychology, part of the dialectic was the renewal of interest in inner experience as legitimate psychological data (Zener, 1958). But the more fundamental thrust came from a growing awareness of the psychological implications of human experiential capabilities, namely, their potential for having a transformational impact on the environment. Among personality theorists, Kurt Lewin was probably the most explicit and systematic on this point, his views reflecting the important influence of the philosopher, Ernst Cassirer (1953): "No longer in a merely physical universe, man lives in a symbolic universe . . . Physical reality seems to recede in proportion as man's symbolic activity advances. Instead of dealing with things themselves man is in a sense constantly conversing with himself [p. 43]." In Lewinian field theory (Lewin, 1951a), this perspective led to an insistence on describing the environment *as it is perceived or experienced by the actor:* ". . . to substitute for that world of the individual the world of the teacher, of the physicist, or of anybody else is to be, not objective, but wrong [p. 62]." Cartwright (1978), in his recent Lewin Memorial Award address, recalls Lewin's premise that behavior cannot be properly explained if one does not understand the way in which individuals view the world in which they live, and he notes that Lewin: ". . . was, in this sense, a subjectivist [p. 174]."

Concern with the environment from the perspective of the actor, that is, concern with its psychological description or its perceived meaning, was a common thread running through the theoretical formulations of the "classical interactionists" (the phrase is Ekehammar's, 1974; see also Jessor, 1956, 1958, 1961; and Jessor & Jessor, 1973). Although rather broadly shared, this phenomenological or subjectivist position remained difficult for psychologists of a behaviorist persuasion to assimilate. It seems to have required the throes of the person–situation controversy over the past decade to bring about a widened consensus in which they could also participate. Contemporary social behavior formulations (Bandura, 1978) now do include such acknowledgments as: ". . . the environment is partly of a person's own making [p. 345]" and "external influences operate largely through cognitive processes [p. 355]" (see also Mischel, 1973). It is sobering to realize, however, that the resolution of the person–situation controversy in interactionism constitutes little more than a rediscovery of the earlier field-theoretical position of Lewin and others (Murray, 1938; Rogers, 1959; Rotter, 1954). In the concluding paragraphs of an historical review of the various issues in the dispute, Ekehammar (1974) notes that the cognitive and perceptual concepts invoked by the more recent interactionists: "... have essentially the same meaning as the classical interactionists' psychological environment. Although the terminology is different, the common main idea is that the individual's psychological representation and construction of the environment is emphasized [p. 1044]."

Coming to terms with subjectivity implies acceptance of a fundamentally phenomenological perspective in psychology and agreement on the importance of dealing with the psychological environment. Despite the progress in this direction, it constitutes only a necessary starting point for conceptualizing the environment of human action. Basic issues persist, among them the relation of the psychological environment to other environments in more traditional descriptions, the relationship of the psychological environment to behavior and development, the formal or structural properties of the psychological environment, and finally, its content. Some comment on each of these conceptual issues is in order before we turn to a set of research findings that have an empirical bearing on them as well.

THE MULTIPLICITY OF ENVIRONMENTS

It was emphasized in an earlier discussion (Jessor & Jessor, 1973) that every human action can be seen as taking place in multiple and various environments *simultaneously*. The context of action can always be dealt with as a physical context, a geographic context, a cultural context, a social structural context, a psychological context, and more. This inherent multiplicity of the environment precludes any hope of arriving at some ultimate or ontologically most real environment. Instead, the environment has to be seen as capable of being continuously and differentially *constituted* depending on such factors as the conceptual orientation of a particular discipline, the explanatory objectives of a particular researcher, or the guiding purposes of a particular actor.

In this view, it would seem quite reasonable to try to link human action to many different kinds of environments or contextual attributes—humidity, radiation, urban density, normative conflict, bureaucracy, marginality, overprotection, threat, etc. But it is precisely its multiplicity that makes for the problematic status of the environment in contemporary psychology. What is needed are principles for organizing the multiplicity and diversity of environments in relation to the disciplinary goal of achieving *psychological explanation*.

Environment–Behavior Mediation

Two related principles can be invoked toward that end. The first principle has to do with the fact that *explanation* of any observed linkage between environment and action requires some theoretical structure to mediate the linkage and to make it psychologically understandable if not logically inescapable. In the absence of a psychologically relevant theoretical network to bridge the explanatory gap, such observed linkages as those of climatic variation with aggression, apartment house dwelling with schizophrenia, low socioeconomic status with apathy, or bureaucracy with conforming behavior, remain merely empirical. The degree to which there exist theoretical structures to account for the causal impact of the various environments on action would be one principle that could be useful in determining which environments to explore. At present, social and cultural environments lend themselves more readily to the specification of a theoretical linkage to action than do physical or geographic or genetic environments.

Experiential Proximity of Environments

The second and more important principle is that the multiple and various environments can be ordered along a dimension of conceptual proximity to experience, to perception, to interpretation, or to psychological response. Some environments are relatively (or even absolutely) remote from direct experience; they are generally described in nonpsychological language and are without specific functional significance for the person. The environments of physics, geography, biology, and institutional sociology are examples that are remote from immediate experience; they would fall, therefore, toward the *distal* end of this dimension. Environments that are closer to being directly perceived or experienced fall toward the *proximal* end of the dimension. These latter employ a psychological or, at least, a psychologically relevant language of description, and they refer to attributes that can be perceived or interpreted or that have rather direct implications for perception and meaning. Along this distal–proximal dimension, *the most proximal environment would be the perceived environment,* the environment of immediate significance for the actor.

The idea that the multiplicity of environments can be ordered in relation to their proximity to perception or experience can be found also in the spatial arrangement of Lewin's topological concepts: The psychological environment is most proximal; next is the boundary zone around the life space; and then there is the further differentiation of the region lying outside the boundary zone into the ''foreign hull'' and the still more remote ''alien factors'' (Lewin, 1951b).

Invariance of Behavior with the Perceived Environment

Several implications follow from the nature of the distal–proximal dimension. First, environmental variables that are distal will require complex, theoretical structures to link them with experience and, thereby, with action; whatever linkage they do have to action, it follows necessarily, must be mediated by more proximal environmental variables. Second, proximal variables, precisely because they mediate the linkage of distal variables to action, make it possible to account for variation in behavior where the distal environment remains constant. Finally, the most important logical implication of the distal–proximal dimension is that *action or behavior is invariant with the proximal or perceived environment* rather than with the distal environment. The search in psychology for invariant relations requires, therefore, a proximal or perceived environment focus (Jessor, 1961; Jessor & Jessor, 1973). The key *empirical* consequence to be derived from these various implications is that correlations between environmental variables and behavior should be greater the more proximal the environment, and they should be greatest for those variables that are in the perceived environment. This is one of the propositions that will be examined in the data to be presented shortly.

The discussion thus far can be made more concrete by consideration of three different kinds of environments that are commonly used in social-psychological studies and that we ourselves have worked with over the past two decades in relation to our own research on deviance and problem behavior. In distal-to-proximal order, they are the demographic environment, the social structural environment, and the perceived environment.

THE DEMOGRAPHIC ENVIRONMENT

The environment of demography is made up of a variety of *descriptive* (rather than theoretical or analytic) concepts referring to quite obvious or phenotypic attributes that serve to classify persons or locate them in positions in societal space. Age, sex, race, religious membership, rural–urban residence, family composition, education, and occupation are the most frequently used, and they lend themselves readily to epidemiological purposes that are of interest to the discipline and to society at large. It is in regard to their *causal or explanatory contribution,* however, that the distal remoteness of such attributes becomes apparent. Demographic concepts do not convey univocal experiential significance, and none of them carries any necessary theoretical significance that would imply a particular influence on behavior. On both of these grounds, demographic concepts need to be seen as highly distal; at best, they can have only indirect and quite uncertain consequences for variation in action.

Perhaps most invoked in psychological research is the demographic concept of social class or socioeconomic status, a position in the hierarchical organization of society that is usually indexed by level of occupation and amount of education. A forceful claim for the importance of this aspect of demography has been made by Kohn (1976): "In actuality, social class embodies such basic differences in conditions of life that subjective reality is necessarily different for people differentially situated in the social hierarchy [p. 179]," and "... members of different social classes ... come to see the world differently ... [p. 180]." If this were in fact the case, the distal environment of social class would constitute an extremely useful concept in accounting for variation in behavior. Its utility, as Kohn makes clear, would derive from the implications it would have for the perceived environment, that is, for differences in "subjective reality." The distal environment of social class has not proved to be useful in this way, however. Social classes are not (or are no longer) insulated from each other; there is mobility between classes; all classes are exposed to the same homogenizing mass communication media; and there have even been secular changes in the defining criteria of class. Further, the complexity of social life and experience is such that it defies summary by a simple index of years of education or status of occupation. Said otherwise, there is enormous heterogeneity of experience *within* class, perhaps as great as that between classes, at least in some areas. In light of these remarks the distal environment of social class is not an appropriate index or map of the perceived environment, and therefore it should have little necessary consequence for behavior.

To sum up this perspective on the demographic environment, it is too distal from experience to yield strong linkages with behavior; it conveys little in the way of analytic understanding of behavioral variation; and whatever linkage can be established between it and behavior must remain essentially empirical unless there is also an account—and, ideally, an assessment—of its mediation by the perceived environment.

THE SOCIAL STRUCTURAL ENVIRONMENT

The second environment to be considered—the environment of social structure—is more proximal to experience and to behavior than is the environment of demography. By virtue of the fact that it is constituted in *theoretical* (rather than descriptive) terms, it does convey particular implications for the perceived environment and, thereby, for behavior. The concepts that are employed in constituting the social structural environment tend to have experience and behavior relevance precisely because they were invented to account for variation in social behavior. They tend to emphasize those properties of the environment that would be expected to shape the perceptual field and the possibilities for action. The distinction being drawn here can be illuminated by a different aspect of Kohn's approach to the work situation. Instead of a demographic concern with the status level of an occupation, Kohn and Schooler (1973) focus on the "structural imperatives" of the job, for example, the actual conditions of work, its substantive complexity, and its routinization, and their findings emphasize: "... the social psychological importance of the structural imperatives of the job that impinge on the man most directly, insistently, and demandingly... [p. 116]." In sum, the social-structural environment is constituted of those attributes of the social context that have a high degree of *potential* significance for experience and behavior.

A major concern of our earlier research in a tri-ethnic community was to elaborate a conceptualization of the social structural (we called it *sociocultural*) environment that would yield a logical account of both interethnic and intraethnic variation in deviant behavior. That environment, defined as a system, is shown in Fig. 19.1 (the personality system and the socialization system that were part of the overall conceptual framework are omitted). Three component environmental structures were designated in the theory—a structure of opportunity, a structure of norms, and a structure of social controls—and the location of a person (or of an ethnic group) in each of these structures specified the likelihood of occurrence of problem behavior (Jessor, Graves, Hanson, & Jessor, 1968). Each structure included variables that had potential significance for perception. For example, the social control structure included three such variables: "exposure to deviance" (the prevalence of models for deviant behavior in the ecology); "absence of sanction networks" (nonparticipation in or exclusion from social interactions, such as those in church groups, that negatively sanction transgression); and "opportunity to engage in deviance" (the availability of time and of access to places and materials [e.g., cars or alcohol] that make certain behaviors possible).

The theory behind this environmental conceptualization is that value-access disjunctions in the opportunity structure tend to instigate deviance, whereas anomie in the normative structure and access to illegitimate means in the social control structure tend to attenuate controls against deviance; the balance among the three structures is what generates the environmental dynamic for behavior. This effort sought to capture a behavior-relevant dimension of the social structural environment—what might be called *its conduciveness to deviance*. (In this connection, see Sells' concern [1963a] that behavior-relevant dimensions of the

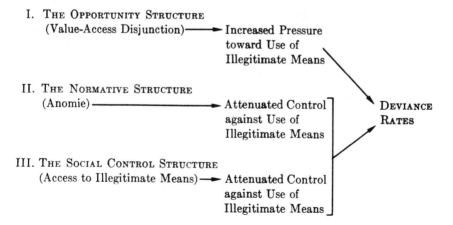

I. THE OPPORTUNITY STRUCTURE
  (Value-Access Disjunction) ⟶ Increased Pressure toward Use of Illegitimate Means

II. THE NORMATIVE STRUCTURE
  (Anomie) ⟶ Attenuated Control against Use of Illegitimate Means

III. THE SOCIAL CONTROL STRUCTURE
  (Access to Illegitimate Means) ⟶ Attenuated Control against Use of Illegitimate Means

DEVIANCE RATES

FIG. 19.1. The sociocultural system and deviance rates. (Reprinted from Jessor, Graves, Hanson, & Jessor, 1968, p. 78.)

environment be identified and his employment of one such dimension which he called "conduciveness to academic achievement.")

Although theoretically relevant to deviant behavior, and although referring to properties of the social environment that are potentially amenable to experience, conduciveness to deviance nevertheless remains distal from the perceived environment. As a description of the environment it is in perceiv*able* but still not in perceiv*ed* terms. Although this approach to the environment was successful for the purposes of the Tri-Ethnic Project and accounted for more of the variance than did the more obvious demographic attributes such as ethnic group membership or socioeconomic status, it still left considerable variance unaccounted for. This was part of the impetus for our move to assessing the perceived environment in our next major research effort.

THE PERCEIVED ENVIRONMENT

The third environment—the one that is the main focus of this chapter—is the perceived environment, the environment that is most proximal to experience along the distal-proximal dimension. The perceived environment refers to the social-psychological constitution of the environment out of the perceptions, definitions, reports, or responses of the actor. To borrow Brunswik's (1943) very apt phrase, it is the environment that is "post-perceptual and pre-behavioral [p. 266]." Reflecting socially organized and shared dimensions of potential meaning as well as personally organized and idiosyncratic dispositions to perceive and to process information, the perceived environment is the one that, logically, is most invariant with or causally closest to action. The notion of "causal closeness" as used here is quite different from physical or biological closeness. For example, a physical-language description of the immediate context in which a person is located, or a description of such biologically close aspects of the person's environment as obesity or skin color, remain causally distal because they do not specify their experiential relevance or the actual significance they have for the person. It is the *meanings* of attributes or the *definitions* of situations that are causally closest because they are most immediately prebehavioral in a chain of causal linkages.

In the empirical portion of this chapter, we deal with essentially the same environmental dimension that was explored earlier in the Tri-Ethnic Study—its conduciveness to problem behavior—but this time the dimension is treated as an aspect of the perceived environment rather than the social structural environment. Before turning to the research, however, it is useful to elaborate some of the formal or structural properties that emerge from an effort to conceptualize the perceived environment. The task of conceptualizing the perceived environment is, in fact, not very different from what has to be done when conceptualizing personality. Questions to be answered concern its structure, its organization, its enduringness, its development, and its content.

The Property of Depth

The first of the properties of the perceived environment needing mention is its *depth*. When a specific behavior or class of behavior is at issue, some aspects of the perceived environment are "closer" to it than others; they are those aspects that directly and obviously implicate that behavior. For example, in predicting the use of marijuana from perceived environment variables, the perception that friends use marijuana is considered conceptually closer to the use of marijuana than the perception that friends are generally warm and supportive. The notion of depth always obtains in relation to specific behavior, and variables can be allocated to a closer or a more remote "region" within the perceived environment depending on the immediacy of their import for that behavior. As might be expected, these closer and more remote regions are referred to, respectively, as proximal and distal regions. The very same logic that was applied to the proximal–distal dimension underlying the different kinds of environments is applied to these two regions, but now *within* the perceived environment. Variables in the proximal region of the perceived environment are those with an obvious connection to behavior. They refer to models for it, or approval for it, or sanctions against it, etc., and all of them actually specify the behavior in the definition of the variable itself, for example, "perceived models for marijuana use." Variables in the distal region of the perceived environment are unconnected to any specific behavior. Whereas they clearly have implications for variation in behavior, those implications depend on theory rather than being immediately obvious, for example, "perceived support from friends."

Depth is an important property because it indicates that even the perceived environment is not homogeneously relevant to a specific action. A consideration of the property of depth enables the ordering of perceived variables in relation to their closeness to specific behaviors. It also clarifies why some perceived variables, namely those that are proximal, are more likely to have powerful associations with behavior than others, namely those that are distal. It is worth pointing out, parenthetically, that the association of a distal perceived variable with behavior, although it is usually weaker, may be more *interesting* than the association of a proximal perceived variable precisely because the connection of the former is so much less obvious.

The Property of Texture

A second property, *texture*, has to do with the degree to which the perceived environment as a whole and its distal and proximal regions are differentiated into component variables and attributes. Texture is thus a direct reflection of the degree of theoretical articulation that has been accomplished for the perceived environment. Instead of lending itself only to global or generalized characterization, the perceived environment can be differentiated according to content (e.g., perceived supports and controls), according to social agents (e.g., perceived parental supports or friends controls), according to opportunities to learn behaviors (e.g., perceived models for it), and according to instigations to engage in behaviors (e.g., perceived social approval for such actions). The more texture it has, the more the perceived environment is likely to yield analytic understanding.

The Property of Enduringness

A third property of the perceived environment is its *enduringness*. It is possible to specify the perceived environment in relation to a given place at a particular moment of time—near the end of a party, perhaps, or just as the instructor is calling on a student in class. This is the usual meaning of the concept of the psychological situation, the situation as it exists at a moment in time, and the situation in which the psychological concern is with understanding the actor's very next behavior. It was this momentary perceived environment that Kurt Lewin sought to represent in his diagrams of the psychological situation in hodological space. But it is also possible to consider a more extended, more generalized, more enduring perceived environment, one that has reference to a broader and longer segment of life. Enduringness refers to quite different perceptions of the environment by the same person. Thus, "I have a lot of support in my marriage" is different from "This particular interaction is threatening." The former example illustrates the perception of a relatively enduring aspect of the environment, and it contrasts sharply with the perception of the momentary situation in the latter example. In interviews and questionnaires, it is usually the more enduring perceived environment we are seeking to characterize rather than the immediate situation of the inquiry. W. I. Thomas seemed to be reaching for this kind of property in relation to his notion of definitions of the situation when he stated in Ball (1972): "Not only concrete acts are dependent on the definitions of the situation but gradually a whole life-policy and the personality of the individual himself follow from a series of such definitions [p. 62]."

The Property of Developmental Change

Fourth, it is useful to conceive of the perceived environment as having the property of *developmental change*. Because the perceived environment reflects socially organized dimensions of potential meaning and personally organized dispositions to perceive, and because there are developmental tendencies in both of these sources of influence, the perceived environment can be expected to evidence systematic and predictable changes over time or at different life stages. In the social environment, for example, the operation of the social process of age grading implies systematic changes in demands, expectations, and opportunities as young people grow older. There will also be a predictable increase in the prevalence of friends who are models for certain behaviors as adolescence is reached and passed. It makes sense even to conceive of "growth curves" for attributes of the perceived environment in the same way as it does for attributes of personality or ability. A similar point has been made by Nesselroade and Baltes (1974), who have introduced the concept of "environmental ontogeny [p. 64]" in their work.

The Question of Content

A final concern with the perceived environment would be with its *content*. Although Lewin never really elaborated the content of the psychological environment, a number of the classical interactionists did propose approaches to formulating content as well as actual systems of content. Murray's (1938) notion of beta press provided perceived environment content in direct analogy to the need concepts in his theory. As another example, Rotter (1954, 1955) has suggested describing the reinforcements or goals in situations, as well as the complexity and the novelty of situations. In the final analysis, content would seem to be partly a matter of theory—both theory of the person and theory of the social environment—and partly a matter of the particular problem the theory is being applied to. There is no single mapping of the content of the psychological environment that would make sense given the diversity of the enterprise of psychology.

THE PERCEIVED ENVIRONMENT AND PROBLEM BEHAVIOR

Our own effort to map the perceived environment has been shaped, as indicated earlier, by an interest in the dimension of environmental proneness or conduciveness to problem behavior. It has involved the specification of both a proximal and a distal set of variables within the perceived environment system, all the variables having theoretical implications for problem behavior. The perceived environment system is shown as Box B in Fig. 19.2 (which also presents the larger conceptual structure for our problem-behavior research).

The content of the distal and proximal variables in Box B of Fig. 19.2 continues the theoretical emphases that had been represented in the social structural system in the earlier Tri-Ethnic Study. The present concern with the compatibility between parents and friends in their expectations, and with the relative influence of these two reference groups, continues our earlier interest in normative consensus and in the degree of anomie that may obtain in the social environment. The present concern with generalized supports and controls, and the focus on models and on approval–disapproval for specific behaviors, reflects a continuity with our earlier interest in social controls and in access to illegitimate means in the social environment. However, all the variables shown in Box B of Fig. 19.2 are now derived from the respondent's perception and are based on direct reports

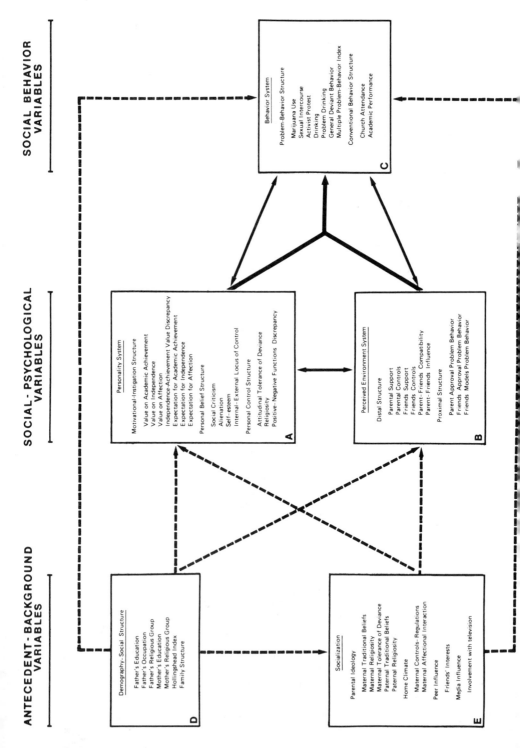

SOCIAL BEHAVIOR VARIABLES

SOCIAL-PSYCHOLOGICAL VARIABLES

ANTECEDENT-BACKGROUND VARIABLES

Behavior System

Problem-Behavior Structure

Marijuana Use
Sexual Intercourse
Activist Protest
Drinking
Problem Drinking
General Deviant Behavior
Multiple Problem-Behavior Index

Conventional Behavior Structure

Church Attendance
Academic Performance

C

Personality System

Motivational-Instigation Structure

Value on Academic Achievement
Value on Independence
Value on Affection
Independence-Achievement Value Discrepancy
Expectation for Academic Achievement
Expectation for Independence
Expectation for Affection

Personal Belief Structure

Social Criticism
Alienation
Self-esteem
Internal-External Locus of Control

Personal Control Structure

Attitudinal Tolerance of Deviance
Religiosity
Positive-Negative Functions Discrepancy

A

Perceived Environment System

Distal Structure

Parental Support
Parental Controls
Friends Support
Friends Controls
Parent-Friends Compatibility
Parent-Friends Influence

Proximal Structure

Parent Approval Problem Behavior
Friends Approval Problem Behavior
Friends Models Problem Behavior

B

Demography-Social Structure

Father's Education
Father's Occupation
Father's Religious Group
Mother's Education
Mother's Religious Group
Hollingshead Index
Family Structure

D

Socialization

Parental Ideology

Maternal Traditional Beliefs
Maternal Religiosity
Maternal Tolerance of Deviance
Paternal Traditional Beliefs
Paternal Religiosity

Home Climate

Maternal Controls-Regulations
Maternal Affectional Interaction

Peer Influence

Friends' Interests
Media Influence
Involvement with television

E

308

or descriptions of those relatively enduring aspects of the perceived environment. (Other aspects of the perceived environment relevant to problem behavior were also assessed, for example, the perception of friends' interests [Finney, 1979], but they are not represented in Fig. 19.2 and will not be discussed further.)

Conduciveness to problem behavior in the perceived environment system was conceptualized as the balance between the perception of social controls against problem behavior, on the one hand, and the perception of models and support for problem behavior on the other. In the distal structure, conduciveness theoretically implies low parental support and controls, low friends controls, low compatibility between parents' and friends' expectations, and low parent influence relative to friends influence. In the proximal structure, conduciveness implies low parental disapproval of specific problem behaviors, and high friends models for and approval of engaging in specific problem behaviors. The more that these separate variables pattern together in a theoretically conducive way, the more likely the occurrence of problem behavior.

The remainder of the chapter is concerned with three major objectives. The first is an empirical appraisal of the explanatory effectiveness of this particular conceptualization of the perceived environment in relation to problem behavior in youth. The second is to demonstrate that the perceived environment, because of its causal closeness to behavior, accounts for a substantially larger portion of the variance in youthful problem behavior than the demographic environment. And the third objective is to show that, within the perceived environment, the proximal variables account for more of the variance in problem behavior than the distal variables. We have the opportunity in these analyses to test some of the logical implications of the preceding discussion.

Measuring the Perceived Environment

Measures of four separate but related behavioral domains will constitute the "dependent" or criterion variables: excessive alcohol use, involvement with marijuana, experience with sexual intercourse, and engagement in protodelinquent actions such as stealing or aggression. Two entirely independent data sets are employed in the analyses, thereby enabling a complete replication of the tests of the major propositions. The first data set is from a four-year longitudinal study of problem behavior and psychosocial development (Jessor & Jessor, 1977) carried out in a small city in the Rocky Mountain region of the United States. It is referred to in this chapter as the *High School Study*. Questionnaires were administered annually to cohorts who were initially in grades 7, 8, and 9; by the fourth testing in 1972, the cohorts had reached grades 10, 11, and 12. It is the cross-sectional data from this fourth testing of 188 males and 244 females that are considered in this chapter. The questionnaires contained a wide variety of measures of personality, the perceived environment, and behavior, but our focus will be restricted to the measures of the demographic environment, the perceived environment, and the four areas of behavior.

The second data set is from a national sample study carried out by the Research Triangle Institute in the spring of 1974 (Donovan & Jessor, 1978; Rachal, Hubbard, Williams & Tuchfeld, 1976; Rachal, Williams, Brehm, Cavanaugh, Moore & Eckerman, 1975). It is referred to in this chapter as the *Nationwide Sample Study*. Over 13,000 students in grades 7-12 in a stratified random sample of high schools in the 48 contiguous states and the District of Columbia filled out questionnaires that included many of the measures that we had devised earlier for use in the High School Study. Although the High School Study was carried out in a local community and was based on a largely middle-class, Caucasian sample, the Nationwide Sample Study, by contrast, included a wide diversity of socioeconomic status, ethnic status, and geographic location. Replication across such different samples can prove especially compelling.

The measures that were obtained for the demographic environment, for the perceived environment, and for behavior were quite comparable in both the High School Study and the Nationwide Sample Study, although the wording and the number of items in a particular scale (and, hence, the score range) could differ in the two studies. The demographic measures included the conventional indicators of socioeconomic status—*father's education, mother's education, father's occupation,* and the *Hollingshead index of social position*—and a measure of the degree of liberalism–fundamentalism of the parents' *religious group membership*. Measurement of the distal structure of the perceived environment was somewhat more elaborate in the High School Study than in the Nationwide Sample Study. It included four two-item scales to measure: perceived *parental support* (e.g., "Would you say that your parents generally encourage you to do what you are interested in doing and show interest in those things themselves?"); perceived *friends support* (e.g., "Do you feel free to talk to your friends about personal problems when you want to?"); perceived *parental controls* (e.g., "If you act in a way your parents disapprove of, are they likely to make things tough for you?"); and perceived *friends controls* (e.g., "Compared to most other students, how strict would you say your friends are about standards for how to behave?"). In both studies, identical scales were employed for the other two variables in the distal structure: perceived *parents–friends compatibility* (e.g., "With respect to what you should get out of being in school, would you say that your parents and your friends think pretty much the same way about it?"); and relative *parents–friends influence*, (e.g., "If you had a serious decision to make, like whether or not to continue in school, or whether or not to get married, whose opinions would you value most—your parents' or your friends'?").

Measurement of the proximal structure of the perceived environment was behavior specific in relation to the different behaviors. It included three scales in both studies. To illustrate for the drinking area, these were: perceived *parental approval–disapproval for drinking* (e.g., "How do your parents (or your family) feel about people your age drinking?"); perceived *friends approval for drinking* (e.g., "How do most of your friends feel about people your age drinking?"); and perceived *friends models for drinking* (e.g., "Do you have any *close* friends who drink fairly regularly?").

Psychometric properties of the various perceived environment measures were at least adequate as far as Scott's homogeneity ratio and Cronbach's alpha reliability are concerned. Because of the longitudinal nature of the High School Study, it is possible also to report on the temporal stability of the measures across the annual testings. The average interyear correlations are very satisfactory, falling for the most part at about .40 or better. Further details about the different scales, the number of items in each, and their score range may be found in Jessor and Jessor (1977) for the High School Study and in Donovan and Jessor (1978) for the Nationwide Sample Study.

Measuring Problem Behavior

With respect to the measures of behavior, the measure of frequency of drunkenness was a single item: "During the past year, about how many times have you gotten drunk?" The measure of marijuana involvement was a four-item Guttman scale: "Have you ever tried marijuana?"; "Have you ever been very high or 'stoned' on marijuana to the point where you were pretty sure you had experienced the drug effects?"; "Do you or someone very close to you usually keep a supply of marijuana so that it's available when you want to use it?"; and "Do you use marijuana a couple of times a week or more when it's available?" The coefficient of reproducibility and the coefficient of scalability were, respectively, .96 and .86 in the High School Study and .94 and .68 in the Nationwide Sample Study. Sexual intercourse experience was not assessed in the Nationwide Sample Study; in the High School Study, the index of virgin–nonvirgin status was based on the single question: "Have you ever engaged in sexual intercourse with someone of the opposite sex?" Finally, the measure of general deviant behavior included 26 items in the High School Study and 12 items in the national study. Items asked how often in the past year the respondent had: "broken into a place that is locked just to look around"; "taken as much as $5 or $10 from your parents' wallet or purse when they weren't around"; and "threatened a teacher because you were angry about something at school," etc. Psychometric properties are good in both studies, and temporal stability is excellent in the High School Study where it could be examined.

LINKING ENVIRONMENTS WITH BEHAVIOR

It is possible now to address the main empirical concerns of the chapter. The strategy we follow is to present Pearson bivariate correlations and multiple correlations of the demographic environment measures and the perceived environment measures with each of the behavioral criteria, by sex, for the two independent

TABLE 19.1

Pearson Correlations and Multiple Correlations of Demographic and Perceived Environment Measures with Four Problem-Behavior Criterion Measures (*High School Study*, Year IV [1972] Data)

Measures	Times Drunk in Past Year		Marijuana Involvement		Deviant Behavior in Past Year		Virgin–Nonvirgin Status	
	Males[a]	Females[a]	Males[c]	Females[c]	Males[c]	Females[c]	Males[d]	Females[d]
A. Demographic Environment								
Socioeconomic Status								
Father's education	−.11	.01	.01	.03	−.04	−.01	−.22**	−.14*
Mother's education	−.24**	−.00	.01	−.05	−.06	−.04	−.28***	−.11
Father's occupation	−.06	.01	.02	.11+	−.14+	.06	−.23**	−.07
Hollingshead index[b]	−.09	.01	.01	.08	−.12	.03	−.25**	−.11
Multiple R	.25**	.02	.02	.17	.16	.12	.30***	.15
Religious Group								
Father's relig. grp.	.02	.08	−.16*	.02	−.06	−.03	.02	.01
Mother's relig. grp.	.01	.01	−.18*	.02	−.06	−.02	.03	−.04
Multiple R	.02	.10	.18*	.02	.06	.03	.03	.06
Combined Demographic								
Multiple R	.26	.10	.19	.17	.19	.13	.30**	.17

312

B. Perceived Environment

Distal Structure

Parental support	-.18*	-.02	-.31***	-.21**	-.28***	-.13*	-.11	-.19**
Parental controls	-.19*	.02	-.15+	-.07	-.04	-.01	-.17*	-.13*
Friends support	.01	.16*	.00	.13+	-.11	.14*	.04	.06
Friends controls	-.19*	-.06	-.43***	-.35***	-.24**	-.22***	-.18*	-.24***
Parent–friends comp.	-.24**	-.07	-.31***	-.33***	-.25***	-.25***	-.08	-.24***
Parent–friends infl.	.05	.11	.29***	.18**	.16*	.25***	.11	.15*
Multiple R	.36**	.22	.52***	.53***	.34**	.43***	.26*	.39***

Proximal Structure

Parent approval	.11	-.06	.36***	.33***	.08	.09	.16*	.16*
Friends approval	.27**	.15*	.68***	.72***	.32***	.42***	.14+	.23***
Friends models	.23**	.20**	.69***	.69***	.40***	.52***	.45***	.54***
Multiple R	.31***	.24*	.74***	.76***	.41***	.55***	.46***	.55***

Combined Perceived

Multiple R	.44***	.30+	.76***	.78***	.45***	.59***	.47***	.59***

C. Demographic Plus Perceived Environment

Multiple R	.50**	.32	.77***	.79***	.49***	.59***	.54***	.60***

Note: Level of significance: $+p \leq .10$, $*p \leq .05$, $**p \leq .01$, $***p \leq .001$.

[a] Data are based on drinkers only; male $N = 142$, female $N = 177$.

[b] The Hollingshead index was deleted from the multiple R that includes its components.

[c] Results are based on all respondents: 188 males and 244 females.

[d] Results are based on 186 males and 242 females.

313

studies separately. The data for the High School Study are shown in Table 19.1. Section A of the table consists of the variables of the demographic environment categorized into socioeconomic status variables and religious denomination variables. Multiple correlations for each category and for the combined demographic variables are shown in italics and underlined in Section A. Section B lists the separate variables in the distal structure of the perceived environment and their multiple R when combined; it also lists the three variables in the proximal structure and their combined multiple correlation; finally, it shows the multiple R for the entire set of variables in the perceived environment. Section C, the last line in Table 19.1, shows the multiple R for the demographic and perceived environment variables combined. Each of the variables listed has been correlated with each of the four behavior measures.

The implications of the findings in Table 19.1 can best be developed by following through the correlations for a single behavior measure. The data for marijuana involvement measure in Table 19.1 are discussed because they represent an almost paradigmatic outcome. With the exception of parental religious denomination for males (the more fundamentalist the parental religious denomination, the less involvement with marijuana), none of the other demographic measures shows a relationship with marijuana use, and the multiple correlation of the combined demographic variables is not significant for either sex. By contrast, most of the measures in the distal structure of the perceived environment show a significant relation in the expected direction with variation in marijuana involvement (lesser parental support and controls, greater friends support and lesser friends controls, less parent–friends compatibility, and greater friends-relative-to-parents influence), and their multiple correlation accounts for slightly over 25% of the criterion measure variance for both sexes. Finally, when we turn to the proximal structure variables, all measures are significant, and friends approval and friends models reach substantial magnitude. The multiple correlation for the combined proximal structure is .74 for males and .76 for females; it accounts for more than twice the variation in marijuana involvement that the distal structure does. When the variables in both structures are combined, the perceived environment as a whole accounts for about 60% of the variance in this drug-use criterion. And as seen in the last line in Section C of the table, there is no real increment achieved by adding the demographic variables.

With some variation in both the patterning of the results and the magnitude of the correlations, the findings for the other three criterion measures in Table 19.1 are consistent with those for the marijuana measure. With respect to the measure of times drunk in the past year, the distal variables of the perceived environment are considerably weaker, especially for the females, and the overall multiple R is only modest; and with respect to the measure of sexual experience, there is a real departure from the general pattern in the significant relations of the socioeconomic variables for the males. On the other hand, the findings for the measure of deviant behavior in the past year are very similar in pattern to those for marijuana use.

In general, these data from the High School Study do provide support for the three empirical objectives that were specified earlier. They make clear that the measures of the perceived environment provide a significant and at times substantial explanation of variation in problem behavior; they sustain the expectation that the perceived environment, being more proximal, will account for more of the variance than the distal demographic environment does; and they confirm the greater explanatory contribution, *within* the perceived environment, of the proximal variables over the distal variables. What was noteworthy was the fact that the demographic environment made almost no contribution to an account of the variation in youthful problem behavior.

Although these findings tend already to be replicated across the two sexes, we have a rather unique opportunity to examine their replication in an entirely different sample with a much larger N and a much wider degree of variation in demographic characteristics. The data from the Nationwide Sample Study are presented in Table 19.2.

Table 19.2 provides even more compelling empirical support for our environmental expectations. In regard to all three of the behavioral criterion measures, the patterning of the findings is clear and consistent for both sexes. The demographic environment accounts for almost none of the variation in problem behavior (although the correlations often do reach significance, it should be kept in mind that, with the sample sizes involved, a correlation of .04 can be significant for each sex and yet account for much less that even 1% of the variance). The distal structure of the perceived environment does better, but it still accounts for less than 10% of the variance even when its variables are combined; and the proximal structure does best, accounting for between about a quarter and a half of the variance across the three different behavior measures. This consistency of the overall pattern is not attenuated by departures of the sort encountered in the High School Study, and it is even clearer here that no increment is gained from independent variance when the demographic measures are added to the perceived environment measures—see the last line in Table 19.2.

CONCLUSION

Taken together, the results of the two independent studies are quite persuasive in their coherence and their import. With respect to delineating proneness or conduciveness to deviance in the perceived environment, the variables derived from problem-behavior theory have been shown to be effective. Generalized support and controls from parents and friends, and the relations perceived between these two most salient reference groups for youth, tend to be linked to problem behavior in a modest but significant way. As distal aspects of the perceived environment, they are variables that suggest something about the operation of the social system in which a young person is embedded and, more particularly, about whether that system is still parent oriented or whether it reflects the de-

TABLE 19.2
Pearson Correlations and Multiple Correlations of Demographic
and Perceived Environment Measures with Three Problem-Behavior
Criterion Measures (*Nationwide Sample Study,* [1974] Data)

Measures	Times Drunk in Past Year		Marijuana Involvement		Deviant Behavior in Past Year	
	Males[a]	Females[a]	Males[b]	Females[b]	Males[b]	Females[b]
A. Demographic environment						
Socioeconomic Status						
Father's education	−.05*	.01	.02	.06***	−.06***	−.01
Mother's education	−.06***	.02	−.00	.05***	−.08***	.01
Father's occupation	−.02	.02	.05***	.05***	−.03+	−.00
Multiple R	*.06**†	*.02*	*.05***†	*.07***†	*.08***†	*.01*
Religious Group						
Father's relig. grp.	.01	−.04*	−.04**	−.05***	−.03*	−.06***
Mother's relig. grp.	−.01	−.03+	−.06***	−.05***	−.03*	−.05***
Multiple R	*.04+†	*.04+†	*.06***†	*.06***†	*.03+†	*.06***†
Combined Demographic						
Multiple R	*.08**†	*.04*	*.08***†	*.08***†	*.09***†	*.06***†
B. Perceived Environment						
Distal Structure						
Parent–friends comp.	−.16***	−.17***	−.19***	−.20***	−.26***	−.29***
Parent–friends infl.	.17***	.21***	.24***	.24***	.26***	.33***
Multiple R	*.22***†	*.24***†	*.28***†	*.28***†	*.34***†	*.39***†
Proximal Structure						
Parent approval	.10***	.10***	—	—	—	—
Friends approval	.31***	.29***	.59***	.60***	.38***	.48***
Friends models	.48***	.49***	.72***	.71***	.43***	.52***
Multiple R	*.49***†	*.50***†	*.74***†	*.73***†	*.45***†	*.55***†
Combined Perceived						
Multiple R	*.51***†	*.52***†	*.75***†	*.73***†	*.50***†	*.60***†
C. Demographic Plus Perceived Environment						
Multiple R	*.52***†	*.52***†	*.75***†	*.74***†	*.51***†	*.61***†

Note: Level of significance of correlations, two-tailed test: +$p \leq$ .10, *$p \leq$ .05, **$p \leq$ .01, ***$p \leq$ .001

[a]Data are based on drinkers only; male Ns range from 3100 to 3700, female Ns range from 3000 to 3700 for the different correlations.

[b]Results are based on all respondents with valid data; degrees of freedom for the correlation range from 4300 to 4900 for the males and from 4700 to 5620 for the females.

velopmental move toward a peer orientation. In regard to the proximal aspects, the strongest to emerge are the models and reinforcements for problem behavior perceived among one's friends, variables that have consistently substantial associations with behavior. As a whole, the variables in the perceived environment seem capable of accounting for between 25 and 50% of the variance depending on the behavior at issue. In light of this outcome, and especially its stability for both sexes in two such diverse studies, it is not unreasonable to claim some support for the particular conceptualization of environmental conduciveness to problem behavior that has been advanced.

As a problematic concept, the environment is amenable to a variety of levels of analysis and alternative conceptual foci. We have argued that distal environments such as demography are too remote to be useful as explanations in social-psychological research. Social structural environments do have explanatory interest insofar as they involve concepts that shape and map the conditions and interactions that persons can experience. But it is the perceived environment, as our data have shown, that is most likely to yield "... the thing that psychology has always been really after throughout its history" (Brunswik, 1943, p. 266)—invariant relations between environment and action.

ACKNOWLEDGEMENT

Preparation of this chapter was supported by Grant No. AA03745-01, R. Jessor, principal investigator. Support for the data collection was provided by Grant No. AA-00232 and Contract No. ADM 281-75-0028. I am grateful to Dr. John Donovan for his contribution in carrying out the analyses of the data.

This chapter is Publication No. 175 of the Institute of Behavioral Science, University of Colorado, Boulder.

IV

PERSON-ENVIRONMENT INTERACTIONS

Most of the chapters in this volume deal with person-environment interactions in the one way or another. Part IV contains five chapters concerned especially with the role of situations and the importance of analyses of situations in person–situation interactions. Hunt emphasizes the person–environment interactions in development and Stokols in concerned with group × place interactions in research on settings, whereas Pervin, Endler, and Nystedt deal with the person–situation interaction process at the level of momentary situations.

Hunt (Chapter 20), against a background of reference to Piaget, emphasizes the impact of situations (environmental circumstances) on the psychological development of infants. Because psychological knowledge and achievements are cumulative and hierarchical, situations that an infant encounters should ideally be within coping range, though still challenging enough to foster development (cf. the discussion of promotive versus restrictive environments). There is a situational basis underlying the plasticity of development rate. Through the introduction of more propitious qualities in infants' environments, development can be persistently and significantly improved and precipitated. Hunt evidences this with several examples from his own research on orphans in Teheran.

Pervin (Chapter 21) focuses on three major points. First, consideration is given to *individual* representations of situations and to the multiple alternative schemata available to the individual for representing situations (compare, for example, Rommetveit's discussion in Chapter 10 of "private worlds" and "referential alternatives"). Second, consideration is given to the relationship of a specific situation to the larger structure of goals–plans residing in the individual. Third, the paper addresses the question of the relationship of situations to behavior in terms of a test of the prediction that situations perceived as similar in their reinforcements will result in similar behaviors.

Endler (Chapter 22) reviews a large number of empirical and theoretical studies concerned with the role and implications of situational factors for interactional psychology, together with conceptual distinctions that have been proposed and are valuable to maintain for effective theorizing and research on person-by-situation interactions. He is concerned with problems connected with description and classification of stimuli, situations, and environments. Endler discusses important methodological problems and suggests directions for further research on situations.

Nystedt (Chapter 23) proposes a process model and discusses its application in the study of the perception of situations. The model is primarily based on Brunswik's lens model and the personal construct theory. The importance of studying the interaction between the characteristics of the external situation and the characteristics of the perceiver is stressed. The *external situation* is described by using three categories: substance, quality and relation. The *person system* is divided into four interactive systems: the *perceptual cognitive system* defined as the cognitive representation of the immediate external situation, the *abstract structure*, defined as the person's knowledge of the past, attitudes, opinions, the common categories and "rules" that he shows with other people in the society, his individual rules and the long term expectations about the future, the *momentary state* which refers to the transitory states of a person at the time of perception, and the *input selector*. Some methodological problems involved in studying persons' perceptual-cognitive structures are discussed.

Stokols (Chapter 24) focuses on the nature of the interface between groups and their physical milieu. Three aspects are given particular attention: (1) the strength and diversity of linkages between groups and places; (2) the degree of compatibility between social, personal, and physical components of settings; and (3) the conditions under which incongruities among the components of settings lead to functional or dysfunctional changes in the physical environment, group organization, and/or personal well-being. To permit an analysis of these issues, the *social imageability* of places—defined as the capacity of a physical environment to evoke shared, sociocultural meanings among the members of a setting—is considered. These meanings comprise the *perceived social field of the physi-*

cal environment. Three dimensions of the perceived social field are discussed: those pertaining to the functional, motivational, and evaluative salience of places. In relation to these dimensions, the concepts of *place dependence, group-environment congruence,* and the *transformational potential* of settings are developed.

20

The Role of Situations in Early Psychological Development

J. McVicker Hunt
University of Illinois

The recent spurt of interest in what is coming to be termed *interactional psychology* (Endler & Magnusson, 1976a; Magnusson & Endler, 1977b) has stemmed from dissatisfaction with two theoretical positions. One is the attempt by clinicians and personologists to explain personality in terms of trait theory. The other may be characterized as the overemphasis by social psychologists and sociologists on the rules (folkways and mores) for behaving in specified situations. Part of this dissatisfaction is theoretical in nature and derives from those emphasizing social learning and cognition as a source of the characteristic behavior of persons (Mischel, 1973) and therapeutic behavioral change (Mahoney, 1974; Meichenbaum, 1977). Part of it has an empirical basis and derives from evidence that neither persons nor situations, objectively defined, account for much of the variance in reported behavioral and subjective indicators of such traits as anxiousness and hostility, whereas person–by–situation interactions account for a very substantial portion of the variance (Endler & Hunt, 1966, 1968, 1969; and Bowers, 1973). The person–by–situation interaction appears to represent idiosyncratic construing of situations by persons. Investigations by others have corroborated these findings (Bowers, 1973) and have extended them to other traits and to objective measures of behavioral indicators (Heffler, 1977, 1978; Heffler & Magnusson, 1978). Moreover, Magnusson and Stattin (1978a) have added evidence that the idiosyncratic cross-situational profiles have considerable stability over time.

At least two kinds of person–situation interactions exist. The one illustrated in the methodology of the S–R Inventories of Anxiousness (Endler & Hunt, 1966; Endler, Hunt, & Rosenstein, 1962 and Hostility Endler & Hunt, 1968) is statistical in nature. Even though the person–by–situation interaction is descriptive

323

rather than causative, it resembles the interaction between various pure heredit- ary lines and characteristics of the environment that resulted in Johannsen's (1909) distinction between genotype (hereditary constitution), phenotype (the observable, measurable outcome of the interaction), and Richard Woltereck's (1909) concept of the "range of raction."

The descriptive person-by-situation interactions illustrated in the S-R Inven- tories must also be characterized as cross-sectional in nature. Overton and Reese (1973) have contended that such cross-sectional, statistical interaction reflects a *mechanistic* view of person-by-situation interaction that is to be contrasted with a *dynamic* one. On the contrary, cross-sectional, statistical interaction need not reflect a mechanistic view. Rather, it constitutes a methodology of measurement through which implications from a dynamic or developmental view of person- by-situation interaction can be confronted with relevant evidence. As Magnus- son (1980b) has pointed out in his excellent empirical and theoretical review, cross-sectional, statistical measurements of person-by-situation interaction re- veal "static moments in what is actually a continuously on-going process." He might have added that this is a process of bidirectional interaction or transactions between the individual and his/her environmental circumstances, both social and inanimate. This paper attempts to clarify the nature and role of those intimate, proximal environmental circumstances involved in early psychological develop- ment.

ENVIRONMENT, SITUATIONS, AND STIMULI

In the history of the long controversy over the relative importance of nature and nurture, a tendency has existed to construe these opposing sources of influence in toto. Such has been the practice of investigators attempting to determine the relative importance of heredity and environment on intelligence by way of indi- ces of heritability for the IQ (Burks, 1928; Jensen, 1969, 1973; Leahy, 1935). This practice has persisted even though experimental embryologists in the last quarter of the nineteenth century already were investigating the effects of specific forms of exercise on specific structures and functions of the nervous system (Oppenheim, 1980). At various times and in various contexts, the environment has been reduced to *stimuli*, i..e. the various types of energy delivered to recep- tors as in the psychophysical studies of Fechner and of Weber (Boring, 1929), or to *situations*, often termed *stimuli* in the experimental psychology of animal and human behavior. Such has been the terminological practice in behaviorists' theory from Watson (1919) to Hull (1943) and Miller and Dollard (1941).

In what follows, the term *situation* will be used generically for that range of environmental circumstances that lie between "the environment as a whole" and "specific kinds of energies delivered to receptors." Many situations can be described physically, to be represented in sound cinemas or in television. These may vary greatly in complexity and may be construed variously by individuals. Some situations are interactive, or transactional, in their nature. These must be defined in terms of both external conditions and the actions, expectations, intentions, and knowledge of the reacting individuals.

It has been my own habit to emphasize the role of *experience* in psychological development. I have contended that the environment, per se, has no direct influence on psychological development. Rather, organisms, including human infants, develop through their functioning, through their exercise or use of their various sensorimotor or symbolic organizations, and through their adaptive modifications of these inner organizations in the course of assimilating newly encountered impressions and information and in the course of making adaptive modifications in those organizations to cope with the demands of the various environmental circumstances encountered. The environment has its influence indirectly by eliciting use or calling forth the adaptive modifications of existing systems. These various environmental circumstances relevant to development constitute the situations, the nature of which I hope, at least in a preliminary fashion, to clarify. The motivation to make this effort is the topic of this volume. Moreover, a sense of the way has come from Magnusson's (1978) attempt to formulate a conception of the psychological situation. Inasmuch as deliberate attempts to foster psychological development must come about through appropriate manipulations of the environmental circumstances, or the situations, that elicit the use of existing systems or evoke adaptive modifications in them, I believe this effort is important both for the theory of early psychological development and for the creation of an effective pedagogy for infancy and early childhood.

"EQUILIBRATION" AND "THE PROBLEM OF THE MATCH"

A mutual interdependence exists between every organism and the environment. This interdependence exists on both the biochemical and the psychological level. In his recent essay on *equilibration*, Piaget (1977) notes that "stimulus–response is not a one-way road . . . A subject is sensitive to a stimulus only when he possesses a scheme [sensorimotor organization] that permits the capacity for response . . . The stimulus–response scheme must be understood as reciprocal [p. 5]." On the same page, Piaget (1977) has written that: "the organism is sensitive to a given stimulus only when it possesses a certain *competence*. I am borrowing this word from embryology in the sense in which Waddington used it . . . if an inductor has no effect at all; thus, it does not modify the structure . . . the phenomena is the same in cognition." This means that for any situation to foster psychological development, the organism must have first, a capacity to sense and respond to it and, as situations become more complex, a child must have a cognitive appreciation or grasp of the situation if it is to be assimilated into his or her achieved competencies or if the situation is to elicit use of the systems comprising the competencies or evoke adaptive modifications, or accommodations, in them.

As an illustration within the cognitive domain, Piaget (1977, p. 7) presents the following:

We asked children first to compare the length of two pencils. Children see that A is smaller than B. We then hide A and show B and C; is very obviously longer than B. We then ask the child, 'Do you think C is longer than the first one you saw? Smaller than the first one you saw, or about the same length?' The little children will say, 'I can't tell. I didn't see them together.' The child does not make the inference we would make from the information that allows for such transitivity. It [the inference] seems to impose itself upon us with the feeling of necessity that C must be longer than A. But small children do not have that same feeling of necessity. This feeling of necessity is tied to the operational structure I have been calling *seriation* or *serial ordering*. . . . . The notion of transitivity is, thus, tied to the operational structuration of a series. Transitivity feels necessary to us and imposes itself upon us because of the nature of the closed operational structure; it is the result of the closing of the structure. And this, of course, means *equilibrium* [emphases added] [p. 7-8].

No theory of psychological development has epitomized dynamic interactionism better than Piaget's, and none has succeeded more completely in making the developing child in his environment the focus of concern. Piaget's concepts of *assimilation, accommodation, equilibrium,* and *equilibration* have emerged from this dynamic interactionistic focus of concern. The troublesome unfamiliarity many educators and psychologists find in Piaget's writings is, in considerable part, a function of a success in focusing on the organism in its environmental situations as the unit for investigation and theory. As already illustrated, Piaget's theorizing about cognitive adaptation and development is based upon an analogy with biological adaptation and development in which assimilation and accommodation tend toward equilibrium through successive coping efforts (Piaget, 1970, 1971, 1977).

In his essay on *Biology and Knowledge*, Piaget (1971) has said: "Cognitive processes seem, then, to be at one and the same time the outcome of organic autoregulation, reflecting its essential mechanisms, and the most highly differentiated organs of this regulation at the core of interactions with the environment [p. 76]." It is this conception that underlies Piaget's (1971) epistemology as exemplified, for instance, in the statement that "knowledge is not a copy of the environment, but a system of real interactions reflecting the auto-regulatory organization of life just as much as things themselves do [p. 27]." Piaget considers these auto-regulations to be analogous to the homeostatic regulations that regulate hunger and eating or thirst and drinking. In Skinner's (1953) system of behavioral technology, these homeostatic regulations are externally influenced by what are termed the *setting conditions,* (hours without food, hours without water, hours without rest, etc). In Skinner's system, these "setting conditions" influence the goal of action and the nature of what will be reinforcing to the organism. Human beings develop goals far removed from these homeostatic regulations. They achieve them in the fashion to be related later. Once intentions have been established, the human organism functions in the fashion of the TOTE (Test-Operate-Test-Exit) unit of Miller, Galanter, and Pribram (1960; see also Hunt, 1963b, pp. 48–55).

With his concept on *equilibration,* Piaget clearly places primary emphasis on cognition even though, when he was faced with a leading question from Hans Furth, (see Appel & Goldberg, 1977), he agreed that: "there certainly is an affective aspect [to intelligence]. Each scheme (sensorimotor or conceptual organization)," he said, "provides its own need to be fed and to act. The scheme seeks to reproduce, so the very existence of a scheme has its motivational aspect which is one with its structural aspect [p. 20]". Despite this admission of affect and motivation in equilibration, Piaget has seldom allowed the affective and motivational aspects of functioning to enter explicitly into his interpretations of his empirical observations. It is for these reasons that I have found myself reformulating what I have learned from our own observations and findings and from a scrutiny of Piaget's empirical observations (see Hunt, 1963a, 1965, 1971).

"The Problem of the Match"

In this reformulation, any organism brings to its encounter with a situation the biological mechanisms programmed by its heredity, its repertoire of existing competencies (motor, perceptual, cognitive, motivational—based on current homeostatic needs, expectations, and learning sets), and its habitual patterns of reaction. These existing competencies, motives, and habits of reaction are included under Piaget's term of *equilibration.* What appears to be important for the outcome of any encounter is the degree of discrepancy between the competancies, the motives, and the habits of reaction that an individual animal or human being brings to any given situation, on the one hand, and the demands of that situation, on the other. A cognitive appreciation of the situational demands is a key factor in the reaction of the individual organism. When, for instance, those demands are completely beyond the cognitive grasp of the animal or child, they will not engage attention or concern and they will evoke no reaction. In such a case, the individual is in the proverbial situation of a pig exposed to a "lecture about Sunday." Such a metaphorical illustration demonstrates the validity of Piaget's (1977) proposition that "a subject is sensitive to a stimulus only when he/she possesses a scheme [understanding] that permits a capacity for response . . . [p. 5]."

When a child has a cognitive appreciation of the demands of a situation, however, there may still be differ*ing* degrees of discrepancy between those demands and the child's competencies. These differing degrees of discrepancy may evoke three kinds of reaction in which the affective and motivational aspects of functioning predominate. Moreover, these affective and motivational aspects are central in determining whether and how a child's encounter with a situation will influence his/her development.

First, if the child has already completely mastered the demands of the situation, and if the situation fits perfectly his/her expectations and requires no adaptive modifications in his/her habitual schemes of reaction, the encounter will be interesting, perhaps even boring. To illustrate the affective impact of such encounters, Hebb (1949) compared their effects to those involved in reading a detective story for the fourth or fifth time. Inasmuch as encounters with such situations elicit no use of and call forth no adaptive modification in competencies or patterns of reaction, they yield no development. The dramatic apathy and retardation so characteristic of infants reared in understaffed orphanages appear to result from a life history from birth in an environment consisting of such unchanging and unresponsive situations.

Second, at the other extreme, when an infant or child encounters situations making demands that he/she appreciates cognitively, but with which he/she cannot cope, the most obvious reaction is emotional distress. Who has not experienced such encounters? In the late sensorimotor phase of development, a child who is still fitting the blocks of various shapes into the holes of a shape box with motor trial and error will make every effort to "leave the field" when presented with the game of matching pictures. If escape is blocked, tears will result. Early psychological development, and perhaps all knowledge (Bickhard, 1980), is hierarchical. Psychological achievements, like embryological transformations, are built one upon another. Thus, certain "entry skills" (information, understandings, strategies) are required if a child or an adult individual is to cope successfully with the demands of any situation, or, in other words, if he/she is to make the appropriate modification in his existing achievements to solve the given problem. Various people concerned with teaching the handicapped have discovered independently this hierarchical principle in psychological development, and some of them have made theoretical capital of their discovery (Bickhard, 1980; Feuerstein, 1979; Gagne & Paradise, 1961). Among these is also Piaget (1952b), for, as he has noted in his autobiography, it was his discovery that the failures of children in the elementary schools of Paris on the tests of Cyril Burt resulted from lack of such understandings that led him to his own life's work. Such developmental predeterminists as Gesell have also emphasized damage that can be done by "pushing" children to hasten their development (Gesell & Gesell, 1912). The validity of such counsel is illustrated by the fact that measures of the developmental level of children show a high inverse correlation with the degree to which their mothers report overestimations of what their children will do on specific tests (Hunt & Paraskevopoulos, 1980). Unless caretakers, parents, and teachers are in a position to intervene helpfully when young children encounter situations posing appreciated demands beyond their coping capacity, beyond their limits for adaptive modification, they should avoid confronting children with such situations. Not only will they hamper the child's development, but the child will become impressed with his own lack of competence and, all too often, his lack of worthiness.

Third, when a child encounters situations affording demands within the limits of his own capacity for modification, demands with which he can cope, the most obvious aspect of the child's reaction is the behavioral sign of his interest. For instance again, children who have learned to look at and discern the shape of a block before attempting to place it through the proper hole in the shape box will take delight in searching among the pictures on a page to find the one which matches that on the card in an examiner's hand. The higher the percentage of situations offering such levels of discrepancy, the more smoothly and joyfully development progresses. Yet, finding and providing such situations for individual children is a problem for caretakers, parents, and teachers. In the light of our still over-abundant ignorance about the details of the order of successive achievements in early development, one usually can know whether a given situation will solve this problem of the match only after a child encounters it, and then by the behavioral signs of interest in it. One use of the ordinal scales of Uzgiris and Hunt (1975) is to provide evidence of levels of achievement already attained on the various branches of sensorimotor development. Knowing these permits a caretaker, parent, or teacher to be in a position to supply for the child's choice a variety of situations offering demands approximately appropriate to foster the child's development. The evidence available suggests the hypothesis that the greater the proportion of waking time an infant or child is in such interesting situations, the more rapidly and the more happily does he/she develop.

THE EPIGENESIS IN INFANT–SITUATION INTERACTION: RECEPTOR SYSTEMS

The human infant arrives, at birth, after roughly nine months of embryonic and fetal development in the programmed environment of the uterus, with a repertoire of receptor systems and a repertoire of action systems. Although it is sometimes contended that these receptor systems are already organized in a fashion that makes them prone to recognize certain patterns, the objects, persons, and places which comprise the intimate, proximal situations that the infant encounters are largely strange. The perceptual ability to recognize them appears to depend upon the establishment through repeated perceptual encounters of a coded representation, or memory, within the firing systems of the infant's brain. Evidence for this hypothesis comes from the work on "imprinting" in birds, from Piaget's observations of his own three children as infants, from the fact that young children typically show more interest in repeated commercials than in the program (Hunt, 1965, 1970), and, on the conceptual side, from the theory of the relation of pleasure to memory formulated by Hebb (1949, p. 229). It follows from this theory, that infants should show an attentional preference for those objects repeatedly encountered before they show such preference for those never encountered. This prediction has now been confirmed by a series of studies (Greenberg, Uzgiris, & Hunt, 1970; Uzgiris & Hunt, 1970; Weizmann, Cohen, & Pratt, 1971; Wetherford & Cohen, 1973). For very young infants, making perceptual contact with a familiar object appears to be a source of pleasure that brings the smile. Charlotte Buhler (1931) and others have contended that the infant's smile is a social reaction to people, but Piaget (1952a, p. 72) demonstrated that "the smile is primarily a reaction to familiar images" by showing that Laurent came regularly to smile at inanimate objects after they had been repeatedly encountered. These studies cited so far concern only visual recognition, but Friedlander (1970) has shown that earlier interest in the familiar holds also for auditory inputs.

Infants soon shift their attentional preference to what is novel. Each of the studies cited in the foregoing has demonstrated this shift. Moreover, I have a clinical impression that the facial expressions of infants encountering something novel differ substantially from the pleased expressions that come in encounters with what is becoming recognitively familiar. Instead of a joyful sort of expression, one signifying what one might verbalize as "I know you," the infant appears to show a strained expression, sometimes even a scowl. It is as if the infant were struggling for recognition, or what Woodworth (1947) identified as the goal to perceptual activity. I have suspected that this shift from attentional preference, defined in terms of *looking time*, for what is recognitively familiar to what is novel in the perceived world appears to come about as the consequence of a kind of generalization, or learning set, that "things should be recognizable." Such is the hypothetical nature of this very early epigenetic shift of perceptual concern in early human infancy. Others will come about later with such conceptual learning-sets as "things have names," "things come in categories," and "certain things are fair." Once an infant has acquired language and has begun to construe the nature of the world, the infant often encounters information that fails to correspond with his/her construings. The consequences appear in epistemic quandaries, and once children have language, these quandaries become evident in children's "Why?" questions, noted in 1930 by Nathan Isaacs (Hardeman, 1974).

This epigenesis in the receptive, or perceptual, interaction of human infants with situations has a motivational aspect which a variety of evidence suggests is highly important in psychological development (Hunt, 1965, 1971). For instance, the interest in what is becoming recognitively familiar helps to explain the repetitive hand and foot watching and vocal cooings and bablings of young infants, and the fact that pseudoimitation, or responding vocally to adult presentations of highly familiar vocal patterns, comes well before genuine imitation. The development of interest in the novel helps to explain the avid interests of infants in exploration, in dropping and throwing objects, and in genuine imitation. Despite his already noted focus on the cognitive, an implicit recognition of the foregoing motivational implications of his observations of infant behavior are reflected in Piaget's (1952a), aphorism that "the more objects [persons and places] a child sees, the more new ones he wishes to see [p. 277]." This development of interest in what is novel creates what I have termed "the problem of the match."

The residues (memories) of experiences are not mere copies of the objects, places, and persons encountered perceptually in the past. They are not mere writings of experience on the blank page of each newborn's mind, according to the famous metaphor in John Locke's (1690) *Essay Concerning Human Understanding*. Nor are the actions of infants merely chains of identifiable S-R bonds or reflexes. Observing the reactions of infants to the eliciting situations arranged by examiners using the ordinal scales of Uzgiris and Hunt (1975) shows them to consist of a combination of active construing on the receptive-cognitive side and intentional coping on the motor side. Moreover, intentionality and goal direction are written increasingly large in these infant construings and actions as development progresses. It is important, I believe, to understand the experiential roots of intentions and of their consequences in cognition, learning, and motivation.

THE EPIGENESIS IN INFANT-SITUATION INTERACTION: ACTION SYSTEMS

Piaget (1952a) considered his own three infants to be essentially responsive organisms until they were about five months of age. At this point, a "reversal transformation" took place wherein the infant began to anticipate the outcome of his actions. From a scrutiny of his published "observations," I gleaned that what Piaget's infants first anticipated was perceptual contact, or a resumption of perceptual contact, with objects, places, or events that were becoming recognitively familiar through repeated perceptual encounters—the second stage of intrinsic motivation as already outlined in the foregoing (Hunt, 1965, 1971). Evidence for their intentional character came from the fact that the infant's actions ceased once the perceptual contact had been attained. Anyone who has ever jounced an infant on a knee is familiar with this behavioral phenomenon. Ceasing the jouncing brings motor efforts to reproduce it or vocal protestations. These efforts and/or protestations cease as soon as the dandler resumes the jouncing.

Several kinds of recent investigation have called for a major change in both this conception of the experiential origins of intention and the age at which intentions first may appear. One such kind of investigation has consisted of assessing the intimate, proximal conditions for infant-situation interaction within the homes of infants by means of two 3-hour periods of observations when the infants were 4 and again when they were 5 months old. The behavior of the infants was assessed by Bayley's scales at age 6 months. Among the highest correlations were those between the responsiveness of the social and the inanimate environments of the infants and the persistence of their goal striving at age 6 months. This suggests that perceptual feedback associated closely with spontaneous actions may be an important situational condition for the origin of intentionality.

Another kind of research has been done by pediatricians on "bonding," or the source of attachment between mother and infant. Leaving infants with their mothers during the first few days following birth in the lying-in hospital has been found to enhance these attachments (Brazelton, Tronick, Adamson, Als & Wise, 1975), and the extra strength of attachment endures (Klaus, Jerauld, Kreger, McAlpine, Steffa, & Kennel, 1972). Observation of the infant–mother interaction shows a high degree of reciprocality to which such metaphorical terms as "communication," "conversation," "dialogue," and "dance," have been applied (Brazelton, *et al.,* 1975; Schaffer, 1977; Trevarthen, 1974, 1977; Uzgiris, 1978). Moreover, in cinematic records of this interaction, neonates begin within 3 weeks of birth to show differing patterns of interaction with their mothers than with inanimate objects. With their mothers, they show cycles in which they act and then hesitate, apparently waiting for a maternal reaction (Trevarthen, 1974) and, in the third month of life, such "conversation" may be well established (Trevarthen, 1977).

Combining the findings from such studies has suggested a new hypothesis of the origins of intentionality (Hunt, 1981a). It is clear from the work of Lipsitt and his collaborators that newborns show something akin to what Skinner has termed "operant conditioning" during the first 4 or 5 days of postuterine life. Also, mothers typically have an especially high level of concern for their neonates on the days immediately following birth (Badger, 1977). Without other responsibilities, the mother is free to interact with her newborn during this lying-in period and her interaction tends to consist of matching her facial expressions and vocalizations to those of her infant (Papousek & Papousek, 1977; Trevarthen, 1977). Matching the infant's facial expressions and vocalizations amounts to providing the infant with feedback from his/her spontaneous actions which would be recognitively familiar, at least to immediate memory, inasmuch as the infant alread has made the face or sound. This evidence suggests that imitating an infant's gestural and vocal behavior may be a situational condition important for not only the development of pseudoimitation but also of intentional behavior. Imitation of the infant's vocalizations seems intuitively more likely to be of importance than imitation of its facial expressions.

The hypothetical scenario takes the following form. If an infant has repeatedly uttered a sound and heard the mother utter one like it in turn, a memory of the sequence of events must become established. Because the central brain processes that account for memory will run off more rapidly than events, the infant must inevitably come to anticipate the outcome of his own utterances, and receiving recognitively familiar feedback is a source of joy. In turn, receiving the response of the infant is a joy to the mother, and the vocal games that go on become the basis for a joyful mutual relationship that leads to mutual understanding. It is in this sense that Papousek and Papousek (1977) have considered such mutural attachments to be the basis for a "cognitive head start."

At the Orphanage of the Queen Farah Pahlavi Charity Society in Tehran, Iran, an intervention planned to foster the development of language served serendipitously to yield evidence supporting this view of the origins of intentionality and also of trust and initiative (Hunt, 1981a).

LANGUAGE ACQUISITION AND EXPERIENCE

The species Homo sapiens is unique in its utilization of vocal and written language. It seems to me that Chomsky (1959) and Lenneberg (1967) are correct in contending that there is a biological basis for language. On the other hand, they are wrong in their additional contention that experience plays little or no role in language acquisition because human infants regularly acquire its main rudiments during the period between the ages of 9 and 30 months. Chomsky (1959) has explicitly considered language to be analogous to "complex innate behavior patterns . . . studied in lower organisms [see footnote 48, p. 58]" and contended, therefore, that human infants must come equipped with an inherent "language acquisition device (LAD)." Such a contention shows an utter lack of appreciation for the epigenetic character of early psychological development. Moreover, the postulation of a LAD has the same circular logic as the postulation of instincts and drives that was discredited long ago (Hunt, 1963b, p. 42).

The plan for an intervention to foster language in the foundlings of the Tehran orphanage was prompted by a finding. We employed a "wave design" in which successive samplings of foundlings were taken from the Municipal Orphanage of Tehran when they were less than a month old (Hunt, Mohandessi, Ghodssi, & Akiyama, 1976). Finding that the 15 foundlings of the first, control wave and the 10 of the second wave that received "abortive audiovisual enrichment" failed to name spontaneously any object by age three and understood no spoken language demonstrated the necessity for experiences to foster language. This finding prompted making language acquisition the focus of the experiences prescribed for a fifth wave of 11 foundlings.

The question was: What kinds of experiences? *Phonology, Semantics,* and *syntactics* constitute three quite separate aspects of language (Hunt, 1981b). I guessed from observations of my own and from others in the literature that mastery of phonological skill, at least some phonological skill, would come first. I believed that this first phonological aspect would be acquired through the process of imitation.

Semantic mastery, I guessed, would come second and would be dependent at least at the beginning upon a process of associating concrete experiences with the sound of the phonological utterances of others. I guessed that at first this association would be largely imposed from without. Once infants have acquired the vocal signs that constitute the names for a number of objects, they typically develop a learning set that "things have names." Thereafter their vocabulary building becomes a matter of intentional actions as is illustrated by their often persistent question, "What's that?"

Syntactics, according to the observations of Brown and Fraser (1963), appears to originate in creative attempts to utilize semantic attainments in communication to obtain wants and to comment on matters cognitively appreciated. These communications are typically telegraphic in their syntactic simplicity. The earliest consist of only single words, then two, and more. The syntax of the parental or caretaker language, however, is established gradually through corrections (Brown, 1973). In these corrections, parents or caretakers supply the functors of sentences to elaborate the infant's telegraphic communications according to the syntactical rules of the language.

If this hypothetical scenario for language acquisition were correct, I reasoned that one might best aid the process by fostering vocal pseudo-imitation and the use of the vocal system first. As pseudoimitation became genuine imitation, it in turn could serve to establish phonology. With this goal in view, I revised the Teaching Guide for Infants (Badger, 1971a) and Toddlers (Badger, 1971b) to include instructions for the caretakers to begin by imitating the cooing and babbling sounds of the foundlings in their charge in order to get interactive vocal games going. The instruction to imitate the infant was based on the already remarked fact that receptor inputs with recognitive familiarity are attractive and could, therefore, be expected to encourage (or reinforce) vocalizing by the infants. The vocal games would foster the coordination of the neuromuscular vocal system through use. Because Earladeen Badger (personal communication) had found a period without progress between the establishment of pseudoimitation and genuine imitation, I interposed a transitional phase the basis of which was merely intuitive. When an infant had been observed to repeat several different vocal patterns, the caretakers were instructed in introduce a game of "Follow the leader." They were to get a vocal game going with one pattern, shift to another pattern, get the game going in the other pattern, and then shift to a third. They were also to decrease gradually the time between shifts from one pattern to another. This procedure obviously owes a debt to Skinner's (1953) shaping procedures. Once an infant had become adept at following his caretaker from one vocal pattern to another, the caretaker was to begin introducing vocal patterns from the Persian language that they had not heard the infant produce and start games of genuine imitation. Such games consisted of repeating models till the infant through successive approximations achieved a good copy of the model. It is probable that in the course of such games, the infants acquired a learning set that motivated them to produce good vocal copies, or to make good vocal copies a goal of their imitative vocal activity.

In order to foster semantic mastery, the caretakers were instructed to talk about the caretaking operations as they conducted them. Probably no experience is more palpable than having a part of the body touched. Thus, in order to simplify the basis for associating heard symbols with touched parts of the body, the caretakers were instructed to *time their utterances of the name for a part with touching it.* According to the paradigm, the caretaker was to say, "Now I am going to wash your *ear.*" As her vocal emphasis hit the word *ear,* her washcloth was to make contact with the anatomic ear.

No instructions were given concerning syntax. Unfortunately, neither were instructions given for games such as "Where is your eye? your nose? or chin?" It must be noted, moreover, that the caretakers failed to ask such questions naturally. Caretakers in orphanages and a good many parents, especially from uneducated families of poverty, seldom indulge in vocal games and talk very little with their children (Bernstein, 1960; Deutsch, 1964; Hess & Shipman, 1965; Milner, 1951). Nevertheless, the outcome was far more successful than expected, and this lends credence to the view that syntactical utterances are originally creative efforts to utilize what has been mastered semantically and phonologically in intentions to communicate wants or comments.

On the Scale of Schemes for Relating to Objects (Uzgiris & Hunt, 1975), all 11 of these foundlings in Wave V spontaneously named objects handed to them in the examination before they were 2 years old, whereas only two of the 25 in the control wave and the second wave, which received the abortive audiovisual enrichment, ever spontaneously named an object before they departed the orphanage at about age 3 years. These foundlings of Wave V were also skillful in producing good copies of vocal sounds uttered for their imitation. They could even imitate English words (e.g., *glasses*) calling for a combining of consonants against which there is a phonological rule in Persian. All 11 of them had vocabularies of more than 50 words. These included names for the parts of their bodies, the pieces of clothing they wore, the utensils involved in their feeding, etc. All knew the names of some of the colors, and one at a little less than 2 years regularly names all four of the Hering primaries (red, yellow, green, and blue) correctly when patches were pointed to in pictures along the wall. Moreover they could and did form sentences in communication. One foundling of less than 18 months was being asked to imitate the names of the other foundlings in her group. When the examiner came to Yass, this infant turned toward the door as she said, "Yass rafteh [Yass gone]." This telegraphic sentence reflected her cognitive appreciation of the fact that Yass was indeed gone. She had been adopted and had been removed from the orphanage during the preceding week. Although there had been little genuine conversation between these foundlings and their caretakers, the foundlings nevertheless used language in their interaction with each other. The contrast between these who received the tutored human enrichment outlined and the controls, who used their voices only for yelling and crying and understood no language at age 3, was exceedingly striking.

Intentions, Trust, and Initiative

That contrast was also striking in an unexpected way, a way that adds credence to the hypothesis of intentionality originating in experiences with pseudoimitation. Whereas the facial expressions of the control foundlings at ages from 18 months to 3 years were persistently glum and apathetic, the expressions of these in Wave V were bright and full of the joy of life and interest in what they were doing. Whereas the controls and those of Wave II tended to withdraw when approached even by caretakers and examiners and even more by strangers, these of Wave V approached adults as if they expected to be welltreated, to obtain the aid wanted, and to have experiences of interest. They trusted people. Whereas the controls and those of Wave II almost never initiated either social contacts or activities on their own, those of Wave V were continually occupied in activities, usually of their own choice and initiative. Moreover, when they hit snags or frustrations in their activities, they sought help from any adult handy. They had not only trust, but initiative in eliciting the attention and help of adults in attractive fashion. Such initiative is the first in the list of social abilities found by White and Watts (1973, p. 10) to differentiate children who are judged to be outstanding from those who are not. The contrast in social attractiveness between those of Wave V and those of Waves I and II is as great as that in language skill. This judgment received confirmation of an essential sort when seven of the eleven foundlings in Wave V were adopted as 2-year-olds. Of the 55 other foundlings in this program, only two were ever adopted. These two were adopted at ages of five or six months because they were pretty babies; the seven were adopted because they were attractive 2-year-olds with interested expressions, trust, and initiative (Hunt, 1981a).

This unexpected finding lends credence to the idea that adult imitations of the spontaneous vocalizations of infants sets in motion the basis for not only the genuine imitations through which phonology is acquired but also for intentions, trust, initiative, and affection. The caretakers claimed that they could not have loved infants of their own bodies more than they loved these foundlings who had been in their care, and the validity of their claims was attested by the tears evident for several days after each adoptee was removed from the orphanage.

In that infant–situation interaction based on the infant's action systems, the role of the situation is different from that interaction based on the infant's receptor systems. It is changes in the perceived situation associated with the spontaneous actions of the infant that lead to expectations of outcome and intentions. These changes must be timed responsively to the spontaneous actions of the infant to be effective, and they also must match the level of development in that progression of pleasure from mere attention to change in characteristics of receptor input, to interest in the recognitively familiar, to interest in the novel, and then to the anticipated goal or intention of the infant. Thus, there is a kind of epigenesis in the nature of the kinds of perceptual situation that satisfies and reinforces the infant. Parenthetically, the role of what Skinner (1953) has termed "setting conditions," such as hours without food or water, may be seen as a means of establishing both the nature of intentional goals and the kind of changes in the situation that will satisfy them.

SITUATIONAL BASIS FOR PLASTICITY

One of the outstanding outcomes of my research during the past two decades has been the abundant evidences of plasticity in the rate of development as a whole and along specific branches. It is possible to indicate the probable situational basis both from the overall rate of development and from the rates along specific brances.

First, however, a comment on the assessment of development and then another on the methodology of investigating early psychological development. Alfred Binet (1909) was interested in the educational cultivation of intelligence. Yet the substitutive averaging that Binet and Simon (1905) employed to obtain the mental age frustrated his purpose by hiding the details of the kinds of experience that foster the various kinds of development. Moreover, once Wilhelm Stern (1912) hit upon the idea of dividing mental age by chronological age to obtain the intelligence quotient (IQ), the hereditary predeterminism and the eugenic faith promulgated by Francis Galton (1869) and Karl Pearson (1901) could readily become the causal interpretation, and the IQ could be viewed a constant characteristic or dimension of each individual.

If investigation is to test the validity of this interpretation, it is important to assess both the intimate, proximal experiences of infants and children and their development in order to determine the influence of the former on the latter. Longitudinal studies by themselves are inadequate unless either the characteristics of the situations are assessed and correlated with measures of development or educational interventions are planned. Moreover, if investigation is to uncover the relationships between kinds of experience and kinds of development that are so important for an effective pedagogy, it is important to assess separately but simultaneously several kinds of developmental advances (Hunt, 1976).

Overall Plasticity

Our own research has employed two strategies One consists of comparing the means and standard deviations of the ages at which groups of children reared under differing conditions achieve the steps on the ordinal scales of Uzgiris and Hunt (1975). The other consists of comparing these same measures of development for samples of foundlings reared under successive interventions at the Tehran orphanage. Yet another approach has been to correlate measures of development with assessments of the rearing conditions (situations) available in the homes of infants and young children (Caldwell, 1964; Wachs, 1976, 1978; Wachs, Uzgiris, & Hunt, 1971; Yarrow, Rubenstein, & Pedersen, 1975).

Such studies have produced evidence of great plasticity in the rate of early development. At the Tehran orphanage, the foundlings of Wave V, who received the tutored human enrichment, achieved the top steps on the 7 Uzgiris–Hunt scales at a mean of the mean ages of attainment, which was 62.43 weeks younger than that of the controls and those in Wave II. When this difference is transformed, for purposes of communication only, into an IQ ratio, it is one of the order of 47 points. Since this transformation averages across the seven branches it can be expected to correspond rather well to a difference between IQs from standard tests. Humphreys & Parsons (1979) have found scores based on a composite of Piagetian tasks correlating + .87 with scores from the Stanford Binet. It should be noted here that the 11 foundlings in Wave V achieved the top steps on five of the seven Uzgiris–Hunt scales at mean ages younger than did home-reared infants from predominantly professional families in Worcester, Massachusetts (Hunt, Mohandessi, Ghodssi, & Akiyama, 1976). Again, in the Milwaukee project, Heber (1978) has enabled, with educational day care, 20 offspring of uneducated Black mothers of poverty with IQs of 75 or below to obtain a mean IQ of 124 at age 66 months. This mean was 30 points above that for a control sample of offspring from comparable mothers.

Such plasticity cuts both ways. Losses can be made up at least partially if the development-fostering quality of the circumstances are improved, and gains can be partially lost if these are worsened. In the Milwaukee project, after the special educational day care ceased and these children became dependent on their families and the public schools for the development of what is measured by tests of intelligence, the mean of the treated group by age 9 had dropped to 109 and that of the controls to 79. The 30 points of advantage from the educational day care persisted even though both groups lost once they were limited to the schools and their homes for the development-fostering quality of their experience.

Specificity Between Kinds of Situations and Kinds of Development

Although I had expected specific relationships between kinds of experience and kinds of developmental advance from remembering the studies of "scatter" on the Stanford–Binet (Harris & Shakow, 1937), nearly all of those uncovered have been unexpected. The first came from the institutional laboratory of Burton L. White. White (1967) had provided a pair of enrichment programs that reduced the median age of achieving the top level of visually directed reaching from 145 days to 89 days. The fact that the home-reared infants serving as subjects in the studies that led to the Uzgiris–Hunt scales were not achieving top-level reaching till they were about 150 days old led us to discuss comparisons. When I noted that the home-reared infants typically were manifesting vocal pseudoimitation at

60 to 80 days of age, White became interested in whether the institutional infants of his study would show this vocal achievement. They did not, not even those as old as 180 days. Thus, providing a complex stabile over cribs for infants to look at and touch encouraged the use of that coordination between looking and reaching, and advanced it, but had no influence on the development of a coordination between hearing and vocalizing.

A second unexpected example of such specificity came in our study of the effects of educational day care on the eight consecutive infants born to the uneducated parents of poverty served by the Parent and Child Center of Mt. Carmel, Illinois. This intervention served to advance the mean age of these eight infants in achieving the top step on our scale of Object Permanence to 73 weeks. It put their mean age of achieving this landmark 25 weeks ahead of that (98 weeks) at which it was achieved by the home-reared offspring of predominantly professional families in Worcester, Massachusetts. Yet this same educational day care left these eight infants of Mt. Carmel 20 weeks, or approximately 5 months, behind the Worcester infants in achieving the top step on the scale of Vocal Imitation. What the intimate, proximal interaction within the educational day care was that effectively advanced the rate of object construction was entirely unclear until questioning brought out the fact that the toy which had been most interesting and most regularly played with from about age 26 weeks to about 73 weeks, was a shape box with five holes in the top (round, square, rectangular, triangular, and irregular) and with blocks of corresponding shape. Once a block went through its hole, it disappeared while making a sound as it hit the bottom of the box. The infant could retrieve the block by lifting the hinged top of the box where he/she could see the block. In the beginning, it was necessary for someone to help the infant lift the box lid and show him that he could see and retrieve the block. Actually, in the first instance, a Ping-Pong ball had to be substituted for the round cylindrical block (Hunt, Paraskevopoulos, Schickedanz, & Uzgiris, 1975). Although this finding has not yet been repeated with another group of infants, it would appear that interested preoccupation with the shape-box situation provides experience highly important for object construction. But such experience has no influence whatever on the development of vocal imitation or language. Two years later, seven of these eight infants were retarded in their performance on the Stanford–Binet, which depends heavily on language achievement, despite their earlier advancement in object construction.

A third unexpected example of such specificity occurred at an orphanage in Athens, Greece (Paraskevopoulos & Hunt, 1971). There, the retardation associated with being reared in the Municipal Orphanage where the infant–caretaker ratio was of the order of 10/1, as compared with being home-reared in working class families, was far greater for vocal imitation that for gestural imitation. In constructing the ordinal scales, we had followed Piaget in conceiving of imitation as a single sensorimotor organization, but it becomes quite clear, once the differing effects of such rearing conditions have appeared, that vocal imitation is a function of auditory experience, whereas gestural imitation is a function of visual experience. Although it is generally true that caretakers in orphanages bathe, clothe, and feed their charges without any vocal interaction, opportunities for the infants to see and imitate human motions are inevitable.

A fourth unexpected instance of specificity occurred at the Tehran Orphanage (Hunt, et al., 1976). Reducing the infant–caretaker ratio from more than 30/3 to 10/3 in what was termed *untutored human enrichment* served to advance the age at which standing and cruising about the cribs occurred by about 8 months, yet these foundlings of Wave III, who received such enrichment, showed no advancement whatever in achieving steps on the Piaget-inspired scales of Uzgiris and Hunt. From observation and inquiry, it turned out that the extra time that the caretakers had as a result of the reduction in the infant–caretaker ratio was spent in carrying their charges about in their arms and placing them in strollers. Being carried permitted the infants to use their balancing mechanisms, and thereby encouraged development of posture. The strollers permitted the infants to use their stepping scheme and to put weight on their legs.

In the sixteenth century, Shakespeare had Hamlet say while urging his mother to "assume a virtue, if you have it not [that] for use almost can change the stamp of nature [Act III, Scene 4]." In the same vein, Piaget (1952a) has emphasized in psychological development the importance of use of existing systems beginning with reflexes and continuing through the more complex schemes or sensorimotor organizations. A major basis for specific relationships resides in the fact that many situations call forth the use of specific schemes, and it is these and these only that advance. It is not unlikely that some of the learning disabilities derive from depending upon such advances while failing to achieve the proper organization to permit the adaptive modifications required. Because such specific relationships have begun to be investigated only very recently, the ignorance of developmental psychologists is immense, and this ignorance generally precludes the prescription of effective recommendations in early education (see Hunt, 1976). The promise of greater knowledge of the epigenesis in infant–situation interaction is illustrated by my hypothetical scenario for language acquisition. It worked well, at least once.

CONCLUSION

In the process of early psychological development, the word *environment* has little meaning except as a generic term for all those intimate, proximal circumstances or situations with which infants interact. Although infants must come by their appreciation of these circumstances via their receptor systems, it is not specific stimuli, defined as energy delivered at receptors, that constitute what is appreciated.

In the infant-environment interaction based on the receptor systems, there is an epigenesis starting with the changes in the characteristics of receptor inputs that evoke attention, or the orienting response. Repeated encounters with perceptual patterns bring motivational attractiveness that appears to account for such autogenic behaviors as repetitive cooing and babbling, hand and foot watching, and pseudoimitation, gestural and vocal. As most of the patterns within an infant's life space become recognizable, he/she seems to acquire a learning set that "things should be recognizable." At this point, it is the novel that comes to attract attention, and this motivates exploration, genuine imitation, such motor schemes as "letting go" and throwing with attention on what happens to the objects. With interest in the novel comes motivation for continual growth that depends upon a proper discrepancy between the demands of situations, as individually appreciated and capacity for coping and adaptive modification. This creates for caretakers, parents, and teachers "the problem of the match."

In the infant-environment interaction based on spontaneous actions, changes in situations associated in time with the actions become effects. When actions leading to hedonically desirable changes in the situation are repeated, they establish memories of the sequence. Because the neural firing systems that comprise the memories run off faster than events, they lead to anticipations of the effects of action and, thereby, to intentions. The intended goals of action change with knowledge of the world and with mastery of language and number systems.

A hypothetical scenario for the acquisition of language was presented with imitation as the source of phonology, association as the first source of semantic mastery, and creative utilization of these for intentional goals as the original source of syntactics. An intervention based on this scenario was exceedingly successful in fostering the development of language. Unexpectedly, this intervention also served to foster social attractiveness based on facial expressions, trust, and initiative.

Situations appear to influence early psychological development in several ways. First, by attracting attention and becoming a source of that information inherent in information processing and in action. Second, by being responsive to the spontaneous actions of infants and thereby fostering the use of such actions and by providing the conditions which satisfy the intentions of infants once intentional action is established. Third, by encouraging the use of one scheme rather than the others; the encouraged scheme develops at a rate much more rapid than the others. Fourth, situations, especially social situations, which make demands recognized by an individual that are beyond his/her coping or adaptive capacity hamper development and damage confidence. The influence of situations is never direct, however; it comes through the use, coping, and adaptive efforts of the infant or child. Achieving an effective pedagogy for infancy and early childhood calls for far more information about the specificities of infant-situation interaction than is now available.

ACKOWLEDGMENTS

Support for the writing of this chapter has come from the Waters Foundation of Framingham, Massachusetts, and I wish to acknowledge this support with gratitude. I am indebted also to Håkan Stattin for challenging me to clarify the ways in which environmental circumstances, which I am subsuming here under the term *situations,* operate to produce the experiences that foster or hamper development.

21

The Relation of Situations to Behavior

Lawrence A. Pervin
Rutgers University, USA

Attention to the role of situations in influencing behavior has varied throughout the history of psychology, both in terms of views concerning its importance relative to person influences and in terms of views concerning the nature of situational influences. Independent of such theoretical differences, situations have been viewed as arousing organisms, eliciting specific behaviors, constraining or precluding specific behaviors, and altering the probabilities of present and future behaviors. Although just about every theoretical position would recognize that each of these situational influences plays a role in most human behavior, we are still without an adequate definition of the situation or an adequate conceptualization of its relationship to behavior (Pervin, 1978b).

This chapter touches on the relation of situations to behavior within three theoretical contexts—trait theory, social-learning theory, and general systems theory. The emerging emphasis is on the varying ways that the single individual can construe situations and on the need for a process-oriented, systems perspective in our efforts to understand behavior–situation relationships.

TRAIT THEORY AND THE CATEGORIZATION OF SITUATIONS

Strange as it may seem, trait theorists did, and do, recognize the importance of situations. This point has been made in a number of places and, hopefully, an otherwise distorted picture of trait theory has now been corrected (Magnusson & Endler, 1977a; Pervin, 1978a). In his 1961 book, Allport (1961) devoted a considerable section to discussion of the relationship of situations to traits and behavior. His view is stated as follows:

We are forced, therefore, to the conclusion that while the situation may modify behavior greatly, it can do so only within the limits of the potential provided by the personality. At the same time, we are forced to concede that traits of personality must not be regarded as fixed and stable, operating mechanically to the same degree on all occasions. Rather we should think of traits as ranges of possible behavior, to be activated at varying points within the range according to the demands of the situation [pp. 180–181].

Similarly, Cattell and Child (1975) emphasizes the role of situational influences in the specification equation that is to be used in the prediction of behavior.

Despite this recognition of the importance of situations, it is true that trait theorists have not explored this area in any systematic way. One of the initial criticisms made by Mischel (1968) of traditional trait theory was that it was ineffective in predicting behavior in situations. When one considers trait personality questionnaires as well as other such questionnaires, it is easy to see why this approach has been criticized for its lack of attention to the importance of situations and for its inability to predict behavior effectively. In a study done by Paul Werner and myself, we did a content analysis of six personality questionnaires including the Sixteen Personality Factor Inventory (Cattell), the Eysenck Personality Inventory, and the Maudsley Personality Inventory (Eysenck). One issue considered was whether the items relate to overt behavior. Here we found that no more than one-third of the items related to overt behavior as opposed to beliefs, values, opinions, preferences, and feelings. As we know, aspects of personality such as attitudes and beliefs have a very complex relationship to behavior and are not always directly predictive of behavior.

More to the point of situations and the prediction of behavior, we found that in one-half to two-thirds of the items either no situation at all was specified or only some very general statement was made. In other words, in the majority of items, individuals are responding to general statements concerning their feelings, attitudes, and behavior rather than to more specific aspects of their functioning. Other illustrations of problems in these questionnaires involve the frequent emphasis on past behavior or hypothetical future behavior rather than on current behavior, and their failure to consider in any systematic way frequencies and probabilities of behavior. Given this structure in such personality questionnaires, it is not surprising that they have had an unimpressive record in predicting behavior, particularly in the prediction of behavior in specific situations.

Would questionnaires more faithfully derived from trait theory do a better job? According to Allport, the trait concept involves three distinguishing characteristics: frequency, intensity, and range of situations. As noted, personality questionnaires generally do not consider these issues in any systematic way. In an effort to do so, Paul Werner and I constructed a questionnaire to study sociability; dominance-assertiveness; and anxiety in terms of frequency, intensity, and range of situations. A questionnaire was developed with items concerning frequency of a situation occurring, probability of the trait response in that situation, and intensity of the trait response in that situation. Six items were written for each of the three traits.

What of range of situations? Each item was written in terms of its occurrence in four settings: home, school, work, recreation–peer relationships. These four settings were chosen on the basis of earlier work suggesting that people often categorize situations in such terms, a point that we return to shortly. In all there were 216 items (three traits; six items per trait; judgments concerning frequency, probability, and intensity for each item; and four settings: $3 \times 6 \times 3 \times 4 = 216$). These items were followed by ratings by the subjects of their sociability, assertiveness, and anxiety in each of the four settings and overall. Ratings also were made of their consistency in behavior as far as these three traits were concerned.

These data still are being analyzed but some conclusions are possible. In terms of the concepts of frequency, probability, and intensity, the latter two concepts appeared to be related to one another and to the final trait ratings whereas the frequency ratings appeared to stand by themselves. In terms of the four settings (home, school, work, recreation–peer relationships), there were not any consistent relationships and a factor analysis of the ratings did not suggest that subjects were more consistent in their behavior within these settings than across the settings. Generally, the data did suggest a basis for considering the three traits as distinguishable characteristics of the subjects, particularly in the case of anxiety, but only at the level of an aggregate response. After that, even the subjective ratings show considerable variability from item to item and from situation to situation.

The fact that the four settings chosen did not turn out to be a useful categorization is worthy of note. As noted, these categories were derived from previous research with subjects and have been suggested by others in the field (Pervin, 1978b). Most people would agree that they make some intuitive sense. Why then the difficulty? If such a categorization of situations is not used, can others be suggested that will show greater consistency within a category and discrimination between categories? One possible basis for the difficulty is that the items did not provide a fair test of the categories. Another possibility is that the categories are applicable to the behavior of some subjects but not others; in other words, there are individual differences in how situations are organized or classified and it may not be possible to develop a generalized classificatory scheme that will be applicable to all subjects. For example, Mischel (1977a) suggests that: "depending on one's purpose, many different classifications are possible and useful. To seek any simple 'basic' taxonomy of situations may be as futile as searching for a final or ultimate taxonomy of traits; we can label situations in at least as many different ways as we can label people [pp. 337-338]."

To continue Mischel's analogy between traits and classifications of situations, we can consider a third possible explanation for the results in the afore mentioned study—the categorization scheme represents more of a cognitive effort to make sense out of and simplify the world rather than a systematic evaluation of behavior–situation regularities. In other words, cognitive classifications of situations may have limited relationships to behavioral regularities. When subjects classify situations, they tend to do so on the basis of characteristics, such as feelings (e.g., emotional, pleasurable, friendly, angry), objective characteristics (e.g., large group, physical exercise, family, work), or something that might be described as qualities of a relationship (e.g., intimate–nonintimate, competitive–cooperative, honest–dishonest).[1] Although partly based on behaviors and probably related to behaviors, such classifications are not systematically tied to the behaviors themselves. Nor are the classifications necessarily based on characteristics of the situations that are tied to behavioral regularities. For subjects organizing their worlds, many classificatory schemes are possible and one based on behavioral regularities or one based on situation characteristics associated with behavioral regularities are just two among many.

THE RELATION OF SITUATIONS TO BEHAVIOR: SOCIAL-LEARNING THEORY

One approach to considering the relation between situations and behavior has been suggested by social-learning theory. This involves an emphasis on reinforcements in the environment. Whereas some suggestions have also been made that situations can be classified in terms of similarities in reinforcements (Rotter, 1955), more recent statements have emphasized behavioral regularities due to situation reinforcements without regard to classificatory efforts. For example, Bandura (1977b) suggests that people will behave similarly in situations perceived to be similar in terms of their implications for particular behaviors. It is suggested that situations be analyzed in terms of the consequences customarily provided for particular behaviors and that in regulating their behavior people must develop multidimensional reinforcement contingencies. Similarly, Mischel (1976) emphasizes the importance of behavior-outcome relations: "'These behavior-outcome expectancies (hypotheses, contingency rules) represent the 'if _____, then _____' relations between behavioral alternatives and expected probable outcomes in particular situations. In any given situation, we generate the response pattern which we expect is most likely to lead to the most subjectively valuable outcomes (consequences) in that situation [p. 503].''

The emphasis on behavior-outcome expectancies goes back to Rotter's (1954) early work on social learning. This work emphasized the relation between behavior and the perception of the likely response consequences of various be-

---

[1]In some research that was reported previously, it was clear that categorizations of situations based on objective characteristics, on feelings, and on behaviors were related to one another but were also clearly distinct and separate from one another (Pervin, 1976).

haviors and the value of these response consequences or reinforcers. However, little work has been done to test the hypothesis that people will behave similarly in situations perceived to be similar in their reinforcement contingencies. The study by Magnusson and Ekehammar (1978) addressed the question of similarity of behavior in relation to perceived similarity of situations. The findings were interpreted as suggesting a relation between the two but the relation was not a strong one and it varied considerably from individual to individual. Furthermore, the situations and reactions were chosen from a limited domain (anxiety-arousing situations familiar to students at college and anxiety reactions) and were not chosen so as to be directly relevant to each individual involved. Finally, there was not an emphasis on, or detailed analysis of, behavior-outcome contingencies and similarity of behavior in relation to the similarity of such situational contingencies.

A study being done by Betty Champagne, a graduate student doing her dissertation with me, attempts to address the social-learning hypothesis more directly. Twelve female college students are the subjects in this study. Each subject begins her participation by listing 20 representative situations in her current life. As in earlier research (Pervin, 1976), a situation is described in terms of *who* is there, *what* is going on, and *where* it is taking place. Next the subject is given a list of 14 behaviors that may occur in a situation. These behaviors were taken from earlier student descriptions of their behavior in social situations and from the literature on interpersonal behavior (Benjamin, 1974). They are reasonably representative of such behavior and range from such global concepts as ''act friendly'' to such specific behaviors as ''smile a lot.'' For each of the 20 situations the subject rates the likelihood of her behaving in that way on a four-point scale (very unlikely, somewhat unlikely, somewhat likely, very likely). In other words, the 14 behaviors are rated in terms of *likelihood of occurrence* for each of the 20 situations.

On another day the subject comes in and fills out a behavior × outcome grid for each of the situations. Along one side of the grid are the 14 behaviors. Along the other side are nine outcomes or reinforcers. Again, these were derived from previous student statements concerning desired and undesired outcomes of behaviors in situations and from a review of the literature. Two points are worthy of note concerning the list of reinforcers. First, they are general enough so that they are applicable to most, if not all, social situations. Outcomes particularly relevant to some situations would not be relevant to others and this would preclude cross-situation comparisons. Second, the list includes both external and internal reinforcers (e.g., self-approval, self-disapproval). An important development in social-learning theory has been the emphasis on self-control mechanisms, in particular the development of internal standards for self-reward. Therefore, any consideration of similarities in behavior-outcome relationships from a social-learning standpoint would have to include outcomes generated from within the person as well as those generated by others in the environment. For each behavior the subject rated the likelihood that each reinforcer would follow if the behavior occurred. Likelihood ratings were again made on a four-point scale. To summarize, then, for each of 20 situations the subject rated her expectation that each of the nine reinforcers would follow if each of the 14 behaviors occurred (2520 judgments in all). Half the situations were completed on one day and half the situations on another day.

Following completion of the behavior-outcome grid, the subject rated the value of each reinforcer for her in that situation. It was felt that the value of a reinforcer likely varies from situation to situation and any general estimate would likely be deficient in this regard. Although additional data were obtained (e.g., semantic differential ratings of the 20 situations, paired comparison judgments in terms of similarity of situations and similarity of behavior in situations, a task involving sorting the situations into groups and continuously combining groups to produce a hierarchical ordering of clusters of situations), the previous three sources of data (probability of behavior ratings, behavior-outcome ratings, and value of reinforcer ratings) are particularly relevant to the discussion that follows. Again, it is worth noting the extent to which these data are idiographic— the situations are generated by the subjects from their own lives and all judgments are in terms of their own expectancies and values.

In terms of the social-learning hypothesis, one has to consider whether behavioral similarities and situation similarities should be considered in terms of individual elements or a total gestalt. The earlier quote from Mischel suggests that response patterns should be considered, but this issue generally is not considered in any detail. Most of the analyses currently in progress are at the pattern level. Thus, multidimensional analyses are being conducted of situations in terms of the rated probabilities for the behaviors and of situations in terms of their behavior-outcome grids. Once this is completed, we can address the question of whether people perceive themselves as behaving similarly in situations they perceive as similar in terms of their behavior-outcome contingencies. Although these analyses are still in progress, some of the preliminary results suggest a reasonably strong relationship between behavior similarity and situation similarity. Further support for this comes from a study conducted by an undergraduate, Robyn Lowin, of paired comparison judgments. Situations rated as similar in terms of their situation characteristics tended to be rated as similar in terms of the way that the subject behaves in those situations.[2] At the same time, it is clear that the relationship is by no means perfect and exceptions do occur. In addition, other data clearly suggest instances where situations are perceived as similar but different behaviors occur and instances where the same behaviors occur in situations perceived as being different.

Although we must await the outcome of these multidimensional analyses, additional consideration can be given to the hypothesis in terms of individual

---

[2]In this paired-comparison study, subjects were making general judgments concerning situation similarities and behavior similarities and behavior–outcome judgments were not considered.

behaviors and the relation of behavior probabilities to reinforcement contingencies. Here too, although the evidence suggests that similar outcomes are associated with similar behavior probabilities, exceptions occur. For example, in one subject the probability of being submissive with one date was rated as four (very likely) although the probability of being submissive with a different date was rated as three (somewhat likely). All the probability of reinforcement ratings for being submissive were the same for the two dates. In both cases, for example, the student felt that she would receive love and affection from her dates for being submissive though she also felt that she would be disapproving of herself for behaving in this way. The ratings of the value of the reinforcers were the same for the two dates except for one rating—the value of receiving love and affection. In the case of the date with whom she acts in a more submissive way, the student also reported valuing his love and affection more. In other words, despite being equally disapproving of her submissive behavior in the two situations, it may be that she is more likely to behave this way in one situation than the other because she values that date's affection more. Some further insight into this difference may be derived from her semantic differential ratings of her feelings in the two situations. These indicate that she feels far more tense, inhibited, and self-conscious with the date associated with more submissive behavior than she does with the other date.

A clearer picture of the data emerging in this study and of the relationship between behavior probabilities and reinforcement contingencies can be obtained from consideration of specific situations. I randomly picked out one subject and then picked out two situations in which there was some distribution of the behaviors in terms of their reinforcement probabilities. I then grouped the behaviors associated with each probability rating and listed the ratings for the probability of each behavior being followed by each reinforcer. A score was then calculated for the sum probability of receiving positive reinforcers and negative reinforcers for individual behaviors and the behaviors in each group. In addition, for each behavior these probability of reinforcement ratings were multiplied by the ratings of the value of the reinforcer in that situation. This led to a probability × value score for positive and negative reinforcers for individual behaviors and for the behaviors in each probability of occurrence group.

The behavior–outcome grid for behaviors of different probabilities for the situation "Going to the Dorm to Visit My Old Friends" is presented in Table 21.1. According to social-learning theory, one would expect the behaviors with high probability ratings to have a more positive reinforcement contingency value than those rated as low in probability of occurrence. This turns out to be clearly the case with the positive–negative difference becoming increasingly more negative as the probability of the behaviors decreases. Multiplying the probability of the reinforcer by its value appears to enlarge the differences between groups of behaviors. The same general pattern can be seen in a second situation for this subject, "Riding in Jim's Car While on a Date With Him" (Table 21.2). Although there is this general pattern, it is clear that the relationship does not

TABLE 21.1
Behavior × Outcome Matrix

Probability Rating	Behavior	Receive love/ affection	Be ignored	Receive recognition/ status/ prestige	Feel anxious/ uncomfortable/ tense	Face conflict
4	Act friendly, supportively, co-operatively	4	2	3	2	1
4	Act informally, openly	4	2	3	2	1
4	Express personal opinion(s)	3	2	2	2	1
3	Act actively	4	2	3	2	1
3	Act passively	3	3	2	3	1
3	Talk a lot	4	1	3	2	1
3	Smile a lot	4	2	3	2	1
2	Act intensely, very involved	3	2	3	2	1
2	Act submissively	3	2	2	3	1
2	Express disagreement	3	2	2	2	2
1	Act aloof, detached, withdrawn	3	2	2	3	1
1	Act formally, rigidly	3	2	2	3	1
1	Act dominantly	2	2	2	3	3
1	Act hostile, unfriendly	1	1	1	4	3
How significant or important is each of these consequences to you in relation to this particular situation?		+4	−4	+3	−4	−4

always hold for individual behaviors. For example, the behavior ''Act Actively'' in Table 21.2 has an outcome value suggesting that it should be likely to occur, yet the subject rates this behavior as somewhat unlikely to occur in that situation.

Whereas these analyses need to be done for all 20 situations for each of the 12 subjects, I have to date analyzed the data for two more situations for another subject. Again the subject was chosen at random and the two situations were picked in terms of their having a distribution of ''likelihood of occurrence'' ratings for the various behaviors. The data for these two situations are presented in Tables 21.3 and 21.4. The behavior–outcome relationships for the four groups of behaviors for the situation ''At the Deathbed of My Grandfather'' follow the same pattern as described in the two previous illustrations. One behavior, how-

TABLE 21.1 (cont.)

Approve of self	Disapprove of self	Receive tangible rewards (money, etc.)	Receive disapproval/ rejection	Sum Probability Positive Outcomes	Sum Probability Negative Outcomes	Sum Probability × Value: Positive	Sum Probability × Value: Negative
3	2	1	1	11	8	38	32
3	2	1	1	11	8	38	32
3	2	1	1	9	8	31	32
			Mean	10.0	8.0	35.7	32.0
			Difference	2.0		3.7	
3	2	1	1	11	8	38	32
2	3	1	1	8	11	27	44
3	2	1	1	11	7	38	28
3	2	1	1	11	8	38	32
			Mean	10.3	8.5	35.3	34.0
			Difference	1.8		1.3	
3	2	1	1	10	8	34	32
2	3	1	1	8	10	27	40
3	2	1	2	9	10	31	40
			Mean	9.0	9.3	30.7	37.3
			Difference	−.3		−6.6	
2	3	1	1	8	10	27	40
2	3	1	2	8	11	27	44
2	3	1	3	7	14	23	56
1	4	1	3	4	15	12	60
			Mean	6.8	12.5	22.3	50.0
			Difference	−5.7		−27.7	
+4	−4	+1	−4				

ever, is particularly worthy of note here. The behavior "smile a lot" is rated as low in likelihood of occurrence, yet it has a highly positive reinforcement contingency pattern. Why should this be the case? Again, the semantic differential ratings may be of assistance. The subject rates herself as feeling sad, emotional, helpless, pessimistic, and confused in this situation. Thus, whereas she may perceive herself as being rewarded for smiling, she is so overcome with feelings of sadness and grief that she cannot express this behavior. The data in the final table, for the situation "Talking on the Phone to My Mother," fit the previous pattern for the behaviors rated as very likely as opposed to all other behaviors, but they do not do so for the remaining three categories. This may be because of rating errors, because of significant missing reinforcers, because of more ex-

TABLE 21.2
Behavior × Outcome Matrix

Probability Rating	Behavior	Receive love/affection	Be ignored	Receive recognition/status/prestige	Feel anxious/uncomfortable/tense	Face conflict
4	Act friendly, supportively, cooperatively	4	1	2	2	1
4	Talk a lot	3	1	2	2	2
4	Express disagreement	3	1	2	2	2
4	Smile a lot	3	1	2	2	1
4	Express personal opinion(s)	3	1	2	2	2
3	Act intensely, very involved	3	1	2	2	2
3	Act submissively	3	2	2	3	2
3	Act informally, openly	3	1	3	2	1
2	Act actively	3	1	3	2	1
2	Act formally, rigidly	2	2	2	3	2
2	Act dominantly	2	2	2	4	2
2	Act passively	2	2	1	3	2
1	Act aloof, detached, withdrawn	2	2	2	3	2
1	Act hostile, unfriendly	2	2	1	4	2
How significant or important is each of these consequences to you in relation to this particular situation?		+4	−4	+3	−4	−4

treme reinforcer value differences than was provided for, or because of the intrusion of other influences such as feelings.[3] How many of the remaining situation analyses show this pattern as opposed to that found in the first three situations remains to be seen.

To summarize what has been said so far, the following may be suggested: (1) In general, situations perceived to be similar in their reinforcement contingencies

_____

[3]Although separate attention is given here to the role of feelings–emotions–affects, it is clear that they could be considered as behaviors that occur in conjunction with or in conflict with other behaviors, or as reinforcers. Thus, for example, expression of grief could be considered as a behavior that has a high positive reinforcement value in the situation and blocks smiling behavior. It could also, however, be considered as a reinforcer in the same way as anxiety is considered. Affects generally present a dilemma for reinforcement theory and, other than anxiety, have received minimal attention by reinforcement theorists.

TABLE 21.2 (cont.)

Approve of self	Disapprove of self	Receive tangible rewards (money, etc.)	Receive disapproval/rejection	Sum Probability Positive Outcomes	Sum Probability Negative Outcomes	Sum Probability × Value: Positive	Sum Probability × Value: Negative
3	2	1	1	10	7	35	28
3	2	1	2	9	9	31	36
3	2	1	2	9	9	31	36
3	2	1	2	9	8	31	32
3	2	1	2	9	9	31	36
			Mean	9.4	8.4	31.8	33.6
			Difference	1.0		1.8	
3	2	1	2	9	9	31	36
2	3	1	2	8	12	27	48
3	2	1	1	10	7	34	28
			Mean	9.0	9.3	30.7	37.3
			Difference	−.3		−6.7	
3	2	1	2	10	8	34	32
3	2	1	2	8	11	27	44
2	3	1	3	7	14	23	56
2	3	1	3	6	13	20	52
			Mean	7.8	11.5	26.0	46.0
			Difference	−3.7		−20.0	
2	3	1	2	7	12	23	48
1	4	1	3	5	15	16	60
			Mean	6.0	13.5	19.5	54.0
			Difference	−7.5		−34.5	
+4	−4	+1	−4				

do appear to be associated with similar patterns of behavior, though exceptions do occur. (2) Individual behaviors associated with similar reinforcement contingencies appear to be associated with similar "likelihood of occurrence" values, although again exceptions clearly occur. (3) Behaviors rated as high in "likelihood of occurrence" generally have a more positive outcome expectancy than behaviors rated as low in likelihood of occurrence. Here too exceptions occur that may be due to rating errors, missing reinforcers, or other influences (e.g., feelings) that are not considered in a behavior-outcome reinforcement matrix. (4) The meaning of the behavior-outcome matrix appears to be enhanced by including data concerning the value of a reinforcer as well as data concerning its probability. In addition, the data clearly indicate that the value of many reinforcers varies not only from person to person but also from situation to situation for the same individual.

TABLE 21.3
Behavior × Outcome Matrix

Probability Rating	Behavior	Receive love/affection	Be ignored	Receive recognition/ status/ prestige	Feel anxious/ uncomfortable/ tense	Face conflict
4	Act friendly, supportively, co-operatively	4	1	4	4	1
4	Act intensely, very involved	4	1	4	4	1
4	Act informally, openly	4	1	4	4	1
3	Act submissively	4	1	4	4	1
3	Act actively	4	1	4	4	2
3	Express disagreement	4	1	4	4	3
3	Express personal opinion(s)	4	1	4	4	3
2	Act dominantly	4	1	4	4	2
2	Act passively	4	1	4	4	1
2	Talk a lot	4	1	4	4	1
1	Act aloof, detached, withdrawn	3	1	4	4	1
1	Act formally, rigidly	3	1	4	4	1
1	Act hostile, unfriendly	2	1	3	4	3
1	Smile a lot	4	1	4	4	1
How significant or important is each of these consequences to you in relation to this particular situation?		+3	−2	+4	−4	−4

CONSTRUCTIVISM AND ALTERNATIVE CONSTRUCTIONS

As most reviews of the field indicate, a consistent issue has been whether situations should be defined in objective or perceived terms (Pervin, 1978b). Most researchers in the field emphasize the subjectively perceived environment, part of a cognitive or constructivist emphasis in the field of psychology generally. Implicit in this approach to situations are some assumptions concerning conceptualization and assessment that need to be examined.

Assessment of the Perception of Situations

Often research on the perception of situations makes use of group data that may ignore the significant individuality of construct systems. For example, in some

TABLE 21.3 (cont.)

Approve of self	Disapprove of self	Receive tangible rewards (money, etc.)	Receive disapproval/ rejection	Sum Probability Positive Outcomes	Sum Probability Negative Outcomes	Sum Probability × Value: Positive	Sum Probability × Value: Negative
4	1	1	1	13	11	45	29
1	1	1	1	10	8	33	29
4	1	1	1	13	8	45	29
			Mean	12.0	9.0	41.0	29.0
			Difference	3.0		12.0	
4	4	1	1	13	11	45	38
4	1	1	1	13	9	45	33
4	1	1	3	13	12	45	45
4	1	1	2	13	11	45	41
			Mean	13.0	10.8	45.0	39.3
			Difference	2.2		5.7	
4	2	1	2	13	11	45	40
1	4	1	1	10	11	34	38
4	1	1	2	13	9	45	33
			Mean	12.0	10.3	41.3	37.0
			Difference	1.7		4.3	
4	4	1	1	12	11	45	38
4	3	1	1	12	10	45	35
1	4	1	3	7	15	20	54
4	1	1	1	13	8	45	29
			Mean	11.3	11.0	38.8	39.0
			Difference	.3		−.2	
+4	−3	+1	−4				

cases situations are presented to subjects that have little relationship to their daily lives. In such cases it may be difficult to know the basis for the subject's response. Some researchers have taken the excellent precaution of first determining the situations that are common to the subjects and then using these situations for presentation (Forgas, Argyle, & Ginsburg, 1979; Magnusson & Ekehammar, 1978). Another possibility, one which I favor, is to use an idiographic approach in which each subject chooses situations that are personally relevant.

A related issue here concerns the choice of scales and factors or dimensions to be used. Again, often the tendency is to use the same scales for all subjects and to use the same factors or dimensions not only for all subjects but for all situations. An illustration of this would be the use of the same semantic differential scales for all subjects and situations and the analysis of all data in terms of the evaluative, activity, and potency dimensions. Obviously, this approach provides for comparisons across subjects and situations. However, it also has significant

TABLE 21.4
Behavior × Outcome Matrix

Probability Rating	Behavior	Receive love/affection	Be ignored	Receive recognition/ status/ prestige	Feel anxious/ uncomfortable/ tense	Face conflict
4	Act friendly, supportively, co-operatively	3	1	2	3	3
4	Act intensely, very involved	3	1	2	3	3
4	Act informally, openly	3	1	2	1	2
4	Talk a lot	3	1	2	1	2
3	Act submissively	2	1	1	4	4
3	Act actively	3	1	2	1	3
3	Act dominantly	3	1	2	2	4
3	Act hostile, unfriendly	4	1	4	4	4
2	Express disagreement	3	1	2	4	4
2	Smile a lot	3	1	2	2	2
2	Express personal opinions	2	3	2	4	4
1	Act aloof, detached, withdrawn	4	1	4	4	4
1	Act formally, rigidly	2	1	3	4	1
1	Act hostile, unfriendly	4	1	4	4	4
How significant or important is each of these consequences to you in relation to this particular situation?		+4	−4	+4	−4	−4

problems associated with it. First, the scales may have differential relevance and significance for the various subjects. Furthermore, scales that are particularly salient for individual subjects may be left out. Second, in a related way, the dimensions determined from group data may not reflect the dimensions used by individuals. Dimensions obtained from group data may mask important subgroup or individual differences, providing only a gross commonality. Third, different dimensions may not only be relevant to different individuals but to different situations. Thus, for example, Forgas, Argyle, and Ginsburg (1979), analyzing group data, found that the number of dimensions and the nature of the dimensions used varied in the perception of each of four different settings. Because both the relevant attributes and the salient dimensions were found to vary from situation to situation, they questioned the assumption of a stable organization of perception regardless of context.

TABLE 21.4 *(cont.)*

Approve of self	Disapprove of self	Receive tangible rewards (money, etc.)	Receive disapproval/ rejection	Sum Probability Positive Outcomes	Sum Probability Negative Outcomes	Sum Probability × Value: Positive	Sum Probability × Value: Negative
4	1	1	2	10	10	33	39
4	1	1	2	10	10	33	39
4	1	1	3	10	8	33	31
4	1	1	3	10	8	33	31
			Mean	10.0	9.0	33.0	35.0
			Difference	1.0		−2.0	
1	4	1	4	5	17	16	64
3	1	1	3	9	9	30	35
1	4	1	1	6	11	20	44
1	4	1	4	10	17	36	64
			Mean	6.0	13.5	25.5	51.7
			Difference	−7.5		−26.2	
4	1	1	3	10	13	33	51
3	1	1	2	9	8	30	31
4	1	1	4	9	16	29	63
			Mean	9.3	12.3	30.7	48.3
			Difference	−3.0		−17.6	
3	1	1	1	12	11	42	43
1	4	1	1	7	11	24	40
1	4	1	4	10	17	36	64
			Mean	9.7	13.0	34.0	49.0
			Difference	−3.3		−15.0	
+3	−3	+1	−4				

Again, these difficulties suggest to me the utility of an idiographic approach in which not only are situations provided by the subject but the data are analyzed in terms of the unique perceptual organization of the individual. In this way we may be able to discover principles concerning the organization of perceptions and their relation to behavior, that are independent of specific content.

Conceptualization of Construct Systems

There is a tendency in much of our current research to assume that individuals use the same constructs to construe all situations. However, just as Forgas et al. found that the structure and complexity of organization of group perceptions were situation specific, we should not be surprised to find that individuals employ alternative constructs and even alternative construct organizations according to the requirements of the situation. In other words, each person may have multiple schemata that are used somewhat interchangeably or under varying circumstances. In George Kelly's terms, we each may have many *templates* with which to construe life. We may tend to favor one or another such template but switch over to others when circumstances dictate or when we want to "get another slant" on what is being perceived.

There is, in fact, considerable evidence concerning this degree of complexity to individual construct systems. Indeed, one of the problems with the cognitive-style dimension of cognitive complexity–simplicity is that it ignores the fact that the same person may organize information in complex or simple ways according to the information being processed. For example, Signell (1966) found that both the content and the complexity of cognitive structure varied for individuals depending on whether they were perceiving people or nations. A full understanding of an individual's construct system involves, then, an understanding of the constructs that are used, the multiple ways in which the constructs may be organized, and the ways in which these organizations are utilized in relation to other behavior.

Recognition of the point that individuals may have multiple construct organizations or classificatiory schemes has important implications for predicting behavior. If the individual has multiple classificatory schemes, then some classifications of situations will relate to overt behavior more directly than others. This is the point that was made earlier in relation to the classification of situations into the categories of home, school, work, and recreation–peer relationships. Although such an organization of situations makes sense for some purposes, it may not for others. In sum, the effort to develop a meaningful taxonomy of situations may be difficult not only because of individual differences and complex relationships between cognitive constructions and behavior but also because people make use of multiple schemes and may constantly be shifting among them—sometimes using a telephoto lens and sometimes a wide-angle lens, sometimes viewing life's situations primarily in terms of feelings and other times viewing life's situations primarily in terms of social norms and rules of behavior.

STATIC AND PROCESS VIEWS OF BEHAVIOR–SITUATION RELATIONSHIPS

One of the aspects of the previous research, as well as much of the research done in psychology generally, is the extent to which it suggests a static model of human behavior. In other words, we tend to consider situations as if they are fixed entities and behavior-situation relationships as if they are isolated events rather than parts of more extended processes and systems. From a systems standpoint, treating events and structures in isolation from one another can result in missing some of their most significant and interesting characteristics.

Some observations from my own experience may serve to illustrate the point. First, I find that if I have spent a great deal of time working alone, I seek out contact with colleagues and friends. On the other hand, if I have been interacting extensively with others, I look forward to spending a day or two by myself. The meaning of these situations depends on where I am in this "introversion-extroversion" cycle and my response really cannot be understood without consideration of the importance of this cycle to me. Second, I find that many situations that I am in change in significant ways despite the fact that the characters, location, and basic content remain the same. Thus, although I can describe a situation in general terms, it may have distinctive phases within it. In part this involves the question of the segment that we choose for investigation, but it goes beyond that because analyzing any segment alone will miss the flow of events and changes in the ways the situation is construed. The third observation is derived from a task set for myself and members of my seminar. The task was to record our daily behavior in terms of situations we were in that lasted for 15 minutes or more. Many of us were surprised to find out just how we spend our time. One particularly interesting aspect of this was the extent to which we spend time in activities that are not intrinsically rewarding but are done in the service of some other goal (e.g., driving to work, taking some course). Again, the meaning of the situation cannot be understood except in the context of other phenomena.

What appears to me to be common to these experiences is that they highlight the importance of a process, systems perspective in studying behavior–situation relationships. Within this general view, it seems to me that increased attention needs to be given to the concept of goals in relation to our understanding of situations and how we organize our perceptions of situations, as well as our behaviors in relation to them. For a considerable time the concept of goals was criticized within the field because of its teleological connotation. With the advent of cybernetics and general systems theory, the concept of goals began to be more acceptable (Miller, Galanter, & Pribram, 1960; Pervin, 1978c). Most recently, Schank and Abelson (1977) have made use of the concept of goals in relation to their model of how information is organized and processed; in fact, their emphasis on concepts such as scripts, plans, and goals would appear to have potential relevance to our efforts to understand behavior–situation relationships.

Schank and Abelson describe a script as a structure that describes appropriate sequences of events in a particular context. A plan represents more generalized information concerning relationships between events and is the basis for developing more specific scripts. Goals speak to the motivational component of behavior. Goals provide a basis for expectations. We predict our own behavior and that of others on the basis of our understanding of the relevant goals. In terms of the behavior–outcome research described earlier, the individual's behavior–outcome matrix for each situation may be considered to be part of the person's script for that situation. Their generalized expectancies concerning behavior–outcome relationships may be viewed as part of their plans or general views concerning relationships between events. Finally, what is left out and remains to be considered is the person's goals. In other words, analyses remain to be done of how situations are organized in relation to one another and in relation to anticipated future events. We do not perceive situations in isolation from one another, nor do we select situations or respond to them in isolation from what has occurred and what we hope will occur. There is, then, the need for conceptual and empirical efforts to understand these process and system aspects of behavior–situation relationships.

22

Situational Aspects of Interactional Psychology

Norman S. Endler
York University, Canada

Compared to the person, the situation has received relatively little attention in personality theorizing and research. This state of affairs is probably due to historical, political, social, and methodological factors. Historically, the early research on personality in this century grew out of the concern with the assessment of individual differences. (Freud's theorizing about personality development and dynamics was concerned with situations, but primarily as a context within which individual impulses were expressed.) The impetus for the study of individual differences stems, to a great extent, from the theorizing and research of Francis Galton (1907). Galton's aim was to assess the inherited abilities of individuals. Hunt and Kirk (1979) have stated: "Galton appears to have hoped that his tests could function as a means of improving the human race through eugenics [p. 1]."

The early work on personality, derived from the research on individual differences (psychometrics), overestimated the role of *person factors* and underestimated the role of *situation factors*. Whereas the research and theorizing in personality focused on person factors, social and experimental psychology focused on situational factors. Ichheiser (1943) suggests that the overemphasis of personal factors at the expense of situational factors has its roots in sociopolitical factors. The focus on personal factors had its etiology in the ideology and social system of nineteenth-century liberalism, which postulated that "our fate in social space depended exclusively, or at least predominantly, on our individual qualities—that we, as individuals, and not the prevailing social conditions shape our lives [p. 152]." The sociopsychological and sociopolitical forces of the last half century (e.g., the depression, unemployment, World War II, the Cold War, inflation, Viet Nam, the revolution of rising expectations, the Third World forces) have shifted the focus in the direction of explaining behaviour as a function of social conditions.

Personality research is, to some extent, influenced by political, social, and personal considerations. It is *not* value-free. According to Pervin (1978a) all "Scientific pursuits have a historical context and a political context [p. 280]." In addition to personality theory and research being influenced by nonscientific factors, personality methodology and research tactics are also influenced by personal and social factors (Endler, 1980). Our aim should be to be aware of and to minimize the effects of these extra-scientific considerations.

Research in personality has been primarily guided by the trait model, which emphasizes traits (inner factors) as the major determinants of behavior. Therefore, there has been more concern with the investigation of *traits* than with the investigation of *situations* in personality research. Much of the research on situations has been concerned with their role as experimental stimuli. One of the sources of the impetus for an investigation of the role of situations in personality research has been the interactional model of personality (Endler & Magnusson, 1976c).

The two basic tasks for an interactional psychology of personality concern: (1) the investigation of how persons and situations interact in evoking behavior; and (2) the description, classification, and systematic analyses of situations (including stimuli and environments) (Endler, 1977, 1980; Magnusson, 1976). The nature of person-by-situation interactions has been discussed in detail by Endler and Magnusson (1976a), Magnusson and Endler (1977b), Magnusson (1976), and Endler (1977). In this chapter we focus on the psychological investigation of the situation in terms of the role of situational factors for interactional psychology. We are concerned with the description, classification, and systematic analyses of stimuli, situations, and environments. Both the *within* situation factors and the *between* situation factors in personality theory are discussed (Magnusson & Endler, 1977b).

STRATEGIES WITH RESPECT TO SITUATIONAL ANALYSES

Sociologists and social learning theorists have focused on situations as the prime determinants of behavior. Ecological psychologists (Barker, 1965) have been concerned with the role of environmental factors in behavior. However, as Endler (1975a) has indicated, there have been few attempts to study situations *psychologically*. Furthermore, there have been few attempts at integrating personality research and ecological psychology. Research by Mehrabian and Russell (1974) points to the relevance of environmental psychology and personality psychology for interactional psychology. Craik (1973) has proposed a personality research paradigm for environmental psychology.

Pervin (1978b) points to the fact that there has been a failure to define and differentiate adequately among the terms *stimuli, situations,* and *environments.* Fredericksen (1972) pointed out that: "We need a systematic way of conceptualizing the domain of situations and situation variables before we can make rapid progress in studying the role of situations in determining behavior [p. 115]."

Ekehammar (1974) discusses five major methods of studying the problem of situational description and classification: (1) a priori defined variables of *physical* and *social* character; (2) need concepts; (3) some *single reaction* elicited by the situations; (4) individuals' *reaction patterns* elicited by the situations; and (5) individuals' *perceptions (cognitions)* of situations [p. 1041-1042].

Moos (1973), in his article on the conceptualizations of human environments, describes six major methods that can be used to characterize environments as they are related to human functioning: (1) ecological dimensions (e.g., geographical-meteorological variables, architectural-physical variables); (2) behavior settings involving both behavioral and ecological properties; (3) parameters of organizational structure; (4) behavioral and personal parameters of the environmental inhabitants; (5) organizational psychosocial and climate variables; and (6) variables relating to reinforcement or functional analyses of environments. Moos (1973) has said: "The six categories of dimensions are nonexclusive, overlapping, and mutually interrelated [p. 652]."

In defining the environment of personality, Feshbach (1978) discusses two levels of this dimension: (1) the *situational* level or environment; and (2) the *sociocultural* environment. "The situational level refers to the immediate social and physical environmental stimuli to which the organism responds and adapts [p. 447]." This level of analysis, according to Feshbach, provides the empirical basis for issues such as the situational specificity versus the cross-situational consistency controversy. Feshbach (1978) continues: "The second category of environmental influence relates to the broader social and physical context that provides situations their meaning and their continuity [p. 447]." Population density, cultural ideologies, and social norms are examples of variables at this level. According to Feshbach (1978) there is also a third class of variables that are part of the environment of personality and a distinct subset of our sociocultural environment. The third class refers to the theories and perspectives that determine an investigator's research. This is analogous to the sociopolitical factors (or ideologies) that we discussed earlier.

Ekehammar (1974), Endler and Magnusson (1976a, 1976b), Magnusson (1978), and Pervin (1978b) have all made the basic distinction between the subjective or psychological aspects and the objective or physical aspects of environments and situations. This distinction is not new and has previously been made using terms such as the *physical* and the *psychological environment.* For example, Kantor (1924, 1926) distinguished between *biological* and *psychological environments;* Koffka (1935) distinguished between *geographical* and *be-*

havioral environments; and Murray (1938) distinguished between *alpha press* (objective) and *beta press* (subjective) situations or environments. These various terms have been used with somewhat different meanings by different investigators. However, the basic conceptual distinction, in all cases, was between the *objective* "external world" that affects the person, and the *subjective* "inner world," as the person perceives it and reacts to it (Magnusson, 1978).

Endler and Magnusson (1976b) state that the subject of the "external world" with which the individual interacts (including both social and physical environmental factors) can be conceptualized as the *ecology* (Brunswik, 1952, 1956). Actual behavior occurs in a *situation,* or the aspect of the ecology that a person perceives and reacts to immediately (Murray, 1938, p. 40), or the *momentary situation* (Lewin, 1936, p. 217].

Both the objective "external world" (i.e., the environment as it actually is, independent of the individual's interpretations) *and* the subjective world (i.e., the psychological meaning or significance of the environment for the individual), can be described and discussed at different levels of generality (Endler & Magnusson, 1976b; Magnusson, 1978). We can describe and discuss both macroenvironments and microenvironments. In terms of the "external world" we can describe and discuss the environment with respect to physical factors, social factors, or some combination of the two.

Cities, lakes, parks, and buildings are examples of the physical *macroenvironment.* Single stimulus variables or objects such as a spoon or a letter opener are examples of the *physical microenvironment.* Cultural values, norms, and roles, common to the whole society, are examples of the *social macroenvironment.* The *social microenvironment* refers to norms, values, habits, and attitudes, common to the specific individual, and groups with whom the person interacts directly at home, school, or work. To some extent it refers to the social environment unique to the individual. Tajfel (1978) points out that there are certain principles that influence how a person structures the social world (environment) that she or he inhabits. We assign: "objects and events in the world at large to separate and discrete categories [p. 320]." There are both similarities and differences with respect to the "systems of categories used to simplify the physical and the social environment [p. 320]." The information received from our social environment is both more ambiguous and fluid than that received from our physical environment. The reaction to our social environment, both people and events, is rarely free of both positive and negative evaluations.

Environments, Situations, and Stimuli

At a general and crude level it is possible to distinguish among environments, situations, and stimuli. The environment is the general and persistent background or context within which behavior occurs; whereas the situation is the momentary or transient background. Stimuli can be construed as being the elements within a situation. This is analogous to the trait–state distinction with environments construed as the enduring background ("traits") and situations construed as the momentary or transient background ("states"). Stimuli are the elements or components within the situation. As we see later, one can compare elements *within* a situation and judge how this affects behavior, or one can do a comparison *between* situations, assessing effects of situations as wholes on behavior.

Although in general one can distinguish among stimuli, situations, and environments, the borderline between any two of them is often fuzzy, as stimuli spill over into situations and situations into environments. One person's stimulus might be another person's situation, and one person's situation may be another person's environment. As we discuss later in this chapter, the individual's perception of the situation (or stimulus, or environment) appears to be an important determinant of behavior. The same environment (or situation or stimulus) can and does have an different impact on different people.

As Pervin (1978b) points out, the terms *stimulus, situation,* and *environment* have been used interchangeably and are frequently used without being defined. According to Pervin (1978b): "The major distinction appears to have to do with the scale of analysis—ranging from the concern with molecular variables in the case of stimulus to molar variables and behaviors in the case of the environment [p. 79]." However, as Pervin goes on to point out, this is not always the case.

Environmental psychologists or ecologists have focused on the environment; personality theorists, who have been concerned with person–situation interactions, have focused on situations; and perception psychologists (and most experimental psychologists) have focused on the stimulus. One important issue is whether we can define the situation (or environment or stimulus) independently of the perceiver. Because the meaning or significance of a situation appears to be an important determinant of behavior, we focus on the perception of situations when discussing the person–situation interaction issue; that is, we are concerned with how persons construe the situations that they select and with which they interact.

Pervin (1978b), in discussing the uses of the concept of situation, points out that Sells (1963b) defines situations on the basis of objectively measured external characteristics; Rotter (1955) and Barker (1965) define situations on the basis of objective characteristics; Fredericksen (1972) defines the situation in terms of the *reactions* or behaviors associated with the situation; and Endler and Magnusson (1976a), Endler (1980), and Magnusson (1978) define the situation in terms of a person's perception of the situation. Pervin (1978b) states that: "The situation-perception approach leads to definitions of situations in terms of their perceived properties or dimensions, as opposed to their objectively defined properties or their behavior-eliciting properties [p. 77]."

Not only do persons react to situations, but they also affect the situations with which they interact. As Bowers (1973) points out: "Situations are as much a function of the person as the person's behavior is a function of the situation [p. 327]." There is a constant and continuous interplay between persons and situations, and, as we see later, we have to examine the ongoing *process*.

Selected Versus Imposed Situations

In many cases, we select the situations we encounter and the situations with which we interact. However, there are instances in which situations are imposed on us. This is a continuous lifelong ongoing process, but, instead of examining situations longitudinally we are prone to observe and examine a cross-sectional slice of situations, at one point in time.

By selecting (or being born in) a city, as opposed to a rural area, we are more likely to encounter subways, tall buildings, and areas of high population density and less likely to encounter farm animals and unpolluted air. By deciding to go to the university we are probably eliminating (manual) labor occupations such as farm hands, assembly line operators, or taxi drivers and minimizing the opportunity of interacting with persons in these occupations. By deciding to go into graduate school, in psychology, for example, we are further limiting the situations (including other persons) we encounter. Most of us are creatures of habit and except for vacations and other unusual events (e.g., sabbaticals, marriage) we routinely interact in the same types of situations from day to day and from weekend to weekend. Therefore, if there is any consistency in behavior, it is due, to a fair extent, to the fact that we encounter similar situations (both at work and during our leisure hours) from day to day. All of us go through similar routines from day to day. Although we shape our environment, our environment shapes us.

We are subject to complex stimuli at various levels. According to Magnusson (1978): "the total environment influencing individuals' lives consists of a complex system of physical–geographical, social, and cultural factors which are continuously interacting and changing, at different levels of proximity to the individual [p. 1]." Stimulation affects behavior not only in terms of information being processed at the moment but also by interacting with previously stored information: "The total environment influences individual development and behavior [but] the influence of environment is always mediated via actual situation [p. 1]."

Differential Psychology: Persons and Situations

The term *differential psychology* has typically and usually referred to individual differences. Magnusson (1978) has recently suggested that we need a differential psychology of situations to complement the differential psychology of persons. What direction should a differential psychology of situations take? Can we scale situations in terms of impact, complexity, relevance, objectiveness, subjectiveness?

There is an inherent danger of overemphasizing taxonomies of situations. Different investigators may focus on different attributes and produce different taxonomies. This has happened with respect to traits, in that different trait theorists have produced different taxonomies or classifications of traits. Any taxonomy of situations and/or environments must fit into a theoretical context and should not be arbitrary. It is our contention that a classification system should be based primarily on the situations that people encounter and on the perception or meaning that the situations have for them. Pervin (1977) has sampled situations ecologically, in terms of natural habitats that persons encounter. Pervin examines free responses of individuals on the basis of their perceptions and behavioral and affective responses to their daily situations, and he classifies his variables via factor analysis. He has concluded that one should focus on the person–situation interaction as the unit of analysis.

Magnusson (1978) believes that the actual situation is central for: "understanding the development process and actual behavior [p. 8]." The *total situation* (as a frame of reference or context) and situational settings should be our major focus according to Magnusson. Brian R. Little (personal communication, 1979) believes that personal projects are appropriate units for understanding behavior. Everyone has certain goals in life and certain projects they engage in (e.g., buying a home or a car, obtaining a degree, going on a vacation). However, projects differ in size, relevance, and intensity; therefore, it may be necessary to ask persons to scale their projects along these dimensions. Runyan (1978) has suggested the investigation of the life course in terms of sequences of person–situation interactions.

It may be desirable to have persons keep daily logs of their activities and the situations they encounter. Perhaps our data base should be in terms of how persons construe their daily life encounters and which situations they consider stressful. We need to examine real-life situations. We discuss this in more detail later when we present some of our anxiety research in various settings.

Situation Perception and Situation Reaction Studies

Earlier we indicated that Ekehammar (1974) had suggested a five-strategy classification scheme for investigating situations. At least two of these strategies provide a psychological perspective for investigating situations, namely *situation perception* and *situation reaction* studies. According to Endler and Magnusson (1976b): "The psychological significance of the environment can be investigated by studying the individual's *perception* of the situation (the meaning he assigns to a situation) and *reaction* to a situation (a specific situation or the general environment) [p. 15]."

According to Magnusson (1971): "individuals differ not mainly with regard to certain stable characteristics of behavior but particularly regarding their specific characteristic ways of adjusting to the varying characteristics of different situations [p. 851]." Magnusson (1971, 1974) has developed an empirical psychophysical method for investigating the perception of situations. Investigating situations common to university students in their studies and using the psychophysical method, Magnusson and Ekehammar (1973) found two bipolar situational dimensions: positive versus negative and active versus passive, which are similar to the semantic differential factors. In addition, they found one unipolar dimension, a social factor. When they extended their research to stressful situations, Ekehammar and Magnusson (1973) found basically the same results as in their previous studies. The meaning or *perception* of the situation seems to be an essential and influential factor that affects a person's behavior.

The *situation reaction* studies have focused on peoples' responses to situations. Both Rotter (1954) and Frederiksen (1972) suggested that situations could be classified in terms of the similarity of behavior that they evoke in individuals. With this approach, the aim is to develop taxonomies of situations. Most of the investigations that have used a situation reaction approach have utilized data from inventories originally constructed for research purposes (e.g., the S-R Inventory of Anxiousness, Endler, Hunt, & Rosenstein, 1962; the Interactional Reactions Questionnaire, Ekehammar, Magnusson, & Ricklander, 1974; Magnusson & Ekehammar, 1975a; and the Stressful Situations Questionnaire, Hodges & Felling, 1970). A factor analysis of subjects' responses to various situations of the S-R Inventory of Anxiousness yielded three situational factors: interpersonal, inanimate physical danger, and ambiguous. With respect to the S-R Inventory of General Trait Anxiousness, Endler and Okada (1975) and Endler and Magnusson (1976d) found similar situational factors. The situation *reaction* studies have investigated the dimensionality of situations on the basis of persons' reactions to situations as wholes.

Magnusson and Ekehammar (1975b, 1978) and Ekehammar, Schalling, and Magnusson (1975) have studied the relationship between subjects' *perceptions* of situations and their *reactions* to situations. Reactions to a situation are to a high degree a function of the individual's perceptions of the situations. Therefore, the relationship between perceptions and reactions have implications for an interactional model of personality. Magnusson and his colleagues, using situation perception *and* situation reaction data, compared the two strategies within a single study because they were interested in assessing the psychological significance of situations and in investigating person-by-situation interactions.

Magnusson and Ekehammar (1975b) collected situation *reaction* and situation *perception* data on 40 subjects. There were four different categories of stressful situations covering a total of 12 situations. The coefficient of congruence between perceptions and reactions for three of the four a priori groups of situations ranged from .89 to .92; for the fourth group of situations the coefficient of congruence was .69. In a similar study, Ekehammar, Schalling, and Magnusson (1975) obtained essentially the same results. The two studies discussed previously used group data. Analyzing individual data, Magnusson and Ekehammar (1978) also obtained results that were congruent with an interaction model of personality.

In exploring the psychological significance of situations, it is essential to distinguish between situation *perception* dimensions and situation *reaction* dimensions. Although two individuals may *perceive* the same situation as threatening, one individual may *react* by attacking the situation, and another person may *react* by withdrawing from the situation. The research in this area by Magnusson and his colleagues provides a promising approach for determining how perceptual factors in situations influence reactions. Another important dimension in the relationship between perception and reaction is the temporal one. At one time the person may react to stress by withdrawing, whereas at another instance in time the same person may react by attacking. In addition to the specific situation, various contextual and motivational factors may mediate the relationship between perception and reaction.

As indicated earlier there are other useful distinctions in addition to the situation reaction versus the situation perception distinction. One of these distinctions refers to objective versus subjective (or psychological) characteristics of situations. Some researchers (Gibson, 1960; Sells, 1963b; Tolman, 1951b) have advocated an analysis of the environment in objective terms. Kantor (1924, 1926) using the terms *biological* and *psychological environment,* Koffka (1935) using the terms *geographical* and *behavioral environment,* and Murray (1938) using the terms *alpha press* and *beta press* have all distinguished between objective and subjective (psychological) environments. However, there have been few systematic analyses of the relationship between objective and subjective (psychological) environments. It is my contention that we should focus on the psychological characteristics of situations and environments and treat the objective characteristics as one of the determinants (in addition to implicit cues, needs, cognitions, and past experience) of the perception (psychological meaning) of situations and of behavior. (Oostendorp, McMaster, Rosen, & Waind, 1978, have examined the relationships between design characteristics of building entrances and peoples' reaction to them.)

Between Situations and Elements Within a Situation

Most of the studies in the area of interactional psychology and most of the research studies on situations have focused on the situation as a *whole* and have compared the effects between different situations. The research on situations as *wholes* has investigated how each situation is experienced or interpreted in its total context (Magnusson, 1971). However, one can also examine the elements or situational cues *within* a situation. In examining the various *cues* within a situation, it is important to determine how they continuously interact with one another and change in the process (Magnusson & Endler, 1977b). For example, at a cocktail party situation, Mary's reaction to George is influenced by George's reaction to Mary and both of their reactions might be influenced and modified when Susan (George's wife) appears. This is a continuing and ongoing process (Endler, 1980; Magnusson, 1976). Endler (1977) says: "One can construe a situation as a dynamic process in which a person selects certain elements or events (primarily other persons) and is in turn affected by these other elements [p. 356]. '' In studying situations we should focus on the various elements within a situation including, e.g., person-by-situation interactions and person-by-person interactions.

Situations, Events, and Units of Analysis

Although we are usually concerned with obtaining representative samplings of persons, we rarely obtain representative samplings of situations and environments. Brunswik (1952, 1956) emphasized the need to obtain representative samplings of situations, lest we bias our conclusions. There are numerous unresolved definitional and conceptual problems. When does a situation begin and when does it end? How long is a situation? What are the differences between events and situations? What impact does a situation have on persons? Are persons in agreement as to whether or not they are operating in the same situation? When does an individual respond directly to a situation, and when does he or she respond independently of the situation?

Skinner's (1938) distinction between operants (reactions independent of observable stimuli) and respondents (direct reactions to stimuli) has relevance with respect to the cross-situational consistency versus situational-specificity issue. Greater consistency would be expected with respect to operant reactions than with respect to respondent reactions. For respondents, the person may have situations imposed on him or her and may well have to respond primarily to the demands of the situations rather than on the basis of his or her own interests and tendencies. For operants, the individual may *select* his or her situations and seek situations similar to those he or she has found rewarding in the past.

Units of Analysis. In general, what *kind* of unit should be used in research in personality, and what *size* of units should be used? More specifically, what kind and size of unit should be used in the scientific investigation of situations? With respect to the kinds of units in personality research, the ones that have been most frequently used have been traits, but some investigators have used motives and defenses. Unfortunately, there has not been much of a parallel research effort with respect to situations. However, there has been a recent upsurge in the role of situations and environments in personality research (Magnusson, 1978). Perhaps the most appropriate unit of analysis with respect to personality research is the person-by-situation interaction unit (Endler, 1980; Pervin, 1977; Raush, 1977).

Although Murray (1938) suggested, over 40 years ago, that need-press units or themas were most appropriate for personality research, to the best of my knowledge, no one has conducted systematic and/or intensive investigation of themas, although there has been systematic longitudinal and/or intensive studies of persons (Block, 1977; Levinson, 1978; White, 1966, 1976). Perhaps the time has come to have longitudinal studies of the situations that individuals encounter and longitudinal studies of person-by-situation interactions. Murray (1938) pointed out that: "much of what is now *inside* the organism was once *outside*. For these reasons, the organism and its milieu must be considered together, a single creature–environment interaction being a convenient short unit for psychology. A long unit—an individual life—can be most clearly formulated as a succession of related *short units* or *episodes* [p. 40]." Murray's call over 40 years ago has gone largely unheeded.

When we focus on the size of units, it is usually very difficult to determine when a situation or event begins or ends. Should we emphasize elements within situations or do we focus on a total situation? Do we study a family of events and their interrelationship or do we merely focus on a specific event? Should we focus on person-by-person interactions (Patterson & Moore, 1978) or person-by-situation interactions? Do certain situations elicit certain responses? Do other situations constrain some responses? Price (1974a) and Price and Bouffard (1974) have discussed taxonomic classification of situations and responses and the problems involved with respect to behavior–environment congruence.

Both personologists and social psychologists (including ecologists) are moving in the direction of a person-by-situation interaction framework. Environmental psychologists (and ecologists) are becoming concerned with how situations and environments are perceived by individuals and the meaning that situations have for persons. Crowding, for example, is now conceived of as a perceptual (phenomenological) variable rather than mere physical density (Stokols, 1972). Density refers primarily to *physical* space limitations, but crowding refers to the person's *perception* of the restrictive characteristics of the space limitations. Crowding is a function of the interactions among environmental, social, and personal variables. Many studies in the area of anxiety, locus of control, and conformity are using a person-by-treatment (situation) experimental design (Endler & Edwards, 1978).

It is important to examine the *dynamic* ongoing chain of events, but it is also necessary to isolate the important personal and situational variables. Although situations have an impact on persons, individuals actively seek and select the persons and situations with whom they interact. Each person is an active intentional stimulus-seeking organism and is not a passive victim of situational encounters. The *process* of interaction is important. There is also a need to investigate real-life situations rather than merely relying on laboratory procedures. Although real-life behavior is more complex and more difficult to study, the potential extra payoff is worth the extra effort (Endler & Edwards, 1978).

Person–Situation Interactions in Real-Life Anxiety Provoking Situations

At this point I want to review briefly some person-by-situation interaction studies on anxiety that we have been conducting in real-life situations. Flood and Endler (1980) have examined the person-by-situation interaction model of anxiety (Endler, 1975b) in the field setting of a major track and field meet in Toronto.

We postulated that there would be a significant interaction between an ego-threatening (social evaluation) track and field meet situation and the (congruent) social evaluation A-Trait, in inducing changes in A-State arousal. The prediction was confirmed. In addition, we examined the subjects' perception of the situation and found that the athletes did indeed perceive the situation as a social evaluation situation.

Diveky and Endler (1977) examined middle-management male bankers in both nonstressful "off the job" situations (as reported by the bankers themselves) and stressful (social evaluation) "on the job" situations (as reported by the bankers). The social-evaluation A-Trait by (congruent) social-evaluation situational stress interaction was significant with respect to increases in A-State arousal; that is, those persons high in social-evaluation A-Trait manifested greater A-State arousal increases in social-evaluation situations than those low on social-evaluation A-Trait.

Endler and Magnusson (1977), studying Swedish college students, and Endler, Edwards, Kuczynski, and King (1979), studying Canadian high school students, found significant interactions between social-evaluation (interpersonal) A-Trait, and congruent classroom-examination (social-evaluation) situations, in evoking A-State arousal.

Endler, Edwards, and McGuire (1979) conducted a study in which they tested actors on anxiety both during rehearsal and before an important stage performance. There was a trend toward an interaction between social-evaluation A-Trait and the situational stress of a live theatre performance in inducing A-State. (With a larger sample size this interaction would have been significant.)

In all the studies reported previously (except for Endler & Magnusson, 1977) we assessed the subjects' perception of the stressful situation, and in all cases (except for Endler, Edwards, Kuczynski, & King) the situation was perceived as a social-evaluation situation. All the previous studies lend support to the interaction model of anxiety (Endler, 1975b).

Kendall (1978) conducted a study in which he compared the Spielberger (1972) state-trait anxiety model with the Endler (1975b) interaction model of anxiety. Kendall used both a social-evaluation stressor situation (failure on an intellectual task) and a physical danger situation (a car accident film). His study supported the interaction model of anxiety. The high social-evaluation A-Trait group (as assessed by the Endler & Okada, 1975, S-R Inventory of General Trait Anxiousness, S-R GTA) manifested a greater increase in A-State after the social-evaluation stressor situation than the low social-evaluation A-Trait group (as assessed by the S-R GTA). Similarly, the high physical danger A-Trait group (as assessed by the S-R GTA) manifested a greater increase in A-State after the physical danger threat (the car accident film) than the low physical danger A-Trait group. None of the other differences between high and low A-Trait groups were significant. These results strongly support the interaction model of anxiety (Endler, 1975b), in that high A-Trait subjects manifested greater A-State responses than low A-Trait subjects only when the facet of A-Trait was congruent to the type of situational stress.

Concluding Remarks

What direction should our research on situations and on interactions take? It is important to look at ongoing *processes* and *dynamic interactions*. We should also focus on subjects' perceptions of situations and on the meaning that situations have for them. The research involved is complex and we may not have the necessary and adequate methodologies. We will probably advance furthest by taking multimethod approaches, including introspection. We should remember that one individual's situation variable is another individual's person variable and vice versa.

Argyle (1977) has suggested that we investigate and analyze the *generative rules* of social interaction, in preference to attempting to make *predictions* about the content of social interaction. Grammatical rules with respect to language behavior provide an excellent analogy. A useful approach for studying person-by-person interactions (or person-by-situation interactions) is to infer the strategies and rules that individuals use in interacting with one another, in various situations.

ACKNOWLEDGMENT

This chapter was revised while the author was on sabbatical and was partially supported by an SSHRC Leave Fellowship (No. 451-790497).

23

A Model for Studying the Interaction Between the Objective Situation and a Person's Construction of the Situation

Lars Nystedt
University of Stockholm, Sweden

Much experimental work in psychology has relied on the objective definition of the situation. Psychological problems have been studied by varying systematically the characteristics of the situation and observing or measuring the variability of the person's reactions. The relationship between the variation in the objective characteristics of the situation and the variation in the person's reaction is used to draw conclusions about the mediating process between input and output. Implicit in this approach is the assumption that persons react on the basis of external stimulation. Therefore one fundamental problem for this approach is to specify and measure the external situation as objectively as possible.

Another way to conceptualize the situation is to define it as the individual's perception and construction of the situation, which can be described in terms of psychological variables (Kelly, 1955; Lewin, 1936; Murray, 1938). For those following this approach, the physical characteristics of the situation are not relevant by themselves but only with respect to their meaning to the person. Implicit in this approach is the assumption that a person does not react to the stimuli as such but to the interpretation of the stimuli. In using this approach, the latent cognitive structure underlying behaviors and the inference process must be a central concern for research. The focus should be on how the person selects, interprets, and treats the information available in a situation and the factors that influence this process.

The goal of science is to understand and explain the real world. Psychology, as a part of the scientific society, has the role of increasing our knowledge and understanding of how people construe and react in a complex environment. To fullfil this purpose neither of the two approaches briefly mentioned is sufficient. What is needed is an approach that combines the two, thereby stressing the importance of studying the interaction between the person and the environment. The present chapter is concerned with such a model. The model makes a distinction between the situation as it is and the situation as it is perceived by the person. Furthermore, it stresses the importance of studying the interaction between the characteristics of the external situation and the characteristics of the perceiver in order to understand and be able to predict human behavior. Before that model is presented, some basic assumptions underlying the model and two other models that constitute the basis for the actual model are briefly discussed. Due to space limitations, relevant research and methodological considerations are considered only superficially.

BASIC ASSUMPTIONS

Based on Kelly's (1955) theory of personal constructs and the notion of constructive alternativism, it is assumed that the most fundamental characteristic of human beings is their capacity to represent the external environment; they are free to construe the situation but bound by their constructions. The person develops a model of the environment and tests this model by predicting what is going to happen in the future. Because people are free to construe the external situation, it can be construed by each in different ways. This means that in order to predict a person's behavior at a certain time in a specific situation one must know that person's *structural representation* of the situation and must base the prediction on that structural representation and not on information about the external physical and social characteristics of the situation. The approach is not completely subjective because it is argued that in order to understand a person's behavior in a situation one must know the physical and social characteristics of the situation; otherwise it is impossible to know to what type of situation the person has given a specific meaning.

The external situation is assumed to exist by virtue of activity or, more precisely, it exists by continual change with respect to itself. Situations can be conceptualized in different perspectives. In the present chapter, the external situation will be conceptualized in a microperspective and will be considered to consist of things, events, persons, processes, and so on that are related to each other in space, in time, or by causal relations. Qualities within the external situation promote or restrict a person's freedom of choice. The properties of a person's cognitive structure limit that person's potential to interpret the situation in different ways. Empirical studies of the cognitive system's way of functioning in interaction with the external situation are necessary in order to increase our knowledge about how people select, interpret, and treat information. An effective study of the cognitive system presupposes, however, a detailed analysis of the external situation. Only by such an analysis of the external situation can one: (1) evaluate a person's performance in relation to a cognitive or situational limit;

(2) compare a person's performances in different situations; and (3) obtain an insight into how people function cognitively (Hursch, Hammond, & Hursch, 1964).

The Lens Model

One model that takes into account a simultaneous analysis of certain aspects of the cognitive system, the external situation, and the interaction between them is Brunswik's (1956) lens model (Fig. 23.1).

The left-hand part of the model represents the situation (ecology) and describes the relations between cues and a distal variable. The environmental system is assumed to consist of a series of elements (or events). Relationships between them are probabilistic. The characteristics of an element (distal event) may be predicted on the basis of information concerning the relationships of other elements (cues) to the distal variables, with a fair amount of certainty. The right-hand part describes the relations between cues and the responses of the individuals. If both the distal variables and cues have metric properties, the relationships between cues and the distal variable may be expressed in the form of correlation coefficients (r_e)—ecological validities. Under the same conditions the relations between cues (r_i) and the relations between cues and an individual's responses (r_s)—utilization coefficients—may be calculated. The coefficient

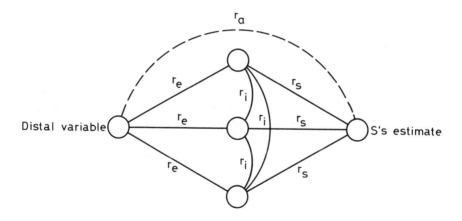

r_e = ecological validity
r_i = intercorrelations between cues
r_s = utilization coefficients
r_a = functional validity

FIG. 23.1. The lens model.

r_a—functional validity—is a measure of the correspondence between the distal variable and the person's estimations of that variable. The lens model, thus, takes into account, simultaneously, certain aspects of the cognitive system, the external situation, and the interaction between them.

The Brunswikian frame of reference has stimulated a lot of research on how individuals combine cues to make a total judgment, how individuals learn to use cues, and how cues affect interpersonal learning and cognitive conflict. The interaction between the cognitive system and the environmental system has been analyzed with the lens model equation originally derived by Hursch et. al., (1964) and modified by Tucker (1964).[1]

With this equation, r_a is analyzed in three related components: degree of matching, degree of linearity, and degree of nonlinearity. Thus research in this tradition is mostly concerned with studying the characteristics of the inference process and the degree of matching between the cognitive system and the environmental system.

The Modified Lens Model

With the lens model as a frame of reference for research, psychological problems are studied by systematically varying the characteristics of the objectively defined situation and observing or measuring the variability of the person's reactions. The conclusion about the cognitive process is based upon an analysis of the relationship between the input and the output and contributes little to the understanding of the nature of cognition.

The modified lens model (Nystedt, 1972a) was developed in the frame of reference of person–perception research and deals with the process involved in knowing the external and internal states of other persons. It consists primarily of an attempt to include in the lens model a multidimensional model for the study of a person's structural representation of a situation. The theoretical frame of reference for that model was based mainly on Brunswik's (1956) probabilistic functionalism; Sarbin, Taft, and Bailey's (1960) cognitive theory of clinical inference, and Kelly's (1955) theory of personal constructs. A description of the model is presented in Fig. 23.2.

---

[1]Tucker's (1964) version of the lens model equation is

$$r_a = R_e R_s G + C[(1 - R_s^2)(1 - R_e^2)]/^{1/2}$$

where

r_a = the correlation between the distal variable and a person's estimations
R_e = multiple correlation between cues and the distal variable
R_s = multiple correlation between cues and the person's ratings
G = the correlation between the variance in the distal variable predicted from R_e and the variance in the person's ratings predicted from R_s
C = partial correlation between the distal variable and the person's ratings with the cues held constant

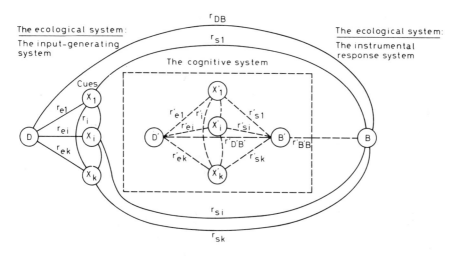

FIG. 23.2. The modified lens model.

where

   D = distal variable. This is a variable in the individual's physical and social environment upon which the individual is focused but not in immediate contact with.

   X_i = ecological stimulus variables. These are variables with which the individual is in immediate contact and that contain information about the distal variable.

   D' = the individual's cognitive representation of the definition of D.

   X_i' = the individual's cognitive representation of the definition of X_i.

   B' = central response in the utilization system.

   B = experimental response.

   r_{ei}^* = relationships of the ecological stimulus variables to the distal variable.

   r_i = relationships between ecological stimulus variables.

   r_{ei}' = the individual's cognitive representation of r_{ei} or anticipation of relationships between ecological stimulus variables and the distal variable.

   r_i' = the individual's cognitive representation of r_i or anticipation of relationships between ecological-stimulus variables.

   r_{si} = utilization coefficients. They denote relationships between ecological stimulus variables and the instrumental response variable.

   r_{si}' = cognitive-utilization coefficients. These symbolize hypothetical relationships between X_i' and B',

   r_{DB} = functional validity (i.e., relationship between a distal variable and the experimental-response variable).

   $r_{D'B'}'$ = the hypothetical relationship between the cognitive representation of the definition of D and the central response that is based on X_i', r_{ei}', and r_i',

   $r_{B'B}'$ = relationship between a central judgment (B') of the definition of D and the experimental response (B) to (D).

*The symbol r is used as a general expression for relationship, which can be expressed in different ways; it does not necessarily imply a correlation coefficient.

In the model the environmental system has been divided into two subsystems: the input-generating system and the instrumental-response system. The far left-hand part of the model, the input-generating system, consists of a criterion variable (D) and a number of stimulus variables (X_i). The relationships between the cues (r_i) and between the cues and the distal variable (r_{ei}) are assumed to be probabilistic. In a judgment situation the X_i's are the actual information that a judge obtains about D. The judge bases his evaluation on X_i and yields an experimental response (B) about D.

The cognitive system likewise is divided into two subsystems. The perceptual–cognitive system, the left-hand part of the cognitive system, is conceived of as a multidimensional space, where the cognitive representations of external elements (D' and X') are seen as points. The relationships r'_{ei} and r'_i between the cognitive representations are assumed to be probabilistic. The position of each element in the perceptual–cognitive system is determined in relation to the cognitive dimensions that the person is assumed to make use of in his selection, organization, and interpretation of the external environment. Thus the modified lens model suggests that relational knowledge affects cognitive representations of D and, by extension, X_1, X_i, X_k.

The utilization system, the right-hand part of the cognitive system, is assumed to describe how the person utilizes properties within the perceptual–cognitive system as a basis for the behavior. This system is part of the process of translating cognition into behavior by integration of the perceived information. The characteristics of the utilization system are assumed to be affected by the characteristics of the perceptual–cognitive system. Furthermore, according to the utilization system, the person will weight the selected pieces of information in forming an impression in accordance with the rank order of the assumed relationship (r'_{si}) between selected information and the judgmental dimension.

For an experimental study of the model and a test of the hypothesis that knowledge of the person's structural representation of the situation would increase the prospects of predicting the person's behavior, it must be possible to estimate the perceptual–cognitive matrix (r'_{ei} and r_i'), representing a certain situation.

According to the general model for the perceptual–cognitive structure, the cognitive dimensions may be regarded as vectors in a multidimensional space. Multidimensional scaling methods that recently have been developed are based on the same model (Ekman, 1970; Torgerson, 1958). These methods appear to be well-suited to the purpose of estimating individuals' perceptual–cognitive structures. Such methods have been used fruitfully in studies on implicit personality theory (Rosenberg & Sedlak, 1972) and perception of situations (Magnusson, 1971). However, with few exceptions (Nystedt, 1972b; Todd & Rappoport, 1964), the predictive validity of such methods has not been studied. The results from the studies cited and results from a study of the predictive power of the notion of implicit personality theory (Nystedt, 1979) suggests that information obtained about a person's perceptual–cognitive structure has predictive validity with regard to the person's behavior and suggests the value of determining relational concepts in person perception.

The modified lens model was developed in the frame of reference of person–perception research. The term *situation* was reserved to represent single distal objects, persons or some covert distal variables such as control of affect and impulses, and the information available about the distal variable or object.

The rest of this chapter is devoted to expanding that model to include situation perception in general, which by an analogy to person perception can be defined as the process that gives us knowledge about the internal and external qualities of situations. In the following process model, the terms *input selector* and *momentary states* are the same as those used in a model of person perception presented by Warr and Knapper (1968).

A PROCESS MODEL OF SITUATIONAL PERCEPTION

An account of the process model is rendered in Fig. 23.3.

The model is similar to the modified lens model in that the external situation is located on a distal–proximal dimension. The distal variable is replaced by a total situation, which is assumed to consist of things, people, events, processes, and so on that have certain qualities; these qualities are related to each other in space, in time, or by causal relations.

The proximal layer consists of the information that the person attends to in construing the external situation. The cognitive representation of the external situation is affected by the person's abstract structure, which is thought to be relatively stable across different situations and the more transitory or momentary states. Both of these structures also are thought to affect the input selector. The person's reactions and behaviors are a consequence of the characteristics of the perceived structure and content of the situation. The model distinguishes between a covert response and an overt response. The covert response is defined as the most probable behavior to express according to the meaning the person attaches to the particular situation. Because of situational constraints, not directly under the control of the person, the relation between the covert response and the overt response is probabilistic.

The External Situation

The model is based on the assumption that it is useful to distinguish between the external situation and the situation as it is perceived by the person. This raises the problem of how to describe a situation in objective terms. It is proposed that the external situation can be described by using three categories; substance, quality, and relation. Substance is concerned with the metaphysical questions of what a

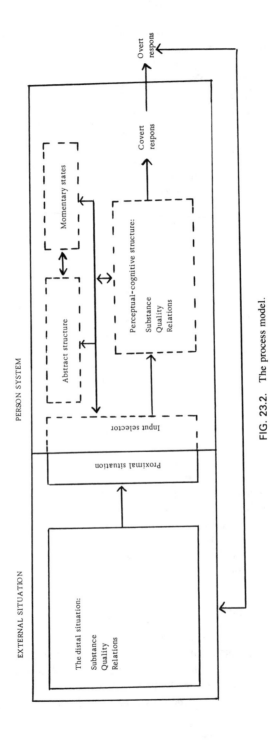

FIG. 23.2. The process model.

situation is and which situation it is. In the present model it is hypothesized that the external situation consists of things, people, events, processes, rules, norms, and so on. Many of these entities have names, can sometimes be pointed to, and can have certain characteristics or qualities. These qualities are sometimes overt and concrete, which means that they are observable (Brunswik, 1956), but sometimes covert or abstract and not directly observable. This creates a problem when we try to describe situations in objective terms. Generally speaking, one can gather knowledge about the external situation only by making successive estimates of the situation. The situation as a whole, or the different entities, does not tell us who or what they are; situations only manifest themselves in our experience as having certain qualities and being related to each other in some way. Thus, knowledge is rational rather than absolute. However, some qualities can be measured by instruments, and in that sense we are able to describe and identify a situation in objective terms; but very often (especially with regard to personal and social characteristics) we have to replace objectivity with intersubjective agreement among observers. The generality of intersubjective agreement, however, is limited by potential errors. In one study (Nystedt & Magnusson, 1973), it was shown that the agreement among judges' conceptualization of the validity of different units of information in a judgment task was very high but did not correspond with the predictive validity of the information. In another study (Nystedt, 1974) the interagreement among judges was also very high but decreased when the amount of information available increased; once again the predictive validity of the judgments was very low. These results and others (Goldberg, 1968; Nystedt, 1972c) raise the problem of how often common constructions about situations obscure the fact that they are wrong. Another problem with the use of intersubjective agreement as a substitute for objectivity is that consensus among observers is often high concerning overt characteristics of situations but becomes lower the more covert the characteristics are (Nystedt, Magnusson, & Aronowitsch, 1975). In as much as it is often more important to know covert than overt characteristics in order to understand and classify social situations, there is a risk that what is objectively measured is trivial.

Despite the fact that an objective description of a situation can not be constructed in the strict meaning of the term *objective,* one should try to describe the external situation as objectively as possible by following the scientific rules that define methodological objectivity.

The entities of a situation do not only have qualities; they are also related to each other; if that were not the case, there could be no situation but only a single stimulus. This means that the external situation can be considered an integrated system and that this integration is not an effect of our construction of the external situation but is a characteristic of the external situation as such. In describing the external situation three common types of relations should be considered: relations of betweenness, relations in time, and causal relations. It is assumed that a situation can be considered as a space in which the different entities are located.

The relation of betweenness is used to describe how different entities are arranged in a space (e.g., that A is between B and C). This is a different configuration from that in which B is between A and C. Furthermore betweenness refers to the association between elements and the distance between the elements refers to the degree of associations between elements. This is in agreement with the assumption underlying some common multidimensional scaling techniques used in studying situational perception. Situations consist of more than things related to each other by the concept of betweenness. Events and processes mean things in action. Action is a form of motion and in order to talk about motions we have to use the concept of time. For example, a person cannot be both young and old simultaneously. If it is true that a particular person is young and that he is also old, these facts must be true of the person at different times. Thus in describing the relations between entities we have to use the concept of time. The fact that an event is happening before another event also can imply that the first event *caused* the second event to occur. Therefore these two events are related to each other by a causal relation. A causal relation is defined such that the cause has the power to generate the effect and is connected to it. The three categories discussed, substance, qualities, and relations, are so-called *within* factors (Magnusson, 1978). Together these within factors can be used to describe and to classify the total situation by means of overall factors.

The proximal situation in the model represents that part of the total external situation that the person pays attention to and includes all external factors that affect the person's responses. This definition of the proximal situation corresponds to Fiske and Rice's (1955) definition of situations.

This means that from a person's point of view the proximal situation can be different from other persons' proximal situations independent of the objective characteristics of the distal external situation.

The Person System

The perceived situation is derived from: (1) our observation of what happens in our immediate vicinity; (2) what we have experienced in the past; and (3) what we expect about the future. This implies that the concept of time is of equal importance in describing the process of perception of situations as it is in describing the external situation and that the process of perception of situations can be defined as a redefining or restructuring of the external situation through the presentation of an alternate description of some situational datum (Levy, 1963). Thus the perceived situation is not a simple function of integration of situational data but a function of the person's constructions of the situation.

In accordance with this the person system is devided into four interactive systems: the perceptual cognitive system, the "abstract" structure, the momentary states, and the input selector. The abstract structure and the momentary states are supposed to have a directive influence on input selection and on the perceptual–cognitive structure. The distinction between the abstract structure and the perceptual–cognitive structure is related to the work of Feather (1971).

The Perceptual – Cognitive System

The focus of the model is upon the perceptual–cognitive system, which is assumed to correspond to a set of assumptions about why a person behaves the way he does in the immediate situation (i.e., contains action dispositions in a specific situation). This implies that in order to predict a person's behavior in a certain situation one must estimate the person's construction of the situation and use the characteristics of this information as a basis for prediction of the person's behavior.

The perceptual–cognitive structure is defined as the cognitive representation of the immediate external situation. More precisely, it is defined in terms of the elements it contains, the qualities of the elements, and the relations between them. The elements are assumed to be the cognitive representations of the covert and overt characteristics of the external situation, and the relations are assumed to be the cognitive representations of the relations between the characteristics of the external situation. Thus, it is not the situation per se but the situation as it is restructured by the person. It refers to the meaning a person attaches to the immediate situation and is dependent on the immediate external situational context, the characteristics of the abstract structure, the momentary states, and the effect of those "systems" on input selection.

By analogy to the external situation, it is assumed that the perceptual–cognitive system can be described as a multidimensional space in which the cognitive representations of external elements are seen as points that are related to each other. The meaning of the perceived elements is derived from the category in which they are placed and from the way the categories are distinguished from each other (Sarbin et al., 1960). The degree of correspondence between the perceptual–cognitive system and the external situation or the degree of representativeness of the perceptual–cognitive system is a measure of the validity of the perceived situation. The terms *content* and *structure* are defined in the same way as by Streufert and Streufert (1978). Content refers to the location of a situational datum or a configuration of situational data on a cognitive dimension to which it is assigned by the person. Thus the content refers to *what* a person thinks. Structure refers to the integrative use of dimensions in the cognitive space (i.e., *how* a person thinks).

The perceptual–cognitive structure contains information about the external situation as it is perceived here and now. It is always referring to a specific situational domain and directly to a specific situation within this domain. This means that the perceptual–cognitive structure is amenable to change and that it cannot be used for prediction of the behaviors of individuals across situations or for long-term predictions, because the external situation is assumed to exist by continually changing with regard to itself.

The Abstract Structure

The abstract structure is assumed to contain a person's knowledge of the past, attitudes, opinions, the common categories and "rules" that he shares with other people in the society, his individual "rules," and the long-term expectations about the future. It is this psychological context or horizon that exerts a directive influence on what cues a person pay attention to and on the way in which the actual situation is perceived. This is based upon the assumption that one of the goals the person has in the interaction with the social reality is to control the reality in some way. Because the social reality is assumed to exist by continual change with regard to itself, one way to gain control of the present situation is to compare the present situation with situations in the past. The situation cannot be exactly similar to a situation in the past, but it can be so similar to a past situation and yet, at the same time, so different from other past situations that we can identify it as similar to one that we have experienced in the past (Kelly, 1955). It is in this context that the abstract structure exerts a directive influence on the cues to which a person pays attention.

The abstract structure contains more elements than the perceptual–cognitive structure, which refers to the immediate situation; the abstract structure refers to the person's life situation. The abstract structure is the person's cognitive universe and contains all categories a person possesses for identification and discrimination of situations. This means that the abstract structure is responsible for the fact that we go beyond the information given when we perceive the situation. The abstract structure involved in the representation of social reality has a normative function. It specifies sets of "rules" that are appropriate in a given situation; it consists of a general structure that the person carries with him from situation to situation. This structure is assumed to be relatively stable and provides continuity and meaning to the person under changing circumstances, but it is amenable to change as new and discrepant information is continually experienced. Thus, the idea of the abstract structure is the same as found in the works of Bartlett, Piaget, and Tolman.

Because the abstract structure: (1) has a directive effect on the selection of information; (2) has a directive effect on the perceptual–cognitive structure; and (3) contains information about a person's characteristic way of perceiving situations; plus the fact that the perceptual–cognitive structure corresponds to a set of assumptions about the way a person behaves in a situation, there is a need for a taxonomy of ways in which structures can differ. This seems to be of fundamental importance for proponents of an interactional model of personality, because they stress (Magnusson, 1980b) that knowledge about the *way* in which individuals perceive and interpret situations provides a basis for understanding individual behavior and interindividual differences in behavior. The problem of studying how structures can differ also has stimulated both theory and research. It is beyond the scope of the present report to give a comprehensive discussion of all the concepts and indices used to describe and measure structural characteristics of a structure. But the most commonly used concepts in describing various relationships between categories in a structure are differentiation, complexity, unit, and organization (Zajonc, 1960); dimensionality and integration (Scott, 1970; and indices derived from the interactive complexity theory (Schroeder, Driver, & Streufert, 1967). However, it is fair to say that research on this important problem has produced more confusion than clarification because, with few exceptions, researchers working with this problem seem to have paid more attention to developing and measuring different indices of poorly defined concepts than to trying to clarify the theoretical assumptions behind the indices. This is particularly true with regard to the research on cognitive-complexity simplicity.

The Momentary State

The following discussion of the momentary state is based on the work of Jones and Thibaut (1958), Sarbin et al. (1960), and Warr and Knapper (1968). The momentary state refers to the transitory states of a person at the time of perception. The dichotomy between the momentary state and the abstract structure is not clear. They can be regarded as two end points on a dimension that influences the perceptual process. However, for analysis and interpretation of the interaction between the person and the environment, it is important to distinguish between these two personal systems.

The momentary state refers to such transitory influences on the perceptual–cognitive process as emotional states, motivation, and intentions that arise during the perceptual sequence. Thus, the momentory state is assumed to affect the nature of the relationship between the person and the immediate situation and is therefore important for understanding and predicting an individual's behavior in the immediate situation. The characteristics of the abstract structure, on the other hand, are important to consider for understanding and predicting individuals' behaviors in both the immediate and future situations.

The momentary state of a person is assumed to influence the identification of the part of the external situation to which a person is paying attention by influencing the input selector and the activity of the abstract structure. One relevant aspect of the momentary state that has such an influence is the needs and intentions of the person.

It is proposed that the main goal of a person's interaction with the environment is to obtain some personally relevant goals. One such goal of the person is to understand and predict the immediate external situation in relation to himself or herself. This goal gives rise to inferential sets that require the person to ask questions like: "What is this situation in relation to me?" or "Why is the situation the way it is?". These inferential sets can be broken down further into more specific questions such as: "Is this situation friendly, hostile, unpredictable, ethical, and so on?". Such inferential sets can limit or broaden the attention of the person and consequently have to be considered in the study of perception of situations.

Another aspect of the momentary state that is related to the more cognitive and inductive inferential sets and that affects the nature of the relationship between the person and the external situation is the intensity or degree of personal involvement in the interaction. The personal involvement can vary from a situation in which the person is highly emotionally involved to a situation in which the person acts as an uninvolved observer.

It is beyond the scope of this chapter to review relevant results, but the need for a systematic study of the effect of the degree of involvement on perception of situations is based on research on the role of motivational and emotional involvement and arousal on cue selection and the impression formed about other persons and the research on inferential sets, stimulated by Jones and Thibaut (1958), and on tuning sets, suggested by Zajonc (1960).

METHODOLOGICAL PROBLEMS

The methodological problems involved in studying persons' perceptual–cognitive structures deals with: (1) data collection technique; (2) methods of data analysis; and (3) interpretation of structures.

Data Collection Techniques.   The problem of data collection techniques in studies of perception of situations is primarily the same as in studies of implicit personality theory. In such studies the experimenter typically has provided the constructs or characteristics the subjects are to use in judgment of other people. Examples of such data collection techniques are checklists, trait sorting, and rating scales. A theoretical background for a critique of the use of provided constructs in research on person perception is given in Kelly's (1955) personal construct psychology. This theory emphasizes the individuality of a person's system of construing events and claims that every individual interprets himself or herself and the environment in accordance with his or her own system of personal constructs. According to the theory, in a specific situation a person selects from an integrated system of personal constructs those that best represent his or her personal dimensions or through which he or she anticipates the greater possibility for elaboration of the system. Furthermore, it is assumed that each construct is suitable for the anticipation of a finite range of events only. Examples of methods by which the subject generates the constructs are naturalistic descriptions and the Repertory Grid technique. In the similarity rating technique the subject is also free to use his or her own constructs. A review of research on the effect of own and provided constructs on different measures of discimination and cognitive complexity if found in Fransella and Bannister (1977). The effect of own and provided constructs on structural representations of other people also has been studied (Nystedt, 1976; Nystedt, Kuusinen, & Ekehammar, 1976). The results from studies of this problem in person-perception research indicate that it is relevant to research on perception of situations as well.

Another problem related to the question of content of methods is whether the techniques used express the types of relations between events that the person perceives. With such techniques as the semantic differential or the similarity rating technique, the relationship between events corresponds to the concept of betweenness as it is defined in the present report. To my knowledge, techniques that allow the person to make judgments of time and causal relations between events or characteristics have not been used in studies of structural representations of people or situations.

Methods of Analysis.   Independently of whether own or provided constructs are used in collection of data, the assumptions underlying the methods of analysis applied to these data must correspond to the conceptualization of the perceptual–cognitive structure. If the perceptual–cognitive structure is regarded as a multidimensional structure, factor analysis and multidimensional scaling methods can be used in studying structural representation of situations. If the perceptual–cognitive structure is assumed to consist of superordinate and subordinate constructs, hierarchical structure analysis models should be used. It is still an empirical question whether a person's perceptual–cognitive structure is best represented by a hierarchical or a dimensional model.

Interpretations of Structures.   Data collection techniques are related to the problem of interpretation of the dimensional or typological structure of a person's constructions of situations. In using provided constructs, the investigator has made some prejudgments about the underlying dimensional or typological structure of a person's perceptual–cognitive framework. But in using data collection techniques that allow the subject to use his own constructs in interpretation of situations, neither the investigator nor the person need be aware of the underlying constructs for interpretation of situations. In multidimensional scaling analysis based on input from similarity ratings of situations, meaningful dimensions are "found" in the multidimensional configuration of the similarity rating data. This means that the researcher relies on his/her intuitions by examination of the solution itself in interpretation of situational dimensions.

A more objective approach to the interpretation of a dimensional structure (Rosenberg & Sedlak, 1972) is to collect ratings of the situational stimuli on some dimensional properties. These ratings are collected independently of the data used as input for the multidimensional scaling. Multiple regression techniques are then used to locate an axis in the situational space, which corresponds to the rated property. This procedure is repeated for each rated property by using the dimensions from the multidimensional solution as independent variables. For interpretation of typological structures, the methods of analysis of variance can be used by employing the property ratings as dependent variables and the clusters from the cluster analysis as the independent factor. The strength of association between the property rating and the clusters at different levels in the hierarchical structure can be computed by means of the index omega squared (Hays, 1963). The level of this index combined with the associated probability value can be used for the determination of which level in the hierarchical structure of each property dimension renders an optimal differentiation between the clusters.

CONCLUDING REMARKS

The process model deals primarily with two broad and related psychological problems. One problem derives from a statement that one characteristic of human beings in the interaction with the environment is that they use the environment to obtain some personally defined goals. The other problem is concerned with prediction of an individual's behavior and with interindividual differences.

Using the Environment

In order to use the environment to reach some goal successfully, the person's construction of the external situation (the perceptual–cognitive structure) must be valid. The validity of a person's perceptual–cognitive structure is defined as the degree of correspondence between the perceptual–cognitive structure and the external situation to which it refers. This means that the model proposes a monotonically positive relation between, on the one hand, the increased degree of matching between a person's perceptual–cognitive structure and the structure of the external situation and, on the other hand, the person's performance in that situation. In terms of the modified lens model the degree of validity of a person's construction of a situation is dependent on the degree of correspondence between r'_{ei} and r_i', on the one hand, and r_{ei} and r_i, on the other hand. Thus, both the characteristics of the external situation and the situation as it is perceived must be measured and described independently, and indices of structural similarities must be developed. Different methods are available to calculate similarity between structures and some of these indices are discussed by Nystedt (1972a).

Prediction of Human Behavior

As stated in the introduction, the individual does not react directly to the characteristics of the external situation but rather to the interpretation of the situation. Therefore, the prediction of a person's behavior should be based on the characteristics of the person's construction of the situation. It also means that individuals are similar if they construe the situation similarly and different if they construe the situation as different (Kelly, 1955).

Structural representations and their interpretative influences on external properties provide useful summaries of data, but methodological analyses of measurement operations alone cannot answer the question of their psychological utility unless their predictive reliability is studied simultaneously in comprehensive research projects. One of the objectives of the presentation of the process model has been to make suggestions for such research.

ACKNOWLEDGMENTS

The study was supported by a grant from the Swedish Council for Research in Humanities and Social Sciences. The author is indebted to Dr. Frank Landy for constructive comments on the manuscript. He also kindly checked the English.

24

Group × Place Transactions: Some Neglected Issues in Psychological Research on Settings

Daniel Stokols
Program in Social Ecology
University of California, Irvine

BACKGROUND

Recent developments in areas such as environmental, social, personality, cognitive, and developmental psychology reflect an increasing emphasis on the importance and complexity of the molar environment. The traditional focus of psychology on the experience and behavior of the person appears to be shifting toward a broader, contextual orientation in which the transactions between people and their sociophysical settings are emphasized.

Psychological research on situations and settings, though still at an early stage, reflects considerable definitional progress, a preliminary empirical base, and a diversity of conceptual and methodological guidelines for future work (Magnusson & Endler, 1977a; Pervin & Lewis, 1978). Distinctions have been drawn, for example, between objective and subjective dimensions of settings and among different levels of the environment ranging from situation-specific stimuli to the multiple settings that comprise an individual's life situation (see Magnusson, 1978 and Pervin, 1978b for recent reviews of this research). Moreover, taxonomic criteria for describing diverse situations and settings have been derived from alternative theoretical orientations (Barker & Schoggen, 1973; Bem & Funder, 1978; Bronfenbrenner, 1977; Fredericksen, 1972; Moos, 1973; Price & Blashfield, 1975).

The continued development of alternative perspectives on situations and settings would seem to be advantageous in light of the enormous range and complexity of person–environment relationships. At the same time, however, an important challenge for future research is to develop linkages among alternative conceptualizations and to move toward more comprehensive analyses of settings.

393

The necessity of developing a "cross-paradigm" approach to the study of environment and behavior (Craik, 1977; Stokols, 1978) becomes increasingly apparent as we move from microlevel analyses of stimuli and events to the conceptualization of molar, sociophysical settings. For it is at the level of the large-scale environment that our theories must begin to integrate geographical, social-structural, and psychological properties of settings. Although architects, sociologists, and planners have focused primarily on the first two facets of the environment, psychologists have paid most attention to the third and (only recently) have begun to consider the nature of the interface among physical, social, and psychological dimensions of settings, (Magnusson, 1978).

Since the late 1960s and early 1970s, increasing interest among psychologists in environmental issues has spawned a large body of research concerning the effects of the physical environment on behavior (Craik, 1973; Proshansky & Altman, 1979; Stokols, 1978). Much of this research has attempted to isolate specific dimensions of the physical milieu (e.g., ambient temperature, spatial restriction, architectural design, noise) and to assess their respective effects on individual and group behavior (Baron & Bell, 1976; Baum & Valins, 1977; Bechtel, 1977; Glass & Singer, 1972). Relatively few attempts have been made, however, to chart the broader sociophysical milieu as it relates to psychological and behavioral issues. Among the exceptions to this trend are Barker's (1960, 1968) theory of behavior settings and Bronfenbrenner's (1977, 1979) analysis of the ecology of human development. Both Barker and Bronfenbrenner have attempted to delineate the ecological context of everyday behavior—structured settings characterized by the interdependence of their physical, social, and personal components. Although focusing on different psychological and developmental questions, Barker's and Bronfenbrenner's analyses of settings reflect a common set of elements, namely, a particular place in which specific individuals share recurring patterns of activity and experience (Argyle, 1977; Magnusson, 1978; Pervin, 1978b; Sells, 1973).

Though the psychological relevance of the molar environment is now widely recognized, the existing research literature provides a rather incomplete basis for understanding the dynamics of behavioral settings. First, most environment–behavioral studies have emphasized unidirectional ($E \rightarrow B$) rather than reciprocal ($E \leftrightarrows B$) relationships. This trend reflects a traditional goal of psychological research, namely, to discern stimulus–response regularities whereby behavior is viewed as the direct ($E \rightarrow B$) or mediated ($E \rightarrow (O) \rightarrow B$) product of environmental conditions. A basic limitation of both the behaviorist and mediational perspectives is that they construe behavior as essentially reactive and neglect the effects of goal-instigated behavior on the environment (Lazarus & Launier, 1978; Overton & Reese, 1973). Thus, although we know much about the impact of physical factors on behavior and well-being, we know considerably less about the conditions under which physical settings are designed, established, or modified, or the processes by which physical environments come to be associated with widely shared social and cultural meanings.

A second limitation of earlier research concerns the restricted role of the physical environment in existing conceptualizations of settings. Whereas previous analyses treat the concept of "place" as a crucial component of settings, none have systematically examined the nature of the linkages between the architectural-geographical environment and the social system. Most of the research inspired by Barker's concept of the behavior setting, for example, has focused on the measurement of social and behavioral phenomena (e.g., adaptive reactions to conditions of undermanning and overmanning in groups) and placed less emphasis on the physical features of settings (Barker & Associates, 1978; Barker & Schoggen, 1973).[1] Similarly, Bronfenbrenner's analysis of human development focuses almost exclusively on the social-structural properties of settings with special emphasis on the developmental consequences of participation in social networks (i.e., interpersonal linkages both within and across settings). The role of the physical environment in the ecology of human development remains unspecified in Bronfenbrenner's analysis.

The general emphasis of environment-behavioral research on unidirectional rather than reciprocal processes and the perfunctory treatment of the physical environment in existing theories of settings suggest an important agenda for future research, namely, the analysis of group × place transactions. Group × place transactions encompass the processes by which groups are affected and, in turn, influence their physical milieu. A transactional approach to the study of settings highlights the active role taken by individuals and groups in creating and modifying their environments. Accordingly, the physical milieu of groups is construed not only as an antecedent of behavior but also as a sociocultural product (i.e., as the material reflection of collective behavior and as a repository of shared social meanings).

Several questions about group × place transactions remain to be examined. For instance, what factors determine the strength of group ties to a particular place? Can settings be characterized in terms of the compatibility of their physical and social components? Under what conditions will modifications of the physical environment or the social structure of settings be most likely to occur? Before such questions can be addressed, it is necessary to develop a set of terms for describing the interface (i.e., degree of interdependence) between social units and their physical milieu. We turn now to a consideration of this issue.

---

[1]More recently, ecological psychologists have begun to examine the connnections between architectural design and conditions of undermanning and overmanning in settings (Bechtel, 1977; Wicker, 1979; Wicker & Kirmeyer, 1976). Also, a recent article by Barker (1979) examines the consequences of undermanning that arise as a result of migration to frontier environments.

THE PERCEIVED SOCIAL FIELD OF THE PHYSICAL
ENVIRONMENT: A MATRIX OF SHARED
SOCIOCULTURAL MEANINGS

A defining characteristic of settings is the interdependence of their physical, social, and personal elements. This attribute distinguishes ongoing, behavioral settings from less socially structured portions of the environment. Various terms have been used in the psychological literature to describe the differential interdependence among environmental elements: for example, the concepts of *causal texture* (Emery & Trist, 1965; Tolman & Brunswik, 1935), *synomorphy* (Barker, 1960), and Ashby's (1960) distinction between *poorly* versus *richly joined* environments.

In Barker's analysis, the behavioral program (recurring patterns of activity) conforms to the shape and requirements of the physical milieu: hence, the term *synomorphy* (or *sameness of form*), denoting the interdependence between environment and behavior. Yet the behavioral and physical components within different settings may not be uniformly synomorphic or linked. Thus, the social activities (e.g., economic functions) of a particular group may rely heavily on the physical resources available within its immediate vicinity whereas those of another group may be less tied to a single locale. Also, one family may grieve bitterly for its previous home following a residential relocation (Fried, 1963) whereas another may be negligibly affected by such a move. And, whereas the residents of certain communities will resist "urban renewal" projects to preserve the historical significance of their neighborhood, others may be less invested in maintaining the existing form of their community (Firey, 1945).

The Social Imageability of Places

In the present analysis, the degree of interdependence between groups and places is indexed in terms of the shared, sociocultural images that are conveyed by physical environments. These images constitute the nonmaterial properties of the physical milieu—the sociocultural "residue" (or residual meaning) that becomes attached to places as the result of their continuous association with group activities. Just as environments can be described in terms of the *imageability* (or *memorability*) of their physical elements (Lynch, 1960), they also can be understood in terms of their *social imageability* (i.e., their capacity to evoke vivid and widely shared social meanings among the members of a setting). As a place becomes increasingly "layered" with social meanings, the interdependence among social and physical components of the setting is assumed to increase. Thus, the sociocultural meanings associated with a setting are viewed as the "glue" that binds groups to particular places.

The present approach is in contrast to earlier taxonomic analyses of environments that have focused either on the objective features of settings (e.g., their architectural features, membership size, overt behavior, and activity patterns) or on the individual's subjective impressions of and reactions to the environment (Magnusson, 1978; Pervin, 1978b). Underlying these analyses is the assumption that the perceived environment is of a personal or idiosyncratic nature (Lewin, 1935), unlike the objective environment that can be described consensually by a variety of observers. This assumption may account for the neglect of an important aspect of environmental perception in psychological research, namely, that portion of the perceived environment that is consensually shared by the members of a setting but not necessarily by outside observers (nonmembers) of the setting (James & Jones, 1974).

The description of sociophysical environments in terms of the perceptions shared among setting members is advantageous for several reasons. Most importantly, because the members of settings comprise organized social units rather than clusters of detached individuals, an analysis of the interdependence among setting components must address the nature of the bonds between groups and places, as distinct from those existing between individuals and their environments.[2] Yet, although psychologists have analyzed the personal ties between individuals and places (Cooper, 1974; Hansen & Altman, 1976; Proshansky, 1978), they have given much less attention to the nature of group–environment linkages (cf. Altman & Chemers, 1979; for sociological and anthropological analyses of this issue, see Duncan & Duncan, 1976; Firey, 1945; Fried, 1963; Gerson & Gerson, 1976; Rapoport, 1976).

The development of environmental taxonomies based on the shared perceptions of setting members is relevant to a number of theoretical and practical issues. First, the behavior and well-being of setting members might be predicted more reliably from their collective perceptions of environmental conditions (e.g., environmental constraints that are blocking the accomplishment of salient group goals) than from the vantage point of single individuals (Katona, 1979). Moreover, the classification of physical environments in terms of the social meanings that are typically associated with them would provide a basis for predicting the impact of architectural/geographical changes on group members across different kinds of settings and for designing future settings that are congruent with the activities and goals of their users.

Dimensions of the Perceived Social Field

The imageability of a place refers to those features of the environment that are highly salient to its occupants. Kevin Lynch's (1960) discussion of the physical imageability of places, for example, emphasizes the dimensions of *perceptual*

---

[2]The subjective nature of the perceived social field distinguishes this concept from Lewin's (1936) "objective social field (i.e., the actual structure, activities, and composition of the group as it exists within the ecological environment) and from Durkheim's (1964) "social facts" (the unperceived yet powerful social forces that guide the behavior of community members).

salience (i.e., the number and intensity of highly noticeable features within an environment [Stokols, 1979; Taylor & Fiske, 1978]). Among the factors that heighten the perceptual salience of environments are stimulus contrast, novelty, and complexity (Berlyne, 1960; Kaplan, 1975; Wohlwill, 1976).

The concept of social imageability, as used in this analysis, refers not to the perceptual prominence of environments but rather to their *functional, motivational,* and *evaluative significance.* These dimensions of environmental salience encompass socially shared images that relate, respectively, to three basic facets of settings: (1) their *functions* (i.e., group-specific activities that occur within the setting, including the norms associated with these activities as well as descriptive information regarding the identities and social roles of setting members); (2) collective *goals* and purposes, each of which is weighted by its relative importance to setting members (these are distinguished from the personal needs and goals that are pursued independently by individuals within the setting); and (3) *evaluations* of occupants, physical features, and/or social functions within the setting (e.g., the negative stereotypes associated with certain neighborhoods relating to the presumed dangerousness of their occupants [Suttles, 1968]).[3]

The actual content of those sociocultural meanings associated with particular places will be referred to in this discussion as the perceived social field of the physical environment. More specifically, the *perceived-social field of a setting is defined as the totality of functional, motivational, and evaluative meanings conveyed by the physical environment to members of the setting.* This matrix of meanings is essentially a set of collectively shared images that evolves as the result of sustained social interaction within a particular place.

To illustrate the communication of sociocultural meanings via the physical environment, consider the example of a Manhattan resident driving along Main Street of a small midwestern town for the first time. As the visitor catches a glimpse of the town's church, post office, and town hall, certain culturally shared information about the social functions (e.g., worship services, town council meetings) of these settings is conveyed. The visitor would not, however, be privy to information about local functions that occur within each setting and are known only by town residents (e.g., the weekly flea market held in the church parking lot every Saturday at 2:00 P.M.). Also, although the American flag in front of the post office would convey to the visitor certain cultural meanings associated with national identity (e.g., evaluative feelings about being an American citizen), the Kiwanis Club sign posted outside Town Hall would communicate little information to a stranger about the townspeople who belong to the organization (e.g., who they are, their standing in the community) or about the reputation of the

---

[3]The dimensions of functional, motivational, and evaluative salience reflect the three factors of semantic meaning identified by Osgood, Suci, and Tannenbaum (1957): activity, potency, and evaluation. The description of situations in terms of these focuses on person × setting rather than group × place transactions.

organization among town residents. These meanings would be noticed only by members of the local community, especially those who participate most directly in its organizations and settings.

The analysis of social meanings generally has been the province of sociology and anthropology (Agar, 1979; Berger & Luckmann, 1966; Garfinkel, 1967; Mead, 1934; Tyler, 1969) though the emphasis of these fields has not been on place-specific meanings per se but rather on the broader set of social rules and meanings (e.g., widely held ethical norms) shared by the members of a community. More recently, psychologists have begun to apply ethnographic methods to the study of social interaction and group structure (Harré, 1977; Harré & Secord, 1972).

The present conceptualization of the perceived social field differs from earlier analyses of related constructs in some important respects. First, in contrast with Argyle's (1977) and Harré and Secord's (1972) analyses of the "generative rules" and "ascribed meanings" of social interaction, the perceived social field refers only to that subset of socially shared meanings associated with the physical environment of a setting. For instance, the members of a church congregation might share the ethic of "doing unto others as you would have them do unto you," as well as a set of norms about what constitutes appropriate dress and behavior at Sunday worship services. Although the "do unto others . . ." ethic is a socially shared rule that would apply across a variety of settings, the latter norms are more specifically associated with social functions of the church and the particular individuals who participate in that setting. The perceived social field of the church setting, thus, would refer to the latter but not the former category of social rules.

The assumption that physical environments convey information about the sociocultural functions associated with them is also similar to Gibson's (1977) "affordance" concept. The affordance of an object refers to the potential uses or activities it suggests to observers by virtue of its physical properties. Kaplan (1978) has extended the concept of affordance to the level of the molar, physical environment and uses the term to refer to the potential actions suggested by a particular place to its current or prospective users. In the present analysis, the concept of social field encompasses those sociocultural functions afforded by the physical attributes of a setting but not the nonsocial activities associated with physical objects or places (e.g., the behavior of "sitting" suggested by the presence of a chair, or that of "swimming" afforded by the seashore).

Another construct that is closely related to the present conceptualization of the social field is "social climate" (Moos, 1976; Pace & Stern, 1958; cf. James & Jones' [1974] discussion of organizational climate). Although both the social climate and social field concepts pertain to collectively shared (versus idiosyncratic) perceptions of a setting, they differ in at least two important respects. First, the perceived social field, as defined here, subsumes only those aspects of social climate that are associated with or symbolized by the physical environment of a setting. The interpersonal cohesiveness of a setting, for example, would be viewed as a dimension of the social field only to the extent that images of cohesiveness (e.g., evaluative memories of prior interactions that have been pleasant or supportive) become attached to a particular place. Second, the concept of social field emphasizes the specific content of those sociocultural meanings associated with an environment, whereas Moos' notion of social climate summarizes the collective perception of a setting in terms of three basic dimensions (social relationships, personal development, and system maintenance/change).

The preceding discussion suggests some possible strategies for measuring the perceived social field of a setting. First, the *content* of the social field can be assessed by having a representative sample of group members list those functional, motivational, and evaluative meanings associated with the physical environment of their setting. This open-ended listing procedure is similar to Harré and Secord's (1972) notion of "accounting" (i.e., the explication of social action in terms of shared social meanings reflected in individuals' accounts of their social experiences) but pertains more specifically to the sociocultural images attached to the physical environment. The *scale* of the social field varies according to whether the listing of setting meanings is completed in relation to the physical milieu as a whole or to specific places comprising the broader milieu (e.g., Main Street of a small town versus the church, post office, and meeting hall located there).

The *complexity* of the social field can be indexed in terms of the number of shared meanings that emerge from the independent listings provided by different group members. The assessment of social-field complexity presumes the availability of criteria for distinguishing among shared meanings and idiosyncratic perceptions (i.e., those that are mentioned only sporadically by members of the setting) and between redundant and nonredundant meanings (i.e., those that are sufficiently different to warrant separate enumeration). Shared meanings might be operationally defined, for example, as those listed by at least a majority of respondents or, less restrictively, as those cited most frequently by respondents irrespective of whether they constitute a majority of the sample.

The more often a particular meaning is cited among setting members, the greater its *clarity*. An additional criterion for judging the relative clarity of shared meanings is the extent to which they are rated by setting members as being slightly or highly characteristic of a particular place. These criteria jointly define the relative clarity of sociocultural images attached to a particular place. Considering the perceived social field as a whole (i.e., as a composite of multiple meanings), an index of the social imageability of a place can be derived by weighting the diverse meanings of the social field (reflecting its content and complexity) by their relative clarity among setting members. An ambiguous social field would be characterized by low imageability (i.e., by a lack [or small number] of vivid images and/or by a lack of agreement among group members regarding the social meanings of the physical environment).

In some situations, the content and clarity of setting meanings may vary according to subgroup membership. Thus, the perceived social field can be characterized in terms of its *heterogeneity*, or the number of subgroups within the setting for whom distinguishable patterns of meaning can be discerned. The social field also can be analyzed in terms of its *distortions*. Distortions are unrecognized discrepancies between the sociocultural images of a place and the nature of the social activities and experiences that actually occur there. Distortions can arise as the result of insufficient exposure to a setting (e.g., among outsiders who have never visited the setting or among group members who are minimally involved in its activities) or from misinformation about the setting. The discriminatory beliefs and negative stereotypes that sometimes become associated with the territories of opposing groups (Allport, 1958; Sherif, 1966; Suttles, 1972) exemplify distortions of the social field to the extent that these stereotypes diverge from reality.

Finally, the perceived social field can be characterized in terms of its consistency with or contradiction of the expectations and preferences of setting members. *Contradictions* (or "disjunctions," cf. Rausch, 1977) between the actual and preferred social meanings of a setting are exemplified by situations in which one's images of a place are negatively toned as a result of earlier unpleasant experiences there or where the actual uses of a setting are contradictory to its intended functions (e.g., a congested and smog-filled Yosemite Valley, a noisy library, a dormitory lounge that is rarely used by residents for socializing). Unlike distortions, contradictions involve recognized discrepencies between actual and preferred conditions within settings.

Having outlined the major dimensions of the perceived social field, an important question remains to be addressed: How useful are the proposed dimensions as a basis for describing, categorizing, and understanding settings? Ideally, environmental taxonomies should provide a framework not only for describing settings but also for predicting the relationships among their components (Mischel, 1977a; Pervin, 1978b). Some of these relationships are considered in the following section.

A THEORETICAL ANALYSIS OF GROUP × PLACE TRANSACTIONS

In this section, the dimensions of functional, motivational, and evaluative salience are employed as a basis for developing the constructs of *place dependence*, *group-environment congruence*, and the *transformational potential* of settings. These concepts suggest a number of hypotheses concerning the transactions between groups and places.

Functional Salience and the Place Dependence of Settings

The dimension of functional salience encompasses descriptive information about the activities, norms, and group members associated with particular places. The description of places in terms of their functional meanings is pertinent to several aspects of group–environment transaction. For instance, an assessment of the sociocultural meanings of places reveals the variety of functions supported by geographical and architectural environments, ranging from the purely physical (e.g., the provision of physical shelter and resources for performing numerous behaviors) to the psychological and social (e.g., the provision of opportunities for aesthetic fulfillment, social contacts, and the establishment of personal and social identity). The range of functions associated with different environments is potentially relevant to predictive as well as descriptive concerns. For example, the complexity and clarity of functional meanings attached to a place may mediate the intensity of group members' reactions to sudden or substantial changes in the physical milieu. Also, to the degree that a physical environment is associated with clear and undistorted functional meanings, it may not only support but, in some instances, may actually substitute for direct participation in group activities. Thus, proximity to areas that convey a high level of supportiveness and cohesion may provide a measure of vicarious social support to group members even in the absence of direct social interaction (Jacobs, 1961; Newman, 1973).

From a transactional perspective, the functional meanings that become associated with places must be understood both as a product as well as an antecedent of social behavior. Once these meanings are established, they become part of the collectively perceived environment that guides social behavior and affects personal and social well-being. The role of functional salience in mediating behavior and well-being is perhaps most clearly revealed through a comparison of two kinds of settings: those in which group functions are strongly tied to a particular place and those in which they are not.

In the ensuing discussion, the concept of place dependence is used to describe the strength of association between group functions and the physical environment. *The place dependence of settings is defined as the degree to which group members perceive the major functions of their setting to be exclusively tied to a particular location.* Major functions are those that are viewed as essential for the existence and/or effectiveness of the setting.

Place-dependent settings are those whose functions and existence are intimately linked to a particular physical environment whereas place-independent settings are those whose major functions could thrive equally well within a variety of alternative locations. For instance, the economic functions of certain businesses (e.g., sawmills, shipbuilding, ski resorts) are highly dependent on the natural resources available within particular geographical areas whereas those of others (e.g., banks, restaurants, pharmacies) are less closely tied to the immediate locale. And at a social–psychological level, the residents of certain ethnic enclaves in urban areas sometimes express greater dependence on their neighborhood for social identity and support than do those of suburban areas (Fried & Gleicher, 1961; Gans, 1967).[4]

To arrive at a more precise conceptualization of place dependence, it is necessary to consider the kinds of functions that occur within settings. Specifically, we can speak of the place dependence of social, cultural, economic, psychological, and physiological functions, or, more simply, of social and personal functions. At the social level, certain interpersonal and organizational processes (e.g., love, friendship, membership in political or professional groups) transcend the boundaries of specific places whereas others are intimately tied to the locations in which they occur (e.g., the economic functions of a setting that are dependent on local resources). Similarly, certain personal functions (e.g., eating, thinking) occur within diverse locations whereas others are more closely linked to specific places (e.g., establishment of personal territory, Altman, 1975; and "place identity," Proshansky, 1978).

Psychological and physiological functions are relevant to the present analysis only to the extent that they are accomplished through the joint efforts of setting members (e.g., the enhancement of psychological security through identification with a particular group). Personal functions that do not depend on the presence of others for their accomplishment (e.g., aesthetic experiences associated with natural environments; Kaplan, 1975; Wohlwill, 1976) are excluded from this analysis.

The place dependence of a setting reflects the degree to which the various social and psychological functions associated with it are, themselves, locationally dependent. Accordingly, the measurement of place dependence at the level of settings involves the following steps: (1) a listing of the major social and psychological functions (F) associated with the setting, compiled by a representative sample of its occupants; (2) the categorization of each function, f, within the set, F, as either place dependent (f_d) or place independent (f_i); (3) the subjective rating of each function according to its relative degree of place dependence (PD_{fd}) or place independence (PI_{fi}) (this step assumes that the dimension

---

[4]In the present analysis, *place dependence* is defined in relation to an ongoing setting, and refers specifically to the degree to which the major functions and actual existence of the setting are dependent on a particular physical environment. Also, place dependence is operationalized in terms of group members' collective perceptions of the connections between setting functions and places. In a subsequent manuscript (Stokols & Shumaker, in press), the concept of place dependence has been broadened to incorporate the following issues: (1) individuals' perceptions of the interdependence between *themselves* and places, as well as between their *group* and places; (2) settings whose functions are oriented toward individuals and aggregates as well as toward organized groups; (3) psychological processes underlying the development of people's subjective attachments to places; and (4) people's dependence on functionally-similar places as well as on a specific geographical area ("categorical" vs. "geographical" place dependence).

of place dependence is more usefully construed as continuous rather than dichotomous); and (4) the weighting of setting functions according to their "relative centrality" (RC), or the degree to which they are viewed by occupants as crucial to the existence and/or effectiveness of the setting. The fourth step assumes that the place dependence of a setting is most closely related to the locational dependence of its major (versus subsidiary) functions. The *place dependence of a setting* (PD_s) can now be represented as the proportion of place-dependent to place-independent functions, where each function is weighted by its degree of locational dependence and relative centrality to the setting:

$$PD_s = \frac{\Sigma_d \ (PD_{fd} \times RC_{fd})}{\Sigma_d \ (PD_{fd} \times RC_{fd}) + \Sigma_i \ (PI_{fi} \times RC_{fi})} \tag{1}$$

The previous formulation suggests some potential determinants of place dependence, including: (1) the length of association between a group and a particular place; (2) the availability of alternative locations in which the key functions of a setting can be carried out effectively; (3) the territorial and population size of settings; and (4) the complexity of settings (i.e., the number and diversity of its major functions). It seems reasonable to assume that the ties between the physical environment and social system of a setting become stronger as their temporal association increases, the availability of suitable alternative locations decreases, and the size and complexity of the setting increase (because such settings are less easily transported to new environments).

A number of hypotheses can be derived from the place-dependence construct. First, place-dependent settings are more likely to be vulnerable to sources of turbulence in the physical environment (e.g., sudden geographical or architectural changes, or the presence of unwanted stimuli such as noise and congestion) than are place-independent settings. This hypothesis is based on the assumption that the physical environment is more closely associated with various social and psychological functions in place-dependent settings. Therefore, abrupt changes in the physical milieu or undesirable environmental conditions are more likely to disrupt social and psychological processes within place-dependent versus place-independent settings.

Second, members of place-dependent settings are more likely to be psychologically committed to and actively protective of their environment than are those of place-independent settings. This prediction derives from the assumption that the members of place-dependent settings perceive that they have fewer alternative settings to choose from. In Thibaut and Kelley's (1959) terminology, they have a lower comparison level for alternative settings (CL_{alt}) and, therefore, tend to have more of an investment in their present situation. To the extent that these assumptions are valid, members of place-dependent settings are also more likely to: (1) overevaluate their own group's products; (2) discriminate against out-group individuals (Allport, 1937); and (3) exhibit greater sensitivity to conditions of overmanning (Barker, 1960; Wicker, 1979) than are those of place-independent settings.

Third, it is predicted that transitions (e.g., relocations) between place-dependent settings will be more difficult for group members than will those involving place-independent settings, even when such moves are anticipated and voluntary. This hypothesis is based on the assumption that disengagement from a familiar environment will be more difficult for members of place-dependent settings, due to their greater investment in the situation (Firey, 1945; Fried, 1963). Moreover, entry into novel, place-dependent settings may be more stressful because the social and psychological meanings of the setting may take longer to decode than in situations where the physical environment is less closely linked to social–psychological functions.

The previous hypotheses reflect some interesting extensions of earlier analyses. First, in relation to Barker's (1960) assumption that the behavioral programs of settings are synomorphic or closely linked to their physical location, the present analysis suggests that settings are not uniformly place dependent, and that this attribute of settings has important implications for the ways in which their members respond to social or physical constraints (e.g., overmanning, geographical change). And within the context of Bronfenbrenner's (1977, 1979) ecological analysis of human development, the present formulation suggests that the existence of "multi-setting linkages" (social networks) may be more crucial as sources of social support to individuals moving between place-dependent rather than place-independent settings. The sharing of setting transitions by two or more individuals may provide each person with a link to the past and a basis for social support in novel, unpredictable situations. One benefit of such support may be the collective translation of subtle, functional meanings embedded in the physical structure of unfamiliar settings. Participation in social networks, particularly among newcomers to place-dependent settings, thus may serve to reduce ambiguity and distortion within the perceived social field.

The gist of the preceding discussion is that place dependence plays an important role in mediating group reactions to conditions of environmental turbulence and/or deterioration. But an analysis of the functional features of settings, by themselves, sheds little light on the more active modes of group–environment transaction (e.g., the attempts of group members to establish new settings or to alter the structure and meanings of existing ones). To address these issues, the motivational and evaluative salience of settings also must be considered. For it is the level of congruence between setting functions (the environment as it is perceived to exist) and salient group goals (images of the environment as it "ought to be") that determines the perception of environmental quality and prompts efforts to establish or restructure settings.

In the following section, the dimension of motivational salience is examined and strategies for assessing group–environment congruence are discussed. Subsequently, the relationship between evaluative salience and environmental change is considered.

Motivational Salience and the Concept of Group-Environment Congruence

The term, *motivational salience*, denotes the degree to which an environment is associated with subjectively important goals. At the level of person-environment transaction, motivational salience, MS, is simply the subjective importance rating assigned by an individual to a specific goal or need, n_i, from among the larger set of situationally relevant needs, N (Stokols, 1979).[5] In the present analysis of group-environment transaction, the motivational salience of a setting, MS_s, denotes a composite score consisting of two basic components: (1) a set of collectively shared goals, G, identified by a representative sample of group (or subgroup) members; and (2) a set of motivational significance (i.e., subjective importance) ratings, MS, each of which is associated with a particular goal, g_i. These ratings reflect the average significance weights assigned to each goal, g_i, by group members. The *motivational salience of the setting* is defined as the sum of the average goal weights for all setting-relevant goals, G, as follows:

$$MS_s = \Sigma_i\ (MS_{gi}). \tag{2}$$

The dimensions of functional and motivational salience, although closely related, are conceptually distinct. As noted earlier, functional salience encompasses a wide array of descriptive information about settings, including the kinds of activities that occur within the setting, the schedules and locations of these activities, the identity of group members and their relationships to each other, as well as the rules and norms that guide social interaction. To the degree that physical environments convey such information to setting members, they are said to be functionally salient. The preceding discussion has focused primarily on the activities component of functional salience and, more specifically, on the extent to which the major activities or uses of a setting are perceived as being restricted to a particular location.

To distinguish between functional and motivational salience, it is necessary to consider the relationship between setting functions and group goals. Often, the

---

[5]The term *needs* refers in this analysis to emotional, physiological, and behavioral states of the individual that are actually advantageous and/or are perceived as being necessary or advantageous for personal well-being. Needs are not restricted to somatically determined drives but also subsume personally chosen goals and plans. Although the terms *needs* and *goals* often are used interchangeably in analyses of person-environment transaction (Stokols, 1979), the present discussion uses only the term *goals* to describe conditions of the group (and/or its environment) that are viewed by setting members as being necessary or advantageous for collective well-being. Thus, the term *needs* is restricted to the analysis of person-environment relations whereas the term *goals* pertains exclusively to group-environment transactions.

major functions of a setting (e.g., activities considered to be crucial for its existence and effectiveness) correspond closely with salient-group goals. For instance, a church provides a context for numerous activities including worship services, Sunday School, adult education classes, weddings, and dances. Participation in these activities enables members of the church to accomplish a variety of religious and social goals. But although members of the setting might agree on its major activities, the motivational significance of these functions (and related goals) would vary considerably. Thus, younger members of the congregation might view the educational, recreational, and social-identity functions of the church as more important than its religious functions, whereas older members might assign greater importance to religious activities. Furthermore, the salient goals of certain subgroups within the setting might be quite unrelated to the major functions of the church. The groundskeepers and janitors employed by the church, for example, would be more interested in earning a decent salary, having a flexible work week, and maintaining the physical appearance of the church, than in the religious and social purposes of the setting.

The dimensions of motivational and functional salience, therefore, are different in at least two respects. First, in those instances where setting goals and functions overlap, motivational salience pertains not only to the content of these goals but also to their relative importance to group members. Second, the motivational and functional meanings of a setting are not always correspondent. This point can be illustrated by considering the concept of *place dependence*. It was hypothesized earlier that members of place-dependent groups (e.g., residents of ethnic enclaves) are more likely to be committed to (or motivationally invested in) their settings than those of place-independent groups (e.g., residents of suburban areas), due to the fewer alternative settings available to the former. But if the level of place dependence is held constant, several other sources of motivational salience become apparent. For example, although the behavioral settings within an ethnic neighborhood (e.g., specialized restaurants, bookstores) may be quite place dependent and, therefore, might not flourish in other parts of the city, the motivational significance or importance of these settings probably would vary among resident groups depending on how committed they are to the cultural-identity functions of the neighborhood. Some families might be highly committed to the culturally supportive activities of the neighborhood whereas others, whose social networks extend to other parts of the city, would be less invested in their immediate residential area.

The description of settings in terms of their motivational salience is directly relevant to the issue of *group-environment congruence (i.e., the degree to which an environment accommodates the important goals and activities of group members)*. The congruence between group goals and perceived environmental opportunities for accomplishing them has a direct bearing on the quality of group-environment transaction and on the behavior and well-being of group members. Although previous analyses of congruence have focused on the degree of fit between individuals and their environment (French, Rodgers, & Cobb, 1974; Hunt, 1963b; Kahana, 1975; Michelson, 1976; Mischel, 1973; Stokols, 1979; Streufert & Streufert, 1978; Wicker, 1979), they have given little attention to the issue of group-environment congruence and the possibility of describing settings along this dimension.

The present discussion extends an earlier analysis of person-environment fit (Stokols, 1979) in which congruence is conceptualized as a function of two basic components: environmental controllability and environmental salience. Controllability is defined in terms of the multiple need dimensions that are relevant to an individual within a given situation and the degree to which the actual facilitation or thwarting of these needs is perceived to be discrepant within ideal or preferred levels of facilitation. Salience refers to the dimensions of motivational and perceptual salience as defined earlier. The ensuing discussion emphasizes the role of motivational salience in mediating group-environment congruence, though it is assumed that perceptual salience also contributes to the congruence equation by intensifying people's awareness of controllable (goal-facilitative) or uncontrollable (goal-constraining) features of the environment (Stokols, 1979).

The present discussion of group-environment congruence retains the key assumptions of the earlier analysis but emphasizes the facilitation of collectively shared goals rather than personally defined needs. A major assumption of this analysis is that group-environment congruence depends not only on the level of goal facilitation (controllability) afforded by a setting but also on the subjective importance (motivational salience) of the goals that are facilitated or thwarted by the environment. A high degree of control over trivial (goal-irrelevant) features of the setting, for example, would be associated with a lower level of congruence than the same degree of control over important dimensions of the environment. The present analysis also assumes that the perceived level of actual/ideal goal facilitation within a setting provides a valid (functionally equivalent) index of the group's capacity to control the environment (i.e., to maintain or modify it in accord with collective preferences).

As a basis for arriving at an operational definition of group-environment congruence, let G represent those goals that are relevant to a group within a particular setting. Further, let g_f denote each goal within the set, G, that is perceived by group members as being facilitated by environmental conditions, and let g_t denote each goal among G that is perceived to be thwarted. The identification of relevant goals, G, and their classification as either facilitated or thwarted, reflect the modal judgments of a representative sample of group members. Each goal, g_f or g_t, is assumed to be weighted by an actual facilitation (AF) or thwarting (AT) score, respectively, and by an ideal facilitation (IF) score. The AF and AT scores reflect the average subjective ratings (across all respondents) of the degree to which a specific goal is either supported or constrained by the environment, whereas the IF score reflects the group's appraisal of the optimal or desired level of facilitation associated with that goal. The *environmental controllability of a setting*, C_s, can be represented as a ratio of actual/ideal goal facilitation as follows:

$$C_s = \frac{\Sigma_f (AF_{gf}) - \Sigma_t (AT_{gt})}{\Sigma_f (IF_{gf}) + \Sigma_t (IF_{gt})} \tag{3}$$

To illustrate the application of this equation, suppose that the members of a company are asked to list those goals (G) that are relevant within the context of a work environment and to rate on seven-point scales the degree to which each goal (g_f or g_t) is facilitated (AF) or thwarted (AT) by the environment. Let us assume that the group identifies company productivity, opportunities for socializing and interesting work assignments as the major goals associated with the setting. Also, suppose that the facilitation scores associated with these goals are 2, 5, and −4, respectively, where the latter number reflects a thwarting score of +4. Assuming that the ideal facilitation (IF) scores for each of the three goals is +7, we can represent the perceived controllability of the work environment as (7 − 4)/(14 + 7) = .14.

Equation 3 emphasizes the multidimensional nature of environmental controllability but it does not reflect the differential importance of various goal dimensions in determining the overall level of congruence. It is assumed in this analysis that motivational salience affects environmental congruence through its adjustment of actual and ideal levels of goal facilitation. In operational terms, the facilitation (AF, IF) and thwarting (AT) scores associated with different goals are multiplied by the respective importance ratings (MS) of these goals, and the sum of these products is used to derive an index of *environmental congruence* (CG) *within a given setting*, s:

$$CG_s = \frac{\Sigma_f (AF_{gf} \times MS_{gf}) - \Sigma_t (AT_{gt} \times MS_{gt})}{\Sigma_f (IF_{gf} \times MS_{gf}) + \Sigma_t (IF_{gt} \times MS_{gt})} \tag{4}$$

To illustrate the effects of motivational salience on goal facilitation, we can return to the previous example of the work setting where the actual facilitation (AF) scores associated with productivity, socializing, and interesting work assignments were 2, 5, and −4 and the ideal facilitation (IF) score for each goal was 7. Previously, we assumed that the relative importance of these goals was equal. Now, however, let us assume that the importance ratings (MS) of the goals, on a seven-point scale, are 1, 6, and 3, respectively. The ratio of actual/ideal goal facilitation is, thus, (2 + 30 − 12)/(7 + 42 + 21), or .29, as compared to the previously unadjusted value of .14.

The proposed formulation of congruence is pertinent to an important facet of group–environment transaction, namely, the vulnerability of groups to physical and social-structural stressors. Recent research on stress has documented the negative effects of uncontrollable stimuli on health and behavior (Averill, 1973;

Glass & Singer, 1972; Holmes & Rahe, 1967; Seligman, 1975). Many programs of stress research, although focusing on the consequences of specific, uncontrollable events, have neglected to consider the sociophysical context in which these events occur. This tendency to overemphasize the impact of isolated, acute stressors has precluded an analysis of issues such as the proportion of uncontrollable/controllable events within a setting and the relative importance of those goals with which a stressor (or set of stressors) interferes.

By considering the multiple goals that are salient to group members within a particular setting, the present analysis offers a basis for describing the ecological context in which stressors occur and for estimating the impact of these events on social organization and well-being. Estimating the impact of a potential stressor can be illustrated in relation to the earlier-mentioned example of the office environment. Suppose, for instance, that a program of Muzak is installed in the work setting by the office manager and that this change in the environment reduces productivity from 2 to 1, increases socializing from 5 to 6, and decreases the interestingness of work assignments from -4 to -6. Also, assuming that the Muzak has been installed against the wishes of the workers, additional goal dimensions relating to workers' autonomy and respectful treatment by superiors are salient and are perceived as being constrained by the environment to the degree of 5 and 7, respectively. With the addition of Muzak, then, the perceived controllability of the work setting (from the employees' point of view) shifts from .14 to $(7 - 18)/(21 + 14)$, or $-.31$, reflecting a net loss of 45 points on a continuum ranging from complete uncontrollability (-1.0) to complete controllability $(+1.0)$. As depicted in Equation 4, the net deterioration in congruence prompted by the addition of Muzak to the setting also depends on the motivational salience of the workers' goals.

In accord with the findings from earlier research, the present analysis suggests that reduced controllability is associated with increased levels of stress (e.g., social conflict, reduced efficiency, psychological and physiological imbalances). The main effects of controllability, however, are mediated by motivational (and perceptual) salience, with higher levels of salience being associated with greater symptoms of stress in relatively uncontrollable environments (where $-1 \leq C_s < 0$) and less stress in relatively controllable settings (where $0 < C_s \leq 1$).

Whereas much of the research literature on stress is directly relevant to the issue of environmental controllability and its implications for personal well-being, little attention has been given to the role of motivational salience in mediating the behavioral and health consequences of controllable events. Nonetheless, certain studies pertaining to urban stress and learned helplessness offer preliminary (albeit indirect) evidence for the interactive effects of salience and controllability. First, a comparison of the findings from several crowding studies conducted in a diversity of settings suggests that high density exerts a more negative impact on health and behavior when it occurs within psychologically important (i.e., "primary") environments than within less salient ("secondary'') settings (Stokols, 1976).[6] As a case in point, a naturalistic study of the consequences of living in "tripled-up" dormitory rooms (originally designed for two rather than three students) found that those students who spent the greatest amount of time and felt most invested in their dorm rooms exhibited more negative reactions to their crowded living conditions (e.g., dissatisfaction with roommates, health problems) than did those who spent less time and felt less involved in their dorm residence (Aiello, Epstein, & Karlin, 1975).

Second, experiments on learned helplessness further suggest that motivational salience mediates the intensity of stress reactions, with exposure to uncontrollable stimuli leading to more extreme symptoms of learned helplessness in situations that are of high rather than low importance to the individual (Roth & Kubal, 1975; Wortman & Brehm, 1975). Although these data pertain to the experiences of individuals, they suggest that the impact of stressors on groups (e.g., roommates sharing a crowded dormitory suite) may be mediated by the motivational salience of shared goals.

The hypotheses discussed previously emphasize the impact of the environment on people rather than the reciprocal influence of groups on the environment. The actual impact of environmental demands on well-being, however, depends on the group's capacity to cope effectively with salient sources of uncontrollability. Within the present framework, coping processes can be understood as efforts to enhance controllability and/or to regulate the salience of group goals and relevant environmental conditions (Lazarus & Launier, 1978). A crucial question pertaining to stress and coping is under what conditions individuals and groups actively attempt to restructure the environment in accord with personal and collective goals. This issue is addressed in the following section.

Evaluative Salience and the Transformational Potential of Settings

The evaluative salience of the physical environment is the degree to which it evokes positive or negative feelings about the occupants, social functions, and physical features of a setting. A setting tends to be associated with positive evaluative meanings when the level of group–environment congruence is high and negative meanings when congruence is low. To the extent that environmental congruence remains low and negative evaluations of the environment persist, group members are motivated to improve or withdraw from the setting.

The *transformational potential of a setting refers to the motivation of group members to modify the physical or social structure of their setting in accord with collective preferences*. The degree of transformational potential reflects the dis-

---

[6]Additional evidence suggesting the interactive effects of density and environmental salience is presented by Altman (1975); Booth (1976); Cohen, Glass, and Phillips (1979); Galle, Gove, and McPherson (1972); and Stokols (1978).

crepancy between present and potential levels of environmental congruence: $[CG_{s(\text{potential})} - CG_{s(\text{present})}]$. *Potential congruence denotes the highest level of goal facilitation thought to be available in the best alternative setting.* The potential congruence of a setting is essentially the collective comparison level of group members for what they perceive to be their best available, alternative setting (Thibaut & Kelley, 1959).

The measurement of potential congruence is similar to that of actual congruence (see Equation 4) except that the actual facilitation or thwarting score (AF or AT) associated with each goal is replaced by a potential facilitation or thwarting score (PF or PT). The resulting index of potential congruence reflects the ratio of potential/ideal facilitation of salient goals perceived to be attainable in the best alternative setting. The "best alternative setting" can be either a transformed version of the existing setting or a completely different setting that has not yet been established or experienced.

To the extent that group members possess clear images of preferred future environments, potential congruence is greater than actual congruence. Images of preferred settings arise from the collective imagination of group members in response to existing environmental conditions.[7] But the salience of preferred environmental arrangements (i.e., a high level of transformational potential) does not necessarily promote structural modification of the setting. For, the accomplishment of environmental change requires not only salient images of the future but also sufficient levels of environmental flexibility and behavioral competence among group members. Thus, assuming that group members are motivated to improve their environment, the greatest amount of change would be initiated by imaginative groups within flexible settings whereas the least change would be accomplished by unimaginative groups within rigid settings. The present discussion suggests certain factors that may promote active efforts to ameliorate negative features of settings. Among these factors are the collective imagination of group members, their behavioral competence, and the flexibility of the existing environment. This list of change–promotive conditions hardly constitutes a theory of environmental change, but it does highlight some intriguing directions for future research.

One implication of the present analysis is that psychology has paid too little attention to the ecological conditions under which generative or creative thought, adaptive social behavior, and functional environmental change occur (Gergen, 1978). Accordingly, it suggests the importance of developing a particular kind of theoretical construct in future research—namely, "transformational constructs," or those relating to conditions within settings that promote observable environ-

---

[7]For an empirical analysis of historical antecedents of innovation, see Hamblin, Jacobsen, and Miller's (1973) mathematical model of social change.

mental change. The focus of transformational constructs is on properties of the setting at time₁ that prompt intrapersonal and intragroup processes, (O), and collective or individual action, B, yielding a modified environment at time₂: $E_1 \rightarrow (O) \rightarrow B \rightarrow E_2$.

At least three categories of transformational $(E_1 \rightarrow E_2)$ constructs can be developed. The first category describes environmental conditions that prompt insight and imagination pertaining to possible environmental change: $E_1 \rightarrow (O) \rightarrow (E_2)$. The enclosure of E_2 within parentheses denotes a "cognitive transformation" (Kelley & Thibaut, 1978; Mischel, 1973) of the existing environment involving the mental representation of an alternative situation(s). The cognitive transformation of environments can be differentiated from those processes within settings that promote actual environmental change via planning and intentional action. This second category of constructs can be summarized as follows: $E_1 \rightarrow (O) \rightarrow B \rightarrow E_2$. Environmental change also can occur unintentionally as the product of unplanned or serendipitous behavior. This sequence of events is depicted by a third category of constructs: $E_1 \rightarrow B \rightarrow E_2$.

Changes occurring within the sociophysical environment between times 1 and 2 can be conceptualized and measured along several possible dimensions. Moreover, the quantity of environmental change can be represented as a composite of $t_2 - t_1$ difference scores along these theoretically relevant dimensions. As for the quality of environmental change, situation-specific criteria must be designated for evaluating the degree to which physical or social-structural changes are functional or dysfunctional for the individual and group. On the basis of these criteria, "generative environments" would be defined as those which promote insight and functional environmental change, whereas "degenerative environments" would be those that discourage insight and/or promote dysfunctional environmental change.

The proposed conceptualization of transformational constructs suggests several questions for future research. First, what properties of settings promote insight as well as functional versus dysfunctional modifications of the environment? Among the possible antecedents of social–environmental change are direct or vicarious exposure to environmental problems (e.g., resource scarcities, community noise, and air pollution) that require creative solutions, socially programmed reinforcers designed to increase aggregate rates of "proenvironmental" behavior (Cone & Hayes, 1977), physical mobility resulting in exposure to unfamiliar cultures and geographical regions, and situations involving interpersonal conflict (Kelley & Thibaut, 1978).

The relative salience of change-inducing circumstances undoubtedly varies across situations and settings. In general, though, it is assumed that those situations that heighten the salience of alternative (preferred) environmental arrangements, although offering behavioral opportunities for achieving those arrangements, are most conducive to change.

SUMMARY AND CONCLUSIONS

The traditions of Lewin (emphasizing the subjective environment of individuals) and Barker (emphasizing the objective environment of groups) generally have remained separate in psychological research on settings. In an effort to bridge these perspectives, the present analysis has focused on the shared, sociocultural meanings conveyed to group members by their physical milieu. These consensually defined images constitute the perceived social field of places—the functional, motivational, and evaluative meanings attached to the physical environment. The perceived social field reflects the linkages between groups and places and plays an important role in mediating the quality and intensity of group–environment transactions.

The description of physical environments in terms of their social meanings is relevant to a number of theoretical and practical issues. At a theoretical level, the concepts derived from the dimensions of functional, motivational, and evaluative salience provide a framework for analyzing several neglected aspects of group–environment transaction, including the strength of group ties to specific locations, the determinants of perceived environmental congruence and quality, and the antecedents of structural changes within settings.

An analysis of the social meanings attached to places also seems germane to various social, political, and community planning issues. The notion of place dependence, for example, seems to be reflected in the behavior of groups living in hazardous areas who often refuse to resettle in a different region, despite recent or imminent disasters (Burton, Kates, & White, 1978). Within the political arena, the fervor of terrorist groups is apparently heightened rather than neutralized by the perception that they have been denied a desired geographical area. In these and other instances of intergroup conflict, the place dependence of groups and the collectively perceived contradiction between existing and preferred functions of an area can have enormous political ramifications. And within the realm of community planning, the identification of conditions that increase the transformational potential of settings (e.g., ecological antecedents of innovation and behavioral competence) could provide valuable guidelines for environmental design.

The present analysis has focused on the development of theoretical terms for describing group × place transactions rather than on the methodological and statistical complexities associated with the measurement of these phenomena.[8] This strategy seems justified in view of the limited attention that has been given in psychological research to the conceptualization and description of settings.

---

[8]These complexities include the development of reliable procedures for measuring shared goals and their salience to group members, an assessment of the statistical relationships among the indices proposed earlier (Equations 1–4), and the drivation of criteria for distinguishing among functional versus dysfunctional modifications of the environment.

Only by developing an adequate vocabulary for the description of settings can we begin to move toward a systematic empirical analysis of group-environment transactions.

ACKNOWLEDGMENT

I would like to thank Roger Barker, Dorwin Cartwright, Baruch Fischhoff, Stephen Kaplan, David Magnusson, Joseph McGrath, Sally Shumaker, and Allan Wicker for their helpful comments on the manuscript.

Preparation of this chapter was supported by the Focused Research Program in Human Stress at the University of California, Irvine.

References

Aarons, L. Sleep—Assisted instruction. *Psychological Bulletin,* 1976, *83,* 1–40.

Abelson, R. P. Situational variables in personality research. In S. Messick & J. Ross (Eds.), *Measurement in personality and cognition.* New York: Wiley, 1962.

Acking, D., & Küller, R. Presentation and judgment of planned environment and the hypothesis of arousal. In W. P. F. Preiser (Ed.), *Environmental design research* (Vol. 1). Stroudsburg, Pa.: Dowden, Hutchinson & Ross, 1973.

Adair, J. G., & Spinner, B. *Subjects' access to cognitive processes: Demand characteristics and verbal report.* Unpublished manuscript, 1979.

Agar, M. H. *Ethnography as an interdisciplinary campground.* Paper presented at the Conference on Cognition, Social Behavior, and the Environment. Vanderbilt University, May 1979.

Aiello, J., Epstein, Y., & Karlin, R. Field experimental research on human crowding. Paper presented at the Eastern Psychological Association Convention. New York, 1975.

Alexander, C. N., & Knight, G. W. *Situated identities and social psychological experimentation. Sociometry,* 1971, *34,* 65–82.

Allardt, E. *Att ha, att älska, att vara.* Having, loving, being. Lund: Argus, 1975.

Allen, V. L., & Greenberger, D. B. An aesthetic theory of vandalism. *Crime and Delinquency,* 1978, *24,* 309–321.

Allport, F. H. Teleonomic description in the study of personality. *Character and Personality,* 1937, *6,* 202–214.

Allport, F. H. Theories of perception and the concept of structure. New York: Wiley, 1955.

Allport, G. W. *Personality: A psychological interpretation.* New York: Holt, 1937.

Allport, G. W. *The nature of prejudice.* Garden City, N.Y.: Doubleday Anchor, 1958.

Allport, G. W. *Pattern and growth in personality.* New York: Holt, Rinehart & Winston, 1961.

Alston, W. P. Traits, consistency and conceptual alternatives for personality theory. *Journal for the Theory of Social Behavior,* 1975, *5,* 17–48.

Altman, I. *The environment and social behavior.* Monterey, Calif.: Brooks/Cole, 1975.

Altman, I., & Chemers, M. M. *Culture and environment.* Monterey, Calif.: Brooks/Cole, 1979.

Amasov, N. M. *Modeling of thinking and the mind.* New York: Spartan Books, 1967.

Andrews, F. Social indicators of perceived life quality. *Social Indicators Research,* 1974, *1,* 279–299.

Andrews, R. N. L., & Waits, M. *Environmental values in public decisions: A research agenda.* Ann Arbor, Mich.: School of Natural Resources, University of Michigan, 1978.

Anochin, P. K. Das funktionelle system als grundlage der physiologischen architektur des verhaltensaktes. Jena: Fischer, 1967.

Appel, M. H., & Goldberg, L. S. *Topics in cognitive development (Vol. 1). Equilibration: Theory, research, and application.* New York: Plenum, 1977.

Appleyard, D. Why buildings are known. *Environment and Behavior,* 1969, *1,* 131–156.

Appleyard, D. *Planning a pluralistic city: Conflicting realities in Ciudad Guayana.* Cambridge, Mass.: MIT Press, 1976.

Appleyard, D. Understanding professional media: Issues, theory and a research agenda. In I. Altman & J. F. Wohlwill (Eds.) Human behavior and environment (Vol. 2) New York: Plenum, 1978.

Appleyard, D., & Craik, K. H. The Berkeley environmental simulation laboratory and its research programme. *International Review of Applied Psychology,* 1978, *27,* 53–55.

Argyle, M. *Social interaction.* London: Methuen, 1969.

Argyle, M. *Bodily communication.* London: Methuen, 1975.

Argyle, M. Personality and social behavior. In R. Harré (Ed.), *Personality.* Oxford: Blackwell, 1976.

Argyle, M. Predictive and generative rules models of $P \times S$ interaction. In D. Magnusson & N. S. Endler (Eds.), *Personality at the crossroads: Current issues in interactional psychology.* Hillsdale, N.J.: Lawrence Erlbaum Associates, 1977, pp. 353–370.

Argyle, M. Interaction skills and social competence. In M. P. Feldman & J. Orford (Eds.), *The social psychology of psychological problems.* London: Wiley, 1980.

Argyle, M., & Little, B. R. Do personality traits apply to social behavior? *Journal for the Theory of Social Behavior,* 1972, *2,* 1–35.

Argyle, M., Forgas, J., Ginsburg, G. P., & Campbell, A. Are different personality constructs used in different situations? In M. Argyle, A. Furnham, & J. A. Graham (Eds.), *Social situations.* Cambridge University Press, 1981.

Argyle, M., Furnham, A. and Graham, J. A. *Social Situations.* Cambridge University Press, in press.

Argyle, M., Graham, J. A., Campbell, A., & White, P. "The rules of different situations." *New Zealand Psychology,* 1979, *8,* 13–22.

Argyle, M., Graham, J. A. and Kreckel, M. The structure of behavioural elements in social and work situations. *In* Argyle, M., Furnham, A. and Graham, J. A. *Social Situations.* Cambridge University Press, 1981.

Arrow, K. J. *Social choice and individual values.* New York, Wiley, 1963.

Arsenian, J., & Arsenian, J. M. Tough and easy cultures. *Journal of Abnormal and Social Psychology,* 1948, *11,* 377–385.

Ashby, W. R. *Design for a brain.* New York: Wiley, 1960.

Ashby, W. R., & Conant, R. C. Every good regulator of a system is a model of that system. *International Journal of Syst. Science,* 1970, *1,* 89–97.

Astin, A. W., & Holland, J. L. The environmental assessment technique: A way to measure college environments. *Journal of Educational Psychology,* 1961, *52,* 308–316.

Atkinson, J. Change in activity. In T. Mischel (Ed.), *Human action: Conceptual and empirical issues.* New York: Academic Press, 1969.

Avedon, E. M. The structural elements of games. In E. M. Avedon & B. Sutton-Smith (Eds.), *The study of games.* New York: Wiley, 1971.

Averill, J. R. Personal control over aversive stimuli and its relationship to stress. *Psychological Bulletin,* 1973, *80,* 286–303.

Bach, K. Analytical social philosophy: Basic concepts. *Journal of Theoretical Social Behavior,* 1975, *5,* 189–214.

Badger, E. *Teaching guide: Infant learning program.* Paoli, Pa.: The Intructo Corporation, 1971.

(a)

Badger, E. *Teaching guide: Toddler learning program.* Paoli, Pa.: The Instructo Corporation, 1971. (b)

Badger, E. The infant stimulation/mother training project. In B. M. Caldwell & D. J. Steadman (Eds.), *Infant education: A guide for helping handicapped children in the first three years.* New York: Walker & Co., 1977.

Baldwin, A. L. A cognitive theory of socialization. In D. A. Goslin (Ed.), *Handbook of socialization. Theory and research.* Chicago: Rand McNally, 1969.

Bales, R. F. *Interaction process analysis.* Cambridge, Mass.: Addison-Wesley, 1950.

Ball, D. W. 'The definition of the situation': Some theoretical and methodological consequences of taking W. I. Thomas seriously. *Journal for the Theory of Social Behavior,* 1972, *2,* 61-82.

Bandura, A. Self-efficacy: Toward a unifying theory of behavioral change. *Psychological Review,* 1977, *84,* 191-215. (a)

Bandura, A. *Social learning theory.* Englewood Cliffs, N.J.: Prentice-Hall, 1977. (b)

Bandura, A. The self system in reciprocal determinism. *American Psychologist,* 1978, *33,* 344-358.

Bandura, A., & Walters, R. H. *Social learning and personality development.* New York: Holt, Rinehart & Winston, 1963.

Bannister, D., & Mair, J. M. M. *The evaluation of personal constructs.* London and New York: Academic Press, 1968.

Barber, T. X., Dalal, A. S., & Calverley, D. S. The subjective reports of hypnotic subjects. *American Journal of Clinical Hypnosis,* 1968, *11,* 74-88.

Barker, M. L. Planning for environmental indices: Observer appraisals of air quality. In K. H. Craik & E. H. Zube (Eds.), *Perceiving environmental quality: Research and applications.* New York: Plenum, 1976, pp. 175-203.

Barker, R. G. Ecology and motivation. *Nebraska Symposium on Motivation,* 1960, *8,* 1-48.

Barker, R. G. Explorations in ecological psychology. *American Psychologist,* 1965, *20,* 1-14.

Barker, R. G. *Ecological psychology.* Stanford, Calif.: Stanford University Press, 1968.

Barker, R. G. The influence of frontier environments on behavior. In J. O. Steffen (Ed.), *The American West: New perspectives, new dimensions.* Norman, Okla.: University of Oklahoma Press, 1979, 61-93.

Barker, R. G., & Associates. *Habits, environments, and human behavior.* San Francisco: Jossey-Bass, 1978.

Barker, R. G., & Schoggen, P. *Qualities of community life.* San Franscisco: Jossey-Bass, 1973.

Barker, R. G., & Wright, H. F. *Midwest and its children: The psychological ecology of an American town.* Evanston, Ill.: Row-Peterson, 1954.

Baron, R. A., & Bell, P. A. Aggression and heat: The influence of ambient temperature, negative affect, and a cooling drink on physical aggression. *Journal of Personality and Social Psychology,* 1976, *33,* 245-255.

Bateson, G. *Steps to an ecology of mind.* Suffolk, Palladin, 1973.

Bauer, R. (Ed.). *Social indicators.* Cambridge, Mass.: MIT Press, 1968.

Baum, A., & Korman, S. Differential response to anticipated crowding: Psychological effects of social and spatial density. *Journal of Personality and Social Psychology,* 1976, *34,* 526-536.

Baum, A., & Valins, S. (Eds.). *The social psychology of crowding: Studies of the effect of residential group size.* Hillsdale: N.J.: Lawrence Erlbaum Associates, 1977.

Bechtel, R. *Enclosing behavior.* New York: McGraw-Hill, 1977.

Beck, A. T. *Depression: Clinical, experimental and theoretical aspects.* New York: Harper & Row, 1967.

Bell, R. T. *Sociolinguistics.* London: Batsford, 1976.

Bem, D. J. Self-perception: An alternative interpretation of cognitive dissonance phenomena. *Psychological Review,* 1967, *74,* 183-200.

Bem, D. J. Self-perception theory. In L. Berkowitz (Ed.), *Advances in experimental social psychology* (Vol. 6). New York: Academic Press, 1972.

Bem, D. J., & Allen, A. On predicting some of the people some of the time: The search for cross-situational consistencies in behavior. *Psychological Review*, 1974, *81*, 506-520.

Bem, D. J., & Funder, D. C. Predicting more of the people more of the time: Assessing the personality of situations. *Psychological Review*, 1978, *85*, 485-501.

Bem, D. J., & Lord, C. G. The template-matching technique: A proposal for probing the ecological validity of experimental settings in social psychology. *Journal of Personality and Social Psychology*, 1979, *37*.

Benjamin, L. S. Structural analysis of social behavior. *Psychological Review*, 1974, *81*, 392-425.

Berger, P., & Luckmann, T. *The social construction of reality*. Garden City, N.Y.: Doubleday, 1967.

Berglund, B. Quantitative approaches in environmental studies. *International Journal of Psychology*, 1977, *12*, 111-123.

Berglund, B., Berglund, U., Engen, T., & Ekman, G. Multidimensional analysis of twenty-one odors. *Scandinavian Journal of Psychology*, 1973, *14*, 131-137.

Bergman, L. R., & Magnusson, D. Overachievement and catecholamine excretion in an achievement-demanding situation. *Psychosomatic Medicine*, 1979, *41*, 181-188.

Berlyne, D. E. *Conflicts, arousal, and curiosity*. New York: McGraw-Hill, 1969.

Berlyne, D. E. (Ed.). *Studies in the new experimental aesthetics*. Washington, D.C.: Hemisphere, 1974.

Bernstein, B. Language and social class. *British Journal of Sociology*, 1960, *11*, 271-276.

Bernstein, N. A. *The coordination and regulation of movements*. Oxford: Pergamon Press, 1967.

Berscheid, E., Graziano, E., Monson, T., & Dermer, M. Outcome dependency: Attention, Attribution and attraction, *Journal of Personality and Social Psychology*, 1976, *34*, 978-989.

Bickhard, M. A model of developmental and psychological processes. *Genetic Psychology Monographs*, 1980 Aug. *102* (1) 61-116.

Bieri, J., Atkins, A. L., Briar, S., Leaman, R. L., Miller, H., & Tripodi, T. *Clinical and social judgment: The discrimination of behavioral information*. New York: Wiley, 1966.

Binet, A. Les idees modernes sur les enfant. Paris: Ernest Flamarion, 1909. Cited from Stoddard, G. D. The IQ: Its ups and downs. *Educational Record*, 1939, *20*, 44-57.

Binet, A., & Simon, T. Methodes nouvelles pour le diagnostis du niveau intellectuel des anormaux. *Annee Psychol.*, 1905, *11*, 191-244.

Bishop, D. W., & Witt, P. A. Sources of behavioral variance during leisure time. *Journal of Personality and Social Psychology*, 1970, *16*, 352-360.

Blauner, R. *Alienation and freedom*. Chicago: University of Chicago Press, 1964.

Block, J. The assessment of communication: Role variations as a function of interactional context. *Journal of Personality*, 1952, *21*, 272-286.

Block, J. *The Q-sort method in personality assessment and psychiatric research*. Springfield, Ill.: Charles C. Thomas, 1961. (Reissued by Consulting Psychologists Press, Palo Alto, Calif.: 1978.)

Block, J. *Lives through time*. Berkeley, Calif.: Bancroft Books, 1971.

Block, J. Advancing the psychology of personality: Paradigmatic shift or improving the quality of research? In D. Magnusson & N. S. Endler (Eds.), *Personality at the crossroads: Current issues in interactional psychology*. Hillsdale, N.J.: Lawrence Erlbaum Associates, 1977.

Block, J. H., & Block, J. The California child Q-set. Unpublished manuscript, University of California, Berkeley, 1969.

Block, J. H., & Block, J. The role of ego-control and ego-resiliency in the organization of behavior. In W. A. Collins (Ed.), *Minnesota Symposia on Child Psychology* (Vol. 13). Hillsdale, N.J.: Lawrence Erlbaum Associates, 1979.

Block, J. H., & Martin, B. Predicting the behavior of children under frustration. *Journal of Abnormal and Social Psychology*, 1955, *51*, 281-285.

Bloom, B. L. *Community mental health: A general introduction*. Monterey, Calif.: Brooks/Cole Publishers, 1977.

Bloom, B. S. *Stability and change in human characteristics*. New York: Wiley, 1966.

Blumer, H. Sociological implications of the thought of George Herbert Mead. *American Journal of Sociology*, 1966, *71*, 535–544.

Blurton-Jones, N. (Ed.). *Ethological studies of child behavior*. London: Cambridge University Press, 1972.

Booth, A. *Urban crowding and its consequences*. New York: Praeger, 1976.

Boring, E. G. *A history of experimental psychology*. New York: Appleton, 1929.

Bower, E. M. Primary prevention of mental and emotional disorders: A conceptual framework and action possibilities. In A. J. Bindman & A. D. Spiegel (Eds.), *Perspectives in community mental health*. Chicago, Aldine, 1969.

Bowers, K. S. Situationism in psychology: An analysis and a critique. *Psychological Review*, 1973, *80*, 307–336.

Bowers, K. S. The psychology of subtle control: An attribution analysis of behavioral persistence. *Canadian Journal of Behavioral Science*, 1975, *7*, 78–95.

Bowers, K. S. *Hypnosis for the seriously curious*. Monterey, Calif.: Brooks Cole, 1976.

Bowers, K. S. There's more to iago than meets the eye: A clinical account of personal consistency. In D. Magnusson & N. S. Endler (Eds.), *Personality at the crossroads: Current issues in interactional psychology*. Hillsdale, N.J.: Lawrence Erlbuam Associates, 1977.

Braun, J. L. & Reynolds, D. J. A factor analysis of a 100-item fear survey inventory. *Behavior Research and Therapy*, 1969, *7*, 399–402.

Brazelton, T. B., Tronick, E., Adamson, L., Als, H., & Wise, S. Early mother-infant interaction. *In parent-infant interaction, CIBA Symposium*, No. 33, Amsterdam: Associated Scientific Publishers, 1975.

Brenner, M. *The social structure of the research interview*. Unpublished PhD. thesis, Oxford University, 1978.

Bridgman, P. W. *The way things are*. Cambridge, Mass.: Harvard University Press, 1959.

Broadbent, D. E. The hidden preattentive processes. *American Psychologist*, 1977, *32*, 109–118.

Bronfenbrenner, U. Toward an experimental ecology of human development. *American Psychologist*, 1977, *32*, 513–531.

Bronfenbrenner, U. *The ecology of human development*. Cambridge, Mass.: Harvard University Press, 1979.

Brown, G. W., Bhrolchain, M. H., & Harris, T. Social class and psychiatric disturbance among women in an urban population. *Sociology*, 1975, *9*, 255–254.

Brown, R. *A first language: The early stages*. Cambridge, Mass.: Harvard University Press, 1973.

Brown, R., & Fraser, C. The acquisition of syntax. In C. N. Cofer & B. Musgrave (Eds.), *Verbal behavior and learning problems and processes*. New York: McGraw-Hill, 1963, pp. 158–201.

Brown, R., & Fraser, C. Speech as a marker of situation, In K. Scherer & H. Giles (Eds.), *Social markers in speech*. Cambridge University Press, 1979.

Bruner, J. S., Goodman J. J. & Austin, G. A. A study of thinking. New York: Wiley, 1956.

Brunswik, E. Organismic achievement and environmental probability. *Psychological Review*, 1943, *50*, 255–272.

Brunswik, E. *The conceptual framework of psychology*. Chicago: University of Chicago Press, 1952.

Brunswik, E. *Perception and the representative design of psychological experiments* (2nd ed.). Berkeley: University of California Press, 1956.

Bühler, C. *Kindheit und jugend* (3rd ed.). Jena: Fischer, 1931.

Burks, B. S. The relative influence of nature and nurture upon mental development: A comparative study of foster parent-foster child resemblance and true parent-true child resemblance. *Yearbook of National Society for the Study of Education*, 1928, *27*, 219–316.

Burton, I., Kates, R. W., & White, G. F. *The environment as hazard*. New York: Oxford University Press, 1978.

Byrne, P. S., & Long, E. L. *Doctors talking to patients.* London: HMSO, 1976.

Caldwell, B. M. The effects of infant care. In M. L. Hoffman & L. W. Hoffman (Eds.), *Review of child development research* (Vol. 1). New York: Russell Sage Foundation, 1964, pp. 9–87.

Campbell, A., Converse, P., & Rodgers, W. *The quality of American life.* New York: Russell Sage Foundation, 1976.

Campbell, D. T. Variation and selective retention in socio-cultural evolution. In H. R. Barringer, G. I. Blanksten, & R. W. Mack (Eds.), *Social change in developing areas.* Cambridge, Mass.: Schenkman, 1965.

Campbell, D. T. Assessing the impact of planned social change. In C. M. Lyons (Ed.), *Social research and public policies.* Hanover, N.H.: Public Affairs Center, Dartmouth College, 1975.

Campbell, J. P., Dunnette, M. D., Lawler, E. E., III, & Weick, K. E., Jr. *Managerial behavior, performance and effectiveness.* New York: McGraw-Hill, 1970.

Cantor, N. *Prototypicality and personality judgments.* Unpublished doctoral dissertation, Stanford University, 1978.

Cantor, N., & Mischel, W. Prototypes in person perception. In L. Berkowitz (Ed.), *Advances in experimental social psychology.* New York: Academic press, 1979.

Cantor, N., Mischel, W., & Schwartz, J. A prototype analysis of a naive psychology of situations. Unpublished manuscript, Princeton University, 1980.

Cantor, N., Smith, E. E., French, R., & Mezzich, J. *Psychiatric diagnosis.* Unpublished manuscript, Princeton University, 1979.

Caplan, N., & Nelson, S. D. On being useful: The nature and consequences of psychological research on social problems. *American Psychologist,* 1973, *28,* 199–211.

Carlsson, G. Random walk effects in behavioral data. *Behavioral Science,* 1972, *17,* 430–437.

Carlsson, G. Crime and behavioral epidemiology. In S. Mednick & K. O. Cristiansen (Eds.), *Biosocial bases of criminal behavior.* New York: Gardner Press, 1977.

Cartwright, D. Theory and practice. *Journal of Social Issues,* 1978, *34,* 168–180.

Cassirer, E. *An essay on man.* Garden City, N.Y.: Doubleday, 1953. (Original publication in 1944.)

Cattell, R. B. *Personality and motivation structure and measurement.* New York: Harcourt, Brace, & World, 1957.

Cattell, R. B. Personality, role, mood, and situation perception: A unifying theory of modulators. *Psychological Review,* 1963, *70,* 1–18.

Cattell, R. B., & Child, D. *Motivation and dynamic structure.* New York: Wiley, 1975.

Cavallo, V. Leistungs—und beanspruchungsbestimmende Figenschaften operativer Abbilder— Untersucht am Montagetätigkeiten. *Informationen der Technischen Universität Dresden,* 1978, No. 22–16.

Chein, I. The environment as a determinant of behavior. *The Journal of Social Psychology,* 1954, *39,* 115–127.

Chomsky, N. *Syntactic structures.* The Hague: Mouton, 1957.

Chomsky, N. Review of verbal bheavior by B. F. Skinner. *Language,* 1959.

Cobb, S. Social support as a moderator of life stress. *Psychosomatic Medicine,* 1976, *38,* 300–314.

Cobb, S. *Dimensions of the social environment that commonly produce strain.* Paper presented at the Meeting of the Psychiatry Department Major Conference Series, University of Michigan, Ann Arbor, Mich., April 18, 1979.

Cohen, C. *Cognitive basis of stereotyping.* Paper presented at the Meeting of the American Psychological Association, San Francisco, August 1977.

Cohen, S., Glass, D. C., & Phillips, S. Environment and health. In H. Freeman, S. Levine, & L. Reeder (Eds.), *Handbook of Medical Sociology.* Englewood Cliffs, N.J.: Prentice Hall, 1979, 134–149.

Collett, R. (Ed.). *Social rules and social behavior.* Oxford: Blackwell, 1977.

Cone, J. D., & Hayes, S. C. Applied behavior analysis and the solution of environmental problems. In I. Altman & J. Wohlwill (Eds.), *Human behavior and the environment: Advances in theory and research* (Vol. 2). New York: Plenum, 1977.

Converse, P. E. The concept of normal vote. In A. Campbell, P. E. Converse, W. E. Miller, & D. E. Stokes (Eds.), *Elections and the political order.* New York: Wiley, 1966.

Cooper, C. The house as symbol of the self. In J. Lang, C. Burnette, W. Moleski, & D. Vachon (Eds.), *Designing for human behavior: Architecture and the behavioral sciences.* Stroudsberg, Pa.: Dowden, Hutchinson, and Ross, 1974, pp. 130-146.

Cottrell, L. S. Jr. The analyser of situational fields in social psychology. *American Sociological Review,* 1942, *7,* 370-387.

Coughlin, R. E. The perception and valuation of water quality: A review of research method and finding. In K. H. Craik & E. H. Zube (Eds.), *Perceiving environmental quality: Research and applications.* New York: Plenum, 1976, pp. 205-227.

Coutu, W. *Emergent human nature.* New York: Knopf, 1949.

Cowen, E. Baby-steps toward primary prevention. *American Journal of Community Psychology,* 1977, *5,* 1-22.

Craik, F. I. M., & Lockhart, R. S. Levels of processing: A framework for memory research. *Journal of Verbal Learning and Verbal Behavior,* 1972, *11,* 671-684.

Craik, K. H. The comprehension of the everyday physical environment. *Journal of the American Institute of Planners,* 1968, *34,* 29-37.

Craik, K. H. Environmental psychology. In K. H. Craik et. al., *New directions in psychology 4.* New York: Holt, Rinehart, & Winston, 1970, pp. 1-22.

Craik, K.H. The assessment of places. In P. McReynolds (Ed.), *Advances in psychological assessment* (Vol. 2). Palo Alto, Calif.: Science and Behavior Books, 1971, pp. 40-62.

Craik, K. H. Appraising the objectivity of landscape dimensions. In J. V. Krutilla (Ed.), *Natural environments: Studies in theoretical and applied analysis.* Baltimore, Md.: John Hopkins University Press, 1972, pp. 292-346. (a)

Craik, K. H. An ecological perspective on environmental decision-making. *Human Ecology,* 1972, *1,* 69-80. (b)

Craik, K. H. Environmental psychology. *Annual Review of Psychology,* 1973, *24,* 403-422.

Craik, K. H. Individual variations in landscape description. In E. H. Zube, R. O. Brush, & J. Fabos (Eds.), *Landscape assessment: Values, perceptions and resources.* Stroudsburg, Pa.: Dowden, Hutchinson & Ross, 1975, pp. 130-150.

Craik, K. H. The personality research paradigm in environmental psychology. In S. Wapner, S. Cohen, & B. Kaplan (Eds.), *Experiencing environments.* New York: Plenum, 1976, pp. 55-80.

Craik, K. H. Multiple scientific paradigm in environmental psychology. *Internal Journal of Psychology,* 1977, *12,* 147-157.

Craik, K. H., & Feimar, N. R. Setting technical standard: For visual assessment procedures. In G. H. Elsner & R. C. Smardon (Eds.), *Our national landscape: Applied techniques for analysis and management of the visual resource.* Berkeley, Calif.: U.S. Forest Service, 1979.

Craik, K. H., & McKechnie, G. E. Editors' introduction: Personality and the environment. *Environment and Behavior,* 1977, *9,* 155-168.

Craik, K. H., & Zube, E. H. (Eds.). *Perceiving environmental quality: Research and applications.* New York: Plenum, 1976.

Cronbach, L. J. Beyond the two disciplines of scientific psychology. *American Psychologist,* 1975, *30,* 116-127.

Csikszentmihalyi, M., & Graef, R. The experience of freedom in daily life. *Journal of Environmental Psychology,* 1979, in press.

Csikszentmihalyi, M., Larson, R., & Prescott, S. The ecology of adolescent activity and experience. *Journal of Youth and Adolescence,* 1977, *6,* 281-294.

Daniel, T. C., & Boster, R. S. Measuring landscape esthetics: The scenic beauty estimation method. Ft. Collins, Colo.: U.S. Forest Service, 1976.

Dansereau, F., Jr., Graen, G., & Haga, W. J. A vertical dyad linkage approach to leadership within formal organizations: A longitudinal investigation of the role making process. *Organizational Behavior and Human Performance,* 1975, *13,* 46-78.

Davidson, D. Agency. In R. Binkley et al., (Eds.), *Agent action and reason.* Toronto: University of Toronto Press, 1971.

Davis, R. C. Physical psychology. *Psychological Review,* 1953, *60,* 7-14.

Dawes, R. N. Suppose we measured height with rating scales instead of rulers. *Applied Psychological Measurement,* 1977, *1,* 267-274.

Dawkins, R. Hierarchical organisation: A candidate principle for ethology. In P. P. G. Bateson & R. A. Hinde (Eds.), *Growing points in ethology.* London: Cambridge University Press, 1976.

Deutsch, C. P. Auditory discrimination and learning social factors. *Merrill-Palmer Quarterly,* 1964, *10,* 277-296.

Deutsch, W. *Sprachliche redundanz und objektidentifikation.* Marburg: Lahn, 1976.

Dickman, H. R. The perception of behavioral units. In R. G. Barker (Ed.), *The stream of behavior.* New York: Appleton-Century-Crofts, 1963, pp. 23-41.

Dittmar, N. *Sociolinguistics.* London: Arnold, 1976.

Diveky, S., & Endler, N. S. *The interaction model of anxiety: State and trait anxiety for banking executives in normal working environments.* Unpublished manuscript, York University, Toronto, 1977.

Dixon, N. F. *Subliminal perception: The nature of a controversy.* London: McGraw Hill, 1971.

Dohrenwend, B. S., & Dohrenwend, B. P. *Stressful life events: Their nature and effects.* New York: John Wiley, 1974.

Donovan, J. E., & Jessor, R. Adolescent problem drinking: Psychosocial correlates in a national sample study. *Journal of Studies on Alcohol,* 1978, *39,* 1506-1524.

Doob, L. W., & Sears, R. R. Factors determining substitute behavior and the overt expression of aggression. *Journal of Abnormal and Social Psychology,* 1939, *34,* 293-313.

Duncan, J. S., & Duncan, N. G. Housing as presentation of self and the structure of social networks. In G. T. Moore & R. G. Golledge (Eds.), *Environmental knowing.* Stroudsburg, Pa.: Dowden, Hutchinson, and Ross, 1976, pp. 247-253.

Duncan, O. D. *Introduction to structural equation models.* New York: Academic Press, 1975.

Duncan, S. Non-verbal communication. *Psychological Bulletin,* 1969, *72,* 118-137.

Duncan, S., Jr., Brunner, L. J., & Fiske, D. W. Strategy signals in face-to-face interaction. *Journal of Personality and Social Psychology,* 1979, *37,* 301-313.

Duncan, S., Jr., & Fiske, D. W. *Face-to-face interaction: Research, methods, and theory.* Hillsdale, N.J.: Lawrence Erlbaum Associates (J. Wiley), 1977.

Dunnette, M. D. *Personnel selection and placement.* Belmont, Calif.: Wadsworth, 1966.

Durkheim, E. *The rules of sociological method.* New York: Free Press, 1964.

Dworkin, R. H., & Kihlstrom, J. F. An S-R inventory of dominance for research on the nature of person-situation interactions. *Journal of Personality,* 1978, *46,* 43-56.

Ebbesen, E. B., & Allen, R. B. Cognitive processes in implicit personality trait inferences. *Journal of Personality and Social Psychology,* 1979, *37,* 471-488.

Eckblad, G. *Schemes and intrinsic motivation. II Scheme theory, a conceptual frame-work for intrinsically motivated behavior.* Department of Psychology, Bergen University, Bergen, 1977.

Ekehammar, B. Interactionism in personality from a historical perspective. *Psychological Bulletin,* 1974, *81,* 1026-1048.

Ekehammar, B., & Magnusson, D. A method to study stressful situations. *Journal of Personality and Social Psychology,* 1973, *27,* 176-179.

Ekehammar, B., Magnusson, D., & Ricklander, L. An interactionist approach to the study of anxiety. *Scandinavian Journal of Psychology,* 1974, *15,* 4-14.

Ekehammar, B., Schalling, D., & Magnusson, D. Dimensions of stressful situations: A comparison between a response analytical and a stimulus analytical approach. *Multivariate Behavioral Research,* 1975, *10,* 155-164.

Ekman, G. *Comparative studies on multidimensional scaling and related techniques.* Reports from the Psychological Laboratories, University of Stockholm, 1970, Suppl. 3.

Emery, F. E., & Trist, E. L. The clausal texture of organizational environments. *Human Relations,* 1965, *18,* 21-32.

Endler, N. S. The case for person-situation interactions. *Canadian Psychological Review,* 1975, *16,* 12-21. (a)

Endler, N. S. A person-situation interaction model for anxiety. In C. D. Spielberger & I. G. Sarason (Eds.), *Stress and Anxiety* (Vol. 1). Washington D.C.: Hemisphere Pub. Corp. (Wiley), 1975. (b)

Endler, N. S. The role of person by situation interactions in personality theory. In I. C. Uzgiris & F. Weismann (Eds.), *The structuring of experience.* New York: Plenum Press, 1977.

Endler, N. S. Persons, situations and their interactions. In A. I. Rabin (Ed.), *Further explorations in personality.* New York: Wiley, 1980.

Endler, N. S., & Edwards, J. Person by treatment interactions in personality research. In L. A. Pervin & M. Lewis (Eds.), *Perspectives in interactional psychology.* New York: Plenum Press, 1978.

Endler, N. S., Edwards, J., Kuczynski, M., & King, P. *State and trait anxiety within a person-situation interaction model: An empirical test in an exam situation.* Unpublished manuscript, York University, Toronto, 1979.

Endler, N. S., Edwards, J., & McGuire, A. *The interaction model of anxiety: An empirical test in a theatrical performance situation.* Unpublished manuscript, York University, Toronto, 1979.

Endler, N. S., Hunt, J. McV., & Rosenstein, A. J. An S-R inventory of anxiousness. *Psychological Monographs,* 1962, 76(17, Whole No. 536), 1-33.

Endler, N. S., & Hunt J. McV. Sources of behavioral variance as measured by the S-R inventory of anxiousness. *Psychological Bulletin,* 1966, *65,* 336-346.

Endler, N. S., & Hunt, J. McV. S-R inventories of hostility and comparison of the proportions of variance from persons, responses and situations for hostility and anxiousness. *Journal of Personality and Social Psychology,* 1968, *9,* 309-315.

Endler, N. S., & Hunt, J. McV. Generalizability of contributions from sources of variance in the S-R inventories of anxiousness. Journal of Personality, 1969, *37*(1), 1-24.

Endler, N. S., & Magnusson, D. Toward an interactional psychology of personality. *Psychological Bulletin,* 1976, *83,* 956-974. (a)

Endler, N. S., & Magnusson, D. Personality and person by situation interactions. In N. S. Endler & F. Magnusson (Eds.), *Interactional psychology and personality.* Washington: Hemisphere Pub. Corp., 1976, (b)

Endler, N. S., & Magnusson, D. (Eds.) *Interactional psychology and personality.* Washington, D.C.: Hemisphere Pub. Corp., 1976. (c)

Endler, N. S., & Magnusson, D. Multidimensional aspects of state and trait anxiety: A cross-cultural study of Canadian and Swedish students. In C. D. Speilberger & R. Diaz-Guerrero (Eds.), *Cross-cultural research on anxiety.* Washington, D.C.: Hemisphere Pub. Corp. (Wiley), 1976. (d)

Endler, N. S., & Magnusson, D. The interactional model of anxiety: An empirical test in an examination situation. *Canadian Journal of Behavioral Science,* 1977, *9,* 101-107.

Endler, N. S., & Okada M. A multidimensional measure of trait anxiety The S-R inventory of general trait anxiousness. *Journal of Consulting and Clinical Psychology,* 1975, *43,* 319-329.

Environmental simulation project. *Environmental adjective check list.* Berkeley, Calif.: Institute of Personality Assessment and Research, University of California, 1972. (a)

Environmental simulation project. *Regional Q-sort deck.* Berkeley, Calif.: Institute of Personality Assessment and Research, University of California, 1972. (b)

Epstein, S. Traits are alive and well. In D. Magnusson & N. S. Endler (Eds.), Personality at the crossroads: Current issues in interactional psychology. New York: Wiley, 1977, pp. 83-98.

Erdelyi, M. H. A new look at the new look: Perceptual defence and vigilance. *Psychological Review,* 1974, *81,* 1-25.

Erdelyi, M. H., & Goldberg, B. Let's not sweep repression under the rug: Towards a cognitive psychology of repression. In J. Kihlström & F. Evans (Eds.), *Functional pathologies of memory*, New York: L. Erlbaum Associates, 1979.

Ericsson, K. A., & Simon, H. A. *Retrospective verbal reports as data*. Unpublished manuscript, 1978.

Evans, F. J. Hypnosis and sleep: Techniques for exploring cognitive activity during sleep. In E. Fromm & R. Shor (Eds.), *Hypnosis: Research, developments and perspectives*. Chicago: Aldine-Atherton, 1972, pp. 43–83.

Fanning, D. M. Families in flats. *British Medical Journal*, 1967, *4*, 382–386.

Feather, N. T. Organization and discrepancy in cognitive structures. *Psychological Review*, 1971, *87*, 355–378.

Feinberg, J. Action and responsibility. In M. Black (Ed.), *Philosophy in America*. Ithaca, N.Y.: Cornell University Press, 1965.

Feshbach, S. The environment of personality. *American Psychologist*, 1978, *33*, 447–455.

Festinger, L., & Carlsmith, J. M. Cognitive consequences of forced compliance. *Journal of Abnormal and Social Psychology*, 1959, *58*, 203–210.

Feuerstein, R. *The learning potential assessment device* (LPAD). Baltimore, Md.: University Park Press, 1979.

Finney, J. W. Friends' interests: A cluster-analytic study of college student peer environments, personality and behavior. *Journal of Youth and Adolescence*, 1979.

Firey, W. Sentiment and symbolism as ecological variables. *American Psychological Review*, 1945, *10*, 140–148.

Fischhoff, B., Slovic, P., & Lichtenstein, S. How safe is safe enough? A psychometrics study of attitudes towards technological risks and benefits. *Policy Sciences*, 1978, *9*, 127–152.

Fiske, D. W. Personologies, Abstractions, and Interaction. In D. Magnusson & N. S. Endler (Eds.), *Personality at the Crossroads, Current issues; Interactional Psychology*. Hillsdale, N.J.: Lawrence Erlbaum Associates, 1977.

Fiske, D. W. *Strategies for personality research: The observation versus interpretation of behavior*. San Francisco: Jossey-Bass, 1978.

Fiske, D. W., & Rice, L. Intraindividual response variability. *Psychological Bulletin*, 1955, *52*, 217–250.

Flanders, N. A. *Analyzing teaching behavior*. Reading, Mass.: Addison-Wesley, 1974.

Flavell, J. H. *The development of role-taking and communication skills in children*. New York: John Wiley, 1968.

Flood, M., & Endler, N. S. The interactional model of anxiety: An empirical test in an athletic competition situation. *Journal of Research in Personality*, 1980, *14*, 329–339.

Forehand, G., & Gilmer, B. V. H. Environmental variation in studies of organizational behavior. *Psychological Bulletin*, 1964, *62*, 361–382.

Forgas, J. P. The perception of social episodes: Categorical and dimensional representations in two different social millieus. *Journal of Personality and Social Psychology*, 1976, *34*, 199–209.

Forgas, J. P., Argyle, M., & Ginsburg, G. P. Person perception as a function of the interaction episode: The fluctuating structure of an academic group. *Journal of Social Psychology*, 1979, *109*, 207–222.

Frank, L. Man's multidimensional environment. *Scientific Monthly*, 1943, *56*, 344–357.

Frankenhaeuser, M. The quality of life: Criteria for behavioral adjustment. *International Journal of Psychology*, 1977, *12*, 88–110.

Frankenhaeuser, M. Sex differences in reactions to psychosocial stressors and psychoactive drugs. In L. Levi (Ed.), *Decease: The productive and reproductive age*. London: Oxford University Press, 1978.

Frankl, V. E. *Psychotherapy and existentialism*. London: Harmondsworth, 1973.

Fransella, F., & Bannister, D. *A manual for repertory grid technique.* London: Academic Press, 1977.

Frederiksen, N. Toward a taxonomy of situations. *American Psychologists,* 1972, *27,* 114–123.

French, J. R. P., Rodgers, W., & Cobb, S. Adjustment as person-environment fit. In G. Coelho, D. A. Hamburgh, & J. E. Adams (Eds.), *Coping and adaption.* New York: Basic Books, 1974. pp. 316–333.

Fried, M. Grieving for a lost home. In L. J. Duh, (Ed.), *The urban condition.* New York: Basil Books, 1963.

Fried, M., & Gleicher, P. Some sources of residential satisfaction in an urban slum. *Journal of the American Institute of Planners,* 1961, *27,* 305–315.

Friedlander, B. Z. Receptive language development in infancy: Issues and problems. *Merrill-Palmer Quarterly of Behavior and Development,* 1970, *16,* 7–51.

Friedmann, A., Zimring, C., & Zube, E. H. *Environmental design evaluation.* New York: Plenum, 1978.

Fuller, J. L. Situational analysis: A classification of organism-field interactions. *Psychological Review,* 1950, *57,* 3–18.

Funder, D. C. *The person-situation interaction in attitude change.* Unpublished doctoral dissertation, Stanford University, 1979.

Gagne, R. M., & Paradise, N. E. Abilities and learning sets in knowledge acquisition. *Psychological Monographs,* 1961, *75* (14, Whole No. 518).

Galle, O. R., Gove, W. R., & McPherson, J. M. Population density and pathology: What are the relations for man? *Science,* 1972, *176,* 23–30.

Galton, F. *Hereditary genius: An inquiry into its laws and consequences.* London: MacMillan, 1869.

Galton, F. *Inquiries into human faculty and its development.* London: J. M. Dent and Sons, 1907.

Gans, H. J. *The levittowners.* New York: Vintage, 1967.

Garfinkel, H. Trust and stable action. In O. J. Harvey (Ed.), *Motivation and social interaction.* New York: Ronald, 1963.

Garfinkel, H. *Studies in ethnomethodology.* Englewood Cliffs, N.J.: Prentice-Hall, 1967.

Garfinkel, H. Studies of the routine grounds of everyday activities. In D. Sudnow (Ed.), *Studies in social interaction.* New York: Free Press, 1972.

Gärling, T. Studies in visual perception of architectual spaces and rooms: IV. The relation of judged depth to judged size of space under different viewing conditions. *Scandinavian Journal of Psychology,* 1970, *11,* 133–145.

Gärling, T. A multidimensional scaling and semantic differential technique study of the perception of environmental settings. *Scandinavian Journal of Psychology,* 1976, *17,* 323–332.

George, J. R., & Bishop, L. K. Relationship of organizational structure and teacher personality characteristics to organizational climate. *Administrative Science Quarterly,* 1971, *16,* 467–475.

Gerbner, G., Gross, L., Jackson-Beeck, M., Jeffries-Fox, S., & Signorielli, N. Cultural indicators: Violence profile no. 9. *Journal of Communication,* 1978, *28,* 176–207.

Gergen, K. J. Toward generative theory. *Journal of Personality and Social Psychology,* 1978, *36,* 1344–1360.

Gerson, E. M., & Gerson, M. S. The social framework of place perspectives. In G. T. Moore & R. G. Golledge (Eds.), *Environmental knowing.* Stroudsburg, Pa.: Dowden, Hutchinson, and Ross, 1976. pp. 196–205.

Gerst, M., & Moos, R. The social ecology of university student residences. *Journal of Educational Psychology,* 1972, *63,* 513–535.

Gesell, A., & Gesell, B. S. *The normal child and primary education.* Boston: Ginn & Co., 1912.

Gibson, J. J. The concept of the stimulus in psychology. *American Psychologist,* 1960, *15,* 694–703.

Gibson, J. J. The theory of affordances. In R. Shaw & J. Bransford (Eds.), *Perceiving, acting, and knowing.* Hillsdale, N.J.: Lawrence Erlbaum Associates, 1977. pp. 76–82.

Glass, D. C., & Singer, J. E. *Urban stress.* New York: Academic Press, 1972.

Glucksberg, S., & Cowan, G. N. Memory for nonattented auditory material. *Cognitive Psychology,* 1970, *1,* 149–156.

Goffman, E. *The presentation of self in everyday life.* Garden City, N.Y.: Doubleday, 1959.

Goffman, E. The neglected situation. *American Anthropologist,* 1964, *66,* 133–136.

Goffman, E. *Frame analysis.* New York: Harper & Row, 1974.

Goldberg, L. R. Differential attribution of trait-descriptive terms to oneself as compared to well-liked, neutral, and disliked others: A psychometric analysis. *Journal of Personality and Social Psychology,* 1978, *36,* 1012–1029.

Goldberg, L. R. Simple models as simple process? Some research on clinical judgments. *American Psychologists,* 1968, *23,* 483–496.

Goldfried, M. R., & D'Zurilla, T. J. A behavioral-analytic model for assessing competence. In C. D. Spielberger (Ed.), *Current topics in clinical and community psychology* (Vol. 1). New York: Academic Press, 1969. pp. 150–196.

Goldfried, M. R., & Kent, R. N. Traditional versus behavioral personality assessment: A comparison of methodological and theoretical assumptions. *Psychological Bulletin,* 1972, *77,* 409–420.

Golding, S. L. The problem of constructual styles in the analysis of person-situation interactions. In D. Magnusson & N. S. Endler (Eds.), *Personality at the crossroads: Current issues in interactional psychology.* Hillsdale, N.J.: Lawrence Erlbaum Associates, 1977. pp. 401–407.

Goldston, S. E. An overview of primary prevention programming. In D. C. Klein & S. E. Goldston (Eds.), *Primary prevention: An idea whose time has come.* Rockville, Md.: Drew Publication (Adm.), 77-447, 1977. pp. 23–40.

Gore, S. *The influence of social support and related variables in ameliorating the consequences of job loss.* Unpublished doctorial dissertation, University of Pennsylvania, 1973.

Görner, R. Vorgestellter und ausgeführter Tätigkeitsvollzug—eine Möglichkeit zur Erfassung von Denkverläufen in der Arbeitstätigkeit. In W. Hacker, W. Skell, & W. Straub (Eds.), *Arbetspsychologie und wissenschaftlich-technische Revolution.* Berlin: Deutscher Verlag der Wissenschaften, 1968. pp. 59–72.

Gough, H. G. Personality and personality assessment. In M. D. Dunnette (Ed.), *Handbook of industrial and organizational psychology.* Chicago: Rand McNally, 1976.

Graen, G. Role making processes within complex organizations. In M. D. Dunnette (Ed.), *Handbook of industrial and organizational psychology.* Chicago: Rand McNally, 1976.

Graen, G., & Schiemann, W. Leader-member agreement: A vertical dyad linkage approach. *Journal of Applied Psychology,* 1978, *63,* 206–212.

Graham, J. A., Argyle, M., Clarke, D. D., & Maxwell, G. The sequential structure of social episodes. *Semiotica,* in press.

Green, A. W. The social situation in personality theory. *American Sociological Review,* 1942, *7,* 388–393.

Green, B. F. Note on Bem and Funder's scheme for scoring Q-sorts. *Psychological Review,* 1980, *87,* 212–214.

Greenberg, D. J., Uzgiris, I. C., & Hunt, J. McV. Attentional preference and experience: III. Visual familiarity and looking time. *Journal of Genetic Psychology,* 1970, *117,* 123–135.

Hacker, W. Zur Anforderungsabhängigkeit der Nutzung von hierarchischer Ordnung in Sequenzen. *Z. f. Psychol,* 1977, *185* (1), pp. 1–33. (a)

Hacker, W. Coding of hierarchical information in human short-term-memory. *Activitas Nervalis Superior,* 1977, *19*(4), 289–290 (Prague). (b)

Hacker, W. *Allgemeine Arbeits- und Ingenieurpsychologie* (2nd ed). Bern/Stuttgart/Wien: Huber, 1978.

Hacker, W., & Clauss, A. Kognitive Operationen, inneres Modell und Leistung bei einer Montagetätigkeit. In W. Hacker (Ed.), *Psychische Regulation von Arbeitstätigkeiten*. Berlin: Deiutscher Verlag der Wissenschaften. 1976. pp. 88–102.

Hacker, W., & Jatzlau, R. *Ermittlung und Bewertung von Arbeitsinhalten*. Informationen der Technischen Universität Dresden. 1978, 22–15.

Hacker, W., & Meinel, M. Kognitive Komponenten beim erlernen interner Repräsentationen: Sind behaltensoekonomische Representationen stets regulativ zweckmässig? In G. Clauss, J. Gutke, & G. Lehwald (Eds.), *Psychologie und Psykodiagnostik lernaktiven Verhaltens*. 1978. Pp. 54–61. Berlin: Gesellschaft für Psychologie der DDR (Tagungsbericht).

Hackman, J. R., & Oldham, G. R. *The job diagnosis survey: An instrument for the diagnostic of jobs and the evaluation of job redesign projects*. Yale University Technical Report, No. 4, 1974.

Hall, R. The concept of Bureaucracy: An empirical assessment. *American Journal of Sociology*, 1963, *69*, 32–40.

Hall, R., Purcell, A. T., Thorne, R., & Metcalfe, J. Multidimensional scaling analysis of interior designed spaces. *Environment and Behavior*, 1976, *8*, 595–610.

Halpin, A. W., & Crofts, D. B. The organizational climate of schools. *Administrators Notebook*, 1963, *11*, 1–4.

Hamblin, R. L., Jacobsen, R. B., & Miller, J. L. *A mathematical theory of social change*. New York: Wiley, 1973.

Hamilton, D. A cognitive-attributional analysis of stereotyping. In L. Berkowitz (Ed.), *Advances in experimental social psychology*. New York: Academic Press, 1979.

Hammond, K. R. Probabilistic functioning and the chemical method. *Psychological Review*, 1955, *62*, 255–262.

Hampshire, S. Review of: "On human nature," by Edward O. Wilson. *New York Review of Books*, 1978, *35*, 64–69.

Hansen, W. B., & Altman, I. Decorating personal places: A descriptive analysis. *Environment and Behavior*, 1976, *8*, 491–504.

Hardeman, M. (Ed.). *Children's ways of knowing: Nathan Isaacs on education, psychology and Piaget*. New York: Teachers College Press, 1974.

Harré, R. The ethogenic approach: Theory and practice. In L. Berkowitz (Ed.), *Advances in experimental social psychology* (vol. 10). New York: Academic Press, 1977.

Harré, R. Accounts, actions and meanings—the practice of participatory psychology. In M. Brenner, P. March, & M. Brenner (Eds.) *The social contexts of method*. London: Croom Helm, 1978.

Harré, R., & Secord, P. F. *The explanation of social behavior*. Oxford: Blackwell, 1972.

Harris, A. J., & Shakow, D. The clinical significance of numerical measures of slatter on the Standord-Binet. *Psychological Bulletin*, 1937, *34*, 134–150.

Hater, J. J. *Agreement among perceptions of psychological climate: A comparison of within-group and between-group designs*. Unpublished masters thesis. Texas Christian University, 1977.

Hays, W. L. *Statistics for psychologists*. New York: Holt, Rinehart & Winston, 1963.

Hebb, D. O. *The organization of behavior*. New York: Wiley, 1949.

Heber, R. Sociocultural mental retardation: A longitudinal study. In D. Forgays (Ed.), *Primary prevention of psychopathology* (Vol. II). *Environmental influences*. Hanover, N.H.: University Press of New England, 1978. Ch. 4.

Heffler, B. Physiological reactions in an interaction model of behavior. *Reports from the Department of Psychology, the University of Stockholm*, No. 513, 1977.

Heffler, B. The generality of behavioral data V: Cross-situational invariance of self- and peer-ratings. *Reports from the Department of Psychology, the University of Stockholm*, No. 528, 1978.

Heffler, B., & Magnusson, D. The generality of behavioral data IV: Cross-situational invariance of objectively measured behavior. *Reports from the Department of Psychology, the University of Stockholm*, No. 521, 1978.

Heider, F. The description of the psychological environment in the work of Marcel Proust. *Character and Personality*, 1941, *9*, 295-314.

Heise, D. R. *Causal analysis.* New York: Wiley, 1975.

Heller, K. The effects of social support: prevention and treatment implications. In A. P. Goldstein & F. H. Kanfer (Eds.), *Maximizing treatment gains.* New York: Academic Press, 1979.

Heller, K., & Monahan, J. *Psychology and community change.* Homewood, Ill.: Dorsey Press, 1977.

Hellriegel, D., & Slocum, J. W., Jr. Organizational climate measure research and contingencies. *Academy of Management Journal*, 1974, *17*, 255-280.

Hemphill, J. K. *Group dimensions: A manual for their measurement.* Columbus: Ohio State University, 1956.

Henderson, S., & Bostock, T. Coping Behavior: Correlates of survival on a raft. *Australian and New Zealand Journal of Psychiatry*, 1975, *9*, 221-223.

Henderson, S., & Bostock, T. Coping after shipwreck. *British Journal of Psychiatry*, 1977, *131*, 15-20.

Hendrick, C., Martyniuk, O., Spencer, T. J., & Flynn, J. E. Procedures for investigating the effect of light on impression: Simulation of a real space by slides. *Environment and Behavior*, 1977, *9*, 491-510.

Hermann, C. F. International crisis as a situational variable. In J. N. Rosenau (Ed.), *International politics and foreign policy* (Rev. ed.). New York: Free Press, 1969. Pp. 409-421.

Hershberger, R. G., & Cass, R. C. Predicting user response to buildings. In D. H. Carson (Ed.), *Man-environment interactions: Evaluations and applications, Part III.* Stroudsberg, Pa.: Dowden, Hutchinson & Ross, 1974.

Hess, E. H. *The tell-tale eye: How your eyes reveal hidden thoughts and emotions.* New York: Van Nostrand Reinhold, 1975.

Hess, R. D., & Shipman, V. Early experience and the socialization of cognitive modes in children. *Child Development*, 1965, *36*, 869-886.

Heuer, H. Uber Bewegungsprogramme bei willkürlichen Bewegungen. Doctoral Dissertation, Marburg University, 1978.

Hintikka, J. *Knowledge and belief.* Ithaca, N.Y.: Cornell University Press, 1962.

Hodges, W. F., & Felling, J. P. Types of stressful situations and their relation to trait anxiety and sex. *Journal of Consulting and Clinical Psychology*, 1970, *34*, 333-337.

Hogan, R., De Soto, C. B., & Solano, C. Traits, tests and personality research. *American Psychologist*, 1977, *32*, 255-264.

Holland, J. L. *The psychology of vocational choice: A theory of personality types and model environments.* Waltham, Mass.: Blaisdell, 1966.

Holmes, T. H., & Rahe, R. E. The social readjustment rating scale. *Journal of Psychosomatic Research*, 1967, *11*, 213-218.

Holsti, O. R. Cognitive process approaches to decision-making: Foreign policy altors viewed psychologically. *American Behavioral Scientist*, 1976, *20*, 11-32.

Horayangkura, V. Semantic dimensional structures: A methodological approach. *Environment and Behavior*, 1978, *10*, 555-584.

Hornick, C. W., James, L. R., & Jones, A. P. Empirical item keying versus a rational approach to analyzing a psychological climate questionnaire. *Applied Psychological Measurement*, 1977, *4*, 489-500.

Hull, C. L. *Principles of behavior.* New York: Appleton-Century-Crofts, 1943.

Hume, D. An enquiry concerning human understanding. In B. Rand (Ed.), *Modern, classical philosophers.* Boston: Houghton Mifflin, 1936. (Originally published in 1748.)

Humphreys, L. G., & Parsons, C. K. Piagetian tasks measure intelligence and intelligence tests assess cognitive development. *Intelligence*, 1979, *3*, 369-382.

Hundeide, K. *Perspectivity, intentionality and development.* Working paper, Department of Psychology, Oslo University, 1978.

Hunt, J. McV. Piaget's observations as a source of hypothesis concerning motivation. *Merrill-Palmer Quarterly*, 1963, *9*, 263–275. (a)

Hunt, J. McV. Motivation inherent in information processing and action. In J. O. Harvey (Ed.), *Motivation and social interaction: Cognitive determinants.* New York: Ronald Press, 1963. (b)

Hunt, J. McV. Intrinsic motivation and its role in psychological development. In D. Levine (Ed.), *Nebraska symposium on motivation*, 1965, *13*, 189–282. Lincoln: University of Nebraska Press.

Hunt, J. McV. Attentional preference and experience: I. Introduction. *Journal of Genetic Psychology*, 1970, *117*, 99–107.

Hunt, J. McV. Intrinsic motivation and psychological developent. In H. M. Schroder & P. Suedfeld (Eds.), *Personality theory and information processing.* New York: Ronald (ch. 5), 1971.

Hunt, J. McV. Utility of ordinal scales derived from Piaget's observations. *Merrill-Palmer Quarterly*, 1976, *22* (1), 31–45.

Hunt, J. McV. The experiential roots of intention, initiative and trust. To appear in H. I. Day (Ed.), *Advances in intrinsic motivation and aesthetics.* New York: Plenum Pub. Corp. 1981. (a)

Hunt, J. McV. Language acquisition and experience. Manuscript in preparation, 1981. (b)

Hunt, J. McV., & Kirk, G. E. *Compliance with supreme court's mandate on the use of tests: The theoretical and social foundations for job-references tests.* Prepublication draft, University of Illinois, Champaign-Urbana, 1979.

Hunt, J. McV., Mohandessi, K., Ghodssi, M., & Akiyama, M. The psychological development of orphanage-reared infants: Interventions with outcomes (Tehran). *Genetic Psychology Monographs*, 1976, *94*, 177–226.

Hunt, J. McV., & Paraskevopoulos, J. Children's psychological development as a function of the inaccuracy of their mother's knowledge of their abilities. In preparation, 1980.

Hunt, J. McV., Paraskevopoulos, J., Schickedanz, D., & Uzgiris, I. C. Variations in the mean ages of achieving object permanence under diverse conditions of rearing. In B. L. Friedlander, G. M. Sterritt, & G. E. Kirk (Eds.), *The exceptional infant* (Vol. 3): *Assessment and intervention.* New York: Brunner/Mazel, 1975. Pp. 247–262.

Hurrelmann, P., & Stach, H. Testanweisung für die Bewertung der Arbeitssituation der Produktionsarbeiter. Wissenschaftlich-Technisches Zentrum Bauwesen Berlin. Technical Report. 1973.

Hursch, C. J., Hammond, K. R., & Hursch, J. L. Some methodological considerations in multiple-cue probability studies. *Psychological Review*, 1964, *71*, 42–60.

Ichheiser, G. Misinterpretations of personality in everyday life and the psychologist's frame of reference. *Character and Personality*, 1943, *12*, 145–160.

Indik, B. P. The scope of the problem and some suggestions toward a solution. In B. P. Indik & F. W. Berrien (Eds.), *People, groups and organizations.* New York: Teachers College Press, 1968.

Inhaber, H. *Environmental indices.* New York: Wiley, 1976.

Insel, P. M., & Moos, R. H. Psychological environment: Expanding the scope of human ecology. *American Psychologist*, 1974, *29*, 179–188.

Ittelson, W. H. Environment perception a:d contemporary perceptual theory. In W. H. Ittelson (Ed.), *Environment and cognition.* New York: Seminar Press, 1973.

Ittelson, W. H., Proshansky, H. M., Rivlin, L. G., & Winkel, G. H. *An introduction to environmental psychology.* New York: Holt, Rinehart and Winston, 1974.

Jacobs, J. *The death and life of great American cities.* New York: Vintage, 1961.

Jahoda, M. A social-psychological approach to the study of culture. *Human Relations*, 1961, *14*, 23–30.

James, L. R., Gent, M. J., Hater, J. J., & Coray, K. E. Correlates of psychological influence: An illustration of the psychological climate approach to work environment perceptions. *Personnel Psychology*, 1979, *32*, 563–588.

James, L. R., Hartman, A., Stebbins, M. W., & Jones, A. P. Relationships between psychological climate and a VIE model for work motivation. *Personnel Psychology*, 1977, *30*, 229-254.

James, L. R., Hater, J. J., Gent, M. J., & Bruni, J. R. Psychological climate: Implications from cognitive social learning theory and interactional psychology. *Personnel Psychology*, 1978, *31*, 783-813.

James, L. R., Irons, D. M., & Hater, J. J. *Causal factors in leadership behaviors: Situational constraints versus reciprocal relationships with subordinate performance.* Fort Worth, Texas: Institute of Behavioral Research, Texas: Christian University, Technical Report, No. 78-16, 1978.

James, L. R., & Jones, A. P. Organizational climate: A review of theory and research. *Psychological Bulletin*, 1974, *81*, 1096-1112.

James, L. R., & Jones, A. P. Organizational structure: A review of structural dimensions and their conceptual relationships with attitudes and behavior. *Organizational Behavior and Human Performance*, 1976, *16*, 74-113.

James, L. R., & Jones, A. P. *Perceived job characteristics and job satisfaction: An examination of reciprocal causation.* (IBR Report No. 79-5). Fort Worth, Texas: Texas Christian University, Institute of Behavioral Research, 1979.

James, L. R., & Singh, K. An introduction to the logic assumptions and basic analytic procedures of two-stage least squares. *Psychological Bulletin*, 1978, *85*, 1104-1122.

James, W. Pragmatism's conception of truth. In W. Barrett & H. D. Aiken (Eds.), *Philosophy in the twentieth century* (Vol. 1). New York: Random House, 1962.

Janisse, P. J., & Palys, T. S. Frequency and intensity of anxiety in university students. *Journal of Personality Assessment*, 1976, *40*, 502-515.

Jencks, Ch. *Inequality.* New York: Basil Books, 1972.

Jensen, A. R. How much can we boost IQ and scholastic achievement? *Harvard Educational Review*, 1969, *39*, 1-123.

Jensen, A. R. *Educability and group differences.* New York: Harper and Row, 1973.

Jessor, R. Phenomenological personality theories and the data language of psychology. *Psychological Review*, 1956, *63*, 173-180.

Jessor, R. The problem of reductionism in psychology. *Psychological Review*, 1958, *65*, 170-178.

Jessor, R. Issues in the phenomenological approach to personality. *Journal of Individual Psychology*, 1961, *17*, 27-38.

Jessor, R., Graves, T. D., Hanson, R. C., & Jessor, S. L. *Society, Personality and Deviant Behavior: A study of a tri-ethnic community.* New York: Holt, Rinehart & Winston, 1968. (Reprinted by Krieger Publishing Co., 645 New York Avenue, Huntington, N.Y., 1975.)

Jessor, R., & Jessor, S. L. The perceived environment in behavioral science: Some conceptual issues and some illustrative data. *American Behavioral Scientist*, 1973, *16*, 801-828.

Jessor, R., & Jessor, S. L. *Problem behavior and psychosocial development: A longitudinal study of youth.* New York: Academic Press, 1977.

Johannsen, W. *Elemente der exakten Erblichkeitslehre.* Jena: Fischer, 1909.

Johnson, J. E. *Wing leader.* London: Chatto & Windus, 1956.

Johnson, J. H., & Sarason, I. G. Recent developments in research on life stress. In V. Hamilton & D. M. Warburton (Eds.), *Human stress and cognition: An information processing approach.* London: Wiley, 1979, 205-233.

Johnston, J. J. *Econometric methods* (2nd ed.). New York: Mc-Graw-Hill, 1972.

Jones, A. P., & James, L. R. Psychological climate: Dimensions and relationships of individual and aggregated work environment perceptions. *Organizational Behavior and Human performance*, 1979, *23*, 201-250.

Jones, A. P., James, L. R., & Bruni, J. R. Perceived leadership behavior and employee confidence in the leader as moderated by job involvement. *Journal of Applied Psychology*, 1975, *60*, 146-149.

Jones, A. P., James, L. R., Bruni, J. R., & Sells, S. B. Black-white differences in job satisfaction and its correlates. *Personnel Psychology*, 1975, *30*, 5-16.

Jones, E. E., & Davis, K. E. From actors to dispositions: The attribution process in person perception. In L. Berkowitz (Ed.), *Advances in experimental social psychology*. New York: Academic Press, 1965.

Jones, E. E., & Gerard, H. B. Foundations of social psychology. New York: Wiley, 1967.

Jones, E. E., Kanouse, D., Kelley, H. H., Nisbett, R. E., Valins, S., & Weiner, B. *Attribution: Perceiving the causes of behavior*. New York: General Learning Press, 1972.

Jones, E. E., & Nisbett, R. The Actor and the observer: Divergent perceptions of the causes of behavior. In E. E. Jones, D. Kanduse, H. H. Nisbett, S. Valins, & B. Weiner (Eds.), *Attribution: Perceiving the causes of behavior*. New York: General Learning Press, 1972.

Jones, E. E., & Thibaut, J. W. Interaction goals as bases of inference in interpersonal perception. In R. Tagiuri & L. Petrullo (Eds.), *Person perception and interpersonal behavior*. Stanford: Stanford University Press, 1958. Pp. 151-178.

Jones, R. A. *Self-fulfilling prophecies: Social psychological and physiological effects of expectancies*. Hillsdale, N.J.: Lawrence Erlbaum Associates, 1977.

Jöreskog, K. G. Structural analysis of covariance and correlation matrices. *Psychometrika*, 1978, *43*, 443-477.

Kahana, E. A congruence model of person-environment interaction. In P. G. Windley, T. O. Byerts, & F. G. Ernest (Eds.), *Theory development in environment and aging*. Washington, D.C.: Gerontology Society, 1975.

Kantor, J. R. *Principles of psychology* (Vol. 1). Bloomington, Ill.: Principia Press, 1924.

Kantor, J. R. *Principles of psychology* (Vol. 2). Bloomington, Ill.: Principia Press, 1926.

Kaplan, A. *The conduct in inquiry*. San Francisco: Chandler, 1964.

Kaplan, S. An informal model for the prediction of preference. In E. H. Zube, R. O. Brush, & J. G. Fabos (Eds.), *Landscape assessment: Values, perceptions and resources*. Dowden, Hutchinson & Ross, 1975. Pp. 91-101.

Kaplan, S. Concerning the power of content-identifying methodologies. In E. H. Zube & T. Daniel (Eds.), *Environmental aesthetics*. Washington, D.C.: U.S. Forest Service, 1978.

Kasielke, E., Moebius, S., & Scholze, C. Der Beswerdenerfassungsbogen als neurosendiagnostisches Verfahren. In Helm, Kasielke, & Mehl (Eds.), *Neurosendiagnostik*. Berlin: Deutscher Verlag der Wissenschaften, 1974. Pp. 198-227.

Kasmar, J. V. The development of a usable lexicon of environmental descriptors. *Environment and Behavior*, 1970, *2*, 153-169.

Kasvio, L. *Strategien beim erlernen funktioneller Beziehungen*. Informationen der Technischen Universität Dresden, No. 22-9, 1978.

Kates, R. W. Experiencing the environment as hazard. In S. Wapner, S. B. Cohen, & B. Kaplan (Eds.), *Experiencing the environment*. New York: Plenum, 1976. Pp. 133-156.

Kates, R. W. (Ed.) *Managing technological hazard: Research needs and opportunities*. Boulder, CO: Institute of Behavioral Science, University of Colorado, 1977.

Katona, G. Toward a macropsychology. *American Psychologist*, 1979, *34*, 118-126.

Kelley, G. A. *The psychology of personal constructs*. New York: Norton, 1955.

Kelley, H. H. Attribution theory in social psychology. *Nebraska Symposium on motivation*. Lincoln: University of Nebraska Press, 1967.

Kelley, H. H., & Thibaut, J. W. *Interpersonal relations: A theory of interdependence*. New York: Wiley, 1978.

Kelley, H. H., Shure, G. H., Deutsch, M., Faucheux, C., Lanzetta, J. T., Moscovici, S., Nuttin, J. M., Rabbie, J. M., & Thibaut, J. W. A comparative experimental study of negotiation behavior. *Journal of Personality and Social Psychology*, 1970, *16*, 411-438.

Kendall, P. C. Anxiety: States, traits-situations? *Journal of Consulting and Clinical Psychology*, 1978, *46*, 280-287.

Kent, G. G., Davis, J. D., & Shapiro, D. A. Resources required in the construction and reconstruction of conversation. *Journal of Personality and Social Psychology*, 1978, *36*, 13–22.

Kessel, F. S. The philosophy of science as proclaimed and science as practiced: "Identity" or "Dualism"? *American Psychologist*, 1970, *24*, 999–1005.

Kessler, M., & Albee, G. W. Primary prevention. *Annual Review of Psychology*, 1975, *26*, 557–591.

Klaus, M., Jerauld, R., Kreger, N., McAlpine, W., Steffa, M., & Kennel, J. Maternal attachment: Importance of the first post-partum days. *New England Journal of Medicine*, 1972, *286*, 460–463.

Klinger, E. Modes of normal conscious flow. In K. S. Pope & J. L. Singer (Eds.), *The stream of consciousness*. New York: Wiley, 1978.

Knox, R. E., & Douglas, R. L. Trivial incentives, marginal comprehension and dubious generalizations from prisoner's dilemma studies. *Journal of Personality and Social Psychology*, 1971, *20*, 160–165.

Koffka, K. *Principles of gestalt psychology*. New York: Harcourt, 1935.

Kohn, M. L. The interaction of social class and other factors in the etiology of schizophrenia. *American Journal of Psychiatry*, 1976, *133*, 177–180.

Kohn, M. L., & Schooler, C. Occupational experience and psychological functioning: An assessment of reciprocal effects. *American Sociological Review*, 1973, *38*, 97–118.

Koneya, M. Location and interaction in row-and-column seating arrangements. *Environment and Behavior*, 1976, *8*, 265–282.

Krauss, R. M., Geller, V., & Olson, C. *Modalities and cues in the detection of deception*. Paper delivered at the American Psychological Association, Sept. 2, 1976.

Kuhn, T. S. *The structure of scientific revolutions*. Chicago: University of Chicago Press, 1962.

Kuhn, T. S. Reflections on my critics. In I. Lakatos & A. Musgrave (Eds.), *Criticism and the growth of knowledge*. Cambridge: University of Cambridge Press, 1970.

Küller, R. The perception of an interior as a function of its colour. In B. Honikman (Ed.), *Architectural Psychology 1970*, 1971. London: Riba publication. 49–53.

Lackner, J. R., & Garrett, M. F. Resolving ambiguity: Effects of biasing context in the unattended ear. *Cognition*, 1972, *1*, 359–372.

Larson, R., & Csikszentmihalyi, M. Experimental correlates of time alone in adolescence. *Journal of Personality*, 1978, *46*, 677–693.

Laumann, E. O., & House, J. S. Living room styles and social attributes: The pattering of material artifacts in a modern urban community. *Sociology and Social Research*, 1970, *54*, 321–342.

Lazarus, R. S. Psychological stress and the coping process. New York: McGraw Hill, 1966.

Lazarus, R. S. Personality. (2nd ed.) Englewood Cliffs; N.J.: Prentice-Hall, 1971.

Lazarus, R. S. *The riddle of man. An introduction to psychology*. Englewood Cliffs, N.J.: Prentice-Hall, 1974.

Lazarus, R. S., Averill, J. R., & Opton, E. M. The psychology of coping: Issues of research and assessment. In G. V. Coelho, D. A. Hamburg, & J. E. Adams (Eds.), *Coping and Adaption*. New York: Basic Books Inc., 1974.

Lazarus, R. S., & Launier, R. Stress-related transactions between person and environment. In L. A. Pervin & M. Lewis (Eds.), *Perspectives in interactional psychology*. New York: Plenum, 1978. pp. 287–327.

Lazarus, R. S., Opton, E., Jr., Tomita, M., & Kodama, M. A cross-cultural study of stress reaction patterns in Japan. *Journal of Personality and Social Psychology*, 1966, *4*, 622–633.

Leahy, A. M. Nature-nurture and intelligence. *Genetic Psychology Monographs*, 1935, *17*, 235–308.

Leff, H. L. *Experience, environment and human potentials*. New York: Oxford University Press, 1978.

Lenneberg, E. J. *The biological basis of language*. New York: Wiley, 1967.

Levinson, B. W. States of awareness during general anesthesia. In J. Lassner (Ed.), *Hypnosis and psychosomatic medicine*. New York: Springer Verlag, 1967. Pp. 200-207.

Levinson, D. J. *The seasons of a man's life*. New York: Knopf, 1978.

Levy, L. H. *Psychological interpretation*. New York: Holt, Rinehart & Winston, 1963.

Lewin, K. *A dynamic theory of personality*. New York, London: McGraw-Hill, 1935.

Lewin, K. *Principles of topological psychology*. New York: McGraw-Hill, 1936.

Lewin, K. Field theory and learning. In D. Cartwright (Ed.), *Field theory in social science: Selected theoretical papers by Kurt Lewin*. New York: Harper, 1951. (a)

Lewin, K. Defining the "field at a given time." in D. Cartwright (Ed.), *Field theory in social science: Selected theoretical papers by Kurt Lewin*. New York: Harper, 1951. (b)

Lewin, K. *Field theory in social science*. New York: Harper, 1951. (c)

Lewis, J. L. Semantic processing of unattended messages using dichotic listening. *Journal of Experimental Psychology*, 1970, *85*, 225-228.

Lewis, M. Situational analysis and the study of behavioral development. In L. A. Pervin & M. Lewis (Eds.), *Perspectives in interactional psychology*. New York: Plenum, 1978, pp. 49-66.

Lippa, R. Expressive control and the leakage of dispositional introversion-extraversion during role-played teaching. *Journal of Personality*, 1976, *44*, 541-559.

Litton, R. B., Jr. Aesthetic dimensions of the landscape. In J. V. Krutilla (Ed.), *Natural environment: Studies in theoretical and applied analysis*. Baltimore, Md.: John Hopkins University Press, 1972, pp. 262-291.

Litwin, G. H., & Stringer, R. A. *Motivation and organizational climate*. Cambridge, Mass.: Harvard University Press, 1968.

Loo, C. M. Behavior problem indices: The differential effects of spatial density on low and high scores. *Environment and Behavior*, 1978, *10*, 489-510.

Lundgren, U. P. *Model analysis of pedagogical processes*. Lund: Gleerup, 1977.

Lynch, K. *The image of the city*. Cambridge, Mass.: MIT Press, 1960.

MacKay, D. Aspects of the theory of comprehension. Memory and attention *Quarterly Journal of Experimental Psychology*, 1973, *25*, 22-40.

Magnusson, D. *Test theory*. Reading, Mass.: Addision-Wesley, 1967.

Magnusson, D. An analysis of situational dimensions. *Perceptual and Motor Skills*, 1971, *32*, 851-867.

Magnusson, D. The individual in the situation: Some studies on individuals' perception of situations. *Studia Psychologica*, 1974, *16*, 124-132.

Magnusson, D. The person and the situation in an interactional model of behavior. *Scandinavian Journal of Psychology*, 1976, *17*, 253-271.

Magnusson, D. On the psychological situation. Report from the Department of Psychology, University of Stockholm, No. 544, 1978.

Magnusson, D. Situational effects of data in empirical personality research. Paper presented at the XXII International Congress of Psychology, Leipzig, 1980. (a)

Magnusson, D. Personality in an interactional paradigm of research. *Zeitschrift für Differentielle und Diagnostische Psychologie*, 1980, *1*, 17-34 (b)

Magnusson, D., Situational factors in research on stress and anxiety: Sex and age differences. In C. D. Spielberger, I. G. Sarason, & P. D. Defares, *Stress and Anxiety* (Vol. 10), Washington, D.C.: Hemisphere, in press.

Magnusson, D., Dunér, A., & Zetterblom, G. *Adjustment: A longitudinal study*. New York: Wiley (Stockholm: Almqvist & Wiksell), 1975.

Magnusson, D., & Ekehammar, B. An analysis of situational dimensions: A replication. *Multivariate Behavioral Research*, 1973, *8*, 331-339.

Magnusson, D., & Ekehammar, B. Anxiety profiles based on both situational and response factors. *Multivariate Behavioral Research*, 1975, *10*, 27-43. (a)

Magnusson, D., & Ekehammar, B. Perceptions of and reactions to stressful situations. *Journal of Personality and Social Psychology*, 1975, *31*(6), 1147-1154. (b)

Magnusson, D., & Ekehammar, B. Similar situations–similar behaviors? *Journal of Research in Personality*, 1978, *12*, 41–48.

Magnusson, D., & Endler, N. S. (Eds.). *Personality at the crossroads: Current issues in interactional psychology*. Hillsdale, N.J.: Lawrence Erlbaum Associates, 1977. (a)

Magnusson, D., & Endler, N. S. Interactional psychology: Present status and future prospects. In D. Magnusson & N. S. Endler (Eds.), *Personality at the crossroads: Current issues in interactional psychology*. Hillsdale, N.J.: Lawrence Erlbaum Associates, 1977. (b)

Magnusson, D., & Heffler, B. The generalization of behavioral data. III. Generalization potential as a function of the number of observation instances. *Multivariate Behavioral Research*, 1969, *4*, 29–42.

Magnusson, D., Gerzén, M., & Nyman, B. The generality of behavioral data: I. Generalizations from observation on one occasion. *Multivariate Behavioral Research*, 1968, *3*, 295–320.

Magnusson, D., & Stattin, H. *How unique and stable are individual cross-situational patterns of behavior?* Report from the Department of Psychology, the University of Stockholm, 1978, No. 534. (a)

Magnusson, D., & Stattin, H. A cross-cultural comparison of anxiety responses in an interactional frame of reference. *International Journal of Psychology*, 1978, *13*, 317–332. (b)

Magnusson, D., & Stattin, H. Situation-outcome contingencies of threatening experiences. Department of Psychology, the University of Stockholm (in manuscript), 1980.

Magnusson, D., & Stattin, H. *Threatening situations: A conceptual and empirical analysis*. Department of Psych., Univ. of Stockholm. Manuscript, 1981.

Mahoney, M. J. *Cognition and behavior modification*. Cambridge, Mass.: Ballinger, 1974.

Mahoney, M. J. Reflections on the cognitive-learning trend in psychotherapy. *American Psychologist*, 1977, *32*, 5–13.

Mahoney, M. J. Psychotherapy and the structure of personal revolutions. In M. J. Mahoney (Ed.), *Psychotherapy process: Current issues and future directions*. New York: Plenum, 1980.

Maier, N. R. F. Reasoning in humans: The solution of a problem and its appearance in consciousness. *Journal of Comparative Psychology*, 1931, *12*, 181–194.

Mann, J. W. Rivals of different rank. *Journal of Social Psychology*, 1963, *61*, 11–28.

Mann, L. Queue culture: The waiting line as a social system. *American Journal of Social Psychology*, 1969, *75*, 340–354.

Mann, R. D., Gibbard, G. S. & Hartman, J. J. *Interpersonal Styles and Group Development*. New York: Wiley, 1967.

Mannheim, K. *Essays on the sociology of knowledge*. Oxford: Oxford University Press, 1952.

Marsh, P., Rosser, E., & Harré, R. *The rules of disorder*. London: Routledge & Kegan Paul, 1978.

Markus, H. Self-schemata and processing information about the self. *Journal of Personality and Social Psychology*, 1977, *35*, 63–78.

Masling, J. The influence of situational and interpersonal variables in projective testing. *Psychological Bulletin*, 1960, *57*, 65–85.

Masterman, M. The nature of a paradigm. In I. Laktos & A. Musgrave (Eds.), *Criticism and the growth of knowledge*. Cambridge: University of Cambridge Press, 1970.

Matern, B. Zum Einfluss der ARt der Signald Arbeitung auf das erlernen funktioneller Beziehungen. In W. Hacker (Ed.), *Psychische Regulation von Arbetstätigkeiten*. Berlin: Deutscher Verlag der Wissenschaften, 1976, pp. 39–52.

Matheny, A. P., Jr., & Dolan, A. B. Persons, situations, and time: A genetic view of behavioral change in children. *Journal of Personality and Social Psychology*, 1975, *32*, 1106–1110.

McCormick, E. J., Jeanneret, P. R., & Mecham, R. C. *The development and background at the position analysis questionnaire (PAQ)*. Occupational Research Center. Purdue University, 1969.

McGrath, J. E. Stress and behavior in organizations. In M. D. Dunette (Ed.), *Handbook of industrial and organizational psychology*. Chicago: Rand McNally, 1976, 1351–1395.

McKechnie, G. E. *Manual for the environmental response inventory*. Palo Alto, Calif.: Consulting Psychologists Press, 1974.

McKechnie, G. E. Simulation techniques in environmental psychology. In D. Stokols (Ed.), *Perspectives on environment and behavior: Theory, research and applications.* New York: Plenum, 1977.

McKechnie, G. E. Environmental dispositions: Concepts and measures. In P. McReynolds (Ed.), *Advances in psychological assessment* (Vol. 4) San Francisco, Calif.: Jossey-Bass, 1978. Pp. 141-178.

McReynolds, P. Introduction. In P. McReynolds (Ed.), *Advances in psychological assessment* (Vol. 2). Palo Alto, Calif.: Science and Behavior Books, 1971. Pp. 1-13.

Mead, G. H. *Mind, self, and society.* Chicago: University of Chicago, 1934.

Medin, D., & Schaffer, M. Context theory of classification learning. *Psychological Review, 1978, 85,* 207-238.

Meehl, P. Schizotaxia, schizotypy, schizophrenia. *American Psychologist, 1962, 17,* 827-838.

Mehrabian, A., & Diamond, S. G. Effects of furniture arrangement. Props and personality on social interaction. *Journal of Personality and Social Psychology, 1971, 20,* 18-30.

Mehrabian, A., & Russell, J. A. *An approach to environmental psychology.* Cambridge, Mass.: MIT Press, 1974.

Meichenbaum, D. *Cognitive-behavior modification: An interactive approach.* New York: Plenum, 1977.

Menzel, H. Meaning—Who needs it? In M. Brenner, P. Marsh, & M. Brenner (Eds.), *The social contexts of method.* London: Croom Helm, 1978.

Merleau-Ponty, M. *Phenomenology of perception.* London: Routledge & Kegen Paul, 1962.

Messick, D. M., & McClintock, C. G. Motivational basis of choice in experimental games. *Journal of Experimental Social Psychology, 1968, 4,* 1-25.

Michelson, W. *Man and his urban environment: A sociological approach* (2nd Ed.). Reading, Mass.: Addison-Wesley, 1976.

Miller, D. R. The study of social relationships: Situation, identity and social interaction. In S. Koch (Ed.), *Psychology: A study of science* (Vol. 5). New York: McGraw-Hill, 1963, pp. 639-737.

Miller, G. A., Galanter, E., & Pribram, K. H. *Plans and the structure of behavior.* New York: Holt, Rinehart & Winston, 1960.

Miller, N. E., Sears, R. R., Mowrer, O. H., Doob, L. W., & Dollard, J. The frustration-aggression hypothesis. *Psychological Review, 1941, 48,* 337-342.

Miller, N. E., & Dollard, J. *Social learning and imitation.* New Haven, Conn.: Yale University Press, 1941.

Milner, E. A study of the relationship between reading readiness in grade one school children and patterns of parent-child interactions. *Child Development, 1951,* 95-122.

Minsky, M. A framework for representing knowledge. In P. H. Winston (Ed.), *The psychology of computer vision.* New York: McGraw-Hill, 1975.

Mischel, W. Theory and research on the antecedents of self-imposed delay of reward. In B. A. Maher (Ed.), *Progress in experimental personality research* (Vol. 3). New York: Academic Press, 1966.

Mischel, W. *Personality and assessment.* New York: Wiley, 1968.

Mischel, W. Toward a cognitive social learning reconceptualization of personality. *Psychological Review,* 1973, *80,* 252-283.

Mischel, W. Processes in delay of gratification. In L. Berkowitz (Ed.), *Advances in experimental social psychology* (Vol 7). New York: Academic Press, 1974.

Mischel, W. *Introduction to personality.* New York: Holt, Rinehart & Winston, 1976.

Mischel, W. The interaction of person and situation. In D. Magnusson & N. S. Endler (Eds.), *Personality at the crossroads: Current issues in interactional psychology.* Hillsdale, N.J.: Lawrence Erlbaum Associates, 1977, pp. 333-352. (a)

Mischel, W. On the future of personality measurement. *American Psychologist,* 1977, *32,* 246-254. (b)

Mitchell, J. V., Jr. The identification of student personality characteristics related to perceptions of the school environment. *School Review,* 1968, *76,* 50-59.

de Montaigne, M. Of the inconsistency of our actions. In D. M. Frame (translator), *Selected essays.* Roslyn, N.Y.: Walter J. Black, 1580, 1943.

Moos, R. H. Conceptualizations of human environments. *American Psychologists,* 1973, *28,* 652-665.

Moos, R. H. *Evaluating treatment environments: A social ecological approach.* New York: Wiley, 1974.

Moos, R. H. Assessment and impact of social climate. In P. McReynolds (Ed.), *Advances in psychological assessment* (Vol. 3). San Francisco, Calif.: Jossey-Bass, 1975.

Moos, R. H. *The human context: Environmental determinants of behavior.* New York: Wiley, 1976.

Moos, R. H. Social environments of university student living groups: Architectural and organizational correlates. *Environment and Behavior,* 1978, *10,* 109-126.

Moos, R. H., & VanDort, B. Student physical symptoms and the social climate of college living groups. *American Journal of Community Psychology,* 1979, *7,* 31-43.

Murray, H. A. *Explorations in personality.* New York: Oxford University Press, 1938.

Murray, H. A. Toward a classification of interaction. In T. Parsons & E. A. Shils (Eds.) *Toward a general theory of action.* Cambridge: Harvard University Press, 1951.

Murray, H. A. Studies of stressful interpersonal disputation. *American Psychologist,* 1963, *18,* 28-36.

Neisser, N. *Cognition and reality: Principles and implications of cognitive psychology.* San Francisco: W. H. Freeman, 1976.

Nemeth, C. A critical analysis of research utilizing the prisoner's dilemma paradigm for the study of bargaining. In L. Berkowitz (Ed.), *Advances in experimental social psychology* (Vol. 6). New York: Academic Press, 1972.

Nesselroade, J. R., & Baltes, P. B. Adolescent personality development and historical change: 1970-1972. *Monographs of the Society for Research in Child Development,* 1974, *39* (Serial No. 154), 1-80.

Newman, O. *Defensible space.* New York: Macmillan, 1973.

Newtson, D., Engquist, G., & Bois, J. The objective basis of behavior units. *Journal of Personality and Social Psychology,* 1977, *35,* 847-862.

Nisbett, R. E. Interaction versus main effects as goals in personality research. In D. Magnusson & N. S. Endler (Eds.), *Personality at the Crossroads: Current issues in interactional psychology.* Hillsdale, N.J.: Lawrence Erlbaum Associates, 1977, p. 235-241.

Nisbett, R., Caputo, C., Legant, P., & Maracek, J. Behavior as seen by the actor and as seen by the observer. *Journal of Personality and Social Psychology,* 1973, *27,* 154-165.

Nisbett, R. E., & Ross, L. D. *Human inference: Strategies and shortcomings of informal judgment.* Century Series in Psychology. Englewood Cliffs, N.J.: Prentice-Hall, 1979.

Nisbett, R. E., & Wilson, T. D. Telling more than we can know: Verbal reports on mental processes. *Psychological Review,* 1977, *84,* 231-259.

Norman, D. A. Memory while shadowing. *Quarterly Journal of Experimental Psychology,* 1969, *21,* 85-93.

Norman, W. T. Toward an adequate taxonomy of personality attributes: Replicated factor structure in peer nomination personality ratings. *Journal of Abnormal and Social Psychology,* 1963, *66,* 574-583.

Nowakowska, M. Quantitative approach to the dynamics of perception. *General Systems,* 1967, *12,* 81-95.

Nowakowska, M. *Language of motivation and language of actions.* The Hauge: Mouton, 1973. (a)

Nowakowska, M. A formal theory of actions. *Behavioral Science,* 1973, *18,* 393-416. (b)

Nowakowska, M. Towards a formal theory of dialogues. *Semiotics,* 1976, *17,* 4.

Nowakowska, M. *Teorie badań: Usecia modelowe.* [Theories of research: Modeling approaches.] Warszawa, PWN, 1977.

,ᴇFERENCES

R. *College and university environment scales: Technical manual.* Princeton, N.J.: Educa-
al Testing Service, 1963.

C. R., & Stern, G. G. An approach to the measurement of psychological characteristics of
ᴊlege environments. *Journal of Educational Psychology,* 1958, *49,* 209–277.

ɴ, C. F. A. Organism and environment. In M. Grene (Ed.), Toward a unity of knowledge.
Psychological Issues, 1969, *6,* 113–126.

ᴐousek, H., & Papousek, M. Mothering and the cognitive head-start. In H. R. Schaffer (Ed.),
Studies in mother-infant interaction. New York: Academic Press, 1977, pp. 63–85.

ᴀraskevopoulos, J., & Hunt, J. McV. Object construction and imitation under differing conditions
of rearing. *Journal of Genetic Psychology,* 1971, *119,* 301–321.

Patterson, G. R., & Moore, D. R. Interactive patterns as units. In S. J. Suomi, M. E. Lamb, & G.
R. Stevenson (Eds.), *The study of social interaction.* Methodological issues. Madison, Wis.:
University of Wisconsin Press, 1978.

Pawlik, K. Umwelt und Persönlichkeit: Zum Verhältnis von ökologischer und differentieller
Psychologie. In C. F. Graumann (Eds.), *Ökologische Perspetiven in der Psychologie.* Bern:
Huber, 1978.

Payne, R. L., & Mansfield, R. Relationships of perceptions of organizational climate to organizational structure, context, and hierarchical position. *Administrative Science Quarterly,* 1973, *18,*
515–526.

Payne, R. L., & Pugh, D. S. Organizational structure and climate. In M. D. Dunette (Ed.), *Handbook of industrial and organizational psychology.* Chicago: Rand McNally, 1976, pp. 1125–
1174.

Pearson, K. National life from the standpoint of science. An address delivered at Newcastle, No. 19,
1900. London: A. & C. Black, 1901.

Pearson, R. E. Response to suggestions given under general anesthesia. *American Journal of Clinical Hypnosis,* 1961, *4,* 106–114.

Persson, L-O., & Sjöberg, L. The influence of emotions on information processing. *Göteborgs
Psychological Reports,* 1978, *8,* No. 7.

Pervin, L. Performance and satisfaction as a function of individual environment fit. *Psychological
Bulletin,* 1968, *69,* 56–68.

Pervin, L. A. A free-response description approach to the analysis of person-situation interaction.
Journal of Personality and Social Psychology, 1976, *34,* 465–474.

Pervin, L. A. The representative design of person-situation research. In D. Magnusson & N. S.
Endler (Eds.), *Personality at the crossroads: Current issues in interactional psychology.* Hillsdale, N.J.: Lawrence Erlbaum Associates, 1977, pp. 371–384.

Pervin, L. A. *Current controversies and issues in personality.* New York: Wiley, 1978. (a)

Pervin, L. A. Definitions, measurements, and classifications of stimuli, situations, and environments. *Human Ecology,* 1978, *6,* 71–105. (b)

Pervin, L. A. Theoretical approaches to the analysis of individual-environment interaction. In L. A.
Pervin & M. Lewis (Eds.), *Perspectives in interactional psychology.* New York: Plenum, 1978,
pp. 67–86. (c)

Pervin, L. A., & Lewis, M. (Eds.). *Perspectives in interactional psychology.* New York: Plenum
Press, 1978.

Peters, R. S. *The concept of motivation.* London: Routledge & Kegan Paul, 1958.

Peterson, D. R. A functional approach to the study of person-person interactions. In D. Magnusson
& N. S. Endler (Eds.), *Personality at the crossroads: Current issues in interactional psychology.*
Hillsdale, N.J.: Lawrence Erlbaum Associates (J. Wiley), 1977, pp. 305–315.

Pheysey, D. C., & Payne, R. L. The Hemphill group dimensions discription questionnaire: A British
industrial application. *Human Relations,* 1970, *23,* 473–497.

Piaget, J. *The moral judgment of child.* London: Routledge & Kegan Paul, 1932.

Piaget, J. *The psychology of intelligence.* London: Routledge & Kegan Paul, 1947.

Nowakowska, M. Formal theory of group actions and its app.
Nowakowska, M. Monopolization and exclusion in scientific co. istrators. In J. W. Sutherland (Ed.), *Management handbook* York: Van Nostrand, 1978. (b)
Nowakowska, M. A theory of social change. In F. Geyer & H. van ⅃ *tics.* Leiden: Nijhof, 1978. (c)
Nowakowska, M. On planning freedom. *Management Science,* 1979, *25.*
Nowakowska, M. Object and its verbal copy: Formal semiotics. Ars Semei.
Nowakowska, M. Empirical foundations of formal semiotics. *Ars Semeiotica,*
Nowakowska, M. Cybernetics and social processes. In R. Trappl (Ed.), *Handbo.* 1980. (b)
Nuckolls, K. B., Cassel, J., & Kaplan, B. H. Psychosocial assets, life crisis, and th. pregnancy. *American Journal of Epidemiology,* 1972, 95(5), 431–441.
Nystedt, L. A modified lens model: A study of the interaction between the individua ecology. *Perceptual and Motor Skills,* 1972, *34,* 479–498. (a)
Nystedt, L. Predictive accuracy and utilization of cues; Study of the interaction between an indi al's cognitive organization and ecological structure. *Perceptual and Motor Skills,* 1972, 171–180. (b)
Nystedt, L. *Judgments in quasi-clinical situations: Accuracy and process. Report from the Psychological Laboratories, University of Stockholm,* 1972, Suppl. 12. (c)
Nystedt, L. Consensus among judges as a function of amount of information. *Educational and Psychological Measurement,* 1974, *34,* 91–101.
Nystedt, L. *Cognitive complexity and structural representation of role figures.* Report from the Department of Psychology, University of Stockholm, 1976, No. 473.
Nystedt, L. *An implicit personality theory approach to the prediction of individuals' judgment.* Report from the Department of Psychology, University of Stockholm, 1979, No. 553.
Nystedt, L., Kuusinen, J., & Ekehammar, B. Structural representations of person perception: A comparison between own and provided constructs. *Scandinavian Journal of Psychology,* 1976, *17,* 223–233.
Nystedt, L., & Magnusson, D. Cue relevance and feedback in a clinical prediction task. *Organizational Behavior and Human Performance,* 1973, *9,* 100–109.
Nystedt, L., Magnusson, D., & Aronowitsch, E. Generalization of ratings based on projective tests. *Scandinavian Journal of Psychology,* 1975, *16,* 72–78.
Olson, D. Language and thought. Aspects of a cognitive of a cognitive theory of semantics. *Psychological Review,* 1970, *77,* 257–273.
Oostendorp, A., & Berlyne, D. E. Dimensions in the perception of architecture. I. Identification and interpretation of dimensions of similarity. *Scandinavian Journal of Psychology,* 1978, *19,* 73–82. (a)
Oostendorp, A., & Berlyne, D. E. Dimensions in the perception of architecture. III. Multidimensional preference scaling. *Scandinavian Journal of Psychology,* 1978, *19,* 145–150. (b)
Oostendorp, A., McMaster, S., Rosen, M., & Waind, P. Toward a taxonomy of responses to the built environment. *Interactional Review of Applied Psychology,* 1978, *27,* 9–18.
Oppenheim, R. W. Preformation and epigenesis in the origins of the nervous system and behavior: Issues, concepts, and their history. In K. Immelmann et al. (Eds.), *Issues in behavioral development.* London: Cambridge University Press, 1980.
Ortony, A. Beyond literal similarity. *Psychological Review,* 1979, *86,* 161–180.
Osgood, C. E., Suci, G. J., & Tannenbaum, P. H. *The measurement of meaning.* Urbana, Ill.: University of Illinois Press, 1957.
Overton, W. F., & Reese, H. W. Models of development: Methodological implications. In J. R. Nesselroade & H. W. Reese (Eds.), *Life-span developmental psychology: Methodological issues.* New York: Academic Press, 1973, pp. 65–86.

Piaget, J. *The origins of intelligence in children, 1936.* (M. Cook. Transl.) New York: International University Press, 1952. (a)

Piaget, J. Jean Piaget: An autobiography. In H. S. Langfeld, E. G. Boring, H. Werner, & R. M. Yerkes (Eds.), *A history of psychology in autobiography* (Vol. 4). Worcester, Mass.: Clark University Press, 1952, pp. 237-256. (b)

Piaget, J. Piaget's theory. In P. H. Mussen (Ed.), *Carmichael's manual of child psychology* (Vol. 1). New York: Wiley, 1970.

Piaget, J. *Biology and knowledge: An essay on the relations between organic regulations and cognitive process.* Chicago: University of Chicago Press, 1971.

Piaget, J. Invited lecture. *International Congress of Psychology,* Paris, 1976.

Piaget, J. Problems of equilibration. In M. H. Appel & L. S. Goldberg (Eds.), *Topics in cognitive development* (Vol. 1). *Equilibration: Theory, research, and application.* New York: Plenum Press, 1977.

Plath, H.-E., & Richter, P. Der BMS-1-erfassungsbogen—ein verfahren zur skalierten erfassung erlebter beanspruchungsfolgen. *Probleme und Ergebnisse der Psychologie,* 1978, *65,* 45-86.

Polanyi, M. *Personal knowledge: Toward a post-critical philosophy.* New York: Harper Torchbook, 1964.

Porteous, J. D. *Environment and behavior: Planning and everyday urban life.* Reading, Mass.: Addison-Wesley, 1977.

Posner, M. I. Coordination of internal codes. In W. Chase (Ed.), *Visual information processing.* New York: Wiley, 1973.

Posner, M., & Keele, S. On the genesis of abstract ideas. *Journal of Experimental Psychology,* 1968, *77,* 353-363.

Price, R. H. The taxonomic classification of behaviors and situations and the problem of behavior-environment congruence. *Human Relations,* 1974, *27,* 476-585. (a)

Price, R. H. Etiology, the social environment, and the prevention of psychological dysfunction. In P. Insel & R. H. Moos (Eds.), *Health and the social environment.* Lexington, Mass.: D. C. Heath & Co., 1974. (b)

Price, R. H. Behavior setting theory and research. In R. H. Moos (Ed.), *The human context.* N.J.: Wiley, 1976.

Price, R. H. The ecology of treatment gain. In A. P. Goldstein & F. Kanfer (Eds.), *Maximizing treatment gain.* New York: Academic Press, 1979.

Price, R. H., & Blashfield, R. K. Explorations in the taxonomy of behavior settings: Analyses of dimensions and classifications of settings. *American Journal of Community Psychology,* 1975, *3,* 335-351.

Price, R. H., & Bouffard, D. L. Behavioral appropriateness and situational constraints as dimensions of social behavior. *Journal of Personality and Social Psychology,* 1974, *30,* 579-586.

Price, R. H., Ketterer, R. F., Bader, B. C., & Monahan, J. (Eds.) *Prevention in community mental health: Research, policy and practice.* Beverly Hills, Calif.: Sage Publications, 1980.

Price, R. H., & Politser, P. (Eds.) *Evaluation and action in the social environment.* New York: Academic Press, 1980.

Proshansky, H. M. The city and self-identity. *Environment and Behavior,* 1978, *10,* 147-170.

Proshansky, H. M., & Altman, I. Overview of the field. In W. White (Ed.), *Resources in environment and behavior.* Washington, D.C.: American Psychological Association, 1979.

Proshansky, H. M., Ittelson, W. H., & Rivlin, L. G. Freedom of choice and behavior in a physical setting. In H. M. Proshansky, W. H. Ittelson, & L. G. Rivlin (Eds.), *Environmental psychology: Man and his physical setting.* New York: Holt, Rinehart, & Winston, 1970, pp. 173-183.

Pruitt, D. G. Reward structure and cooperation: The decomposed prisoner's dilemma game. *Journal of Personality and Social Psychology,* 1967, *7,* 21-27.

Pugh, D. S., Hickson, D. J., & Hinings, C. R. An empirical taxonomy of work organization structures. *Administrative Science Quarterly,* 1969, *14,* 115-126.

Rabkin, J. B., & Struening, E. L. Life events, stress, and illness. *Science,* 1976, *194,* 1013–1020.

Rachal, J. V., Hubbard, R. L., Williams, J. R., & Tuchfeld, B. S. Drinking levels and problem drinking among junior and senior high school students. *Journal of Studies on Alcohol,* 1976, *37,* 1751–1761.

Rachal, J. V., Williams, J. R., Brehm, M. L., Cavanaugh, B., Moore, R. P., & Eckerman, W. C. *A national study of adolescent drinking behavior attitudes, and correlates* (Rep. No. PB-246-002; NIAAA/NCALI-75/27). Springfield, Va.: U.S. National Technical Information Service, 1975.

Rahe, R. H. Life change and illness studies: Past history and future directions. *Journal of Human Stress,* 1978, *4,* 3–14.

Rand, B. *Modern classical philosophers.* Boston: Houghton Mifflin, 1936.

Ransen, D. L. The mediation of reward-induced motivation decrements in early and middle childhood: a template matching approach. *Journal of Personality and Social Psychology,* 1980, *39,* 1088–1100.

Rapoport, A. Environmental cognition in cross-cultural perspective. In G. T. Moore & R. G. Golledge (Eds.), *Environmental krowing.* Stroudsburgh, Pa.: Dowden, Hutchinson, and Ross, 1976, 220–234.

Rapoport, A. *Human aspects of urban form: Towards a man-environment approach to urban form and design.* New York: Pergamon Press, 1977.

Raush, H. L. Paradox, levels, and junctures in person-situation systems. In D. Magnusson & N. S. Endler (Eds.), *Personality at the crossroads: Current issues in interactional psychology.* Hillsdale, N.J.: Lawrence Erlbaum Associates, 1977, pp. 287–304.

Reed, S. K. Pattern recognition and categorization. *Cognitive Psychology,* 1972, *3,* 382–407.

Report to the President from the president's commission on mental health (Stock 040-000-00390-8). Washington, D.C.: U.S. Government Printing Office, 1978.

Richardson, F. C., & Tasto, D. L. Development and factor analysis of a social anxiety inventory. *Behavior Therapy,* 1976, *7,* 453–462.

Riesman, D. (in collaboration with N. Glaser & R. Denney). *The lonely crowd: A study of the changing American character.* New Haven: Yale University Press, 1950.

Rogers, C. R. A theory of therapy, personality and interpersonal relationships as developed in the client-centered framework. In S. Koch (Ed.), *Psychology: A study of a science* (Vol. 3). New York: McGraw-Hill, 1959.

Rogers, T., Kuiper, N., & Kirker, W. S. Self-reference and the encoding of personal information. *Journal of Personality and Social Psychology,* 1977, *35,* 677–688.

Rokeach, M. *Beliefs, attitudes and values.* San Francisco: Jossey-Bass, 1968.

Rokeach, M. Long-range experimental modification of values: Attitudes and behavior. *American Psychologist,* 1971, *26,* 453–559.

Rokeach, M., & Kliejunas, P. Behavior as a function of attitude-towards object and attitude-towards situation. *Journal of Personality and Social Psychology,* 1972, *22,* 194–201.

Rommetveit, R. *On message structure. A framework for the study of language and communication.* London: Wiley, 1974.

Rommetveit, R. On negative rationalism in scholarly studies of verbal communication and dynamic residuals in the construction of human intersubjectivity. In M. Brenner, P. March, & M. Brenner (Eds.), *The social contexts of method.* London: Croom Helm, 1978. (a)

Rommetveit, R. Language and thought. *Cornell Review,* 1978, *2,* 91–114. (b)

Rommetveit, R. *The role of language in the creation and transmission of social representations.* Paper presented at the Colloque sur les Representationes Sociales, Paris. January, 8–10, 1979.

Rommetveit, R. On ''meanings'' of acts and what is meant by what is said in a pluralistic social world. In M. Brenner (Ed.), *The structure of action.* Oxford: Blackwell and Mott, 1980.

Rosch, E. Principles of categorization. In E. Rosch & B. B. Lloyd (Eds.), *Cognition and categorization.* Hillsdale, N.J.: Lawrence Erlbaum Associates, 1978.

Rosch, E., & Mervis, C. Family resemblances: Studies in the internal structure of categories. *Cognitive Psychology,* 1975, *7,* 573-605.

Rosch, E., Mervis, C., Gray, W., Johnson, D., & Boyes-Braem, P. Basic objects in natural categories. *Cognitive Psychology,* 1976, *8,* 382-439.

Rose, A. M. *Human behavior and social processes: An interactionist approach.* Boston: Houghton Mifflin, 1962.

Rosenberg, M. J. When dissonance falls: On eliminating evaluation apprehension from attitude measurement. *Journal of Personality and Social Psychology,* 1965, *1,* 18-42.

Rosenberg, M. J. The conditions and consequences of evaluation apprehension. In R. Rosenthal & R. W. Rosnow (Eds.), *Artifacts in behavioral research.* New York: Academic Press, 1969.

Rosenberg, S., & Sedlak, A. Structural representation of implicit personality theory. In L. Berkowitz (Ed.), *Advances in experimental social psychology* (Vol. 6). New York: Academic Press, 1972.

Rosenthal, R. *On the social psychology of the self-fulfilling prophecy: Further evidence for pygmalian effects and their mediating meachnisms.* M. S. S. Modular Publications, 1974.

Ross, L. The intuitive psychologist and his shortcomings: Distortions in the attribution process. In L. Berkowitz (Ed.), *Advances in experimental social psychology* (Vol. 10). New York: Academic Press, 1977.

Ross, M., & Sicoly, F. Egocentral biases in availability and attribution. *Journal of Personality and Social Psychology,* 1979.

Roth, S., & Kubal, L. Effects of noncontingent reinforcement on tasks of differing importance: Facilitation and learned helplessness. *Journal of Personality and Social Psychology,* 1975, *32,* 680-691.

Rothe, S. Arbeitsinhalt und Möglichkeiten zur selbständigen Zielsetzung. *Informationen der Technischen Universität Dresden,* 1978, No. 22-17.

Rotter, J. B. *Social learning and clinical psychology.* Englewood Cliffs, N.J.: Prentice-Hall, 1954.

Rotter, J. B. The role of the psychological situation in determining the direction of human behavior. In M. R. Jones (Ed.), *Nebraska Symposium on Motivation.* Lincoln: University of Nebraska Press, 1955, pp. 245-268.

Rotter, J. B. Psychotherapy. In P. R. Farnsworth (Ed.), *Annual Review of Psychology.* Palo Alto, Calif.: Annual Reviews, Inc., 1960.

Rotter, J. B. Generalized expectancies for internal versus external control of reinforcement. *Psychological Monographs,* 1966, *80,* No. 1(Whole No. 609).

Rotter, J. B., Chance, J. E., & Phares, E. J. *Applications of a social learning theory of personality.* New York: Holt, Rinehart and Winston, 1972.

Rumelhart, D. E. Understanding and summarizing bried stories. In D. LaBerge & S. J. Samuels (Eds.), *Basic processes in reading: Perception and comprehension.* Hillsdale, N.J.: Lawrence Erlbaum Associates, 1976.

Runyan, W. M. The life course as a theoretical orientation: Sequences of person-situation interaction. *Journal of Personality,* 1978, *46,* 569-593.

Russell, J. A., & Mehrabian, A. Distinguishing anger and anxiety in terms of emotional response factors. *Journal of Consulting and Clinical Psychology,* 1974, *42,* 79-83.

Russell, J. A., Ward, L. M., & Pratt, G. *The affective quality of environments.* Vancouver, B.C.: Department of Psychology, University of British Columbia, 1978.

Saarinen, T. F. Environmental planning: Perception and behavior. Boston: Houghton Mifflin, 1976.

Sackheim, H. A., & Gur, R. C. Self-deception, self-confrontation, and consciousness. In G. E. Schwartz & D. Shapiro (Eds.), *Consciousness and self-regulation* (Vol. 2). New York: Plenum, 1979.

Sarason, I. G. Test anxiety and cognitive modeling. *Journal of Personality and Social Psychology,* 1973, *28,* 58-61.

Sarason, I. G. The growth of interactional psychology. In D. Magnusson and N. S. Endler (Eds.) *Personality at the crossroads: Current issues in interactional Psychology.* Hillsdale, N.J.: Lawrence Erlbaum, 1977.

Sarason, I. G. The test anxiety scale. Concept and research. In C. D. Spielberger & I. G. Sarason (Eds.), *Stress and anxiety* (Vol. 5). Washington, D.C.: Hemisphere, 1978, pp. 193-216.

Sarason, I. G. *Lifestress, self-preoccupation, and social supports.* Office of Naval Research Technical Report No. Scs-Ls-008. Seattle, Wash., 1979.

Sarason, I. G., Johnson, J. H., & Siegel, J. M. Assessing the impact of life changes: Development of the life experiences survey. *Journal of Consulting and Clinical Psychology,* 1978, *46*(5), 932-946.

Sarason, I. G., & Stoops, R. Test anxiety and the passage of time. *Journal of Consulting and Clinical Psychology,* 1978, *46*(1), 102-109.

Sarbin, T. R., Taft, R., & Bailey, D. E. *Clinical inference and cognitive theory.* New York: Holt, Rinehart and Winston, 1960.

Schacter, S. The interaction of cognitive and physiological determinants of emotional state. In L. Berkowitz (Ed.), *Advances in Experimental Social Psychology.* New York: Academic Press, 1964.

Schachter, S., & Singer, J. E. Cognitive, social, and physiological determinants of emotional state. *Psychological Review,* 1962, *69*, 379-399.

Schaffer, H. R. (Ed.), *Studies in mother-infant interaction.* New York: Academic Press, 1977.

Schank, R., & Abelson, R. *Scripts, plans, goals and understanding.* Hillsdale, N.J.: Lawrence Erlbaum Associates, 1977.

Schatzman, L., & Strauss, A. Social class and modes of communication. In A. G. Smith (Ed.), *Communication and culture. Readings in the codes of human interaction.* New York: Holt, 1966, pp. 442-455.

Scheibe, K. The psychologist's advantage and its nullifications: Limits of human predictability. *American Psychologists,* 1978, *33*, 869-881.

Schleicher, R. Die intelligenzleistung erwachsener in abhängigkeit vom niveau beruflicher tätigkeit. *Probleme und Ergebnisse der Psychologie,* 1973, No. 44, pp. 25-56.

Schneider, B. Organizational climate: An essay. *Personnel Psychology,* 1975, *28*, 447-479.

Schneider, B., & Bartlett, C. J. Individual differences and organizational climate: II. Measurement of organizational climate by the multi-trait multi-rater matrix. *Personnel Psychology,* 1970, *23*, 493-512.

Schroeder, H. M., Driver, M. J., & Streufert, S. *Human information processing.* New York: Holt, Rinehart and Winston, 1967.

Schutz, A. On multiple realities. *Philosophical and Phenomenological Research,* 1945, *5*, 533-576.

Schutz, A. Choosing among projects of action. *Philosophical and Phenomenological Research,* 1951, *12*, 161-184.

Schwarz, J. C. Contribution of generalized expectancy to stated expectancy under conditions of success and failure. *Journal of Personality and Social Psychology,* 1969, *11*, 157-164.

Scott, W. A. Conceptualizing and measuring structural properties of cognition. In P. B. Warr (Ed.), *Thought and Personality.* Middlesex: Penguin Books, 1970, pp. 145-159.

Searle, J. *On speech acts.* Cambridge: Cambridge University Press, 1974.

Seaton, R. W., & Collins, J. B. Validity and reliability of ratings of simulated buildings. In W. S. Mitchells (Ed.), *Environmental design: Research and practice.* Los Angeles, Calif.: University of California Press, 1972.

Seligman, M. E. P. *Helplessness.* San Francisco: W. H. Freeman, 1975.

Sells, S. B. An interactionist looks at the environment. *American Psychologist,* 1963, *18*, 696-702. (a)

Sells, S. B. Dimensions of stimulus situations which account for behavior variances. In S. B. Sells (Ed.), *Stimulus determinants of behavior.* New York: Ronald Press, 1963. (b)

Sells, S. B. General theoretical problems related to organizational taxonomy: A model solution. In B. P. Indik & K. K. Berrien (Eds.), *People, groups and organizations*. New York: Teachers College Press, 1968.

Sells, S. B. Prescriptions for a multivariate model in personality and psychological theory: Ecological considerations. In J. R. Royce (Ed.), *Multivariate analysis and psychological theory*. New York: Academic Press, 1973, pp. 103-123.

Sells, S. B. Organizational climate as a mediator of organizational performance. In E. I. Salkovitz (Ed.), *Science, technology, and the modern navy*. Arlington, Va.: Department of the Navy, Office of Naval Research, 1976.

Shalit, B. Structural ambiguity and limits to coping. *Journal of Human Stress*, 1977, *3*, 32-45.

Shalit, B. Perceived perceptual organization and coping with military demands. In N. Milgram (Ed.), *Psychological stress in peace and war*. Washington, D.C.: Hemisphere Publishing Co., 1979.

Shapiro, D. *Resources required in the construction and reconstruction of conversation*. Mimeo, 1976.

Sheldon, R. C. Some observations on theory in the social sciences. In T. Parsons & E. A. Shils (Eds.), *Toward a general theory of action*. Cambridge, Mass.: Harvard University Press, 1951, pp. 30-46.

Sherif, M. *In common predicament: Social psychology of intergroup conflict and cooperation*. Boston: Houghton Mifflin, 1966.

Sherif, M., Harvey, O. J., Hoyt, B. J., Hood, W. R., & Sherif, C. W. *Inter-group conflict and cooperation: The robbers' cave experiment*. Norman: University of Oklahoma. Book Exchange, 1961.

Sherif, M., & Sherif, C. W. *An outline of social psychology*. New York: Harper & Row, 1956.

Siegel, J. M., Johnson, J. H., & Sarason, I. G. Life changes and menstrual discomfort. *Journal of Human Stress*, 1979, *5*(1), 41-46.

Signell, K. A. Cognitive complexity in person perception and nation perception: A development approach. *Journal of Personality*, 1966, *34*, 517-537.

Simon, A., & Boyer, E. G. (Eds.). *Mirrors for behavior* (3rd ed.). Classroom interaction Newsletter, Wyncote, Penn.: Communication Materials Center, 1974.

Sivik, L. Colour meaning and perceptual colour dimensions: A study of exterior colours. *Göteborg Psychological Reports*, 1974, *4*, No. 11.

Sjöberg, L. The new functionalism. *Scandinavian Journal of Psychology*, 1971, *12*, 29-52.

Sjöberg, L. Self esteem and information processing. *Göteborg Psychological Reports*, 1976, *6*, No. 14.

Sjöberg, L. *Beliefs and values as attitude components*. Paper read at International Symposium on Social Psychophysics, Mannheim, Germany, October 9-11, 1978.

Sjöberg, L., & Johnson, T. Trying to give up smoking: A study of volitional breakdowns. *Addictive Behaviors*, 1978, *3*, 149-164.

Sjöberg, L., & Samsonowitz, V. Volitional problems in trying to quit smoking. *Scandinavian Journal of Psychology*, 1978, *19*, 205-212.

Sjöberg, L., & Samsonowitz, V. Success and failure in trying to quit smoking. *Scandinavian Journal of Psychology*, 1978, *19*, 205-212.

Sjöberg, L., Svensson, E., & Persson, L.-O. The measurement of mood. *Scandinavian Journal of Psychology*, 1979, *20*, 1-18.

Skinner, B. F. *The behavior of organisms*. New York: Appleton-Century-Crofts, 1938.

Skinner, B. F. *Science and human behavior*. New York: MacMillan, 1953.

Smedslund, J. Meanings, implications and universals: Toward a psychology of man. *Scandinavian Journal of Psychology*, 1969, *10*, 1-15.

Smelser, N. J., & Smelser, W. T. Analyzing personality and social systems. In N. J. Smelser & W. T. Smelser (Eds.), Personality and social systems. New York: Wiley, 1968, pp. 1-32.

Smith, E. E., & Medin, D. *Representation and processing of lexical concepts*. Unpublished manuscript, Stanford University, 1979.

Smith, E. R., & Miller, F. D. Limits on perception of cognitive processes: A reply to Nisbett and Wilson. *Psychological Review*, 1978, *85*, 355-362.

Smith, R. E., Johnson, J. H., & Sarason, I. G. Life change, the sensation seeking motive and psychological distress. *Journal of Consulting and Clinical Psychology*, 1978, *46*, 348-349.

Sneath, P. H. A., & Sokal, R. R. *Numerical taxonomy*. San Francisco, Calif.: W. H. Freeman, 1973.

Snyder, M. The self-monitoring of expressive behavior. *Journal of Personality and Social Psychology*, 1974, *30*, 526-537.

Snyder, M. Cognitive, behavioral, and interpersonal consequences of self-monitoring. In P. Pliner, K. R. Blankstein, I. M. Spiegel, T. Alloway, & L. Krames (Eds.), *Advances in the study of communication and affect* (Vol. 5). New York: Plenum Press, 1979.

Snyder, M., & Cantor, N. *Thinking about ourselves and others: Cognitive processes in self-monitoring*. Unpublished manuscript, University of Minnesota and Princeton University, 1979.

Snyder, M., & Monson, T. C. Persons, situations, and the control of social behavior. *Journal of Personality and Social Psychology*, 1975, *32*, 637-644.

Snyder, M., & Swann, W. Behavioral confirmation in social interaction: From social perception to social reality. *Journal of Experimental Social Psychology*, 1978, *14*, 148-162.

Snyder, M., & Tanke, E. Behavior and attitude: Some people are more consistent than others. *Journal of Personality*, 1976, *44*, 501-517.

Snyder, M., Tanke, E., & Berscheid, E. Social perception and interpersonal behavior: On the self-fulfilling nature of social stereotypes. *Journal of Personality and Social Psychology*, 1977, *35*, 656-666.

Sommer, R. Small group ecology. *Psychological Bulletin*, 1967, *67*, 145-152.

Sommer, R. *Personal space*. Englewood Cliffs, N.J.: Prentice-Hall, 1969.

Sonnenfeld, J. Equivalence and distortion of the perceptual environment. *Environment and Behavior*, 1969, *1*, 83-100.

Spielberger, C. D. Anxiety as an emotional state. In C. D. Spielberger (Ed.), *Anxiety: Current trends in theory and research* (Vol. 1). New York: Academic Press, 1972.

Spielberger, C. D. State-trait anxiety and interactional psychology. In D. Magnusson & N. S. Endler (Eds.) *Personality at the Crossroads: Current issues interactional Psychology*. Hillsdale, N.J.: Lawrence Erlbaum Associates, 1977.

Spielberger, C. D., Gorsuch, R. L., & Lushene, R. E. *Manual for the state-trait anxiety inventory*. Palo Alto, Calif.: Consulting Psychological Press, 1970.

Stagner, R. Traits are relevant: Theoretical analysis and empirical evidence. In N. S. Endler & D. Magnusson (Eds.), *Interactional psychology and personality*. New York: Wiley, 1976.

Stagner, R. On the reality and relevance of traits. *The Journal of General Psychology*, 1977, *96*, 185-207.

Stattin, H., & Magnusson, D. *The individual organization of behavioral reactions and its relation to situation perception*. Reports from the Department of Psychology, University of Stockholm, 1978, No. 525.

Stebbins, R. A. A theory of the definition of the situation. *The Canadian Review of Sociology and Anthropology*, 1969, *4*, 148-164.

Stephenson, W. The study of behavior. Chicago: University of Chicago Press, 1953.

Stern, G. G. *Scoring instructions and college norms: Activities index and college characteristics index*. Syracuse, N.Y.: Psychological Research Center, Syracuse University, 1963.

Stern, G. G. *People in context: The measurement of environmental interaction in school and society*. New York: Wiley, 1970.

Stern, W. *The psychological methods of testing intelligence 1912*. (G. N. Whipple, trans.) Baltimore: Warwick & York, 1914.

Stokols, D. On the distinction between density and crowding: Some implications for future research. *Psychological Review*, 1972, *79*, 275-277.

Stokols, D. The experience of crowding in primary and secondary environments. *Environment and Behavior*, 1976, *8*, 49–86.

Stokols, D. Origins and directions of environment-behavioral research. In D. Stokols (Ed.), *Perspectives on environmental and behavior*. New York: Plenum Press, 1977.

Stokols, D. Environmental psychology. Annual Review of Psychology, 1978, *29*, 253–295.

Stokols, D. A congruence analysis of human stress. In I. G. Sarason & C. D. Spielberger (Eds.), *Stress and anxiety* (Vol. 6). Washington, D.C.: Hemisphere Press, 1979, in press.

Stokols, D., & Shumaker, S. A. People in places: A transactional view of settings. In J. Harvey (Ed.), *Cognition, social behavior, and the environment*. Hillsdale, New Jersey: Lawrence Erlbaum Associates, in press.

Stotland, E., & Canon, L. K. *Social Psychology: A cognitive approach*. Philadelphia: Sanders, 1972.

Stratton, T. T., & Moore, C. L. Application of the robust factor concept to the fear survey schedule. *Journal of Behavior Therapy and Experimental Psychology*, 1977, *8*, 229–235.

Streufert, S., & Streufert, S. C. *Behavior in the complex environment*. Washington, D.C.: Winston & Sons, 1978.

Stryker, S. Developments in "two social psychologies": Toward an appreciation of mutual relevance. *Sociometry*, 1977, *40*, 145–160.

Suttles, G. D. *The social order of the slum: Ethnicity and territory in the inner city*. Chicago: University of Chicago Press, 1968.

Suttles, G. D. *The social construction of communities*. Chicago: University of Chicago Press, 1972.

Tagiuri, R. Executive climate. In R. Tagiuri & G. H. Litwin (Eds.), *Organizational climate: Exploration of a concept*. Cambridge: Mass.: Harvard University Press, 1968.

Tajfel, H. Experiments in intergroup discrimination. *Scientific American*, 1970, *223*, 96–102.

Tajfel, H. The structuring of our views about society. In H. Tajfel & C. Fraser (Eds.), *Introducing social psychology*. Hardmondsworth, Middlesex, England: Penguin Books Ltd., 1978.

Task Panel Report on Prevention. Submitted to the President's Commission on Mental Health, 1978. Vol. 4.

Taylor, S. E., Fiske, S. T., Etcoff, N. L., Ruderman, A. J. Categorical and contextual bases of person memory and stereotyping. *Journal of Personality and Social Psychology*, 1978, *36*, 778–793.

Taylor, S. E., & Fiske, S. T. Salience, attention, and attribution: Top of the head phenomena. In L. Berkowitz (Ed.), *Advances in experimental social psychology* (Vol. 11). New York: Academic Press, 1978.

Tedeschi, J. T., Schlenker, B. R., & Bonoma, T. V. Cognitive dissonance: Private ratiocination or public spectacle? *American Psychologist*, 1971, *26*, 685–695.

Thibaut, J., & Faucheux, C. The development of contractual norms in a bargaining situation under two types of stress. *Journal of Experimental Social Psychology*, 1965, *1*, 89–102.

Thibaut, J. W., & Kelley, H. H. *The social psychology of groups*. New York: Wiley, 1959.

Thomas, W. A (Ed.). *Indicators of environmental quality*. New York: Plenum, 1972.

Thomas, W. J. The behavior pattern and the situation. Publications of the American Sociological Society: Papers and Proceedings (Vol. 22), 1927, 1–13.

Thomas, W. I. *The child in America*. New York: Knopf, 1928.

Toda, M. What happens at the moment of decision? Meta decisions, emotions and volitions. In L. Sjöberg, T. Tyszka, & J. Wise (Eds.). *Decision processes*. Lund, Sweden: Doxa, 1979.

Todd, F. J., & Rappoport, L. A cognitive structure approach to person perception. *Journal of Abnormal and Social Psychology*, 1964, *68*, 469–478.

Tolman, E. C. A psychological model. In T. Parsons & E. A. Shils (Eds.), *Toward a general theory of action*. Cambridge, Mass.: Harvard University Press, 1951, 279–364. (a)

Tolman, E. C. Psychology versus immediate experience. In E. C. Tolman (Ed.), *Collected papers in psychology*. Berkeley: University of California Press, 1951. (b)

Tolman, E. C., & Brunswik, E. The organism and the causal texture of the environment. *Psychological Review*, 1935, *42*, 43–77.

Tomaszewski, T. Die Struktur der menschlichen Tätigkeiten. *Psychologie und Praxis*, 1964, *8*, 145-155.

Torgerson, W. S. *Theory and methods of scaling*. New York: Wiley, 1958.

Trevarthen, C. Conversations with a two-month-old. *New Scientist*, 1974, *62*, 230-235.

Trevarthen, C. Descriptive analyses of infant communicative behavior. In H. R. Schaffer (Ed.), *Studies in mother-infant interaction*. New York: Academic Press, 1977, pp. 227-270.

Trist, E. L., Higgin, G. W., Murray, H., & Pollock, A. B. *Organizational choice*. London: Tavistock, 1963.

Trower, P., Bryant, B., & Argyle, M. *Social skills and mental health*. London: Methuen, 1978.

Trustman, R., Dubovsky, S., & Titley, R. Auditory perception during general anesthesia—myth or fact? *International Journal of Clinical and Experimental Hypnosis*, 1977, *25*, 88-105.

Tucker, L. R. A suggested alternative formulation in the developments of Hursch, Hammond, and Hursch and by Hammond, Hursch and Todd. *Psychological Review*, 1964, *71*, 528-530.

Tversky, A. Features of similarity. *Psychological Review*, 1977, *84*, 327-352.

Tversky, A., & Kahneman, D. Availability: A heuristic for judging frequency and probability. *Cognitive Psychology*, 1973, *5*, 207-232.

Tversky, A., & Kahneman, D. Judgment under uncertainty: Heuristics and biases. *Science*, 1974, *185*, 1124-1131.

Tyler, S. A. (Ed.). *Cognitive anthropology*. New York: Holt, Rinehart and Winston, 1969.

U.S. Office of Management and Budget. *Social indicators*. Washington, D.C.: Government Printing Office, 1973.

Uusitalo, H. *Class structure and party choice*. Helsinki: Research Group for Comparative Sociology, 1975, No. 10.

Uzgiris, I. C. The many faces of imitation in infancy. In L. Montada (Eds.), *Fortschritte der entwicklungspsychologie*, in press. Paper presented for the International Seminar on Developmental Psych., Trier, W. Germany, August 1978.

Uzgiris, I. C., & Hunt, J. McV. Attentional preference and experience: II. An exploratory longitudinal study on the effects of visual familiarity and responsiveness. *Journal of Generic Psychology*, 1970, *117*, 109-121.

Uzgiris, I. C., & Hunt, J. McV. *Assessment in infancy: Ordinal scales of psychological development*. Urbana: University of Illinois Press, 1975.

Vaillant, G. E. Natural History of male psychological health: II. Some antecedents of healthy adult adjustment. *Archives of General Psychiatry*, 1974, *21*, 15-22.

Vaillant, G. E. *Adaptation to life*. Boston: Little, Brown Co., 1977.

van Hooff, J. A. R. A. M. A structural analysis of the social behaviour of a semi-captive group of chimpanzees. In M. von Cranach & I. Vine (Eds.), *Social communication and movement*. London Academic Press, 1973.

von Wright, G. H. *An essay in deontic logic and theory of actions*. Amsterdam: North Holland, 1968.

Wachs, T. D. Utilization of a piagetian approach in the investigation of early-experience effects: A research strategy and some illustrative data. *Merrill-Palmer Quarterly*, 1976, *22*, 11-30.

Wachs, T. D. Relationship of infants physical environment to their binet performance at 2.5 years. *International Journal of Behavioral Development*, 1978, in press.

Wachs, T. D., Uzgiris, I. C., & Hunt, J. McV. Cognitive development in infants of different age levels and from different environmental backgrounds: An exploratory investigation. *Merrill-Palmer Quarterly*, 1971, *17*, 283-317.

Wachtel, P. L. Psychodynamics, behavior therapy, and the implacable experimenter: An inquiry into the consistency of personality. *Journal of Abnormal Psychology*, 1973, *82*, 324-334.

Wachtel, P. L. Interaction cycles, unconscious processes, and the person-situation issue. In D. M. Magnusson & N. S. Endler (Eds.), *Personality at the crossroads: Current issues in interactional psychology*. Hillsdale, N.J.: Lawrence Erlbaum Associates, 1977.

Walker, J. H. Real-world variability, reasonableness judgments, and memory representations for concepts. *Journal of Verbal Behavior,* 1975, *14,* 241-252.

Wallace, J. What units shall we employ? Allport's question revisited. *Journal of Consulting Psychology,* 1967, *31,* 56-64.

Walsh, W. B. *The theories of person-environment interaction: Implications for the college student.* Iowa City, Iowa: American College Testing Program, 1973.

Wapner, S., Kaplan, B., & Cohen, S. B. An organismic-developmental perspective for understanding transactions of men and environments. *Environment and Behavior,* 1973, *5,* 255-289.

Ward, L. M., & Russell, J. A. *Psychological dimensions of molar physical environments.* Vancouver, B.C.: Department of Psychology, University of British Columbia, 1978.

Warr, P. B., & Knapper, C. *The perception of people and events.* London: Wiley, 1968.

Watson, J. B. *Psychology from the standpoint of a behaviorist.* Philadelphia: Lippingcott, 1919.

Weinstein, N. D. Human evaluations of environmental noise. In K. H. Craik & E. H. Zube (Eds.), *Perceiving environmental quality: Research and applications.* New York: Plenum, 1976, pp. 229-252.

Weizmann, F., Cohen, L. B., & Pratt, R.J. Novelty, familiarity, and the development of infant attention. *Developmental Psychology,* 1971, *4*(2), 149-154.

Wetherford, M., & Cohen, L. B. Developmental changes in infant visual preferences for novelty and familiarity. *Child Development,* 1973, *44,* 416-424.

White, B. L. An experimental approach to the effects of experience on early human development. In J. P. Hill (Ed.), *Minnesota Symposia on Child Development.* Minneapolis: University of Minnesota Press, 1967, pp. 201-226.

White, R. W. *Lives in progress* (2nd ed.). New York: Holt, Rinehart and Winston, 1966.

White, R. W. *The enterprise of living: A view of personal growth* (2nd ed.). New York: Holt, Rinehart and Winston, 1976.

White, B. L., & Watts, J. *Experience and environment: Major influences on the development of the young child.* Englewood Cliffs, N.J.: Prentice-Hall, 1973.

Whitfield, T. W. A., & Slatter, P. E. The effects of categorization and prototypicality on aesthetic choice in a furniture selection task. *British Journal of Psychology,* 1979, *70,* 65-76.

Whyte, W. F. *Human relations in the restaurant industry.* New York: McGraw-Hill, 1948.

Wicker, A. W. *An introduction to ecological psychology.* Monterey, Calif.: Brooks/Cole, 1979.

Wicker, A. W., & Kirmeyer, S. L. From church to laboratory to national park. In S. Wapner, S. B. Cohen, & B. Kaplan (Eds.), *Experiencing the environment.* New York: Plenum, 1976, pp. 157-185.

Wiggins, J. S. *Personality and prediction: Principles of personality assessment.* Reading, Mass.: Addison-Wesley, 1973.

Willows, D. M. Reading between the lines: Selective attention in good and poor readers. *Child Development,* 1974, *45,* 408-415.

Willows, D. M., & MacKinnon, G. E. Selective reading: Attention to the "unattended" lines. *Canadian Journal of Psychology,* 1973, *27,* 292-304.

Wilson, T. P. Conceptions of interaction and forms of sociological explanation. *American Sociological Review,* 1970, *35,* 697-710.

Wish, M., & Kaplan, S. J. Toward an implicit theory of interpersonal communication. *Sociometry,* 1977, *40,* 234-246.

Wittgenstein, L. *Philosophical investigations.* Oxford: Blackwell, 1968.

Wohlwill, J. F. Environmental aesthetics. The environment as a source of affect. In I. Altman & J. F. Wohlwill (Eds.), *Human behavior and environment: Advances in theory and research* (Vol. 1). New York: Plenum Press, 1976, pp. 37-86.

Wohlwill, J. F., & Kohn, I. Dimensionalizing the environmental manifold. In S. Wapner, S. B.

Cohen, & B. Kaplan (Eds.), *Experiencing the environment*. New York: Plenum Press, 1976, pp. 19-54.

Wolfgang, M. E., Figlio, R. M., & Sellin, T. *Delinquency in a birth cohort*. Chicago: University of Chicago Press, 1972.

Wolk, S. Situational constraint of the locus of control-adjustment relationship. *Journal of Consulting and Clinical Psychology*, 1976, *44*, 420-427.

Wolpe, J., & Lang, P. J. A fear survey schedule for use in behavior therapy. *Behavior Research and Therapy*, 1964, *2*, 27-30.

Woltereck, R. Weitere experimentelle undersuchungen über artveränderung, speziell über das wesen quantitativer artunterschiede bei daphniden. *Verhandlungen der Deutschen Zoologischen Gesellschaft*, 1909, *19*, 110-173.

Woods, W. A. What's in a link: Foundations for semantic networks. In D. G. Bobrow & A. Collins (Eds.), *Representation and understanding. Studies in cognitive science*. New York: Academic Press, 1975, pp. 35-82.

Woodworth, R. S. Reinforcement of perception. *American Journal of Psychology*, 1947, *60*, 119-124.

Wortman, C. B., & Brehm, J. W. Responses to uncontrollable outcomes: An integration of reactance theory and the learned helplessness model. In L. Berkowitz (Ed.), *Advances in experimental social psychology* (Vol. 8). New York: Academic Press, 1975, pp. 277-336.

Wyer, R. S. *Cognitive organization and change: An information processing approach*. Potomac, Md.: Lawrence Erlbaum Associates, 1974.

Yarrow, L. J., Rubenstein, J. L., & Pedersen, F. A. *Infant and environment: Early cognitive and motivational development*. Washington, D.C.: Hemisphere Publishing Co., 1975.

Zajonc, R. B. The process of cognitive turning in communication. *Journal of Abnormal Psychology*, 1960, *61*, 159-167.

Zener, K. The significance of experience of the individual for the science of psychology. In H. Feigl, M. Scriven, & G. Maxwell (Eds.), *Minnesota studies in the philosophy of science* (Vol. 2). *Concepts, theories, and the mind-body problem*. Minneapolis: University of Minnesota Press, 1958.

Zube, E. H. Perception of landscape and land use. In I. Altman & J. F. Wohlwill (Eds.), *Human behavior and the environment: Advances in theory and research* (Vol. 2). New York: Plenum, 1976, pp. 87-121.

Zube, E. H., Pitt, D. G., & Anderson, T. W. Perception and prediction of scientific resource values of the northeast. In E. H. Zube, R. O. Brush, & J. Fabos (Eds.), *Landscape assessment: Values, perception and resources*. Stroudsberg, Pa.: Dowden, Hutchinson & Ross, 1975, pp. 151-167.

Zuckerman, M., Kolin, E. A., Price, L., & Zoob, I. Development of a sensation seeking scale. *Journal of Consulting Psychology*, 1964, *26*, 250-260.

Author Index

Subject Index